MW00341263

OCEAN PASSAGES AND LANDFALLS

OCEAN PASSAGES & LANDFALLS

CRUISING ROUTES OF THE WORLD

Rod Heikell and Andy O'Grady
With contributions by Warwick Clay and others

Imray Laurie Norie & Wilson

Published by
Imray Laurie Norie & Wilson Ltd
Wych House The Broadway St Ives
Cambridgeshire PE27 5BT England
℡ +44(0)1480 462114
Fax +44(0)1480 496109
Email ilnw@imray.com
www.imray.com
2009

All rights reserved. No part of this
publication may be reproduced,
transmitted or used in any form by any
means – graphic, electronic or
mechanical, including photocopying,
recording, taping or information
storage and retrieval systems or
otherwise – without the prior
permission of the Publishers.

© Rod Heikell 2009
© Andrew O'Grady 2009

Rod Heikell and Andrew O'Grady have
asserted their right under the
Copyright, Designs and Patents Act
1988 to be identified as the authors of
this work.

© Photographs are all by Rod Heikell,
Andy O'Grady, Lucinda Michell and
Ulla Norlander unless otherwise stated.

1st edition 2005
2nd edition 2009

A catalogue record for this book is
available from the British Library.

ISBN 978 184623 155 1

CAUTION

Every effort has been made to ensure
the accuracy of this book. It contains
selected information and thus is not
definitive and does not include all
known information on the subject in
hand; this is particularly relevant to the
plans, which should not be used for
navigation. The authors believe that
their selection is a useful aid to
prudent navigation, but the safety of a
vessel depends ultimately on the
judgement of the navigator, who
should assess all information, published
or unpublished.

PLANS

The plans in this guide are not to be
used for navigation. They are designed
to support the text and should at all
times be used with navigational charts.

CORRECTIONAL SUPPLEMENTS

This pilot book will be amended at
intervals by the issue of correctional
supplements. These are published on
the internet at our web site
www.imray.com and may be
downloaded free of charge. Printed
copies are also available on request
from the publishers at the above
address.

Printed by Star Standard Industries
(PTE) Ltd in Singapore.

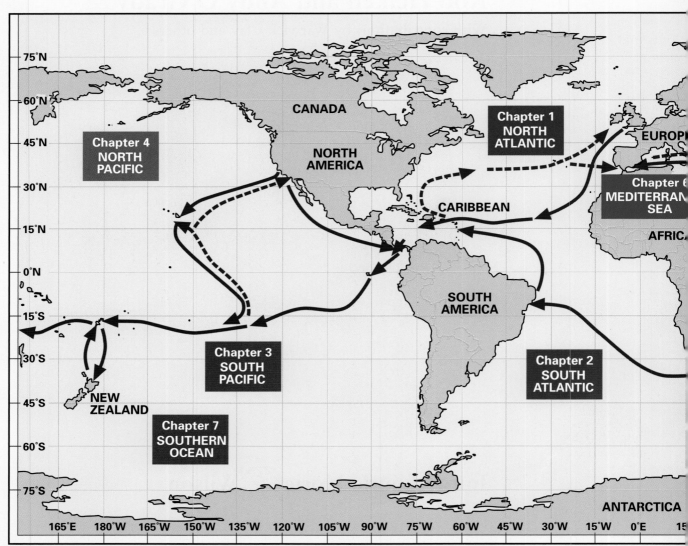

CHAPTER AREAS AND COMMON CIRCUMNAVIGATION AND CRUISING ROUTES

CONTENTS

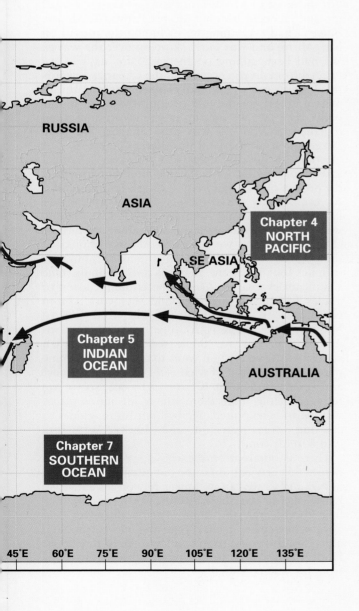

PREFACES

ROD HEIKELL

PREFACE TO FIRST EDITION

This book has been a long time coming. I first proposed a book along these lines to Imray in 1985 and they agreed that I should start work on it. Somehow over the next few years the project slipped away as I researched and wrote books about the Mediterranean, got on with the business of living on board and cruising the coasts and islands of the Mediterranean and a few other places, got married and got divorced, fell in and out of love, worked to put bread on the plate, and then one day picked up the files for this book again.

In the mid 1990s, nearly a decade after the first proposal, I finally got back to the book again and eventually signed a contract with Imrays. The only slight problem was getting some first-hand information on other areas, so I set about contacting people who cruised and wrote about other parts of the world and managed to put together a team of people who knew the ins and outs of the parts of the world they cruised in. By the end of the millennium I had cruised to SE Asia and back, around the Caribbean and back to the Mediterranean. Still the task looked daunting and though I had files stuffed full of information, chunks of chapters ready to go (notably from the doyen of cruising in the Pacific, Warwick Clay), I still lacked some vital pieces of the whole nautical jigsaw.

It was Willie Wilson at Imray who suggested I get in contact with Andy O'Grady, who had spent two years in Chile cruising and writing about this snow-driven cruising ground before heading for South Africa for a refit. Somewhere along a rhumb line on a windy night watch on *seven tenths* it hit me: there was some sort of wonderful symmetry here. Andy liked to cruise in high latitudes, cold places or at least places that were not in the high teens temperature-wise. I liked lower latitudes where the weather was warmer. Andy had cruised in all sorts of places that I hadn't and vice versa. At the time Andy was working as a GP in New Zealand to top up his cruising kitty before returning to his boat in South Africa and I was due for a visit back to Godzone to see family and friends (just coincidentally the Americas Cup was on as well), so I drove up to the remote hospital in Northland where he was working with a proposal on this book. He would edit the book with me on equal terms and deal with those high latitudes while I stuck mostly to low latitudes. Out of the deep blue it was all coming together.

Of course, things are never that easy. There has been a lot of cross-fertilisation between us over all the areas in the book and we have criss-crossed paths on the ocean a few times. More importantly, input from dozens of cruising folk, delivery skippers, and other writers have added to the nitty-gritty detail of the book. We have emailed chunks of the book all over the place and in the final stages, as I charged up through the Caribbean to Florida and back across to the Mediterranean and Andy battled through the fog and drizzle off the Labrador coast, we would both be cutting and pasting chunks of text and maps and plans to email to each other and exchanging views on weather windows for the bits of the world we were sailing in. A quite strange and wonderful camaraderie grew between us, a sort of virtual sailing in company, despite the fact that nearly 2,000 miles separated my tropics from Andy's tundra.

This book can never be complete. We have put it together with all the firsthand information we know about from our cruising and have hassled countless cruising friends and acquaintances, and even people we have never met in the flesh, to get all the bits in between. We owe them all a big debt.

PREFACE TO SECOND EDITION

Off the coast of Mindelo in the Cape Verdes a small tan sail emerged heading at speed towards *Skylax*. *Balaena* had everything up including the topsail on her gaff rig and was fairly skipping over the waves. We had been talking on the radio for days as we headed from divergent ports in the Canaries towards the Cape Verdes and had planned for months to meet up there for the first time on the water in our boats. The fact we met up in the ocean and sailed together to Mindelo was pure chance. We have talked often on the land in different countries, but meeting up on the water was a token, a special sartori, of how far we had come after embarking on the project of writing *Ocean Passages and Landfalls*. As usual Andy was heading south to the higher latitudes of Chile and Antarctica while I was sailing west for the Caribbean and Pacific along lower lats.

For this edition we have revised large chunks of the original book and have sailed tens of thousands of miles looking at the passages and landfalls. One significant change to this edition is the inclusion of guides to cruising areas around the world. From Greenland to Antarctica and the Red Sea to Vanuatu, we have put together the sort of information that we think will be useful when choosing just where you want to go as well as some photos to give a hint of what is there. It's a big planet and seven tenths of it is covered by sea, so we are fully conscious that there are a lot more places waiting to be explored. We will put future guides to cruising areas up on the Imray web site (www.imray.com).

There is one blot on the seascape to this edition. Before this new edition came out Warwick Clay died in NZ and so we can no longer rely on his extensive knowledge of the South Pacific. We have done our best to research the South Pacific ourselves and *Skylax* has spent a busy year and more trundling along South Pacific routes to landfalls in this book. Hopefully Warwick is looking down benignly on us from his watery Valhalla.

ACKNOWLEDGEMENTS

A lot of people contributed knowledge of passages, weather, and landfall information to this book. Without them the information here would be less complete. Lu was my shipmate for much of the additional research we carried out for this book and she has more miles under her belt than most. She has always brought good cheer and lightly voiced wisdom to our passages and without her on board I would be the poorer. She also helped edit parts of the book and took many of the photos. Graham and Katrina Sewell on S.Y. *Songline* provided information and comfort and cheer in the SW Pacific. Bob McDavitt, NZ weather guru provided clear explanations on weather in the SW Pacific and has a wonderful way with words. Wal and Barb Cole on S.Y. *Bloody Mary* provided wonderful anecdotes and good down to earth info from their two circumnavigations. Many thanks to Rosemary Ralph who provided valuable information on Mexico and I'm only sorry I can't use it all here. Thanks also to Bob the 'brainscratcher' on S.Y. *Boomerang*. Roy Dixon and Irene on S.Y. *Peggywest* provided good old fashioned information on areas and delightful craic. Clive and Norma Garner on S.Y. *Sanyassa* provided valuable info on passages as did Alan and Fiona Poole on S.Y. *Seabiscuit*. Fenton Hamlin on S.Y. *Pateke* provided lots of info on the Indian Ocean and SE Asia from his wonderful 29ft Lyle Hesse design. Peter and Jan Metherall on S.Y. *Penyllan* provided information from their circumnavigation and good food to boot. Sam Coles on S.Y. *Ramprasad* has sailed many miles and contributed solid information as well as incredible tales of small boat explorations in the Indian Ocean in former years. Professor Peter Seary and Fiona on S.Y. *Sayonara* threaded Shakespeare and Dryden through the ocean chain. Don Street provided solid information on Atlantic routes and landfalls. Thanks also to James Ingle on S.Y. *Kaama*, Steve and Di Evans and Paul on S.Y. *Independent Freedom*, Paul and Margueritte Jackson, Murray Pereira for the academic views, Rodney Keenan of Evolution Sails, Graeme and Judith MacKay, Nan Harris, Karen Whelan, Andy and Linda on S.Y. *Coromandel Quest*, Bill and Sharon Stephens on S.Y. *Sunrise*, Tito and Roger at the sadly demolished PCYC, Paul Gelder and Dick Durham at *Yachting Monthly*, Dr Chassefaire in Atuona, and Phil Ash at Gulf Harbour Riggers.

At Imray Elinor Cole and Clare Georgy laboured over proofs from both ends of the world, and along with Willie Wilson and the crew at Imray put this book together into what you hold in your hands. To you all my thanks.

Rod Heikell
Cairns 2009

ANDY O'GRADY

PREFACE TO FIRST EDITION

Sailing among the glaciers and fiords of Tierra del Fuego and the Beagle Canal, an email reached me asking if I could provide a chapter on the South Atlantic for this book. As we were about to set course into that ocean and were eagerly collecting information on sailing in Brazil and South Africa, it seemed an easy task. As the chapter grew, so did my enthusiasm and commitment to the book. Later, Ulla and I met Rod in New Zealand and to my astonishment Rod asked me to become a partner in the venture of preparing this book.

There was a lot of work to do, and sketches and chapters gradually took shape as we sailed from Cape Town towards Brazil. The final months, when we were ready to begin a cruise to Labrador, brought the rewards of seeing the work come together in a surprisingly smooth way and a growing friendship with Rod.

This book gave me an opportunity to share with others the experience gained and knowledge passed on to me over many years of sailing. I am a dreamer, one who likes to live out his dreams. I hope the book will help the reader to do both and to derive as much pleasure as I have from cruising and meeting people who follow the ocean passages to faraway places.

PREFACE TO THE SECOND EDITION

Since the publication of the first edition of this book both Rod and I have sailed many thousands of miles. Despite very different cruising plans we managed to meet along the way in the memorable encounter that Rod describes. Rod has visited *Balæna's* New Zealand and Pacific home waters while I have kept mainly to the higher latitudes with short interludes in Spain, the Atlantic Islands and Brazil. It has been enormously gratifying to meet people who are using the book and hear their comments. I have also enjoyed following many of the routes described gaining new experience that I am now able to pass on and correcting errors that I hope have not caused any inconvenience. Like Rod I have added new details of favourite cruising areas and hope that you will come to enjoy them as much as me.

ACKNOWLEDGEMENTS

Without the trust and confidence of Rod Heikell and Willie Wilson I would not be writing this. Ulla Norlander supported and helped me in everything and is responsible for drawing over 100 of the sketch charts in the book. Yachtsmen of more than 10 different nationalities have assisted my work. Kitty Van Hagen of *Duet* and Dominique and Nicholas Drury of *Chaski* provided much of the material on which the North Pacific chapter is based. Cruising companions from our years in Chile continue to keep in contact and provide information and answer questions. Foremost amongst these are Gustaf and Tina Thomsson of *Caminante*, Jim and Lina Gallop of *Mist*, Brian and Althea Elliot of *Althea*, Bjørn Bratlie and Marit Aasdal of *Kuven* and Noel Kerebel of *Enez*. Many of the friendly and experienced members of the Port Owen Yacht Club and Traditional Boat Association in South Africa, particularly Jan Neelmeyer, Robin Ellis and Gordon Webb, contributed information on the South Atlantic. In Scandinavia I met with unstinting hospitality and assistance, once again from Bjørn Bratlie and Marit Aasdal of *Kuven*, from Armin Mueck of *Eja af Slussen* and Leif Frejdestedt of *Nieta*, and many more. Countless others over the last 40 years have been unstinting in their advice and assistance, such is the spirit of cruising. The staff at Imray have once again done a remarkable job of turning my imperfect text and some far from tidy sketches into a wonderful book. Thanks also to María Clemencia Valencia Uribe who encouraged me to visit Cartagena and gave me a warm haven to work on the new text. To you all: thank you, and may you cruise on for ever.

Andy O,Grady,
Isla Jaime, Chilean Patagonia 2009

THE AUTHORS

ROD HEIKELL

Rod Heikell was born in New Zealand and sailed hesitantly around bits of its coast in a variety of yachts. He tried racing in the Hauraki Gulf but was really not much good at it. In England he abandoned academic life and for no good reason other than curiosity bought *Roulette*, a 1950s plywood JOG yacht nearly 20ft long, and sailed it down to the Mediterranean. He worked on charter here and delivered yachts until, in ignorance of the scale of the task, he set off to write a yachtsman's guide to Greece. This was followed by guides for other countries in the Mediterranean. He has sailed back and forth between England and the Mediterranean, including a trip down the Danube and on to Turkey in *Rosinante*, an 18ft Mirror Offshore. In 1996 he took his fourth yacht, his beloved *Tetra*, to SE Asia and back for the research for *Indian Ocean Cruising Guide*. Apart from sailing the 'wrong' way and back again the 'right' way across the Indian Ocean, he has done four transatlantics on his own yachts and also cruised extensively in other parts of the world on other yachts. He is currently in the Indian Ocean on his way back to the Mediterranean at the end of a circumnavigation collecting information for this edition.

Other books by Rod Heikell
Imray Mediterranean Almanac (editor)
Mediterranean Cruising Handbook
Mediterranean France & Corsica Pilot
Mediterranean Sailing
Greek Waters Pilot
Ionian
West Aegean
East Aegean
Italian Waters Pilot
Turkish Waters and Cyprus Pilot
The Turquoise Coast of Turkey
The Danube – A river guide
Yacht Charter Handbook
Indian Ocean Cruising Guide
Dorling Kindersley Eyewitness Companion Sailing (contributor)
Mediterranean Islands (contributor)
Sailing in Paradise: Yacht Charter Around the World

Skylax

ANDY O'GRADY

Andy O,Grady grew up sailing dinghies on the Isle of Wight in the south of England and later graduated to his father's 28-foot cruising boat. In this and friends' boats he sailed European waters between Sweden and Greece. After graduating from medical school in 1980 he sailed to New Zealand, via the Caribbean, Panama and Polynesia, in a 26-foot, 40-year-old wooden boat. He built *Balaena*, a 42ft gaff cutter, while working full time as a doctor in New Zealand. Aboard *Balaena* he has cruised extensively in New Zealand, the southwest Pacific, New Guinea and Indonesia and circumnavigated Australia. Since 1999 the boat has been his home and has visited Patagonia and South Georgia, then via the Caribbean to Labrador, Greenland, Scandinavia, Spain, Brazil, Argentina and Antarctica. Andy is once again cruising in his beloved Chilean Patagonia.

With Ulla Norlander, as well as writing for magazines, he has edited the RCC Pilotage Foundation's *Chile and Argentina* and written a short guide for South Georgia.

Other books by Andy O'Grady
Chile RCC Pilotage Foundation

Balaena

WARWICK CLAY

Warwick Clay was born in New Zealand. He grew up beside the sea in Auckland and was briefly in the New Zealand Navy. Following many years of yacht cruising and racing in his own yachts, success in ocean racing led him and his wife Janet to build an ocean cruising yacht. The designer, Laurie Davidson, was asked to modify his 10.7m design for ocean cruising in remote areas. *Transcender* proved to be a very fast cruiser. He sailed three circuits in the South Pacific in this yacht, as well as a circumnavigation, and circuits of the Mediterranean and the Caribbean. While sailing the Pacific he found many beautiful anchorages uncharted, in fact whole coastlines uncharted or with very bad errors. This led him to draw up chartlets of these anchorages and eventually led the the publication of these in his book, *South Pacific Anchorages*.

Sailing Books by Warwick Clay
South Pacific Anchorages
Downwind around Australia and Africa.

KEY TO SYMBOLS USED ON PLANS

3 5 2 : depths in METRES

<1 : shallow water with a depth of 1 metre or less

: drying (mud or sand)

: coral

: rocks with less than 2 metres depth over them

: rock just below or on the surface

(2) : a shoal or reef with the least depth shown

: wreck partially above water

: eddies

: overfalls

: wreck

4 Wk : dangerous wreck

: rock ballasting on a mole or breakwater

: above-water rocks

: cliffs

: harbour with yacht berths

: yacht harbour/marina

: anchorage

: prohibited anchorage

: mosque

: church

: windmill

: chimney

: castle or fort

: airport

: ruins

: houses/buildings

: harbour master or port police

: fish farm

: customs

: travel-hoist

: yacht club

: water

: fuel

: post office

: Telecommunications

: Tourist information

: mangroves

: palms

: electricity

: waypoint

: yacht berth

: Local boats (usually shallow or reserved)

: bn

: port hand buoy

: starboard hand buoy

: mooring buoy

Characteristics

: Light

: Lighthouse

F : fixed

Fl. : flash

Fl(2) : group flash

Oc. : occulting

R : red

G : green

W : white

m : metres

M : miles

s : sand

m : mud

w : weed

r : rock

co : coral

Welcome aboard!

Like everything to do with the study of the oceans, we do not consider this a completed work. We have got this far with the help of many people, and now it is over to you, the people who make these passages, to add to the total body of information and opinion. We will partly judge the success of the book by the amount of feedback received. Even letters confirming that our information was correct or of use are invaluable. In particular, we will welcome the pointing out of errors and corrections of items that have gone out of date. Corrections and improvements will be available at the Imray website (www.imray.com) and later in a second edition. Please send your comments to either author at: ilnw@imray.com

INTRODUCTION

USING THIS BOOK

This book was a rewarding collaboration between the two authors who pulled together information from over 60 years of combined experience with contributions from other cruising yachtsmen in every corner of the world.

Below there is a complete schema for the book. It is important to note that the extent and depth of the description under each title or sub-title depends on the importance attached to it in terms of passage-making and on the subsequent landfall. Some entries will have a full description and additional maps whereas others will have a comparatively meagre description. To some extent this is a subjective appraisal by the authors, although we have endeavoured to research the subject and discuss our findings with as many cruising yachtsmen and women out there on the water as possible.

CHAPTER CONTENTS AND ORDER

The book starts in the Atlantic and follows a common circumnavigation via the Pacific and Indian Oceans and back into the Atlantic via the Mediterranean or South Africa. The exception is that the North and South Pacific and Atlantic are grouped together. Trans-equatorial passages and passages from the Southern Ocean towards the equator will require a bit of page-turning to sort out some routes. The text is illustrated by maps (of winds, gales, tropical storms, currents, etc.) which illustrate the subject. The maxim that 'a picture is worth a thousand words' applies here.

Note When we refer to seasons such as summer or winter, this is the 'local' hemispheric season. Remember that the northern hemisphere summer is the winter in the southern hemisphere and vice versa.

Each chapter describes the following:

Weather and Sea

Prevailing winds Describes the general oceanic circulation of winds and specific descriptions of trade winds and monsoonal winds and the Intertropical Convergence Zone (ITCZ).

Gales Describes the typical passages of depressions and instances where the prevailing winds can get up to a yachtsman's gale (Force 7) or more.

Tropical storms The season for tropical storms often limits when passages are made. Tropical storms can develop into hurricanes and passages are normally made out of the hurricane season for pretty obvious reasons. Hurricanes are called cyclones in the Indian Ocean and South Pacific and typhoons in the NW Pacific.

Currents Describes the general oceanic circulation of currents. On many passages a route which detours from the rhumb line can often pay dividends by making use of a favourable current or avoiding an unfavourable current.

Ice Describes the likely limits of pack ice and icebergs where applicable.

Fog Describes areas where fog is common.

Routes and passages

Each route has the following information (where applicable) and then a general description of the route. The example given below is for NAW1 route in the North Atlantic.

Name of the route (e.g. **NAW1** Western Europe and the Mediterranean to the Canaries.)

Distances between key ports or anchorages (e.g. Falmouth to Cape Finisterre 450M/Porto to Las Palmas 840M/Gibraltar to Madeira 610M/Madeira to Las Palmas 265M/Gibraltar to Las Palmas 710M)

Season The typical season for a cruising yacht to sail this route (e.g. May to November)

Best time The best time (if different) within the season to sail this route (e.g. Northern Europe to Spain and Portugal July-August/Spain and Portugal to Madeira and Canaries August–mid-October/Gibraltar to Canaries August–October)

Tropical storms The time of year when tropical storms can affect this route. (e.g. None for NAW1)

The text describes routes going westwards, the 'normal' direction of a circumnavigation, with an acronym relating to the ocean and the direction. So NAW1 describes a route for the North Atlantic going westwards. These descriptions contain very basic information on the route and any incidental information the authors consider useful. The description should be used in conjunction with information on prevailing winds, gale frequencies, tropical storm information and currents. Pilot charts will give additional information. Although, as has often been pointed out, pilot charts only give an average over a monthly period collated over the last hundred years or so, that is to some extent misleading. It pays to remember that an average wind strength like the Force 4–5 typically given for the NE Trades in the North Atlantic in November and December is made up of the steady trades plus frequent squalls with winds up to Force 6–7 and days of calm. In the end, this information and experience is the best we have to go on. In the text the sort of weather conditions you are likely to encounter will be mentioned.

Country and port guide

This section contains a description and plans for the common destinations on the routes described above. Country details are only given where a nation's ports or anchorage are described and not for all the countries along the way. The country information is necessarily condensed so that this book does not get too big and we hope that you will flesh it out with local cruising and land guides.

Country details are as follows:

National flag (or ensign)

General A brief description of the country with the emphasis on visiting under sail.

Coastline Where useful, a brief description of the coastline and islands for that country.

Formalities Clearing in and out and any other information pertinent to boat and crew.

Telecom IDD code and whether there is a GSM network and internet access.

Currency Unit of currency and whether there are ATMs and credit cards are accepted.

Sailing season Normal sailing season and some pointers to the usual conditions to be expected.

Routes and harbours Brief description of cruising areas and routes in and out of the country.

The section detailing ports and/or anchorages contains only those places commonly used on various routes. There is a subjective element to this although the authors have tried to canvas opinion from other cruisers. In some cases they may be the only practical port, such as Galle in Sri Lanka. Others are detailed because a regatta like the ARC starts and finishes there (Las Palmas in the Canaries and Rodney Bay in St Lucia respectively). Some are considered a better option by the authors rather than a more commonly known harbour nearby (Piriapolis gets the vote over Punta del Este in Uruguay). There is bound to be debate over ports that have been included and those that have been omitted. We have tried to include places where a yacht could find a comfortable marina or anchorage, change crew, re-provision or undertake repairs. Those not in need of such facilities may well prefer to visit less developed locations, bearing in mind the almost universal requirement to arrive at a Port of Entry for completion of formalities. The authors recommend that cruisers make a small investment in cruising guides for the areas they intend to visit, on the basis that this will make your cruising in the area more informed and a lot more enjoyable.

Port and/or anchorage details are as follows:

Waypoints are listed for each port and are included on the plans.

Tidal range (the range is at springs only).

Navigation Approaches and dangers to navigation.

Berths Harbour data. Unless otherwise mentioned it can be assumed the harbour is well sheltered in settled weather conditions.

Anchorage Possible anchorages, shelter and holding.

Facilities Harbour and shore facilities. Necessarily brief and not meant to be all-inclusive.

Remarks Any other general remarks.

Resources A selection of cruising guides and web addresses we think are useful.

In places there may be brief notes relating to security, piracy, and other important information.

The key for the plans, as well as general notes on using the maps and plans in this book, can be found opposite page 1.

CRUISING DESTINATIONS PAGES

Throughout the book we have included pages on cruising areas and some popular passages like the 'Coconut Milk Run' and the 'Atlantic Circuit'. These pages supply additional information on cruising in areas from Greenland to Antarctica with some warm bits in between. They contain a diverse amount of information based on our experiences in these areas and we have also included some photos to give you a taste of what an area is like. There is a more or less standard format described below, although because of the diversity of the areas covered, the pages often stray from this format to accommodate the sort of information we think will be useful there.

During the life of this edition we will be putting more of these pages up on the Imray website in the annual supplement at www.imray.com.

Cruising destination page structure

Seasons and winds
Normal season to cruise the destination and what sort of weather to expect.

Ashore
Provisions and restaurants and bars and a few things to see and do.

Facilities
Yacht facilities in the area.

Reading
Pilotage for the area.

My gem
One non-pilotage book we would take to read for the destination described. The choice is personal and we only allowed ourselves one book for an area.

Photographs are all by Rod Heikell, Andy O'Grady, Lu Michell and Ulla Norlander unless otherwise stated.

Cruising strategies
Getting to and from the destination and getting around the cruising area.

Weather resources for an Ocean Passage

An invaluable resource for weather information via radio and Internet is the US National Weather Service (NWS) Worldwide Marine Radiofacsimile Broadcast Schedules. This is available for download at www.nws.noaa.gov/om/marine/rfax.pdf Many yachting magazines have also published good articles on this subject.

The authors know of the following methods of obtaining weather information (in order of complexity and cost) on the high seas:

WWV AND WWVH

These two stations, in Colorado and Hawaii, can be received on a simple short wave radio without SSB and often without an external antenna; their main purpose is to provide time checks. They also provide information on the position and expected movement of major weather systems. Broadcasts are continuous on 2.5, 5, 10, 15 and 20MHz. WWV broadcasts Atlantic information at eight and nine minutes past the hour and for the Pacific at 10 minutes past. WWVH provides Pacific information between 48 and 50 minutes past the hour.

NAVTEX

A NAVTEX receiver works for most of the world on 518KHz with a nominal range of 400M from the coastal station. In practice the range is often greater, up to 1,000M+ for Miami in the Atlantic in one author's (RJH) experience. Weather forecast details can vary according to the shore station, but are often comprehensive with gale and tropical storm warnings. It is relatively cheap to buy, and once installed can be left on and programmed to receive selected information.

SSB VOICE BROADCASTS

Many nations broadcast these; some are mentioned in the text. More details can be found in the Admiralty *List of Radio Signals*. A SSB receiver is required.

HAM AND SSB NETS

Several of these are listed in the book. The information given is often very relevant, as the person giving the forecast may be a yachtsman with experience of the waters in question. An SSB receiver is required (many people listen without transmitting).

SSB FACSIMILE RECEPTION

Given a simple software program, faxes can be received with an SSB receiver and PC. Some stations are given in the ocean chapters but you will find much more detail in the NWS schedule. Modern programs use the sound card of the PC to receive the fax from an SSB capable radio, so no extra hardware is required. Suitable programs include JVCOMM32, and Xaxero Weather Fax 2000, which are available as trial versions from www.jvcomm.de or www.xaxero.com

Many people experience problems with fax reception. The best thing you can do is to find a sailing radio amateur to help you. Failing this, the following may help. Remember that the set is usually tuned about 1.7kHz below the published frequency on upper sideband. At sea, broadcasts are often heard best on frequencies between 10 and 16MHz. Choose a much lower frequency when close to the station. It helps to have a choice of frequencies for a particular station programmed into the receiver. Reception is often better around dusk and dawn. Inverters are a common source of interference; if a clear signal is not received use a laptop run from its batteries and try turning off all other electrics on board. The need for a good antenna (often a stay or shroud) is obvious; grounding a metal part of the frame of the receiver can also make a big difference. Get used to the sound of a good fax signal and don't be afraid to try fine adjustment to the tuning to make the picture clearer.

SATELLITE WEATHER SERVICES

Users of Inmarsat will receive weather information as part of some service packages.

EMAIL DOWNLOADS

Many yachts have the ability to send and receive email via SSB, HAM radio, Inmarsat or other satellite phone. It is possible to request specific weather products from a variety of sources. The two most useful are the catalogue of products available to Hams on the Winlink system and ftp downloads from the US NWS. Both have forecasts, weather maps and other information covering the world's oceans. Instructions on how to use the NWS are found in the *Worldwide Marine Radiofacsimile Broadcast Schedules,* or can be obtained by sending the following email: To: ftpmail@weather.noaa.gov Subject: blank, Message: Help. Though the format of a requesting email is complex and must be correct in every detail, in practice it is quite a simple system as the requesting email can be saved and a copy sent whenever the information is required.

GRIB FILE DOWNLOADS

Grib files are a collection of weather information for a specified area and squares of latitude and longitude selected by the user. Information is for up to 14 days in advance and is often uncannily accurate, especially out at sea and away from the disturbing influence of land. Requests can be made to automatically receive the files daily for up to 14 days. The Airmail program, used by those who connect on the Winlink and Sailmail systems, has a neat way to request grib files. Otherwise *Email* query@saildocs.com with the message: Send gribinfo for a detailed description on how to subscribe. If not using an automated program to request files, the sending email can be saved for future use. Grib files need a program to display them. Several common PC navigation programs (e.g. Raytech, Maxsea) have the ability to request and display grib files, as does a nice little add-on to airmail.

Although grib files are handy for looking at weather they do have limitations. Most cruisers reckon you can add between 5 and 8 knots to the predicted windspeeds. Grib files are also poor at showing squall activity and in particular small lows developing in convergence zones. Its worth using them in conjunction with weather faxes showing isobars where small 'bumps' in the isobars are more easily picked up indicating that there may be something a bit nasty around.

ROUTEING SERVICES

Several individuals and organisations provide professional advice on weather and routeing to yachtsmen. Communication may be via satellite phone, SSB or email. A short internet search will find several possibilities.

DIRECT INTERNET ACCESS

Using Inmarsat (not Inmarsat C or Mini-M but the much larger and more costly systems intended for big ships), some yachts may have access to the internet. A very wide range of weather services is then available in addition to many of those mentioned above. A good place to start looking is www.nws.noaa.gov

OTHER RESOURCES

www.sailmail.com/smprimer.htm
www.airmail2000.com/rfi.htm
Intended for users of radio email systems, these sites have links to weather routeing services and many useful hints on connecting radios to computers and dealing with interference.

http://buoyweather.com/
Buoy weather provides a very economical, user pays, service for forwarding weather forecasts for a specified region to an email address.

ITCZ

The Intertropical Convergence Zone (ITCZ), can be simply defined as the convergence zones of northern and southern weather systems around the equator. More properly, the ITCZ is a complex interaction of weather and oceanic factors demarcating a meteorological equator. The ITCZ lies around the equatorial trough where the prevailing winds in the northern and southern hemisphere meet to form a low pressure feature. These prevailing (trade) winds, laden with heat and moisture after their passage across the sea, converge to form a zone of increased convection, rain and cloudiness. Although the prevailing winds provide the engine for the ITCZ, oceanic factors like the prevailing surface currents and deep ocean bottom-currents causing an upwelling of colder water, and the warm surface water carried by the prevailing swell, also influence the formation of the ITCZ. The ITCZ plays a critical role in the global weather picture, restoring equilibrium by the release of latent energy generated by the prevailing winds in their passage over the sea.

In sailing terms the ITCZ is neither simple to pin down nor well understood. Let us get a few misconceptions out of the way and make some general comments on the ITCZ.

- The ITCZ is not always a well defined area. It can be a zone perhaps 50 miles wide with well-established limits, or it can extend over 300 miles with ill-defined boundaries.
- The ITCZ does not stay in the same place at any given period. Although the maps show the average position of the ITCZ for the time of year, this is only an average as the ITCZ is continually shifting in response to weather systems and can be a long way N or S of its given position before moving back again.
- Although the ITCZ is called the 'doldrums' (specifically in the Atlantic), it is not always a windless zone with calm seas. There will frequently be violent thunderstorms and sometimes only a few days of calm. You can have wind from variable directions, often strong, and awkward seas for long periods. The wind will often be variable, although towards the boundaries of the zone the winds become more consistent and more or less from the direction of the prevailing wind outside the ITCZ zone.
- There can be frequent squalls with torrential rain, sometimes continuous for days on end. We have both experienced crossings with days of continuous solid torrential rain, squalls up to 50 knots and continuous cloud cover in the Atlantic, Pacific and Indian Ocean ITCZs. The effects on morale of sailing in the ITCZ should not be underestimated.
- The lightning displays can be dramatic and scary. We have seen ball lightning and St Elmo's fire in the ITCZ, most of us do not want to witness these weird displays of atmospheric ionisation.
- Weather faxes and to some extent 'grib' files show the position of the ITCZ but you should not be surprised to find that by the time you get to the reputed position it is somewhere else entirely.
- In some of the oceans there are effectively two convergence zones which may converge at times. This has been reasonably well documented for the Pacific and Indian Oceans and recent satellite photos have demonstrated the existence of an Atlantic double convergence zone.

In truth, getting through the ITCZ, whether you are stuck in it on an outer edge or cutting across it, is a matter of luck. Because the ITCZ zone changes not just seasonally but also daily, you may have just a day or so of variable winds and calms or you can get a week of variable winds, thunderstorms, rain and awkward seas. It pays to keep in touch with other yachts on HF to get an exact picture of what is going on, although even a few days later ITCZ boundaries can change dramatically.

Tropical storm avoidance

WARNING SIGNS

If you are not on the receiving end of HF communications or a weatherfax warning of a developing cyclone, there are a number of warning signs of a developing cyclone which can give some indication of what is going on. In practice, though, it can all be a bit vague.

- If you have a barometer corrected for height, latitude, and temperature and you are equipped with tables for the diurnal variation, then a sudden drop of three millibars below the mean pressure for the time of year should put you on your guard. If there is a drop of five millibars or more then it is definitely time to take avoiding action and the likelihood is that you are already experiencing an increase in wind strength.
- If there is an abrupt change in wind direction and strength this is a good indication of an approaching tropical storm, assuming you are not in the ITCZ or there is a thunderstorm in the vicinity. Buys Ballot's Law states that if you face into the wind the centre of the storm will be around 100°–125° on the right-hand side in the northern hemisphere and on the left-hand side in the southern hemisphere. This will be when the eye of the storm is about 200 miles away. As the centre gets closer the angle becomes nearer to 090°.
- A long low swell, usually with a long period, contrary to the prevailing swell, will sometimes emanate from the eye of the storm. Most yachties are pretty tuned in to the pattern of swell when on passage and contrary swell with a long period can be a useful indicator.
- Solid amounts of cirrus followed by altostratus and then broken cumulus advertise the approach of a tropical storm.

AVOIDING ACTION

If a tropical storm is known to be forming or the signs are that one may, it is necessary for all sailing yachts to take avoiding action in the early stages. Basically the action is to head for the equator if you are on a typical east or westabout passage along the principal sailing routes.

In the northern hemisphere the storm revolves in an anticlockwise direction and travels somewhere between W–NW and possibly recurving to the NE. If you are to the E of the storm, it is necessary to head towards the equator in whatever fashion you can. This will be difficult because the winds will be predominantly SW–S, but you will just have to do the best you can. Even making little progress and heaving to and making headway to the S is better than 'following' the storm which will only bring you closer to stronger winds. If you are W of the storm, proceeding S towards the equator will be easier because winds will be mostly N–NW.

Quarterly wind charts for the world

EXPLANATORY NOTES FOR PAGES 6–13

The charts have been prepared using the data in the DMA pilot charts which is provided for each month, with the exception of the South Atlantic which is given for each quarter. This meant three months wind data had to be condensed into one. In places, such as the Indian Ocean with its monsoons this may give rather confusing results (see the Introduction to the chapter for Indian Ocean for more details of the Monsoons). It is hoped that the format will provide a more easily understood display of wind trends for the oceans. Obviously those wishing to obtain more detail should refer to the original pilot charts.

The single arrow is intended to give a representation of the most predominant quadrant from which the wind blows. In temperate areas there is a great deal of variability and the direction given may not occur that often. The figure represented by the length of the arrow indicates the percentage of time wind blows from that direction and 45° to either side. Where this figure is small (short arrows) winds from other directions are fairly frequent.

The thickness and colour of arrows represents average wind strength from the given quadrant. Again, especially in temperate and equatorial areas, there is much variability. Where the figure is over Force 5 stronger winds may be very frequent, where it is below three calms may occur frequently.

Figures for calms and gales are percentages in the range 0–5, 5–10, 10–15 and so on.

In high latitudes the data from pilot charts becomes unreliable because few boats have reported weather observations in these areas. In places the data on the official charts does not make sense. Data has been interpolated from adjacent areas, these figures are indicated by a double exclamation mark and grey background but in most cases the data is omitted. In any case very few yachts will venture into these waters.

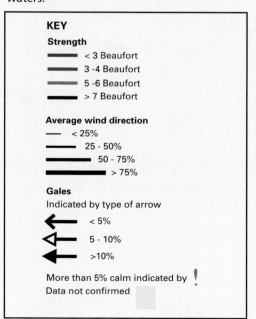

KEY

Strength
— < 3 Beaufort
— 3 -4 Beaufort
— 5 -6 Beaufort
— > 7 Beaufort

Average wind direction
— < 25%
— 25 - 50%
— 50 - 75%
— > 75%

Gales
Indicated by type of arrow
← < 5%
← 5 - 10%
← >10%

More than 5% calm indicated by !
Data not confirmed ▨

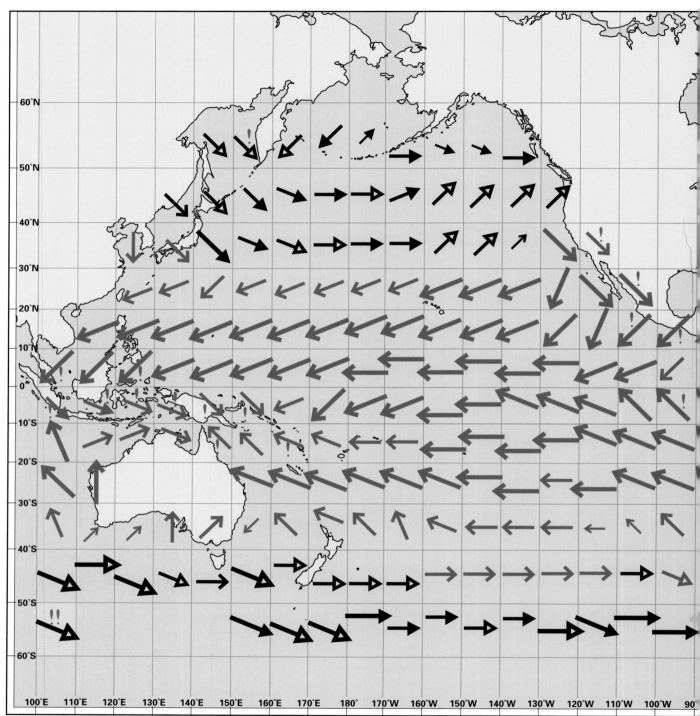

WINDS - SUMMARY OF OBSERVATIONS JANUARY - MARCH

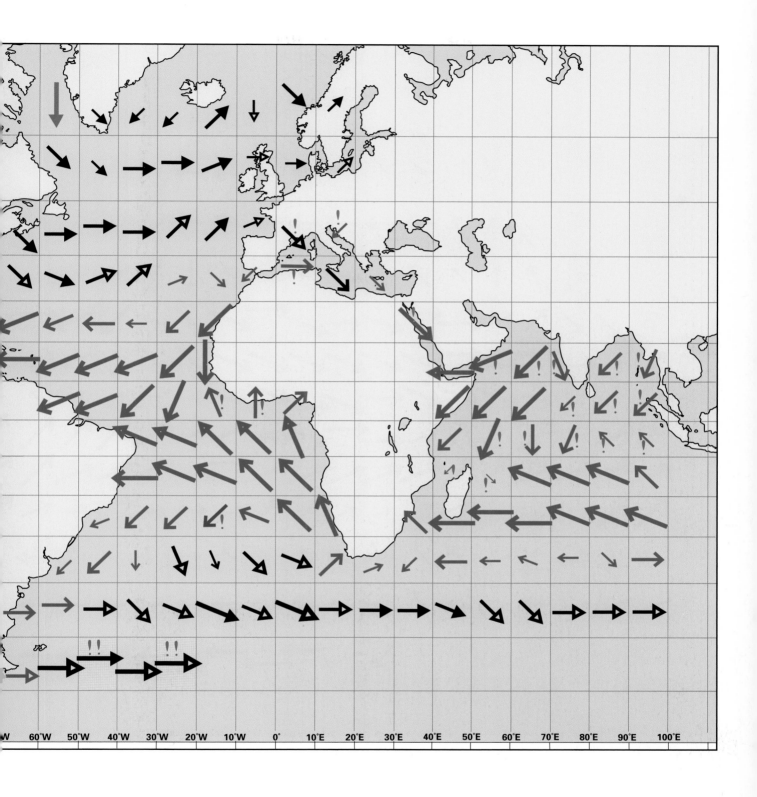

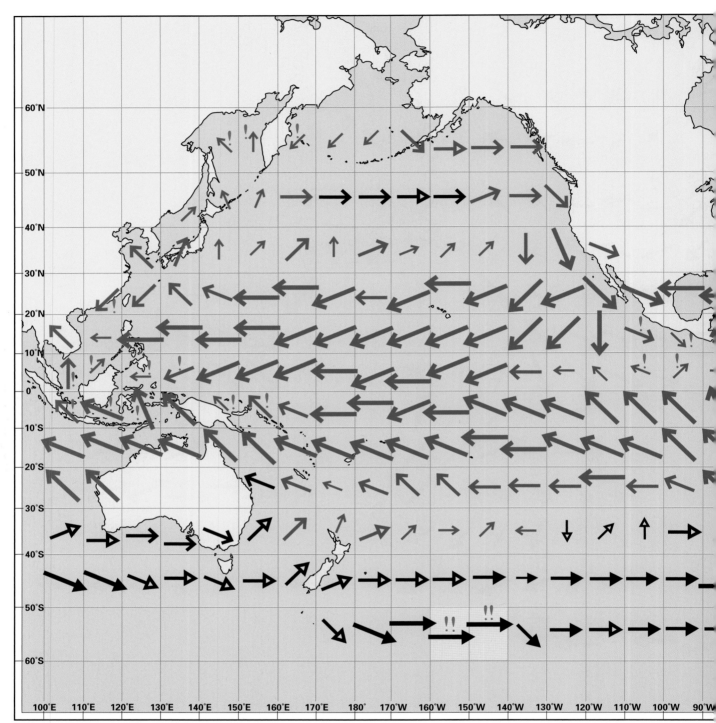

WINDS - SUMMARY OF OBSERVATIONS APRIL - JUNE

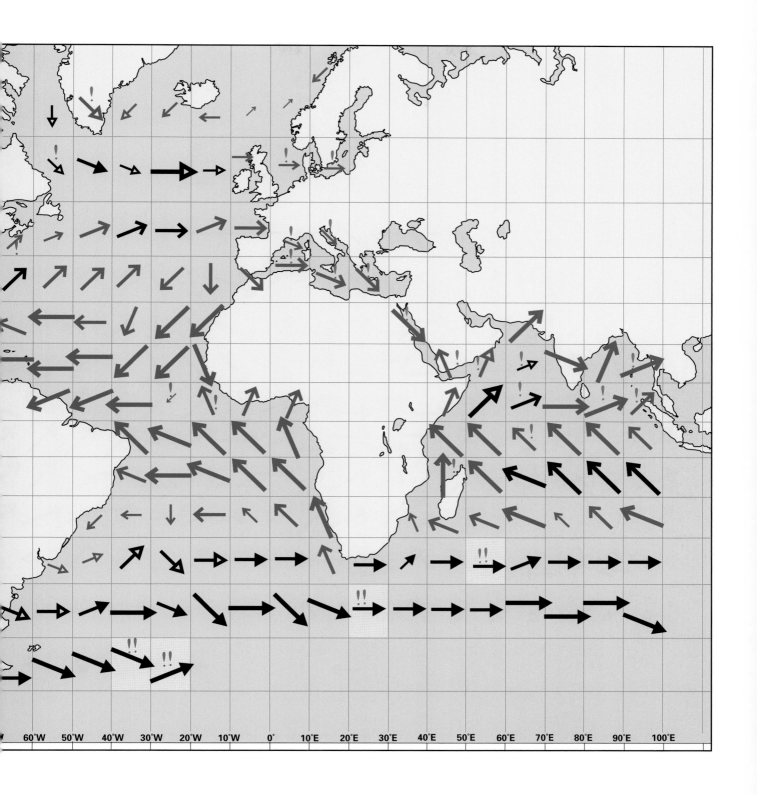

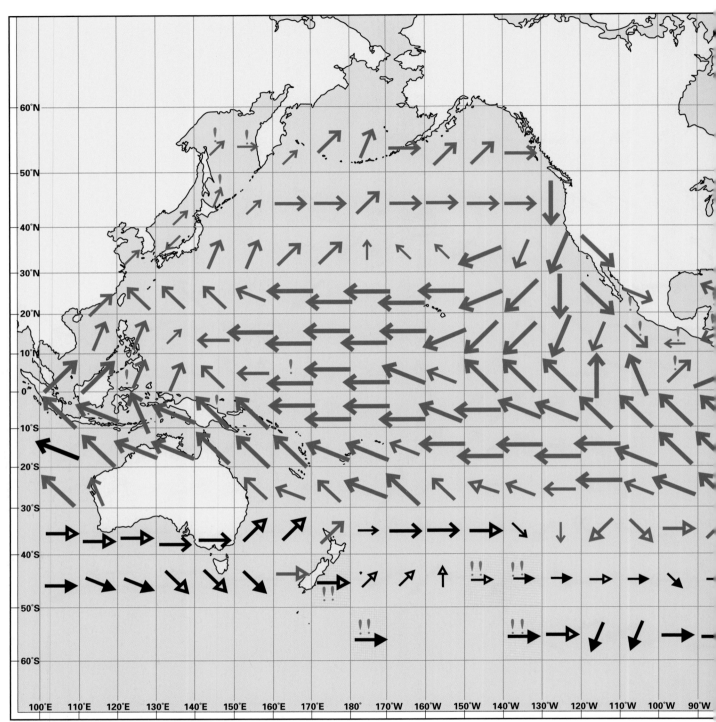

WINDS - SUMMARY OF OBSERVATIONS JULY - SEPTEMBER

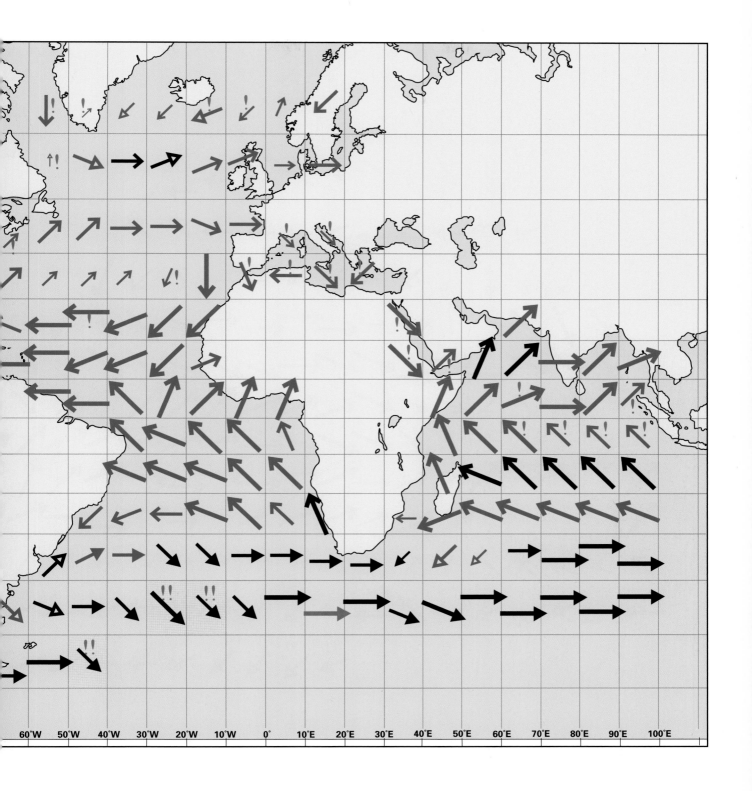

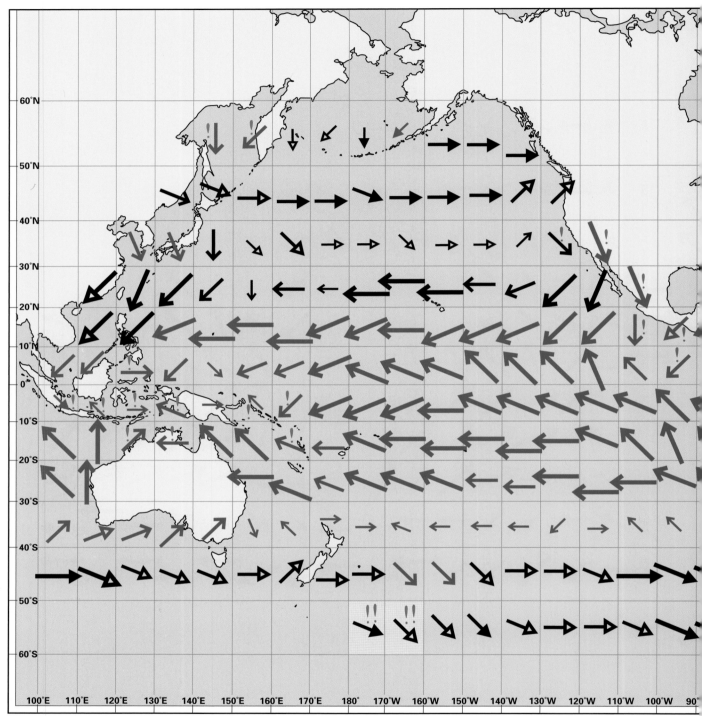

WINDS - SUMMARY OF OBSERVATIONS OCTOBER - DECEMBER

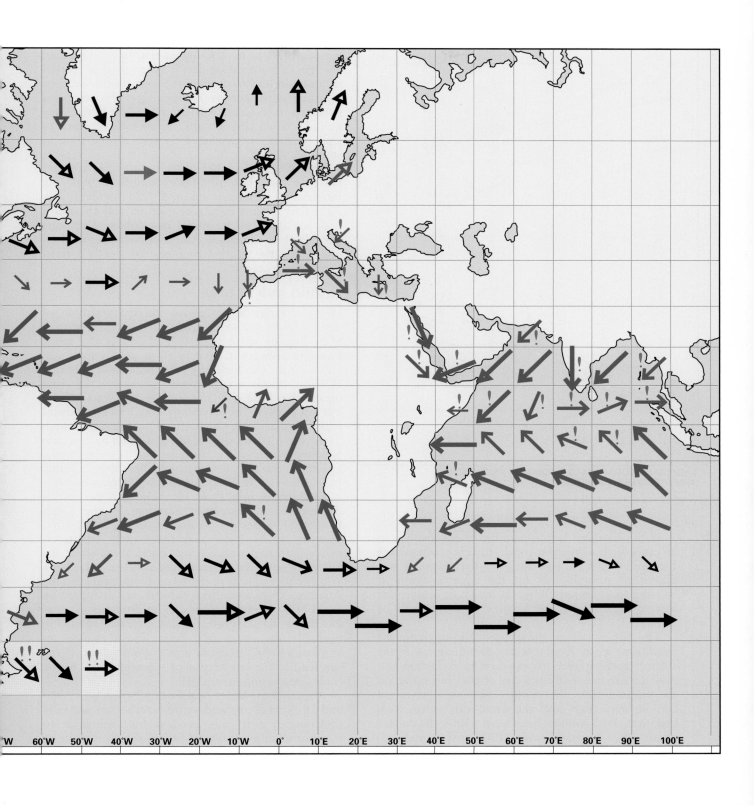

60°W 50°W 40°W 30°W 20°W 10°W 0° 10°E 20°E 30°E 40°E 50°E 60°E 70°E 80°E 90°E 100°E

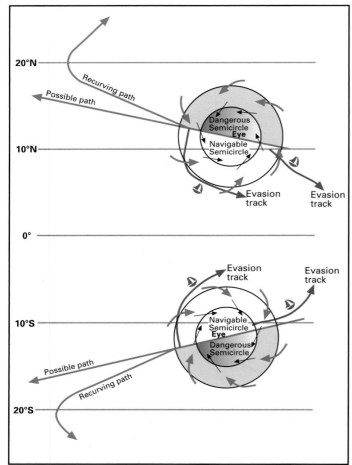

TROPICAL STORM TRACKS FOR NORTHERN AND SOUTHERN HEMISPHERES

In the southern hemisphere the storm revolves in a clockwise direction and travels somewhere between W–SW. If you are E of the storm, it is a matter of struggling N for the equator again or heaving to. If you are W of the storm, it is an easier matter to head for the equator as winds will be S–SW.

The diagram shows the scenario, although not the conditions at sea. Even towards the equator with the storm travelling away from you it is likely that you may have to heave-to for a day or two depending on the distance from the storm. The waves generated can be very high and the swell can travel long distances. Both authors have been within the danger sector of a tropical storm (<200 miles) and can vouch for the seas generated and the cross-seas that result.

For weather information on tropical storms and forecasts see the relevant section in each chapter.

CLIMATE CHANGE

Most climatologists believe that global warming is occurring and that some general conclusions can be drawn from the data that is available. Studies of El Niño off the South American coast from 1990–1995 point to the longest period of warming in 130 years of records. In the last century the average global temperature rose by 0.5°C. A conservative estimate of the rise in global warming by 2100 is for temperatures to be 2°C higher than in 1990. Small changes in temperature over a relatively short period of time can lead to dramatic changes in the weather. Warming of the oceans (not melting of the icecaps) is expected to cause sea levels to rise 50cm in the same period. When the oceans' temperatures start to change, they are predicted to take a long time to stabilise.

The effects of global warming are that weather patterns may become more disturbed, with big fluctuations between hot and cold temperatures. Rain may be less evenly distributed and there is a high likelihood of torrential rain followed by long periods of no rain at all. And in terms of depressions and storms the weather becomes less clearly defined between the seasons.

EL NIÑO AND LA NIÑA

El Niño refers to an above average warming of equatorial Pacific waters and, conversely, La Niña to a cooling of these waters. El Niño is the name Peruvian fishermen gave to these events long ago and it means the 'little boy' or 'Christ child', because El Niño usually occurs around Christmas. La Niña means the 'little girl' and usually follows El Niño, but not always. The warming of the waters produces high cloud activity which affects the jet stream high in the earth's atmosphere and this leads to dramatic weather events as far away as the western Pacific coastline, the Indian Ocean and northern Atlantic. In recent years El Niño events have increased.

El Niño is important to yachtsmen because it disrupts normal weather patterns. In the South Pacific the trades are weakened during an El Niño year. In an El Niño year the North Atlantic is believed to experience fewer hurricanes, while the Eastern Pacific has an increased number. A La Niña year is believed to give rise to more hurricanes in the Atlantic. Tropical rainfall patterns are disrupted by an El Niño year and there can be droughts in areas like Indonesia and Australia and increased rainfall in normally dry areas like Peru. These changes in tropical rainfall patterns affect wind patterns and can lead to the late arrival of monsoons and to the trades decreasing in strength.

Although the exact relationship between El Niño and La Niña events and world weather are not fully understood, it is only prudent for yachtsmen to monitor whether or not an El Niño event is going to happen and look at possible predictions for unusual weather events. At its simplest, El Niño can point to the possibility of fewer early or late season hurricanes in the North Atlantic and light trade winds in the South Pacific.

ENSO

El Niño and La Niña events lead to a see-saw oscillation of sea level pressure in the western and eastern Pacific. This is called the Southern Oscillation (SO). The SO is usually measured

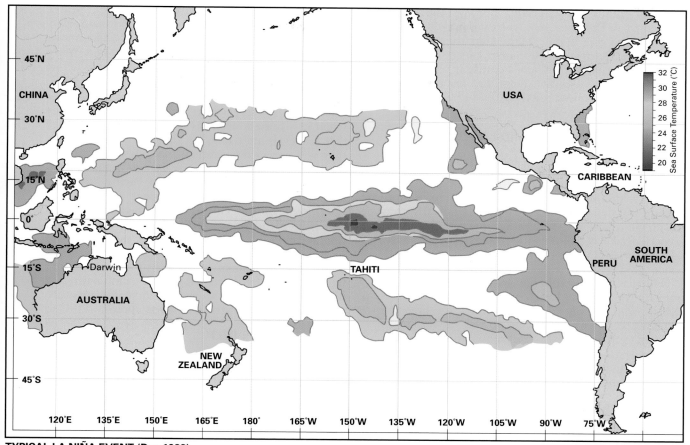

TYPICAL LA NIÑA EVENT (Dec 1988)

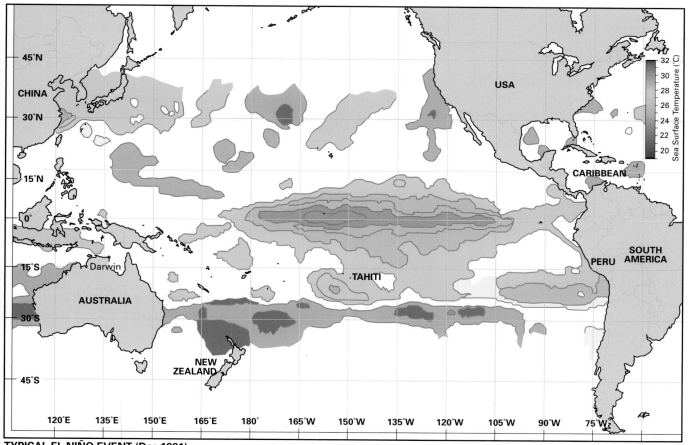

TYPICAL EL NIÑO EVENT (Dec 1991)

between Tahiti and Darwin. Because the SO is related to an El Niño event, the two terms are often combined to give ENSO. Many climatologists agree that the usage of all these names can be confusing and we mention ENSO here because it has become fashionable to use the term to describe what everyone else has been referring to as El Niño and La Niña events.

TROPICAL STORMS AND MID-LATITUDE HURRICANES

Changes of frequency have occurred in El Niño years. There does not appear to be an increase in intensity, although hurricane tracks seem to be more erratic and there is evidence of more tropical storms in previously low risk months. One author (RJH) experienced a North Atlantic tropical storm in early December 2003, the first recorded in this month since 1887.

Hurricanes and typhoons grab the headlines, but mid-latitude hurricanes or extratropical storms which originate outside normal hurricane breeding grounds are of more concern to the yachtsman or woman as they affect seas and coasts not normally in hurricane areas. Studies point to an increase in storm intensity and a trend to increasing winds and wave heights in the North Atlantic since the 1980s.

SAILING SEASONS

One consequence of global warming is likely to be less settled weather in the temperate summer and tropical winter. Normally predictable trade winds and monsoonal winds could be delayed and there may be more gales than the norm. At a gut level the authors and other experienced yachtsmen believe that weather patterns are shifting.

WATERSPOUTS AND TORNADOES

These have wind speeds in the 50–100 knot band. Double-funnel spouts with possible wind speeds up to 400 mph have recently been recorded and studied, notably on the east coast of the USA. These water tornadoes are significantly bigger and more violent than waterspouts and do not appear to break up when moving from the land to the sea or vice versa. Whether they are connected to global warming is difficult to know, but theoretically it would seem likely that localised patches of hot and cold air resulting from global warming could produce bigger and more violent waterspouts.

RAINFALL

Rainfall already appears to be conforming to predictions, with heavy precipitation over short periods becoming common and a shift in regional precipitation patterns occurring. Global warming means that there will be more rain overall and it will fall in different regions and in heavy downpours.

Flooding of river estuaries will become more common and flash floods can cause a lot of damage to vessels and to marinas within rivers and estuaries. While global warming brings more rain, it will mostly be distributed in high northerly latitudes. For yachtsmen cruising to lower latitudes, water shortages are likely to become a real problem, as is already a reality in some areas of the Mediterranean and Caribbean, and it will be more and more difficult to find good potable water.

SEA LEVELS

The rise in sea level occurs because water expands when it is heated. There is no dispute over the fact that sea levels are rising, but there is over how much they will rise in this century. Nations which live on atolls like the Maldives (rarely more than 2.5m above sea level) and a number of Pacific atolls are concerned that they may disappear off the map. Large areas of low-lying and reclaimed land such as the Netherlands and the east coast USA could become unusable because of storm surges coupled with the increased sea level.

For the yachtsman it is likely that some yacht harbours will be destroyed by the combination of higher sea levels and storms of increased intensity producing highly destructive storm surges.

THE 'CONVEYOR BELT'

This is the clockwise circulation of water in the Northern Atlantic. The warm Gulf Stream flows up the east coast of the USA and then turns eastwards towards Britain. This keeps northern Europe warm when on the opposite side of the ocean there is an icy wilderness where the sea ices over in winter. Off Europe the heavy salt-laden current sinks and travels clockwise down to the Tropics where it warms up, crosses the ocean and begins its circulation along the east coast of the USA again. Fresh water from the melting polar ice sheets dilutes the Gulf Stream in the north and at some (unknown) dilution this can act to turn the current off. Meteorologists believe that if the 'conveyor belt' is turned off or damaged, the climate of northern Europe may cool dramatically over a period as short as a decade. It should be mentioned that this theory is disputed by some climatologists who believe the fresh/salt oscillation is a normal event that would not affect the 'conveyor belt'.

DESTRUCTION OF NATURAL HABITATS

Increased sea levels also affect natural habitats like estuarine wetlands and it is likely that many of these will disappear along with the bird and marine life associated with them. Coral reefs are formed over tens of thousands of years, and although they look robust, especially if you accidentally nudge them with the boat, in fact they are delicately balanced ecosystems. Reefs are being affected by global warming as warmer tropical waters kill the algae, which reef animals use for food. They are already disappearing at a frightening rate from man-made causes (one tenth of all reefs have been destroyed and the WWF predicts that another third will be lost in the next couple of decades) and global warming will exacerbate this destruction. A few years ago in the Seychelles one author (RJH) noticed that large areas of reef were dead and the other (AO'G) noticed a severe degradation in reefs in Grenada when he returned after a 20-year absence.

In other areas algal blooms have occurred, some of which can result in the build-up of toxins in shellfish, the so-called 'Red Tide'.

DIRECT COSTS

As weather patterns become more variable and storm damage more frequent, the costs of yachting are likely to escalate. One area is marine insurance, which may become unobtainable in some areas. Already some large companies have stopped providing cover for long passages and others have tightened up on the sort of cover they provide, with yet more exclusion clauses. Cyclone *Val* in 1992 prompted the withdrawal of insurance agencies in the Samoan Islands, and after Hurricane *Andrew* in the Caribbean eight insurance companies went bankrupt. In 2004 many insurance companies predicted global warming could increase general insurance premiums by up to 30%.

In 2004 Hurricane *Ivan* (cat. 4–5) swept through the Caribbean and devastated Grenada before making landfall on the W coast of Florida. The S end of Grenada had previously been thought a safe area to spend the hurricane season as the last hurricane to hit here was *Janet* in 1955 and it did comparatively little damage. One of the authors' (RJH) boats was ashore for the summer hurricane season and was damaged by *Ivan*. In the future the costs of *Ivan* alone may mean that this area is not covered by insurance in the hurricane season and the costs will certainly increase premiums.

Cruising in coral

MORPHOLOGY

Coral grows at just below the surface down to 70 metres. From just below the surface down to 20 metres you get the widest variety of species and the best conditions for growth. Contrary to popular belief, coral grows very slowly, at around 0.3–0.6 metres (1–2ft) every hundred years on the ocean side and 0.5–1.5 metres (1.6–5ft) every hundred years in sheltered reef areas. These are maximum rates and are frequently slowed by storm damage or conditions that are less than ideal. Charts made from old surveys 50 or even a 100 years ago will pretty much reflect what is down there now (assuming the survey was correct in the first place). In some areas the charts are known not to be reliable, whereas in others the surveys are meticulous and are wonderful pieces of work. What has usually been missed in a survey are isolated coral heads or 'bommies'.

NAVIGATION

Both authors are surprised by how few yachtsmen go aloft when approaching coral. It is essential to keep a good lookout: going aloft not only increases your range of sight but makes the angle of the eye with the water surface less acute, which allows more detail to be seen below the surface. A pair of polarised sunglasses is essential to navigating through coral (or in relatively shallow water anywhere, for that matter). Other sunglasses will not do: only polarised glasses cut out the light from one plane and so remove much of the reflected light from the surface, making it much easier to see the relative depths in shallow water.

When approaching a reef anchorage always time the approach for between 0900 and 1400 or 1500 at the very latest. For reef approaches towards the west the approach should probably be made no later than 1300–1400, although we are nearly all guilty of later approaches. After 1400 the sun is starting to dip lower in the sky so that it is in your eyes and identifying reefs becomes a lot more difficult. For reef approaches towards the E, 1500 is OK, although time it earlier if possible. It constantly surprises us how many boats make an approach through coral late in the afternoon and for many it is sheer luck that they do not hit anything. Even with someone conning you in over the radio and utilising GPS positions, it is dangerous to approach through coral late in the afternoon. You may misunderstand an instruction or there may be bommies that the person conning you in did not see.

As a general rule the following colour coding applies for the depth of water: brown to yellow-brown means two metres or less, green 2–5 metres, blue-green 5–25 metres and dark green-blue 25 metres plus. This is in relatively calm water with the sun overhead. On days when there is scattered cloud identification is more difficult, as you will get dark shadows moving over the water which make it difficult to see what is going on. Under 10–15 metres the nature of the bottom also confuses the scheme, with sandy bottoms giving the clearest indication while rock and weed make things look darker and shallower. Weed clumps on the bottom can give you a heart attack as they look closer to the surface than a sandy bottom or light coral and it can be difficult to judge whether a patch of weed is a coral outcrop or what it actually is – weed. In disturbed water where the sand has been whipped up or blown off the shore, the water is murkier and it is more difficult to work out the depths.

Coral reefs are not normally exposed except for a few hours at MLWS. Coral cannot survive being exposed to the hot sun for more than a few hours, so in most places the coral will be just under the water or at the surface for most of low water. At high water it may well be a couple of metres under the surface. Where coral is above water it has generally been raised by the land underneath being pushed up by the tectonic plates and this is dead coral. In places coral boulders may be thrown up by storms onto the reef and these are a useful visual indication of a part of the reef.

Under 20 metres great care is needed when navigating in coral as it is in these depths that coral grows most prolifically and irregularly. Bommies grow anywhere they can, on old coral accretions, on the higher parts of submerged land, on wrecks, and can vary in size from a pillar to a fair-sized clump or small isolated reef. If you are under 20 metres and see the depth sounder fluctuating wildly, slow down and send someone aloft.

CURRENTS

Currents around the reefs are generally strong and variable in direction and it can be alarming to watch your boat being sluiced sideways through the reefs when in fact your heading is elsewhere. Currents outside reefs of any type will often have a set towards the reef (a benign phrase that could be replaced with 'reef-sucking currents' however you say it). Constant attention must be paid to currents when near to reefs as they can be as much as 2–3kn in places and inattention to your navigation can lead to catastrophic results.

LAGOON PASSES

Passes are often rather too constricted to allow the tide to readily fill and empty the lagoon so there can be strong currents and tidal races, particularly at spring tides. Some passes must only be entered at or near slack water, or at times of minimum flow in those with a constant outflow. The flow is complicated by an outflow of water from surf breaking over the reef. In small lagoons there may be a constant outgoing current and no slack water because of this factor. The current strength will vary with the state of the tide and the height and direction of the swell. This may still be a major factor in big lagoons, with the ingoing current being of short duration and perhaps weak, and the outgoing current correspondingly strengthened.

Slack water is often of short duration, about half an hour. If the times of high and low water are used for estimating the time of slack water, be aware that the time may vary greatly from the turn of the tide. This applies particularly when a high swell is pushing water over the reef to windward or in passes with strong currents. The low water slack may occur long after low water and be very short. The high water slack may occur before high water. In extreme cases the high and low water slacks combine into one slack during the rising tide. Alternatively, a minimum current may occur at this time in the case of lagoons with a constant outflow. Under normal wind and swell conditions, the ingoing stream can be expected to begin at approximately four hours after moonrise and one hour before the moon's lower meridian passage.

The more dangerous tidal race is that of the falling tide. Not only is the current stronger but the race is outside the pass in the open sea where the current flows into deeper water and has to lose its energy by forming standing waves. Any ocean waves will be opposing the race and dangerous breaking waves can result.

On the rising tide the current is weaker and the race is now in the calmer water of the lagoon. Standing waves are not so large, but if a yacht enters from the side, steering control can easily be lost and there is a risk of being swept on to dangers.

Marine perils

JELLYFISH

Jellyfish stings are the most common injury encountered in the marine world. All jellyfish sting as that is the way they immobilise their prey and it is also their defence against predators. They will only sting if you bump into them or inadvertently become entangled in their trailing tentacles. Some jellyfish, like the Portuguese man-of-war and some sea wasps, are vicious stingers and the sea wasp causes a number of fatalities in Australia every year. Other jellyfish such as the more common *Aurelia aurita* and *Pelagia noctiluca,* are stingers but never fatal. Different people have different reactions to jellyfish stings. For some there is a violent allergic reaction with loss of breath and increased heart rate, while for others the symptoms are just a mild irritating reaction on the skin. There are various treatments although none are 100% effective. Those likely to have a violent reaction should use anti-histamine creams and something like Waspeze. Other treatments are dilute ammonium hydroxide, neat alcohol, vinegar, lemon rubbed on the sting, and even meat tenderiser, which is said to break down the protein base of the venom. One tip is to wear gloves when hauling up an anchor as jellyfish tentacles can become wrapped around it and will still sting you even if detached from the body of the jellyfish.

SEA URCHINS

These can be a problem when wandering around rocky areas if you tread on one and get the spines embedded in your foot. Always wear shoes or sandals when walking in shallow water around rocky areas or reefs and watch where you put your feet. The spines themselves are not venomous but are difficult to remove and usually cause an infection.

CORAL

Coral cuts are common when you go swimming or walking around reefs, and for some reason they take an age to heal. Coral does sting mildly, but this is not the cause of cuts taking a long time to heal. Any cuts should be washed with an antiseptic solution and then kept dry. If necessary put a plastic bag on the foot with a rubber band around the ankle when going ashore in a dinghy or anywhere else the foot is likely to get wet. A tube of antibiotic ointment and, failing that, a course of broad-spectrum antibiotic may be needed if the cut becomes septic.

CIGUATERA

One of the biggest worries for cruisers in tropical waters is ciguatera poisoning. This is due to a toxin that builds up in fish that inhabit coral reefs and in predatory fish that eat them. There is no way to tell whether fish may be affected or not, other than by taking local advice. Sometimes the fish that was safe in one atoll is unsafe in an atoll 40M away. Fish caught on a line trolled behind a boat are seldom affected. Local fishermen normally know if ciguatera is around and consequently will not deliver certain types of fish to market at certain times of year. If you have been fishing around a reef ask the locals if the fish is OK to eat.

Poisoning symptoms are initially nausea, vomiting, cramping, abdominal pain, and diarrhoea. Later symptoms include intense itching, joint and muscle pain, tingling of the lips, burning or pain when cold liquids touch the tongue. Poisoning is unlikely to cause death but may result in several months or longer of severe malaise. There is talk of the development of kits to detect the toxin, but we do not know of any that are yet available. Well equipped hospitals may be able to provide treatment that will limit the severity of cases, but there is no cure.

These fish are commonly known to have ciguatera: Horse-eyed Jack, Parrotfish, King Mackeral, Yellowtail Snapper, Dog Snapper, Black Grouper, Hogfish, Barracuda, Amberjack, Moray Eel.
www.rehablink.com/ciguatera

SHARKS

These are always a concern, but attacks are rare and usually avoidable if sensible precautions are taken, such as not spearfishing with a large collection of bleeding fish hanging from the waist.

RED TIDE

In temperate areas such as Alaska, Nova Scotia, New Zealand and the S of Chile toxic shellfish poisoning (Red Tide) can be a problem, so be sure to check with locals before gathering shellfish.

CROCODILES

In N Australia and parts of the SE Asian archipelago these can be a danger, particularly close to estuaries and mangroves.

Malaria

Cruising people are sometimes remarkably cavalier about malaria, which is common in many excellent cruising areas. If you are going to visit a malarial area, seek proper medical advice beforehand. This disease is one of the world's biggest killers and the situation is getting worse as resistance to drugs increases. Yachtsmen and women die from malaria probably far more often than from sharks or piracy.

Misinformation is common. Many think that because of drug resistance, there is no point in bothering with prophylactics; this is far from true. We are rich enough to afford effective drugs that are often unobtainable by indigenous people. And drug resistance tends to be relative, so that a case of malaria occurring in someone who is taking a drug tends to be less severe than one in a person with no protection at all. Locals often deny that there is a problem, but take a look at the number of infant graves in the local cemetery. Many of these are the ones who did not acquire immunity and perished, while the living are those who have immunity. Do you want to risk seeing which you would be?

Piracy

The question of piracy is one often asked and too little backed up by reliable reports. In general, piracy is on the increase again worldwide after a period when there was a marked decrease in the numbers of

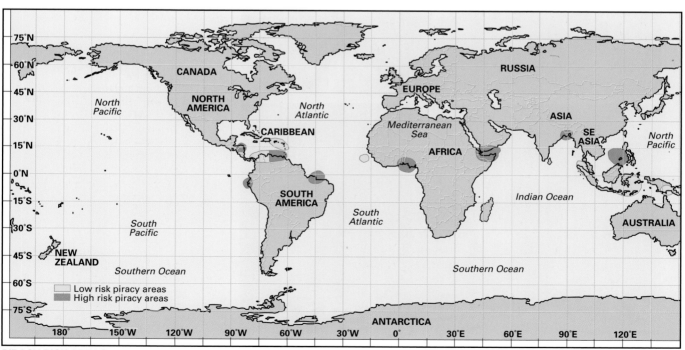

PIRACY RISK AREAS

Navigating in ice

It is possible to encounter ice in several of the sea areas mentioned in this book. This adds enormously to the beauty of the cruising ground but can also pose a very significant risk to safe navigation. The memory of being in the vicinity of dense pack ice or icebergs in heavy weather is enough to send shivers down the spine.

Ice arises from two main sources:

1. Actual freezing of the water surface that occurs with sufficiently cold temperatures, often this is in the form of thick ice flows formed by freezing of the sea surface but may also be encountered as a superficial layer of varying thickness in still and sheltered waters with a high concentration of fresh water.

2. From the calving of glaciers or ice shelves resulting in icebergs, large pieces that can vary from the size of a big house to that of a small country; bergy bits, smaller lumps the size of a small house or a car and growlers, nasty little pieces that are too small to spot easily but liable to cause an expensive bang if hit at speed.

Ice flows can be metres in thickness and vary from small pieces to very large 'islands', accumulations are generally known as drift ice or pack ice. Encountering pack ice at sea is a very dangerous situation as it is very mobile and the concentration of flows can vary suddenly. A conventional yacht trapped in pack ice is likely to be crushed and sunk. Because most of the ice is underwater the effect of tide and current is generally greater than that of the wind – it is not uncommon for the movements to be very irregular, illogical and unpredictable, though the overall movement will probably be in the direction of the prevailing current unless a very strong wind is blowing. It is not unusual for the channels, known as leads, between the flows to suddenly narrow and close. In addition, when pack ice is in the vicinity the navigator has to be aware that even if there is no ice in sight it may appear

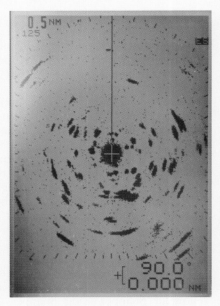

Radar display of four tenths drift ice (originating from frozen sea – pack ice)

Two tenths drift ice (originating from a glacier)

Three tenths drift ice (originating from a glacier)

quite suddenly. The concentration of drift or pack is generally expressed in tenths describing the amount of the water surface covered by ice as a fraction of the whole area. Ice charts issued by Denmark and Canada mark the density of ice as a number between one and 10 in the upper section of an 'egg' symbol (a full explanation can be viewed at www.natice.noaa.gov/egg_code/index.html.

The following terms are used by the Canadian Ice Service (there is much useful information on their site: http://ice-glaces.ec.gc.ca)

- **Very open drift:** the concentration is $\frac{1}{10}$ to $\frac{3}{10}$ – more water than ice. Navigation for yachts possible in good weather when the extent of ice is not great.

- **Open drift:** the concentration is $\frac{4}{10}$ to $\frac{6}{10}$, with many leads and open areas (polynyas). Floes are not usually touching. Navigation is dangerous but possible – it is essential to have an exit route in view before entering as it can quickly change to:

- **Close pack:** the concentration is $\frac{7}{10}$ to $\frac{8}{10}$, mainly floes touching each other. Navigation out of the question for yachts in these and the following conditions:

- **Very close pack:** Floating ice in which the concentration is $\frac{9}{10}$ to less than $\frac{10}{10}$.

- **Compact ice:** Floating ice in which the concentration is $\frac{10}{10}$ and no water is visible.

- **Consolidated ice:** Floating ice in which the concentration is $\frac{10}{10}$ and the floes are frozen together.

In short no yacht should ever enter anything that could be defined as pack ice – drift ice will provide you with all the adrenalin you could desire.

In addition to ice flows it is not uncommon, especially when the ice has originated from glaciers in the vicinity, to encounter much smaller pieces of ice that are very mobile. Even when these are quite dense it is usually possible to push through them at slow speed without doing any damage as long as conditions are calm.

When in the vicinity of ice flows or pieces broken from glaciers it is important to remember that even when no ice is visible there may be isolated pieces floating so low in the water that they are very

difficult to see even when a good lookout is being kept. Most of my (A O'G) collisions with ice have occurred in these circumstances.

Icebergs are much larger, sometimes kilometres in length, and generally much easier to spot, they are usually no great problem when coastal sailing, keeping a good lookout and sailing by day. In shallower waters bergs may be aground even in hundreds of metres and therefore stationary. However, at sea the situation can be very different unless the watch keeper is very alert. At night or in poor visibility with snow, fog or rain it can be very hard to spot them. Even quite large bergs can fail to show up on radar until you are within a few miles. My rule is to heave-to at night if bergs have been spotted in the last few hours. Downwind from icebergs it is common to meet bergy bits and growlers and a close watch needs to be kept when passing them. Remember that even when sailing in perfect visibility it may be very difficult to judge the distance from icebergs as you don't know if it is a small berg very close or a large one far away. This is a situation where the radar can assist.

Forward scanning sonar may assist at times. It is capable of spotting ice on the surface up to several hundred metres ahead. Unfortunately this only works when it is calm and there is no surface interference - in these conditions there is usually no problem seeing the ice by eye. However, if obliged to motor at night the sonar may be very useful.

When choosing an anchorage it is wise to think about the possibility of ice trapping the boat against the shore. For this reason shallower anchorages, or those with a bar at the entrance, may be preferable as large pieces cannot enter. However, there is a real danger of ice stranding at the entrance and blocking it for a few days. A wind setting in to the anchorage may carry dense ice and necessitate an unplanned departure to avoid being trapped. When it is not possible to avoid a large amount of floating ice it may be preferable to swing to the anchor rather than tie to the shore. Hopefully this way the ice being carried by the current will collide with the bow and be washed to the sides of the vessel.

In short, ice is pretty and looks good on your photos but should be avoided wherever possible.

Five tenths drift ice

Pushing through small pieces between larger floes

pirate attacks reported. There are some areas in the world where care is needed and a few areas to be actively avoided. One of the problems in assessing threats to small craft is that the most reliable statistics are gathered for commercial shipping and there is no doubt that in some areas there is a very real increase in piracy and, worse, deaths on board resulting from piracy, on commercial ships. In some of the areas where there is a threat to commercial shipping there appears to be only a slight risk to yachts. The picture gets more complicated because much of what passes between cruising boats is often fourth or fifth hand, much embellished, and in the worst cases totally insubstantial. (Some cruising folk seem to make an industry out of dissembling rumour and paranoia as reliable reports).

Some of this comes from local craft approaching yachts, not to attack them, but out of mere curiosity or in some cases to get something to eat or medical attention. There are a lot of poor people on normal cruising routes around the world and life on the water is a hard business. Many of the fishermen look like something out of a pirate movie and your first impulse is to take evasive action and tell them to go away. With a little care you can have some wonderful encounters with locals on the water and avoid the few locals who engage in piracy. In many places the threat comes not from local fishermen or others on the water but from land-based pirates who use a dinghy or swim out to boats to rob them. Whether to call this piracy or not is a moot point, but the result is really the same whether you are threatened and robbed some distance offshore or at anchor, so as far as the authors are concerned it all amounts to piracy.

On the world map the hotspots for piracy are circled to give some indication of the threat. This is in no way the whole story and you are urged to do your own research. A lot of boats have sailed in some of these hotspots and with a little vigilance and care there should be no problems. For the unlucky few who do encounter armed and dangerous pirates, the lessons of previous encounters is that you should give them everything they ask for (or at least appear to do so) and in no way try to engage in a firefight. Pirates will normally be better armed, more versed in training firearms on people and less worried about the consequences of killing someone. The tragic death of Peter Blake in Brazil should underline this. Neither author carries firearms on board and both would discourage the practice for all sorts of reasons we cannot go into here.

www.yacht-piracy.org

About the plans and pilotage notes

CHARGE BANDS

Charge bands are included to give some idea of the cost of a marina. The charge band cost is in Euros and a GBP and US$ equivalent.

Charges are the daily high season rate for a 12-metre (40ft) yacht. It must be stressed that rates out of the high season can be appreciably less and long term rates can be negotiated on a sliding scale which will be substantially less than the daily rate for short-stay visitors.

Charge band 1	No charge
Charge band 2	Under €25 (c.£21 / $35)
Charge band 3	€25–40 (c.£21–34 / $35–56)
Charge band 4	€41–55 (c.£35–47 / $57–77)
Charge band 5	€55+ (c.£47+ / $77+)

WEATHER AND CURRENT MAPS

These maps are designed to show the prevailing winds and currents over the sea area covered. As anyone who sails on ocean passages knows, these maps can conceal as much as they reveal for the ocean navigator.

Maps which show a monthly average of Force 4 from an easterly direction can be made up of winds of Force 2, Force 6–7 and some calms. It would be good to know about the weather which is the exception to the prevailing averages, but of course that would mean a confusing mass of statistics and for the most part the best we have is monthly averages for a sea area. In the text for each passage described we have tried to give a general picture of the weather you will encounter, such as the incidence of squalls and how consistent the trade or monsoonal winds are.

Currents can also be variable and a daily rate of one knot can be made up of a whole host of differing currents, including even currents from an opposite direction. I am sure that we are not the only ones who with the advent of GPS have found an opposing current where the pilot tells you there is a favourable current. Again in the text we try to indicate how consistent a current may be.

HARBOUR PLANS

The harbour plans and charts are designed to illustrate the very brief pilotage detail for the places mentioned. It is stressed that many of these plans are based on the authors' sketches and therefore should only be used in conjunction with the official charts. They are not to be used for navigation.

BEARINGS

All bearings are in 360° notation and are True.

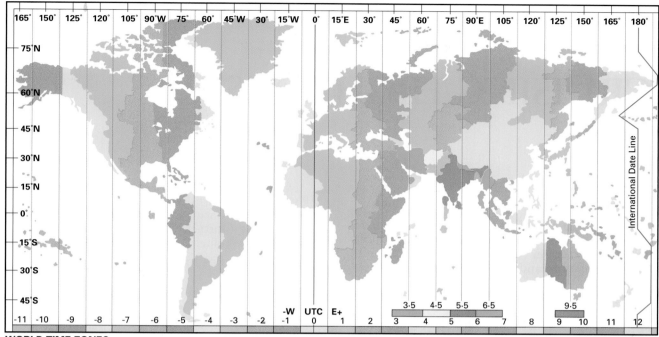

WORLD TIME ZONES

SOUNDINGS

All soundings are in metres and are based on mean low-water springs. In the case of the authors' and others' soundings there will sometimes be up to half a metre more water than the depth shown when the sea bottom is uneven, but in most cases there is the depth shown.

For those used to working in fathoms and feet the use of metres may prove difficult at first, and there is the danger of reading the depths in metres as the depths in fathoms. For all practical purposes one metre can be read as approximately three feet and two metres is approximately equal to one fathom. As an instant check on the depths in fathoms without reference to conversion tables, it is possible to divide the depth in metres by two and that will be approximately equal to the depth in fathoms. e.g. three metres = 1½fathoms (whereas accurately three metres = one fathom 3.8ft).

WAYPOINTS

Waypoints are given for all harbours and anchorages. If given waypoints are used for navigation the navigator must ensure that he/she has plotted them and the boats position on a chart and has safe water on the proposed route. The origins of the waypoints vary and in a large number of cases the datum source of the waypoint is not known. Where the authors have taken waypoints for a harbour or anchorage it has a note after it reading WGS84. All these waypoints are to World Geodetic Survey 1984 datum, which it is intended will be the datum source used throughout the world. Most GPS receivers automatically default to WGS84.

It is important to note that plotting a waypoint onto a chart will not necessarily put it in the position shown. There are a number of reasons for this:

1. The chart may have been drawn using another datum source. Many charts use a national datum source which differs from other datums and will affect where a GPS position ends up. Most hydrographers are converting their charts to WGS84 datum, though the end result is not always satisfactory for a number of reasons.
2. All charts, including those using WGS84, have errors of various types. Most were drawn in the 19th century and have been fudged to conform to WGS84 (the term 'fuzzy logic' could aptly be used).
3. When a harbour plan is drawn there is still a significant human element at work and mistakes easily creep in.

The upshot of all this is that it is important to eyeball your way into an anchorage or harbour and not just sit back and assume that all those digits on the GPS display will look after you. In the case of waypoints we have taken and which are appended WGS84, the waypoint is indeed in the place shown. Other waypoints may be derived from the light position, from reports in our files, or from other sources.

All waypoints are given in the notation:
degrees   minutes   decimal place of a minute

It is important not to confuse the decimal place of a minute with the older 60-second notation.

We have purposely not given waypoints to be used on ocean passages. This is because the precise course to be steered will always vary, even in the trade winds, depending on the wind, weather, shipping and preferences such as keeping the sun on one's solar panels for more hours of the day. Also, for obvious reasons, we strongly discourage the practice of large numbers of boats all heading to the same waypoint with an accuracy of a few metres.

CRUISING HIGHWAYS

Cruising Highways

As an aid to familiarity with the various routes to cross the oceans, a selection of passages have been linked together in tabular form to make a circumnavigation and illustrate possible cruises within each ocean. These illustrations are not presented as the best ways to cruise the oceans (a subject of endless debate amongst cruising folk). They are given to help you visualise how world cruisers link passages together with regard to the seasons and prevailing winds to make a successful cruise. Quite a lot of variation is possible in the timing of many of these cruises allowing for a faster, slower or more extended circuit.

Yachts may join these routes at many different points and there are, of course, an almost infinite variety of alternative routes.

*Passages forming the circumnavigation route
These are marked with a red star *. At the end of the passage notes a further red star will lead to the next passage on the route. For example:

*NAW2   Canaries to the Antilles
Following text:
See * CAR1

*CAR1   Windward islands to Panama
Following text:
See * SPW1

*SPW1   Galapagos to French Polynesia
Following text:
See * SPW3

*SPW3   Marquesas to Tahiti and Isles sous Le Vent
Following text:
See * SPW7

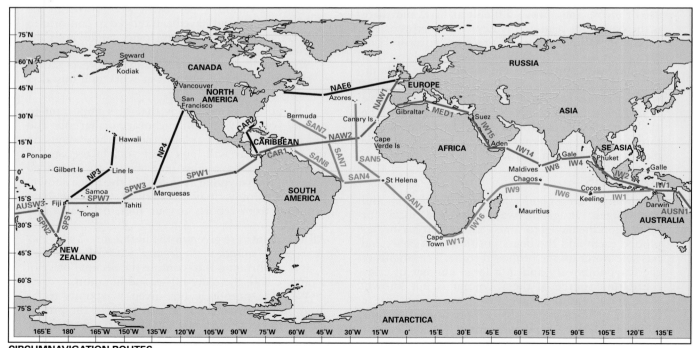

CIRCUMNAVIGATION ROUTES

*Alternative circumnavigation via South Africa

For those originating in Southern Africa or who choose not to sail in the Red Sea, passages have been marked in the same way with green stars *.

*Passages joining the main circumnavigation passages

A blue star * similarly marks routes to or from the yachting centres of Northern Europe and the East and West coasts of N America and Hawaii. For example:

*NAW1   Western Europe and the Mediterranean to the Canaries
Following text:
See * NAW2

Circumnavigation (Red * in chapters)

Month of Departure	Passage number		Approx distance and comment
September	NAW1	Falmouth to Las Palmas	1,420
December	NAW2	to St Lucia	2,850 Middle passage
February	CAR1	to Panama	1,110
April	SPW1	to Marquesas	3,920
June	SPW3	Marquesas to Tahiti	760
July	SPW7	French Polynesia to Fiji	1,830
November	SPS1	Fiji to New Zealand	1,060 Spend the southern summer in NZ
May	SPN2	to Noumea	910
July	AUSW3	to Brisbane	790 Head for more N'ly destination if time is short
August	AUSN1	to Torres Strait	1,210
September – early October	IW1	to Darwin	600
	IW2	to Phuket	2,510
December – January	IW4	to Sri Lanka	1,100
January	IW8	to Maldives (Male)	430
February	IW14	to Yemen (Aden) and the Red Sea	1,850
March	IW15	to Suez	1,300
June	MED1	to Gibraltar	2,000 (+1,050 to Falmouth)

Total distance approximately 27,000M (Start and finish at Falmouth)

Alternative Circumnavigation via South Africa (Green* in chapters)

Month of Departure	Passage number		Approx distance and comment
June	IW1	to Cocos Keeling	2,220
July	IW6	to Chagos	1,520
August/September	IW9	to Madagascar	2,180
November	IW1§6	to Durban	1,390
January	IW17	to Cape Town	775
February–March	SAN1	to St Helena	1,690
March–April	SAN4	to Brazil	1,800 (for those heading to the Caribbean or N America)
April–May	SAN5	to Azores and NAE5 to Europe	4,900 (to Falmouth)
April	SAN7	to Bermuda	2,940
October	SAN8	to Caribbean	1,930 Anytime if staying S of 11°N

Total distance approximately 34,700M (Start and finish at Newport, USA – via W Europe)

Passages joining the Circumnavigation (Blue * in chapters)

Month of Departure	Passage number		Approx distance and comment
June	NAE6	Newport to Falmouth	3,040
February	CAR2	Florida to Panama	1,250
April	NP3	Hawaii to Tonga	2,600 Don't sail S of 10°S before mid-May
April	NP4	W coast N America to Marquesas	2,810

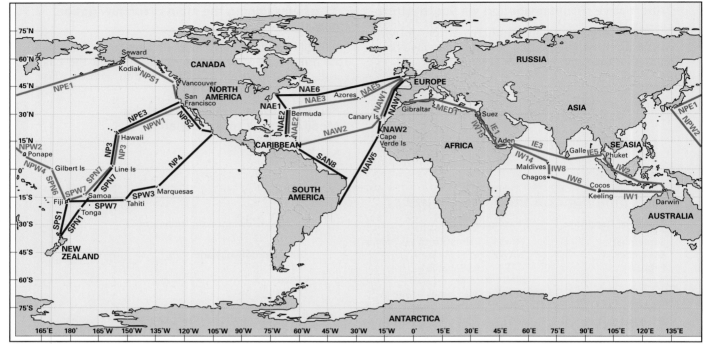

OCEAN CIRCUITS

North Atlantic circuit with winter in the Caribbean

Month of Departure	Passage number		Approx distance and comment	
September	NAW1	Falmouth to Las Palmas	1,420	
November	NAW2	to St Lucia	2,850	Middle passage
May	NAE2	to Bermuda	840	(from Virgin Is)
May-early June	NAE3	to Azores	1,700	
July	NAE5	to W Europe	1,200	(to Falmouth)

Total distance approximately 8,000M (Start and finish at Falmouth, excluding cruising miles in Caribbean)

North and South Atlantic circuit with winter in Brazil and the Caribbean

Month of Departure	Passage number		Approx distance and comment	
May-August	NAE6	Newport to W Europe	3,040	Spend summer in Europe or take passage via Azores
September	NAW1	to Las Palmas	1,420	(from Falmouth)
October	NAW2	to Cape Verde Is	850	
November	NAW3	to Brazil	1,870	(to Salvador)
February	SAN8	to Caribbean	1,930	(to Trinidad) +570 to Virgin Is.
May	NAE2	to Bermuda	840	(from Virgin Is)
May-June	NAE1 (reversed)	to E coast N America	655	(to Newport) Later departures incur hurricane risk.

Total distance approximately 10,600M (Start and finish at Newport, USA, excluding cruising miles in Brazil and Caribbean)

Pacific Circuit 1

Month of Departure	Passage number		Approx distance and comment	
October to January	NPS2 W coast USA	to Vallarta, Mexico	1,040	(San Diego to Vallarta) Depart anytime during the winter.
March	NP4	From W coast of N or Central America to Marquesas	2,810	Could leave earlier if willing to accept a very small cyclone risk in the Marquesas
June	SPW3	Marquesas to Tahiti	760	
July	SPW7	French Polynesia to Fiji	1,850	
November	SPS1	Fiji to New Zealand	1,060	Spend the southern summer in NZ
May	SPN1	New Zealand to Tonga	1,030	Leave following cyclone season
July	SPN7	Tonga to the Line Islands	1,600	Leave earlier if eventual destination is Alaska or BC
August–Sept	NP3	to Hawaii	950	Leave earlier if eventual destination is Alaska or BC
August–September	NPE3	Hawaii to W of USA	2,600	

Total distance approximately 13,700M

Pacific Circuit 2

Month of Departure	Passage number		Approx distance and comment	
Any time	NPW1	West Coast of N America to Hawaii	2,200	Depart anytime during the winter
March	NP3	Hawaii to Line islands	950	
May	SPN7	Line Islands to Samoa	1,260	Don't arrive in Samoa before the end of May
July	SPW7	Samoa to Fiji	670	It is not difficult to sail via Tonga
September	SPN6	to the Gilbert Islands	1,330	To avoid the cyclone season, aim to reach Tuvalu by November
January	NPW4	to Ponape	1,170	Alternative to Japan is to return via Midway Is.
April	NPW2	to Japan	2,050	Leave earlier if planning to cruise in Alaska the same season.
June-July	NPE1	to Alaska or W coast N America	3,300	(to Kodiak) – an alternative would be to spend the whole summer in Japan and return to Hawaii for the winter.
September	NPS1	to W coast N America	1,670	(Seward to San Francisco)

Total distance approximately 14,600M

Indian Ocean Circuit

Month of Departure	Passage number		Approx distance and comment	
June	MED1	to Suez	2,000	
July	IE1	to Bab el Mandeb	1,200	
August	IE3	to Sri Lanka	2,280	Alternative is to sail via Mina Raysut (Oman), Bombay and Cochin
January	IE5	to Thailand (Phuket)	1,100	
March	IW2 (reversed)	to Darwin	2,510	Stay clear of Aus. waters until mid-April
June-July	IW1	to Cocos Keeling	2,220	Alternative is to go via Bali
August- October	IW6	to Chagos Arch.	1,520	
January	IW8	to Maldives	600	
February	IW14	Maldives to Yemen (Aden) and the Red Sea	1,850	
March	IW15	to Suez	1,300	
June	MED1	to Gibraltar	2,000	

Total distance approximately 16,800M

1
NORTH ATLANTIC OCEAN

Anchoring Baltic style

General

The North Atlantic circuit is one of the most popular ocean passages for yachts to do. (This is not surprising given the numbers of yachts to be found in Europe and along the east coast of the USA.) Every winter there are literally hundreds of yachts around the Canaries getting ready for the westabout crossing to the Caribbean. The ARC (Atlantic Rally for Cruisers) alone has nearly 300 yachts all setting off at the same time (the third Sunday in November), and other rallies also have significant numbers of yachts. In addition there are at least as many, if not more, yachts crossing independent of organised rallies. The return eastabout leg has significant numbers of yachts crossing, though there never seem to be as many as there are on the westabout route from the Canaries, perhaps because yachts often spend several seasons in the Caribbean and some continue on through Panama into the Pacific.

Although the Atlantic crossing is popular, that doesn't mean it is always an easy passage. It is a bit of a misnomer to call it 'the pond' given that average wind strengths can be high on the trade wind route and the possibility of bad weather is always there. And it isn't always one of the most comfortable ocean passages you can do.

Weather and sea

PREVAILING WINDS

Essentially there is a clockwise circulation of winds in the North Atlantic basin. North of 35°N winds are predominantly SW–W. South of 35°N winds are predominantly NE–E. Between 30°N and 40° there is an area of variable winds (the variables or 'horse latitudes') which oscillates N or S depending on the time of year. This clockwise circulation results from two notable features in the North Atlantic: the Azores High and the Icelandic Low.

The Azores High, centred on or around the Azores and mostly stretching in a NE–SW direction, gives rise to the NE Trades, and observation of the Azores High, its position and extent, can be useful for predicting the strength of the trades. It is at its greatest extent in the winter months and from November to March the trades blow strongest, with January and February being the peak months. In the summer the Azores High moves north and influences weather over Europe.

NE Trade winds The trades extend from the ITCZ to the Azores High, around 2–4°N to 30–35°N. The trades blow from the NE around the Canaries to ENE over the Caribbean. Pilot charts show around Force 4–5 (15–25kn) over the winter months, but this average covers everything from Force 3–7

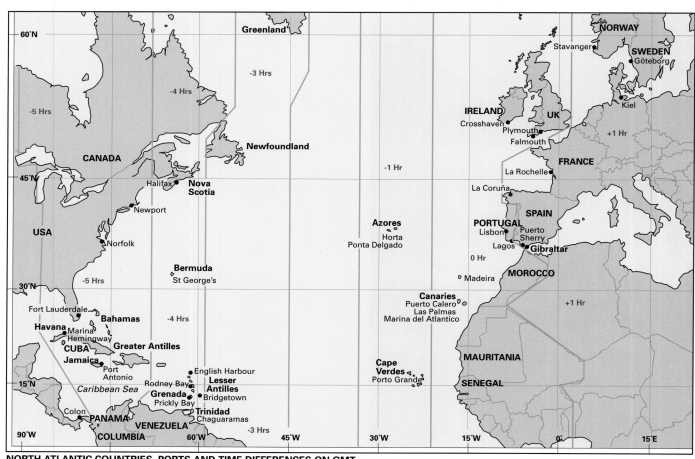

NORTH ATLANTIC COUNTRIES, PORTS AND TIME DIFFERENCES ON GMT

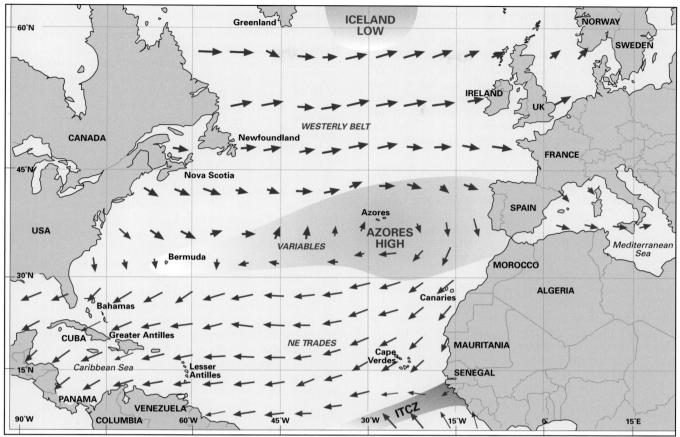

NORTH ATLANTIC PREVAILING WINDS - NOVEMBER

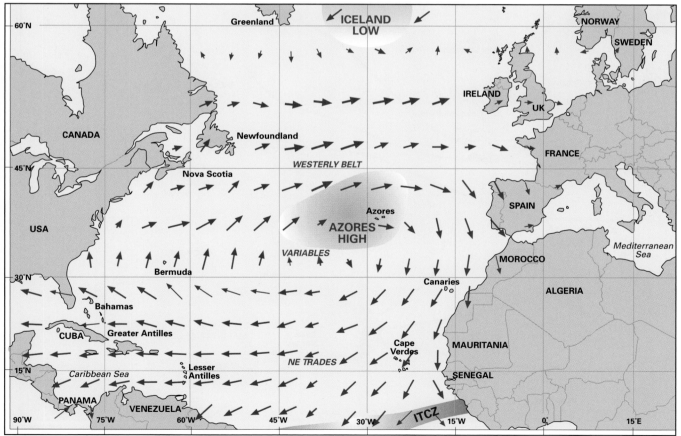

NORTH ATLANTIC PREVAILING WINDS - MAY

(5–35kn) with some calm patches as well. In general the most consistent trade winds will be found between 10° and 20°N in the winter. There are always squalls. There is some evidence that the wind is more easterly in the day and backs to the NE at night so that many yachts will go downwind through the day and gybe onto the quarter at night. There also seems to be a lighter belt of trades about three-quarters of the way across going W, though this does not necessarily show up in pilot charts and may be apocryphal.

Westerlies The westerly winds N of the Azores High extend from around 35°N right up to 55°N. They are not as consistent as the NE Trades because of the passage of depressions across the Atlantic which continually disrupt the westerly circulation of the wind. This means that you can expect more contrary winds on an eastabout crossing than on to the westabout trade wind route.

SW Monsoon Off the African coast between around 20°W and below 15°N the SW monsoon blows onto the African coast from the S–SW. This anomaly is caused by the ITCZ and the Coriolis Effect on the SE Trades further S. It generally blows at Force 3–4 (10–15kn) and the weather can be squally with a fair amount of rain.

ITCZ

The ITCZ (Intertropical Convergence Zone, Equatorial Trough, doldrums) moves N or S according to the time of year. In winter it is around 0–2°N and in summer moves further N to around 5–10°N. Its exact position and width varies on a daily basis, but generally it is 200–300 miles wide and fatter at the eastern end than at the western end. Weather in the ITCZ is characterised by calms and squalls and most yachts elect to have a good supply of fuel on board so that they can motor through it to get to the trades on the other side. Yachts on a trans-equatorial route will generally try to cross it as far to the W as possible, which pretty much makes sense for the main routes to Brazil.

GALES

Depressions typically come off the mainland of the USA between 30°N and 55°N and proceed on an E–NE track across the Atlantic. The principal tracks for depressions are across the Great Lakes and off the Carolinas. Depressions will then usually track NE towards Newfoundland and then continue on a E–NE course towards the UK and Iceland. Out of hurricane season the lower the latitude, the less likely you are to encounter a depression, which explains the new-found popularity of the eastabout

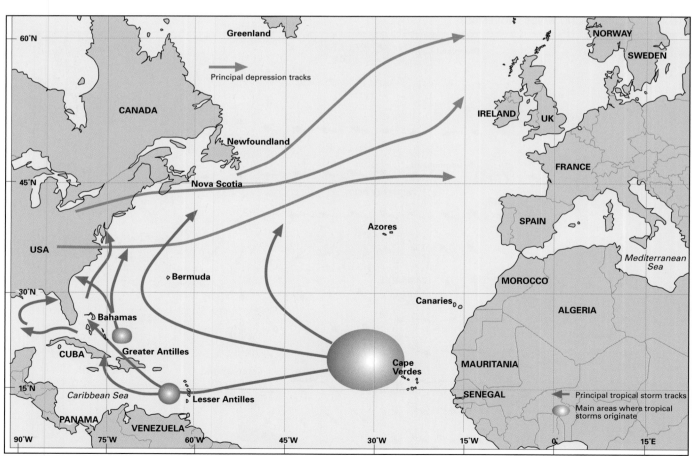

TEMPERATE AND TROPICAL STORM AND HURRICANE TRACKS

route from the Antilles to the Azores through the 'horse latitudes'.

In April there are few gales under 30°N and by May there is only a 2–3% chance of gales under 40°N. By June the frequency of gales under 40°N is very low, although it is now the start of the hurricane season.

Forecasting for depressions crossing the Atlantic is now much more advanced than it was and although seven-day forecasts have a variable predictive rate once over three days, nonetheless they are most helpful. There are various sources of forecasts including SSB, weatherfax, email and internet grib files, internet weather sites and Navtex.

TROPICAL STORMS

Tropical storms in the North Atlantic typically breed in the sea area off the Cape Verdes between 7°N and 15°N. Most are associated with the African easterly wave (a tropical wave or frontal system moving W through the Tropics) which seeds around a nucleus of a localised depression to form a tropical storm. Sea surface temperatures of around 25–26°C are required. The tropical storm then typically moves in a W to WNW direction at around 10kn. Around 25°N the storm may re-curve to the NE or carry on until it hits the Antilles or the continental USA and in some cases as far N as Nova Scotia and Newfoundland.

This is a simplified picture which is confused by the fact that tropical waves in and around the Antilles can also breed tropical storms, though most originate on the eastern side of the Atlantic. In the active La Niña year of 2004 there were 16 tropical or sub-tropical storms of which nine became hurricanes, including Ivan which reached category five on the Saffir Simpson scale three times. Five of these tropical storms formed off the E coast of the

USA or in the Caribbean Sea, though most of the hurricanes showed the classic formation off the Cape Verdes before heading W and NW. The percentage likelihood of encountering a tropical storm varies by month and by sea area. The sea areas with the highest percentage likelihood of encountering a tropical storm over a year are NE of the Virgin Islands (50%) and in the sea area off the E coast USA between 75°W and 55°W (50–60%). In any one year the statistics for tropical storms and hurricanes are given in the table above. They are only statistics, as one of the authors (RJH) can attest – having weathered Tropical Storm Peter (60kn) in 2003, which was the first time since 1887 that two tropical storms had developed in December.

CURRENTS

Currents in the North Atlantic primarily follow the prevailing wind direction and revolve around the basin in a clockwise direction.

North Equatorial Current This flows in a general W-going direction between around 10°N and 20°N. On the eastern side the current will be mostly SW-going until it swings to a more westerly direction around 30°W. The current is constant throughout the year, although greater in the winter when the trades are stronger. In the Antilles it splits, with one stream flowing NW up the E side of the Antilles (the Antilles Current) and the other stream pushing W into the Caribbean Sea and curving N up to the W end of Cuba. It mostly averages around 0.5kn.

North Subtropical Current A mostly W-going current N of the North Equatorial Current between 20°N and 30–32°N. On the E side it can be S-going tending to SW-going further W. This current is mostly less than 0.5kn. Between the Azores and Bermuda (32°N to 40°N) currents are variable in direction and rate although there is a general clockwise oscillation.

Florida Current and Gulf Stream The Florida Current follows the coast of Florida, turning N where it merges with the Antilles Current to become the Gulf Stream. (The Florida Current is often referred to as part of the Gulf Stream in most literature.) The Gulf Stream flows N and NE and then E along the coast of the USA until around 50°W where it becomes the North Atlantic Current. The Gulf Stream is a clearly defined current of warm water (27°C in the S) around 50 miles wide with an average speed of 3–4kn. N of Cape Hatteras. Where it turns NE, damp air from over the Gulf Stream is cooled by the cold Labrador Current, producing some of the densest concentrations of fog in the world. Because of the strength of the current care is needed of wind over tide conditions when strong northers blow down and produce exceptionally steep and disturbed seas.

AVERAGE NUMBER OF TROPICAL STORMS AND HURRICANES PER YEAR

	Min	Average	Max
Tropical storms (F 8-11)	4	9	19
Hurricanes (F12 +)	2	5	12

TROPICAL STORMS AND HURRICANES BY MONTH (1944-2000)

Month	Tropical storms and hurricanes		Hurricanes	
	Total	Annual average	Total	Annual average
Jan–April	3	0.1	0	0.0
May	8	0.1	2	<0.05
June	31	0.5	11	0.2
July	50	0.9	22	0.4
August	151	2.6	95	1.6
September	198	3.5	129	2.3
October	100	1.8	60	1.1
November	26	0.5	16	0.3
December	4	0.1	2	<0.05

(Data from NOAA)

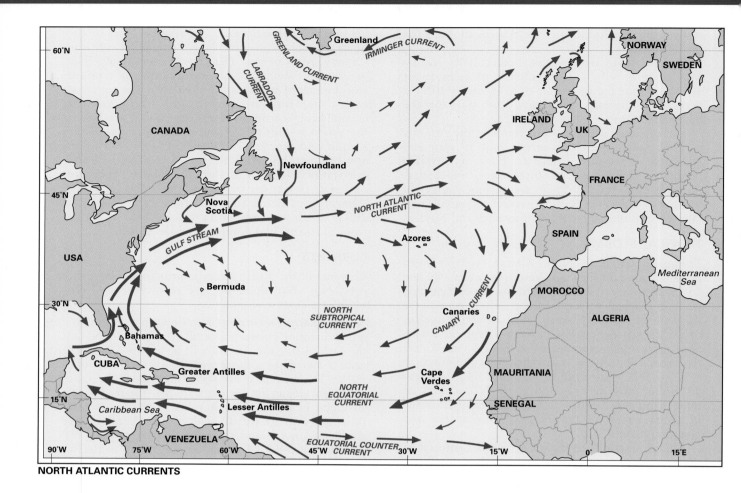

NORTH ATLANTIC CURRENTS

North Atlantic Current This is the continuation of the Gulf Stream across the N of the Atlantic basin between 38°N and 50°N in an E–NE direction. It then fans out around the Bay of Biscay and runs up the W coast of Ireland and the UK. Though not as warm after its passage across the Atlantic, it still brings relatively warm temperatures to the Bay of Biscay and Ireland and the W coast of the British Isles and Scandinavia. Off Spain and Portugal the current is deflected to the SE–S to flow into the Canary Current. The current flows at around 0.8kn in the W decreasing to 0.5kn in the E.

Labrador Current This flows down the coast of Labrador bringing ice and cold water from Greenland to its confluence with the North Atlantic Current on the Grand Banks of Newfoundland.

Equatorial Counter-current Under 10°N and E of 45°W a counter-current flows E–SE onto the African coast. Speeds are variable from 0.8–1kn on the western edge to 0.5kn off the African coast. *See note under Currents in Chapter 2 South Atlantic.*

ICE

In winter, pack ice extends from the W side of Iceland around Greenland and down to the southern end of Newfoundland. In summer this is only a problem off Greenland and the Labrador coast (which is generally clear after July). On the Greenland coast the pack ice is densest on the E coast and on the W coast between Kap Farvel and Kap Desolation. These areas usually become navigable sometime in July. Between Kap Desolation and Disko Bugt pack ice is not a problem. Icebergs and bergy bits are always present on the Greenland coast. Icebergs may be found in an extensive area to the SE of Newfoundland, especially in the early summer months and may extend as far S as 38°N. *See maps for more details.*

FOG

Fog is a major problem SE of Newfoundland, where SW winds have blown across the warm waters of the Gulf Stream and then meet the cooler water of the S-going Labrador Current.

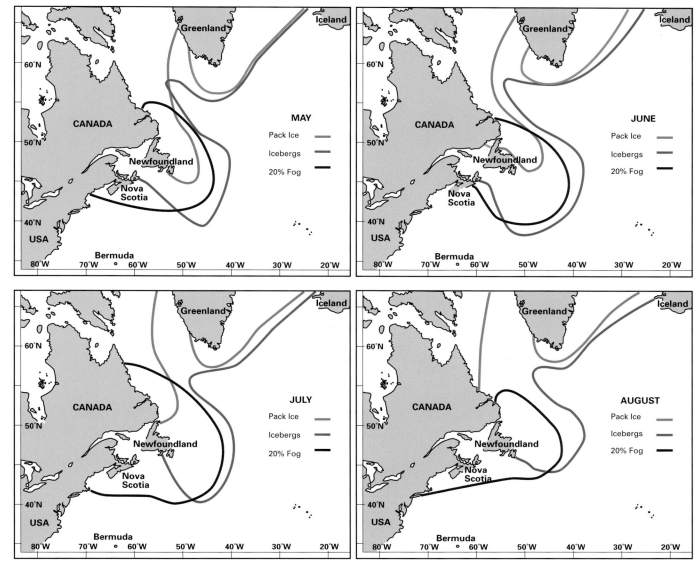

MAXIMUM LIMITS OF PACK ICE, ICEBERGS AND 20% FOG

Atlantic Circuit

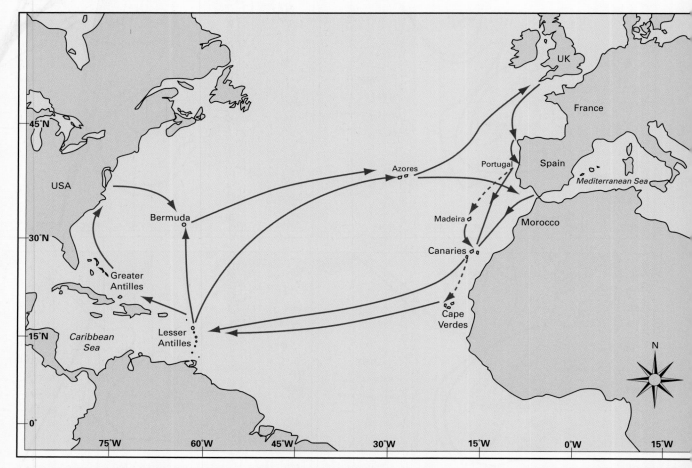

Start of the ARC in Las Palmas

Gathering of the clan in Sint Maarten before the exodus east

Yachts in Europe, and yachts on the East coast of the US will often do an Atlantic Circuit which can be completed in a sabbatical year from work. From Europe this involves getting down to the Canaries in the late summer before crossing to the Caribbean for the winter season. The return is via the Azores the following spring, and then on back to a home port in the summer. From the E coast US it involves crossing to Europe via Bermuda and the Azores in spring, before a summer cruise in either N Europe or the Mediterranean. The return via the Caribbean to the E coast needs consideration (see Routes and Passages section), but some will leave the boat in the Caribbean for a season before completing the trip home. For information on leaving a boat in the Caribbean see the section on the Lesser Antilles.

Strategies

For more information see the *Routes and Passages section*.

Westabout

Most yachts will start the Atlantic crossing from the Canaries in November to February. Some boats leave from Gibraltar. The old adage (several centuries old) was to head SW until the butter melted around 20°N 25°W and then head due W to the Lesser Antilles. This still makes sense. Some boats will take the rhumb line route from the Canaries and others will head for the Cape Verdes, stopping in Mindelo, and then head west to the Lesser Antilles.

Eastabout

Yachts will leave from the Lesser Antilles to Bermuda or direct to the Azores in April and May. The direct route will almost certainly involve some light winds and wind on the nose compared to stopping in Bermuda first and then heading for the Azores.

Typical puffy tradewind clouds in the Atlantic

Radio nets

Informal nets run every year and it is a matter of checking around to see what frequencies and times are used. These are often the best nets as the people on them will generally be in your vicinity and crossing at around your pace.

Herb Hilgenberg's Southbound II WX Net. 12359kHz at 2000 UTC. Check-in at 1930 UTC. Long-standing net and the guru on Atlantic weather.

HAM Nets

Trans Atlantic Net	21400kHz at 1300 UTC.
UK Maritime Mobile Net	14303kHz at 0800 & 1800 UTC.
European Maritime Mobile Net	14297kHz at 1900 UTC.

Not all a grind on an Atlantic crossing

Provisioning

Leaving the Mediterranean

Spain

Almerimar Low cost marina with a good supermarket within the marina and you can trolley provisions back to the boat. Good chandlers and boatyard.

Ceuta Secure marina with good supermarkets nearby and a general market as well.

Gibraltar

Can be some difficulty finding a berth here. You will need a hire car to go to the large Morrisons and also to go to the supermarkets across the frontier in Spain where there is excellent shopping.

Leaving Europe

Portugal

Cascais Good supermarket near the marina and you can visit Lisbon as well.

Portimão Supermarket nearby.

Canaries

Lanzarote Excellent supermarkets out of town so you will need a hire car if you are in Puerto Calero or Puerto Rubicon.

Gran Canaria Excellent supermarkets near the marina in Las Palmas. They will deliver large loads to the marina.

Packing away provisions for the Atlantic in Las Palmas

Skylax in the Atlantic swell

Twin headsail rig in the Atlantic

Provisioning up in the Caribbean

If you are setting off to go back across the Atlantic some islands are better than others for provisioning up. The following list gives some indication of places to stock up but is in no way definitive.

Road Town BVI Supermarket on the outskirts of town and speciality provisioning in the Moorings marina.

Sint Maarten One of the best places to provision up. Duty free with large well stocked supermarkets. French supermarkets on the French side and Dutch on the Dutch side. You will really need a hire car to go to the largest supermarkets (there is one before you get to Phillipsburg from the Lagoon). Also the best stocked chandlers (Budget Marine and Island Waterworld) in the Caribbean and a whole range of yacht services from rigging to hauling.

Antigua Epicurean supermarket in Jolly Harbour is well stocked and convenient. Also chandlers and hauling.

Martinique Le Marin. Good French supermarkets a dinghy ride away from the anchorage. Chandlers and yard.

Guadeloupe Good supermarket a short distance from the marina in Pointe à Pitre though you really need a hire car.

Curaçao (ABCs) Good supermarket.

In all of the islands you can find a reasonable selection of the basics in small supermarkets and local shops. If you are heading off for Panama the provisioning in Colon and Balboa is excellent with large American style supermarkets and a good selection of everything including quaffable cheap Chilean wine. If you are heading for the USA then there will of course be large supermarkets in all the larger towns and cities although you generally need a car to get to them.

Fuel

There are few problems around the Atlantic Circuit getting fuel. On the outward bound trip there are fuel quays throughout European marinas, in the main marinas in the Canaries, and in Mindelo in the Cape Verdes. In Mindelo there will occasionally be shortages but generally only for a few days.

On the return trip you can easily fill up in the main islands of Antigua, St Maarten and the BVI's. In Bermuda there is a fuel quay and in the marinas in the Azores there are fuel quays.

Gas

Spain & Portugal Most propane bottles can be refilled here, though sometimes you have to find a 'friendly' agent. Camping Gaz bottles can be exchanged everywhere.

Gibraltar No gas available here.

Canaries Like Spain most bottles can be refilled at some petrol stations and Camping Gaz is easily available.

Cape Verdes Most bottles can be refilled through a 'fixer'.

Lesser Antilles Most bottles can be refilled with a little investigation. Sometimes it will be the chap who helps out in the boatyard or a chandlers who does it as a sideline. Camping Gaz bottles can be exchanged in the French Islands although at times there are shortages. American propane bottles can be filled in most places. Consult a pilot or a local for advice.

Bermuda Most propane bottles can be filled.

Azores Most bottles can be filled. Camping Gaz bottles can be exchanged or filled.

Hauling and repairs

Around the entire circuit there are good hauling and repair facilities with the exception of the Cape Verdes. See separate sections on the cruising areas around the circuit for more detail on hauling and repairs.

Changing crew

Spain and Portugal International and internal flights. Budget airlines run to many airports.

Canaries Flights to Europe and internal flights to the islands. Charter and budget airlines run to many airports. Regular ferry service between the main islands.

Cape Verdes Flights to Portugal and UK from Sal, Santiago, and Boa Vista and internal flights including Mindelo. Ferry services between the main islands.

Lesser Antilles Scheduled international flights from Europe and the USA fly all year around to many of the major islands. Puerto Rico is the main hub for flights from the USA. USVI, St Martin, St Kitts, Antigua, Guadeloupe, Martinique, St Lucia and Grenada all have airports with regular international flights from the USA and Europe. In the winter there are a number of charter flights running from Europe to some of these airports (principally Antigua, St Lucia and Grenada) in addition to scheduled flights. There are also international flights to Barbados and from there inter-island flights to places like St Vincent.

If you need to get between the islands then it is wise to book in advance for inter-island flights. To get to BVI you will need to fly to one of the main hubs like St Martin or St Lucia and take an inter-island flight to BVI from there. Likewise to get to St Vincent you will likely fly to Barbados and get an inter-island flight from there. There are no real inter-island ferry services except between St Vincent and Grenada and the USVI and BVI.

Bermuda Flights from the USA from several hubs and flights from the UK and Canada.

Azores Most flights are via Lisbon. Some direct flights to the UK.

Reading

Atlantic Crossing Guide RCCPF / Anne Hammick, Gavin McLaren and John Lawson. Adlard Coles Nautical
Sailing an Atlantic Circuit Alistair Buchan. Yachting Monthly Books.
Your First Atlantic Crossing: A Planning Guide for Passagemakers Les Weatheritt. Adlard Coles Nautical

My gem

Adrift: 76 Days Lost at Sea Steven Callahan. Ballantine Books.

Atlantic sunset en route to the Caribbean

If you are leaving the boat in the Caribbean (or elsewhere) it's a good idea to get a custom cover made

Shipping the boat back is one way of doing half an Atlantic circuit

ROUTES AND PASSAGES

PASSAGES WESTABOUT

Passages westabout are usually on the trade wind belt anywhere between 30° and 10°N. Probably 98% of yachts crossing the Atlantic westabout take the trade wind route from the Canaries across to the Antilles in the Caribbean. It is a popular route with several organised rallies, among which the ARC (Atlantic Rally for Cruisers) is the most popular. A number of yachts head from the Canaries for the Cape Verde Islands and then on to the Antilles and this is arguably one of the best routes for a reliable trade wind crossing.

*NAW1 Western Europe and the Mediterranean to the Azores, Madeira and the Canaries

Falmouth to Cape Finisterre 450M
Porto to Las Palmas 840M
Gibraltar to Madeira 610M
Madeira to Las Palmas 265M
Gibraltar to Las Palmas 710M

Season May to November

Best time Northern Europe to Spain and Portugal: July–August/Spain and Portugal to Madeira and Canaries: August–mid-October/Gibraltar to Canaries: August–October

Tropical storms None

Essentially this is a feeder route to get to the Canaries for the trade wind crossing to the Antilles. Most yachts from northern Europe will potter down to Spain and Portugal in the summer months before crossing to the Canaries sometime between August and November. The later you leave the trip the more likely you are to encounter bad weather from depressions sweeping in from the west. It is best to get the Biscay part of the trip out of the way sometime between June and September, even if this means leaving the yacht in Spain or Portugal or in the Canaries and returning to it later. Yachts on passage across Biscay will usually make some westing to ensure they are not caught on a lee shore if westerlies blow up.

A small number of yachts go via the Azores. Winds are generally W–WSW in the summer so a yacht will be close-hauled for much of the trip. Any depressions passing across the Atlantic will disturb the overall pattern and it is essential to watch the weather and pick a suitable weather window. The AZAB (Azores and back) race, run every four years (next race 2011), starts from Falmouth in early June and runs to Ponta Delgada and then back in late June.

Crossing from Spain or Portugal or the western Mediterranean should ideally be made before October. The later you leave it the more likely it is that you will encounter strong winds which often blow from the SW. Depressions often track north of 40°N in the autumn, but south of this you will still get caught by the tail end of these depressions. Care is needed along the African coast as it is a long lee shore with SW winds and ports of refuge are few and far between.

Crossing from the Azores to Madeira and on down to the Canaries should be made in August to September at the latest.

See *NAW2.

*NAW2 The Canaries to the Antilles

Season November to March

Best time December–January

Tropical storms June to November

This is far and away the most popular route for westabout crossings. Yachts can cross with the ARC or one of the other organised rallies or there are many informal radio NETs operating which often include fifty or more yachts with a roll-call and weather information. Essentially this trade wind route can be divided into three.

1. Northern route Las Palmas to Antigua 2,660M.

This is the rhumb line route from the Canaries to the Antilles. On this route there is more likelihood of unsettled weather from fronts coming in, especially on the first half of the route. There is also the possibility of tropical storms moving across the route on a NE track at the beginning and end of the season. The trade winds are less likely to be as consistent or as strong as further S and some unsettled weather can be expected from the southern edges of weather systems further N. Reports also indicate a higher frequency and stronger winds from squalls compared to more southerly passages.

Note One of the authors (RJH) experienced a tropical storm (60kn) on this route in early December 2003, though the statistical chances are slim as this was the first tropical storm since 1897.

2. Middle route Las Palmas to St Lucia 2,800M.

This is the most popular route and involves heading S-SW from the Canaries before heading more or less due W to the Antilles. The nautical lore cited in earlier days was that you headed S from the Canaries until the butter melted and then turned W for the Caribbean. Most yachts will try to get down to 20°N at around 25°W, though exactly where you get to 20°N is dependent on weather and a lot of yachts will cut the corner more towards 30°W. From around 20°N you can take a rhumb line towards your destination in the Caribbean. The idea is to get down into consistent trade winds S of the Canaries where winds are not only more consistent but temperatures are warmer as well. There is also a slightly stronger W-going current. Leaving the Canaries you may encounter contrary winds for a few hundred miles, but the further S you go the more likely you are to pick up consistent easterly trade winds.

3. Southern route Las Palmas to Cape Verdes 850M.
Cape Verdes to Barbados 2,050M

From Las Palmas to the Cape Verdes is an easy ride with the wind on the quarter. In the Cape Verdes there are sufficient facilities to refuel and take on water and arrange for some repairs. From the Cape Verdes to the Antilles the trade winds blow consistently and yachts invariably report good passage times with regular seas.

See *CAR1*

NAW3 Canaries to Senegal

Los Cristianos, Tenerife to Dakar, Senegal 850M

Season Year round

Best time May to October

Tropical storms June to November - mainly W of Cape Verdes.

During the winter months the NE Trades can be very strong but they tend to be calmer with more N component when near to the African coast. Keep at least 90M off Cap Blanc. Visibility can be affected by dust blowing from the desert.

NAW4 Senegal to Cape Verdes and reverse

Cape Verdes to Senegal 475M

Season Year round

Best time May to October

Tropical storms June to November - mainly W of Cape Verdes.

It is usually possible to sail direct in both directions. If the trend is more E, sailing from the Cape Verdes to Senegal can be difficult and certainly wet and boisterous. Winds tend to be calmer and with more N component when near to the African coast.

NAW5 Cape Verdes or Senegal to Brazil

Season November to February

Best time December to January

Tropical storms June to November around the Cape Verdes.

Yachts on passage to Brazil must decide where to cross the ITCZ. In general the ITCZ is thinner at the western end and most yachts will aim for somewhere around 24–28°W to pass through the ITCZ. In December–January the NE Trades are as low as 4°N so yachts can carry a good wind this far S. After that it is a matter of where to cross the ITCZ, bearing in mind that you will pick up the SE Trades at some time (usually not far S of the equator).

(See Chapter 2 South Atlantic Ocean routes for more detail.)

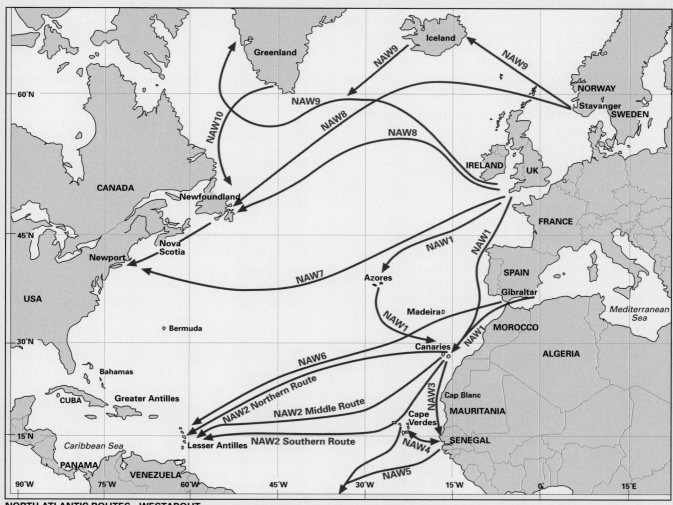

NORTH ATLANTIC ROUTES - WESTABOUT

NAW6 Mediterranean direct to the Lesser Antilles

Gibraltar to Antigua 3,200M

Season November to April

Best time Mid-November to December

Tropical storms June to November

This direct route to the Lesser Antilles is used by a few mostly larger yachts. You need to pick your weather window carefully when leaving the Mediterranean. Yachts will often drop south to Madeira and then angle down to a course above or on the rhumb line course from the Canaries. You can expect to have some bad weather en route from depressions moving east in the Atlantic, and some periods of calm weather out of the trade wind area.

NAW7 Western Europe to USA east coast

Falmouth to Azores 1,200M Azores to Newport 2,070M
Falmouth to Newport 3,040M

Season May to September

Best time July to August

This direct route to the USA is the least favoured as yachts are likely to have head winds for much of the way. Yachts on transatlantic races such as the OSTAR will perforce take this route, but for cruising yachts there is no good reason to do so, and given the likelihood of headwinds and the risk of meeting fog and ice SE of Newfoundland, there are very good reasons for not doing so. Cruising yachts will often make for the Azores and then head directly for the east coast USA from there, though the prevailing winds are still likely to be westerlies.

NAW8 Western Europe to Newfoundland and USA east coast

Stavanger to Reykjavik 870M
Reykjavik to St John's 1,470M
Falmouth to St John's via 55°N 30°W 1,950M

See notes on ice and fog.

Season May to August

Best time May to June

For hundreds of years, starting in the Viking age and extending through pre-Columbian Basque whalers, to Wilfred Grenfell in his mission vessel, sailing ships from Northern Europe made this passage every year. However, this route can be stormy and one of the authors (AO'G) had to turn back half-way following a knockdown.

The direct route to Newfoundland is against the wind, but by arcing N towards Iceland, aiming to reach the latitude of Northern Ireland in mid-ocean or to visit Iceland, it is possible to pass N of the depressions and experience predominantly E winds. This is especially true of passages from Norway to Iceland and on to Newfoundland. Fog and ice will still be a problem closing Newfoundland or Labrador, but the distance passed through icy and foggy waters will be less than on more southerly routes. In May and June there will still be pack ice off the N shores of Newfoundland and there is always an iceberg risk.

NAW9 Europe to Greenland

Crosshaven to Prins Christians Sund 1300M
Reykjavik to Nuuk 1250 (Via 57°35'N 046°38'W)

Season May to August. *See Greenland country guide*

Earlier in the year there will be a lot of ice off the S and E of Greenland. After checking latest ice information (Danish Met service) sail well south and W of Kap Farvel (this could be around 150M or more) before heading N to Nuuk or Disko Bugt.

NAW10 Greenland to Newfoundland

Nuuk to St Anthony 870M

Season June to September (depending upon ice conditions). *See Greenland country guide*

Returning to Newfoundland in August or September ice will not be a problem and a direct course can be steered. However, there is a risk of meeting deep depressions resulting from Caribbean hurricanes on the direct route, by steering a little N towards St Mary's Harbour on Labrador before heading S it should be possible to stay clear of the strongest blows.

PASSAGES EASTABOUT

Passages eastabout are usually made above 35°N to utilise the prevailing westerlies. Most yachts cruise up to Bermuda and then across to the Azores, although an increasing number sail direct from the Lesser Antilles to the Azores through the light and variable wind belt between the trade winds and the westerly circulation further N. This latter option has become more popular as yachts now have a greater range under power and can generally sail better in the lighter winds that will be encountered. Some yachts take a more northerly route although there is a greater likelihood of encountering gale force winds on this route.

NAE1 East coast USA to Bermuda

Newport to Bermuda 655M
Miami to Bermuda 900M

Season April to June

Best time May

Tropical storms June to November

Yachts from east coast USA use Bermuda as a stepping stone on the eastabout crossing. From here yachts invariably head for the Azores. The Newport to Bermuda Race is held in mid-June. Winds between the east coast and Bermuda are predominantly SW at around Force 4–5 (15–25kn) so from ports in the N of the USA east coast there is likely to be more windward work compared to ports further S. It may be worthwhile chugging S down the Intracoastal Waterway for a bit to get a better slant across to Bermuda. There is also a fair proportion of winds from the N–NE which can be strong at times. The earlier you make this passage, the more likely you will encounter a depression moving NE off the coast, bringing strong winds and rain with the associated front.

Apart from winds the other factor to be taken into account is the Gulf Stream flowing N off the coast. Rates average around 1–1.5kn, though at times much stronger flows have been recorded. Strong northerly winds blowing over the N-going Gulf Stream can set up horrendous seas so care is needed planning when and where to cross.

Note: this passage can be sailed in the opposite direction.

NAE2 Antigua to Bermuda

Antigua to Bermuda 935M

Season March to May

Best time April to May

Tropical storms June to November

Yachts heading for the Azores or returning to east coast USA use Bermuda as a stepping stone to get back. From Antigua, or further south, yachts island hop up towards the BVIs before jumping off towards Bermuda. Winds are typically easterly for the first half of the trip going light and anywhere from S–SW as you get nearer to Bermuda. You can expect a fair percentage of calms around Bermuda except if a

depression tracks across to Bermuda from the E coast USA. In general most yachts reckon on motoring for a part of this trip.

NAE3 Bermuda to the Azores

Bermuda to Horta 1,700M

Season April to May

Best time May

Tropical storms June to November

Yachts leaving here will wait for a break in the weather as depressions often pass over or close to Bermuda from the east coast USA. Once out of Bermuda yachts will typically head NE until around 38°N when they should pick up westerly winds and can head directly for the Azores. Some yachts head directly for the Azores on the rhumb line and there is no real consensus as to whether the more northerly course will give you a quicker and easier passage. You can expect some periods of calm and light weather on the route and if the Azores high is in place there will often be calms or light weather up to 200–250M around the Azores.

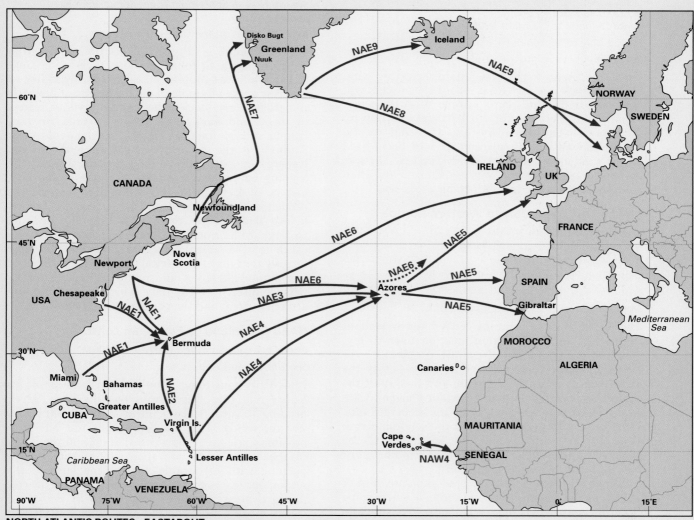

NORTH ATLANTIC ROUTES - EASTABOUT

NAE4 Leeward Islands to the Azores

Antigua to Horta: rhumb line 2,160M
Antigua to Horta: N route 2,270M

Season April to May

Best time May

Tropical storms June to November

The direct route from the Leewards to the Azores is becoming increasingly popular. It is a relatively light wind passage with a fair number of calms, but for yachts which can sail in light winds it is fairly easy passage. You will need to carry a good fuel load for the calms en route. Winds on the passage vary from easterlies when leaving the Leewards to winds of variable direction though there is a fair percentage of S–SW winds. Depressions crossing the Atlantic will influence winds and you can expect some frontal activity. There is some debate over whether you curve north through waypoints around 25°N 60°W and 33°N 45°W to the Azores or take a direct rhumb line route. There appears not to be much in it, although one author (RJH) favours curving N for this passage.

NAE5 Azores to western Europe and the Mediterranean

Horta to Falmouth 1,200M
Ponta Delgada to Gibraltar 980M

Season May to September

Best time July to August

Once the Azores High is established the wind blowing clockwise around it means that yachts will have to beat N until there is some W in the wind. Some yachts elect to cross to Portugal and hop up the coast to northern Europe. Crossing to the Mediterranean will often mean days of being hard on the wind until it shifts to the NE and N. The seas between the Azores and western Europe are often confused, with some uncomfortable cross-seas.

*NAE6 East coast USA to Western Europe

Newport to Falmouth 3,040M
Newport to Horta (Azores) 1,940M
Horta to Falmouth 1,200M

Season June to August

Best time July to August

Tropical storms June to November (S of 47°N)

This is the reverse route of NAW5 for westabout routes. Serious consideration must be given to fog, commonly encountered until well E of Newfoundland where SW winds blow across the warm waters of the Gulf Stream and then meet the cooler water of the S-going Labrador Current. Care is also needed to keep south of the iceberg limits. Icebergs may be encountered SE of Newfoundland, as far S as 38°N in May and June. Scattered pack ice may be encountered in May over the Grand Banks of Newfoundland (See plans page 35).

Winds on this passage are predominantly W–SW as long as the route is not too northerly where some easterlies may be encountered (between Greenland and Norway, for instance). Depressions do pass along this route so you will need to be prepared for some bad weather on passage and occasionally severe hurricanes will reach Nova Scotia and the Grand Banks (generally late in the season).

If proceeding directly to Europe, head towards 40°N 45°W before setting course to the destination. This course avoids the greatest concentrations of ice and fog and is only about 200M longer than going via the SE tip of Newfoundland, which is the closest to the great circle course.

Alternatively head for the Azores, which on the rhumb line route should have predominantly W–SW winds in the summer except when patterns are disturbed by depressions passing through. One thing to watch out for is the remnants of tropical storms curving around to a NE–E passage from the E coast USA and becoming extra-tropical but still very active depressions in the northeastern Atlantic. A friend of one of the authors (RJH) lost his boat to just such an extra-tropical depression (Charlie) in August 2004.

*See *NAW1*

NAE7 Newfoundland to Greenland

St Anthony to Nuuk 870M

Season May to September (depending upon ice conditions)

Refer to notes on the Greenland pages

Newfoundland is a good departure point from North America. St John's is a logical choice because of availability of supplies and facilities. By sailing to the west of Newfoundland via the Straits of Belle Isle (unless they are blocked by ice) the perilous waters of the Grand Banks (fog, gales, icebergs, oil rigs, fishing and commercial vessels) can be avoided. St Anthony is the departure point using this route. Icebergs are carried down the Labrador coast by the S going Labrador current, so it is wise to sail E or just N of E for 100–200 miles until outside the influence of the current and ice (check ice reports before departure – there is a helpful Canadian Coastguard Station in St Anthony). Thereafter steer north for the Greenland coast. Most people make directly for Nuuk, the capital of Greenland, however one author (AOG) would prefer to make a longer passage direct to Disko Bay, which is a much more attractive area, and then cruise south from there.

NAE8 Greenland to European coast

Prins Christians Sund to Crosshaven 1300M

Season July and August

Prins Christians Sund is unlikely to be clear of ice before mid July. Depressions pass by Kap Farvel, heading towards Iceland, in an almost continuous stream, winds N of the depressions are NE. It is possible to tie up at the weather station at the E end of the sound and with their help watch for an opening with favourable winds. The later in the season one leaves the departure the greater is the risk that a depression will be augmented by a tropical storm moving N from the West Indies. It would require great luck to avoid bad weather completely, the trick is to be as far as possible from Kap Farvel before it arrives. Once at sea steer a great circle course for the destination, with predominantly W winds.

NAE9 Prins Christians Sund to Europe via Iceland

Prins Christians Sund to Reykjavik 640M
Reykjavik to Stavanger 850M

See NAE8, The first part of this trip needs careful timing to avoid being caught in a NE gale. After visiting Iceland the winds are likely to be favourable and the Faeroe and Shetland islands break it into shorter sections if desired.

CARIBBEAN ROUTES

*CAR1 Windward Islands to Panama

Grenada to Colon (Panama Canal) 1,110M

Season March to May

Best time May

Tropical storms June to November

This can be a very bumpy passage as the trades are reinforced as they blow onto Central America and can blow at gale force for days. Wave heights in the sea area between Colombia and the approaches to Panama are generally higher and a large swell more frequent than elsewhere in the Caribbean Sea. You will need to be well reefed down for most of this trip and the later you can leave it (towards May) the less wind there is likely to be. Most yachts elect to coast

west along Venezuela, the Dutch Antilles (the ABCs), and then along the Colombian coast to Panama. Some yachts cruise the Colombian coast and there are now fewer yachts around the Venezuelan coast because of the unrest and an increase in piracy. A lot of yachts head for the San Blas islands before heading to Colon.

Important note The reverse leg of this route from Colon to the Windward islands should not be attempted in the winter. It is a gruelling slog to windward against steep seas and most yachts give up the unequal battle. If it is necessary to make this passage in winter, the winds tend to be lighter at night which facilitates motor sailing; also, by watching the passage of fronts to the N it may be possible to choose a time when the wind is more northerly. In the summer it is possible by hugging the coast of Colombia and Venezuela when the trades blow less strongly and there can be days of calm. Although you are theoretically S of the hurricane zone, strong winds and seas will be encountered if a hurricane passes to the N so it pays to monitor the progress of any hurricanes carefully. See CAR4 for routes to the Virgin Islands.

See *SPW1

*CAR2 Florida to Panama

Fort Lauderdale to Colon (Panama Canal) 1,275M

Season December to May

Best time April to May

Tropical storms June to November

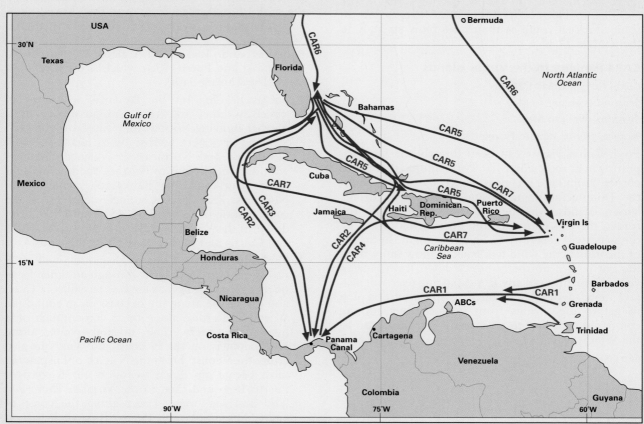

CARIBBEAN ROUTES

This is mostly a downwind route with a number of places you can stop off en route. From Florida you need to decide if you are going round the W or E end of Cuba. The W end is favourite as you will have the prevailing wind with you and the Gulf Stream can be avoided by keeping closer to the Cuba side of the passage, where the current flows to the SW. Most yachts will head down the Keys as far as Key West before heading off round the W end of Cuba. Going round the E end means beating against the trade winds until you get to the windward passage (see CAR5). Some yachts will want to cruise around Cuba en route and it makes sense to get some easting by cruising inside the reefs from the W end of Cuba before shaping a course to Panama. From the W end of Cuba you can head directly for the passage between Rosalind Bank and Gorda Bank (15°45'N 81°00'W) and then head directly for Colon. Passage can also be made via the Cayman Islands and Jamaica and down the E coast of Central America. The trades are quite brisk for most of this trip and it can be a wet and windy ride down to Colon.

See *SPW1

CAR3 Panama to Florida

Colon to Key West 1,095M

Season December to May

Best time May

Tropical storms June to November

On the reverse route of CAR2 you can head directly for the passage between Rosalind Bank and Gorda Bank and then up to the W end of Cuba before crossing to Florida. It makes sense to schedule in some stops en route as the trades blow strongly in the winter.

CAR4 Panama to the Virgin Islands

Colon to St Thomas 1,265M

Season December to May

Best time April to May

Tropical storms June to November

From Colon yachts can head directly for Jamaica, putting in at somewhere like Port Antonio on the NE corner. From here it is possible to coast along Haiti, the Dominican Republic and Puerto Rico to the Virgin Islands. Although you are beating into the trades, there is a sea and land breeze effect whereby the wind will generally be lighter at night. In the lee of the islands the wind will back to blow more from the north. If a northerly blows down from Florida you can use this and any fronts passing over will also give more favourable winds. It is still a bit of a slog to get to the Virgins from Jamaica, but nothing compared to trying to go directly E from Colon to the Windwards

See CAR1

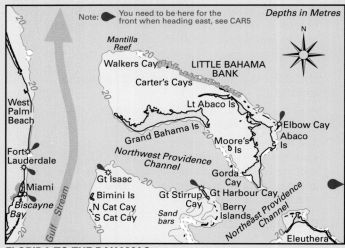

FLORIDA TO THE BAHAMAS

CAR5 Florida to the Antilles

Fort Lauderdale to Virgin Islands via the Bahamas and Turks and Caicos c.1,000M

Fort Lauderdale to Virgin Islands via Cuba, Hispaniola and Puerto Rico c.1,050M

Fort Lauderdale to Virgin Islands direct from Bahamas.

Season December to May

Best time April to May

Tropical storms June to November

Basically there are two ways to attempt this passage. Delivery skippers will advise that the quickest way is to head E into the Atlantic from Fort Lauderdale on the back of a weather 'front' and then head S once you can shape a course with the easterly trades. Most cruising yachts will opt for a passage via the Bahamas and Turks and Caicos or via Cuba, Hispaniola and Puerto Rico which is often referred to as 'The Thorny Path'.

1. Yachts heading for the Bahamas will leave in settled weather to avoid the possibility of a norther blowing, so that they can cross the Gulf Stream in safety. Most will head through Northwest and Northeast Providence Channels with maybe a detour to Nassau. Shallow draught yachts can cross the Banks to Exuma. From Northeast Providence Channel yachts can make some easting (to around 68–65°W)and then drop down to the Virgin Islands or head for the Turks and Caicos and then onto the Virgin Islands.

2. Yachts heading for Cuba or Hispaniola will often wait for a norther to blow through and then leave on its coat-tails to get as far E as possible. In Cuba you can cruise along the N coast or go round the W end and cruise along the S coast, much of it inside the reefs. The normal route along Hispaniola is on the N coast, but you can also cruise the S coast. From the N coast of Hispaniola most yachts dip down to follow the S coast of Puerto Rico and then to the Virgins. There is a land and sea breeze effect along the coast of Cuba, Hispaniola and Puerto Rico such that at

night the trades are moderated and may back to a greater or lesser degree to give you an advantageous slant along the coast. It is not an easy route, but there are lots of places to stop en route.

3. Yachts heading directly for the Virgin Islands from Florida can use a front coming through to get as far east as possible. It pays to monitor fronts coming through so you get a feel for when a front 'lite' is coming along. You need to be on your way and parked on the eastern side of Northeast Providence Channel when the front comes through and hope that there is not too much lightening associated with the front. The Bahamas has one of the highest incidences of lightening strikes in the world. Once the front is coming through you will find the wind swings to the SW and then W and then NW over several days. Head directly E to around 65°W or even 60°W if you can make it before heading down to the Virgin Islands. It might be tempting to cut the corner, but resist as the wind will suddenly snap back to the NE–E Trades quickly. As long as you are far enough E you should have a close reach to the Virgins.

CAR6 East coast USA to the Antilles

Newport to St Thomas via Bermuda 1,510M
Norfolk to Fort Lauderdale via Intracoastal Waterway 1,090M

Season October to November

Best time October

Tropical storms June to November

There are two main ways to do this passage. One is by an open water passage via Bermuda or direct. Yachts leaving from Newport will often stop at Bermuda whereas yachts leaving Chesapeake will often go S of Bermuda before turning further S to the Antilles. The other is using the Intracoastal Waterway (ICW) running down the E coast USA.

1. *Open water passage* The timing for this passage is critical so as to avoid winter gales from depressions moving E off the USA and tropical storms off the Atlantic. Most yachts will leave sometime in September or October, aiming to arrive after the worst of the hurricane season. Some leave in the spring in May or June and aim to be in the Antilles before the peak hurricane season in August to September. Most tropical storms tend to track up the E coast of the USA and few hit Bermuda, though it can happen. It is important to keep an eye on any tropical storms developing in the Atlantic and monitor their progress before setting out for Bermuda or the Antilles.

2. *ICW* Depths in the ICW are stated to be minimum 12ft (3.7m) from Norfolk to Fort Pierce, minimum 10ft (3m) on to Miami. In practice there are several sections where, depending on how recently they have been dredged, depths drop to 6ft (2m) at HW. It is not difficult to make a short hop in the open sea to bypass these shallower spots. Air height under fixed bridges is min. 56ft (17m) at Julia Tuttle in Miami and 64ft elsewhere. Yachts come down the ICW in the spring or more usually in the autumn (Fall) to arrive after the hurricane season. Although hurricanes do hit the E coast USA, there will be plenty of warning and lots of places to hole up in. From Fort Lauderdale or Miami yachts can follow the Cuba, Hispaniola, Puerto Rico route described in CAR5.

Note One of the authors (AO'G) started N on the ICW in late February. It was sometimes cool but on the whole the weather was good with very little other traffic on the water. Leaving early avoids the summer season rush and the risk of storms.

CAR7 Leewards to Florida

BVI to Fort Lauderdale N or S of Greater Antilles
1,200M (N) 1,425M (middle) 1870 (S)

This route with the trades to Florida is a comparatively easy passage. Yachts in a hurry can take the northern shorter route and make the passage with fair winds to Florida. The middle route going S of Puerto Rico, Dominican Republic and Haiti has the disadvantage that the trades are accelerated and blow down from the NE and even N through the Windward Passage which means a bit of a slog to get up here. The passage around the W end of Cuba is easy until you turn the corner and need to beat up around to Havana or up to Florida. The route you take will really depend on whether you want to stop and cruise around any of the Greater Antilles. For more information see the pages on *The Greater Antilles*.

ROUTES TO SCANDINAVIA

See plan on page 52 for routes

S1 North of Scotland to Skagerrak and return

Inverness to Gothenburg 520M

Season April to September

Coming from Ireland or the W coast of Scotland one can sail around Cape Wrath and the Pentland Firth or traverse the Caledonian Canal. Maximum dimensions for the canal are the Length 45m, Beam 10.5m, Draught 4.08m, height 34.44m.
www.waterscape.com/canals-and-rivers/caledonian-canal.
It makes sense to steer directly for the S coast of Norway or the Skagerrak. Winds are variable, mainly W, and often light in summer, out of season heavy gales are common. Shipping is not so much of a problem as further S but there are many oil rigs and their tenders to be avoided.

S2 E coast of England to Danish coast and return

Great Yarmouth to Thyborøn 350M

Season April to September.

Coming from the E coast of England (or even from the English Channel and staying to the N and W of the shipping lanes) it makes sense to steer for about 53°58'N 003°04'E before heading for the Danish coast, this keeps you clear of all the separation zones. There will be a lot of shipping and oil rigs. Steer for Thyborøn to enter the Limfjord or for the Skagerrak. (Note: Thyborøn has a bar and lies on a very inhospitable coast – do not approach in heavy weather). This route is one author's (AOG) preference for returning to the S of England from the Baltic.

S3 English Channel and Low Countries to Kiel Canal

Plymouth to Brunsbüttel 580M

Season March to October

This is probably the most popular route. It involves steering along the Dutch and German coasts inside the separation zones. The German authorities are very particular about yachts being well clear of these and will be watching you on radar, try not to approach within 1M. This makes the return journey against the prevailing W wind a little tricky as tacks will be very short, for this reason is recommended S2 for the return trip. Many of the harbours along the route are either busy commercial ports or difficult to enter in heavy weather. From continental ports it will not be necessary to cross the separation zones whereas coming from the English side it will be necessary to cross them. My preference is to cross somewhere to the N of a line drawn W from Hook of Holland, thus avoiding some of the heavy traffic off the Rhine delta.

ROUTES WITHIN THE BALTIC

Sailing in the Kattegat and Baltic is straightforward. Winds are often light and variable and there are many good ports and anchorages. There are three important short cuts:

Kiel Canal

From Brunsbüttel to Holtenau the canal can be traversed in a long day, or two days with a pleasant stop-over in the pretty town of Rendsburg, and saves a considerable distance if heading for the Southern Baltic. There is a moderate fee, there are no limits to the size or height of yachts and navigation and locking are very simple. It is compulsory to have a copy of the rules for navigation and light signals and the authorities have little tolerance for those who do not obey them in this busy waterway.

www.kiel-canal.org/english.htm

(This is an exceptionally good site and the regulations are published here).

Limfjord

This is a beautiful way to reach the Baltic and is worth taking your time time as the route is via natural waterways through the Danish countryside. The waterway is 100M. All significant bridges are lifting so there are no size limits (a minimum depth of 4m is maintained by dredging). If in a hurry it can be traversed in two days (some bridges close at night). There are plenty of good anchorages along the way.

Göta Canal

This route provides a shortcut between the W coast of Sweden and the central Baltic and is a very attractive cruise in its own right taking you across two of Europe's largest lakes, Vänern and Vättern and past some fascinating and historical towns and fortresses.

Strictly speaking the Göta Canal starts at the E end of Lake Vänern, the stretch between Gothenburg and Vänersborg on the W side of Vänern is a separate canal (Trollhätte Canal) sufficiently large for commercial traffic and charging a separate fee. Locks and bridges on this stretch are controlled by remote video, don't expect anyone to greet you or even answer on VHF except for the locks at Trollhättan where they will collect your fee. Sometimes, especially in Gothenburg, when road traffic is heavy you may have to tie up near the bridges and wait for the lights to indicate that there will be an opening.

The Göta canal is only open in summer, 1 May to 27 September with limited hours and days for navigation except 8 June – 23 August (dates are for 2009). Maximum dimensions for passage are: length 30m, beam 7m, height 22m and draught 2.8m. We recommend avoiding the high summer months, particularly July, when traffic can be very heavy. However, the 58 locks can be very social places and the lock keepers are mainly cheerful and helpful young students, so this can be a good place to discover something about Sweden.

www.gotakanal.se

COUNTRY AND PORT GUIDE

See map at beginning of the chapter for ports and anchorages covered.

EU COUNTRIES

The relevant EU countries in this sea area are: **Finland, Sweden, Denmark, United Kingdom, Ireland, Lithuania, Estonia, Poland, Germany, Netherlands, Belgium, France, Spain**, and **Portugal**. The Azores and Madeira are Portuguese and the Canaries are Spanish, but these island groups have special status within the EU, including tax exemptions.

EU regulations

Entry formalities

All yachts entering from outside the EU should fly the courtesy flag of the country they are entering and a Q flag. All yachts must visit Customs and Immigration upon entry and conform to the regulations for that specific country as well as EU regulations. Passports and boat registration documents will be requested, as will a number of crew lists. Proof of VAT status, insurance cover, radio licence, and certificates of competence may also be requested.

VAT

EU registered yachts

Since 1 January 1993 all yachts registered in EU countries are required to have proof that VAT has been paid or that the yacht is exempt from payment. The only exemption is for yachts built before 1 January 1985 which were in an EU country before 1 January 1993. All yachts built after 1 January 1985, and older craft imported into the EU after 1 January 1993, are liable for VAT payment.

If liable, VAT may be paid in any EU country.

Non-EU registered yachts

From 1 July 2002 yachts registered in countries outside the EU and owned by someone who is established outside the EU, are allowed 18 months Temporary Importation (TI) into the EU without incurring VAT liability. At the end of the 18-month period the yacht must leave the EU to discharge its TI liability. Once the TI liability has been discharged by exit from the EU, the vessel may re-enter the EU to begin a new period of TI. There doesn't seem to be an official minimum time that a vessel needs to be out of the EU before it may re-enter to start a new TI period, but it is important that a yacht has established a recognisable time gap, backed up with documentary proof, before attempting to re-enter the EU. Proof of clearing customs out of the EU, into and out of, a non-EU country, such as Norway, Turkey or Tunisia, with official documents, and, say, dated berthing receipts from the non-EU country. The lack of an official time limit means that the law is open to a certain amount of interpretation from country to country, and possibly from port to port.

Notes

1. VAT, if payable, will have to be paid in the country where it falls due.
2. Evidence of VAT payment, or exemption from VAT must be retained for inspection by customs officers.
3. Yachts registered in non-EU countries, but with an owner who is an EU resident, have a much more limited TI period of just one month.
4. The Channel Islands, Gibraltar, Ceuta, Melilla and the Canary Islands are not part of the EU VAT area. These places may be visited to discharge your TI liability.
5. If a yacht is hauled out and placed under customs bond in an EU country, it is probable that this time will not count against the 18-month limit. Thus a non-EU yacht can remain within the EU for up to 2 years, as long as it is hauled out and under customs bond for a period of 6 months. Yacht owners who are not EU nationals must also leave the EU for this 6-month period. It is essential that these terms be agreed with the relevant customs officials before assuming this interpretation of the ruling.
6. Obviously any non-EU nationals' visa obligations must be observed over and above the VAT regulations.

Insurance

Many of the EU countries now require a minimum of third-party insurance in their waters. Some EU countries have stipulated a minimum amount of third-party cover and also cover for liability against things like pollution. Some EU countries will also require a translation into their language of the cover provided in the policy – most insurance companies can supply this.

Recreational Craft Directive (RCD)

On 15 June 1998 the Recreational Craft Directive came into existence. There is still a lot of wrangling about the exact interpretation of the directive, but a brief summary is outlined below.

- The RCD applies to all recreational craft in the EU between 2.5 and 24 metres LOA.
- Any craft built after 15 June 1998 must have a CE mark and rating.
- Craft built before 15 June 1998 are exempt, as long as they were in the EU before this date.
- If they were imported into the EU after 15 June 1998 they should apply retrospectively. (This is the main point of contention).
- Home built craft are exempt if not sold for five years. Historical replicas are also exempt.

It appears that the original brief, to have certain common standards of construction for the EU market so that trade within the EU could be facilitated by one kitemark, has been extended to exclude a large number of craft from being sold on in the EU market.

Norway

General Norway is one of the foremost commercial maritime nations in the world. It also has a large yachting fraternity and an exciting coastline for cruising. The cost of living is high, which is most obvious if eating out or buying drinks. Basic foodstuffs are reasonable and marina charges are low by European standards. Norway is not an EU member state.

Coastline This is much indented by beautiful fjords and protected by countless offlying islands. It has every claim to be a sailor's paradise.

Formalities Main commercial harbours are ports of entry. Visas are not required for nationals of EU, USA and Commonwealth countries; others should enquire. The normal length of stay for immigration is three months, renewable, and six months for the boat, which must then leave the country for six months.

Telecom IDD code +47. GSM network. Internet cafés in larger centres.

Currency Norske kronor. Major credit cards widely accepted. ATMs everywhere.

Sailing season The sailing season is from April to October.

Routes and harbours We have chosen Stavanger as a destination as from here you can either cruise N along the Norwegian coast, S about towards Oslo Fjord or set off for the Baltic via Göteborg and the Göta canal or via the Danish archipelago.

STAVANGER

Tidal range 0.6m

Navigation

The approach from the open sea is straightforward and well marked via Skudanes Fjord (Skudanesfjorden), Kvitsoey Fjord (Kvitsøyfjorden) and By Fjord (Byfjorden).

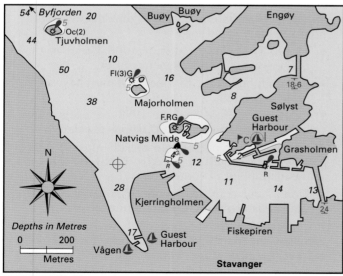

STAVANGER (Norway)
⊕58°58'·5N 5°43'·65W

Berths

Vågen – Vestre havn (West harbour)
There is a fishing harbour and a small guest harbour at the head of the inlet. This is close to the centre of the city and exceedingly convenient.

*Sølyst – Østre havn (*East harbour)
At Stavanger Yacht Club guest harbour. Less convenient for the city but better facilities.

Facilities

All the facilities of a modern city and yachting centre.

Remarks

Stavanger is the main port for Norway's oil industry but remains an attractive city with fine old architecture.
www.stavanger-seilforening.org

Denmark

One author (AOG) meeting a Danish cruiser in Greenland asked him why, considering that sailing is immensely popular in Denmark, he had met so few cruising yachts in other parts of the world. 'The cruising in Denmark is so good that we don't need to sail elsewhere,' was his reply. In fact there are around 500 Danish yachts cruising the oceans of the world at any one time, but one can understand that it must be hard to tear yourself away from this land of peaceful waterways and pretty towns.

Formalities Denmark is in the EU and if coming from Norway or a neighbouring EU country there are no formalities.

Telecom IDD code +45, GSM network, Internet facilities widespread – good free service in public libraries.

Currency Danish kronor. Overseas credit cards are often not accepted by businesses. ATMs widespread and do take credit cards.

Sailing season April to November.

THYBORØN

Tidal range 1m

Navigation

The seaward entrance and channel into the Limfjord are well marked and lit. In onshore winds over 25 knots the seaward bar can break dangerously and no attempt should be made to approach the coast.

Berths

Alongside the harbour wall in the N basin (charge band 3 – one of the only ports in Denmark that charges for daytime stays).

Anchorage

There are many anchorages in the Limfjord nearby but none with access to the town.

Facilities

No specific yachting facilities but it is a major fishing port with an excellent infrastructure for repair and maintenance.

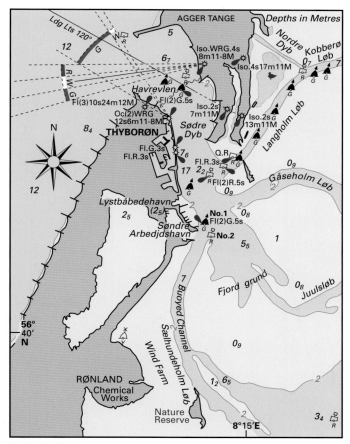

THYBORØN (Denmark)

Remarks

This is probably one of the least attractive ports and towns in the whole of Denmark and is included only because it is an important landfall for yachts arriving in or leaving from Scandinavia.

Sweden

General Sweden has one of the world's largest yachting fleets per capita yet, apart from the Bohuslän coast (Göteborg – Gothenburg – to the Norwegian border) between mid-summer and the middle of August, it is always easy to find a good anchorage or berth. It is a very beautiful country with many interesting historical and cultural sites and is surprisingly warm in summer.

Coastline The interesting sailing is in the island archipelagos (*skärgårdar*) which are very extensive areas of sheltered water where the lack of tide makes tying up to the shore practical. The *skärgårdar* of Bohuslän and Stockholm are the most visited but those in Blekinge (on the SE coast) and in the Gulf of Bothnia are also very good cruising grounds.

Formalities Sweden is in the EU and if coming from Norway or a neighbouring EU country there are no formalities.

THE SCHENGEN AGREEMENT

The Schengen Agreement allows citizens of the signatory countries free movement between these countries. It also allows free movement of all EU passport holders, and holders of a 'Schengen Visa'. This visa allows a maximum stay of 90 days in 180 days in the Schengen area.

Certain non-EU passport holders, such as Canadian and US, may also travel freely without a visa, but they should check the maximum length of permitted stay without a visa. It is often also 90 days. Schengen countries: All EU countries with the exception of the UK, Ireland, Cyprus, Romania and Bulgaria. Non-EU Schengen countries: Switzerland, Norway and Iceland.

Thus within the Schengen area it is possible to travel freely across borders. However, there are several other points to consider:

1. Visitors arriving by private yacht are generally more likely to have to clear immigration than those crossing internal European land borders. Immigration officials in any country can request passport/visa checks.

2. Individuals are responsible for not over-staying the visa limit in each country or area. Multi-entry visas allow you to leave the Schengen area and re-enter, but time restrictions are usually based on 90 days in 180 days rolling limit. Likewise those who do not require a visa will have a similar maximum stay.

3. When travelling by yacht you have the separate responsibility of ensuring that you comply with each country's VAT regulations regarding temporary importation of the vessel (see VAT notes). For example when sailing from Italy to Greece, although they are both within the EU and Schengen area, you are required to obtain a Transit log (effectively a customs record) when entering Greece. This may be further complicated if travelling within the Schengen area, but between EU and non-EU countries. For example sailing from Norway to Sweden.

4. Different countries within the EU and Schengen area have different rules regarding cruising permits. For example, again when sailing from Italy to Greece, you are required to obtain a DEKPA (cruising permit) when entering Greece.

5. The UK is not part of the Schengen area. Many visitors from North America and Australasia do not require a visa and may stay as a visitor for up to six months.

6. It is likely that future plans for Advance Passenger Information will make entry into EU countries more complicated in the future.

Telecom IDD code +46, GSM network, internet facilities widespread.

Currency Swedish kronor. Overseas credit cards are often not accepted by businesses. ATMs widespread and do take credit cards.

Sailing season April to November.

Scandinavia

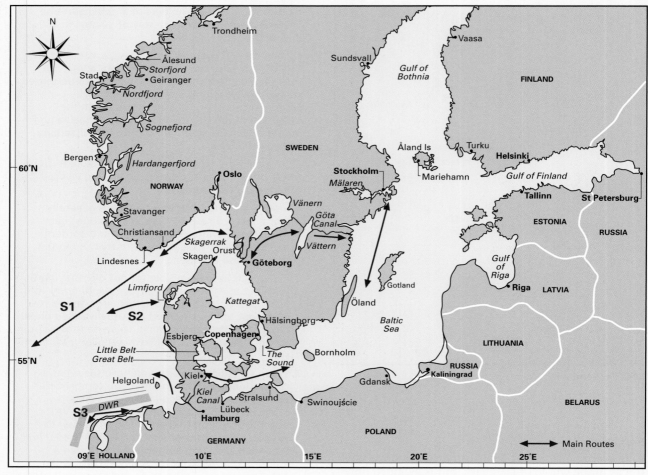

The coastline of Norway is double the length of the UK and four times more spectacular. Denmark has some of the finest sheltered sailing waters and waterside towns in the world. Sweden could easily rival New Zealand as the home of the most sailing boats per head of population. It is surprising how few world cruisers seem to include this area on their travels.

Sailing in Scandinavia is not considered to be a rich man's pastime but a part of the way of life for ordinary people. This is immediately apparent from the reasonable fees charged for visitors' berths, most of which are provided by local authorities who see them as public amenities similar to car parks. Indeed in many places in Norway one pays the mooring fees at a parking meter. Denmark and a few towns in Sweden and Norway have the charming custom of not charging visitors mooring fees during working hours. They would rather we spend our money with local businesses. From the Viking days onward Scandinavians have liked to build their towns around harbours and the visitor often finds his/herself near the centre alongside a lively and friendly waterfront.

Prize winning scenery

With considerable justification Norwegians don't ask if you think that their land is the most beautiful on earth, they just take it for granted. Tens of thousands of miles of fjords and sheltered waterways inside the coastal islands make for safe sailing in almost all conditions for very nearly the entire length of their coastline. Sweden is blessed with many fine archipelagos. The most popular for sailors are off the Bohuslan coast and right outside Stockholm. In both places there are countless possibilities for peacefully mooring amongst

Norway

the rocky islands. There are also many large lakes and quite sizeable cruising boats can access the inland sailing via the Göta Canal. Denmark is a country made up of islands and the sheltered waterways are a delight to sail. The rural scenery with windmills and ancient towns makes a fascinating backdrop to the excellent sailing. Åland is a semi autonomous group of tens of thousands of islands lying between Sweden and Finland and provides some splendid cruising in the surprisingly warm summers. Finland's woods and sheltered waters make for enticing cruising. A refreshing sauna at the end of the day is not unusual.

Windmills and water in Denmark

Weather and sailing season
Strangely the longest sailing season is in the far north. Thanks to the Gulf Stream there is very little ice above the Arctic Circle on the Norwegian coast and boats stay in the water all year round. There is precious little light in mid winter. However, when the light returns in March, there are many who say that this is the best time to cruise in Lofoten when there is still plenty of snow on the mountains and the scenery is at its most spectacular. Further S and in the Baltic ice generally prohibits sailing from January to April though amounts vary from year to year and from Denmark which is rarely affected to the Gulf of Bothnia which can be blocked well into May. The Norwegian coastal weather is often dominated by depressions that sweep across the Atlantic, though, like the British Isles there can be long periods of fair weather in summer. Denmark, the west coast of Sweden and south of Norway tend to oscillate between unstable weather from the west and settled continental high pressure. Once in the Baltic the continental systems predominate and sunny settled weather is the norm in summer. In settled weather land and sea breezes provide the force that drives the sails.

Ashore
Cycling is popular in all the Scandinavian lands and a bike is possibly more useful than the dinghy. There are many fascinating old towns and some very exciting museums. For those interested in maritime history and the development of sailing vessels each Scandinavian country houses one of the finest museums in the world. Oslo and Roskilde have the Viking Ship Museum's with Viking craft over 1,000 years old, fascinating reconstructions and other exhibits. Stockholm has the Vasa, an almost intact 18th-century warship that sends shivers down the spine when you come into the building and see the huge craft and her beautiful carvings for the first time. In Åland the ship museum concentrates on the very last square rigged sailing ships that plied the grain trade between Australia and Britain right up to the end of the 1930s and the four-masted barque Pommern still lies at the wharf, the last ship of her type in the world to remain in her original state.

Facilities
Not surprisingly these are first rate and relatively inexpensive. Boatyards abound, though hauling out can sometimes be a problem as in many places all the boats in a harbour come out at once for the winter and a large crane is jointly hired for the purpose. There are chandlers and fuel berths everywhere. There is never any problem finding food and the usual amenities of town life.

Bohuslan: island cruising world on the west coast of Sweden

Reading
Cruising Guide to Germany and Denmark Brian Navin. (Imray)
The Baltic Sea RCCPF / Ed. M. Lewin-Harris. (Imray)
Norway RCCPF / Judy Lomax (Imray)

My gem
The Knight Templar (Crusades trilogy) Jan Guillou

Lock on Göta Canal

Parking meter, Stavanger harbour

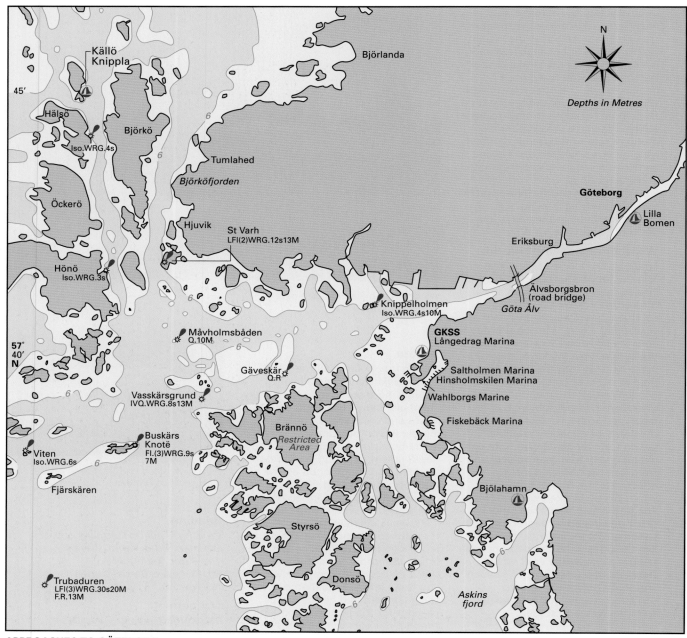

Depths in Metres

Källö
Knippla

45'

Björlanda

Hälsö

Björkö

Tumlahed

Björköfjorden

Öckerö

Hjuvik

St Varh
LFl(2)WRG.12s13M

Hönö
Iso.WRG.3s

Göteborg

Lilla
Bomen

Eriksburg

Knippelholmen
Iso.WRG.4s10M

Älvsborgsbron
(road bridge)

Göta Älv

57°
40'
N

Iso.WRG.4s

Måvholmsbåden
Q.10M

GKSS
Långedrag Marina

Gäveskär
Q.R

Saltholmen Marina
Hinsholmskilen Marina

Vasskärsgrund
IVQ.WRG.8s13M

Wahlborgs Marine

Buskärs
Knotë
Fl.(3)WRG.9s
7M

Brännö
Restricted
Area

Fiskebäck Marina

Viten
Iso.WRG.6s

Fjärskären

Bjölahamn

Styrsö

Trubaduren
LFl(3)WRG.30s20M
F.R.13M

Donsö

Askins
fjord

APPROACHES TO GÖTEBORG

Resources

PILOTS AND GUIDES

Atlantic Crossing Guide Anne Hammick, Gavin McLaren,
    RCCPF / John Lawson (Adlard Coles Nautical)
Atlantic Pilot Atlas James Clarke (Adlard Coles Nautical)
Street's Transatlantic Crossing Guide Donald M Street
Sailing an Atlantic Circuit Alastair Buchan (Adlard Coles
    Nautical)
Imray Chart 100 North Atlantic Passage Chart

WEBSITES

ARC www.worldcruising.com/arc/english
Blue Water Rallies: www.yachtrallies.co.uk
Tropical storms and hurricanes: NOAA www.nhc.noaa.gov
Caribbean Weather Centre: www.caribwx.com
Gulf Stream: Jennifer Clark's Gulf Stream
    users.erols.com/gulfstrm

SSB

Herb Hilgenberg's Southbound II WX Net (VAX498)
    12359kHz at 2000 UT
    www3.sympatico.ca/hehilgen/vax498.htm
Transatlantic Maritime Net (Trudi/8P6QM) 21400kHz at
    1300 UT
Caribbean Weather Net 8104kHz 0830-0900 AST 12359kHz
    0900–0930 AST
USCG text broadcasts of the Ocean Prediction Centre's
    Offshore, NAVTEX and High Seas forecasts 4426, 6501,
    8764, 13089, 17314kHz. Times vary, check webstie:
    www.opc.ncep.noaa.gov/broadcast_schedule/
    uscgbroadcast.html

GÖTEBORG

Tidal range 0.5m

Navigation

There are several easy and well marked routes through the maze of outer islands, there is generally sufficient water to stay out of the big ship channel.

Berths

Use one of the marinas on the outskirts (good public transport to town) or tie up downtown next to the Opera House at Lilla Bomen (Charge band 3).

Anchorage

There are many possible anchorages in the vicinity but none are convenient for accessing the city.

Facilities

This is one of the world's major yachting centres and every conceivable need for yachts is catered for. Lilla Bomen is just a short walk from one of Sweden's major shopping centres.

Remarks

The city is vibrant and well worth visiting.

 # Germany

The German coastline is short compared to the size of the country but well worth visiting. One of the most pleasing things in this land of super friendly people is the way in which ancient towns that have suffered devastating bombing have been lovingly restored. The Kiel Canal is a major waterway and authorities have gone out of their way to make it accessible to yachts. Apart from being a short cut the canal is also a good way to see a bit of the country.

Formalities Germany is in the EU and if coming from a neighbouring EU country there are theoretically no formalities, however, particularly in what used to be East Germany, the harbourmaster may insist on calling immigration who will then make a visit and stamp passports – even though this is a nuisance in practice it takes little time as everything is conducted with the legendary German efficiency.

Telecom IDD code +49, GSM network, internet facilities widespread.

Currency Euro. ATMs widespread.

Sailing season April to November.

BRUNSBÜTTEL

Tidal range Outside lock 4m

Navigation

Approach via the river Elbe. Unless absolutely essential yachts should stay just outside the buoyed channel (there is plenty of water) on the starboard side (somebody will be watching you on radar and the police launches are efficient about imposing spot fines for transgressions). This means that when arriving at the locks you will have to cross the main, busy, shipping channel to Hamburg. Cross at right angles and stay just upriver of the locks and outside

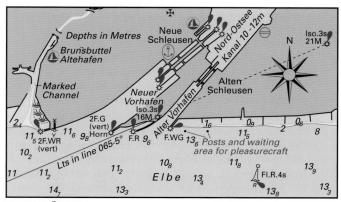

BRUNSBÜTTEL

the channel which is the waiting area. Wait for an occulting white light at the lock entrance which indicates that you can enter. It is wise to tell the authorities of your intentions on Ch 13.

Note yachts are prohibited from travelling on the canal in the night or poor visibility but use of the locks to reach the yacht harbour is permitted at night.

Berths

In the Kanal-Yachthafen which lies directly to port after passing through the locks. The entrance is narrow and maneuvering difficult, yachts longer than 15m will probably have to proceed a little upstream to the next yacht harbor.

Anchorage

None

Facilities

Water fuel and supermarkets.

Remarks

See the section on *Kiel canal* under routes.

 # United Kingdom

General The UK has a large resident yachting population and almost everything you need to buy or do to a yacht is available here. UK customs is strict about EU regulations, particularly on VAT, so ensure you understand the time limits and comply.

Coastline The coastline has harbours and anchorages all around it, with the biggest concentration of yacht harbours and facilities on the south coast. The Scottish coast is the least populated boat-wise and has a much indented coast with off-lying islands, making up a superb cruising area. It is pretty well possible to circumnavigate the UK without doing an overnight passage.

Formalities EU formalities. Customs ☎ 0345 231110 (national no.)

Telecom IDD code +44. GSM network. Internet cafés in larger centres. Wi-Fi in marinas.

Currency Pound sterling. Major credit cards widely accepted. ATMs everywhere.

Sailing season The sailing season is traditionally from April to October. The summers can be unpredictable and the spring and autumn more so. There are good weather forecasts available everywhere so it is a matter of picking your weather window and, should things go wrong, there are always ports of refuge a short distance away.

Routes and harbours Cruising yachts tend to hop around the south coast and as far up as London and the Thames. Some yachts will cruise up to Scotland and then across to Norway while others cruise to or from Ireland. It should be noted that some marinas on the south coast are rated among the most expensive in Europe.

SOLENT (SOUTHAMPTON WATER TO PORTSMOUTH AND ISLE OF WIGHT)

Tidal range 3.7m (Southampton Water)

Navigation

The ports in this area have a lot of shipping movements including ferries as well as commercial shipping. Care is needed not to impede shipping in the recognised channels. There is usually enough water outside the main channels for yachts to safely navigate around. Care also needs to be taken of the strong tidal streams which are complicated (there is a double high tide) and can reach four knots in places. All dangers in the Solent are well buoyed and lit and navigation is straightforward with a little planning.

Berths

VHF Solent Coastguard Ch 67. Southampton Ch 12, 14. Portsmouth Ch 11. Most of the marinas can be contacted on Ch 80 (M).

Marinas around the Solent are busy in the summer and it is useful to book ahead for a berth. Weekends are the busiest. Marinas with berths for visitors are likely to be:

Yarmouth (IOW)
250 berths. 38 moorings. Visitors' berths. Max LOA 25m depending on draught. Charge band 4/5. www.yarmouth-harbour.co.uk

Lymington
300 berths. Visitors' berths. Max LOA 45m. Charge band 5. www.berthongroup.co.uk

Cowes Yacht Haven
260 berths. Visitors' berths. Max LOA 15m. Charge band 4. www.cowesyachthaven.com

Ocean Village Marina (Southampton)
375 berths. Visitors' berths. Max LOA 90m. Charge band 4/5. www.mdlmarinas.co.uk

Gosport Marina (Portsmouth)
575 berths. Visitors' berths. Max LOA 25m. Charge band 4/5. www.premiermarinas.com

Facilities

All the marinas are full service marinas with all facilities.

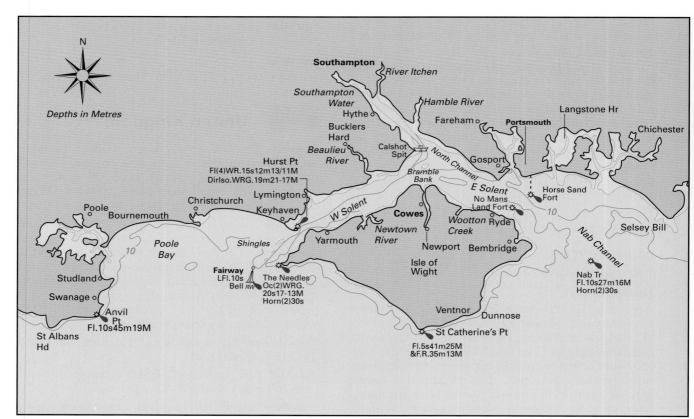

SOLENT AREA

Anchorages

There are numerous anchorages around the Solent that can be used depending on wind and sea conditions, although the most useful anchorages have moorings which are charged for if you pick one up. Just remember you will be competing with all the resident yachts in the area.

Remarks

The Solent is the most populated yachting area in the UK and all facilities will be found here. There are also more than enough pubs, restaurants and bars to keep you happy for a long time.

PLYMOUTH

Tidal range 4.7m

Navigation

Western Channel can be used in all weather. Leave Drake's Island to port and make for one of the four marinas. Strong tidal streams in the channels.

Berths

VHF Queen's Harbourmaster Ch 16 working Ch 14 All the marinas use Ch 80 (M).

Mayflower Marina
270 berths. 30 visitors' berths. Max LOA 30m. Charge band 4.
www.mayflowermarina.co.uk

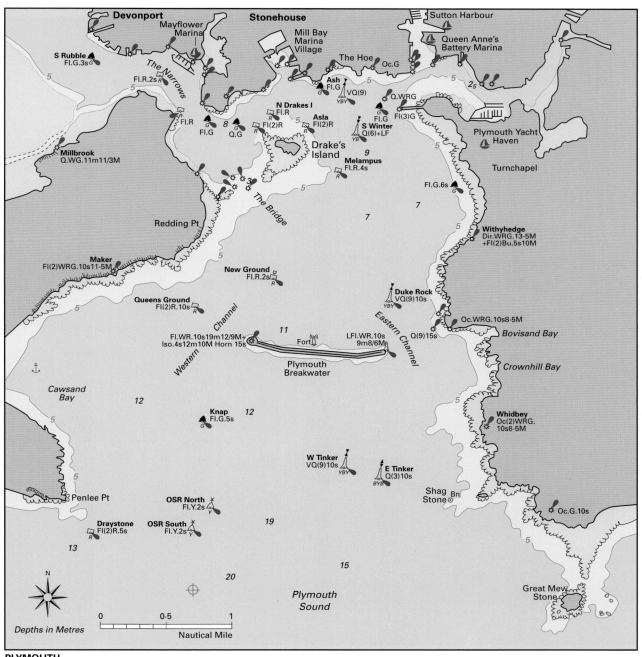

PLYMOUTH
⊕ 50°18′N 04°10′W

Queen Anne's Battery
245 berths. 50 visitors' berths. Max LOA 45m.
Charge band 4.
www.mdlmarinas.co.uk

Sutton Harbour Marina
Visitors' berths. Max LOA 15m. Charge band 3

Plymouth Yacht Haven
Visitors' berths. Depths min. 2.25m.
Charge band 3/4
www.yacht-havens.ltd.uk

Facilities

Usual facilities and amenities in the marinas. Fuel quay. Yards and excellent repair facilities.

Resources

PILOTS AND GUIDES

The Cruising Almanac (Cruising Association/Imray)
Reed's Nautical Almanac (Adlard Coles Nautical)
The Shell Channel Pilot Tom Cunliffe (Imray)
East Coast Pilot Jarman, Cooper and Holness (Imray)
Irish Sea Pilot David Rainsbury (Imray)
West Country Cruising Companion Mark Fishwick
    (Nautical Data)
East and North Coasts of Ireland Sailing Directions and
    South and West Coasts of Ireland Sailing Directions
    (both by Irish Cruising Club Publications Ltd)
Norway RCC Pilotage Foundation (Imray)
Cruising Cork and Kerry Graham Swanson (Imray)

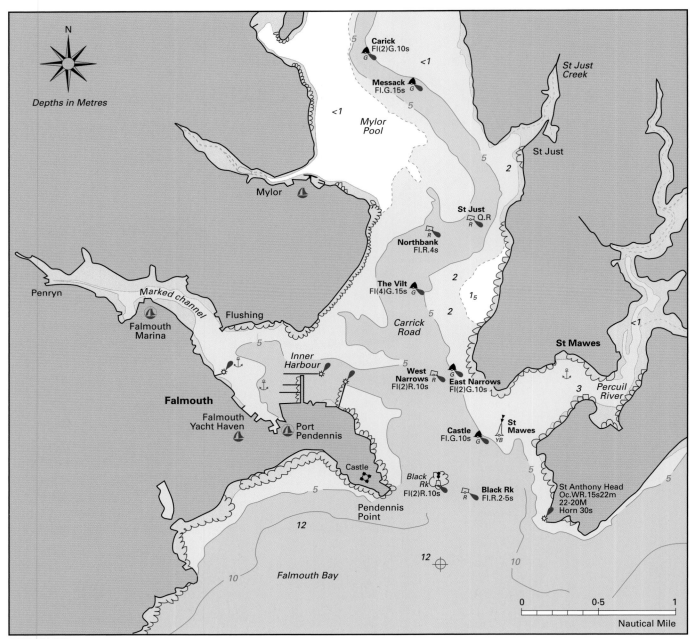

FALMOUTH
⊕50°08'N 05°02'W

Anchorage

Some moorings may be available. Limited space for anchoring. Cawsand Bay is open to southerlies.

Remarks

Historic city with long yachting associations, including many ocean races. All yacht facilities.

FALMOUTH

Tidal range 4.6m

Navigation

Care needed of The Manacles in the western approaches. Harbour entrance wide and can be entered in all weather.

Berths

VHF Falmouth Harbour Radio Ch 16 working Ch 11, 12, 14.
All marinas use Ch 80 (M)

Visitors Yacht Haven
c.100 berths. Visitors' berths. Max LOA 15m.
Depths min 2.5m. Charge band 3.

Falmouth Marina
325 berths. 70 visitors' berths. Max LOA 25m.
Depths min. 2m. Charge band 3/4.

Port Pendennis Marina
60 berths. 20 visitors' berths. Max LOA 50m+.
Depths 2–3m. Charge band 4.

Facilities

Usual amenities in the marinas. Fuel quay. Excellent repair facilities.

Anchorage

Off the town clear of moorings. Good shelter. Some visitors' moorings available and a pontoon is laid in the summer.

Remarks

Most yacht facilities can be found in the town and at Penryn. Good shopping and pubs and restaurants ashore. Convenient setting out or arriving point for Atlantic routes.

Ireland

General Yachting is popular in Ireland and there are well developed facilities, if on a smaller scale than in neighbouring countries.

Coastline The west and north coasts of Ireland are rugged with some magnificent deep inlets providing good cruising and shelter. The south coast is more benign but also has some excellent natural harbours. The east coast is less interesting and beset by sandbanks, but has some excellent man-made harbours.

Formalities EU formalities.

Telecom IDD code +35. GSM network. Internet cafés in larger centres.

Currency Euro. Major credit cards widely accepted. ATMs everywhere.

Sailing season The sailing season is traditionally from May to September. You need to keep a careful eye on lows coming across the Atlantic, especially on the western Atlantic coast.

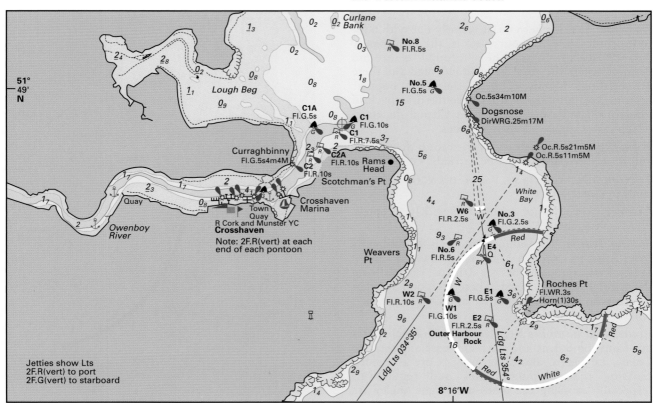

CROSSHAVEN AND APPROACHES
⊕ 51°48'·8N 08°17'W

Routes and harbours Many North American yachts make the south coast of Ireland their first landfall in Europe. From there it is an easy hop to the English Channel ports. The more adventurous cruise up the W coast and cross to Scotland.

CROSSHAVEN

Tidal range 3.7m

Navigation

Simple, well marked, all-weather entrance.

Berths

Crosshaven Boatyard Marina
Salve Marina
Royal Cork Yacht Club Marina
Anchorage possible in the Owenboy River.

Facilities

Fuel quays at marinas. All yacht repairs and facilities. National trains, international airport and ferries.

Remarks

Cork is an interesting and historic city, reached by an easy bus or taxi ride. The Royal Cork was the first Yacht Club in the world.

France

General Like the UK, France has a large resident yachting population. There are yacht harbours dotted all around the coast and every sort of facility is available. The French go on holiday en masse in July and August and the coast can be crowded at this time.

Coastline The northern coast is fairly flat with a lot of purpose-built harbours, as is the low sandy Atlantic Biscay coast. The exception is around Brittany where the coast is much indented and there are offshore islands. This is the most popular cruising area although it does have the drawback of massive tides (7.5m at springs in Chenal du Four) which cause some vicious tidal races.

Formalities EU formalities. Registration documents and insurance papers must be carried.

Telecom IDD code +33. GSM network. Internet cafés in larger centres.

Currency Euro. Major credit cards widely accepted. ATMs everywhere.

Sailing season The sailing season is traditionally from April to October. You need to keep a careful eye on lows coming across the Atlantic, especially on the western Atlantic coast. There are good weather forecasts so it is really a matter of picking a weather window to go.

Routes and harbours Regular cross-Channel routes are from the Solent and harbours east and west to Calais, Le Havre and Cherbourg. Care is needed crossing the shipping routes and regulations (especially crossing the lanes at a right angle) are strictly enforced. Yachts drawing less than about

1.8m (consult a guide) can take the French waterway system from Le Havre to Paris and then on down into the Rhône and the Mediterranean. Once round to the W Brittany coast a lot of yachts elect to make a direct passage across to somewhere like La Coruña in Spain, but there is no reason why you cannot coast-hop around the French Biscay coast. Yachts drawing less than 1.5m can take a short-cut from Bordeaux down to Sète through the French waterways system.

LA TRINITE

Tidal range 4.6m

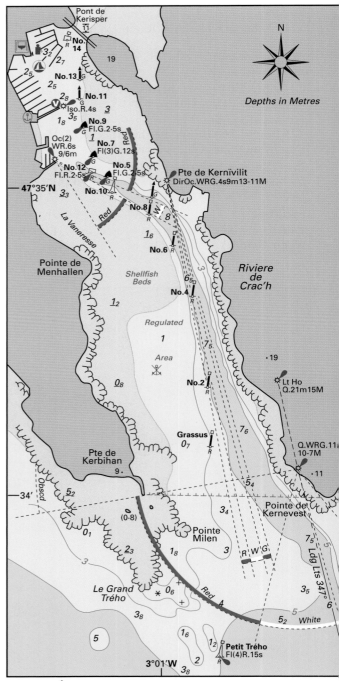

LA TRINITÉ

Navigation

A large marina at the head of the Crac'h River. A buoyed channel leads up the river to the marina. Entrance in all weather and at night with care.

Berths

VHF Ch. 09

1050 berths. 80 visitors' berths. Max LOA 25m. Charge band 3.

Facilities

All marina facilities. Fuel quay. Yard. Provisions and restaurants and bars nearby. Rail connections.

Remarks

La Trinité is usefully situated when on passage through Biscay and can be entered in all weather.

LA ROCHELLE

Tidal range 5.1m

Navigation

From the N the navigable channel under Ré bridge (30m air height) is buoyed with least depths of 2.2m. From the S transit on 059° on the two lighthouses and follow the buoyed channel. Minimes Marina entrance channel is to starboard near Tour Richelieu and the Vieux Port and Bassin à Flot are further up the buoyed channel in the middle of town. Least depths of 0.5m (MLWS) to Minimes and 1m (MLWS) in the dredged channel to the Vieux Port and Bassin à Flot. The approaches are well lit.

Berths

VHF Minimes Marina and La Rochelle Vieux Port Ch 09.

Minimes Marina
3290 berths. Visitors' berths. Depths 2m (MLWS). Charge band 3.

Vieux Port
115 berths. Visitors' pontoon. Max LOA 12m. Depths 1m (MLWS). Charge band 3.

Bassin à Flot
90 berths. Visitors' berths. Max LOA 14m. Depths 3m (sill 1.2m MLWS access −2hr +30min MHWS). Charge band 3.

Bassin des Chaleutiers
Max LOA 60m. Max width 12m. Depths 5m (access −2hr +45min MHWS).

Facilities

Water. 220/380V. Fuel quay. All yacht repairs. Excellent provisioning, restaurants and bars.

Remarks

Minimes is some distance from the city centre but a water bus runs from the marina. The old trawler basin (Bassin des Chaleutiers) is being developed as a super-yacht basin.
www.portlarochelle.com

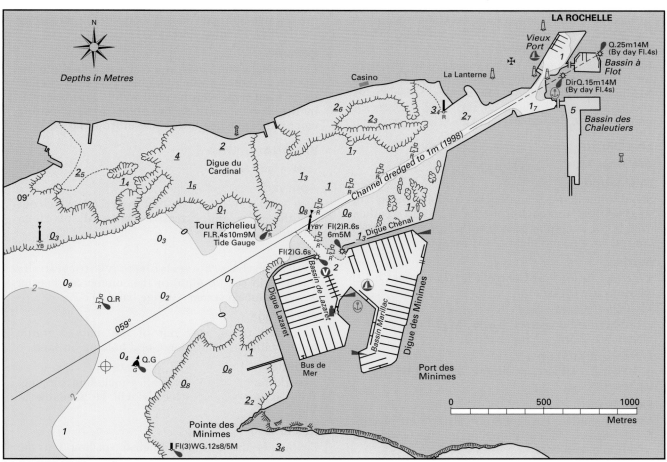

LA ROCHELLE (France)
⊕46°08'·3N 01°11'W

Spain
(Galicia and Andalucia)

General Around the Atlantic coast Spain has a significantly lower population of resident yachts than nearby France and a very large fishing fleet (the third largest in the world). Most facilities can be found, although not on the scale found in the UK and France.

Coastline This Atlantic coast has a lot of fishing harbours, a few yacht harbours and well sheltered natural rias. It is for the most part a rocky forbidding coast (except for some of the southern part which is flatter) and although there is good shelter at intervals, there is always a big Atlantic swell breaking along the coast which can make some entrances to harbours and rias difficult and at times dangerous.

Formalities EU formalities. Registration documents and insurance papers must be carried.

Telecom IDD code +34. GSM network. Internet cafés in larger centres.

Currency Euro. Major credit cards widely accepted. ATMs everywhere.

Sailing season The sailing season is traditionally from April to October, although around the southern part of the coast towards Gibraltar the season is extended to November and later. Keep a careful eye on lows coming across the Atlantic. In spring and autumn fog is quite common and, given the amount of shipping and the resident fishing population, care is needed.

Routes and harbours Yachts cruising this coast are for the most part on passage to or from the Mediterranean or the Atlantic Islands. Some yachts choose to use a harbour in the S as a place for jumping off to the Canaries and an Atlantic crossing.

LA CORUÑA

Tidal range 3.9m

Navigation

Shoal water in the N approaches troublesome in bad weather. Best approach from the W in bad weather. Well lit for a night approach with Torre de Hercules conspic by day and night (23M range).

Berths

VHF La Coruña Port Control Ch 16 working Ch 12. Marinas use Ch 09.

Real Club Nautico and Club Casino
c.250 berths. 50 visitors' berths. Max LOA 15m. Depths <1–2.5m. Charge band 2.

Darsena de la Marina
c. 40 berths. 10 visitors' berths. Max LOA 17m. Charge band 2.

Facilities

Usual amenities. Fuel (pontoon shallow in places). Some repairs. Good shopping in the town and restaurants and bars.

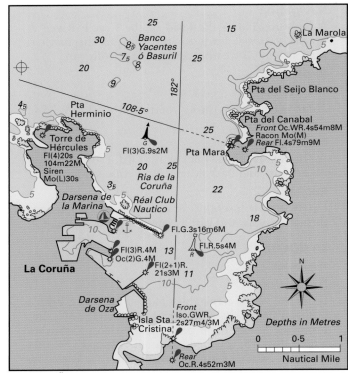

LA CORUÑA
⊕43°24′N 08°25′W

Anchorage

Some visitors' moorings. Anchorage under the breakwater although it is uncomfortable in strong southerlies. Holding unreliable.

Remarks

La Coruña is often used as a convenient harbour for the Biscay crossing going N. Generally yachts should try to keep some westing until well N into Biscay as in the days of yore sailing ships dreaded getting embayed here when lows came in from the W.

BAYONA/BAIONA

Tidal range 4.6m

Approach

Easy from seaward, if coasting from the N watch out for the islets and extensive banks SE of Punta Lameda

Berths

Many berths are available to visitors at the Yacht Club (up to 40m) or the commercial marina www.puertobaiona.com (Charge band 3).

Anchorage

Restricted room, stay out of the marked traffic routes within the harbour. Good holding on sand.

Facilities

A wide range of good facilities including slipping. What is not available locally will be available in Vigo.

Remarks

Bayona is the common English spelling but the official name is now Baiona. For long this has been

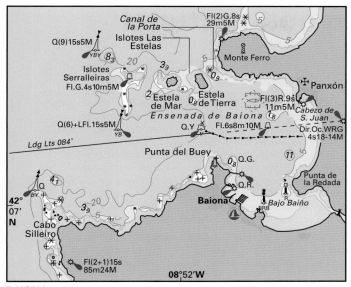

BAIONA

a jumping off point for Atlantic voyages and is a very pleasant town. Don't miss a walk around the walls of the fortress above the Yacht Club (now a luxury hotel).

PUERTO SHERRY

Tidal range 2.8m

Navigation

From the N keep clear of shoals off Pta Santa Catalina del Norte. From the S use buoyed channel off Cadiz. Puerto Sherry approaches min. 4.5m. Night approach straightforward although lights at Cadiz can be confusing and difficult to identify against the background loom.

Berths

VHF Cadiz Practicos (Pilots) Ch 16, 12, 14.
Puerto Sherry Ch 09.

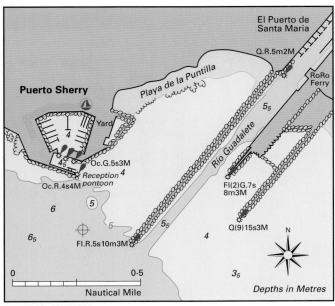

PUERTO SHERRY
⊕39°34'·3N 06°15'·2W

800 berths. Visitors' berths. Max LOA 60m. Depths 3–3.5m. Charge band 3.

Facilities

Usual amenities. Showers and WC. Fuel quay. Good repair facilities. Limited provisioning and restaurants and cafés around the marina.

Remarks

Popular marina to leave a yacht before heading down to the Canaries.
www.puertosherry.com

Portugal

General Portugal has a relatively small population of resident yachts and the marinas around the Algarve largely cater for other European yachts (largely British and German) permanently based here. The Portuguese authorities can be sticklers over EU regulations so make sure your paperwork is in order.

Coastline Like the adjacent Spanish coastline this is a rocky coast cut by a lot of natural rias which provide good shelter.

Formalities EU formalities, although yachts often required to check in at every harbour. Registration documents and insurance papers must be carried. VAT papers often checked.

Telecom IDD code +351. GSM network. Internet cafés in larger centres

Currency Euro. Major credit cards accepted, though less widely than Spain. ATMs common in larger centres and tourist areas.

Sailing season April to October. Like Spain keep an eye on lows coming across the Atlantic and be prepared for fog.

Routes and harbours Like Spain yachts are usually on passage to and from Northern Europe and the Atlantic Islands. It is perfectly feasible to do day trips down the coast and some yachts winter over in the relatively benign (compared to northern Europe) climate.

LISBON

Tidal range 3.3m

Navigation

Approach towards Fort São Juliao on the N entrance point where there are no dangers and least tide. Shoal water off the S entrance point. Care needed of commercial traffic entering and leaving. Cascais Marina at Estoril can be used, as well as Doca de Alacantra in Lisbon centre. Ponte de 25 Abril has 70m air height.

Berths

VHF Lisboa Port Control Ch 16 working 12
Cascais Marina Ch 16 and 62.

Cruising Atlantic Spain and Portugal

Atlantic swell meets the coast
of Galicia

The entire Spanish coast between France and Portugal is a sailors' dream with countless anchorages and many good ports. It deserves many months of exploration. For those sailing S across the Bay of Biscay the NW coast, formed by the Spanish province of Galicia will be the usual destination. Despite a major improvement in living standards and communications, Galicia is every bit as delightful now as it was over 30 years ago. People are happy and friendly, facilities and infrastructure are good and where previously it was rare to meet a Spanish boat there is now a growing fleet of local sailors who are appearing on the ocean passages of the world. Anchorages abound but new marinas are also easy to find and there is a total lack of restrictive officialdom.

Further S the Portuguese coast is lacking in natural harbours but there are several good ports and an increasing number of first rate yachting facilities. In particular the old town of Oporto (best visited from the large artificial harbour at Leixões) and the area around Lisbon should not be missed.

Muros in the evening

Combarro, near Pontevedra

GALICIA - SPAIN

Baiona: the two marinas and anchorage with the old fortress in the background

Almost every boat leaving northern Europe will make a stop on this coast and a stay of at least a month is recommended, working down the coast between La Coruña and Lisbon. This will offer some of the best cruising anywhere and be a good opportunity to test crew and vessel in an area where equipment and facilities are inexpensive and readily available.

Weather and sailing season
The N Spanish coast is influenced by the same frontal systems that affect the British Isles to the N, and SW winds are common. S of Cabo Finisterre the winds are increasingly from the N and during the summer months it is common for the wind and current to be from the N – the 'Portuguese trades'. However, inshore winds are often light to variable and passage makers need to go out to sea to find the breeze (or stay inshore if heading N). With the onset of winter the weather becomes more variable further S with even the southern part of Portugal occasionally affected by large depressions to the N. I met a boat that had sailed from Canada to the Mediterranean and back via Greenland whose only bad experience was being capsized off the Portuguese coast in December. Locals sail all year around and, with careful monitoring of the weather forecasts, there is no reason not to do this.

Ashore
One of the charming things about Spain is the unobtrusiveness of bureaucracy for the short term visitor, in half a dozen visits to the NW coast, spread over 30 years, I have never been approached by an official and when I have needed to seek them out for help I have been received with great courtesy and helpfulness. However, especially in the yachting centres of the Med, those seeking to stay longer than six months are likely to be required to import their vessels and even EU vessels with VAT paid will be subject to special taxes. Unfortunately Portugal has a much more daunting bureaucracy, that now (2008) seems to be relaxing somewhat in its interest for foreign cruising boats. The N coasts of the Basque country and Cantabrica are steep-to with many fine natural harbours where rivers meet the sea. The countryside is lush and towns are mainly old and interesting to visit. In Galicia the beautiful waters of the Rias make for peaceful sheltered cruising with charming villages, each with a picturesque ancient centre, and economical restaurants serving tasty seafood and delicious wine. There are also some marvellously preserved medieval cities such as Santiago de Compostella and Pontevedra, which are well worth a visit. Once into Portugal the character of the land changes and becomes hotter and drier, but still with fascinating old villages and cities and Lisbon has a special charm that makes it a major destination.

Cruising strategies
From Northern Europe this coast makes an excellent first offshore destination with a 2–3 day crossing of the Bay of Biscay (best to pass through the Chenal de Four and Raz du Seine and stay inside the very busy shipping lanes). The best way to cruise the N coast is from W to E, with the SW winds and perhaps return via the French coast. W and S of Cabo Finisterre the coast is best cruised N to S, perhaps returning via the Azores, which would provide an excellent test of crew and boat or working N close inshore where winds are often light. If heading on to the Canary Islands and West Indies be sure to allow plenty of time in this area before setting off across the ocean.

Reading
South Biscay RCCPF / John Lawson (Imray)
Atlantic Spain and Portugal RCCPF / Martin Walker & Anne Hammick (Imray)
Cruising Galicia Carlos Rojas & Robert Bailey (Imray)
CA Cruising Almanac (Imray)

My gems
The films of Pedro Almodóvar.

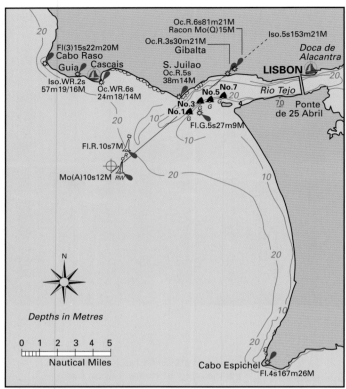

LISBON APPROACHES
⊕38°37'·31N 09°23'·44W WGS84

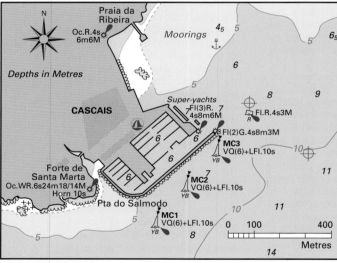

CASCAIS MARINA
⊕38°41'·67N 09°24'·79W WGS84

Cascais Marina
650 berths. Visitors' berths. Max LOA 40–50m. Depths 3–7m. Charge band 4.

Doca de Alacantra
250 berths. Visitors' berths. Max LOA 45m.

Marina Expo
550 berths. Visitors' berths. Max LOA 50m. Charge band 2/3. Go alongside the first pontoon inside the entrance to complete paperwork and be assigned a berth.

Anchorage

E of Cascais Marina. Open S.

Facilities

Usual amenities. Fuel. Good repair facilities. Excellent provisioning at Cascais and Lisbon and numerous restaurants and bars.

Remarks

The attractive city of Lisbon is well worth the visit. Lisbon can be reached quickly and cheaply from Cascais by regular fast trains in 30 minutes. There are a number of other basins along the Tagus River that have berths for visiting yachts and a new marina at Oerias between Cascais and Lisbon proper. Good public transport from Cascais to Lisbon centre.
Email Cascaismarina@mail.telepak.pt

PORTIMAO

Tidal range 2.6m

Navigation

A marina just inside the Rio Arade. Some care

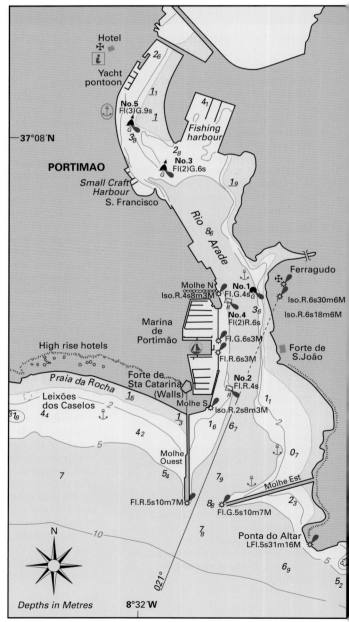

PORTIMAO (Portugal)

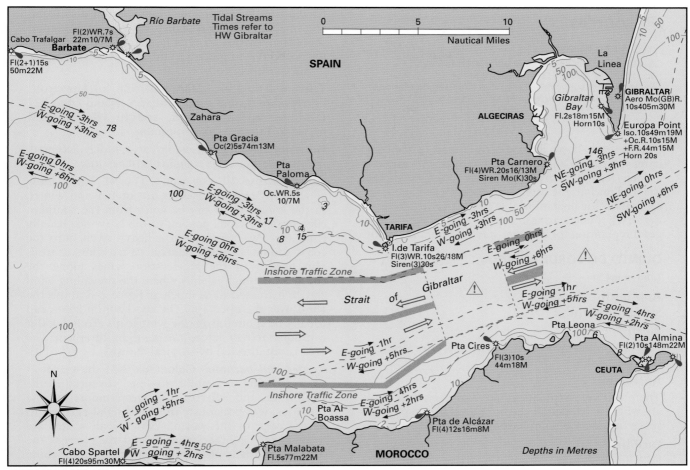

GIBRALTAR STRAIT

needed over tide and river currents in the entrance. This port is a lot easier to enter in bad weather than Lagos, although care is still needed with onshore winds. A night entry is possible as it is well lit. Care needed of fishing boats going in and out of the fishing harbour further up the river.

Berths

VHF Ch 11.
620 berths. Visitors' berths. Max LOA 50m. Charge band 3.

Anchorage

Inside the E breakwater to the river.

Facilities

All marina facilities. Fuel quay. 50/300-ton travel hoists and hard standing. Most yacht repairs can be arranged. Provisions and restaurants and bars within the marina.

Remarks

Portimao is a useful marina to make for when en route down the Portuguese coast to the Mediterranean or the Canaries or on the way back to Europe from the Azores.
www.marinadeportimao.com

GIBRALTAR

For details see entry in the Country and port guide of *Chapter 6 Mediterranean Sea,* page 317.

MADEIRA

Madeira has not been so popular with yachts as the Canaries because of a lack of mooring possibilities. The recent development of a number of marinas has

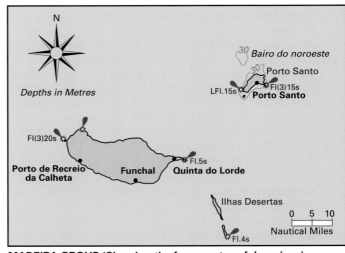

MADEIRA GROUP (Showing the four most useful marinas)

Resources

PILOTS AND GUIDES
North Biscay RCCPF / Mike & Gill Barron (Imray)
South Biscay RCCPF / John Lawson (Imray)
Secret Anchorages of Brittany Peter Cumberlidge (Imray)
Atlantic Spain and Portugal RCCPF / Anne Hammick (Imray)

changed this. Porto Santo on the island of the same name is a secure anchorage and marina, however it is a long ferry trip from the more interesting main island. Funchal, the capital is very crowded and has a reputation for uncomfortable swells, as do several of the newly built marinas. The only place with a very good reputation for a longer stay is Quinta do Lorde.

QUINTO DO LORDE MARINA

Tidal range 3m

Approach
Straightforward.

Berth
264 in marina up to 45m LOA and 4.5m draught. Charge band 4.

Anchoring
There are no possibilities here and very little hope anywhere in Madeira except for a small and exposed space outside the main harbour of Funchal.

Facilities
Full facility marina including travel lift, good supermarkets nearby (taxi ride) for provisioning.

Remarks
This marina is a long way from Funchal but is not far from the international airport. Car hire can easily be arranged for touring the island – a must.

Canary Islands (Islas Canarias)

General The Canaries are part of Spain, though they enjoy special tax privileges including exemption from VAT on most items. This means that many boating items are not appreciably more expensive than in mainland Europe, and in some cases cheaper. The islands are a popular winter destination for sun-starved northerners and the islands have been massively developed for tourism. In the autumn the islands are invariably crowded with yachts getting ready for the annual migration across the Atlantic and it can be difficult to find a berth. ARC participants are guaranteed a berth in Las Palmas. Yachts anchor off in Las Palmas until the ARC participants leave and then move into the marina.

Coastline The islands are the peaks of old volcanoes and for the most part are steep-to basalt and granite with some tufa. The vegetation is largely North African although the lack of natural water means that they are largely arid.

Formalities EU formalities. Registration documents and insurance papers must be carried. Skippers should endeavour to obtain clearance papers from the port office to present to the authorities on arrival in the Caribbean.

Telecom IDD +34. Island code 928 for Lanzarote, Fuerteventura, and Gran Canaria. Island code 922 for Tenerife, La Gomera, and El Hierro. GSM network. Internet cafés common.

Currency Euro. Major credit cards widely accepted. ATMs in larger centres and tourist resorts.

Sailing season All year round. The NE Trades blow consistently over the islands in summer and winter. In the winter there can be gales from the southern edge of depressions passing to the N (winds usually from the SW) which send a heavy swell onto the coast and have caused damage to harbours. Care is also needed of the acceleration zones along the coasts of the high islands where the prevailing wind can be increased to as much as Force 2–3 above the wind over the open sea. The acceleration zones can usually be spotted from the white caps around and it is prudent to reef before you get right into them. The area is not affected by tropical storms.

Routes and harbours Columbus used the Canaries as a jumping off point for his voyages to the Caribbean and Hierro, the westernmost of the Canaries, was previously thought by flat-earthers to be the edge of the world. Virtually all routes are from Europe to the Canaries and then across the Atlantic and it is often said that the quickest route from the Canaries to Europe is via the Caribbean. Around the islands there are large commercial harbours, usually with a yacht basin, a number of marinas and some fishing harbours. Well protected natural anchorages are few and far between.

Tidal range (for Canaries) 2.2m.

GRACIOSA

Navigation
Approach from the N can be on either side of Isla Graciosa. A good lookout is needed for Isla Alegranza (lit on the NE corner) and Roque del Este (unlit). A night approach to the anchorage is possible and also into the harbour with care (entrance lit).

Berths
Two pontoons with finger pontoons in the harbour off the W breakwater can be used by visiting yachts on an ad hoc basis. If there is a berth you can use it, otherwise anchor off. Good shelter. Charge band 2.

Anchorage
Anchor off in either of the two bays to the E of the harbour. Reasonable holding and good shelter from the prevailing NE winds. The bay under the SE corner is a marine reserve and the holding is also uncertain here.

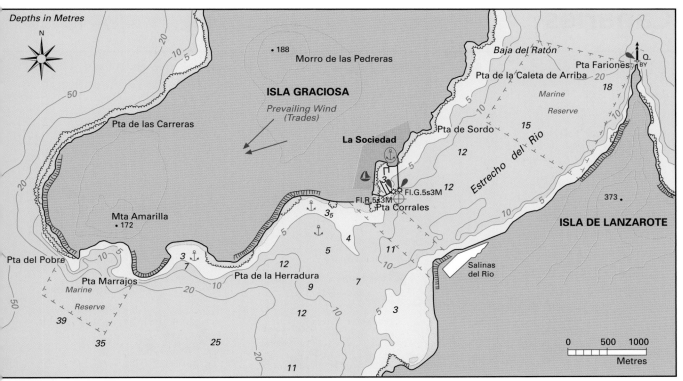

GRACIOSA AND LA SOCIEDAD
⊕ 29°13′·60N 13°30′·12W WGS84

Facilities

The two pontoons have no water or electricity. To fill up with water and fuel you need to make arrangements to go on the quay inside the E breakwater. 64-ton travel hoist. Hardware shop. Restaurants and bars in the village. Ferry to Lanzarote.

Remarks

Graciosa is an excellent arrival point in the Canaries and indeed is one of the best things about the Canaries. This is a simpler more gracious place away from the tourist extravagances of some of the other islands.

PUERTO CALERO (Lanzarote)

Navigation

Difficult to identify exact position by day, and night approach needs to made with caution. Characteristics of light at Puerto del Carmen (small fishing port) nearby are easily confused with lights for Puerto Calero. Care needed of tight turn to starboard at entrance (shoal water buoyed). Berth at reception quay near Torre di Control to be allotted a berth.

Berths

VHF Ch 09, 16.
420 berths. Visitors' berths. Max LOA c.40m. Depths 2.5–10m. Charge band 3.

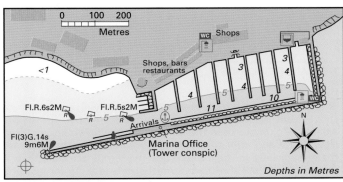

PUERTO CALERO (Lanzarote)
⊕ 28°54′·88N 13°42′·40W WGS84

Facilities

Usual amenities. Fuel quay. Limited yacht repairs. Limited provisioning. Restaurants and bars.

Remarks

Up-market marina. The harbourmaster will usually try to find yachts a berth here, although it is very busy when yachts are getting ready to cross.
www.puertocalero.com

LAS PALMAS (Gran Canaria)

Navigation

Approach straightforward in all weather. Care needed of ferries and commercial shipping entering and leaving harbour. In the marina go on the fuel quay to enquire for a berth. Alternatively berth and then walk to marina office to check in.

Canaries

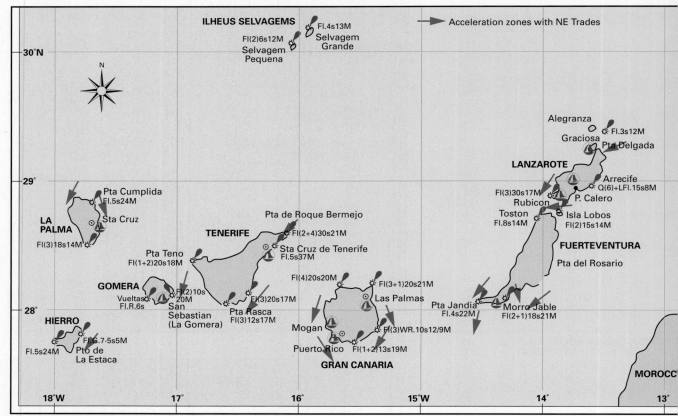

The map shows the Canary Islands with the following labels:

ILHEUS SELVAGEMS
Fl.4s13M Selvagem Grande
Fl(2)6s12M Selvagem Pequena

Acceleration zones with NE Trades

30°N

N

Alegranza
Fl.3s12M
Graciosa
Pta Delgada
LANZAROTE
Arrecife
Fl(3)30s17M
Q(6)+LFl.15s8M
Rubicon
P. Calero
Toston
Fl.8s14M
Isla Lobos
Fl(2)15s14M

29°

Pta Cumplida
Fl.5s24M
Sta Cruz
LA PALMA
Fl(3)18s14M

Pta de Roque Bermejo
Fl(2+4)30s21M
TENERIFE
Sta Cruz de Tenerife
Fl.5s37M

FUERTEVENTURA
Pta del Rosario

Pta Teno
Fl(1+2)20s18M

GOMERA
Fl(2)10s20M
Vueltas
Fl.R.6s
San Sebastian (La Gomera)
Fl(3)20s17M
Pta Rasca
Fl(3)12s17M

Fl(4)20s20M
Fl(3+1)20s21M
Las Palmas
Pta Jandia
Fl.4s22M
Morro Jable
Fl(2+1)18s21M

28°
HIERRO
Fl.G.7·5s5M
Fl.5s24M
Pto de La Estaca

Mogan
Puerto Rico
Fl(3)WR.10s12/9M
Fl(1+2)13s19M
GRAN CANARIA

MOROCC

18°W   17°   16°   15°W   14°   13°

THE CANARY ISLANDS

The Canaries are a group of volcanic islands lying off the African coast and strategically placed at the top of the tradewind belt for sailing across the Atlantic. Columbus used the islands as stepping stones on his voyages to the New World and prior to that they were known to the Romans and possibly the Phoenicians. In the modern age the temperate climate in the winter has attracted all those sun-starved northerners looking for winter sun to their shores and the islands are devoted to tourism, some would say over-devoted.

The Canaries are home to a significant number of yachts who cruise around the islands and also enjoy the sub-tropical temperatures and sun in the winter. Some hardy souls will spend the winter here and then beat back up to the Atlantic coast of Spain and Portugal or into the Mediterranean for the summer. Although this trip is against the prevailing NE trades and the Portuguese trades (also NE), the winds can often be light once you get clear of the Canaries up as far as the Strait of Gibraltar.

The increased number of boats basing themselves in the Canaries and the annual influx of cruisers in the autumn for an Atlantic crossing mean that facilities are well developed and there are marinas around most of the islands and good infrastructure ashore for the care and repair of yachts.

Seasons and winds

The prevailing winds are the trades blowing from the N-NE at 10–20 knots. These are reliable for most of the summer and around 80% of winter observations. From around October to January there is an increase in NE over N winds. In the winter there are periods of SW winds when a depression passes close to the islands and these can be strong at times.

Hurricane season for the north Atlantic is June to November and for the most part do not affect the Canaries. One of the breeding areas for tropical storms is around the Cape Verdes between 7°–15° N and these will normally travel in a NW direction before curving N and then NE. Sometimes a tropical storm will

Puerto Calero Lanzarote

curve back early on in its track and travel E–NE and it is then possible for it to travel over the Canaries. In recent years there have been tropical storms and even the odd hurricane developing in December. This happened in December 2005 with TS *Delta* which caused some damage through the islands. The occurrence of tropical storms in December (RJH was in TS *Peter* in December 2003) needs to be watched for those cruising the Canaries and also for the Atlantic crossing.

One other thing needs to be watched around the islands and that is the acceleration zones that occur where the prevailing NE trades are squeezed into a channel or deflected by the high mountains. When this occurs the wind speed in the zone can significantly increase, sometimes up to 10–15 knots more than the wind over the open sea. The significant acceleration zones are shown on the map of the Canaries.

Ashore

The popularity of the Canaries with land-based tourists means there are more than enough bars and restaurants around the islands to satisfy everyone. Because of the benign winter climate these all remain open when most yachts will be passing through between November and February.

To get around the islands you will really need a hire car. For some its debateable whether the popular islands (I'm thinking of Lanzarote, Gran Canaria and Tenerife in particular here) are worth a tour at all as they are stupendously built up with pseudo-local style white cube houses and apartments littering the coast and hinterland. For those who want to party hard you won't have to move far from the marina. Some of the other smaller islands like Graciosa, Gomera and La Palma are less developed and more rewarding ashore.

Nautical chapel on Graciosa

Facilities

Provisioning is also good with large supermarkets that can supply everything needed for stocking up to go trans-Atlantic. In some places where a marina is not near the main centre you will need a hire car to get to the supermarkets, usually on the outskirts of the main town, to do any major stocking up. In other places like Las Palmas on Gran Canaria, Santa Cruz on Tenerife and Santa Cruz on La Palma there are good supermarkets near the berths.

Yacht facilities are fairly well developed with good chandlers and repair services in the big ports like Las Palmas and Santa Cruz on Tenerife. When the ARC is in Las Palmas a lot of specialised service facilities are arranged with the European suppliers of marine hardware. Usually the service agents are busy enough with the ARC and it is unlikely that they will have any spare time for non-ARC boats, but it may be worth enquiring. Spares can be flown out to most places around the islands and there are few problems clearing goods in.

Useful ports

Yachts sailing down from the Atlantic coasts of Spain and Portugal and the Mediterranean will usually make for the eastern islands first so they can easily sail westwards to the others if they want to. Below is a list of useful ports used by cruising yachts arriving in the Canaries for the Atlantic crossing. They are not by any means exhaustive and concentrate on places where yachts stop to get ready and provision up for the Atlantic crossing.

Graciosa An enchanting first stop and you can anchor off or try to find a place in the harbour at La Sociedad.

Puerto Calero East coast Lanzarote. A popular spot to get ready and relax. Used by the Bluewater Rally but the helpful staff always try to fit you in.

Marina Rubicon A new marina on the bottom of Lanzarote. Normally has plenty of room.

Las Palmas NE corner of Gran Canaria. Good marina close to all facilities and with the best yacht services in the Canaries. The ARC more or less fills the marina until they leave at the end of November. From December onwards there is normally no problem finding a berth.

Graciosa

Drying sardines on Graciosa

Santa Cruz de Tenerife Yachts normally go to Marina Atlantico or Marina Tenerife. There have been a few problems with the authorities in years past. Excellent shopping and good yacht facilities ashore.

San Sebastian East side of Gomera. Always gets good reports from cruisers and consequently is usually crowded. Good shopping nearby.

Santa Cruz de La Palma A marina has been built at the head of the harbour and is run by Señor Calero from the marina of the same name on Lanzarote. Wonderful town ashore and good shopping nearby.

Reading

Atlantic Islands RCCPF/Anne Hammick. (Imray)

My gem

The Four Voyages of Christopher Columbus: Being His Own Log-book, Letters and Dispatches with Connecting Narrative Drawn from the 'Life of the ... and Other Contemporary Historians' (Classics) by Christopher Columbus. Prentice Hall

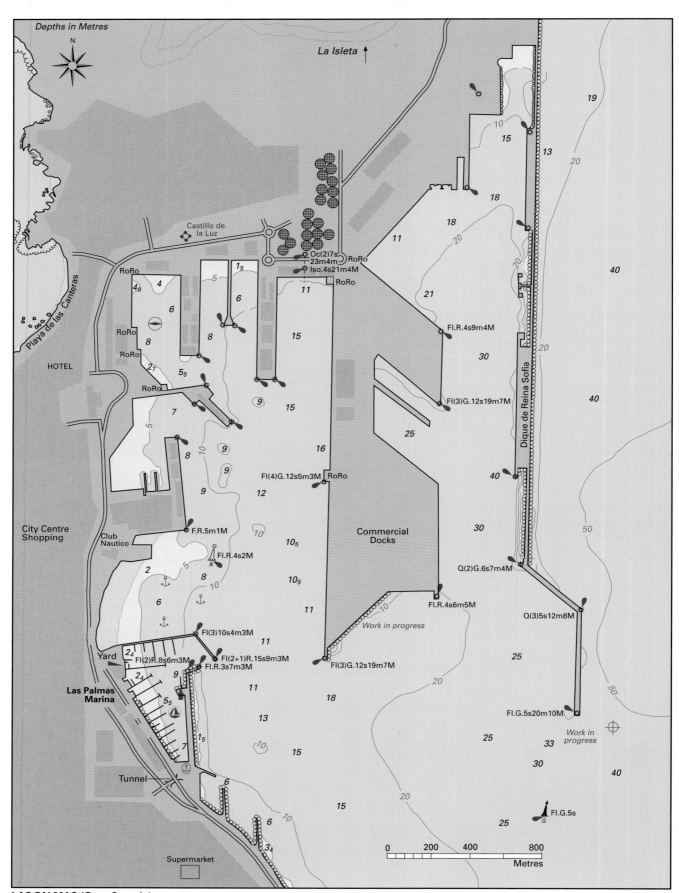

Depths in Metres

N

La Isleta ↑

19

10

15

13

20

18

18

40

11

21

20

20

Castillo de
la Luz

Oc(2)7s
23m4m
Iso.4s21m4M

RoRo

RoRo

RoRo

4₈ 4

6

6

1₅

5

11

Fl.R.4s9m4M

30

RoRo

8

8

2₁

5₅

7

15

15

9

15

Fl(3)G.12s19m7M

25

Playa de las Canteras

HOTEL

RoRo

RoRo

RoRo

Dique de Reina Sofia

40

40

9

8

9

9

12

Fl(4)G.12s5m3M

RoRo

16

30

50

City Centre
Shopping

Club
Nautico

F.R.5m1M

Fl.R.4s2M
R

10

10

10₅

10₅

Commercial
Docks

Q(2)G.6s7m4M

Q(3)5s12m8M

25

2

8

11

Fl.R.4s6m5M

6

Fl(3)10s4m3M

11

Work in progress

18

Yard

2₄

Fl(2)R.8s6m3M

Fl(2+1)R.15s9m3M

Las Palmas
Marina

2₄

9

Fl.R.3s7m3M

11

Fl(3)G.12s19m7M

20

Fl.G.5s20m10M

Work in
progress

33

5₅

13

25

Tunnel

7

1₅

15

30

40

6

15

25

6

Fl.G.5s
G

3₄

Supermarket

0   200   400   800

Metres

LAS PALMAS (Gran Canaria)
⊕28°07'·45N 15°23'·85W WGS84

Berths

VHF Port control Ch 16, 12

Las Palmas Marina
Ch 16, 09. 550 berths. Visitors' berths. Max LOA c.30m. Depths 2–8m. Charge band 2.

Anchorage

N of the marina. Can get crowded before the ARC leaves but a space will usually be found. Good holding and good shelter.

Facilities

Usual amenities. Fuel quay. Most yacht repairs. Good chandlers. Several large supermarkets which deliver and lots of restaurants and bars.

Remarks

Most popular port to depart for the Caribbean. Cannot reserve in advance and berths allotted on first come, first served basis. The ARC leaves on the third Sunday in November (or close) and for up to a month before this the marina is booked solid so yachts need to anchor off. When the ARC boats leave the marina is half empty and there is plenty of room to berth and provision for the trip.
www.grancanaria.com
(deals generally with the island).

MARINA DEL ATLANTICO (Tenerife)

Navigation

Approach straightforward, although care needed of ferries and commercial shipping. Use the eastern entrance to the basin as the western entrance has a wave-breaker pontoon across it.

Berths

VHF Ch 16, 09
360 berths. Visitors' berths. Max LOA 15m. Depths <1–6m. Charge band 2.

Facilities

Water. 220/380V. Showers and WC. Fuel nearby. Some yacht repairs.

Remarks

Useful port for the Atlantic crossing. Good shopping for provisions nearby.

Cape Verde Islands

General Until the last couple of decades the Cape Verdes were rarely visited by yachts, but now a lot more yachts shorten the passage to the Caribbean by stopping here. Lying squarely in the tropics, the climate is hot and humid and frequently very dusty from the trades blowing Saharan dust over the islands. The islands are an independent republic and poor.

Coastline The islands lie in a horseshoe cluster off the African coast (Mauritania and Senegal) and, like the Canaries, are the peaks of volcanoes. They are mountainous except for Sal, Boa Vista Island, and Maio Island. Pico do Cano (2,829 metres/9,281 feet) on Fogo, is still an active volcano.

Formalities Yachts must clear in at a port of entry: Palmeira (Ilha do Sal), Porto Grande (São Vicente), Praia (Ilha de Santiago). Clearance papers from last port required and yachts can be fined for not clearing in on arrival. You must go to the harbourmaster with clearance papers and then to immigration. When clearing out you need to pay a harbour dues fee, and see the harbourmaster and immigration again. It is all very friendly and you have 24 hours to leave after getting stamped out. Clearance papers for the onward passage should be asked for.

Resources

PILOTS AND GUIDES

Atlantic Islands RCCPF/Anne Hammick (Imray)
Canary Islands Cruising Guide Jimmy Cornell (World Cruising Publications).
Street's *Transatlantic Crossing Guide* (Available through Imray)

MARINA DEL ATLANTICO SANTA CRUZ DE TENERIFE
⊕ 28°27′·20N 16°14′·87W

Cape Verdes

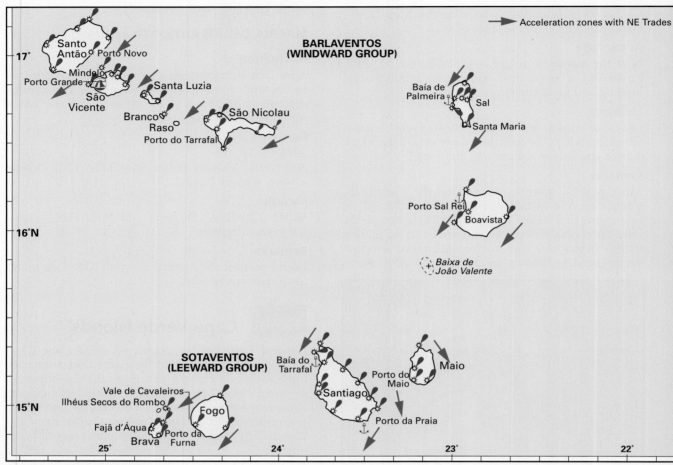

Acceleration zones with NE Trades

BARLAVENTOS
(WINDWARD GROUP)

17°

Santo
Antão — Porto Novo

Mindelo
Porto Grande
São
Vicente

Santa Luzia

Branco
Raso

São Nicolau

Porto do Tarrafal

Baía de
Palmeira — Sal

Santa Maria

Porto Sal Rei
Boavista

16°N

⊕ Baixa de
João Valente

SOTAVENTOS
(LEEWARD GROUP)

Baía do
Tarrafal

Maio

Porto do
Maio

Vale de Cavaleiros
Ilhéus Secos do Rombo

Fogo

Santiago

15°N

Fajã d'Áqua
Brava

Porto da
Furna

Porto da Praia

25°   24°   23°   22°

CAPE VERDE ARCHIPELAGO

The Cape Verdes have become popular in recent years as part of the trans-Atlantic circuit. Most yachts will make for Mindelo on São Vicente from the Canaries and from there head off for the Caribbean or in a few cases to Senegal and Brazil. The islands are a gem and most people enjoy the experience. Ashore the people are friendly and vibrant, the landscape is spectacular though mostly fairly dry, the food in the restaurants is good, and the music is out of this world. Cape Verde musicians are renowned the world over from the wonderful sad melodies of Imorna, think Cesaria Evoia who came from the Cape Verdes, to the acoustic *funana* and *batuque* melodies, all of it an exotic blend of Portuguese, Brazilian and African elements. Many of the restaurants will have a local live band playing and you shouldn't miss it.

Mindelo fish market

Seasons and winds

The season in the Cape Verdes is year round with consistent trade winds from the E and near tropical temperatures. The trades here are well developed and one of the problems of sailing around the islands is that the trades will consistently blow at 20 knots and more from an easterly direction which makes going east a nightmare. You will have strong winds and big seas to beat into. For this reason the logical route for yachts heading to Senegal and the Cape Verdes is to go to Senegal first and then cross to the Cape Verdes. The strong trades here mean that you must take anchoring seriously and ensure the anchor is well in with lots of scope. The holding is not always the best in some of the anchorages including at Mindelo and with the trades often gusting in at 25 knots or so care is needed making sure you are securely anchored.

Mindelo in the Cape Verdes

Music galore

The strong trades also bring in a lot of dust off Africa which impairs visibility around the islands and also deposits a gritty red patina over the boat.

Routeing

Most boats will leave Mindelo for the Caribbean. Once you are out of the wind shadow of Santa Antao which can extend for 10 miles or so, you will have the wind on the quarter for around half of the trip. There also seem to be less squalls on the passage from the Cape Verdes compared to passage from the Canaries.

Boats on passage to Brazil will have to pick where to cross the ITCZ which means a rhumb line passage will not always be the best option. There can be a lot of squalls, some of them prolonged and vicious, when going through the ITCZ, so spend some time monitoring where it is so you can plot to cross it where it is thinnest and least developed. This is complicated by the fact that it constantly moves and expands and contracts, but the general consensus is that you should cross it around 25°–30° W where it is thinnest, or at least as close to that as you can get on the route from the Cape Verdes.

Music in Café Yacht

Facilities

You should stock up on all the staples before leaving the Canaries. In the Cape Verdes you will be able to get a reasonable selection of fresh fruit and vegetables and some frozen meat and poultry. Other basics can be found although at times there will be shortages of some items.

Fuel and water are available. Water may not be available all the time as it is mostly made by reverse osmosis and the plant will not run all the time. Fill up when you can. Other yacht supplies are few and far between and even quite basic items like epoxy, other adhesives, glass cloth and fillers will often not be available. Specialised yacht equipment is virtually unobtainable and you will need to get it brought in and cleared by an agent.

Reading

Atlantic Islands RCCPF / Anne Hammick (Imray)

My gem

Café Atlantico Cesaria Evora (CD).

Mindelo market

Telecom IDD code +238.

Currency Cape Verde escudo. Major credit cards accepted in a few places (can be used to obtain cash in Porto Grande).

Sailing season All year round. Tropical storms are born to the W of the Cape Verdes but always move off to the W-NW.

Routes and harbours The Cape Verdes are little cruised and yachts usually stop in Porto Grande before crossing to the Caribbean or Porto de Praia before crossing to Senegal.

Note Theft happens and all precautions should be taken. Employ a boatman to look after the boat and make sure the dinghy and outboard are securely locked when ashore. Some care is also needed ashore in places.

PORTO GRANDE (MINDELO) (São Vicente)

Tidal range 0.9m

Navigation

Straightforward approach. Care needed of dust causing bad visibility around the islands. Aids to navigation are poorly maintained and should not be relied on to be working or in place.

Anchorage

VHF Port control Ch 15.
Anchor off in the bay in convenient depths. Good holding and adequate shelter. See note on security.

Berths

VHF Ch 09.
120 berths. Visitors' berths. Max LOA 30m. Charge band 3.
Yachts can go stern or bows-to or alongside as directed. Laid moorings tailed to the pontoon or a pick-up buoy. Good shelter although there is some ground swell.

Anchorage

Anchor in the bay on mud and sand, good holding once the anchor is in. The bay has old hulks at anchor and a few wrecks on the bottom. Dinghies can safely be left in the marina near the office.

Facilities

Electricity. Water can be metered on request. The water is from a reverse osmosis plant and is potable. Fuel by jerry can or from the Fishing Harbour in the

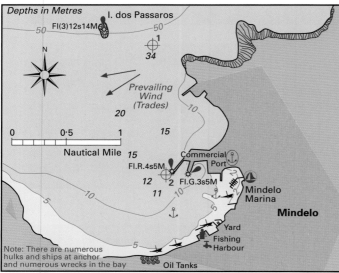

APPROACHES TO PORTO GRANDE MINDELO
⊕₁ 16°54′·67N 25°00′·27W WGS84
⊕₂ 16°53′·24N 25°00′·14W WGS84

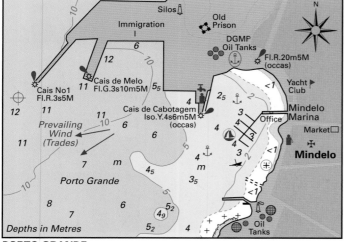

PORTO GRANDE
⊕ 16°53′·24N 25°00′·14W WGS84

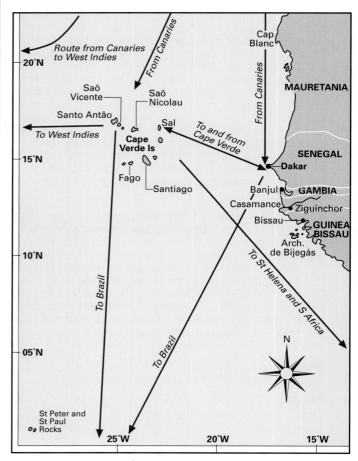

bay. Wi-Fi ashore in the Yacht Club restaurant. Good market with fruit and vegetables. Basic provisions in small supermarket.

Remarks
Local advice was to remove loose items from the deck in the anchorage and you would have few problems. Ashore the locals are friendly, the food good and the music superb.
www.marinamindelo.com *Email* Kai@boatcv.com

Senegal

General Senegal is the mainland African country nearest to Cape Verde. Fortunately it is also one of the more stable nations of the continent and has earned a good reputation with visiting yachtsmen. Nevertheless many visitors, without previous experience of Africa, are shocked by the poverty and primitive conditions. Many boats enjoy navigating several of the long rivers leading into the great continent. (Gambia is a small nation that lies along one of these rivers and is almost encircled by Senegal).

Formalities These are best described as tedious, but are not all that restrictive and with local advice it is fairly easy to comply. US and EU citizens do not require Visas.

Telecom IDD +221, reasonable facilities in Dakar and major centres.

Currency CFA

Sailing season Year round

Routes and harbours Dakar is a good base from

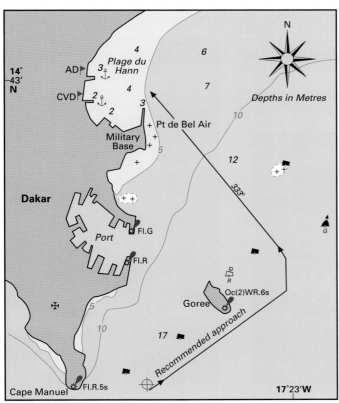

DAKAR - SENEGAL
⊕14°38′·8N 17°25′·0W

which to start a cruise to the rivers of Senegal and the Gambia and even further south into Guinea Bissau. This area is fairly popular and you will meet sailors in the area with extensive local knowledge.

DAKAR
Tidal range 2.2m

Navigation
Approach is straightforward, head for the anchorage in Hann. Lights are said to be well maintained. Viability is often poor, especially if the *Hamartan* is blowing dust from the Sahara.

Berths
None available.

Anchorage
Off the two YCs in Hann, good holding. The YCs provide showers and meals.

Facilities
Fairly good facilities for provisioning. Fuel and water and a few yacht supplies are available. Boats up to 16 tonnes can be slipped at the clubs.

Lesser Antilles

General This is the Caribbean island chain running from the Virgin Islands to Trinidad. It encompasses the Leeward Islands (USVI and BVI to Dominica) and the Windward Islands (Martinique to Grenada) as well as Trinidad and the Dutch Antilles (Aruba, now independent, Bonaire and Curaçao, usually referred to as the ABCs). Most of the old colonial islands are now independent, with the following exceptions.

British dependencies: BVI, Anguilla, Montserrat.
Netherlands dependencies: Saba, St Eustatius, Sint Maarten, Curaçao and Bonaire.
French dependencies: St Martin, St Barthélémy, Guadeloupe, Martinique.

   The islands are home to a large number of yachts, principally from northern Europe and the USA, attracted by clear warm water (sea temperatures are around 25°C–29°C), palm fringed beaches and steady trades blowing across the islands. Scheduled flights from Europe and the USA to many of the islands also helps. These boats are kept here year-round, although insurance for the summer hurricane season is now harder to obtain after the large number of yachts damaged by Hurricanes *Hugo*, *Lenny* and *Ivan*. Most insurance companies exclude the area N of 12° and S of 36°. In the Antilles this means you need to be on the S end of Grenada, or further S in Trinidad or the ABCs, or in Venezuela, to get cover.

Note It is possible that Grenada may be excluded by some insurance companies after it was devastated by Hurricane *Ivan* in September 2004.

Coastline The islands are mostly mountainous, with the exception of some of the Leewards (Anguilla, St Martin and Antigua and Barbuda), Barbados and the Tobago Cays. On the windward side most of the

Lesser Antilles

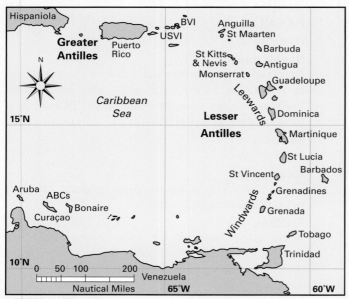

LESSER ANTILLES

Jolly Harbour on Antigua, a popular jumping-off point for the direct route to the Azores

Caribbean Leewards and Windwards

The lesser Antilles stretch in a crescent chain for over 400 miles in a roughly north to south direction. The islands are grouped into the Virgin Islands in the north, the Leeward Islands and the Windward Islands. There are also the ABCs, Abaco, Bonaire and Curacao along the top of the South American coast.

The Caribbean island experience is different things to different people. Throughout the Caribbean there is tradewind sailing at its best with consistent 10–20 knot trades blowing over the islands. For some it is the life ashore and depending on the island and where you are on an island, it is possible to find sophisticated cuisine that would not be out of place anywhere in the world. Alternatively, there are local beach bars and restaurants that serve simple tasty food in wonderful locations. For some it is all white sandy beaches, coconut palms and a turquoise sea like warm soup and you are spoilt for choice through the Caribbean chain. For others there is the racing scene and the Caribbean hosts a number of important races through the year of which Antigua Race Week is probably the best known.

Catamarans are a popular choice for cruising the Lesser Antilles

Rain coming through in the Windwards

Safe havens in the Caribbean

Yachts sailing an Atlantic Circuit, whether starting from Europe or from the East Coast of the US, will consider leaving the yacht for an extra season in the Caribbean before heading onwards. (For more details on Atlantic Circuits see the box near the beginning of the chapter). You will need to find somewhere safe to leave the boat afloat if the crew are returning home during the winter for any time.

Popular harbours to leave a boat afloat in the winter (N–S):

BVI Road Town Marina. Nanny Cay Marina.
St Martin Fort St Louis Marina.
Sint Maarten Simpson Bay Marina. Lagoon Marina.
Yachts also left on anchor here.
Antigua Jolly Harbour. At anchor in Falmouth.
Guadeloupe Pointe à Pitre Marina.
St Lucia Rodney Bay Marina.
Martinique Marin Yacht Harbour.
Grenada Clarkes Court Bay Marina. Port Louis Marina.
Trinidad Crewsinn Marina.
Note This is not a definitive list.

If a boat is to be based in the Lesser Antilles for a year or two then somewhere needs to be found to leave it during the hurricane season from June to November. Yards to leave a boat during the hurricane season:

Trinidad Chaguaramas boatyards including Coral Cove, Peakes, Power Boat Services, IMS.
Grenada Grenada Marine. Spice Island Marine.
Antigua Jolly Harbour*.
BV Nanny Cay*.
Puerto Rico Marina del Rey*.

* These yards have tie-down points and are acceptable to some insurance companies, but not all. Check with your insurance company first to see if they are acceptable. You may also be required to take the mast down. Remember that Grenada was hit by Hurricane *Ivan* which damaged 100% of boats in Spice Island and around 50% of boats in Grenada Marine.

Rodney Bay Marina on St Lucia - the finish point of the ARC

Nelson's Dockyard, Antigua

Hauling for the summer hurricane season in Grenada

Seasons and winds

Autumn

October to mid-November. This is at the tail end of the hurricane season and so a weather eye needs to be kept for the possibility of hurricanes developing. November is generally safe. The easterly Trades blow at around 15–20 knots with some squalls bringing rain.

Winter

Mid-November to March. This is the favoured season for cruising and inevitably the most crowded.

Spring

March to May. This is arguably the best time to go sailing in the Caribbean as the weather has settled down with the easterly Trades blowing at a manageable 12–18 knots and less rain than earlier on.

Summer

The tropical storm and hurricane season officially runs from June to November and this is the least favoured time to go sailing in the Caribbean for obvious reasons. In fact June and even July are pleasant months to sail here and the risk of tropical storms is relatively low. Later on in August through to October the risk of tropical storms is much higher and this is also the wet season to boot, so there is relatively little sailing going on. If you are sailing at this time you need to keep a close watch on the weather. If there is any possibility of a hurricane brewing then you will need to find a hurricane hole or run off south to Grenada or Trinidad if you have time. Most cruisers will have migrated south to Grenada and Trinidad anyway.

The easterly trades blow steadily throughout the year at 10–20 knots. On the lee side of the islands there will be calm patches and less sea where the wind is blocked and at either end of the islands there will be increased winds where it blows around either end. The Windwards being higher than the Leewards means there are more flat spots there where the wind is blocked.

Over Christmas and New Year the Trades can be blustery and stronger than normal – the so-called 'Christmas Trades'. Between the islands the sea rolls in clear across the Atlantic so there is a large swell to deal with.

Currents are variable but mostly west-going and where the wind meets the current at a bit of an angle (going north out of Deshaies on the northern end of Guadeloupe is one notorious area) there can be large confused seas and breaking crests.

Crime and piracy

Theft is common in some of the islands and all precautions should be taken. Take local advice in all matters and remove all loose items from the deck.

Fuel and water barge in Bequia

Its good policy to haul the dinghy up on a halyard at night

Dinghies and outboards should be locked and at night haul them up clear of the water on a halyard or on davits if you have them. Ashore dinghies should be locked up and outboards locked onto the dinghy. Most chandlers in the Caribbean will make up stainless strops with an eye in each end to lock the dinghy onto something solid ashore and aboard.

There have been instances of crime ashore in some of the islands in both the Leewards and Windwards. Mostly this has been of the mugging variety although there have also been instances of death in aggravated robbery. Cruisers need to heed local advice on shore-side activities which usually means not going into certain areas at night.

Piracy or attacks on yachts have also occurred. These have all been on yachts at anchor. There have been incidents around St Vincent, Carriacou, Marigot on St Lucia, Falmouth and English Harbour on Antigua, and Chaguaramas on Trinidad. Yachts should take advice on areas from other cruisers and in some cases lock yourself in the boat at night. In some anchorages a security watch is kept on VHF through the night.

Venezuela One area yachts should keep away from is Venezuela where there have been repeated attacks on yachts at anchor and underway. These have resulted in injury and death in a significant number of cases. Areas that were once considered safe are now not so. Take advice from other cruisers and also check for recent developments on the Caribbean safety and security net.

It is important to stress that many of us have cruised the length and breadth of the Caribbean, (in the case of RJH four tours of the Caribbean), without incident. It is all too easy to get worked up about security and safety issues when in all probability you will never come close. Bearing this in mind you can always check on the Caribbean safety and security net www.safetyandsecuritynet.com.

Reading
See separate box on Resources

My gem
Omeros Derek Walcott. (Faber & Faber)

Beach restaurant

Martin on *Providence*, one of the boat 'boys' in Portsmouth on Dominica

Fruit and vegetables delivered to the boat. Portsmouth on Dominica

Ferrying people and goods around in Grenada

islands are fringed by coral reefs. Most of the leeward sides of the islands do not have extensive coral reefs, with the exception of the low islands mentioned above. The reason for this is that most rainfall hooked by the higher land runs off on the leeward side, bringing down silt and inhibiting the growth of coral.

Formalities Yachts must clear in and out of the respective islands. This usually only requires the boat papers and passports, but in some countries the insurance papers will be requested. Clearance papers must be obtained when leaving the island for the next island. All islands have ports of entry and it is generally advisable to go straight to a port of entry and not to anchor overnight before clearing in. Many of the islands will charge a cruising tax which may be calculated on your intended length of stay or may be a set amount for a given period, usually anything between five days and a month. For the USVI all those on board must have a valid US visa in advance.

Telecom IDD codes vary throughout the islands, although many have the US IDD code +1 followed by a 3-digit NDD number.

Electricity Many of the marinas will have dual voltage sockets so European and US boats can be accommodated. Care is needed over reversed polarity in many installations.

Currency Euro in the Dutch and French islands. East Caribbean dollar (EC$) in Anguilla, St Kitts and Nevis, Antigua and Barbuda, Montserrat, Dominica, St Lucia, St Vincent, and Grenada. The EC$ is pegged to the US dollar which is also common currency throughout the islands, with many places showing dual prices in EC€ and US$. USVI and BVI use the US dollar. Trinidad uses the Trinidad dollar.

Major credit cards accepted in most places and ATMs in the larger towns.

Sailing season Winter (November to April) is the most popular time of year. This is the dry season (read 'less rain') with slighter cooler but still tropical temperatures. The summer (May to October) is the wet season (read 'lots of rain') and, more importantly, the hurricane season. It is rare for a tropical storm/hurricane not to hit somewhere along the island chain in any one year (see notes on insurance above).

Routes and harbours Yachts normally sail up and down the chain on the leeward side where there are flatter seas in the lee of the islands from the easterly trades. Because of the geography of the islands it is easier sailing up the leewards compared to sailing down, and conversely it is easier sailing down the windwards compared to sailing up. Often yachts will have to motor for part of the way in the lee of some of the islands where the wind is shut out altogether. There are harbours and anchorages all along the island chain, meaning you do not have to do overnight passages.

Note Theft is common in some of the islands and all precautions should be taken. Take local advice on the matter and remove all loose items from the deck. Dinghies and outboards should be locked onto something solid.

ROAD TOWN

Tidal range 0.2m

Navigation

Any approach to the BVI's must be made in daylight as there are numerous unlit dangers to navigation. Agneada and Horseshoe Reef is called the 'boat cemetery' of the Virgin Islands. From the S you can use Salt Island Passage between Cooper Island and

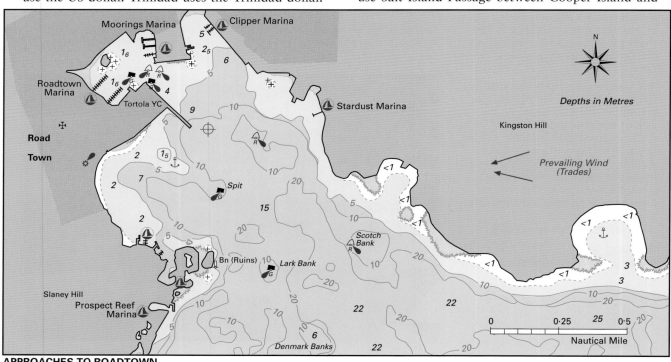

APPROACHES TO ROADTOWN
⊕18°25'·25N 64°36'·6W

Peter Island or Round Rock Passage between Ginger Island and Fallen Jerusalem. From the N keep well clear of Agneada and head down the W side of Jost Van Dyke and then in through The Narrows between Great Thatch Island and St John. The immediate approaches to Road Town are buoyed though care must still be taken. Clear in at Road Town before proceeding elsewhere in the BVI's.

Berths

VHF Ch 16 for *Village Cay Marina*.
100 berths. Visitors' berths. Max LOA 25m. Depths 2–3m. Charge band 5.
It's quite tight in here to manoeuvre and the trades blowing in don't make it any easier so have everything ready for berthing.

Anchorage

Anchor off to the N of Burt Point and S of the commercial dock keeping clear of the ferry channel. Good holding on mud. There is a bit of slop from the trades blowing in though it is entirely tenable. All yachts should anchor here and dinghy in to clear immigration and customs from here before berthing in the marina

Facilities

Water and electricity in the marina. Fuel dock. Travel hoist and repair services on Wickham Cay 2. Chandlers and sailmakers. In Road Town there is a good supermarket and restaurants and bars.

Remarks

If you need anything fixed or a good chandlers this is the place to head for. Apart from Village Cay there is also the large Moorings marina which may have berths for visitors (VHF Ch 12).
www.igy-villagecay.com

Antigua

IDD +1-268

FALMOUTH HARBOUR AND ENGLISH HARBOUR

Tidal range 0.3m

Navigation

Straightforward, although it can be difficult to determine exactly where the harbour is. The best clue is usually the masts of yachts inside and yachts

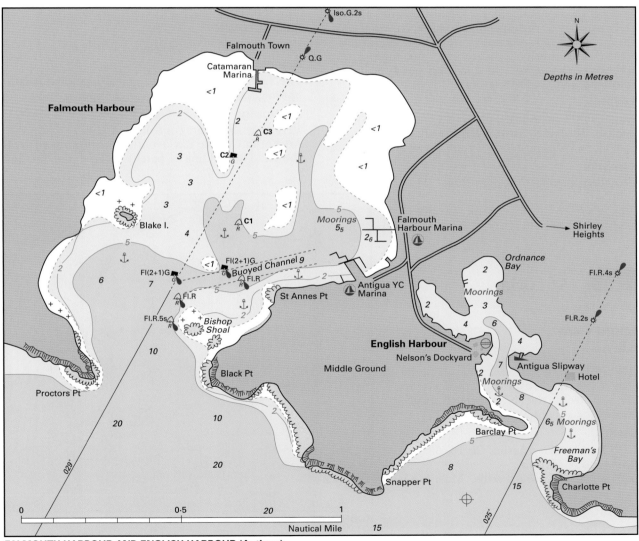

FALMOUTH HARBOUR AND ENGLISH HARBOUR (Antigua)
⊕17°00'·0N 61°45'·9W

coming and going. By night the approach is difficult for the first time. Inside Falmouth Bay care is needed of shoal areas which, although buoyed and lit, can be difficult to identify outside daylight hours.

Berths

VHF English Harbour Radio Ch 16, 68
Antigua Yacht Club Falmouth Harbour Marina, Catamaran Club Ch 16, 68.

English Harbour
c.45 berths. Visitors' berths. Max LOA c.50m. Charge band 2.

Antigua Yacht Club
c.40 berths. c.25 visitors' berths (mostly super-yachts). Max LOA c.60m. Depths 1–7.5m.

Falmouth Harbour Marina
c. 50 berths. Visitors' berths (super-yachts). Max LOA c.70m. Depths 2–5.5m.

Catamaran Marina
c.50 berths. Visitors' berths. Max LOA c.35m.

Anchorage

Falmouth Bay offers good protection from all winds. Good holding. There are a number of mooring buoys administered by the National Parks Authority. In English Harbour most yachts anchor off in Freemans Bay as the inner anchorage is crowded and has numerous mooring buoys. Yachts are charged by the Parks Authority for anchoring and there is an additional charge for the mooring buoys in both Falmouth and English Harbour.

Facilities

Water at the marinas. Fuel at Antigua Slipway in English Harbour. Most yacht repairs. Boatyards. Some provisions and lots of restaurants and bars.

Remarks

Crowded during Antigua Race Week although it is usually possible to find somewhere to anchor. Major Caribbean base for super-yachts.

 St Lucia

IDD +1-758

RODNEY BAY

Tidal range 0.2m

Navigation

Straightforward, although difficult to identify from the N approach. Care needed for a night approach.

Berths

VHF Rodney Bay Marina Ch 16, 68.
Rodney Bay Marina
230 berths. Visitors' berths. Max LOA

c.50m. Depths 3–4m in channel. Charge band 4/5.

The marina has been expanded and tidied up under ICY, though prices have inevitably gone up.

Anchorage

Limited anchoring in the lagoon where there is good holding and shelter. Anchorage in the bay outside where there is good shelter although NE Trades send some swell in, more uncomfortable than dangerous. Best anchorage is under Pigeon Island at the N end of the bay.

Facilities

Water and electricity. Fuel quay. Yacht repairs and boatyard. Most provisions. Restaurants and bars.

Remarks

Full during the ARC and for a couple of weeks after, although there is room in the anchorage. Good shelter in bad weather in the lagoon.
www.igy-rodneybay.com

 Barbados

IDD +1-246

BRIDGETOWN

Tidal range 0.6m

Navigation

The approach to the island and Bridgetown is clear of dangers and well lit for a night approach.

Anchorage

VHF Barbados port control Ch 16, 12
Anchor in Carlisle Bay avoiding the prohibited areas shown. The holding is patchy in here and the best

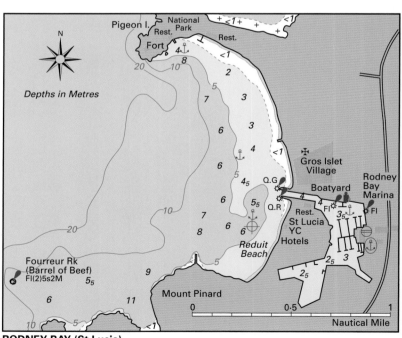

RODNEY BAY (St Lucia)
⊕ 14°04'·5N 60°57'·5W

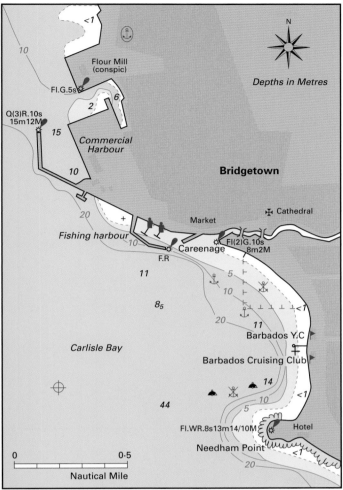

BRIDGETOWN AND CARLISLE BAY (Barbados)
⊕13°05'·0N 59°38'·0W

Grenada

IDD +1-809

PRICKLY BAY

Tidal range 0.8m

Navigation

Approach is simple from the S. Beware of the Porpoises Rocks and of the reefs off Prickly Point.

Anchorage

Anchor where possible in the bay. It gets crowded in the season and there are some laid moorings towards the beach. Some care is needed of shallow patches near the entrance of the cove where Spice Island Marine is located. Good shelter although it can be rolly in here at times.

Facilities

Spice Island Marine has a large yard and travelhoist. Chandlers. Other services including sailmakers and electrical and mechanical repairs. For worthwhile shopping get the bus into Grand Anse.

holding will be found in the S of the bay between the large hotel jetty and the yacht club. The holding in the N of the bay is not good. It can be a bit rolly in the anchorage but is otherwise safe once your anchor is well in. Care needed when going ashore in the dinghy if there is any surf.

Facilities

Water in the commercial harbour and at the fuel quay in the fishing harbour. Some yacht repairs. Good shopping for provisions. Restaurants and bars.

Remarks

Yachts often make landfall here after the Atlantic crossing as it would otherwise entail a 60-mile beat to windward to get here from the Windward islands if you wanted to explore Barbados.

Note Port St Charles Marina further N of Carlisle Bay is an apartment-marina complex and yachts are not welcome here. You can go on the reception quay and check in and get fuel and water, but you are unlikely to be allowed to stay here. Occasionally you can get a berth in the marina but don't count on it. Moorings in the bay and you can anchor off here although it is not comfortable.

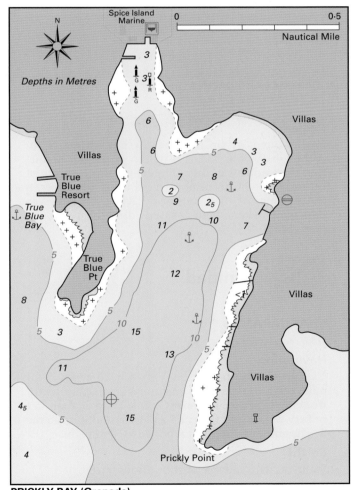

PRICKLY BAY (Grenada)
⊕11°59'·00N 61°46'·00W WGS84

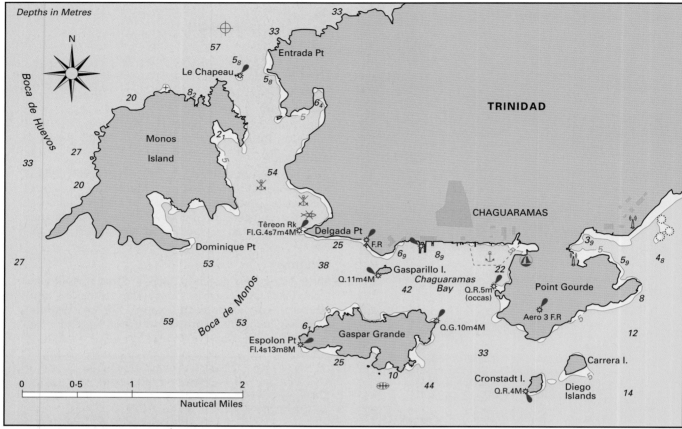

CHAGUARAMAS APPROACHES (Trinidad)
⊕10°43'N 61°40'·5W

Remarks

Yachts often lay up here for the hurricane season. Although Prickly Bay is S of the magic 12°N line, that does not mean it is immune from the effects of hurricanes, as Ivan demonstrated to deadly effect in 2004 (one of the authors' (RJH) yachts was damaged when Ivan passed directly over the boatyard).

 # Trinidad

IDD +1-868

CHAGUARAMAS

Tidal range 0.9m

Navigation

Call up the coastguard on VHF Ch 16 when 5–10 miles off. Entrance to Chaguaramas is straightforward from the N between Gaspar Grande I and Gasparillo I or between Gaspar Grande I and Cronstadt I, from the S. The entrances are lit but not advised at night.

Berths

Some berths available at the various yards.

Anchorage

Anchor off in 8–10m in the buoyed off anchoring area.

Facilities

Chaguaramas is a major laying up area for the hurricane season and has just about every repair facility you could want. Yachts laying up for the summer are usually wrapped in plastic because of the high humidity here. There are several firms in the area which will do this.

Remarks

Flights to Europe and the USA. Trinidad is a popular place to leave a yacht for the hurricane season. There have been reports of increased muggings and robbery in Trinidad.

Resources

PILOTS AND GUIDES

Grenada to the Virgin Islands Jacques Patuelli (Imray)
Cruising Guide to the Leeward Islands Chris Doyle (Cruising Guide Publications)
A Sailor's Guide to the Windward Islands Chris Doyle (Cruising Guide Publications)
Cruising Guide to Trinidad and Tobago plus Barbados Chris Doyle (Cruising Guide Publications)
Martinique to Trinidad Don Street

Greater Antilles

General The Greater Antilles encompass Cuba, Jamaica, Hispaniola (Haiti and the Dominican Republic) and Puerto Rico. All of the islands are independent except for Puerto Rico which is part of the commonwealth of the USA (for all intents and purposes an 'unofficial state'). Cuba remains a thorn in the side of the Americans although Europe, Canada and many other countries long ago renewed ties with the island. Cuba is the largest island in the Caribbean and Hispaniola the second largest. This island chain is little frequented compared to the Lesser Antilles, and has comparatively little in the way of dedicated marinas and yacht facilities except on the E side of Puerto Rico.

Coastline The coastline is everywhere mountainous, in places spectacularly so. There are extensive coral reefs around all of the islands, some enclosing huge lagoons, especially on the S coast of Cuba. There are also numerous offshore islands which make up wonderful and comparatively little-frequented cruising areas, in particular the Spanish Virgins E of Puerto Rico and the islands and cays off the N and S sides of Cuba.

Formalities The paperwork for these countries is more convoluted and tedious than for the Lesser Antilles, partially because fewer yachts travel this route. Yachts will need the boat papers and passports, and in some countries the insurance papers will be requested. Clearance papers must be obtained when leaving one island for the next island. All islands have ports of entry and it is generally advisable to go straight to a port of entry and not to anchor overnight before clearing in. This applies especially to Puerto Rico and Cuba. In the other islands things are more laid back and it is sometimes difficult to know if you are dealing with a bona fide official or a 'Mr Fix-it'. For Puerto Rico all those on board must have a valid US visa in advance. In Cuba you must purchase a cruising permit and submit a cruise plan for each leg of the journey.

Telecom IDD codes are Puerto Rico +1-787 or +1-939, Dominican Republic +1-809, Haiti +509, Jamaica +1-876, Cuba +53.

Electricity Some of the marinas will have dual voltage plugs so European and US boats can be accommodated. Care is needed over reversed polarity in most of these countries.

Currency US dollar is the official currency for Puerto Rico and is accepted almost everywhere. In Cuba US$ are no longer officially accepted for purchases. They must be exchanged for convertible pesos which are equivalent. If using US$ to obtain convertible pesos, a 10% commission will be charged. Commission is avoided if Euros, Pounds sterling, Canadian dollars or Swiss francs are used. It is not worth obtaining any other foreign currency in advance. ATMs in Puerto Rico, Cuba and Dominican Republic. Major credit cards accepted in Puerto Rico and Cuba and less so in the other countries (hardly at all in Haiti).

Sailing season As for the Lesser Antilles winter (November to April) is the most popular time of year. At times a norther may blow down from the Continental USA, but over most of the Greater Antilles its effect is weakened this far S and some yachts will intentionally leave on the coat-tails of a norther to make progress to the E when headed down the Thorny Path to the Caribbean. The summer (June to October) is the wet season and the hurricane season. As for the Lesser Antilles it is rare for a tropical storm/hurricane not to hit somewhere along the island chain in any one year.

Routes and harbours The trades blow along the island chain from the E so it stands to reason that passages W are easy downwind runs, while making progress to the E involves a lot of beating to windward. In places the wind accelerates between the high mountains and increases in strength through the channels between the islands. Along the way shelter must be found either in man-made harbours or in the few bights that exist in the coast. Around Cuba once you are behind the reefs the water is comparatively flat and there are numerous places to bring up for the night.

Note Theft is common in some places and small gifts will often be requested. Haiti is politically unstable and parts of the country are unsafe. Cuba, although safe, is also subject to theft despite reports to the contrary.

Jamaica

PORT ANTONIO

Tidal range 0.5m

Navigation

Entrance hard to see in approaches. Once identified the channel into the lagoon is deep and free of dangers. Caution needed at night.

Berths

Errol Flynn Marina
VHF Ch 16
32 berths. Visitors' berths. Max LOA 40–50m. Charge band 3.
Stern-to berths on the pontoon running out from the E side of West Harbour.

Huntress Marina
A couple of alongside berths outside a restaurant on the dock.

Anchorage

Anchor where convenient on sticky mud. Excellent shelter.

Facilities

Errol Flynn Marina
Water and electricity (220V/380V). Toilets and showers. 24-hour security. Clearance procedures. Bar and internet. 100-ton travel hoist.

Huntress
Water. Restaurant. Gates locked at night.
In town: Some provisions and restaurants and bars. Excursions arranged around the island.

Remarks

This is a comparatively settled place to arrive in what is a violent and troubled island. Many think it is geographically the most beautiful island in the Caribbean, including of course Errol Flynn and Ian Fleming of James Bond fame who both lived here. You will still need to keep your wits about you, but most yachts find it a convivial and useful stop.

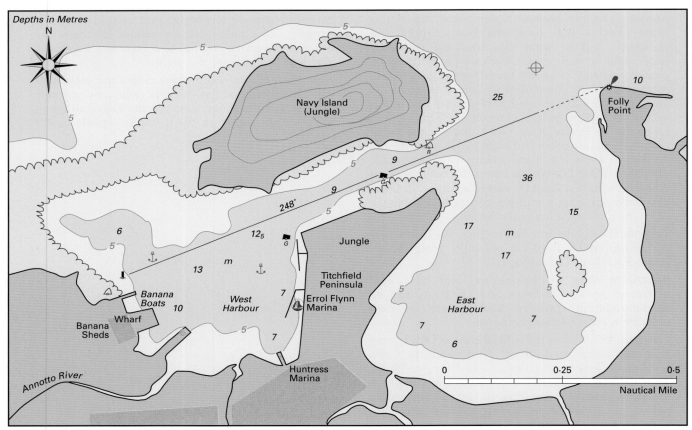

PORT ANTONIO (Jamaica)
⊕18°11'·3N 76°26'·95W

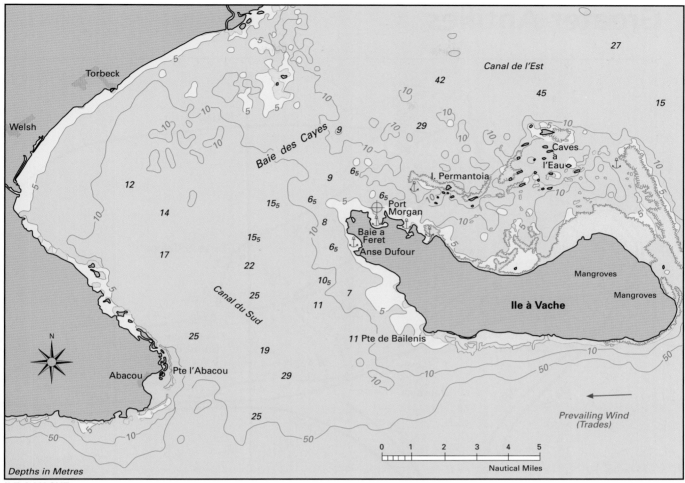

ILE A VACHE
⊕18°06'·63N 73°41'·78W

Haiti

ILE À VACHE

Tidal range 0.6m

Navigation

The approach is best made between Pte l'Abacou and the W side of Ile à Vache. At night anchor off the W side of Ile à Vache (Anse Dufour is a good place) where there are convenient depths and proceed around into Baie a Feret in daylight.

Berths

VHF Ch 16, 09 for *Port Morgan*
Pick up a mooring in Port Morgan or go stern-to off the mini-hotel. You can also anchor in the bay. Good holding on mud. Excellent shelter inside Baie a Feret.

Facilities

Water and fuel can be arranged. Market in Trou Milieu. Meals by arrangement in the mini-hotel.

Remarks

Most yachts arrive here without clearing in (or out), but take local advice. Visits to Haiti need to be judged according to the political situation on the island, but Ile à Vache is well away from what is going on on the main island. It is an idyllic if very poor place. The local boats here sail everywhere and sailing skills that have long disappeared in the rest of the Caribbean still survive here. Port Morgan, the 'marina' and mini-hotel are welcoming and a mine of useful information.
www.port-morgan.com

Greater Antilles

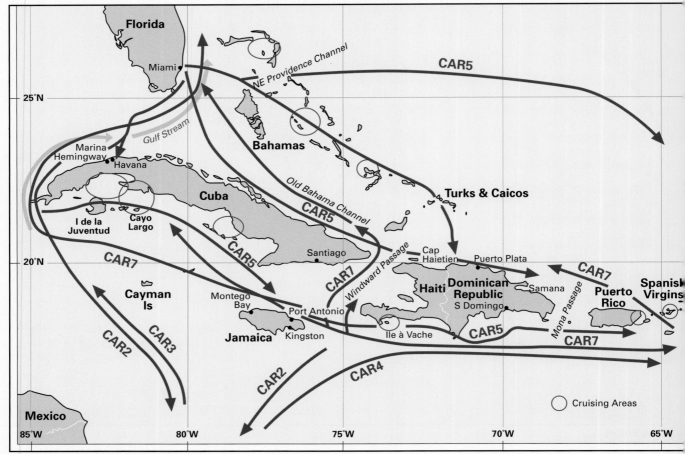

GREATER ANTILLES CRUISING ROUTES

The Greater Antilles comprising the island chain from Cuba to Puerto Rico is the lesser known Caribbean. For most people this is an insurance black hole and normal premiums for the Caribbean exclude Cuba, Haiti and the Dominican Republic. If you ignore the lack of insurance or pay an additional premium and disregard a lot of the stories that circulate about piracy and other goings on, then this is a wonderful and largely uncrowded cruising area that is like stepping back into the Caribbean of 50 years ago.

Cuba

Cuba is a huge island some 700 miles long with more than 2,000 miles of coastline. It has a fascinating history and a vibrant culture that few fail to be enchanted with whatever you think of its folk-communism and the last days of Castro. It is surrounded by coral reefs extending up to 50 miles off the coast on the south side and it is largely untrammelled by cruising boats. Marina Hemingway near Havana is the only place you will see any real concentration of yachts and many of them don't go anywhere else. Around the south side I saw fewer than a dozen yachts sailing around in a six week cruise.

Havana old harbour

Sunset in Cayo Largo on Cuba

Maria La Gorda on the SW corner of Cuba

Book market in Havana

Marina Hemingway near Havana

Havana taxi

Jamaica

Jamaica is one of the most beautiful islands in the Caribbean, but is a troubled place with a lot of violence away from places like the gated holiday compounds in Montego Bay. There are a number of good anchorages around the island, but you are probably best going to Port Antonio, Montego Bay or the Royal Jamaica Yacht Club in Kingston.

Haiti

Haiti is a difficult one to pick and although I have cruised there without incident, other yachts have come to grief. You need to pick just one or two spots to go to that are safe and leave the rest. On the north coast most yachts will put into Cap Haitian. On the south coast Ile à Vache is the best destination and here a French couple run a small 'hotel' and have moorings with a guard. You need

Port Antonio in Jamaica

Local sailing boat in Port Morgan in Haiti

Port Morgan on Ile à Vache in Haiti

Local boats off Ile à Vache in Haiti

Local house on Ile à Vache in Haiti

to carefully judge the political situation there and determine whether things are relatively settled, at least as settled as they get in Haiti, or whether it's best to give the country a miss. If you do go there it's a bit like stepping back 50 years with fishing boats working under sail alone and dug-out canoes all over the place.

Dominican Republic

The Dominican Republic has a limited number of marinas around the coast and recent developments have tended to be marina/apartment complexes. Luperon and Puerto Plata on the north coast are popular stops while on the south coast there are a couple of small marinas with berths and a few deserted anchorages.

Puerto Rico

Puerto Rico has the most developed infrastructure for yachts with marinas concentrated around the eastern end of the island, though there are anchorages and small marinas scattered around the other coasts of the island. It also has the island group off the eastern end known to cruisers as the Spanish Virgins and there are some wonderful anchorages around the group that are just as beautiful as any around the US and British Virgins but without the crowds.

Sailing strategies

Yachts will be on three general tracks: coming north from Panama and Central America, south and east from the USA, or west from the Lesser Antilles.

- From Panama yachts will have a hard time getting north against the northeasterly trades until at least around 15ºN when the trades start to get a more easterly component (see CAR3)

- From the Lesser Antilles it is an easy downwind run along the Greater Antilles and the only real choice will be whether to go north or south of the Greater Antilles. If you are interested in cruising this area it is best to go south of the islands and then make a decision on whether to go north or south of Cuba. Going south of Cuba would be my favoured option leaving it late in the winter season to round the western end of Cuba when the trades are a lot lighter

- From Florida the commonly used route via the Bahamas (CAR5) touches on the northern coasts of Dominican Republic and Puerto Rico, but for an extended cruise in the Greater Antilles I have crossed to Marina Hemingway and then cruised east along the southern side of the island chain. It is not always easy against the prevailing easterly trades, but you are helped at times by fronts passing to the north which will disrupt the trades. At times there are also land breezes off the large islands which effectively 'hold-up' the trades so there is less wind and there can be a northeast or even northerly breeze at night on the southern side of the islands.

Seasons and winds

The Greater Antilles lie in the North Atlantic hurricane belt and so the seasons are effectively the same as anywhere else in the Caribbean: yachts cruise in the winter months from December to May and move out of the area in the summer from June to November. Hurricanes regularly hit the Greater Antilles when they start curving NW up towards Florida and in recent years with increased hurricane activity there has been much damage, especially in Haiti, Jamaica and Cuba.

In the winter the prevailing winds are easterly along the southern side of the island chain and east-northeast along the northern side.

The trades blow anything from 15–25 knots and push fairly big seas along the northern and southern sides of the islands. In the channels in between the islands, especially the Windward Passage between Cuba and Haiti and the Mona Passage between the Dominican Republic and Puerto Rico, the northeast trades are accelerated and these can be very windy places indeed.

In the winter months with the brisk trades temperatures are in the mid-20s to 30ºC range and the humidity is not excessive. In the summer it is hotter, but it is really the higher humidity which makes life less pleasant.

Regulations

Puerto Rico You need a US visa *BEFORE* entry if you do not have a US passport. Clear in at the first customs area where you can get a cruising permit valid for a year. Immigration will stamp your passport. Upon leaving telephone customs and post the immigration docket back.

Dominican Republic You must clear in and out of every port where there are customs and immigration. A tourist visa is issued for 60 days. Small 'gifts' are appreciated.

Haiti Clear in at Cap Haitian where there are customs and immigration. Things are 'looser' at Ile à Vache. Small gifts are almost mandatory though large gifts will be requested.

Jamaica Clear in at Montego Bay, Port Antonio or Kingston where there are police and customs. A small gift is often requested and worth paying.

Cuba You must clear in at a major port with a marina with Marina Hemingway near Havana, Santiago in the southeast and Cayo Lago on the south coast the most popular. Yachts must submit an itinerary and check in and out of ports with any officials. Checking out of Cuba must again be from a port with a marina. Despite the cumbersome paperwork it is well worth cruising the island. Small gifts will often be asked for.

Ashore

Puerto Rico Good American style supermarkets and a wide choice of restaurants and bars.

Dominican Republic Reasonable shopping and a good choice of restaurants and bars at reasonable prices.

Haiti Little in the way of restaurants and bars and don't bargain on finding anything in the way of provisions though there are some interesting local markets.

Jamaica Some good restaurants and bars though you need to be careful of where you drink at night. Mediocre shopping for provisions.

Cuba You will find small simple restaurants and cafés serving simple meals depending on availability, but don't come to Cuba for the food. There are also official and semi-official *paladars* where you eat in someone's home and where the food is generally better. Bars are excellent and so is the rum. Shopping in Cuba is poor because of the American embargo and you should not bargain on finding anything more than the basics and some fruit and veggies.

Facilities

Yacht facilities are limited until you get to Puerto Rico and the marinas and yards on the eastern end of the island. The exceptions are Port Antonio in Jamaica and some developing facilities around the Dominican Republic. Elsewhere you will have to fend for yourself and in places you will need to ferry fuel by jerry can.

Reading

The Gentleman's Guide to Passages South Bruce Van Sant. (Cruising Guide Publications)
Cuba: A Cruising Guide Nigel Calder. (Imray)
Cruising Guide Puerto Rico and Spanish Virgin Islands Steve Pavlidis. (Seaworthy Publications)
Puerto Rico, the Spanish, U.S. and British Virgin Islands (Street's Cruising Guide to the Eastern Caribbean) D M Street. (iUniverse)

My gem

Travellers Literary Companion: The Caribbean Ed. James Ferguson. (In Print Publishing)

Local working boats in Ile à Vache in Haiti

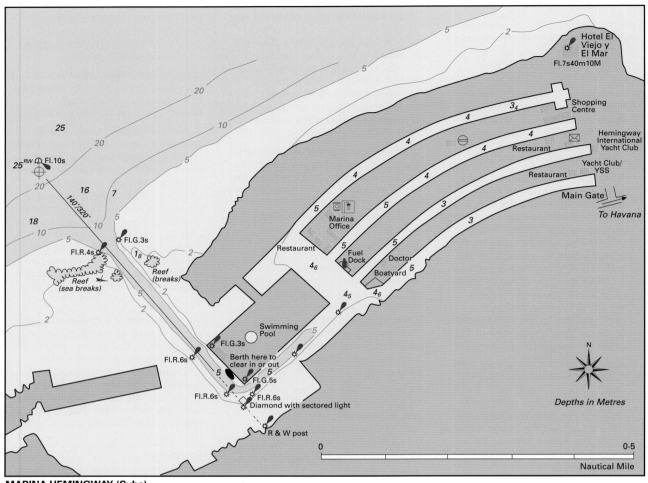

MARINA HEMINGWAY (Cuba)
⊕23°05′·4N 82°30′·5W

Cuba

MARINA HEMINGWAY

Tidal range 0.7m

Navigation

Contact the port authorities 12 miles out on VHF Ch 16 or 68, MF 2760kHz or 2790kHz. The fairway buoy for the channel and the entrance channel itself is difficult to identify. With a norther there the swell rolls straight into the entrance and it could be dangerous to enter (a yacht was pushed onto the reef while one of the authors (RJH) was there in 1999. Once into the dredged basin the water is flat. Tie up on the arrivals quay, or as directed, and the marina will probably have the officials waiting for you to complete all the paperwork for clearing in.

Berths

Visitors' berths are always available in the marina. Yachts usually go alongside in one of the canals though care is needed of the rough concrete. Depth 3–4m although there are obstructions close to the quays in places.

Facilities

Usual amenities. Fuel quay. Basic repairs and engineering. Most provisions are available although the selection and quality may be limited.

Remarks

The marina is secure though theft occurs (remove items from the deck and cockpit). It is an easy taxi ride into Havana itself.

SANTIAGO DE CUBA

Tidal range 1.1m

Navigation

Approach is very straightforward. Best to inform the port authorities on radio of your arrival.

Berths

The marina is the only permitted option. It is in a poor state of repair and was recently closed temporarily for unknown reasons.

Anchoring

Not permitted.

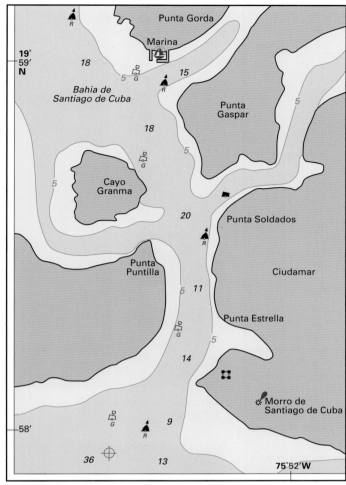

SANTIAGO DE CUBA - CUBA
⊕15°57'·9N 75°52'·5W

Facilities

Very basic provisioning, otherwise almost nothing, but the staff are helpful and like everywhere in Cuba will try and find solutions to your problems.

Remarks

After Cartagena, one author (AOG) ranks this as the second best city in the Americas. The lack of motor cars make wandering the streets a pleasure. This is a wonderful place to hear Cuban music and learn to dance Salsa Cubana.

Colombia

General Colombia has a dreadful reputation, many years of civil war, terrorism, drug barons and misgovernment have contributed to this. However, it is one of the culturally most vibrant countries in the Spanish speaking world, has more biological diversity than any other land on the planet and scenery varying from tropical beaches to glaciated mountain wastes. Music and dancing are very important to Colombians who love to let their hair down. Despite tales of murder and kidnappings the people are open, friendly and very welcoming to outsiders. Even in the worst days of violence, thankfully now much less frequent, yachts were reporting that Cartagena was one of the best cruising destinations in the Caribbean. One outstanding feature is that no hurricanes occur here. On a recent visit to Cartagena one author (AOG) heard no bad stories from the many yachts in the harbour. In short this is a cruising destination that deserves to be much more popular and in terms of safety (in the areas commonly visited) is possibly less dangerous than countries such as South Africa, Brazil, Venezuela and Mexico.

Formalities The coastguard are friendly and helpful and have a voluntary yacht reporting system and will advise on areas considered to have a risk of piracy. In the two major ports visited by yachts, Cartagena and Santa Marta, the authorities will only deal with yachts through an agent (*Email* motoresyvelas@hotmail.com). The agent's costs are reasonable, they completely eliminate the usual nightmare of dealing with South American bureaucracy and can arrange for very prolonged customs and immigration clearance as well as knowing how to help in virtually every way that a yacht requires. Citizens of the USA, Canada, Australia and EU do not require visas.

Telecom IDD +57 GSM network is good. Internet cafés everywhere. Post mainly through courier companies.

Currency Colombian Pesos – be prepared to reckon sums in hundreds of thousands! ATMs widespread, credit cards commonly accepted.

Sailing season All year, driest and most comfortable November–May.

Routes and harbours We have no information on cruising the Pacific coast, but have heard that some yachts have cruised here without incident. Santa Marta and Cartagena are logical stops when sailing W towards the Panama canal, there are many beautiful bays and anchorages along the Caribbean coast, but local advice should be taken before using them.

www.destinationcartagena.com

Has useful internet addresses (in English with a section for visiting yachts)

CARTAGENA DE LAS INDIAS

Tidal range 0.5m

Navigation

Approach: Offshore there are reefs and islands, simply avoided, that are not shown on the sketch. Entry is simple via Boca Chica, Boca Grande should only be entered in settled weather with good visibility – the lights were functioning in 2009, but are said to be unreliable.

San Blas

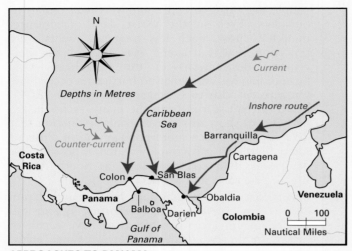

APPROACHES TO PANAMA

Navigating through a shallow pass in the San Blas

The San Blas Islands are a string of small cays scattered along the Caribbean coast of Panama. There is hardly anyone who does not remember the islands with affection and regret not having more time to spend cruising the area. The cays are low, usually with white sandy beaches shaded by coconut palms and fringed by coral reefs. The waters around are emerald clear and soupy warm. Numbers of yachts are now basing themselves in this part of the world and cruising the coast and islands of Panama. When you get done with the Caribbean side you can go through the canal and cruise the islands and coast on the Pacific side.

The San Blas are inhabited by the Kuna Indians, stocky tough characters who have defended their lands against all incomers and retain a traditional way of life. The women wear costumes with molas, reverse appliqué and embroidered squares in traditional motifs, which they also sell to tourists. Most of the tourists are cruisers and everyone comes away with at least a couple of molas. Transport between the islands is usually by dug-out canoes, ulus, which are rowed or sailed. When sailing one of those on board needs to be on a trapeze to keep it upright, the trapeze usually being a bit of old rope off the short mast. The other one on board steers with a paddle and bails with the other hand.

San Blas cay

Puerto Yate in the San Blas

Ulu in the San Blas

The islands are governed by a Kuna committee and council meetings are called regularly to make judgements about village life and to exorcise devils. When the council is meeting a red flag flies over the village and you should refrain from going ashore. Most of the islands are uninhabited or only sparsely inhabited, with just a few of the islands densely populated. For the populated islands I mean densely populated. The houses, built of reeds and timber and a few coral and concrete jobs, cover a few of the main islands entirely. The alley ways in between are sometimes so narrow you have to sidle sideways to pass. Toilets are little huts on stilts over the water so don't go swimming near the village islands. Not that you need to when so many of the islands are like something out of Robinson Crusoe with barely a soul around.

Cruising strategies

Yachts will usually be coming along the coast of Colombia towards Panama or direct from the Leewards.

If you are coming along the coast of Colombia from the ABCs you will be in for a bit of a rough ride as there seem to be upwelling currents and counter-currents to the main W-going current that kick up steep seas, especially around the capes. The consensus seems to be that it is best to sail along the coast in late March to June when winds are lighter. In January and February winds are stronger and conditions can be boisterous on this passage.

Yachts coming from the Leewards (or northerly Windwards) should keep 200 miles off where seas are less and the currents more favourable. As you close Panama you will likely pick up a contrary E–SE-going current of around one knot. Its worth checking in with someone like Herb Hilgenberg (see Resources) to see if you can get any indication of favourable currents and where counter-currents will be for this trip (Herb managed to find RJH a two knot favourable current and avoid the worst of the counter-currents on passage from St Maarten to Panama).

From Colombia yachts will generally make for Puerto Obaldia, a port of entry at the E end of the Comarca or Porvenir, a port of entry at the W end. The approach must be made in daylight as the cays are low and the coral reefs are not well charted.

Yachts intending to transit the Panama Canal should check to see if there is a back-log of boats waiting to go through. In April and May there can be long queues for the transit, up to a month in some cases, so it may pay to go direct to Colon and book the transit and then cruise up to the San Blas afterwards. From Colon you can day-hop all the way up the coast to the San Blas islands.

Seasons and winds

The trades blow down onto the islands in the winter months from December to April, generally at 10–15 knots, but at times up to 20–25 knots. After April the wind dies off a good deal and are variable. If you are heading back to the Windward Islands then try to time it for after April when winds are lighter and you may even get favourable winds at times.

From January to April is the dry season and the wet season is May to December. During the wet season it rains a lot, often torrential, and there can be thunderstorms as well with quite spectacular lightening. The rain and thunderstorms originate from small lows coming off Columbia bringing rain, lots of rain and thunder and lightening, but nothing wind-wise to worry about although you get occasional light westerlies.

San Blas Islands

The San Blas Islands and adjacent mainland coast are a semi-autonomous region, the home of the Kuna Indians who have retained their culture and life-style by keeping speculators and non-Kunas out. When you enter the San Blas you must obtain a permit to cruise the islands ($US12 per person 2009). You can get the permit at Porvenir and at some other islands.

The islands are more cays than islands with fringing coral protecting anchorages. As long as the sun is reasonably high in the sky you can see the reefs and passages through them. It is no place to rely on electronic charts.

Provisions are few and far between in the San Blas Islands so you need to take most things that you will need. Water and fuel are also hard to come by. You will get excellent fish and crayfish from local fishermen who will come alongside in their dug-out canoes (*ulus*) to sell their catch. You will also get lots of Kuna ladies (and the kids) coming out to sell you *molas*, the distinctive reverse appliqué and embroidered covers

Portobello on the coast between Colon and the San Blas

depicting traditional Kuna motifs. If you want to give gifts in exchange take sweets (*caramello* or *bob-bon*) and things like baseball caps and pens and pencils.

There are anchorages everywhere through the cays and yachts can and do spend a whole season here. If you decide to stay and cruise the San Blas remember your permit is for three months and may be difficult to renew at the moment – unless the law is changed again. You can safely leave a yacht in Shelter Bay Marina if you are flying out or sail across to Cartagena. The San Blas and the coast of Panama are a huge cruising area with lots to see and do afloat and ashore. And it's out of the summer hurricane area.

Reading
The Panama Guide: A Cruising Guide to the Isthmus of Panama Nancy Schwalbe Zydler and Tom Zydler. Partners Publishing Group.
A Complete Sailors Guide to The Isthmus of Panama Eric Bauhaus

My gem
The Fruit Palace Charles Nicholl. Vintage

Mola ladies in the San Blas

Panama Canal

This section deals with clearing in from the Caribbean end going into the Pacific. For the reverse route from the Pacific at Balboa into the Caribbean the process is the same.

The canal

Locks The three sets of locks at either end lift ships up 25.9m (85 ft). The dimensions of the locks are 33.53m (110 ft) wide by 320.0m (1,050 ft) long, with a usable length of 304.8m (1,000 ft). The usable lock size determines the maximum sized ship that can fit the locks. These ships are known as Panamax vessels. The new locks under construction will be 427m (1,400 ft) long, 55m (180 ft) wide, and 18.3m (60 ft) deep and will take ships to super-Panamax size.

Miraflores Lock in the Panama Canal
Peter Metherall

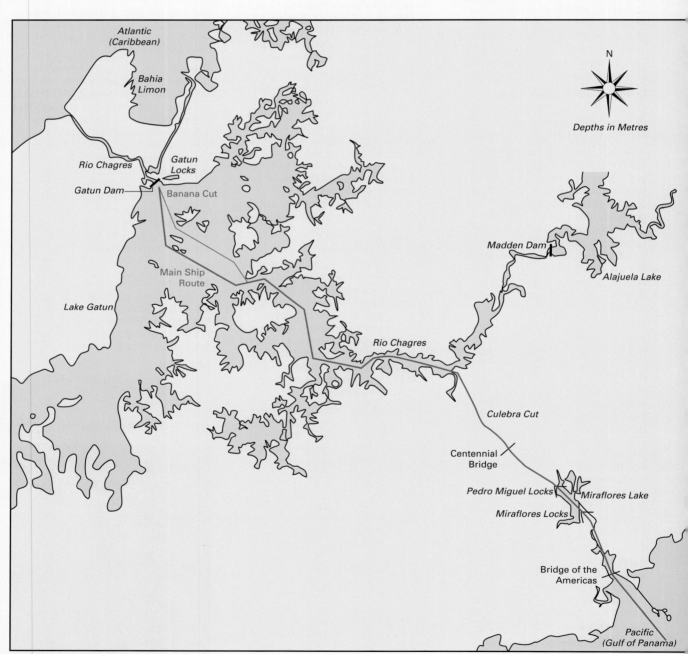

PANAMA CANAL

Anchorage behind the causeway in Balboa with Panama City in the background

Pilot boat from the Panama Canal Authority

Distance The canal is 48 miles long. The short-cut through the canal saves between 5,000 to 8,000 miles over the alternative route around Cape Horn depending on the final destination port.

History A canal was first mooted for Panama in the 17th century. The French started to build a canal in 1880 under the supervision of Ferdinand de Lesseps who had built the Suez Canal. The design for this canal was similar with no locks and basically amounted to an excavated ditch from the Atlantic to the Pacific. The project was abandoned after some 21,000 workers had died of disease including malaria and yellow fever. The Americans took over the project in the early 1900s although it is still a contentious issue of whether it would have been easier to construct a canal through Nicaragua. The American Canal with triple locks at either end was opened in 1914.

Panama bus

The future A plan to widen and straighten parts of the canal and to install super-Panamax locks alongside the old locks was approved in 2006 and work is in progress. Completion is planned for 2015.

Further information Go to the ACP site where there are live webcams at the locks. www.pancanal.com

Arriving in Colon

Yachts arriving in Colon will either anchor out in the Flats Anchorage Area F or in Shelter Bay. All yachts must wear a 'Q' flag and clear in with Immigration (see Formalities).

To transit the Panama Canal you need to do the following. While it is possible to do it all yourself, this will entail walking around in Colon which is a dangerous occupation. Some cruisers will use an official agent and these are all reliable. You can engage an agent and book your transit in advance. Search the internet for agents and a number of names dealing with yachts will come up. Most cruisers use an unofficial agent or 'Mr Fix-It' who formerly operated around the PCYC and now operates at Shelter Bay. Numbers of yachts have used Tito in the past and have been happy with his service. Tito also operates a water taxi to yachts that anchor in the Flats. For all the steps below your agent will drive you to the various offices and sort out the paperwork for you. You will need to present boat documents and passports and fill in the occasional form and of course, sign them. It really is very easy and worth every bit of the US$50–100 fee you will be charged.

The order below may change depending on which offices are open at the time, but don't worry, the agent or his helper will walk you through it all.

The initial paperwork

Note All fees are for 2009. They *WILL* change so get an update on revised costs when you can.

1. Clear in with immigration in Colon or at Shelter Bay Marina.

2. Clear in with customs and the port captain. Firearms will be put in bond and returned when you leave Panama.

3. Go to the Panama Canal office (the large tower building at the commercial docks) where you present your papers and get an appointment with the admeasurer. He will usually come out to the boat the next day.

Panama Canal lock

4. Go to immigration (another immigration office) to get a visa for all crew. Visas are issued for 90 days to most foreign nationals. Nationals of some African, Asian and Middle East countries need a visa prior to arrival. Check with your own embassy and the Panamanian authorities.

5. Get a *zarpe* (properly a *consentimiento de zarpe* (consent to clear).

6. Get a Cruising Permit. You need a Cruising Permit if you are going to be in Panama for more than two days, so basically everyone needs a Permit. The Permit can be obtained for 30 days or 90 days. It's worth getting a permit for 90 days in case there are delays transiting the canal or if you wish to cruise the coast and islands. There have been rumours regarding difficulties in renewing permits, but in practice this is not the case.

7. Go to Citibank to pay the Canal Transit fees. For boats under 50 feet (which includes all overhanging appendages like davits and self-steering gear) the fees were $US600 and a 'buffer' fee of $US850. The 'buffer' fee is taken if you damage the canal, need a tug or inconvenience the authorities including the pilot advisor accompanying you. If using a credit card (Visa only for some reason) the 'buffer' fee is only taken out of your account if it is used and for most people this doesn't happen. If you pay in cash then the 'buffer' fee will be reimbursed approximately 2–4 months after you have transited the canal.

All fendered up for the Panama Canal.

8. Fees for yachts over 50ft are $US850 with the same buffer fee. For yachts over 65ft and up there is an increased fee. For over 50ft you get a full blown pilot rather than a pilot advisor for the additional fee. Yachts over 65ft must have a Class B AIS transponder. If you don't have one you can hire one.

9. The admeasurer will come to the boat and measure it – he really does measure it. He will check on safety equipment including a horn (an aerosol horn will do) and that the necessary line-handlers and lines will be on board (see below).

10. You then check back with the canal authorities (you can phone) for a transit time. It is worth checking with the authorities on a regular basis as your transit time may come forward. You can buy cheap mobiles ($US20 for a phone and $US10 for credit) in Colon or Balboa.

Requirements for the transit

1. In the canal authority office you will be asked how fast your boat can motor. If you say less than eight knots then you will be charged an additional fee (usually $US1,000). The agents, official and unofficial, will all urge you to say you can do eight knots and not surprisingly nearly every boat, however small, signs up to say they can do eight knots. In practice it is unlikely you will have to do more than 6–7 knots and most of the transit will take place at around six knots.

2. You are required to have four line-handlers besides the skipper and pilot advisor or pilot. The crews on other boats waiting to go through normally help out other boats and this also gives them a chance to see what the transit entails. Line-handlers can also be hired at around $110 a day.

3. You will need four 110ft (34m) lines of at least ⅞ inch (22 mm) diameter for the transit. The ropes must be a single continuous line with no joins. You can hire the lines from the agent.

4. It's advisable to have as many fenders as possible and you can hire car tyres wrapped in plastic from the agent. Most boats will take somewhere between 10–12 up to 50ft.

5. You must provide a meal for the pilot advisor.

Loaded up with tyres for fenders and long lines for the Canal

Things to do to ease the transit

1. Make sure you have plenty of drinks (bottled water, sodas, beer, etc.) on board for your line-handlers and the pilot/advisor.

2. A lot of thought goes into food and you need to make an effort for the goodwill of your line-handlers and pilot/advisor. For the evening meal on the first night its best to have something made up that you can re-heat because you cannot be exactly sure when you will eat. Something like a ragout, stew, casserole, etc. will work.

3. Your line-handlers will be sleeping on board the first night (and maybe the second) so sort out berths in advance.

4. Brief your line-handlers on the jobs they will have to do. Basically this means knowing where the lead for the lines will be and where a winch is to tighten or slack the lines. If there is no anchor winch forward that can be used then put your strongest line-handlers forward. Aft you should be able to lead the line to a cockpit winch.

5. If you know who you are going through with talk to them about hand signals for motoring forward or astern or going into neutral. This will save a lot of shouting.

The transit

1. When you go through the canal you basically have the choice of rafting up two or three abreast in the middle of the lock, tying alongside, or tying alongside a tug. Large yachts or very wide catamarans will lock through tied in the middle without anyone else tied alongside. Most boats will go through three abreast.

2. From Colon boats will normally leave in the evening and go up through the Gatun Locks to Gatun Lake. These are a set of three consecutive locks that lift boats up 25.9m (85 ft).

3. Depending on the lock operator and which set of locks you are in the ascent can be relatively smooth or may be turbulent. The left hand set of locks (going up) is generally quieter then the right hand side.

4. If the line handlers are on the ball there is no problem with the ascent and few yachts have suffered damage over the years. Most damage involves a few bent

Ship passing on Gatun Lake

stanchions or a damaged rub-rail where yachts have been rafted together.

5. In the Gatun Lake you tie alongside a large plastic covered mooring buoy. Its so big you can walk on it though it is a bit slippery. Some yachts choose to anchor off.

6. The pilot/advisor leaves and in the morning, usually around 0700–0800, a new pilot/advisor arrives to take you through the lake and down the other side.

7. Most yachts will go via the Banana Cut which is shorter than the main ship channel. It's a wonderful trip winding through islands in the lake. The main channel and the Banana Cut are well buoyed.

8. The first set of locks going down is the single Pedro Miguel lock. A short distance after this is the double Miraflores lock. Going down is a lot smoother than going up and there is rarely any turbulence at all.

9. The pilot/advisor will get off at the Balboa Yacht Club or be taken off further down the channel.

10. The reverse route is the same except that you get some turbulence going up through the Miraflores and Pedro Miguel locks and very little coming down the other side at the Gatun locks.

Reading

The Panama Guide: A Cruising Guide to the Isthmus of Panama Nancy Schwalbe Zydler and Tom Zydler. (Partners Publishing Group)
A Complete Sailors Guide to The Isthmus of Panama Eric Bauhaus

My gem

The Path Between the Seas: The Creation of the Panama Canal 1870–1914 David McCullough (Pocket Books)

Miraflores Lock *Peter Metherall*

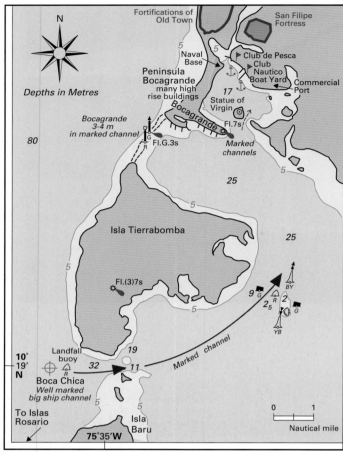

CARTAGENA
⊕10°19'N 75°36'·5W

Berths

Visitors' berths are available at two marinas. Club de Pesca has the most modern facilities and high security. Club Nautico is more relaxed, a little run down but has a very nice atmosphere and cruising yachties feel very much at home. Charge band 2.

Anchorage

There is plenty of room off the two clubs, good holding and the coastguard patrol regularly.

Facilities

There are several yards that haul and store yachts. They have a good reputation for safety, price and quality. The town provides every facility of a large modern city and the airport has good connections to Panama City and Bogotá for flights to USA and Europe.

Remarks

Cartagena is a very fine natural harbour, the old town is magnificent – probably the finest colonial city in all the Americas. There are many islands in the area that provide a quiet getaway from the city.

Panama

General The long skinny peninsula of Panama joins North and South America. The Panama Canal bisects the country and provides a short cut for vessels crossing between the Atlantic and Pacific, so avoiding a long passage round Cape Horn. From the Caribbean yachts often cruise the San Blas Islands before going to Colon for the canal transit.

Coastline The coast is mostly low-lying and care is needed when being blown down onto this dead-end by the trades.

Formalities See Box on the **Panama Canal** for details.

Telecom IDD code +507.

Currency Panama dollar. US dollar widely accepted. Major credit cards accepted in most places. ATMs.

Sailing season Most yachts arrive for the transit through the canal around March to May, although in effect the season is year-round. Yachts usually leave before the beginning of the hurricane season in the Caribbean and at the end of the hurricane season in the S Pacific.

Routes and harbours Most yachts are aiming for the canal with maybe a week or two in the San Blas Islands. The Panama Canal is about 40M long with a minimum depth of 12m. From the Atlantic, vessels travel south to the Gatún Locks where they are lifted 26 metres (c.85 feet) to Gatún Lake. This is a double lock so one vessel can be raised while another is lowered. From Gatún Lake vessels then travel along the canal proper to a lock which lowers vessels 9 metres (c.30 feet) to Miraflores Lake, and then another set of locks lowers vessels to the Pacific. From here the canal runs past Balboa out into the Gulf of Panama.

Note Theft is common in Colon and the town is a muggers' paradise.

COLON

Tidal range 0.6m

Navigation

The approach should be made in daylight even though the approaches are well lit. Contact Cristobal Control on VHF Ch 12 when 10M off and again when 5M off. You may be advised to wait while large ships manoeuvre for the canal.

Berths

Now the Panama Canal Yacht Club has been demolished Shelter Bay Marina is, for the time being, the only really viable place to go.

Shelter Bay Marina: VHF Ch 74. When you enter the commercial harbour from the Caribbean turn to starboard and proceed along the breakwater keeping the green buoys to port (IALA System B). Around 09°22'·23N 79°56'·86W there are two concrete posts marking the entrance to the basin the marina is situated in. Call on VHF Ch 74 for a berth.
100 berths. Visitors' berths. Max LOA 70m. Max draught 10m. Charge band 3.

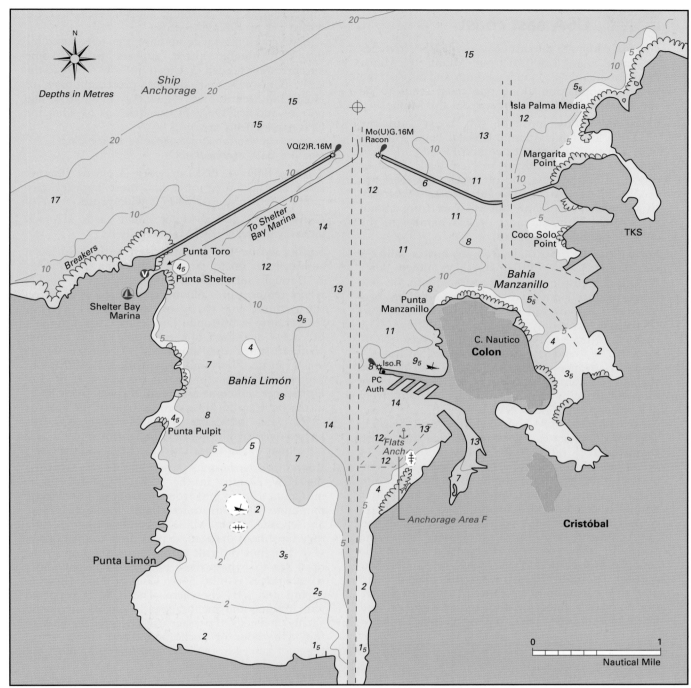

ATLANTIC APPROACHES TO PANAMA CANAL AND COLON
⊕09°23′·8N 79°55′·1W

Facilities
Water and electricity. Fuel barge. 60-ton travel hoist and large hard standing area. Some yacht repairs. Wi-Fi. Laundry. Restaurant and bar. Mini-market. Courtesy shopping bus to Colon.
www.shelterbaymarina.com

Anchorage
Yachts can still anchor in Anchorage 'F' (the Flats) but there is not really a safe place to leave the dinghy (Pier 16 has been used). Tito (VHF Ch 74) supplies a water taxi to ferry anyone from the Flats back and forth. One other possible option is to anchor in Portobello and take a bus or taxi into Colon.

Remarks
The Panama Canal Yacht Club (PCYC) has now been demolished. Whether it will be re-built in a new location is unknown at this time. Colon itself has a deserved reputation for mugging and armed robbery and you should take a taxi everywhere. It does have excellent large American-style supermarkets which are safe and is a good place to provision up for the Pacific.

USA east coast

General Although the east coast of the USA stretches for more than 1,600M from Miami to Maine (without including too many bumps and curves), the yachting population along this coast tends to be concentrated in Miami, Chesapeake and Maine.

Coastline Along most of this coast runs the relatively low-lying Atlantic Coastal Plain which is widest in the Gulf of Mexico and Florida and then runs in a narrower belt up to New York. Most of this coast is low-lying and off much of it there are shoals and sandbanks. The Intracoastal Waterway (ICW), which small craft can use, runs from Miami to Norfolk, Virginia, more or less parallel to the coast (it jigs inland in places).

Formalities All those on board must have a valid US visa in advance. A 'Q' flag should be flown. After 9/11 the US customs was incorporated into the new Department of Homeland Security and customs was renamed Customs and Border Protection. All non-US flagged yachts must now comply with the ANOA (Advance Notice of Arrival). Details and an ANOA form can be found at www.nvmc.uscg.gov. At least 24 hours in advance of the expected ETA in the USA yachts must contact the Captain of the Port where they will arrive by phone, fax or email. Alternatively you can contact the NVMC (National Vessel Movement Center) 96 hours before ETA in the USA. The NVMC operates a 24- hour service and can be contacted at ① (800) 7089823 *Fax* (800) 5478724 *Email* sans@nvmc.uscg.gov There is some confusion over whether the ANOA applies to yachts under 300 grt, with some port captains enforcing it and others not. It is recommended in any case that you do comply with the ANOA as there are heavy fines and imprisonment for non-compliance and the possibility that you will be escorted out of the country. Normally foreign yachts get a one-year cruising permit. Registration documents and insurance papers must be carried. Yachts in the US can be heavily fined for discharging waste oil and black (and in some cases, grey water) (black water =

toilet/greywater = washing, shower, etc.) in areas where it is prohibited to do so.

New reporting regulations have been introduced for the USA though there appears to be some interpretation needed. Yachts must now report to the CPB (Customs and Border protection/part of Homeland Security) every time they move from one port to another. On arrival enquire as to what the CPB requirements are.
www.cbp.gov/xp/cgov/travel/pleasure_boats/boats/pleasure_boat_overview.xml

Telecom IDD +1. GSM network in places. Internet cafés are becoming rare, but most libraries give public internet access. Wi-Fi is widespread.

Currency US dollar. Major credit cards accepted virtually anywhere. ATMs everywhere.

Sailing season The Atlantic coast of the USA has a continental climate varying from tropical in the far S, through sub-tropical, to continental in the N where temperatures plummet and there is snow on the ground for much of the winter (average temperature in Boston in January is 1°C). A number of yachts migrate S in the autumn to the warmer southern states (the 'snowbirds'). Consequently the season in the N around New York is April/May to September/October. In Florida the season is all year. Hurricanes can come ashore all the way from Texas in the far S up to Nova Scotia. One of the authors (RJH) was in Miami when Hurricane Georges passed over the Florida Keys in September 1998 and most boat owners evacuated the Keys and the city.

Routes and harbours A large number of yachts use the ICW. Depths in the ICW are stated to be minimum 12ft (3.7m) from Norfolk to Fort Pierce, minimum 10ft (3m) onto Miami. In practice there are several sections where, depending how recently they have been dredged, depths drop to 6ft (2m) at HW. It is not difficult to make a short hop in the open sea to bypass these points. Air height under fixed bridges is min. 56ft (17m) at Julia Tuttle in Miami and 64ft elsewhere. The ICW is peppered with marinas and anchorages all along its length and yachts on a coastal passage usually enter the ICW to find a harbour or anchorage. There are a whole range of guides to the ICW and to get the most out of it you should buy one.

Note You will need a car or bicycle to get about, even just for shopping, in most places in the USA. Some marinas have courtesy cars or hire cars are relatively cheap.

Resources

PILOTS AND GUIDES

There are more guides to the east coast of America than anywhere else. Some of the popular guides are the *Cruising Guide* series, Maptech *Embassy* series and Richardson's guides. There are many more.
Cruising Guide to the Nova Scotia Coast (Cruising Club of America and RNSYS Pilot Press, Dedham, Mass)
A Cruising Guide to Nova Scotia Peter Loveridge (International Marine)
www/bluewaterbooksweb.com

Note: ● You need to be here for the front when heading east, see CAR5
Depths in Metres
Mantilla Reef
Walkers Cay
LITTLE BAHAMA BANK
Carter's Cays
West Palm Beach
Lt Abaco Is
Elbow Cay
Abaco Is
Grand Bahama Is
Moore's Is
Fort Lauderdale
Northwest Providence Channel
Gorda Cay
Miami
Gt Isaac
Bimini Is
Gt Stirrup Cay
Gt Harbour Cay
Biscayne Bay
N Cat Cay
S Cat Cay
Sand bars
Berry Islands
Northeast Providence Channel
Eleuthera
Gulf Stream

FLORIDA TO THE BAHAMAS

FORT LAUDERDALE (Florida)

Tidal range 0.9m

ANOA The Miami Port Captain authority covers the area from Malabar to Cape Romano including the Florida Keys. ✆ (305) 535-8701 *Fax* (305) 535-8761.

Navigation

The approach is straightforward although it is difficult to identify exactly where the entrance to Lauderdale is. The entrance channel is deep and

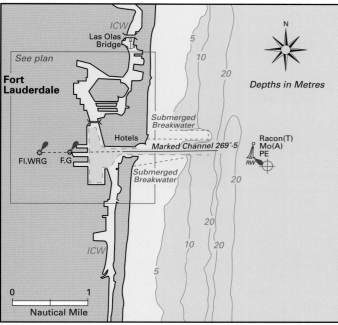

PORT EVERGLADES AND FORT LAUDERDALE APPROACHES
⊕ 26°05′·5N 80°04′·5W

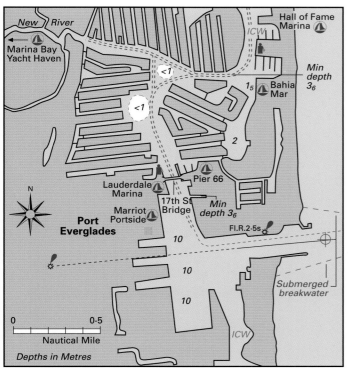

FORT LAUDERDALE (Florida)
⊕ 26°05′·6N 80°06′·1W

buoyed. Once into the port turn to starboard and call up on VHF Ch 09 for the Causeway Bridge (17th Street) to open (the bridge opens on the hour). Numerous marinas in Stranahan River and New River.

Berths

VHF Most marinas monitor Ch 16. For other frequencies consult a local guide.

Lauderdale has a stupendous number of yacht berths. In Stranahan River there is Pier 66, Lauderdale Marina, Portside, and further up the Intracoastal Waterway (ICW) Bahía Mar Marina and Hall of Fame Marina. On New River there are numerous marinas, with Marina Bay and Yacht Haven Marina probably the most popular with transient yachts. There are a number of docks where liveaboards can find long term berths around Los Olas (Bruno's Zoo is popular) and many of the homes on the various canals running off New River have docks that can be rented, though you cannot usually live aboard.

Anchorage

There are no proper anchorages here although yachts sometimes anchor or pick up a mooring S of Las Olas Bridge in the ICW.

Facilities

All the marinas have the usual facilities and most of them an in-house bar and restaurant. Lauderdale has more repair facilities than anywhere else in the USA and possibly the world. Large supermarkets and all the other shops you would expect in a large city. You will need a car to get around.

Remarks

Marina charges vary dramatically depending on location and season, so it is worthwhile doing some homework to check charges. In general Marina Bay and some of the smaller marinas up New River are cheaper than the larger marinas on the ICW.
www.cruiseguides.com

NORFOLK (Virginia)

Tidal range 0.9m

Navigation

Buoyed channel leading through gap in Chesapeake Bay Bridge Tunnel into Thimble Shoal Channel and through Hampton Roads. Chesapeake Channel has another gap through the Chesapeake Bay Bridge Tunnel further to the N. The ICW from the S leads into Portsmouth and Norfolk (Mile 0 on the ICW) before continuing N into Chesapeake Bay. There are strong currents in the approaches and in the channels themselves. The approaches are well lit for a night approach.

Berths

VHF All the marinas listen on Ch 16.

There are numerous marinas at Norfolk and Portsmouth. Some of them are reached by a buoyed channel so consult your guide for access and prices. At Hampton behind Old Point Comfort is Hampton

Cruising the New England coast

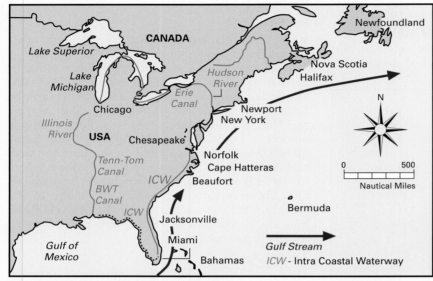

EAST COAST USA TO NEWFOUNDLAND

Statue of Liberty, New York

Few sailing in this area will be able to avoid stopping to visit New York, it is possible to moor on the Hudson side of Manhattan or even anchor in Great Kills Harbour, Staten Island. The sail through the harbour, passing the Statue of Liberty and traversing Hells Gate to reach Long Island Sound is spectacular. Overseas yachts rarely seem to make landfall N of New York. Yet this is a large and attractive cruising ground, justifiably popular with local sailors.

Long Island Sound provides a lot of good cruising with many anchorages, tranquil out of season, and yacht harbours. Despite the proximity of the big city much of the waterfront is relatively green and the further E one sails the greener and wilder it becomes. The sound leads down to the waters of Newport, Nantucket and Cape Cod where a cruising boat could loose herself

Star Island, Isles of Shoals, New Hampshire

for months. Traversing the Cape Cod Canal one can easily reach funky Provincetown or historic Plymouth or Boston. I found Boston an attractive place to visit, it offers the attractions of one of the world's great cities while retaining a civilised pace of life – it is even feasible to cycle down town and the experience of being tied up in the centre of this bustling city is unforgettable. www.bostonwaterboatmarina.com.

Just N of Boston and a short way offshore lie the Isles of Shoals (42°58'N 70°36'W) a small collection of islands that make a peaceful getaway (on weekdays) from the bustle and activity of the mainland. They are right on the border with Maine which provides a maze of islands, sheltered bays and rivers with many thousand miles of coastline. The area is home to countless beautiful yachts, lobster pots and fishing boats. Famous for its fogs and big tides, it is also an enchanting cruising area.

Weather

Summer winds are light and variable with a predominance of SW offshore and a strong land and sea breeze effect inshore. Fog is common with onshore breezes blowing over the warm waters of the Gulf Stream. From August onwards there is a risk of hurricanes. These usually pass offshore and are very accurately forecast, in the event of a storm affecting the coast there are many good anchorages available. The season is June to early September,

primarily July and August. However, there are those who say that fall (autumn) is the best time to visit because of the vibrant colours.

Winter sailing is probably not to be recommended but there can be very good sailing at either end of the season when waters will be free from other boats.

Cruising strategies

Sailing in this area can accommodate any budget. Most towns have marinas though berths may not be available in high season. Anchoring is free and there are unlimited possibilities, even crowded ports have designated anchoring areas. Many overseas yachts visiting this area will be heading back to Europe after a winter in the Caribbean and a trip north through the ICW and will find a S to N cruise the most logical route.

Reading

The Cruising Guide to the New England Coast: Including the Hudson River, Long Island Sound and the Coast of New Brunswick, Twelfth Edition, Edited by Roger F. Duncan

My gem

Ahab's wife, Sena Naslund

Transiting New York

Smuttynose Island, Isles of Shoals, Maine

Waterboat marina – downtown Boston

Cedar Island, Isles of Shoals, Maine

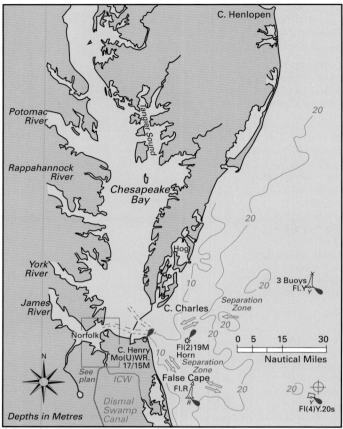

CHESAPEAKE APPROACHES
⊕36°35'·0N 74°50'·0W

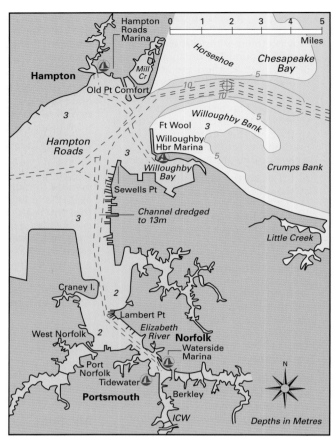

HAMPTON ROADS TO PORTSMOUTH
⊕37°00'·5N 76°15'W

Roads Marina. Opposite in Willoughby Bay is Willoughby Harbour Marina. In Norfolk there is Waterside Marina and on the Portsmouth side Tidewater Yacht Agency.

Facilities

All the normal services you would expect in the marinas and most have an in-house bar and restaurant. Most yacht repairs can be carried out somewhere in the vicinity. Good shopping for everything in Portsmouth.

Remarks

Yachts are often left here because it is N of Cape Hatteras and satisfies insurance requirements to be N of 35°N.

www.cruiseguides.com

NEWPORT (Rhode Island)

Tidal range 1.2m

Navigation

This whole area is prone to fog and is also a busy shipping area. Yachts must keep clear of the Nantucket Shoals which break in bad weather (min. depth 1.25m) and most make for the buoy off the Shoals (40°45'·0N 69°17'·5W) and then for Narragansett Bay: be aware of the separation zones in this area. There are numerous islands and shoals in the area and you will need a detailed chart for the approaches.

Note there are several separation zones in the area.

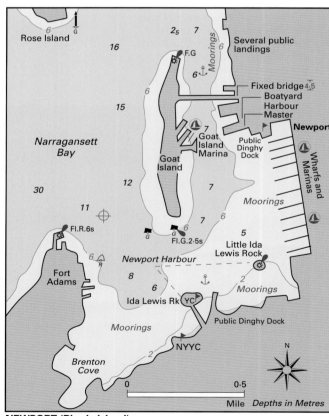

NEWPORT (Rhode Island)
⊕41°29'·00N 71°20'·00W WGS84

Berths

VHF Newport harbourmaster Ch 16 working 14. The marinas listen on Ch 16 and use either Ch 09 or 11.

There are numerous marinas along the waterfront and a large marina on Goat Island. Charges are generally high for berthing in the season. Enquire in advance for charges and availability.

Anchorage

Yachts anchor to the N of Goat Island bridge or in the SE of the bay, W of Little Ida Lewis Rock and S of the cable area shown on the charts. The rest of the area is taken up by moorings and you may be able to pick up a mooring by arrangement with the harbourmaster or one of the yards.

Facilities

All services in the marinas. Excellent facilities for yacht repairs. Good shopping for provisions and everything else ashore.

Remarks

This is the starting point for the Newport-Bermuda Race held in mid-June.
www.newportharborguide.com

Bermuda

General Bermuda is a group of relatively low islands joined by causeways which are the world's most northerly coral islands. The warm Gulf Stream passes nearby and the resulting mild climate attracts lots of tourists from the USA. Prices here (everything has to be imported) are very high.

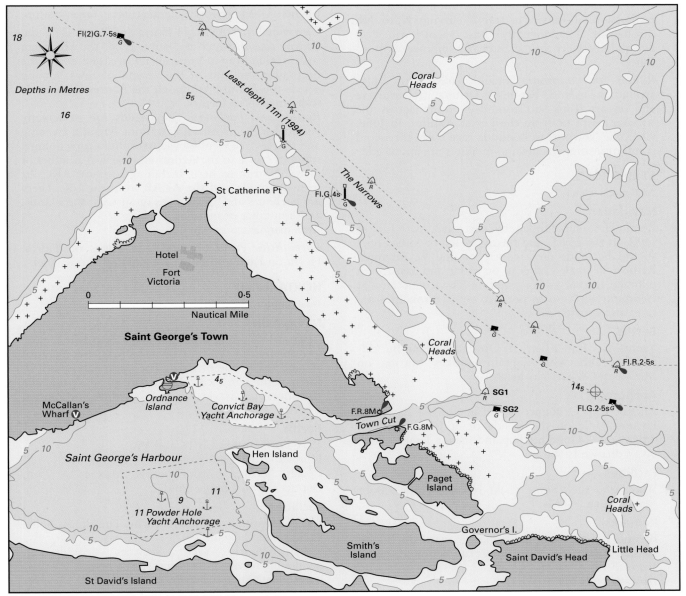

ST GEORGE'S HARBOUR AND APPROACH (Bermuda)
⊕32°22'·8N 64°39'W

Coastline The low islands are fringed by extensive coral reefs, up to 10M off in places.

Formalities A yacht should attempt to contact *Bermuda Radio* on VHF Ch 16 or 27 when in range (20–30M). Details of the boat will be taken and you call again once off St George's. Registration documents and insurance papers must be carried. All crew must have a valid passport. Entry is completed at the Customs Dock in St George's from 0800–2400.

Telecom IDD +1-441. GSM network. Internet cafés.

Currency Bermuda dollar=US dollar. Major credit cards accepted in most places.

Sailing season Most yachts will visit Bermuda on a south-going passage from the northern USA en route to the Caribbean or on an eastabout passage across the Atlantic. Hurricanes do hit Bermuda at times and the corridor between Bermuda and the east coast of the USA is a hurricane alley with a high proportion of hurricane tracks curving N to NE through it. Consequently most yachts will visit Bermuda between spring and early summer (April to June).

Routes and harbours Yachts based here cruise around the island, but most visiting yachts arrive and depart from St George's en route across the Atlantic or to or from the Lesser Antilles. In June, when the Newport to Bermuda race is on, the island is full of visiting yachts and facilities are stretched.

ST GEORGE'S

Tidal range 0.9m

Navigation

Bermuda is surrounded by extensive reefs (up to 10M off the coast) and the approach to St George's should be made on a course of due W. Bermuda Radio will track yachts in on radar and assist with pilotage directions for entering Town Cut into St George's Harbour. In practice entry formalities are brief and courteous.

Berths

Yachts may find a berth at Ordnance Island but this is rare. Otherwise Captain Smokes Marina on McCallan's Wharf has berths.

Anchorage

Anchor E of Ordnance Island in Convict Bay or in Powder Hole on the S side of St George's (long dinghy ride). Good holding and shelter. Dinghy dock on Ordnance Island.

Facilities

Water and fuel. Some yacht repair facilities. Poor provisioning. ATMs.

Remarks

Bermuda is the stepping-stone for many yachts on passage eastwards. Most things can be found, but at a price.
www.bermuda.com

Azores

General The Azores are part of Portugal (see EU regulations), although there are special tax privileges for the island group. Compared to the Canaries these islands are relatively little developed for tourism and Horta has more tourists arriving on yachts than it does by plane. One of the oft-heard complaints from yachts visiting the islands is that they should have budgeted to spend more time here.

Coastline The islands are submerged volcanic peaks and there are a number of active volcanoes throughout the group, including an underwater volcano W of São Miguel. Pico is the highest mountain in Portugal. The approaches to all the islands are generally steep-to and there are few off-lying dangers around the island chain.

Telecom IDD code +351 NDD 292 (Faial) & 296 (São Miguel). GSM network. Internet cafés in larger centres.

Currency Euro. ATMs in Horta and Ponta Delgada.

Sailing season Much the same as for the European season from May to September. Care is needed at the beginning and end of the season of lows coming across the Atlantic, although the Azores High tends to bounce these further N.

Routes and harbours The islands are principally visited by yachts on an eastabout Atlantic crossing and to a lesser extent by yachts from Europe doing a summer cruise to the Azores and back. A number of races also run to here, including a return ARC leg from Bermuda and the AZAB from the UK. There are harbours and anchorages on most of the islands, and a number of marinas.
www.marinasazores.com

Formalities Ports of entry are: Lages on Flores, Horta on Faial and Ponta Delgada on São Miguel.

HORTA (Faial)

Tidal range 1.2m

Navigation

Approach is straightforward with deep water close inshore. Horta will not be seen from the W until around the E side of Faial. The approach is well lit for a night entrance. On arrival go alongside the reception quay to clear in and (hopefully) be allotted a berth.

Berths

VHF Port captain Ch 16 and 11.
Horta Marina Ch 16 and 10.
c. 220 berths. Visitors' berths. Max LOA 25m. Depths 1–4m. Charge band 2.

Facilities

Usual amenities. Laundry nearby. Fuel quay. Some yacht repairs. Chandlers.
Mid-Atlantic Yacht Services provide an invaluable service to cruising yachts here.
www.midatlanticyachtservices.com

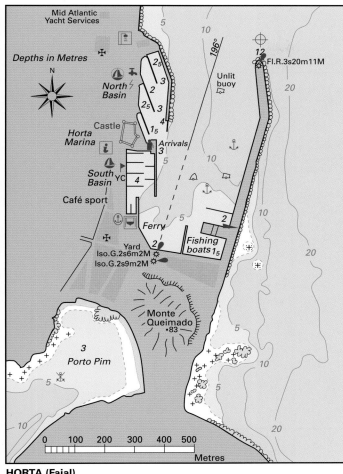

HORTA (Faial)
⊕38°32'·10N 28°37'·14W WGS84

Remarks

Everyone loves Horta: it is a friendly and attractive place. With the new marina extension the yacht berth situation should be eased although in practice it seems just a crowded. Flights to Lisbon and connections from there to other countries.

PONTA DELGADA (São Miguel)

Tidal range 1.4m

Navigation

Straightforward, with just a few rocks along the coast including Baixa da Negra off the airport. There can be a rolling swell at the entrance to the marina, but inside it is quiet although tight for manoeuvring.

Berths

VHF Ponta Delgada Marina Ch 16 and 62.
Recently expanded to 240 berths. 50 visitors' berths. Max LOA 18m. Depths 3–8m. 3m depths in entrance MLWS. Charge band 2. Berth at the reception quay to be allotted a berth. Good shelter inside.

Facilities

Usual amenities. Fuel quay. Limited yacht repairs. Good provisioning and restaurants and bars ashore.

Remarks

The AZAB runs from Falmouth to Ponta Delgada and back.
www.marina.jappdl.pt

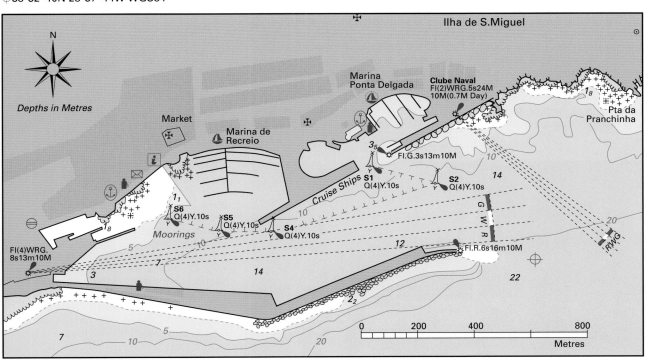

PONTA DELGADA (S.MIGUEL)
⊕37°44'·20N 25°39'·09W WGS84

Azores

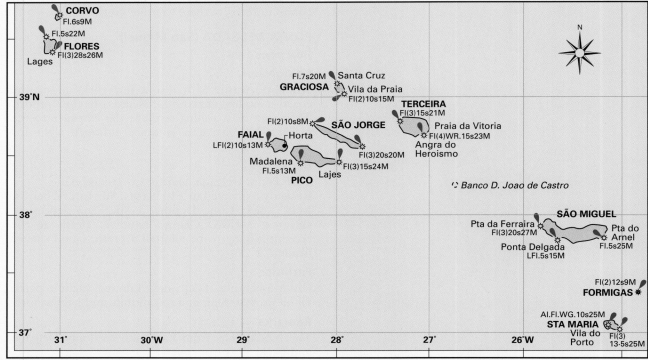

THE AZORES

One of the most common things you will hear from boats arriving and getting ready to depart the Azores is 'why didn't we budget more time for these islands'. I would hazard a guess that there is almost no one who doesn't enjoy the Azores and wish they had longer to spend there. The islands themselves are spectacular. The volcanic peak of Pico is Portugal's highest mountain. The islands are green verdant places with a semi-tropical climate that encourages a wide range of species to grow here. The islanders are a warm and hospitable people. The architecture is enchanting with small towns and villages dotted around the green slopes of the islands. The waters around the islands are full of wildlife and the chances are you will see more whales around the Azores than anywhere else on an Atlantic circuit.

Horta

Cruising strategies

On an Atlantic circuit boats will often pull into Flores first as it is some 60 miles west of the main group including Faial. From Flores yachts will usually head for Horta on Faial and then cruise through São Jorge, Terceira and Graciosa to São Miguel and maybe Santa Maria. Yachts leaving for northern Europe may head north from Graciosa while yachts heading to Atlantic Spain and Portugal and the Mediterranean will usually leave from São Miguel.

Marinas and yacht harbours

Flores Harbour with anchorage.

Faial Horta. Marina often crowded in April/May.

São Jorge Velas Marina.

Terceira Praia da Vitoria Marina and Angra do Heroismo Marina.

São Miguel Ponta Delgada. Marina. Crowded when the AZAB runs.

Sta Maria Vila do Porto. Marina.

Seasons and winds

The winter winds are basically W and the summer winds NE-E-SE. That's easy to say but in fact hides more than it reveals. The Azores high and its influence on the weather in Europe and even in the USA when it extends westwards is well known. It has an influence on Mediterranean weather and on weather in the UK.

The Azores high tends to be more stable and move further N in the summer bringing fine dry weather to Europe. The average pressure is around 1024mb, but it is more variable in the winter than in the summer. In the winter it tends to move further S and weaken. It's the compression zones between lows coming across the Atlantic and the Azores high which brings bad weather and at times this weather will influence the Azores. From mid-April through May the Azores high will establish itself closer to the summer pattern over time and when cruising in the area it is a matter of keeping an eye on weather systems coming across the Atlantic and if they look like they will come close to the high then you will need to seek shelter. Any swell from the systems will affect the Azores and you need to be careful of surges in the harbours.

See charts of Prevailing Winds for May and November at the beginning of North Atlantic chapter.

Ashore

The islands are fertile places and there is an abundance of fresh fruit and vegetables, cheeses, and local lamb and beef. The restaurants in the towns serve excellent food at very reasonable prices. Cruisers arriving in Horta from across the Atlantic have a big appetite and even bigger thirst and this is the place to celebrate the crossing. You have to pay a visit to the famous Café Sport aka Peters Bar, but after that there are lots of other bars and

Crammed into Horta in the Azores on the great eastwards migration

restaurants to mull over the voyage and swap stories. You will also need to contemplate the design of your painting for the famous harbour wall in the harbour which is covered in paintings from ocean travellers who have passed through.

Ponta Delgada on São Miguel is the capital of the Azores and the biggest town, but all of the others have shops and basic services like laundries and internet cafés. There are flights from Faial, Terceira and São Miguel to Lisbon and some direct flights from São Miguel to the UK.

Facilities

Faial In Horta Mid-Atlantic Yacht Services does an amazing job sorting out problems and getting spares in. 22-ton travel hoist. www.midatlanticyachtservices.com

Terceira Basic services. 35-ton travel hoist.

São Miguel In Ponta Delgada there are several chandlers and some yacht services. 25-ton travel hoist.

Reading

Atlantic Islands RCCPF / Anne Hammick. (Imray)

My gem

Barnacle Love Anthony de Sa

Murals on the harbour wall in Horta in the Azores

Painting that mural in Horta

Horta: all yachts and murals

Canada

See Chapter 4 North Pacific for country information.

HALIFAX (Nova Scotia)

Tidal range 2m

Navigation

The approach is straightforward and well marked; however, it is a busy shipping channel with a separation zone in effect. *Halifax Traffic*, VHF Ch 12 and 14, welcomes calls from yachts and will advise on the traffic situation. It is wise to try and stay just outside the marked channel. Poor visibility is common, especially in early summer. Modern charts can be relied upon when using GPS (not universally true on this coast).

Berths

There is no commercial marina, but the Royal Nova Scotia Yacht Squadron (RNSYS) and Armdale Yacht Club in the NW Arm and Dartmouth Yacht Club in Bedford Basin welcome visitors and will almost certainly make a berth available.

Anchorage

It is possible to anchor off the Dartmouth Yacht Club and in Bedford Basin, but the most convenient and secure spot is at Dingle Cove in the NW arm.

Facilities

Both YCs have the usual facilities. Everything a yacht could want is available in this city.

Remarks

Halifax is an interesting destination in its own right and is a good jumping off place for marvellous cruising grounds in Nova Scotia and Newfoundland.
www.armdaleyachtclub.ns.ca

ST JOHNS

Tidal range 2.5m

Navigation

Entrance is simple; icebergs are sometimes grounded in the approaches.

Berths

There are no long term yacht berths, the best position is the Port Authorities pontoon where shown. Yachts can also tie up to the quay in the SE extremity of the harbour. Charge band 2. Both positions can be uncomfortable in E winds. For longer stays it is recommended to use one of the club marinas on the E side of the peninsula (Conception Bay South). There is no anchorage.

Facilities

All the facilities of one of the world's main seaports including all the requirements of yachts. Slipping in one of the smaller ports in the area. Water is available alongside. There is no fuel berth but it is easy to arrange delivery by tanker.

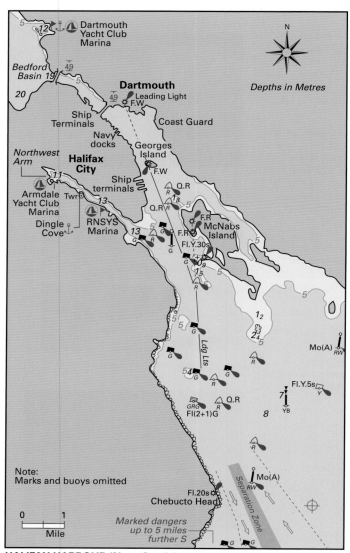

HALIFAX HARBOUR (Nova Scotia)
⊕ 44°30'·00N 63°28'·00W WGS84

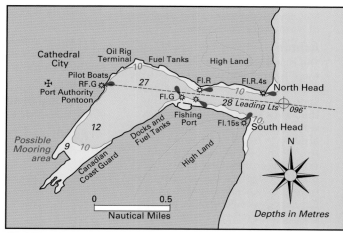

ST JOHN'S NEWFOUNDLAND
⊕ 47°33'·9N 52°40'·5W

Formalities

A port of entry and a good place to do business with the customs who are very close to the mooring area. The Port Authority should be called before entering and when making any movement in this busy harbour.

Remarks

St Johns has been a hub of sea traffic on the North Atlantic for five centuries and is still a stepping stone for voyages to the Arctic and Greenland. Don't miss the Irish music and pub on Water Street (late at night unfortunately).

Greenland

General Only a few weeks sail from Europe, Greenland is one of the world's most rewarding cruising destinations.

Coastline Indented by long and complex fjord systems. On the W coast an island chain, *skærgard*, gives a considerable amount of cruising in sheltered waters. Prins Christians Sund, in the S cuts off the dangerous waters around Kap Farvel.

Formalities There is refreshingly little interest shown in yachts. Alcohol prices are high so that it would be unwise to carry more than reasonable requirements for the crew. Usually the formalities are completed by a courtesy visit to the harbourmaster.

Telecom IDD +299 Public telephones available and internet services widespread in larger settlements, in case of difficulty try in a hotel or tourist office. Good postal service via Denmark.

Transport Greenland has two international airports with regular flights to Iceland and Denmark. Both are accessible from the sea, though Sødre Strømfjord lies almost 100M up a narrow fjord. Narssarssuaq in the S is more easily reached by yacht. Internal flights are expensive, some being by helicopter only.

Currency Danish Kronor

Sailing season Most boats visit between May and September. The inshore stretch between Nuuk and Disko Bugt is relatively ice free in winter so year round cruising may be possible (in the dark!). Much of the outer western coastline is well lit for the regular coastal traffic that operates even in the Arctic night.

Routes and harbours See the **Greenland** pages.

Resources

PILOTS AND GUIDES

Iceland, Greenland and Faeroes RCCPF / Willy Ker (Imray)
Danish meteorological service Greenland forecast
www.dmi.dk/dmi/index/gronland/gruds.htm
My translation of Danish weather terms:
www.sailor.co.nz/Dansk.htm

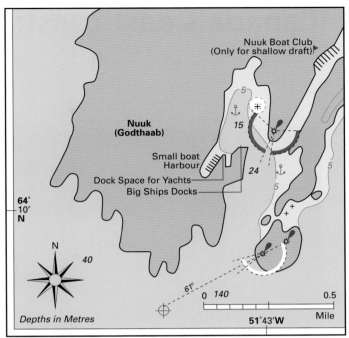

NUUK GREENLAND
⊕64°09'·55N 51°43'·99W

NUUK

Tidal range up to 7m

Navigation

Nuuk is at the centre of an extensive fjord system which looks intimidating on the chart but approaches from seaward or the fjords are straightforward and, in the channels, clear of dangers. The main approach from seaward is called Nordloeb and is deep and well lit.

Berths

It may be possible to tie up for short periods on the inside of the main quay and yachts often tie between the dock and a buoy where marked.

Anchorage

In the main bay, good holding, and, in settled weather, where shown to the E of the main approach, poor holding – keep away from traffic.

Facilities

There is a friendly and helpful Yacht Club where shown, unfortunately it is exclusively used by power boats and low power cables make it inaccessible to yachts. Much chandlery, appropriate to motor boats of all sizes, is available. There are yards capable of slipping a yacht.

Remarks

This is the capital of Greenland and has a good museum, hotels and shops. However, it is an uninteresting town and is only really worth visiting if visiting the splendid Nuuk fjord system.

Canada's east coast: an unspoiled delight

Saglek Fjord,
Magnus with Arctic Char

Tikigatsiak Cove,
Balaena and *Tamara*

Nearly half of Canada's provinces reach the waters of the Gulf of St Lawrence and Atlantic. They all have distinct customs, traditions and linguistic variations of English, French, Gaelic, German and aboriginal languages. There are many picturesque small communities but most of the area is wild and covered in forest or tundra-like rocky landscapes. The summers are warm with settled weather, the fishing is superb and there are plenty of sheltered harbours and anchorages to welcome a yacht. One disadvantage is the fog that sweeps in from the warm Gulf Stream. But with radar, GPS and Canadian digital and paper charts, which are first rate, that is not a great inconvenience. This cruising ground is not very far from the coast of New England. Over the years many boats from the United States have found a warm welcome and a secure spot for over-wintering in one of the excellent boatyards on Cape Breton Island which is within a few days sail of most places south of the Strait of Belle Isle.

North of the Strait of Belle Isle lies the Labrador, another world altogether, close to so-called civilization but in reality sharing more in common with Patagonia and Greenland than with major Canadian

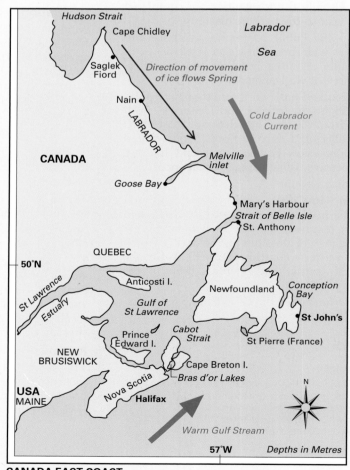

CANADA EAST COAST

centres. Cruising 'down the Labrador': Warm winds blowing off spectacular mountains, wild flowers, bears and caribou in abundance, crystal clear water, almost complete absence of footprints, more fish on the hook than you have ever dreamt of, sunshine almost twenty four hours a day. These are some of the attractions. Of course, there are also icebergs and days when the wind blows from the sea, bringing fog and near freezing temperatures. And, in the far N, there are polar bears that make shore going a bit more exciting than usual. A summer trip to Labrador is a tradition that goes back beyond the days of Columbus. Way back then, people were coming to exploit the fish, seals and whales that abound. Many of them stayed and their descendants are amongst the most welcoming people you will meet anywhere in the world.

Weather and ice
(See also *Weather and Sea* at the beginning of Chapter 1)
Summer
On the whole, summer weather is pleasant and influenced by the heat of the N American continent. The S part of Canada's maritime provinces are dominated by the Gulf Stream. Where this meets cold water flowing S the result is a lot of fog. Depressions also follow this track so that the weather off the Atlantic coast of Nova Scotia and Newfoundland is more unstable than the Gulf of St Lawrence and much of the Labrador coast where light winds and smooth seas are common. Another favourite depression track follows the St Lawrence Valley, however, such systems are not common in summer but start to become more frequent after the beginning of September. Depressions (occasionally unknown to the weather forecasters – it is a long way between observation stations) also often pass over the N tip of Labrador. Tropical cyclones start to pass offshore in August and occasionally come ashore in Nova Scotia or SE Newfoundland.
Winter
After October cruising is largely confined to the few hours of quiet weather between major storms and the few patches of open water between miles of ice flows. This is one part of the world where winter cruising is almost impossible; apart from the areas bathed by the Gulf Stream most of these waters freeze over and are only navigable by large icebreakers. Storms of unbelievable ferocity are also common.

Cruising strategy
In Nova Scotia and SE Newfoundland the season starts in April or May. By late May the Gulf of St Lawrence should be free of ice (varies from year to year) and as you go N the ice is present later and later in the season. In the far north of Labrador the ice is unlikely to be entirely gone before the winter storms begin. Icebergs and fog off the Atlantic coast of Newfoundland are less common towards the end of the season.

A good strategy would be to start in the S of Nova Scotia at the end of April or early May and cruise through the Bras D'Or lakes before entering the Gulf and spending June and July cruising the coasts of New Brunswick, Prince Edward Island and Quebec. Later in July and August cruising on the S coast of Labrador and E coast of Newfoundland should be at their best. Aim to be back in base by the end of September. To visit the N coast of Labrador an encounter with ice (both bergs and pack) is inevitable. A strategy many have found successful is to leave the Strait of Belle Isle towards the end of June and get out to sea, possibly up to 100M, depending upon ice conditions, and sail N to the desired latitude and then try and find a way through the pack ice to the coast. Attempting to sail N along the coast will almost certainly be slow and frustrating until late in the season because of the presence of pack ice.

Reading
Cruising Guides to the Nova Scotia Coast, Newfoundland, The Labrador and the The Gulf of St Lawrence Published by members of The Cruising Club of America. See http://www.puffin-press.com/
Cruising information for Labrador www.annie-hill.blogspot.com/search/label/Labrador

My gem
The Boat Who Wouldn't Float by Farley Mowat.

Balaena in Saglaek Fjord

Harrington Harbour, Quebec

Ironbark in D'Escousse, Cape Breton

Petit Rigolet, Quebec

Greenland

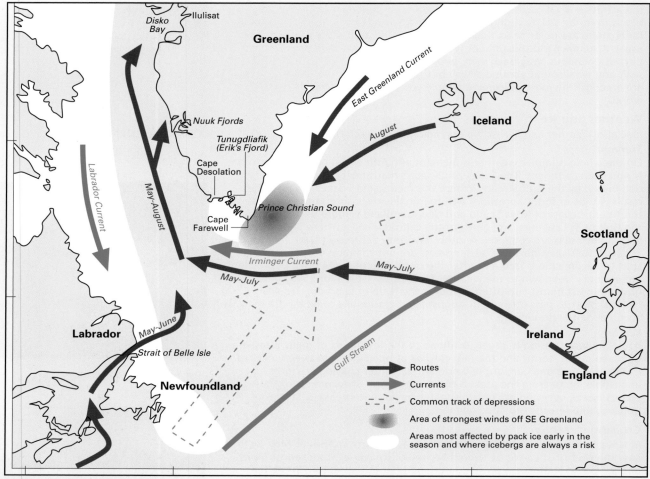

GREENLAND CRUISING ROUTES

This is a great wilderness cruising destination. It offers some of the most spectacular scenery anywhere, safe anchorages, friendly people, unobtrusive and helpful officials, good charts and navigation aids, fascinating history and, in summer very long and sunny days. Considering how close it lies to the major cruising nations of Europe and North America, it is surprisingly less visited than Patagonia and the Cape Horn. I would hazard a guess that more yachts visit Antarctica each year than cruise in Greenland.

Ice

This is the dominant factor in planning a Greenland cruise and is probably what puts most people off. However, with foresight and careful planning it is not such a fearsome obstacle. The worst pack ice is concentrated off the east coast, much of which is only accessible in the late summer and then not every year. Up until July there is usually a lot of ice off Cape Farewell and the SW coast as far N as Cap Desolation. Further N the W coast is mainly free from pack ice all year round though icebergs and the occasional floe are common. Disko Bay has huge numbers of icebergs that break off the glacier at Illulisat and that is one of the major attractions of a visit.

Cruising strategies

Getting to Greenland is not simply a matter of steering a great circle course for Cape Farewell. However, it is a practical enterprise for a summer sailing season. The easiest approach is from North America when around the end of May a yacht can avoid the worst icebergs by creeping up inside Newfoundland and then sail due east from the Strait of Belle Isle to get clear of the Labrador current which carries most of the icebergs S. Then steer N

Balæna in Prince Christian Sound

towards Nuuk or the coast further N, I would recommend a direct course towards Disko Bay. Working S through the summer the SW coast should be accessible by late July and August. Sailing back to Labrador and then further S is practicable in late August and September. There is a risk of hurricanes late in the season but these almost always pass S of Cape Farewell.

From Europe the traditional route is to Iceland and then on to Prince Christian Sound, just N of Cape Farewell. This strategy means that it is usually impractical to visit before August which severely restricts the time available for a Greenland cruise. I would suggest sailing direct from Europe to a point about 150 miles S of Cape Farewell and then steering northwards to come in to the coast in June as mentioned above. It would be necessary to study the ice charts put out by the Danish meteorological service to see exactly how far south and west of the cape to sail (see also my note on weather below). An even better strategy would be to sail direct to Newfoundland and then up to Greenland.

The cruising

The W coast of Greenland is comparable to Norway in the extent of its off-lying islands, fjords, mountains and potential anchorages. Most places are rarely or never visited by yachts. It would require many years to explore this coast in detail. I was particularly impressed with the areas of Disko Bay, Nuuk Fjord, Tunugdliarfik (Eriks fjord to the Vikings) and Price Christian Sound. It is a great experience to anchor in bays where Viking ships once offloaded supplies from Europe and bartered for ivory and fur, where Norsemen thrived for 500 years before Columbus and where their ruins are still very visible and thrilling to explore. Though there are many good harbours and anchorages (see the RCCPF guide to *Faroe, Iceland and Greenland*), there is often ice drifting about and a careful watch needs to be kept for flows that may drive the boat ashore or tear out the anchor.

Weather

The towering mountains and tumbling glaciers of Prince Christian Sound are often compared with the Beagle Channel in Patagonia. Nearby Cape Farewell deserves to be compared to Cape Horn, in fact aboard *Balæna*, we found it just as

challenging. It was respected by the whalers and fisherman who sailed the Greenland seas but lies off the beaten track for most Atlantic shipping so has not acquired the fearsome reputation of its southerly sister. The bad weather here is a much more local phenomenon than at the southern tip of South America where storms can cover vast swathes of ocean.

Even in summer, depressions can sweep out of the Gulf of St Lawrence and intensify to the S of Greenland. During the hurricane season the remains of tropical storms travelling up the Eastern seaboard of North America often aggravate the situation. The combined presence of relatively stable high pressure from the cold air of the Greenland icecap and the high mountain chain running down its coast compresses the isobars dramatically in a belt about 100 miles wide to the S and E of the cape. Even quite minor depressions can follow each other like pearls on a string every few days giving a constant stream of gale to hurricane force winds between SE and NE, making this a lee shore, with the accompanying rain and low cloud. Add the ever present icebergs, even in late summer (in early summer dense pack ice stretches far out to sea), and you have the makings of a real hell's corner in the oceans.

One of the surprising things about Greenland's weather is that, due to the depressions being deflected S and E of the cape, the weather can change for the better very rapidly as you sail up the W coast and away from Cape Farewell. In the fjords it can be calm and sunny when severe storms are raging to the S.

Luckily weather forecasting is very accurate and when leaving Greenland waters there are good places to shelter and wait for an auspicious moment to cast off and run the gauntlet.

Supplies

In the towns all foodstuffs are available from very well stocked Danish supermarkets, but prices for fresh products, which have to be flown in, are very high. Alcohol is prohibitively expensive, though nobody sees to mind if a boat takes sufficient for her own crews needs.

Boat facilities

The good news is that there is almost no tax on diesel and boat supplies, which are surprisingly easily available

Illulisat glacier ice meets the sea at Disko Bay

as there are plenty of local boats. There are no facilities that are directed towards a cruising yacht. However, there is a very large fleet of pleasure motorboats. There are marinas for motor boats in several places but low power cables or bridges make them inaccessible to yachts. In the Nuuk area the local boat club has laid heavy moorings in the fjords and invites visitors to use them. Most of the large settlements have a crane capable of lifting a light displacement yacht and there are fishing boat yards with large slipways in many places. A boat in need of repair or storage overwinter should be able to find help without great difficulty. Marine engineering and motor workshops are also common and run to a high standard.

Reading

Faroe, Iceland and Greenland Guide RCCPF / Willy Ker (Imray)
Land under the Pole Star Helge Ingstad. A classic account of cruising the SW coast in a small boat in the 1950s by the man who found the only proven Viking site in North America.
Viking – The North Atlantic Saga (Smithsonian Institution Press). A scholarly and authoritative text on the Viking period with a very heavy emphasis on the Greenland colonies and exploration of Vinland.

My gem

The Greenlanders by Jane Smiley.

A little ice with your sunshine on the Greenland coast

2
SOUTH ATLANTIC OCEAN

Enseada de Jurujuba, Brazil, showing marina of Club Naval Charitas, Rio in the background, Niteroi is to the right of the picture

General

After the Southern Ocean this is possibly the least cruised of all oceans. With the exception of the coast of Brazil, most people seem to regard the South Atlantic purely as a route to somewhere else. Yet there is some very good cruising. Argentina is a friendly and interesting country with some spectacular destinations along its long Atlantic coastline and in the far south. The W coast of Africa is highly praised by those brave enough to visit. South Africa is on the main highway for circumnavigators, though few visit the coast N of Cape Town. Namibia does not offer interesting cruising, but it has two excellent ports where those wishing to travel in this fascinating country may leave a vessel.

The Falkland Islands and Tierra del Fuego are exotic destinations for those who are able to stomach some rough weather and South Georgia has one of the planet's most pristine wildernesses. Refer to *Chapter 7 Southern Ocean* for more details of cruising in the far S.

Because they are associated with true S Atlantic passages, some of the routes below cross into the N Atlantic up to 10°N.

Weather and sea

PREVAILING WINDS

The overall pattern is dictated by the South Atlantic High, which is generally an area of light and variable winds. Prevailing winds blow in an anticlockwise direction around this. These are the trade winds to the N of the high and the Roaring Forties to the S. Southern Ocean depressions tend to pass well to the south of 50°S in summer and have little effect in the region N of 35°S. In winter they often pass north of 50°S and may influence weather as far N as 25°S.

Trade winds N of 20°S the SE Trade wind blows with great regularity. In summer the trades extend to about 3°S and in winter they reach the equator. In the equatorial region they blend into a band of doldrums. Conveniently, the doldrums are least pronounced along the N coast of Brazil (across the mouth of the Amazon). Most vessels heading from S to N will follow this coastline as they head up towards the Caribbean and find that the SE blends into the NE Trade wind with little loss of strength.

In summer, south of approximately 15°S, the trade wind is deflected to NE along the Brazilian coast.

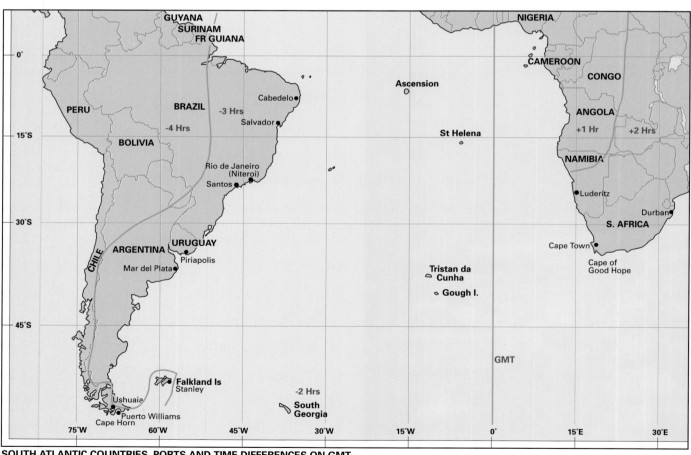

SOUTH ATLANTIC COUNTRIES, PORTS AND TIME DIFFERENCES ON GMT

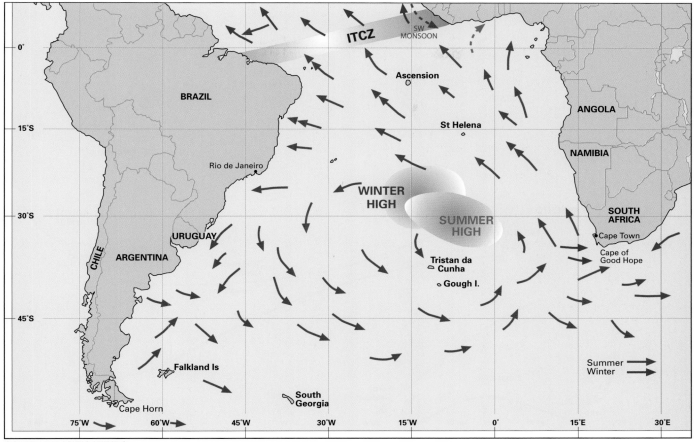

SOUTH ATLANTIC WINDS

Winds of the oceanic circulation Between 20°S and 35°S the winds are predominantly SE off the African coast and NE off the American coast, where they are more changeable in winter with regular (generally weekly) frontal systems extending N from the southern ocean bringing S–SW winds.

The passage of winter depressions also brings occasional northerlies to the African coast.

Variables Light winds are found within the permanent high-pressure system lying in mid-ocean. The high is centred at about 31°S in summer and 26°S in winter. The direct course on the Cape to Rio race (January) lies through the variables and competitors (many of whom are in the cruising division) are often frustrated by calms.

Westerlies Predominant westerlies are the rule south of 35°S. They are strongly influenced by Southern Ocean depressions, which produce frontal weather. In winter their influence may be felt as far N as Luderitz in Namibia or Rio de Janeiro.

Seasonal Winds: SW Monsoon (W coast of Africa – actually in N hemisphere) In the northern summer, intense heat in the Sahara causes a SW flow onto this coast between the equator and 15°N.

GALES

To the N the variables and trade winds are perhaps the most benign on the planet as tropical storms are rare. Note: in March 2004 a vigorous cyclonic system was observed by satellite off the S coast of Brazil. There was argument amongst forecasters about whether or not this was the first hurricane ever observed in the S Atlantic. However, it was unquestionably a storm of great severity. Statistics for gales on this coast are: N of Rio less than 0.2%. In the far S of Brazil the maximum incidence is 2.6% in August. However, quite strong winds can blow at times.

In the S are the Roaring Forties, which seem to blow with particular violence and create exceedingly disturbed seas in the vicinity of Tristan da Cunha. The area of the Cape of Good Hope is renowned for its ferocious gales, particularly in winter when the South Atlantic High has weakened.

Similarly, in the winter months, gales regularly affect the S coast of Brazil. These gales produce winds from W or S and are favourably looked upon by yachtsmen wishing to progress northwards on the South American coast, as they provide a respite from the prevailing NE winds.

On the Argentinian coast the frequency of gales varies from less than 2% in the Rio de la Plata to over 6% winter and 4% summer off the east coast of Tierra del Fuego. However, winds between 30 and

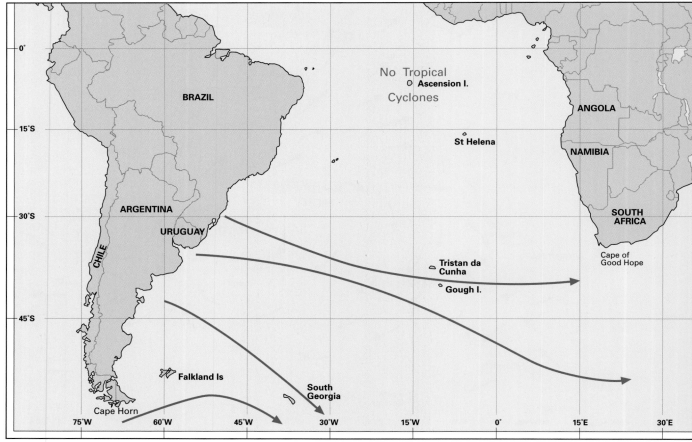

SOUTH ATLANTIC COMMON STORM TRACKS

40kn are very common S of Rio de la Plata and are often intensified by local geography. Put simply, this is a windy place.

Of particular note are the pamperos, violent SW squalls that blow off the Patagonian pampas. These are common in the Rio de la Plata and all the way down the coast. A line of dark cloud on the western horizon usually precedes the wind. The change in weather typically occurs with great rapidity so all precautions should be taken immediately the signs are observed. They are usually preceded by a rapid fall of the barometer.

TROPICAL STORMS

This is the only ocean in the world that does not suffer from tropical storms (but see the note above). Tropical circumnavigators make use of this fact by crossing the South Atlantic in the summer when the Indian and South Pacific Oceans are not open to them. This means that they can plan to leave the Indian Ocean at the beginning of its cyclone season, round the Cape of Good Hope in summer, and spend a few months on the Brazilian coast before reaching the Caribbean at the end of the northern hurricane season.

CURRENTS

The currents follow the same general anticlockwise pattern as the prevailing winds. The Benguela current, which can exceed 2kn close to land, flows N along the SW coast of the African continent. (Beware of an onshore set that occurs frequently.) To the N, the current in the trade wind zone is known as the South Equatorial Current. This current splits off Cabo de São Roque, the NE corner of Brazil. The N part heads towards the West Indies and may reach two knots off the N coast of Brazil in July-September. The southern part turns SW to become the Brazil current. To the S the Roaring Forties give rise to the E-going Southern Ocean Current.

Some important currents do not conform to the overall anticlockwise circulation:

- The N-flowing Falkland Current that runs up the E side of South America to Rio de la Plata. In winter (May-July) the Falkland Current extends north as far as Cabo Frio and is called the Brazil Inshore Counter-current. This current is most noticeable close inshore. Beware of a shoreward set that frequently occurs.
- Between August and December the Equatorial Counter-current, which sets SE, is only just outside the continental shelf of S America, N of 5°N. This coincides with the doldrums and can be

extremely frustrating for yachts bound towards the West Indies that stray too far offshore.

- Though it is actually in the North Atlantic, the Equatorial Counter-current is of particular importance to yachts heading S towards South Africa. By sailing with this current into the Gulf of Guinea (here called the Guinea Current) they can make a relatively comfortable, though mainly windward, passage and avoid the notorious seas in the westerlies further S. Near the African coast this current lies between 0°–10°N in July, and 2°–6°N in January.

FOG

Fog is common on the coast of South Africa and Namibia between 20°S and 32°S when moist onshore winds blow over the very cold Benguela current.

SWELL

N of 30°S swell is rarely a problem when at sea and is generally less than 1.5m and regular. Coastal roadsteads, notably that of James Bay on St Helena, can become untenable at times in winter due to swell produced by Southern Ocean gales.

S of 30°S swells increase. In the vicinity of Tristan da Cunha and S of 40°S, swell can reach dangerous proportions. Yachts frequently report that on Southern Ocean passages from S America to S Africa the combination of multiple swells causes seas of horrifying irregularity. One of the authors (AO'G) experienced a violent knockdown in this area and knows of a skipper whose boat broke up in almost the same place.

SEASONS

Once in the trade winds, a passage can be made at any time of year. Most sailors in Cape Town would not recommend a winter departure from the Cape, as winter storms can be very bad. However, by carefully watching the weather a vessel should be able to leave the Cape, heading northwards, at any time of year.

Winter is a good time for sailing northwards from the River Plate along the S Brazilian coast (see winds and currents – above). Winter can be magnificent for cruising around Tierra del Fuego, but summer is the season for making ocean passages in high latitudes, although some people sail there in purpose-built vessels in the winter.

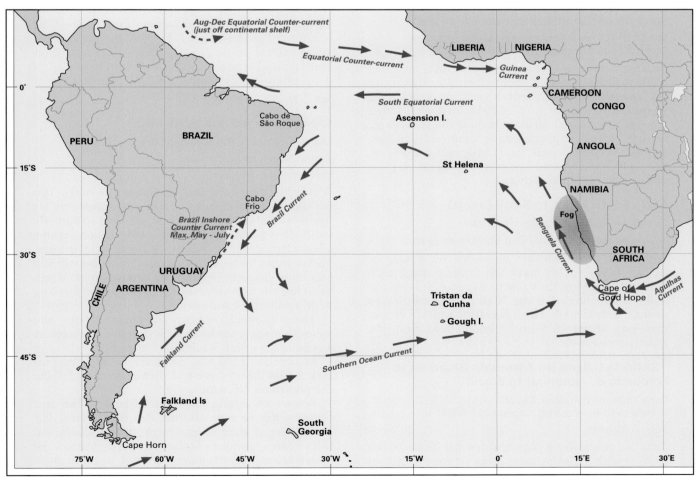

SOUTH ATLANTIC CURRENTS

ROUTES AND PASSAGES

NORTHERLY AND WESTERLY PASSAGES

These are generally taken by circumnavigators who have chosen to leave the Indian Ocean by way of the Cape of Good Hope and are almost the final legs for many yachts returning to Europe or North America.

*SAN1 – South Africa (or Namibia) to St Helena

Cape Town to St Helena 1,690M

Season November to April (but possible all year)

Circumnavigators often arrive in Cape Town early in the New Year. SE winds are predominant in summer and are reliable until at least April.

The course to steer is directly for St Helena. Most yachts will hardly notice the transition from the SE winds of South Africa to the SE Trade wind. Later in the year strong NW winds are associated with the fronts which reach the coasts of S Africa. Departing at that time of year the skipper should watch the forecast carefully, try to leave immediately after the passage of a front, when the next one appears a long way off, and stay well offshore.

See * SAN4

SAN2 South Africa to Namibia

Cape Town to Luderitz 475M

Season November to April (but possible all year)

See SAN1 for comments on winds. The Benguela Current generally gives a lift of 1–1.5kn on this passage.

Because Southern Ocean swells can become steep while in shallower seas, yachts should endeavour to get outside the continental shelf as quickly as possible (it extends up to 130M offshore). Other reasons to stay well offshore include the many large fishing boats, semi-stationary diamond dredges, seismic survey vessels and frequent dense fog. (Coastal VHF radio stations broadcast regular updates on maritime activity.)

SAN3 South Africa to Brazil (direct)

Cape Town to Rio De Janeiro 3,660M

Season November to April (but possible all year)

See SAN1 for comments on winds on E side of Ocean. Many yachts make the direct passage each year in January on the Cape to Rio race. It is best to make a large curve to the N of the rhumb line to avoid the doldrums. Head for 20°S and 10°W and then stay above 20°S until about 600M from the Brazilian coastline.

*SAN4 St Helena (to Ascension Island on to Fernando de Noronha) to Brazil

Cape Town to St Helena 1,690M
St Helena to Rio Paraiba (Cabedelo) 1,800M

Season All year

This is generally a straightforward trade wind passage with a direct course being set for the desired destination. If planning to sail directly to southern Brazil or Rio de la Plata then it may be worth sailing in an arc to the NE of the rhumb line in order to avoid the light winds often found nearer to the centre of the S Atlantic High.

See * SAN5 for Europe
      * SAN7 for US/Canada
      * SAN8 for Caribbean

*SAN5 North-going, from Ascension Island towards the Azores and thence to European destinations

Ascension Island to Azores 3,040M

Season March to July

Best time April to May

While this passage is possible at any time of year, the safest time is early in the northern summer, after the winter gales in the North Atlantic have abated but before the West Indies hurricane season has reached its peak. (This time fits in well with a summer rounding of the Cape of Good Hope).

Leaving Ascension Island head for a point about 5°N and 25°W. The doldrums are less predominant to the W so a weatherly yacht, unwilling to motor far, may steer further west to achieve a faster doldrums passage, but there is a payback by having to sail closer to the wind after crossing them. Once into the NE Trades it is then a long fetch on starboard tack towards the Azores.

If attempting to make this passage late in the season, it is important to stay on the E side of the ocean to avoid hurricanes. The SW monsoon is felt at least 500M off the coast of West Africa and means that favourable winds can be kept until nearly 10°N if steering towards about 22°W. See NAE5.

See * NAW1

SAN6 Rio de la Plata to NE Brazil

Mar de la Plata to Rio Paraiba (Cabedelo) 2,313M

Season March to September

Best time May to June

Winter is definitely the best time to make this passage. The Falklands Current may extend as far north as Cabo Frio and there are more southerly winds. The passage is generally made inshore, taking advantage of lighter winds, sea and land breezes. Yachts trying to make the passage non-stop will still encounter frequent head winds and it may be worth breaking the trip into shorter passages and sailing with favourable conditions.

There is much inshore shipping, oil rigs and fishing activity and the coast is dangerous, therefore a reasonable offing is advisable at night.

In summer it may be necessary to take the port tack for 600M offshore and then make a fetch N in the prevailing NE winds.

Beware of getting too close to land in the area between Rio Grande and the Rio de la Plata. The water here is shallow and with strong winds and tides can produce fearsome seas. Stories of knockdowns and strandings are not uncommon in this area.

*SAN7 North-going, from NE Brazil, towards the Azores and thence to European destinations or the NE coast of USA and Canada

Rio Paraiba (Cabedelo) to Azores 2,950M
Rio Paraiba to Bermuda 2,940M

Season March to July

See comments on season under SAN5.

Leaving the coast of Brazil try to make as much easting as possible. Heading for a point about 5°N and 25°W. Using the motor in the doldrums to make further easting as well as heading north is a good idea. Once into the NE Trades it is then a long fetch on starboard tack towards the Azores.

Yachts bound for the NE North American seaboard need not make so much easting and can generally steer N until meeting the NE Trades, then they can steer for their destination.

*SAN8 North-going, from NE Brazil towards the Caribbean

Río Paraiba (Cabedelo) to Tobago 1,931M

Season All year

Along the NE coast of S America the trade wind is generally steady and the current favourable. A direct course can be steered. Between August and December avoid sailing more than 50M off the 100m line in order to stay out of the Equatorial Counter-current (up to 2kn SE have been reported by yachts) which almost meets the coast at 6°N. (This current is not shown on all Pilot charts and

routeing software. One of the authors (AO'G) noticed that he gained four days on a vessel without this information that took a course less than 50M further to seaward.) The rest of the year it is possible to sail further offshore. If sailing over the continental shelf a lookout must be kept for oil platforms.

Venezuela and Trinidad are just outside the hurricane belt. Passages to those destinations can be made at any time of year, though the weather will be hotter and calmer with squalls in the northern summer.
See *CAR1*

SOUTHERLY PASSAGES

Circumnavigators going westabout will often visit Brazil for a season before sailing to the Caribbean. Others, after arriving in Brazil, will head S in the direction of Cape Horn or E to South Africa.

SAS1 South going from Canaries, Senegal or Cape Verdes to Brazil

Tenerife to Cape Verde to 25°W on equator to Rio Paraiba 2,490M

Season October to June

On this passage the dilemma to be faced is that the doldrum belt is narrower on the western side of the ocean, but a yacht crossing the equator too far to the W may have to beat to weather the NE corner of Brazil. (Bear in mind the predominance of the W-setting equatorial currents on this route.) For a yacht with good range under power it would be best to stay to the E, crossing the equator E of 25°W, motor

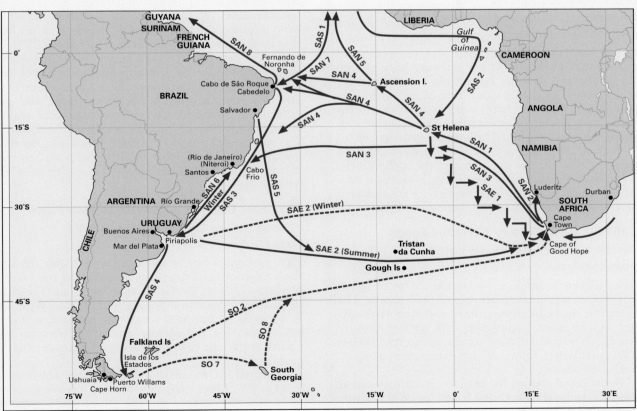

SOUTH ATLANTIC CRUISING ROUTES

due S in the doldrums and then lay a course, reaching, to the destination. Yachts with better windward capability and less motoring range could cross the equator between 25°W and 30°W and should be able to lay their destination.

If choosing to make this passage between June and September, a very weatherly boat would be needed as the wind will be forward of the beam much of the time off the African coast S of 15°N. Once over the equator the SE Trades will also have a more southerly tendency. The yacht would be obliged to keep on the E side of the ocean because of the West Indies Hurricane season.

SAS2 South from the Canary Islands into the Gulf of Guinea to St Helena

Tenerife to St Helena by route described 3,990M

Season All year

Best time June to September

Much of this route is to windward, however it is generally possible to lay the course, and the wind and sea tend to be moderate. After leaving the Canary Islands, sail about 200 miles off the coast, passing inshore of the Cape Verdes. The wind in this area is moderate and variable, mostly from the W. At the Bulge of Africa the wind goes more into the SW and strengthens a little (see seasonal winds). Let the wind push the yacht around the bulge and into the gulf until E of 5–7°E. Turn towards Saint Helena; the wind will be mostly SE. Sailing close hauled the trip may be accomplished in one tack. (*See SAE1.*)

SAS3 Brazil to Rio de la Plata

Rio Paraiba to Mar del Plata 2,310M

Season All year but best November to May

Apart from the obvious dangers of the coast and much shipping, this is a straightforward passage with the winds and currents favourable. In winter there will be some moderate gales from ahead when a S-going yacht would probably want to stay in port. S of Cabo Frio in winter a good offing should be kept to avoid the N-setting Brazil inshore counter-current.

Beware of getting too close to land in the area between Rio Grande and the Rio de la Plata. The water here is shallow and with strong winds and tides can produce fearsome seas. Stories of knockdowns and strandings are not uncommon in this area.

SAS4 Rio de la Plata to Tierra del Fuego

Mar del Plata to Le Maire Strait 1,040M

Season November to March

Cruising yachts heading S have the choice of coast-hopping or staying well off Argentinean shores. The coast has many interesting bays and river harbours but can be quite challenging with strong offshore winds. Of particular note are the pamperos, violent SW squalls that blow off the Patagonian pampas. *See Gales above.*

Some vessels taking the offshore route may call at the Falklands (see Argentina for notes on the effects of the British – Argentinian dispute on yachts).

Entering the Straits of Magellan is not recommended, as it is a difficult trip to windward without good anchorages until S of Cape Froward. Punta Arenas, in Chile can be a dangerous port for yachts because there is no secure berth or anchorage. Most yachts prefer to pass through the Straits of Le Maire and enter the E end of the Beagle Canal, where anchorages are superb.

From the S a vessel either doubles back to the Rio de la Plata by the same route, goes S about via the Chilean Canals (eventually joining SPW10), or follows the westerlies to the Cape of Good Hope.

SAS5 Coast of Brazil to South Africa

Salvador to Cape Town 3,900M

Season all year

Leaving the Brazilian coast, sail slightly E of S until reaching 30°–37°S, and then pick up route SAE2 according to season.

This is the traditional route for sailors returning to South Africa, however there is a high risk of bad weather once the region of westerly winds is reached.

PASSAGES EASTWARDS

Cruisers returning to S Africa or yachts heading towards the Southern Ocean will use these routes.

SAE1 St Helena to South Africa

St Helena to Cape Town, direct 1,690M

Season All year but may be better in winter

This is a windward passage, however the winds and seas are generally regular and several yachts have reported fast and comfortable passages.

Cape Town is directly to windward. However, the wind direction can vary, especially in winter when fronts pass to the S giving SW winds and, S of about 27°S, NW gales. The best plan is to use SE winds to progress S on port tack and S or SW winds to progress towards the E. Do not approach the coast closer than about 600M otherwise the Benguela Current will make the going difficult. It is best to stay well offshore until reaching about 37°S by which time W winds will predominate. Stay well S until the landfall, as it is not uncommon for the current and a SE blow to force yachts well to the N of the Cape of Good Hope in the last days of their passage.

SAE2 East Coast of S America to Cape Town

Piriapolis to Cape Town as described 3,560M

Season November to April

This passage is best made in summer. After departing the S American coast, a yacht should make for a latitude of about 37°S on the Greenwich Meridian. The course should then be set to a point about 500M SW of Cape Town in 37°S. Stay well S until the landfall, as it is not uncommon for the current and a SE blow to force yachts well to the N of the Cape in the last days of their passage.

In winter the frequency of gales on the above course reaches 8%. More variable winds with fewer gales may be found by staying to the N of 30°S until the Greenwich meridian.

COUNTRY AND PORT GUIDE

South Africa

General Yachtsmen receive a very warm welcome in South Africa. The infrastructure and facilities are first-rate and the people are kind and hospitable. An awareness of crime is part of everyday life but in general rural areas are safe to visit and Cape Town and its surrounds are safer than other major cities.

Coastline As a cruising destination the coast of South Africa is rather uninteresting. There is a lack of natural harbours. Several otherwise beautiful destinations, such as Knysna, can be dangerous to enter. However, there are good harbours and a few open roadsteads all around the coast so that coastal sailing is possible.

Formalities These are rather cumbersome. Yachts are treated the same as overseas merchant vessels. Customs and immigration (and sometimes the Port Captain) will have to be visited and it will be necessary to clear in and out with all officials at each port. Be careful about following local advice, as procedures are different for local yachts. However, it is likely that the system will change, making procedures simpler, but meaning that yachtsmen will be limited to a 3-month stay. Citizens of the EU, US and Commonwealth countries do not require visas.

Telecom IDD +27. GSM network. Internet connections are common.

Currency South African Rand. ATMs are plentiful and most credit cards are accepted.

Sailing season Though local yachts make passages at all times of year, summer is considered to be the best sailing season, particularly in the area between Durban and Cape Town.

Normal routes and harbours It is essential to take local advice and follow well-tried guidelines when navigating between Durban and Cape Town. East London, Port Elizabeth and Mossel Bay provide safe harbours en route. Knysna is an attractive destination but has a bar and cannot be entered in adverse conditions or swell. See IW17 Durban to Cape Town and the Atlantic.

CAPE TOWN

Tidal range 1.8m

Navigation

This is one of the world's major ports so expect to encounter large ships in the approach and find many anchored in Table Bay. Vessels of all sizes are constantly entering and leaving port. Entry is easy day or night. Port Control monitors Ch 14 but yachts are not expected to make radio contact. Do not enter if larger vessels are entering or leaving. Proceed to the Royal Cape Yacht Club Marina in the far SE of the harbour.

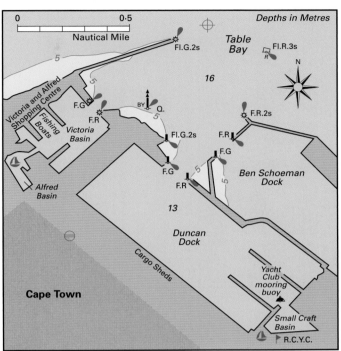

CAPE TOWN (South Africa)
⊕35°53′·8S 18°26′·2W

Berths

VHF Ch 14 and 16.

RCYC always has berths available, up to 20m. Charge band 2. Berths, capable of taking very large yachts, but with fewer facilities, are available at the V & A waterfront marina at the NW end of the harbour. Charge band 3.

Facilities

RCYC is a major club that puts itself out to assist visitors. The club has a boatyard with slip and crane and all repairs can be undertaken. There is a range of excellent chandleries, many boat-builders and several sailmakers. Another heavy-duty slip is available in Granger Bay. Every possible facility and all provisions are available in Cape Town. The Victoria and Alfred (V&A) shopping mall and restaurant complex is conveniently located at the W end of the main harbour.

Remarks

The yacht basin tends to accumulate a lot of dirt and oil from the harbour. The SE wind blows strongly here, especially in the summer months so that manoeuvring in the harbour can be difficult.

Cape Town and its hinterland are major tourist destinations and offer the visitor many possible activities. Prices for goods and services in South Africa are very competitive.
www.rcyc.co.za
V&A www.waterfront.co.za

Cape Town area

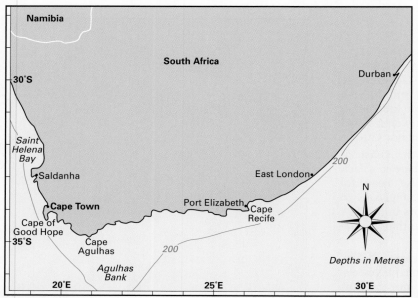

SOUTH AFRICA

Paddling on the Orange River

Cape Town is without doubt one of the world's major sailing destinations. A substantial amount of the worlds shipping passes this way and for those not wanting to sail in the Red Sea it is an essential stop over. Luckily the South Africans are amongst the most welcoming people anywhere and the facilities for cruising yachts could hardly be better. Harbours such as Hout Bay, S of Table Mountain, or Saldahna, 60 miles to the N, also welcome cruisers and allow the visitor a chance to see a little more of this entrancing land. There are many safe places to leave a boat while making a visit to the interior with its spectacular scenery and wildlife.

The skipper of a charter boat in South America complained of being a pack mule at the beginning of each season when, after a winter refit in Cape Town, he fills the boat with inexpensive high quality South African products for the return to Argentina. The sailing industry here is very well developed

Cape Town and Table Mountain seen from the north

and everything needed by yachts is available with good prices and quality. Cape Town has become a centre for yacht construction, particularly of catamarans as prices are low and the skill level is high. Cruising boats can easily refit and repair the wear and tear of a long circumnavigation or Southern Ocean cruise. They usually depart Cape Town low in the water from all the stores they take aboard.

Weather

The weather is dominated by stable low pressure over the continent (created by the heat of the African deserts) the position of the S Atlantic high to the NE and depressions passing from W to E in the Southern Ocean to the S. In summer the S Atlantic high tends to dominate and give settled, usually strong, SE winds which blend imperceptibly into the trades as one sails N. Fronts still brush the far S shores giving regular W winds. In winter the high is further N and frontal systems bring regular strong W winds, though between fronts the high often re-establishes itself with SE winds.

Cruising strategies

Cape Town is one of the major stopping points on a round the world cruise. (*See IW17*) Summer, when cruisers round the Cape from the Indian Ocean, can be very hot and the strong winds are often a great relief. It is possible to sail E as well in the settled periods between fronts. Winter is the time for nature lovers: the desert flowers bloom thanks to the rain that comes with passing fronts and Southern Right Whales come inshore to give birth and raise their young. A coastal cruise at this time of year can be very rewarding.

Reading

South African Nautical Almanac Tom Morgan.
www.onboardpublications.co.za/sanaup.html

Port Owen

Table Mountain and the
Royal Cape Yacht Club

Namibia

General Like South Africa, Namibia has a good infrastructure and facilities are first rate. A friendly greeting is almost guaranteed and crime is much less of a problem here than further S.

Coastline Namibia has one of the least attractive coastlines in the world for a sailor. The well named Skeleton Coast, strictly the coast between the Kunene and Ugab rivers, is long and straight with only two natural harbours of note. In between lie hundreds of miles of exposed beaches backed by inhospitable desert. Though the sailing is uninteresting, Namibian ports can provide a stopping place when on route N and give access to some fascinating desert scenery and wild game.

Formalities Citizens of the EU, US and Commonwealth countries do not require visas. Customs, immigration and the port authority must be visited, but formalities are much more relaxed than in South Africa.

Telecom IDD +264. GSM network. Internet cafés are common.

Currency Namibian dollar (equivalent to SA Rand). ATMs.

Sailing season It is possible to sail the coast at all times of year. On-shore NW winds that create dense fog where they meet the cold Benguela current inshore are more common in winter.

Routes and harbours Sailing is generally up and down the coast, to and from Luderitz and Walvis Bay. There is intense inshore activity on the shelf with many large fishing boats, semi-stationary diamond dredgers and seismic survey vessels.

LUDERITZ

Tidal range (springs) 1.7m

Navigation

Entry is straightforward, the yacht anchorage is in Menai creek. Harbour authorities may direct the yacht alongside for clearance.

Anchorage

Anchor in 3–4m. Moorings may be available for hire.

Facilities

The club provides ablution facilities. Water can be obtained alongside. Engineering repairs are available in the port where it may be possible to arrange for a yacht to be lifted out in an emergency. Spares can be shipped rapidly from South Africa. The town of Luderitz can supply most provisions.

Remarks

Luderitz is a charming town that retains a colonial German flavour. The hinterland is desert where diamonds are mined and there are several interesting visits to be made within a day's drive.

Resources

PILOTS AND GUIDES
South African Nautical Almanac Tom Morgan
South Atlantic Circuit Tom Morgan (www.rccpf.org.uk)

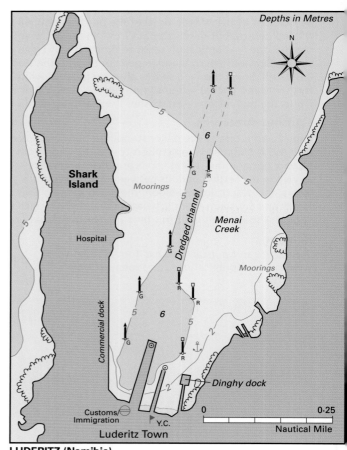

LUDERITZ (Namibia)
⊕26°36′·5S 15°08′·0E (c.1M N of Angra Pt - not shown)

St Helena

General St Helena, a British possession, is a popular stop for vessels crossing the South Atlantic. The island occupies a special place in history as it was the place of confinement of Napoleon after the Battle of Waterloo. The island covers 47M² (122km²), 10 and a half miles (17km) long and six and a half miles (10km) wide. It is an extinct volcano and rises to 823m.

Formalities A fee of £25 per boat and £12 per person is charged. Proof of medical insurance is required for a stay of more than 48 hours.

Telecom IDD +297. Internet, email and facsimile services available.

Currency Pound sterling. There are no international banks on the island. Credit cards (MasterCard & Visa) are accepted by major shops and businesses for the payment of goods. Solomon & Co. PLC also allow you to draw cash from credit cards. Traveller's cheques are recommended and can be cashed at the Cash Office, The Castle, Jamestown.

Sailing season It is possible to visit all year round. During the winter months swell can make the anchorage, which is never still, even more uncomfortable.

JAMESTOWN

Tidal range 1.3m

Navigation

The coast is steep-to and presents no obstacles to navigation.

Anchorage

The anchorage is an open roadstead and prone to rolling. Holding is not good. Vessels of any size can use the anchorage. Charge band 3. Passengers can be ferried by ship's tenders or local boats. Well sheltered from the prevailing wind but open to other directions. Swell can make dinghy landings wet and difficult. Alternative anchorages may be found around the island according to wind and swell.

Facilities

There are no facilities for yachts. However, there is a 40-ton crane which has been used by yachts in an emergency. Basic supplies can be obtained but fresh produce is very limited.

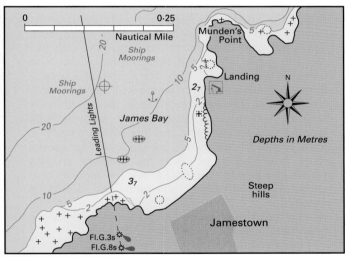

JAMESTOWN (St Helena)
⊕15°52'·2S 05°43'·2W

 ## Ascension Island

General The island is a British possession and is a dependency of St Helena. It has a fascinating flora and fauna and some excellent snorkelling. There is no indigenous population; however, just over a thousand people live here to service the various communications facilities and airfield. Both Britain and the USA maintain a small military presence in the communications facilities. The island covers 35M². It is a dormant volcano and has 44 distinct craters.

Formalities All visitors to Ascension Island need the Administrator's written permission. They must complete and return the Ascension Island Entry Permit prior to travelling. The form is available from: The Administrator, Georgetown, Ascension Island, South Atlantic Ocean, ASCN 1ZZ. However, yachtsmen without prior approval will still be allowed to visit. A fee of GBP £11 is payable for all visitors over twelve years disembarking, plus a fee of GBP £10 for the yacht. Proof of medical insurance (covering medical evacuation) is required before landing.

Telecom IDD +247. Internet, email and facsimile services available.

Currency Pound sterling. There are no banks on the island. Sterling and US currency or traveller's cheques are accepted. Credit cards cannot be used to obtain cash, though a few businesses, such as Cable and Wireless, will accept them for payment. In 2003 no provisions could be obtained by credit card.

Sailing season It is possible to visit all year round. www.ascension-island.gov.ac

GEORGETOWN

Tidal range (springs) 1.3m

Navigation

The coast is steep-to and presents no obstacles to navigation.

Anchorage

The anchorage, Clarence Bay, is an open roadstead and prone to rolling. Holding is good. Well sheltered from the prevailing wind but open to other directions. Swell can make dinghy landings wet and difficult. Alternative anchorages may be found around the island according to wind and swell.

Facilities

There are no facilities for yachts. Basic supplies can be obtained, but fresh produce is very limited. Fuel and water are also available, but would need to be carried to the vessel.

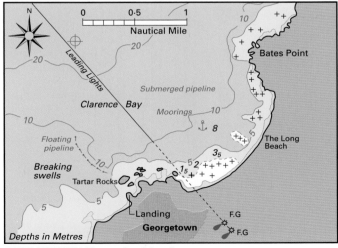

GEORGETOWN (Ascension Island)
⊕07°55'·0S 14°26'·0W

Brazil

General Brazilians are charming, friendly and helpful. Away from the major centres the anchorages are beautiful and safe. Many people return over and over again and regard Brazil as a great cruising destination. Sadly, crime is a large part of everyday life. Yachts are regarded as fair game and many people have bad stories to tell. It pays to be eternally vigilant when on shore and never to take valuables or money along unless necessary. Brazilians also advise against the wearing of jewellery in public. In the centres it is safer to use a guarded marina facility, though this is not an absolute guarantee of security. Away from the centres there is far less trouble and the visitor can relax in safety in many areas. Formerly Brazil has had a reputation for being inexpensive. With changing currency values this is no longer true. Food, drink and eating out is a little cheaper than Europe but boating gear and marina berths are very expensive indeed.

Coastline Brazil has a long coastline, all bordering on the Atlantic Ocean. In the N the mouth of the Amazon is the predominant feature, offering intriguing prospects to the adventurous. S of Recife there are numerous harbours, often on navigable rivers, and many delightful inshore islands and bays for the cruiser.

Formalities EU citizens do not need a visa. Other nationalities, including US, Australia and New Zealand, require visas prior to entry. Entry is normally granted for 90 days and one extension for a further 90 days may be applied for. Procedures are cumbersome and tiresome. It is important to have written clearance from the last port. The offices of customs, immigration and port captain must all be visited on arrival and departure and a health inspection (often no more than a visit to a hospital to complete a form and pay a fee) is frequently required. It is unusual to find any of the offices within easy walking distance of the others.

Telecom IDD +55. GSM network. Internet cafés are found in all but the smallest towns.

Currency Real. ATMs are common.

Sailing season It is safe to sail in Brazil all year round. The summer is very hot and most foreign cruisers prefer the winter climate.

Routes and harbours Brazil is a huge country and there are many beautiful harbours and anchorages for cruising yachts. The ports chosen here are centres where crime and official procedures have not presented too many difficulties for visitors. They are good places to clear in and make arrangements for more protracted cruising. Some other centres, in particular Rio de Janeiro, have gained a poor reputation.

Most yachts arrive from Europe in the N and then work their way down the coast. As these tend to be fleeing the northern winter, they will usually arrive near to mid-summer in the southern hemisphere. This makes it convenient to cruise S with the prevailing NE winds and then return to the N in winter when the NE winds are lighter and may at times give way to offshore winds with the passage of fronts. In general, when heading N, there is a choice between staying close inshore and working with land and sea breezes, and heading offshore to the E until the trade winds are picked up. The coastal route is not often practical for ordinary cruising yachts in summer. The trades may be picked up at about 150M offshore in winter and 450M in summer.

Note that the trade wind varies between predominantly NE in the S to SE in the N.

Those wishing to sail on to South Africa or Tierra del Fuego would be wise to depart Brazilian waters by the end of March as the Southern Ocean is best avoided in winter.

RIO PARAIBA (CABEDELO)

Tidal range 3m

Navigation

Entrance is straightforward through the marked. Buoys may be unlit.

Anchorage

The most popular anchorage for yachts is off Jacaré, about 6M up the river. Good shelter, but currents can be strong in the river.

RIO PARAIBA - JACARÉ (Brazil)
⊕06°56´·2S 34°48´·3W

Facilities

Brian Stevens' yard at Jacaré will help with repairs and paper work. They have good facilities for GRP work and can arrange to haul out if needed. Fuel, water and basic spares are available at the yard. Other supplies available from nearby town João Pessoa, 20 minutes by bus, where most things are available. If more advanced yacht facilities are required, they can be found in nearby Recife.

Remarks

A popular stop for cruising yachts, especially because of the presence of Brian Stevens yard. Authorities are now all available in Cabedelo.

SALVADOR

Tidal range 3m

Navigation

When approaching from N and E the Banco de Santo Antonio (S of Ponta de Santo Antonio and marked by N and S cardinal buoys) is best passed to the S unless entering in daylight and settled conditions.

Berths

Marina berths at Centro Nautico in the old harbour or Bahia marina just to the S. Also at Centro Nautico in Itaparica or the Yacht Club in Baía Aratú.

Anchorage

Anchor between the fort and Centro Nautico in the old harbour (very little room) or between Bahia marina and the old harbour (land only at one of the

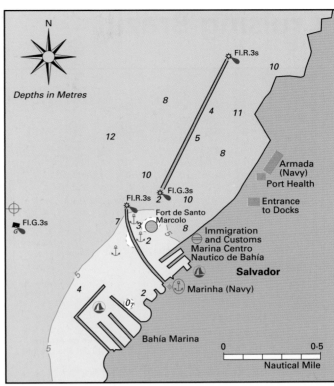

SALVADOR (Brazil)
⊕12°58'·3S 38°31'·7W

marinas due to danger of robbery on the beaches). Also off the town at Itaparica (exposed to SW in winter), off YCs at Baía do Aratú or S of Salvador.

Facilities

Travel-lift, and chandlery, engine, electric and structural repairs and sailmaker, all available at Bahía Marina. Fuel at both places. All Brazilian charts and navigational publications are available from the navy office on the harbourside.

Remarks

Centro Nautico gives the best access to the old town, which is noisy and crowded. There are almost no provisions obtainable near to the harbour and a bus trip is required. Ask in the marina to see a map showing the locations of Port Captain, Customs, Port health and immigration, all have to be visited on arrival and necessitates a considerable amount of walking.

Apart from the facilities, Salvador is not a pleasant place to visit. I would recommend using Itaparica or Baía do Aratú and taking the ferry or bus to Salvador only to complete formalities. Lovely cruising in the bay, especially inside of Ilha de Itaparica and in the Rio Paraguacu.

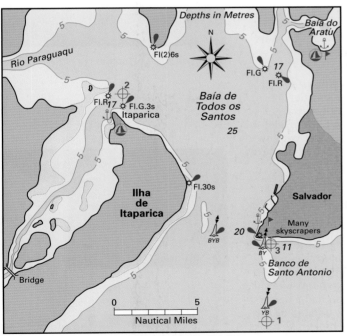

BAÍA DE TODOS OS SANTOS AND SALVADOR
⊕1 13°05'·4S 38°31'·8W
⊕2 12°52'·0S 38°40'·4W
⊕3 13°01'·0S 38°31'·8W (mid channel)

Cruising Brazil

BRAZIL

Sailing on the Río Tapajos

For many world cruisers Brazil is the ultimate destination. The country offers scorching sun, endless beaches, spicy food and beautiful, friendly people. Scattered along its 4,600 mile coastline are numerous welcoming rivers, bays and islands. In addition the Amazon has a length of navigable waterways greater than would be travelled in a circumnavigation.

Given the size of the country it is not surprising that there are many sailing areas to choose from. Many locals and visiting sailors flock to Baía del Ilha Grande, neatly placed between Rio de Janeiro and Santos. With several natural reserves, hundreds of islands and abundant anchorages, it provides fine cruising. At the W end of the bay, Parati, a world heritage site, with it's charming colonial Portuguese buildings, open air cafés and restaurants, makes a good base from which to explore.

Santarem – on the Amazon

The scale of the Amazon is breathtaking. There are said to be 50,000 miles of navigable waterway – twice around the globe. From Alter de Chao, near Santarem (the furthermost point reached by the Iles du Soleil rally) the Rio Tapajós is thirteen miles wide. I visited this area with a cruising friend who is a doctor working from river boats that can cruise the rivers in much the same way as a yacht would. We travelled for 130 miles along the adjoining Rio Arapiuns to reach the first clinic. Even then it was another two hours by speedboat to the furthest community. Sometimes the boatman had a hard time to follow the main stream. In places the river was clearly defined by the edge of the trees, but it was rainy season and had long since broken its banks and the forest on either side was flooded, making it very hard to know where land began. I had the feeling that we were on a huge ocean of fresh-water

Local transport – Salvador

Amazon Village *Marcio Franco*

with scattered islands all linked together in a baffling maze.

Sailing is practical on the wider river sections where there is often a nice breeze and lots of deserted, golden beaches for a lunch stop. Surprisingly disease and dangerous animals are not a major problem on the Tapajós or Arapiuns. Crocodiles are confined to well known areas, piranhas are not a risk to the swimmer and there are only a few places with malaria. In fact we were impressed by the absence of mosquitoes that are such a pest on the Brazilian coast. We slept on deck most nights in hammocks and had no troublesome bites. There are charts over most of the region, though the sandbanks shift constantly and careful navigation with the echo sounder is important.

Amazon practicalities
The Amazon is the world's largest tropical cruising ground that is as yet visited by only a handful of yachts. Pirates, treacherous tides and sandbanks near the river mouth are the major obstacles in the way of reaching the safe cruising areas in your own boat. By joining the Iles du Soleil rally (www.Ilesdusoleil.com) the sailor will have the benefit of careful planning, experienced pilotage and a naval escort. However, it is possible to sail independently and a few people do it successfully every year. The season is important, in the heat of midsummer the water levels are low so locals recommend July to September. This is just after the rainy season, there is plenty of water to visit some of the remoter rivers and temperatures are very pleasant.

Weather
As Brazil is centred in the trade wind belt, breezes are steady and predictable, predominantly SE, and violent storms are rare. Sailing is year round, the winter is cooler and less humid and occasional fronts can bring W winds that help the navigator sail N. In the Amazon water levels are higher between March and September making navigation in the smaller waterways easier. In the drier season water levels can drop many metres exposing vast mud or sand banks.

Cruising strategies
Customs and Immigration restrictions limit cruising in Brazil to a maximum of six months. A common strategy is to visit the NE coast for a few months before continuing to the Caribbean (*see NAW5 and SAN8*), this route will have fair winds at almost all times. A visit to the Amazon can be made on the way. Alternatively the coast can be cruised from Cabo San Roque southwards with a destination of Uruguay or Argentina (both of which have far more generous customs and immigration rules) and after a stop there it is possible to return to the Brazilian coast. (*See SAS3 and SAN6*).

Reading
Brazil Michel Balette (Imray)
South Atlantic Circuit Tom Morgan (www.rccpf.org.uk)
Havens and Anchorages Tom Morgan (www.rccpf.org.uk)

My gem
Voyage of the Liberdade by Captain Joshua Slocum

Sunset on the Rio Arapiuns

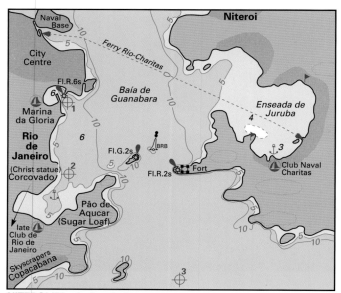

NITEROI (Rio de Janeiro)
⊕₁ 22°55'·1S 43°10'·0W
⊕₂ 22°56'·4S 43°09'·9W
⊕₃ 22°58'·0S 43°03'·0W

NITEROI (Río de Janeiro)

Tidal range 1.3m

Navigation

Entrance is straightforward.

Berths

Club Naval Charitas currently welcomes visitors and is a safer alternative to the expensive marina Gloria in Rio (where crime is a problem just outside the gates). However, policies change with club officers and there have been times when the club has not welcomed overseas boats. If this should happen, there are other clubs in the area that could be tried. Marina Gloria is commercial and very expensive but can be relied upon to accept visitors and there are likely to be many spare berths.

Anchorage

Possible to anchor off Club Nautico Charitas and for a small fee use their facilities. Also possible to anchor in Enseada de Botofogo but risk of theft is great and only sensible landing place is the Rio Yacht Club which is currently not welcoming and charges a very high fee for dinghies.

Facilities

Excellent recreational and social facilities at the club, which also has a small chandlery and a slip for vessels up to 10 tonnes. Fuel and water is available at the club. Larger yachts can be slipped at other yards in the town, but for the most comprehensive facilities it would be necessary to go across the bay to Marina Gloria in Rio (where everything is available). Reasonable shopping, via taxi or bus, in the town.

Remarks

Niteroi is quiet, friendly and safe compared to the hyperactivity of Rio. It is an inexpensive launch ride across the harbour to Rio. Many yachts have recommended mooring here and going to Rio on the launch. Even if berthing in Niteroi it will be necessary to visit the authorities in Rio, located conveniently close to the ferry terminal.

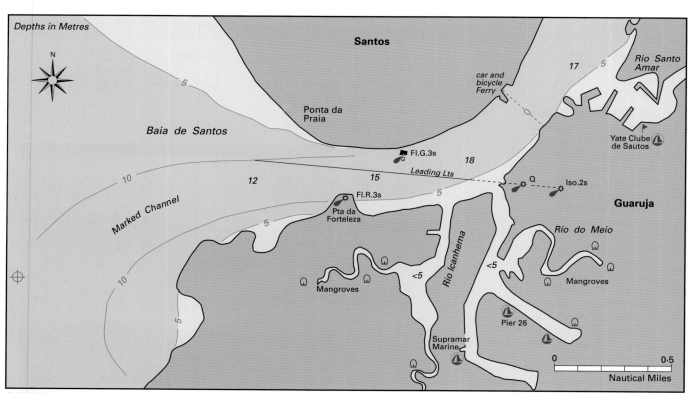

SANTOS (Brazil)
⊕ 24°00'·2S 46°20'·1W

SANTOS

Tidal range 1.3m

Navigation

Entrance is straightforward. Stay clear of the busy big ship channel and watch out for the frequent ferries.

Berths

There are many marinas able to cope with any size of yacht. The following have been recommended:

Yate Clube de Santos
All marina facilities, very expensive and luxurious.

Supramar Marine
Helpful, English-speaking manager, busy boatyard.

Pier 26
Helpful, English speaking, efficient.

Facilities

Travel-lifts up to 50 tons at both marinas. 150-ton slip at Supramar, which also has facilities for every conceivable repair. Fuel, water and all boating supplies.

Remarks

This is Brazil's main yachting centre; everything is obtainable and the wider facilities of São Paulo are the best in South America. However, the urban sprawl is enormous and accessing resources may not be so easy. Distances in Santos are considerable as all the yachting centres are away from town; a bicycle is a great asset here.
www.portodesantos.com (in Portuguese).

RIO GRANDE

Tidal range 2m

Navigation

Approach and Entrance: There are no dangers offshore. Make the landfall mark and enter via the buoyed channel. The entrance is protected by two major breakwaters and as it is a big ship port the depths are around 13 metres. However, with strong onshore winds and an outgoing current the swells in the entrance can be dangerous. Call the *Pilots* on VHF Ch 16 for information in English.

Note that this is an entrance to a lagoon and not a river, thus the currents are dependent upon the wind direction blowing over the lagoon. Strong offshore or NE winds produce an outgoing current of 3–5 knots.

Follow the channel to the town and then along the N shore to the Oceanographic museum and Yacht Club.

Berths

At the Oceanographic Museum that has a dock capable of accommodating three cruising yachts and will make them very welcome. Berths for yachts under 12m may be available at the Yacht Club.

Anchorage

There are several possibilities for anchorage to the sides of the buoyed channel but none with shore access.

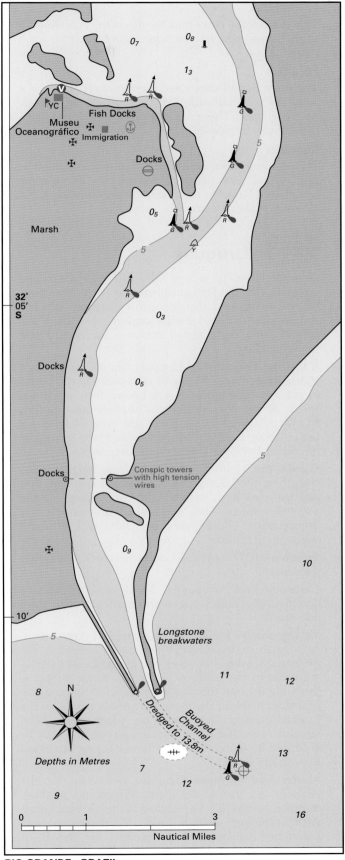

RIO GRANDE - BRAZIL
⊕35°12'·37S 52°03'·03W

Formalities

This is a port of entry and all offices are represented, though unfortunately at some distance from each other.

Facilities

The town has all shops and conveniences. There is a small Yacht Club with a marine railway for vessels up to 10 tons. There are shipyards in the area with capabilities for hauling larger vessels.

Remarks

This is a very convenient first or last port of call. The town is not particularly interesting but the welcome from Lauro Barcellos the director of the Oceanographic Museum makes it extremely attractive.

Uruguay

General Uruguay is a stable and well developed country, though the gulf between rich and poor follows the usual Latin American extremes. It is not a destination chosen for its cruising, but there are several good ports and it makes a useful and safe stopping place.

Coastline The coast of Uruguay lies on the N shore of the River Plate. To the W it runs along the banks of the river and to the E it is bounded by open sea. Much of the coastal water is shallow and muddy. Many otherwise good ports are too shallow for ocean-going yachts. The Río de la Plata forms the boundary between Uruguay and Argentina.

Formalities Visitors, other than from neighbouring countries, the USA and EU, require visas. The first point of contact is with the Armada (Navy) via the *prefectura naval.* They will assist with customs and immigration. Procedures are fair and efficient without corruption.

Telecom IDD +598. GSM network. Internet common.

Currency Peso Uruguayo. Most credit cards are accepted in ATMs (*cajeros automaticos*), which are common.

Sailing season For the Uruguayan and Argentinian yachtsman or woman the summer is definitely the preferred season. However, the incidence of gales in winter is in the order of only 3%. Early winter is probably the best time for starting a northbound trip in order to obtain the most favourable winds on the Brazilian coast (see notes on pamperos). Tidal streams in the Rio de la Plata are strong and may be modified by heavy rainfall inland causing increased flow in the river.

Routes and harbours Uruguay is known for the harbour of Punta del Este. Piriapolis, a short distance to the W, has gained a better reputation with cruising yachts and is therefore our recommended port. If proceeding to the E of Piriapolis there are numerous shallows and great care must be taken to stay in navigable channels.

PIRIAPOLIS

Tidal range 0.8m

Navigation

Entrance is straightforward. The large, white Hotel Argentino is a good landmark from offshore. In a pampero the approach can be rough, but there is calm water in the entrance.

Berths

70 pleasure boats, stern to the N quay with a line tailed to a buoy. There is generally a berth available in summer and always vacant berths at a reasonable rate in winter. Charge band 2.

Facilities

The *prefectura* is close to the harbour behind the hydrographic office. The usual hygienic facilities are available as is a travel-lift with a capacity of 30m and 100 tonnes. Fuel (reported to be closed April–November.) and water are available in the harbour. Marine services may be better at Punta del Este.

Remarks

Prices are reasonable. Vessels have been left here unattended over the winter without problems. There is a very good market about 15 minutes' walk from the marina. Unfortunately in 2008 there seems to have been an increase in petty bureaucratic rules that make slipping and working on the boat more complicated. Check carefully as to the rules before hauling (for instance you may be required to undergo a survey in order to obtain a permit to launch the vessel after a period on the hard).

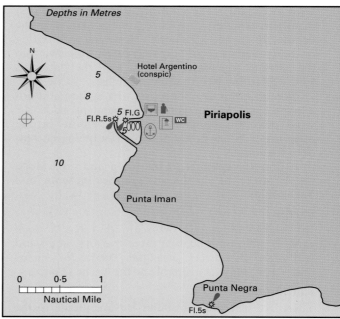

PIRIAPOLIS (Uruguay)
⊕34°52´·5S 55°18´·0W

Argentina

General There is a large yachting fraternity and a good attitude to cruisers. The nation has an excellent infrastructure.

Coastline It is a huge country and the coastline reflects this in its variety. In the N the Rio de la Plata forms the border with Uruguay and Paraguay. S of the Rio de la Plata the coastline appears uninteresting to a casual glance, but actually boasts some superb wilderness anchorages in lonely bays and moderately good ports in river estuaries. The Magellan Strait breaks the southward run of the coast. The E coast of Tierra del Fuego is inhospitable. Lying to the E of Tierra del Fuego is Isla de los Estados which has one or two exceptionally good anchorages. Argentina then turns W and runs along the S coast of Tierra del Fuego, along which are several good places for shelter. The Strait of Le Maire (separating Tierra del Fuego from Isla de los Estados) has very strong tidal flows, which may combine with strong winds to produce fearful seas.

Maritime claims and disputes Argentina is involved in two long-running maritime disputes, neither of which has been resolved to its satisfaction. These are as follows:

- With Chile over the possession of several small islands to the SE of the Beagle Channel. Argentina would also like to assert a right to navigate in some channels within Chile's territorial waters. The effect of this is that there is a degree of tension within these waters which means that a yacht's movements will be monitored carefully and she will frequently be challenged by radio from shore posts or by naval vessels. However, unlike Chile, Argentina does not appear to restrict navigation within these waters provided formalities are complied with.

- With Great Britain over the sovereignty of the Falkland Islands and South Georgia. Under the name of Islas Malvinas, these islands are treated as though they were an integral part of the territory of Argentina. This can affect a yacht's cruising plans. Argentina will not restrict navigation in any way. However, the important point is that, as far as Argentina is concerned, a yacht in the Falkland Islands or South Georgian waters is navigating within Argentina and therefore subject to their laws, customs and immigration regulations. A vessel sailing directly to mainland Argentina from the Falklands may find that it is considered to have entered the country already, but failed to comply with customs and immigration procedures. Likewise, if sailing from Argentina to Falklands and back again, the vessel and her crew may all have over-stayed their customs and immigration periods. To avoid these problems, most skippers make the trip via Puerto Williams in Chile.

- Argentina also claims a large part of the coastline of Antarctica.

Formalities There are a lot of formalities and much confusion about how they are applied, with different yachts reporting contrasting experiences. The best first point of contact is the *prefectura naval* who will probably advise as to what needs to be done. Otherwise yacht clubs will help.

Telecom IDD +54. GSM network. Internet connections common.

Currency Argentine Peso. Most credit cards are accepted in ATMs (*cajeros automaticos*), which are common.

Sailing season Winds blow strongly, mainly offshore, on the Atlantic coast. The wind strength in winter is appreciably lighter (about 33%). Unfortunately it is also colder and short days can make entering the river estuaries difficult, though they are generally well lit. In winter the eastern end of the Beagle Channel can be very pleasant, though cold, and several boats make successful cruises there each winter.

Routes and harbours Passages are up and down the coast. Sailing down this coast in summer may be one of the best ways to approach Patagonia. The main harbours for yachts are Mar del Plata in the N and Ushuaia in the S.

MAR DEL PLATA

Tidal range 1.3m

Navigation

Entrance is straightforward, but stay clear of the bank that lies NE of the S breakwater. The yacht harbour is entered through a swivel bridge, which is normally opened on the approach of a yacht – if not, give a toot.

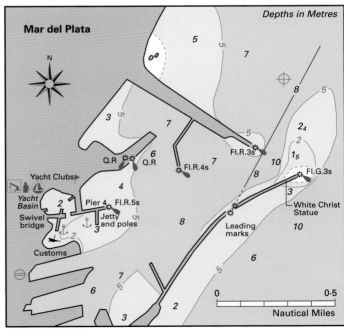

MAR DEL PLATA
⊕38°02′·0S 57°31′·2W

Berths

There is generally space in one of the clubs located in the yacht basin. (Yacht Club Argentino has been reported to be very helpful.)

Anchorage

It is possible to anchor just outside the yacht harbour.

Facilities

The usual facilities are available. It is possible to slip small vessels in the yacht basin and large vessels elsewhere in the harbour. Fuel in the basin. There is a crane in the yacht basin. Marine services are good (it is a major fishing port) and there is a sail loft. Good shops for provisioning. Charge band 2.

Remarks

Prices are reasonable. Officials here are pleasant and helpful. Yachts planning to stay longer in the area should not miss the visit to Buenos Aires where facilities are excellent and visitors are generally given an unforgettable welcome.

> For Ushuaia see *Chapter 7 Southern Ocean*
> For Chile (Puerto Williams) see *Chapter 7 Southern Ocean*.

Resources

Pilots and guides

South Atlantic Circuit Tom Morgan (www.rccpf.org.uk)
Havens and Anchorages Covering the East Coast of South America Tom Morgan (www.rccpf.org.uk)
Downwind around Australia and Africa Warwick Clay (available from Imray)

BUENOS AIRES

Tidal range 3m

Navigation

See notes in **Rio del Plata** box. Entry to the main harbour is simple, either by the main channel or over the shallows, watching out for wrecks of which there are many. Entry to the Delta area (where there are many club marinas offering long stays and first rate hospitality to visitors) is via Canal Emilio Mitre.

Berths

Downtown at the YCA or Yacht Club Puerto Madero good facilities in both. The first week at YCA is free (*cortesía*) and thereafter Charge band 2. Many berths available in the club marinas in the delta, but any individual club may have limited space so it is best to enquire ahead of time. A good plan is to take a berth in the city at YCA and take the train, *Tren de la Costa*, out to the area between San Isidro and San Fernando and visit the clubs to arrange a berth. The hospitality extended to visitors is exceptional.

Anchorage

None except in outer areas of the delta.

Facilities

With over 30,000 yachts in the area, all conceivable facilities are available, usually at very attractive prices and local yachtsmen will go out of their way to help find items. There are many well-stocked chandlers.

Remarks

Buenos Aires is a highly recommended cruising destination. As well as the excellent yachting facilities it is one of the world's landmark cities and lives up to its reputation.

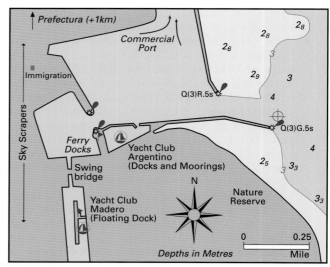

BUENOS AIRES - ARGENTINA
⊕34°36′·67S 58°21′W

Cruising the River Plate

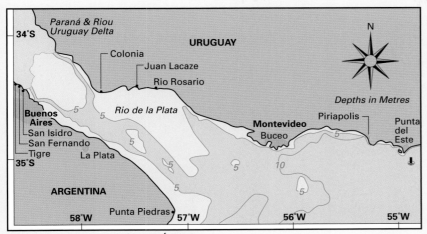

RIO DE LA PLATA AND PARANÁ DELTA

I expected the waters of the Rio de la Plata to be silver (*plata* in Spanish), but they are a vibrant brown in the sunlight and just plain muddy in the shade. The name derives from the treasure convoys that used to arrive from the interior bearing the mineral wealth of the continent to an insatiably greedy Europe. The waters are very shallow and littered by wrecks (the masts of the *Graf Spee* are still visible just outside Montevideo) and navigation can be complicated by the need to avoid dangers, including high speed ferries that cross between Argentina and Uruguay. It is probably best to stay out of the big ship channels.

Sailing is popular in Argentina and there are tens of thousands of yachts. The coast of Uruguay has many attractive destinations with anchorages and harbours that can be very crowded in summer but tranquil and comfortable out of season. Colonia, almost opposite Buenos Aires, stands out with its quaint old town and lazy streets and good restaurants.

At the head of this huge inlet (180M from Punta del Este to Buenos Aires) lies the delta formed by the rivers Uruguay and Parana. Most of the delta is wild and undeveloped, much is national park, and with many small islands and waterways provides interesting cruising away from the crowds. However many of the waterways are shallow and power cables in places make passage difficult. From the delta the two rivers lead into the continent, the waters of the Parana are navigable by yachts up to Asunción in Paraguay.

The main sailing centre of Buenos Aires is on the southern edge of the delta, located between the suburbs of San Isidro and Tigre. There are many club marinas here, some are located on the peaceful islands across the Rio Lujan and all facilities can easily be found. You can moor economically in delightful surroundings but within 45 minutes train journey of one of the world's most vibrant cities.

Weather

Winds are mainly light and the weather settled and warm, even in winter. The direction is very variable with a strong land and sea breeze effect. *Pamperos* (see *Gales* in Introduction chapter) occur several times a year and are usually well forecast. Rain is scarce, even in winter.

Cruising strategies

Apart from those wanting to cruise one of the main rivers, cruising is mainly along the Uruguay coast and in the Delta. A visit to Buenos Aires is a very worthwhile detour from a direct passage from Punta del Este to Mar de Plata and for those wishing to take a break from prolonged cruising and perhaps leave the boat in safety for a period this is the logical place.

Because there are many wrecks and the shallow sounding are rather intimidating it is quite common here to navigate using known waypoints. The following is a route used by *Balæna* (draught 1.7m) which carries a minimum of 3m, names refer to buoys and marks along the way:

Waypoints: Piriapolis to Buenos Aires

Piriapolis
34°52'.4961S 055°16'.8541W
Flores
34°58'.8050S 055°56'.2136W
Calpean
34°58'.0099S 056°13'.7000W
Panela
34°56'.3000S 056°26'.5001W
Tabare
34°51'.4001S 057°00'.3001W
KM55
34°33'.1000S 057°55'.5998W
Paso07
34°30'.5700S 058°18'.6300W
Exp8
34°30'.3600S 058°22'.7998W

Reading

South Atlantic Circuit Tom Morgan (www.rccpf.org.uk)
Havens and Anchorages Tom Morgan (www.rccpf.org.uk)

My gem

Alone through the Roaring Forties, Vito Dumas

Buenos Aires – the the main harbour. YCA is just left of centre and the canal leading to Puerto Madero is near the right hand border

3

SOUTH PACIFIC OCEAN

(Including Coral and
Tasman Seas and
East coast of Australia)

Anchorage off Nuku in the Vava'u group, Tonga

General

This is the ocean that every sailor dreams of sailing. It is common to think just of Polynesian islands, white coral beaches and waving palm trees; the bordering nations of Australasia and South America with their diverse and fascinating geographies, coastlines, environments and people are all too easily forgotten. A lifetime would not be sufficient to do justice to the cruising that this ocean offers.

Weather and sea

PREVAILING WINDS

The main cruising area of the tropical South Pacific does not have quite such consistent trade winds as other oceans. The South Pacific convergence zone (SPCZ: mean position from Papua New Guinea to French Polynesia along a NW–SE axis), causes winds to be more variable than in other oceans, but E and SE are the most common in the N. Winds are stronger at the SPCZ but seldom gale force. Between 15° and about 25°S, a high to the S usually brings fresh to strong winds and depressions light to moderate winds and sometimes a short-lived swing to the W. Trade winds are more regular N of the SE Pacific High centred about 30°S 100°W.

The Intertropical Convergence Zone (ITCZ) is noted for light winds and squalls. It generally lies around 10°N, from around 80°W to New Guinea. The ITCZ and SPCZ come together north of Papua New Guinea. The lowest atmospheric pressures occur in this region, where there is the highest cloud cover and rainfall and the hottest and most desalinated surface water. Between November and February this area may be subject to strong or gale force westerlies. N of the equatorial convergence NE Trade winds can be expected.

In the vicinity of the Solomon Islands the winds are usually light.

On the Australian coast N of Brisbane (26°S) the SE Trade wind is predominant. South of this, winds are variable in direction and strength in the summer, with E winds more prevalent in the N and W winds in the S.

The S Island of New Zealand reaches the Roaring Forties and W winds are predominant.

The Tasman Sea has variable wind direction and strength. SW winds are more common in winter.

GALES

Gale force winds are uncommon in the tropical cruising season but can occur in squalls and with tropical depressions. These depressions are very shallow and hard to pick up on weather maps and can develop into cyclones during the cyclone season.

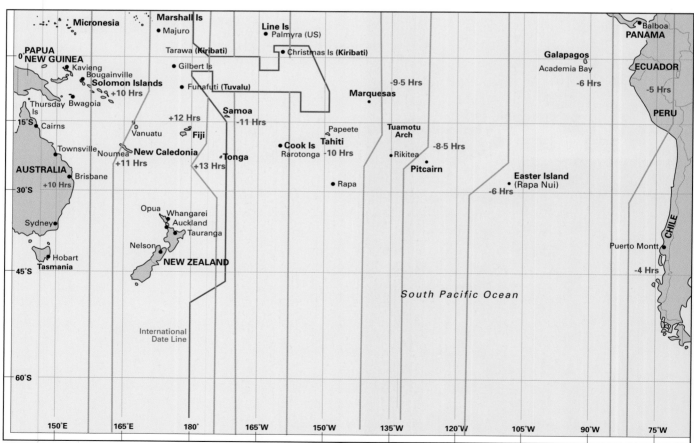

SOUTH PACIFIC COUNTRIES, PORTS AND TIME DIFFERENCES ON GMT

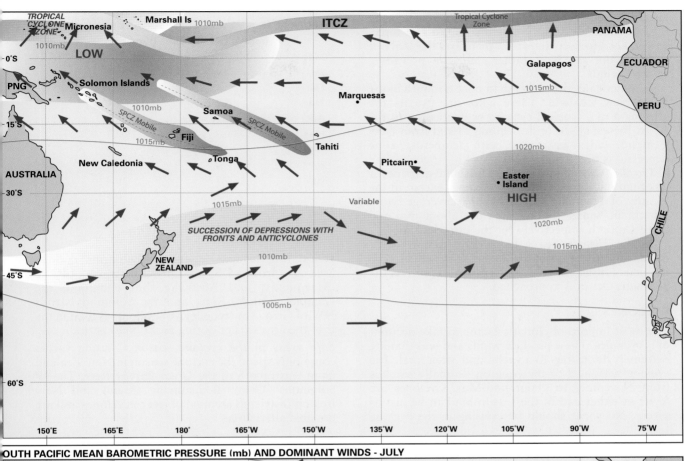

SOUTH PACIFIC MEAN BAROMETRIC PRESSURE (mb) AND DOMINANT WINDS - JULY

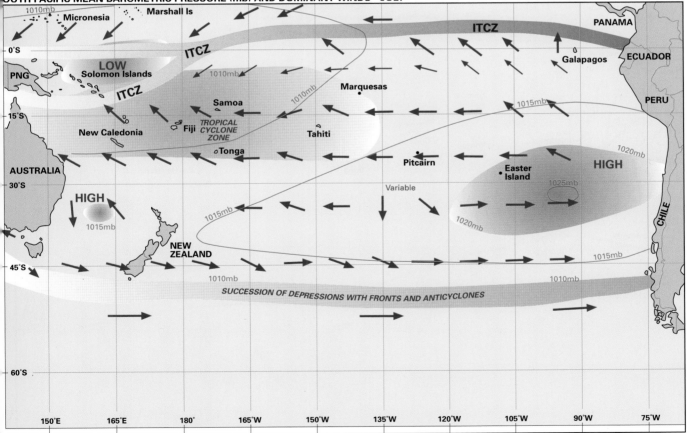

SOUTH PACIFIC MEAN BAROMETRIC PRESSURE (mb) AND DOMINANT WINDS - JANUARY

Small tropical depressions in the winter can bring unseasonable westerlies, sometimes up to gale force, so you need to keep an eye on them and think about shelter from the west rather than the prevailing easterly winds.

Summer gales occur less than once a month in the N of New Zealand. These gales are usually the aftermath of a tropical cyclone or depression to the N. At the usual season for sailing to and from New Zealand, gales associated with temperate zone depressions may occur.

On the Australian coast S of Brisbane gales occur less than once a month in the summer except in the vicinity of Tasmania where they may average two a month. In winter the averages are about two and three a month respectively for the same localities.

In the Tasman Sea gales average about two a month and three a month further S in winter. The frequency of gales increases to four a month as the Southern Ocean is approached.

CYCLONES

The most important climatic factor to take account of is cyclones. These produce winds and seas that are extremely hazardous to a yacht, and often fatal. The cyclone season, S of the equator, normally extends from November to about mid-May. Cyclones are fewer at either end of the season but can be just as severe. No yacht should be cruising in the cyclone

TROPICAL STORMS AND HURRICANES BY MONTH		
	Tropical storms >35K	Hurricanes >64k
Month	Annual average	Annual average
Jan	3.4	0.7
Feb	4.1	1.1
Mar	3.7	1.1
Apr	1.7	0.3
May	0.3	0.05
Jun	2	0
Jul–Oct	0	0
Nov	0.7	0.3
Dec	2	0.5
(Data from DMA)		

area during the cyclone season. The normal cyclone area is from 5°S to 30°S between 140°W (Marquesas) and Australia, but excluding the Gambier Islands, Rapa and the Solomon Islands NW of Gizo. The frequency of cyclones is least in the E of the area except during an El Niño period.

Safe areas in the cyclone season Cruising yachts commonly spend the cyclone season in New Zealand or in Australia S of the Great Barrier Reef. The W Solomons (Gizo), Bougainville (Kieta) and New Ireland (Kavieng) are not subject to cyclones and are possible alternatives.

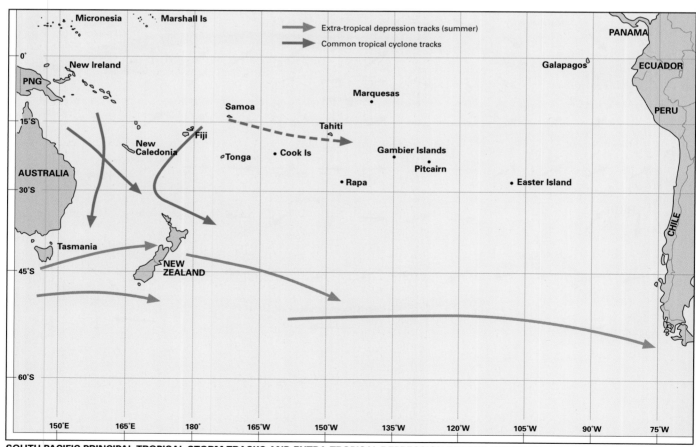

SOUTH PACIFIC PRINCIPAL TROPICAL STORM TRACKS AND EXTRA-TROPICAL DEPRESSION TRACKS (SUMMER)

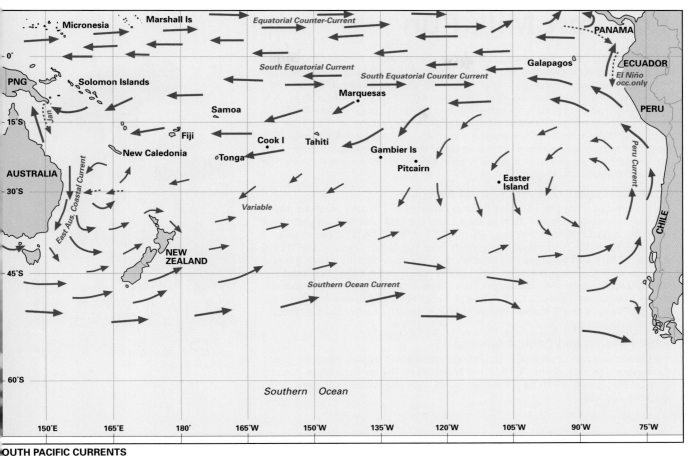

SOUTH PACIFIC CURRENTS

CURRENTS

Ocean currents are seldom more than a knot and they follow the prevailing winds in an anticlockwise circulation. The Equatorial Counter-current is in the N Pacific.

South Equatorial Current This is W-going and is predominant in the tropical area up to about 0°–5°N.

South Equatorial Counter Current This is E-going between 05°–10°S and flows at unpredictable rates, but normally 0.5 knot or less. In El Niño years, this current intensifies in the Pacific Ocean. This current is a bit of a mystery as it is usually given further N, at around 05°N in some sources and 05°–10°S in other sources. The note that it is unpredictable is pertinent.

East Australian Coast Current In the Coral Sea the currents are less than one knot going S to SW. In the Tasman Sea the current is S-going on the Australian side at less than one knot and N-going on the New Zealand side at less than half a knot. There are E-going currents between these two streams of less than one knot.

Southern Ocean Current This sets to the E in waters S of 40°S. Where it meets the coast of S America it forks, at about 48°S, with the S portion running SE towards Cape Horn and the N portion forming the Peru, or Humboldt, Current.

Peru Current (Humboldt Current) This runs at up to 2kn inshore and at its N extremity curves to the W to rejoin the South Equatorial Current.

A small offshoot of the Peru Current runs at up to 1kn into the Gulf of Panama. This is often reversed in January to March when it is called the El Niño (Holy Child) Current, which may be of assistance to passage-makers heading towards the Galapagos. Prolonged reversals are associated with an El Niño year: see Introduction. The name El Niño may have been bestowed in acknowledgement of divine intervention in what Pizzaro, the conquistador, saw as a holy cause. In 1532 he sailed south to overcome the Inca empire, a trip that would normally have been almost impossible in his unwieldy ships.

In the central part of the ocean, between 25°S and 40°S, the currents are more variable, though there is a pronounced S flow in the area between Pitcairn and Easter islands.

Coconut Milk Run

Yachts coming from west coast USA and Central America and those coming from Panama via Galapagos will usually meet up in the Marquesas. The route from the Marquesas through French Polynesia, the Cook Islands, Tonga and Fiji down to New Zealand has long been termed the 'Coconut Milk Run'. It is a fairly well-trodden route with some 300 plus boats in Tonga in late 2008 heading down to New Zealand. There are lots of variations on the route including those who head for Australia via Vanuatu and New Caledonia. The principal reason for heading to New Zealand and Australia, apart from cruising these two wonderful areas, is to avoid the cyclone season (November to May) in the South Pacific.

From west coast USA and Central America

Yachts coming from the USA and Central America will usually leave for the Marquesas between March to mid-May. From the USA and Mexico yachts will head for around 05°N 130°W to cross the ITCZ. Above the ITCZ yachts will normally have 15–25 knots of tradewinds from the N-NE. Crossing the ITCZ is a matter of luck and weather information, but the co-ordinates above generally work so that you cross between 125°–135°W. Once you hit the ITCZ head S until you pick up the SE Trades and then shape a course for your destination in the Marquesas (likely to be Taiohae on Nuka Hiva or Atuona on Hiva Oa). It is better to take this S-shaped course through the ITCZ rather than a direct rhumb line passage.

From Panama and Central America

Yachts coming from Panama and Central America will usually head for the Galapagos and then from there to the Marquesas. The passage from Panama and Central America can be a slow one with light headwinds, contrary currents and rain.

In the Pacific you will do a lot of runs ashore for water and fuel
Graham Sewell

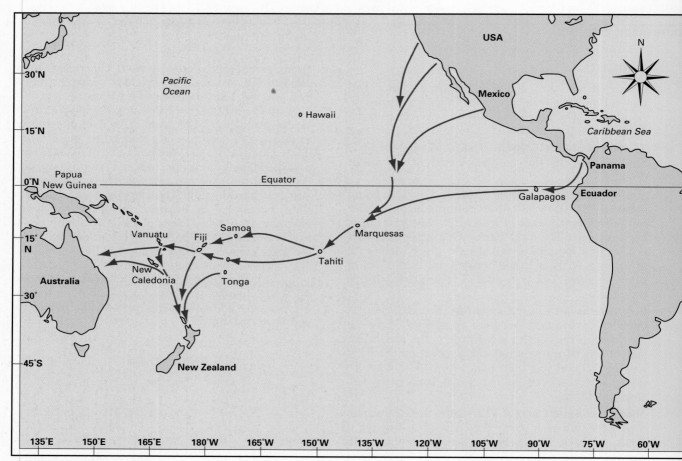

COCONUT MILK RUN

From Galapagos yachts will leave for the Marquesas with May to July being the optimal months. If you are too early the SE Trades may not be fully developed although yachts have made good passages at this time. Like yachts coming from further N yachts shape their passage for Taiohae on Nuka Hiva or Atuona on Hiva Oa. In general yachts should stay slightly N of the rhumb line where, despite old routing information to go S for the tradewinds, you will get good tradewinds and favourable current and generally make a better passage than diving S. Going S you will likely pick up a contrary current.

This is generally a fast passage taking between 20 and 25 days when the Trades are brisk. The SE Trades often blow at 20–25 knots with few squalls, but you can get calm patches, especially as you close the Marquesas.

Moorea in French Polynesia

Routes to New Zealand and Australia

From the Marquesas yachts will generally head down to:

Tuamotus

Tahiti

Iles Sous Le Vent to Bora Bora (see section on French Polynesia)

Rarotonga, Aitutaki or Suvarov in the Cook Islands.

Palmerston Island (Cook Islands) or up to Samoa.

Niue and Vava'u group in Tonga

To New Zealand (and maybe Minerva Reef) from Nuku'alofa in Tonga. (see section on Tonga and Passage to NZ)

Or to Fiji and Vanuatu/New Caledonia and then to NZ.

Or from Vanuatu/New Caledonia to Australia.

Bob McDavitt's Weathergram

The NZ Metservice 'Weather Ambassador' writes a weekly overview of the weather which is available by email, suitable for low bandwidth systems. The weathergram covers routes from the Galapagos to NZ and Australia, and Bob will give personal routing info for a reasonable fee. To subscribe and for more information see www.pangolin.co.nz/ yotreps/list_manager.php

Radio nets

Informal nets run every year and it is a matter of checking around to see what frequencies and times are used.

These are often the best nets as the people on them will generally be in your vicinity and crossing at around your pace.

Panama Pacific Net 8143kHz at 1400 UTC. Operates both sides of Panama. On Pacific side from Panama to Galapagos.

Coconut Breakfast net 12365kHz at 1330 UTC. Covers French Polynesia.

Rag of the Air Net 8173 kHz at 1900 UTC. Covers Marshalls, Samoa, Solomons, Vanatu and Fiji.

Opua Offshore Des Renner 4417kHz at 0700–0715   4429kHz at 0730-0800 and 1900–1930, 6516kHz at 0715–0730 and 1930–2000, 13101kHz at 0800–0830 and 1600–1630 *Email* opuaoffshore@xtra.co.nz. Approaches to NZ.

HAM Nets

Pacific Maritime Mobile Net 14300kHz 24 hours. Non-licensed (HAM) operators can use it in an emergency and this is probably the first base to touch in an emergency.

Pacific Seafarers Net 14300kHz at 0230 UTC. Roll call 0325 UTC.

Comedy Net 7087kHz at 2040 UTC. Australian based.

Provisioning

When leaving from the USA or Mexico the boat should be fully provisioned up as French Polynesia is relatively expensive and you won't be able to get much apart from the basics until you get to Tahiti. Yachts coming from Panama should provision up there as prices in Panama are some of the cheapest along the Coconut Milk Run.

French Polynesia There is good shopping in Papeete, Huahine and Raiatea with all sorts of goodies from France like cheeses, salamis and hams as well as basic goods. The cost of provisioning is on the high side as nearly everything is shipped or flown in. On all the islands there are of course wonderful baguettes available. Outside the supermarkets in the centres above and Papeete covered market there is limited fruit and vegetables and even staples may be hard to come by if the supply ship has not been in for a while.

Cook Islands Good shopping in Rarotonga only. Most items are imported from NZ.

Tonga Reasonable shopping in Neiafu on Vava'u with some local fruit and vegetables in the market. Better shopping in Nuku'alofa with an excellent fruit and vegetable market and most staples in the medium sized supermarkets. Most items are imported from NZ.

American Samoa Good shopping in supermarkets with many American products. Good fruit and vegetables.

Fiji Good supermarkets in the main centres like Suva, Nadi and Lautoka. Small grocery shops in Savusavu. Good fresh fruit and vegetable markets in Suva and Lautoka with a good selection of natural produce.

Vanuatu Good supermarket in Port Vila and fresh fruit and vegetable market. Most staples are imported from Australia or NZ and are moderately expensive. Excellent local beef.

Fishing along the Coconut Milk Run is generally pretty good

Loading the lockers up for provisioning

Fuel

Leave the USA, Central America and Panama with full tanks and full spare cans. This will be some of the cheapest fuel you will get anywhere except for Galapagos.

Galapagos Fuel is subsidised for the islands and is very cheap. The only problem is that it must all be ferried out in cans.

French Polynesia In the Marquesas you can get it by can in Atuona and Uapou and can go on the dock at Taiohae. In Papeete there is a fuel dock at the Tahiti Yacht Club and Marina Taina. When you clear in make sure you get a form for duty free fuel which can be used straight away at either fuel quay. At Fare/Huahine and Uturoa/Raiatea you can go on the dock to get fuel. In Bora Bora you will need to ferry it to the boat in cans.

Cook Islands Fuel station across the road in Rarotonga. For large quantities you can get a fuel truck.

Tonga In Neiafu by can from Safari or for duty free (only when you leave Tonga) you can order the fuel truck onto the customs dock and berth there after you have completed the paperwork. In Nuku'alofa by can or for duty free (again only when you leave) by 44 gallon drum delivered to the small boat harbour.

Fiji Fuel docks in Savusavu, Suva (draught restriction), Denerau Marina and Vuda Point Marina near Lautoka. Fuel by cans in a few other places on the large islands only. Duty free fuel is available by arrangement with customs, but the marinas can help you with the paperwork.

Vanuatu Fuel dock in Port Vila with max. 30 metre mast height clearance. Larger yachts can use the commercial wharf by arrangement. Fuel in Luganville by jerry cans only. Duty free fuel available.

New Caledonia In Noumea there are three fuel docks. The dock at Port Moselle is easiest and there are two fuel docks in the CNC port.

Australia and NZ At the major entry ports you will find fuel docks. In Australia that will commonly be Bundaberg or Cairns. In NZ at Opua, Whangarei, Auckland or Tauranga. Duty free fuel available in NZ.

Gas

Panama Most gas bottles (butane and propane) can be filled.

USA and Central America American style propane bottles.

Diesel supplies for the Pacific

New Caledonia Supermarkets in Noumea with a wide range of products from France and Australasia. Like French Polynesia prices are not cheap. Good fresh fruit and vegetable and fish market.

Australia and New Zealand Excellent supermarkets and wide choice of fresh fruit and vegetables in the larger centres. Either NZ or Australia (or both if continuing on from NZ to Australia and the Indian Ocean) are the places to do major re-stocking before heading on into the Indian Ocean.

Isle des Pins, New Caledonia

Galapagos Most bottles (butane and propane) can be filled in Puerto Ayora.

French Polynesia At present no gas filling in the Marquesas and Tuamotus. In Tahiti most bottles can be filled (butane and propane). Camping Gaz bottles can be exchanged.

Cook Islands Most bottles can be filled in Rarotonga with butane.

Tonga Most bottles can be filled in Neiafu and Nuku'alofa. Butane only and propane bottles will be emptied if they have any gas in them.

Fiji Most bottles can be filled in Suva, Nadi and Lautoka.

Vanuatu Gas bottles can be refilled in Port Vila (propane).

New Caledonia Some propane bottles can be refilled in Noumea. Camping Gaz bottles can be exchanged.

New Zealand Only NZ certified bottles will be filled and many boats will have to buy a certificated NZ bottle for the stay. Gas is a butane-propane mix.

Australia Australian or NZ certified bottles will be filled and many boats will have to buy an Australian bottle. Gas is propane.

Hauling and repairs

In general once you leave USA/Central America/Panama you will find hauling and repairs difficult until you get to Tahiti. After that New Zealand and Australia are your best bet although you can also haul in Fiji, New Caledonia and Vanuatu. Most yachts crossing the Pacific plan to do refits in NZ or Australia where there are excellent skills of all types, access to most spares and good yards for hauling.

Galapagos Few skills and no real chance of hauling. Problems getting spares sent through customs and if possible wait for French Polynesia.

French Polynesia You really need to get down to Papeete for spares and repairs. Most items can be flown in and it is often worth looking in New Zealand for spares to be sent to Papeete as there are direct flights. Chandlers and good skills including a sailmaker. Good yard for hauling with a travel hoist. Raiatea also has a good boatyard with travel hoist and a skill base for repairs.

Tonga Small to medium sized yachts can be hauled on a fairly Heath Robinson marine railway in Vava'u. Some skills and spares can be flown from NZ.

Fiji Travel hoist and yard at Denerau Marina and Vuda Point Marina near Lautoka. Slipways at Suva. Good skills at the two marinas and at Suva. Reasonable chandlers and most items can be flown in from NZ and Australia.

Vanuatu Haul out in Port Vila. Some skills and repair facilities. Spares can be flown in from Australia and NZ.

New Caledonia Two yards with travel hoists in Noumea. Good repair skills and chandlers. Spares can be flown in from Australia and NZ.

New Zealand A number of yards are popular with cruising boats in NZ. All have travel hoists. From the north these are: Opua, Whangarei, Gulf Harbour, several yards close to Auckland, and Tauranga. There are others but these are the popular options for skills. There are nearly all the specialist skills you could need in NZ.

Australia A number of yards are popular with cruising yachts heading for Queensland. All have travel hoists. From the south these are:

Brisbane, Bundaberg, Mackay, Townsville and Cairns. There are others as well. Like NZ there are nearly all the specialist skills you could need.

Changing crew

Galapagos International flights to Ecuador and then onto Galapagos.

French Polynesia Tahiti is the hub for international flights linking with the USA, Europe and Australasia. Regular internal flights to most of the islands.

Cook Islands Flights from NZ and Australia to Rarotonga.

Tonga Flights from NZ and Australia to Nuku'alofa. Internal flights to Ha'apai and Vava'u group.

Fiji Flights from NZ, Australia and USA to Nadi. Internal flights to the main islands.

Vanuatu Flights from Australia, NZ and Fiji.

New Caledonia Flights from Australia, NZ, USA and Europe. Internal flights on mainland and outlying islands.

Australia and New Zealand Main hubs for flights around the world. Internal flights. There are budget airlines and good deals on tickets available in both countries.

Reading

Pacific Crossing Guide RCCPF. Michael Pocock and Ros Hogbin. (Adlard Coles Nautical)

My gem

Over the Edge of the World: Magellan's Terrifying Circumnavigation of the Globe Laurence Bergreen. (Harper Perennial)

Huahine in French Polynesia

ROUTES AND PASSAGES

It may help to consider the Bay of Islands in New Zealand and Papeete in Tahiti as hubs from which many routes radiate. (This view fits with the history of European exploration and exploitation of the Pacific. Along with Hawaii these places gained major importance as bases for the great whaling fleets that cruised the Pacific in the early 19th century.) The favoured routes as far as New Zealand are from the NE to the SW, which on the average is a reach – but average conditions are not always experienced. W of New Zealand there is more flexibility in direction due to more variable winds, but in general the favoured routes are from SE to NW. Routes to and from Australia are grouped separately.

Because of the large size of the South Pacific and the number of places of interest, it takes most yachts the whole cruising season to reach New Zealand. Here they stay for the cyclone season before cruising the areas N and NW of New Zealand and on to Australia. A lay-over in Australia for another cyclone season is generally necessary before proceeding. The trip can be speeded up by sailing beyond Australia after leaving New Zealand or by heading directly to Australia in the first cruising season, and so having only one cyclone season lay-over. Even this can be avoided by sailing N of New Guinea towards the end of the South Pacific tropical cruising season and continuing to sail in the Northern Hemisphere. Passages for all three possibilities are described.

SW-GOING PASSAGES

(Some of these passages can be made in either direction but E to W is the most commonly travelled direction so they are classified this way).

*SPW1 Panama to French Polynesia

Balboa to Academia Bay 950M
Academia Bay to Taiohae 2,960 M
Academia Bay to Papeete 3,640 M
Season Year round (to Marquesas)
Best time March to June
Tropical storms November to May

Yachts aim to enter French Polynesia just after the end of the cyclone season to make maximum use of the coming cruising season. Between Panama and the Galapagos there is likely to be a lot of calm weather; conventional wisdom is to curve to the S of the rhumb line in hope of picking up a favourable push from the currents. For one author (AO'G) this leg was the slowest, hottest sail he has experienced anywhere. For the other author (RJH) this leg was hard on the wind for almost the whole way to the Galapagos. After the Galapagos, most sail to the S of the rhumb line course until regular trade winds are encountered and then head directly for their destination. However, see the section guide on the *Coconut Milk Run*. Typically this passage is a broad reach or a run with gentle to moderate winds from port. The wind becomes a little more variable after the Marquesas Islands but it will generally be a run.

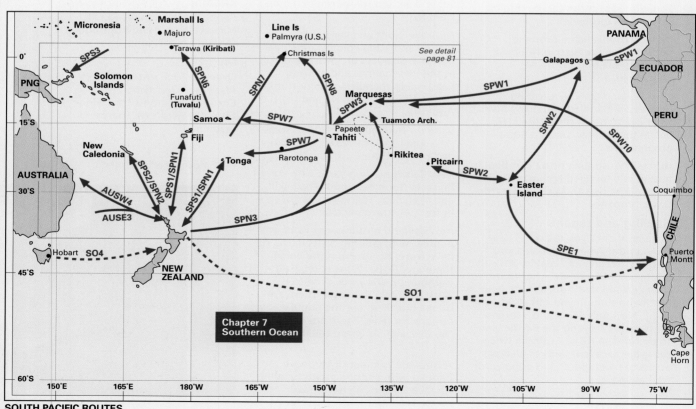

SOUTH PACIFIC ROUTES

A direct course from Galapagos to Tahiti would lead through the Tuamotus; see the comments on this in SPW3.

See *SPW3

SPW2 To and from Easter Island and Pitcairn Island

Academia Bay, Galapagos, to Easter Island 1,930M
Easter Island to Pitcairn Island 1,200M
Pitcairn islands to Rikitea, Gambier Islands 290M

Season All year

Best time January to March

Tropical storms None

From Galapagos to Easter Island or Pitcairn, the passage is generally a reach or a run. From Easter Island to Pitcairn Island and Gambier Islands it is generally a run, with mainly variable winds, but SE predominating near the Gambier Islands. In summer there is a better chance of being able to land on these islands.

PASSAGES WITHIN FRENCH POLYNESIA

(See plan page 81)

In most of French Polynesia the predominant winds are moderate E, swinging between SE and NE. In the Austral Islands the winds are variable from May to August. To some extent this is also true in the S Tuamotus.

*SPW3 Marquesas to Society Islands

Taiohae to Papeete 761M
Papeete to Borabora 140M

Season April to November

Tropical storms November to May

Passages from the Marquesas Islands through the Tuamotus and on to Tahiti will be a run or a broad reach. This also applies from Tahiti to Borabora past Huahine and Raiatea.

Many yachts have been wrecked in the Tuamotus. Currents in this part of the ocean are notoriously unpredictable and variable. If a stop is not planned at one of the atolls then consideration should be given to making a detour to the N to avoid the archipelago, or ensuring that the passage through the narrowest stretches of water is made by daylight. Keep a good lookout all the time, preferably climbing the rigging when in the vicinity of atolls to make a visual sighting, and plot the vessel's position very frequently. Because of uncertainty about the date and datum of surveys, GPS plots should be used with extreme caution. One of the authors (RJH) knows of several yachtsmen with tens of thousands of miles under their belts who have lost yachts here using GPS waypoints.

See *SPW7

SPW4 Gambier Islands to Tahiti

Rikitea (Mangareva Island) to Papeete 890M

Season April to November

Tropical storms November to May

The passage from the Gambier Islands to the Tuamotus and Tahiti varies between a broad reach and a close reach. The reverse passage is more to windward. The direct route passes through the S of the Tuamotu group; if a stop is not planned then a small detour to the S will avoid dangerous waters.

SPW5 Austral Islands to Tahiti

Tubuai to Papeete 350M

Season April to November

Tropical storms November to May

Passages among and to and from the Austral Islands will be subject to variable winds until approaching Tahiti, except later in the season when the northbound route is favoured. The route is free from dangers. Steer well to the E of Tahiti to avoid being forced to leeward. Cyclones are rare in the Australs but do occur occasionally.

SPW6 Marquesas to Tuamotu group and on to Tahiti

Taiohae to Rangiroa 590M
Rangiroa to Papeete 190M

Season April to November

Tropical storms November to May

If it is intended to visit several atolls rather than just pass through, the Tuamotu Islands are best cruised from the SE. Yachts should sail from the Marquesas or Gambier Islands to their SE starting point. The passage in either case will generally be a reach. Great care is needed when cruising the Tuamotus because the windward side of each atoll is submerged and may not be seen at night or in bad weather. Some night sailing is almost inevitable, because the passes into the lagoons can only be used near slack water and they are often too far apart to be sailed between consecutive daylight slack waters. See section guide on the *Tuamotus*.

*SPW7 French Polynesia to the Cook Islands, Tonga, Samoa & Fiji

Papeete to Rarotonga 590M
Rarotonga to Vava'u 810M
Papeete to Vava'u 1,400M
Borabora to Pago Pago 1,110M
Pago Pago to Suva: 670

Season May to October

Tropical storms November to May

In the season, E and SE winds are the most common, except in the S Cook Islands and S Tonga where winds are variable until late in the season. It is therefore likely to be mostly a broad reach or a run from French Polynesia to the N Cooks, N Tonga, Samoa and Fiji. However the winds in this area are fresher and more variable than further E. There is also more risk of a gale, particularly early in the season towards the S, or in squalls on the SPCZ, but they are still uncommon. Heading westwards from French Polynesia there are any number of routes to take, depending on how much time you have, and ultimately where you want to end up. Firstly it is really a question of deciding which of the Cook Islands you would like to visit. Typically the choice, from N to S is Suvarov, Palmerston, Aitutaki or Rarotonga. Some consideration should be given to the position of the SPCZ and general weather conditions, as some of these places offer little shelter from stronger winds. It is possible you will have to continue onwards without stopping at your chosen atoll. The northern route would logically lead on to Samoa, N Tonga or Tuvalu and points N, whilst the central or southern routes head towards Niue and central Tonga. There are numerous tiny atolls and reefs in this part of the S Pacific which make interesting stops in calm weather, but you will need good charts and a bit of nerve to explore them. The passage from Samoa to Tonga and vice versa is likely to be mostly a reach.

See *SPS1

SPW8 Samoa to Wallis, Vanuatu & New Caledonia

Apia to Gahi 260M
Gahi to Port Vila 940M
Port Vila to Noumea 300M

Season Mid-May to October

Tropical storms November to May

Passages on this route are mostly broad reaches in moderate winds with a low risk of gales. However, earlier in the season the winds are sometimes variable in the E part of the route.

SPW9 Fiji to Vanuatu & New Caledonia

Lautoka to Port Vila 530M
Lautoka to Noumea 690M

Season Mid-May to October

Tropical storms November to May

The route to Port Vila is mostly a broad reach or a run. However, earlier in the season the winds may be variable in the vicinity of Fiji. The passage to Noumea is mostly a broad reach in moderate winds with a low risk of gales.

PASSAGES TO AND FROM NEW ZEALAND AND TO THE W ISLAND GROUPS

*SPS1 Tonga & Fiji to New Zealand

Neiafu to the Bay of Islands 1,200M
Suva to the Bay of Islands 1,060M

Season May to November

Best time September to early November

Tropical storms November to May

This passage needs good timing if it is to be at all pleasant. The average wind pattern is a predominant SE in the N, variable in the centre and a slight dominance of SW in the S. However, it may be variable all the way and the wind strength may range from calm to strong and occasionally gale. The passage S is best started with a depression to the S and a high on the way. Leaving the tropics, the winds will be more moderate because of the depression to the S. Mid-passage will be through the high with some motoring in the calm. With luck the destination is reached before a front from the following depression arrives.

As a general rule head somewhat to the W of the rhumb line to around 30°S 175°E. This is to allow for the likelihood of SW winds approaching New Zealand. Some yachts will go to Minerva Reef to wait for a weather window and this gives you a 250NM advantage over the 1100–1200M passage to New Zealand.

See section guide on *Passage from the Tropics to NZ.*

*See * SPN2*

SPS2 New Caledonia and Vanuatu to New Zealand

Port Vila to the Bay of Islands 1,100M
Noumea to the Bay of Islands 910M

Season May to November

Best time September to early November

Tropical storms November to May

See description of passage SPS1. It is easier to make this passage in pleasant conditions than those from Fiji or Tonga. This is because the approaching high and its following depression are moving E, as is the yacht.

(See more tropical area S-going passages below).

N-GOING PASSAGES

SPN1 New Zealand to Tonga & Fiji

Bay of Islands to Neiafu 1,200M
Bay of Islands to Suva 1,060M

Season May to November

Best time May and June

Tropical storms November to May

Hopefully the cyclones will be over in May, but this is not guaranteed. It is safer to leave in June, but even this month can have gales caused by tropical depressions and will have a higher likelihood of being affected by winter gales in the Tasman. The winds at this season are variable until the tropics are approached when SE is more common. This passage should be started a few hours after the passage of a front with a high aproaching. After passing through the high, more moderate winds may be encountered to the N of the following depression. Delay leaving if there is any sign of a trough or depression in the New Caledonia to Fiji area: it can rapidly deepen and move S as a tropical depression or storm. It is easier to make this passage in settled conditions than those to New Caledonia and Vanuatu; this is because the anticyclone is moving with the boat. Weather information in New Zealand is generally sufficient to plan the above trip, though the Australian weatherfaxes may give a better picture of fronts approaching from the Indian Ocean which can affect the passage after a few days at sea. New Zealand Customs, especially in the Bay of Islands, are generally understanding about the need to clear when a front is anticipated and tolerate a delayed departure, particularly if there is no contact with the shore or if they are kept informed about the vessel's movements.

*SPN2 New Zealand to New Caledonia & Vanuatu

Bay of Islands to Port Vila 1,100M
Bay of Islands to Noumea 910M

Season May to November

Best time May and June

Tropical storms November to May

See description for SPN1.

*See *AUSW3*

SPN3 New Zealand to French Polynesia

Auckland to Rikitea 2,660M
Auckland to Raivavae 1,970M
Raivavae to Papeete 350M

Season March to May

Tropical storms November to end May (full cyclones are unlikely to be encountered along this route but degenerating storms from the tropics often end up in this area).

Staying below 30°S until reaching approximately 160°W, the wind direction will be truly variable. As French Polynesia is approached SE is predominant. It will be best to start with an anticyclone arriving as this reduces the chance of meeting a gale. The chance of meeting a gale is about 50% with a random departure at this season. However, the passage is too long to sail with an anticyclone all the way. It is likely that there will be some head winds. This may drive the yacht S or N of the desired course. With a more S course the winds will tend to be stronger with colder conditions and higher risk of W gales but with a reduced possibility of having to tack to windward at the end of the passage. On a more N course the opposite will be true. The N course may have better weather and be an option for a yacht that sails well to windward or is willing to motorsail.

If the destination is Tahiti, the best landfall is Raivavae or Tubuai, where the cyclone risk is very small. Wait until the weather is favourable for the final leg to Tahiti. If the destination is the Marquesas Islands then the best landfall is the Gambier Islands. However, there should not be too many headwinds if landfall is made at Tubuai or Raivavae and the passage to the Gambiers is continued from there. It is not recommended to sail directly from the Australs to the Marquesas through the Tuamotus: the numerous atolls and reefs, combined with unpredictable currents make it a dangerous proposition.

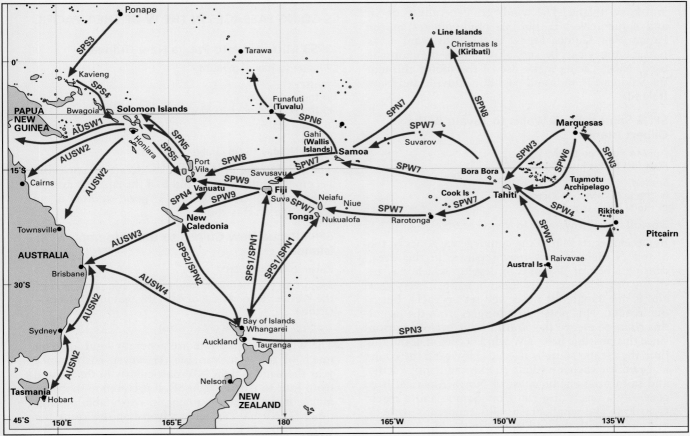

SOUTH PACIFIC ROUTES AND PASSAGES W TO AUSTRALIA - DETAIL

SPN4 New Caledonia to Vanuatu

Noumea to Port Vila 300M

Season Mid-May to October

Tropical storms November to May

This is, on average, a close reach with moderate to fresh winds and little chance of a gale. Great care is needed when navigating through the Loyalty Island chain. There is the possibility of visiting Ouvea if permission has been obtained (see notes on New Caledonia).

SPN5 Vanuatu to the Solomon Islands and Papua New Guinea

Port Vila to Honiara 740M
Honiara to Gizo 210M
Gizo to Bwagoia 290M
Gizo to Kieta 140M
Kieta to Kavieng 370M

Season Mid-May to October

Tropical storms November to May

The W Solomons (Gizo), Bougainville (Kieta) and New Ireland (Kavieng) are not subject to cyclones. These cyclone-free areas are possible alternatives to New Zealand or S Australia during the cyclone season.

The wind is usually moderate to fresh near Vanuatu, moderate near the Santa Cruz Islands, light to moderate in the Louisiade Islands, and light with the odd squall, near the Solomon Islands, Bougainville and New Ireland. The winds are generally E or SE and sometimes NE, but SE predominates in the Papua New Guinea areas. In the light wind areas passage times can be very slow unless the motor is used. Most yachts make use of the motor through the Solomon Islands and past Bougainville and New Ireland.

SPN6 Samoa, Fiji & Wallis to Tuvalu & The Gilbert Islands

Apia to Funafuti 620M
Funafuti to Tarawa 700M

Season
In the S: Mid-May to October
In the N (Kiribati): All year

Tropical storms November to May (S of 5°S)

In December to March the convergence zones of the S and N Hemispheres may separate in this area, causing a belt of W winds to develop which may be strong or gale force. This does not happen every year and is not dangerous for a well set-up yacht, but is unpleasant. This possibility detracts from the use of this route to escape the South Pacific cyclone season since this possible belt of W wind occurs at about the time the escape route is needed. However, the route is useful for yachts wishing to exit the South Pacific and sail to the Pacific coast of North America. It is generally a reach or a run from Samoa and a reach from Fiji. The winds are usually moderate in the S but lighter, with the odd squall, in the N.

SPN7 Tonga or Samoa to the Line Islands

Vava'u to Christmas Island: 1,600M

Season
In the S: Mid-May to October
In the N: All year

Tropical storms
In the S: November to May
In the N: None

This passage can be sailed in either direction. It is generally a close reach going N; to sail S it will be a broad reach. The winds are often SE in the S and NE in the N. The passage leads to or from the Hawaiian Islands.

SPN8 French Polynesia or the Cook Islands to the Line Islands

Papeete to Christmas Island 1,270M

Season
In the S: Mid-May to October
In the N: All year

Tropical storms
In the S: November to May
In the N: None

This is generally a broad to close reach with moderate E winds which become lighter with the odd squall in the N. The winds are often SE in the S and NE in the N. This route leads on to the Hawaiian Islands.

S-GOING PASSAGES IN THE W OF THE S PACIFIC

SPS3 Micronesia to Papua New Guinea

Ponape to Kavieng 730M

Season
In the S: All year
In the N: December to May

Tropical storms
In the S: None
In the N: May to November – low risk

The wind in the N is usually moderate NE or E but becomes light further S, and S of the equator may be a light NW or variable. A good motor is an advantage on this route.

SPS4 Papua New Guinea to the Solomon Islands

Kavieng to Gizo 500M

Season All year between New Ireland, Bougainville and the Western Solomons. E of Gizo the season is June to October

Tropical storms None (W of Gizo)

The winds on this route are generally light and, for much of the year, variable. However, early in the year the wind is light NW particularly in the W, and from June to August light SE. It is common to motor much of this route to maintain reasonable passage times. The usual current is adverse on this route but is less then one knot.

SPS5 The Solomon Islands to Vanuatu

Honiara to Graciosa Bay 360M
Graciosa Bay to Santos 300M

Season June to October

Tropical storms November to May

The wind is on average from the SE and moderate but becomes lighter N of Vanuatu as the season advances. The route is therefore a windward sail but not a hard one. It is usual to sail from the Solomons to the Santa Cruz Islands on the starboard tack and from there to Vanuatu on the port tack. If sufficient fuel is available the W side of Espiritu Santo provides flat calm conditions for motoring, but very slow sailing. The W side of Malekula is also well sheltered but generally there is enough breeze to sail.

PASSAGES E – BACKWARDS ACROSS THE SOUTH PACIFIC

It is sometimes desirable to sail opposite to the normal flow of yachts. In the tropics this must be expected to be mainly windward sailing. A modern sloop may be able to sail quite fast to windward and passage times may be acceptable. Advantage may be taken of the regular wind shifts between SE and NE (corresponding to the passage of depressions in the Southern Ocean), especially in the S part of the trade winds.

Incidentally, and contrary to the theories of Thor Heyerdahl, it is believed that this is how the Polynesians explored and colonised the South Pacific. Sailing to windward gave them the opportunity of an easy run back to a known island if new land was not discovered. Recent archaeology demonstrates a chronological sequence of settlement that largely confirms this theory. The well known Kiwi yachtsman the late David Lewis did much to stimulate modern thinking on this subject by his demonstration of highly developed sailing and navigational practices of Polynesian Peoples. See *We the Navigators* David Lewis (Hawaii University Press).

If a yacht sails badly to windward and the distance to be travelled is great it may be worth considering sailing out of the tropics into the variables or even the westerlies and sailing back to the tropics nearer the longitude of the destination.

From Gambier Islands to Pitcairn and Easter Islands the winds are mainly moderate and variable but with windward sailing predominating. The best season is September to January. From Easter Island to Galapagos loop toward the South American coast. The best season is September to March. Initially the passage will be in variable winds, later a broad reach.

ROUTES ON THE E SIDE OF THE SOUTH PACIFIC

SPE1 Galapagos – Chile

Galapagos to Easter Island 1,914M
Easter Island to Puerto Montt 1,945M

Season October to March

Best time January and February

Tropical storms None

The Galapagos are easily reached from Panama or the W coast of N America. From there it is an easy reach to Easter Island. Leaving Easter Island the vessel should head towards the Chilean coast, taking a course that carries her S of 40°S. In summer the wind is predominantly from the S for at least 300M off the Chilean coast. It is best to approach Puerto Montt on the same latitude, 42°S, or even a little S of this, in order to take advantage of a greater frequency of W winds and avoid being carried N by the Humboldt Current.

*SPW10 Chile – Tropics

Coquimbo to Marquesas, 3,955M

Season All year

Best time April

Tropical storms November to May in the Marquesas, but low risk.

Vessels use the prevailing S wind on the Chilean coast to carry them N, often stopping at Coquimbo (30°S). The SE Trade winds start at this level, though the initial course needs to be NW in order to avoid the S Pacific high-pressure zone (*see weather charts at the beginning of this chapter*).

PASSAGES W TO AUSTRALIA

Passages in the Coral and Tasman Seas

For W-going routes see plan page 157
For E-going routes see plan page 161

If starting from New Zealand or further S in Australia the cruise will start in the summer, since sailing is more pleasant then, with arrival in S Queensland in time to make an early start into the cyclone area when the cyclone season is over.

Yachts sailing W from the South Pacific usually cross the Coral Sea or the N Tasman Sea to the Queensland coast to first ports of call at Thursday Island, Cairns, Townsville, Gladstone, Bundaberg, or perhaps Brisbane. The Coral Sea route from the Louisiade Islands or the Solomon Islands is to be preferred over the rougher seas further S. However, many local yachts, particularly racing yachts, do sail directly between Auckland and Sydney.

AUSW1 Solomon and Louisiade Islands to Torres Strait

Bwagoia to Thursday Island 585M

Season Mid-May to October

Best time September to early October

Tropical storms November to May

Either island-hop through the beautiful Louisiades or pass well to the S of them. Beware of passage-making through the group as they are not well charted, are unlit, have variable currents, extensive reefs and are often obscured by a heat haze even on days when visibility appears excellent. Sail for Bramble Cay at the NE entrance to the Torres Strait, passing N of the Eastern Fields and Portlock Reefs. In the days before GPS, this was one of the most challenging landfalls in the world. One of the authors (AO'G) knows of two notable yachtsmen who have landed on reefs here. Even with GPS, the intricate navigation, poor visibility of the low lying Cay and strong currents mean that the position should be plotted frequently. It is best to arrive at the Cay shortly after dawn and sail down the Strait in daylight. However, this is a major shipping route and is well lit. If stopping overnight on the way, do not land as the Australian authorities will monitor the yacht closely from the air and impose severe penalties for landing prior to clearance.

AUSW2 Solomon and Louisiade Islands to N Queensland

Honiara to Cairns 950M
Honiara to Townsville 970M
Bwagoia to Cairns 560M
Bwagoia to Townsville 630M

Season Mid-May to October

Best time September to early October

Tropical storms November to May

The prevailing wind is a moderate E to SE, making this passage a reach. There are encircling reefs in the Louisiades (see above) and the Queensland Great Barrier Reef has to be navigated through.

The approach to Townsville is through Palm Passage, in the Great Barrier Reef, which has light beacons near each end. A slow yacht may have to make part of this passage at night.

The approach to Cairns is best through the Grafton Passage, which has a light beacon on a reef near the outer end and a directional light for the passage, though it should be possible to sail the whole route by daylight.

Note that the SPCZ can park itself over the Solomon/Louisiade area during the southern winter, and this, combined with frequent 'squash zones' caused by high pressure systems moving off Australia, can make this a rough, wet, windy and generally unpleasant passage.

*AUSW3 Vanuatu and New Caledonia to S Queensland

Noumea to Brisbane 790M
Port Vila to Brisbane 1,030M

Season Mid-May to October

Tropical storms November to May

The wind is mostly moderate E to SE but more variable near Brisbane.

These passages are likely to be a broad reach. There are massive reefs in the Coral Sea and N of New Caledonia to be avoided on passage from Port Vila. From Vanuatu (Vila or Luganville) yachts heading for Cairns will sail to a point N of Sand Cay (around 15°20'S 149°40'E) to clear the reefs S of here. You can then angle down under Bougainville Reef to the Grafton Passage. The alternative of wending your way through the reefs S of Sand Cay has tripped up numbers of boats and electronic charts should not be relied on in this area. One author (RJH) knows of several yachts lost here when relying on electronic charts.

*See * AUSN1*

AUSW4 New Zealand To Australia

Bay of Islands to Brisbane 1,190M
Bay of Islands to Sydney 1,150M

Season All year in the N, November to March in the S

Best time January to March

Tropical storms None S of Brisbane

The Tasman is a notoriously rough sea and spawns depressions and fronts at all times of year. Passages in this direction are against the flow of depressions, so it is unlikely they can be avoided. The wind direction will be variable and so will the strength. Strong winds must be expected. The wind is on average stronger in the W than the E Tasman on the Sydney passage. The winds are more uniform on the Brisbane passage. There is a 25% chance of meeting a gale on either passage. From this description it is easy to see why most foreign cruising yachts sail to Australia by way of New Caledonia or further N.

PASSAGES E FROM AUSTRALIA

(See plan opposite)

AUSE1 North Queensland to Solomon and Louisiade Islands

Townsville to Honiara 970M
Townsville to Bwagoia 630M
Cairns to Honiara 950M
Cairns to Bwagoia 560M

Season Mid-May to October

Best time Late May and June.

Tropical storms November to May

The prevailing wind is a moderate E to SE, making this passage a close reach. The Queensland Great Barrier Reef has to be navigated through and there are encircling reefs in the Louisiades (see AUSW1/2). The route from Townsville is though Palm Passage, in the Great Barrier Reef. It is straightforward and has light beacons near each end. The route from Cairns is best through the Grafton Passage, which has a light beacon on a reef near the outer end and a directional light for the passage.

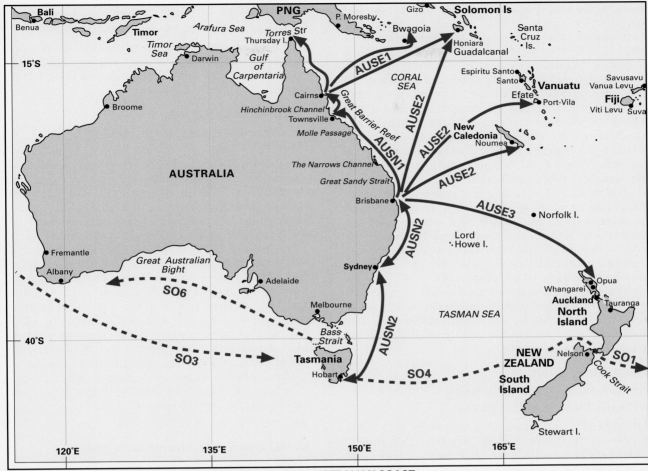

PASSAGES E FROM AUSTRALIA AND PASSAGES ON THE AUSTRALIAN COAST

AUSE2 South Queensland to New Caledonia, Vanuatu & Solomon Islands (Gizo)

Brisbane to Noumea 790M
Brisbane to Port Vila 1,030M
Brisbane to Gizo 1,190M

Season Mid-May to October

Best time Late May and June

Tropical storms November to May

The wind is mostly moderate E to SE but more variable near Brisbane and light approaching Gizo. This is likely to be a windward sail to Noumea, a close reach to Port Vila and a reach to Gizo. There are massive reefs in the Coral Sea and N of New Caledonia to be navigated on passage to Port Vila.

AUSE3 Australia To New Zealand

Brisbane to Bay of Islands 1,190M
Sydney to Bay of Islands 1,150M

Season December to April

Best time January to March

Tropical storms November to May N of Brisbane

A well-planned passage in this direction could be in good weather all the way, because the yacht and the anticyclones are moving in the same direction. A passage started with an anticyclone approaching

may have the luck to reach the destination before the anticyclone passes.

See AUSW4.

PASSAGES ON THE AUSTRALIAN COAST

*AUSN1 Queensland E Coast

Brisbane to Thursday Island 1,210M
Brisbane to Townsville 620M
Townsville to Cairns 160M
Cairns to Thursday Island 440M

Season
In the N: Mid-May to mid-October
In the S: The usual season is November to April

Best time
N-going April to June,
S-going: September to November

Tropical storms November to May in the N

Cruising yachts from the South Pacific usually arrive in Queensland near the beginning of the cyclone season and sail S to Brisbane, the Gold Coast, or Mooloolaba to be clear of the cyclones. There they remain for the cyclone season. Some yachts brave the rougher seas of the New South Wales coast and perhaps Tasmania. Those sailing N along the Queensland coast do so when the cyclone season is over. (*For E–W passage S of Australia see Chapter 7 Southern Ocean*).

Cruising yachts virtually never sail the length of this coast non-stop. It would be necessary to have two competent navigators doing watch and watch about for continuous day and night sailing within the Barrier Reef. Navigating outside the Reef in the Coral Sea is simpler but the passage will not be so smooth. Virtually all cruising yachts anchor for a rest each day when sailing this coast.

The wind is favourable for sailing N in April, May and June. The usual wind is a moderate, sometimes fresh, SE. At the time when yachts are sailing S in September, October and November the wind is somewhat more variable and lighter. Yachts are frequently under power. Visibility can be low at this time and radar is an advantage.

The route inside the Great Barrier Reef is well marked for day and night sailing and should present little difficulty to a competent navigator. The following passages are commonly used deviations from the shipping route.

Great Sandy Strait

Off Wide Bay Bar 25°49'·5S 153°10'E

N Fairway buoy 25°08'·7S 152°49'·8E

Great Sandy Strait is an attractive short cut. It has ample depth, except at Wide Bay Bar. The strait is well marked with lit buoys and beacons. The tidal flow can be up to 4kn in places.

The S entrance, Wide Bay Bar, can only be crossed near high water in good weather. It must be used with considerable caution. Seas break on it with a large swell in bad weather. It is best entered on a rising tide and in the morning for better visibility of the leading lines. The tidal flow can reach 4kn between the headlands.

The Narrows Channel

S Fairway to Gladstone 23°53'S 151°31'E

This channel is an interesting and protected alternative to the route on the E side of Curtis Island. The N Narrows Channel lies between Curtis Island and the mainland. It can only be used around high water (the channel is dry at low water – spring range 3.9m at Gladstone) and for most yachts only near high water springs. The Admiralty *Pilot* states that it dries 0.3m and that vessels with a draft of 2.7m navigate the channel. On the other hand, the beautiful chart prepared by the Queensland Government shows a drying height of 2m. Whichever is correct, there is little difficulty passing through on a rising spring tide with a draft of 2m. The tide height at the narrows is greater than at Gladstone. The best water is reasonably well marked with white leading beacons and port and starboard beacons. The starboard beacons are on the Curtis Island side for the usual direction of travel N.

Molle Passage

S entrance to Long Island Sound 20°25'S 148°52'E

This is a comparatively narrow passage and is more sheltered than the Whitsunday Passage. The tidal flow can reach 5kn at The Narrows in Long Island Sound.

Hinchinbrook Channel

Seaward end of Lucinda leading marks 18°30'.1S 146°24'E

This channel is an interesting and protected alternative to the route on the E side of Hinchinbrook Island. There are possibilities for anchoring, though they are not particularly good. The channel is a deep-water ship channel from the north entrance as far as Lucinda at the south end. It is buoyed and has leading lines; the marks assume a ship enters from the N end. E of Lucinda and beyond the channel proper is a bar with a charted depth of 1.3m so tide and sea must be considered to cross the bar. The preferred course across the bar is buoyed and there is a leading line on a course of 067° leaving. If coming from the S the course entering is 247° and the entrance is nearly a mile N of the outer end of the long wharf projecting E from Lucinda.

Hinchinbrook Island is a rugged mountainous national park. There are very big, biting flies along the channel, so be well dressed.

See *IW1

AUSN2 East Coast – New South Wales – Tasmania

Sydney to Brisbane 450M
Sydney to Hobart 620M
Sydney to Melbourne 570M

Season December to April.

Tropical storms None

This coast has variable winds with the possibility of a gale every month of the year. In the S there is an average of two or more gales per month. There are many ports and anchorages along the coast but few can be entered or used in adverse conditions. There are a number of ports with bars at their entrances. The result is that while some foreign cruising yachts visit this coast, most opt to spend the summer in S Queensland. Passages should be planned to fit with the expected duration of favourable wind and weather.

COUNTRY AND PORT GUIDE

Local customs

In many islands, especially in the west part of the ocean, people may be offended by casual dress and the upper legs should generally be covered. It is wise to dress conservatively until local customs have been observed. In many places there is the expectation of some form of formal visit to the local headman, possibly with the presentation of a ritual gift, as in the Fijian Kava ceremony. Be aware that politeness may mean that offences to traditional customs will not be pointed out, though they will probably result in a cool or unhelpful reception. Minimal compliance will often result in an unforgettably warm reception.

Panama

See Chapter 1 North Atlantic for country information. For information on transiting the Panama Canal see Panama in Chapter 1 North Atlantic Ocean.

BALBOA

Tidal range 5m

Berths

On moorings off the Balboa Yacht Club or at Flamenco Marina. There is also a small marina off the Miramar Hotel in Panama City and another larger marina under construction off the waterfront.

Balboa Yacht Club

VHF Ch 06. Visitors' moorings on a first come first served basis. Moorings are secure but it can be very choppy here. Water and fuel on the pier. A bumboat runs 24 hours to take you ashore and back (it's forbidden to use your dinghy). Charge band 2. Wi-Fi. Clubhouse with bar and restaurant. Taxis and buses into Balboa and Panama City.

Flamenco Marina

190 berths. Visitors' berths. Max LOA 60m. Max

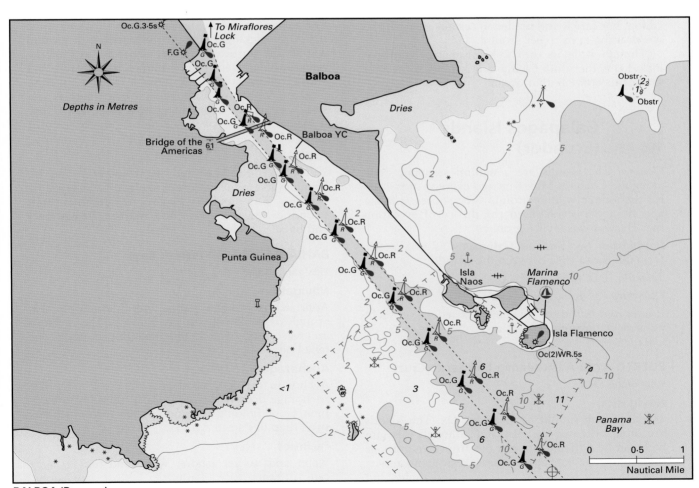

BALBOA (Panama)
⊕08°53'·30N 79°31'·29W WGS84

draught 7m. Charge band 4. VHF Ch 10. Finger pontoons. Good shelter although there can be a surge with easterlies. Water and electricity. Fuel dock. 150-ton travel hoist but limited hard standing. Chandlers. Wi-Fi. Laundry. Restaurants and bars. *Email* mlp@fuerteamador.com

Anchorage

Yachts normally anchor tucked under the W side of Isla Flamenco or on the E side of the causeway depending on wind and swell. You should not leave a boat unattended as strong SW winds can blow into here during March to June. There is a dinghy dock tucked under Isla Naos for the W anchorage and at Marina Flamenco for the E anchorage. These are charged for but do not leave your dinghy anywhere else.

Facilities

Apart from the marina facilities above, nearby Balboa has good facilities as well. Islamorada is a very good chart and pilot agent in Balboa (www.islamorada.com). There is a large supermarket and other shops at the Albrook Mall at the main bus terminal. Agents for marine engine spares and other marine equipment in Panama City and good hardware shops.

Remarks

Balboa and Panama City are not as dangerous as Colon, but care is still needed in certain areas and its worth using taxis to get around.

Though it is in the N hemisphere, Balboa is included in the South Pacific as it is a logical stop for the yachts crossing that ocean.

Galapagos Islands (Ecuador)

General The islands are a natural stepping stone along the Coconut Milk Run and exert an attraction for the unique wildlife around their shores, a fauna and flora that crystallised the theory of evolution that Darwin was working on.

Formalities See box on **Galapagos** as in practice formalities can vary between the islands.

Telecom IDD +593

Currency US dollars are used.

Routes and harbours There are restrictions on yacht movements around the islands. See the box on Galapagos.

PUERTO AYORA (Academia Bay Santa Cruz)

Tidal range 1.6m

Navigation

The approach should be made by day. The islands are often obscured by mist and although they are high can be difficult to make out from five miles or so. In the immediate approaches Isla Comano and its light structure stand out quite well and yachts and tripper boats in the anchorage will be seen. The

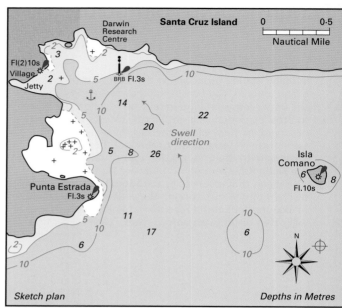

ACADEMIA BAY (Galapagos)
⊕00°45'·88S 090°16'·75W WGS84

isolated danger buoy marking the shallows on the N side will be seen and then it is a matter of sniffing around the anchorage.

Anchorage

The anchorage is crowded and its worth taking some time over picking a spot. A stern anchor at around 45° off the starboard quarter is needed to hold the bows into the swell. The bottom is coarse black sand and excellent holding. If possible anchor as close into the W corner as possible where there is less swell, keeping clear of tripper boat moorings. There is inevitably some swell rolling into the bay and it takes a bit of time to get used to it.

Facilities

Water taxis run day and night to ferry you in. Dinghies left in the water are likely to be annexed by sea lions. Water and fuel by jerry can. Internet cafés. Laundries. Supermarkets and market. Restaurants and bars.

BAHIA NAUFRAGIO (Wreck Bay)

Tidal range 1.6m

Navigation

Approach is straightforward and although possible at night is best made by day. Buoys in the entrance are reasonably well maintained but shouldn't be relied on.

Anchorage

Anchor in the designated area on the E side. The anchorage does spill over in April through to early June. Good holding and good shelter with much less swell than in Puerto Ayora.

Facilities

Water taxis to get ashore. Water and fuel by jerry can. Internet café. Laundries. Most provisions. Restaurants and bars.

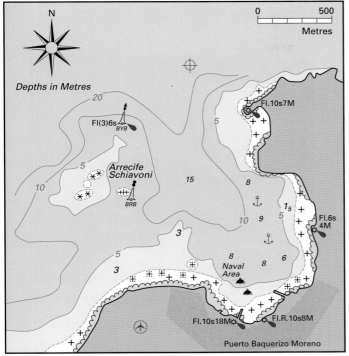

BAHIA NAUFRAGIO (Wreck Bay)
⊕0°53'·3S 89°37'·0W

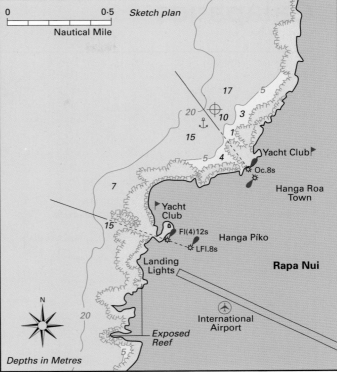

HANGA ROA (Easter Island) (Rapa Nui)
⊕27°08'·7S 109°26'·2W

 # Easter Island (Rapa Nui) (Chile)

See Chapter 7 Southern Ocean for country information.

Sailing season All year, but summer is best if a landing is to be made.

HANGA ROA

Tidal range 1m

Anchorage

The anchorage is off the township. There is a leading line marking it. Anchor in 20m, sand. Further in is foul. The shelter is poor and only tenable in winds from E. There is a landing place through a narrow passage between rocks but it may be rough. Smaller yachts may be able to use Hanga Piko, a small basin nearby, but this is not tenable in some conditions. Swell is generally a problem all around the island and may make landing impossible.

There are alternative anchorages for all wind directions around the island.

Facilities

Basic supplies and transport to tourist sites are available in Hanga Roa. No ATM, US dollars are welcome.

Remarks

Hanga Roa is the township for the island. Formalities are arranged with the *armada* (navy) here.

 # Pitcairn Island

This is a British possession, administered from New Zealand.

General Pitcairn Island is known for its association with the mutiny of the *Bounty* and some of the descendants of the mutineers live here.

Formalities None.

Telecom Via Inmarsat satellite phone with limited hours.

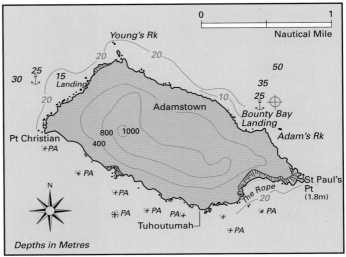

PITCAIRN ISLAND
⊕25°04'·0S 130°06'·0W

Galapagos

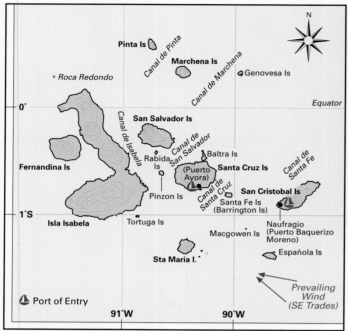

GALAPAGOS ISLANDS

Map labels: Pinta Is, Canal de Pinta, Marchena Is, Genovesa Is, Roca Redondo, Canal de Marchena, Equator, San Salvador Is, Canal de San Salvador, Baltra Is, Canal de Isabela, Rabida Is, Santa Cruz Is, Canal de Santa Fe, Fernandina Is, (Puerto Ayora), Pinzon Is, San Cristobal Is, Canal de Santa Cruz, Santa Fe Is (Barrington Is), Naufragio (Puerto Baquerizo Moreno), Isla Isabela, Tortuga Is, Macgowen Is, Española Is, Sta Maria I., Prevailing Wind (SE Trades), Port of Entry, 91°W, 90°W, 0°, 1°S, N

Giant tortoise in the highlands

Panama to Galapagos

This is often a windward leg and a rainy one as well. There will often be entirely overcast days and rain and the winds can be variable. Although you are theoretically out of the ITCZ, it is usually further N, it seems like the ITCZ influences weather here. There are also usually contrary currents on this leg and you can have over one knot of current against you.

Most yachts will plan to go east of Malpelo Island on starboard tack and then hopefully flop over onto port and make it close to the Galapagos on the opposite tack. In fact it is best to keep going on starboard tack well SW of Malpelo Island, at least 100–150 miles, where there may be the possibility of picking up the SE Trades.

Yachts which don't go well to windward may have to motor-sail for some of this passage, though it is possible to sail it if you so desire. The approach to Puerto Ayora or Bahia Naufragio should be made in daylight. The misty haze that usually hangs over the islands can reduce visibility to 2–3 miles so care is needed even in daylight.

Long-line fishing boats

Between Panama and Galapagos you will likely come across long-line boats fishing for tuna. These long-lines are really long, often a kilometre or more and there will be lots of them laid out like a spiders web across your path. Although they are buoyed, it can be difficult to see some of the small buoys and the likelihood is you will run into the line before you see them. This is not too much of a problem if you are sailing, but if you are motoring you need to make sure you put the engine into neutral straight away so the line doesn't wrap around your propeller.

There will usually be a mother boat and one or two long dories, usually around 40ft, with a big outboard on the back. If they see you they will attempt to guide you around the end of the long-line. If there is no-one around you will have to try and get the long-line off the best way you can and this may mean cutting

Puerto Ayora

it. Lift it up with a boathook and if you can't work it free, cut it as a last resort. I'm not sure if the lines are out at night as most boats seemed to encounter them in the day-time.

The fishermen in the dories are amiable types and are not pirates. They may come close to the boat, but this is curiosity and a wave and a smile goes a long way. Once you see a dory a look around the horizon will usually locate the mother ship and you need to steer clear of it as the lines are normally somewhere between the mother ship and the dory.

Galapagos formalities

A yacht is allowed to enter at one of the ports of entry, commonly Puerto Ayora (Academia Bay) on Santa Cruz or Bahia Naufragio (Wreck Bay) on San Cristobal. Once cleared in a yacht may NOT go to another port without authorization, except in special circumstances (say medical or boat repairs) and for this you will need to supply written documentation to the port captain and await his decision.

While this all sounds very officious, in fact when yachts arrive the port authorities, customs and immigration are friendly and helpful.

WHILE YOU DO NOT NEED A YACHT AGENT TO CLEAR IN AND OUT IN THEORY IN PRACTICE YOU MAY NEED TO EMPLOY AN AGENT.

In Puerto Ayora it appears to be easier to clear in without an agent than it does in Bahia Naufragio. When you arrive you need to take your boat papers, clearance from the last port, and passports to the port captain. He will fill in the requisite forms and request payment.

You pay the following fees:
Boat tonnage Paid to Port Captain. (Currently around $US8.60 per ton in 2009).

Immigration You then go to the immigration police where there is a charge per person for clearing in and out. ($US30 2009).

Agent If you use an agent his fee should be in the $US80–100 range (2009). Ricardo Arenas Sail'n Galapagos has a good reputation. www.sailingalapagos.com VHF Ch 05, 16. Search the internet for other agents.

Once you are cleared in then you are free to wander around the island and to take trips on excursion and dive boats going to other islands. If you wish to take your own boat to another island then a national park

The fish market with local customers in Puerto Ayora

guide must accompany you at a charge of $US100 per day. Few yachts do this as it is a lot cheaper and less hassle to take one of the excursion/dive boats (and they are numerous).

Seasons and winds

The prevailing wind is the SE Trades which blow fitfully over the islands. At times they can blow at 15–20 knots but mostly they are lighter at around 10 knots or so. Occasionally northerly winds will blow and there can be days of calm or nearly calm weather. It is the prevailing swell from the SE and pushed by the Trades that causes most bother and will often be two metres or so between the islands and occasionally more.

There are basically two seasons in the Galapagos. The colder dry season runs from July to December and is known as the *garua* season after the mist over the islands. The hot and wet season, though wet is a relative term as very little rain falls anyway, runs from January to June.

For islands lying just under the equator the temperatures are surprisingly temperate and at night you will need a sweatshirt. To a large extent the temperatures are controlled by the sea temperatures and of the three ocean currents that converge on the Galapagos, the Peru (or Humboldt) Current is the most powerful and the coldest (see Current map at the beginning of this chapter). The Peru Current shrouds

the islands in a misty haze (the *garua*) reducing visibility and cools the islands significantly. Temperatures around the coast are generally 20°–25°C although with the haze and grey skies it feels less, especially after the tropical temperatures of Central America. At night temperatures drop to under 20°C.

The Peru Current causes an ocean upwelling around the Galapagos and sea temperatures are on the chilly side for those used to the Tropics. The temperatures will often be under 20°C and much less if you are diving, depending on depths. You will need a full wet-suit when diving and these are easily hired. Despite the sub-tropical temperatures the diving is world class around the Galapagos. The upwelling currents bring nutrients to the surface starting off a food chain that goes all the way to the top with lots of sea mammals like sea lions and whales and big fish like tuna and lots of sharks. Sea birds are everywhere.

Ashore

Water Most of the water in the Galapagos is from reverse osmosis water plants and is expensive. Currently it is around $US40 per 100 gallons. In Puerto Ayora some of the water taxis can put a large polyethylene container in the taxi and come alongside. An electric bilge pump then pumps it into your own tanks. Alternatively you can send jerry cans ashore.

Galapagos pelican

Marine iguana

Sally lightfoot crab

All supplies are brought ashore in small lighters in the Galapagos

Fuel Diesel is subsidised in the Galapagos and is very cheap (around $US1 per gallon), but you cannot buy it yourself. An agent will usually charge around $US2–2.50 per gallon delivered. Alternatively you may be able to take jerry cans ashore and contract a taxi to go to the petrol station and fill them. He will charge $US5–10 plus the cost of the diesel.

Provisions Most things are shipped into the Galapagos and then brought ashore on small lighters. Consequently anything shipped in, which is nearly everything except for some fruit and vegetables and a bit of beef or goat, is expensive. Often there will be shortages of items until the supply ship arrives. There is a fresh fruit and veggie market in Ayora on Tuesdays and Saturdays in the morning. It seems everything is a

dollar a bag (they supply the bags) so whether you put six limes or a dozen in, it is still a dollar. Potatoes, onions, limes, passion fruit, tomatoes, peppers, and lots of other things are fresh and mostly good quality. There is also a fish market most mornings.

Eating out Eating out in the local restaurants is excellent and good value. In Puerto Ayora there is a restaurant street where you could get the set lunchtime menu for $US3–4. It usually included excellent soup, a choice of a rice dish or something like fried chicken with rice and salad, a fruit juice, and sometimes a dessert. The up-market restaurants like 'The Rock' in Ayora offered superb food at good prices. Alcohol is a little more expensive.

Other Taxis, which are all twin cab pick-ups (commonly a Toyota Hi-Lux) will take you anywhere in the town limits for $US1 a go. Outside town limits you need to negotiate a price. Laundries, Internet cafés, hardware shops and tour operators for excursions.

Puerto Ayora

Ayora has the best facilities for small boat repairs, provisions and eating out. It is also a most uncomfortable anchorage and can have up to a metre of swell rolling in. The holding in coarse black sand is excellent and you will need to lay a kedge anchor off the starboard side at around 45° to hold you into the swell. The anchorage is also very busy with excursion boats, particularly at turn-arounds on the weekend. Fortunately the excursion boat skippers are well skilled in the fine art of anchoring in small spaces.

To get ashore you use water taxis to run back and forth (VHF Ch 14). There is nowhere to leave your dinghy on the dock. Costs are around

60 cents per person in the day and $1 at night. They operate 24 hours. The water taxis will also supply water and fuel and are helpful getting kedges up etc.

Bahia Naufragio

The anchorage here is much better protected and you will have a less stressful time of it. Anchor on the E side of the bay clear of the naval area. The holding is good on black sand and you can lay a kedge if you need to.

Restaurants and bars ashore and adequate shopping. Like Ayora it is best to go ashore in a water taxi.

Ecuador mainland

A number of yachts coming through Panama or down the west coast of Central America hole up in Ecuador for a season to wait until the next season to cross the Pacific. There are two places that are popular.

Puerto Amistad 00°35'.780S 080°28'.300W (off the entrance). Situated in Bahia de Caraquez but usually known as just 'Bahia'. You need to take a pilot into the bay as the channel changes all the time. Call Puerto Amistad on VHF Ch 69. Inside you are on moorings and ashore there is the office/bar/restaurant with all facilities including Wi-Fi. Go to www.puertoamistadecuador.com for information.

Puerto Lucia 02°13'.01S 80°55'.28W (marina entrance). A marina associated with an apartment complex at La Libertad, close to Salinas. All facilities and close to supermarkets and restaurants. Go to www.puertolucia.com.ec for information.

My gem

Fossils, Finches and Fuegians
Richard Keynes. (Harper Collins)

Currency New Zealand dollar. The Island Secretary changes money and traveller's cheques.

Sailing season All year, but summer is best if a landing is to be made.

BOUNTY BAY

Tidal range 1m

Anchor in Bounty Bay if possible, about 350–400m offshore in 22m. Very poor shelter. It may be best to stand off or tack back and forth while some of the crew go ashore. It is unwise to leave the yacht unattended. The main landing is in Bounty Bay, but it is not easy to use; there is a good landing in a cove on the NW coast.

Formalities There are now moderate fees for the use of local ferry service and per person for landing.

French Polynesia

See plan page 170

These islands (Marquesas, Gambier Islands, Tuamotu Islands, Society Islands and Austral Islands) are French overseas territories.

Formalities The main port of entry is Papeete (Tahiti). Report to the gendarmerie at the first port of entry and complete the required paperwork. *See the section guide on French Polynesia for details.*

Telecom IDD +689. GSM network. Internet cafés easy to find.

Currency Central Pacific Franc (CPF). There are ATM machines in the main centres on the larger islands and even some smaller islands. US dollars or Euros can be used on most islands. Banks on most of the islands and post offices which can change money and may have an ATM.

Sailing season All year (though with a small risk of cyclones) in the Marquesas and Gambier Islands, and from April to November elsewhere.

Routes and harbours A general discussion of each group is given here and specific information on a representative anchorage follows.

Marquesas

See plan page 174

TAIOHAE (Nuka Hiva)

Tidal range 1.3m

Navigation

Approach from seawards is straightforward with no dangers to navigation. You won't see the village until you have opened the bay. A night approach is possible, but remember there will yachts in the anchorage without anchor lights.

Anchorage

Anchor where convenient. Don't anchor too close to the landing dock or the gendarmerie will move you along. Good holding on mud and sand. Use a kedge

anchor to hold the boat into the swell or you will roll around a lot as the wind tends to gust into the bay from different directions. Good shelter.

Facilities

Water ashore (reported unpotable). Fuel on the new wharf where you can go stern-to if there is not too much swell running. Wi-Fi. Some provisions. Good quality veggies are brought down from market gardens in the mountains and sold on the waterfront. Fruit trees are everywhere, but fruit is not often seen on sale; if you ask many locals will be happy to trade or donate a generous amount. A few restaurants in town.

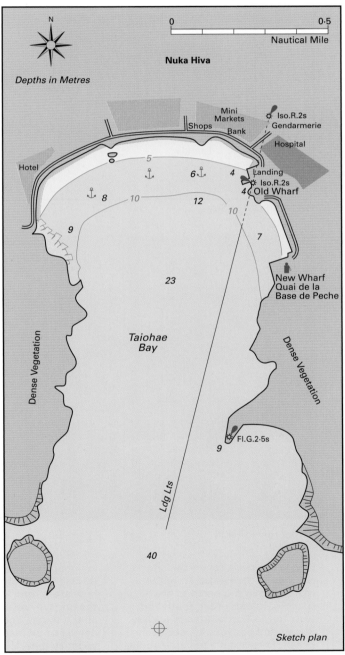

TAIOHAE (Nuka Hiva, Marquesas)
⊕08°56'·47S 140°05'·90W WGS84

French Polynesia

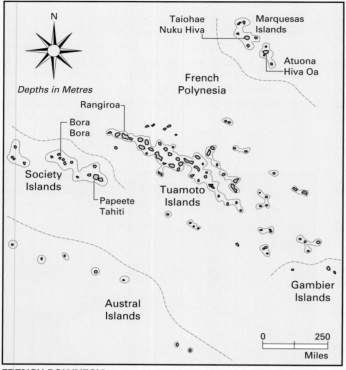

FRENCH POLYNESIA

French Polynesian flag under the tricolour

Barrier reef in Tahiti

French Polynesia covers the largest sea area in the Pacific. From the Marquesas in the north to the Gambier Islands in the south and west to the Austral Islands, Society Islands and Iles Sous le Vent, French Polynesia encloses a sea area about the size of Europe. The islands that

make up French Polynesia gave Darwin the ideas for his theory of how atolls form and his theory is still the one we use today. The group has all the stages from the birth to the demise of an island and although you may think this is a bit of academic trivia, in fact

understanding how atolls form gives us lots of clues for navigating around the islands.

The Marquesas are the newest islands that have been thrust up from the sea bottom through volcanic activity. If you look on the chart there are others that are still coming up either through the thrust of tectonic plates and/or volcanic activity. Actually the best example of this is in Tonga where an island keeps popping up and then disappearing through volcanic activity. There are few reefs around the Marquesas and those that exist are fringing reefs immediately off the coast. The water here is so deep just a short distance off that coral can only grow in the short shallow band adjacent to the coast – coral grows from around 20 metre depths up.

Tahiti, Moorea and the Iles Sous le Vent (Leeward Isles) are the intermediate stage of atoll formation. The fringing reef has grown and the islands have started to sink back into the ocean. Much of the fringing reef has become a barrier reef with deep water between the reef and the island.

Deep here means anything from 10 to 50 metres. Tahiti and Moorea are at the beginning of this stage where the islands have started to sink and Bora Bora is the most advanced with a wide lagoon and *motus* (small sandy islets, usually with vegetation) on parts of the barrier reef.

The Tuamotus are the final stage in atoll formation where the island has completely submerged leaving just the barrier reef with *motus* and a large lagoon inside the barrier reef. The lagoons vary in depth depending on the topography and can be anything from a metre to 50 metres and more deep.

It's disturbing to think that in a short space of time (geologically speaking) man will likely see the demise of atolls with global warming. Not only will the rise in sea level submerge these *motus* which are only a few metres above sea level, but global warming also inhibits coral growth and all around these islands you can already see much bleached coral.

Cruising strategies

Yachts on a westward crossing will usually arrive in the Marquesas and cruise down through the Tuamotus to the Society Islands, clear in at Papeete and then proceed westwards through the Iles Sous Le Vent to Bora Bora and on. Alternatives are to go to the Gambiers instead of the Marquesas and then proceed west. For more detail on Cruising Strategies, Seasons

Captain Cook's Bay on Moorea

and Winds and Facilities see The Coconut Milk Run and the sections on the island groups in French Polynesia.

Buoyage

The islands are amazingly well buoyed, in fact the buoyage is better than many parts of the world I can think of.

BUOYAGE IS IALA SYSTEM 'A' WITH GREEN TO STARBOARD AND RED TO PORT.

There are either buoys or beacons conforming to IALA system 'A'. There are also cardinal marks in places where the buoyage might be confusing. Buoyage in the channel behind the barrier reef is in the direction such that you always have red buoys/beacons on the LAND side and green buoys/beacons on the REEF side. One small thing to be aware of is that some of the beacons are situated on a coral outcrop so don't skim by too close to the channel markers. And remember to wear your polarised sunglasses which show up the reefs well.

The passes through the reefs will also usually have leading marks. All of the leading marks and buoys/beacons are lit and for the most part reliable, although I don't recommend coming through the passes at night.

All Buoyage in French Polynesia is IALA System A and is well maintained

On Tahaa in the Iles Sous Les Vent

Uturoa Pass into Raiatea

Customs boat in Huahine

Customs checking boats in Papeete

Formalities

Papeete is the main port of entry and you need to go here to make a final clearance even if you have cleared in at one of the other ports of entry on other islands. This will commonly be the Marquesas but can be the Gambiers or in fact any island you choose that is a port of entry.

When you clear in at one of the outlying ports of entry the gendarmerie will fill out an entry form, give you a copy and request that you buy a postage stamp so the original can be sent to Papeete. Non-EU nationals must deposit the requisite bond (see below). You will be stamped into the country and you have 30 days to get to Papeete to do the formal check-in.

Ports of entry are as follows:
Marquesas Hiva Oa, Nuka Hiva, Ua Pou.
Tuamotus Rangiroa
Gambiers Mangareva
Society Islands Papeete, Huahine, Raiatea, Bora Bora.
Australs Tubuai, Raivavae

EU nationals
Anyone from an EU country will not have to pay a bond. You go to the gendarmerie who will fill out the requisite form and you will be given the original to post to headquarters in Papeete and a copy you keep with the ships papers. There is no charge apart from the cost of a stamp for the form to go to Papeete (you need to go to the Post Office and get this). You will be given a 90 day visa for French Polynesia from the time of your arrival.

Non-EU nationals
All non-EU nationals must pay a bond equivalent to a one-way plane ticket to their country of residence. You need to either deposit a bond to

that value (assessed by customs) or have a return ticket already in your possession. Bonds will be returned in Papeete or Raiatea, Huahine or Bora Bora. It's useful to make sure that the bank you deposit the bond with has a branch in the island you are departing from.

90 day visa: EU, Australia, Monaco, Norway, Switzerland, Brazil.

30 day visa: Argentina, Canada, Japan, NZ, USA.

Once you have cleared in you will need to check in with the gendarmerie (if there is one) at any other port you go to until you get to Papeete. In Papeete you need to go to the yacht clearance station at the harbour and complete formalities. This is quick and friendly. Here also you should ask for the duty free form so you can get duty free fuel.

CAUTION

You are prohibited from bringing in more than two litres of spirits and two litres of wine per person into French Polynesia. If customs searches your boat and discovers more it will be confiscated and you will have to pay a fine of anywhere between €200 to €500. We are not talking 'cruiser myth' here as I have been in the same anchorage as a boat that was searched, 80 litres of wine confiscated and a fine levied. On *Skylax* we were boarded by customs but explained that we had drunk most of our wine stock on board (nearly true). You are also limited to 200 cigarettes or 250gms of tobacco.

Reading

Charlies Charts of Polynesia Charles & Margo Wood. (Charlies Charts)

Guide to Navigation & Tourism in French Polynesia Patrick Bonnette & Emmanuel Deschamps. (A. Barthelemy)

My gem

Captain James Cook Richard Hough. (Coronet)

Le Truck in Papeete

Papeete market

Marina Taina in Papeete

Marae on Huahine

Bastille Day French Polynesian style

Point Venus on Tahiti

Marquesas

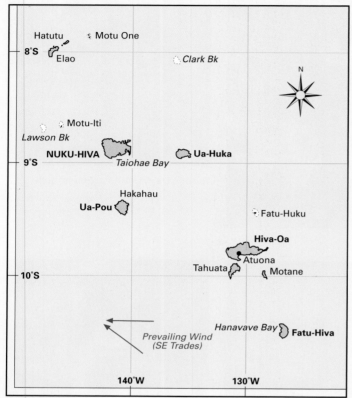

MARQUESAS

Anaho Bay on Nuka Hiva

The Marquesas are a lonely outpost under the equator seemingly miles from anywhere and the reality is that when you arrive here it feels like that. The high volcanic mountains jut up out of the sea in spectacular fashion with the pinnacles and razor-backed ridges lending a savage air to the islands. The islands first leapt into the western orbit with Herman Melville's *Typee* in 1846, a tale that has everything from sex and naked wahines to cannibalism and war. It defined the Marquesas as a savage South Sea paradise and Gauguin reaffirmed the idea of the islands as the last paradise when he settled in Atuona for his final years. He is buried here.

For the sailor from west coast USA or the Galapagos the Marquesas are a welcome landfall after a 3,000 mile plus passage. The islanders take it all in their stride, after all their ancestors made long ocean voyages all around the Pacific centuries ago in the Polynesian catamaran, and in fact the Marquesas has now been identified as one of the main hubs of Polynesian exploration and emigration in the Pacific. Despite the laid back attitude in the islands, the formalities must be adhered to and there has been a tightening of the regulations by the authorities in recent years.

Cruising strategies

From Galapagos the trick, it appears, is to stay in the W-going North Equatorial Current between the E-going North Equatorial Counter Current and the E-going South Equatorial Counter Current so as to get at worst no current and hopefully some W-going current. From reports from boats on passage it appeared that staying just north of the rhumb line route between Galapagos and Hiva Oa or Nuka Hiva would keep you in favourable current for most of the way. We had some current against us for the first 3–4 days, maybe 0.2-0.3 knots of E-going current, and then after that 0.2-0.5 knots of SW-going current all the way to Hiva Oa. One yacht which hove-to several times reported drifting 5 miles in 11 hours in a SW direction which would bear out our observations. Boats that went south of the rhumb line did experience contrary current and usually gybed over to come back north.

Because the North and South Equatorial Counter Currents do shift, staying north of the rhumb line route is not going to be an infallible rule, but as a general rule of thumb it should work. It's unlikely that yachts will go north of the equator and so encounter the North Equatorial Counter Current although yachts on passage to the Marquesas from central America or west coast USA will have to cross it at some time (see Coconut Milk Run).

Seasons and winds

Most yachts will be making the passage to the Marquesas some time between March to July so they can cruise the South Pacific outside the cyclone season (November to May). Cyclones rarely affect the Marquesas and some French yachts spend the summer cyclone season there. There seems to be some evidence that later (in June–July) will ensure better trade winds than earlier (March–April). The reliability of the trades also depends on whether the year is a La Nina, El Nino or neutral year. A neutral year seems to be best for consistent trades.

Old advice used to be go S to find consistent trades on passage from the Galapagos to Marquesas. Looking at wind reports over several months and talking to yachts on passage at different times of the year between February to June showed little difference between winds around 10–15°S and winds 0–10°S. If the trades were blowing then they would likely be blowing much the same at 5°S as at 15°S. Add to the general equation that going S means you will likely encounter adverse E-going current from the South Equatorial Counter Current and there seems every reason to take a more or less rhumb line route, or a route just to the N of it, say between 20–80 miles N depending on how you can shape your course.

From Galapagos you will likely encounter SE winds and occasionally S winds just S of the equator at around 20 knots for around five days to a week. That means the wind will be on the quarter for passage to the Marquesas. After that the wind will become a bit lighter at 12–20 knots and become more easterly which means running wing-and-wing much of the time, although occasionally it will go ESE and you will have the wind on the quarter.

Formalities
(See **French Polynesia** for full details).

Most yachts will head for Atuona on Hiva Oa to clear in. The reason for this is that it will be off the wind when cruising the other islands in the group. If you go to Taiohae on Nuka Hiva to clear in then you will need to beat back down the islands against the SE Trades and fairly big seas. The other ports where you can clear in are Taiohae on Nuka Hiva and, less commonly, Hakahau on Ua Pou.

The Fatu Hiva question Some yachts will make landfall on Fatu Hiva and spend time there before going to Atuona, but if the patrol boat does arrive while you are there and you haven't cleared in, then a fine will be levied. The days when French customs were more laid back with yachts is long gone.

Provisions
Provisions around the Marquesas are much dependent on the supply ship. If it has not been for a while then the islands will often start to run short of commodities. Some vegetables are grown on the islands but a surprising amount of vegetables are imported from Papeete. On Nuka Hiva where there are two small market gardens a pick-up will come down to Taiohae at around 0700 to 0730. Fruit can often be found in little stalls or word of mouth. The locals all have fruit trees so there is no great demand for it in the shops.

Gauguin museum in Atuona *Sam Coles*

Meat will often be frozen, though there is sometimes fresh meat available. Fish of course is fresh from the fish stall on the quay, but will often all be reserved for the hotels and restaurants.

Most basic stores can be found although there will be shortages of this or that depending on what there has been a run on. Fresh baguettes are made most days although in some places (Taiohae for example) the bakery closes at 0730 so you need to get there early.

Other facilities
The island capitals will have an ATM at the local bank or the PO. Wi-Fi can be found at the PO or for the anchorage in Taiohae on Nuka Hiva. Taxis are few and far between but the locals will often give you a lift if you stick your thumb out or not. Yacht repair facilities are virtually nil until you get to Papeete. Fuel is available in Atuona, Taiohae and Hakahau. In all these places you need to jerry can it back to the boat.

Anchoring
In nearly all of the anchorages the holding on sand or mud is excellent. In a lot of places you use a stern anchor to hold the boat into the swell. The only place I can think of where you don't need to do this is Anaho Bay on the NE corner of Nuka Hiva.

In the major towns there is usually a bit of quay or a pier where you can tie up the dinghy. In a lot of these it is useful to use a kedge to hold the dinghy off as there can be a fair amount of surge in places that will push the dinghy onto the rough concrete of the dock.

Reading
Exploring the Marquesas Joe Russell. (Fine Edge Productions)

My gem
Typee Herman Melville. (Penguin)

Atuona on Hiva Oa

Remarks

Taiohae grows on you and most cruisers stop here a while after the long passage from the USA or Galapagos. It is one of the centres of Marquesan tattooing and if you are interested this is the place to get your tattoo.

ATUONA (Hiva Oa)

Tidal range 1.2m

Navigation

The approach should be made by day. There is a bit of a tricky dog-leg to negotiate going into the harbour and there is little room to manoeuvre once inside.

Anchorage

Anchor fore and aft where possible. Keep clear of the area needed by the supply boat to berth on the dock. There is a yellow 'no anchoring' sign on the dock and a rock painted yellow on the NW side of the bay which you should keep behind. The bottom is mud with some rocks and old moorings, good holding. Good shelter although some swell curves around into the inlet and rebounds off the steep sides so you need the stern anchor to keep the bows pointing into the swell.

Facilities

Dinghy dock at the end of the commercial harbour. Use a kedge to keep your dinghy off the sharp rocks. Water tap near the dinghy dock. Petrol station (diesel and petrol) with a small shop on the commercial dock. It is about a 3km walk into Atuona itself (there is a shortcut across the beach) although you will frequently get a lift from the locals. In town there is the PO, bank, ATM, internet, several mini-markets and a café. The gendarmerie is also here,

Remarks

Atuona is a thoroughly friendly place where the locals will often just stop to give you a lift into town. You should visit the Gauguin Museum where all of his paintings are reproduced and a replica of his 'House of Pleasure' where he painted and … pleasured. He is buried here along with Jacques Brel, the Belgian chanteur.

Gambier Islands

The Gambier Islands are in the SE corner of the main South Pacific cruising area, SE of the Tuamotu Islands. They are the logical place to begin a downwind cruise of the South Pacific. They are enclosed within a reef, which is submerged in places.

RIKITEA (Mangareva Island)

Tidal range 1m

Navigation

Most islands in the group are high and should be seen well before arriving at the barrier reef. There is a well-marked channel through the reefs. Note that one of the leading lines takes you across a shoal.

Anchorage

Off the settlement as shown and well protected by reefs.

Facilities

Main settlement of the Gambier Islands but facilities are basic.

Remarks

Port of Entry. There are some notable churches on these islands, but their history is tragic.

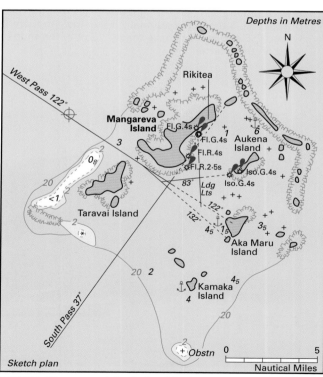

RIKITEA (Mangareva Island, Gambier Islands)
⊕23°05'S 135°05'W

ATUONA
⊕09°48'·52S 139°02'·0W WGS84

Tuamotu Islands

See plan page 178

The Tuamotu Islands are all atolls (bar one) with lagoons and motus of varying sizes. It is possible to navigate into all the larger lagoons ideally at slack water. To minimise windward sailing, any routes through the group should start at the easternmost desired atoll and work W from there.

TIPUTA (Rangiroa)

Tidal range 1m

Navigation

Of the two passes in Rangiroa the Tiputa Pass is bigger and better marked than the more westerly pass. Approaching the pass the red and white iron girder is easily seen and a number of other buildings on the plan can be identified. The two beacons showing the way in are easily identified once up to the pass: the front white tower is four metres high and the rear white tower seven metres high. The back markers for the second transit will be seen on the way in. Proceed around the sandy cay and coral reef with the markers and into the anchorage off the Kia Ora Hotel.

Anchorage

Where convenient on sand, good holding. There are a number of buoys and a couple of isolated bombies on the E side of the anchorage which are easily identified. Good shelter except from southerlies when a chop is set up across the large lagoon. In the event of southerlies (S-SW–WSW) let out more scope or lay a second anchor. It is rarely untenable in here. Dinghy dock on the W side of the pass or at the Kia Ora Hotel. Use a kedge for the dinghy.

Facilities

Limited provisions. Fuel can be arranged. Limited water from the dinghy dock. Garbage disposal ashore.

Remarks

The anchorage is one of the more popular but is rarely crowded. You can take a free tour to a pearl farm from the Kia Ora Hotel and the gendarmerie is conveniently close to the farm so you can clear in and out as well. The snorkelling over the reef in the pass is good and various companies run drift dives here which rams home the extent of the current flowing in and out of the pass.

Other atolls with relatively straightforward passes

These are not definitive but the following atolls have good passes (depending on the weather) and are popular with yachts cruising the Tuamotus.

Manihi, Ahe, Takaroa, Tikehau. Apataki, Aratika, Kauehi, Raroia, Makemo, Fakarava.

There are others and for adventurous souls there is a lot of interesting cruising through the group.

Society Islands

Tahiti, Moorea and Bora Bora are particularly famous. Landfalls are easy since all ports of entry are on high islands and will be seen long before arriving at reefs. The usual route is from Tahiti downwind to Moorea, Huahine, Raiatea/Tahaa, and Bora Bora, and perhaps to Maupiti and/or Maupiha. There are many possible anchorages.

The major base is Papeete and its associated anchorages extending W and E.

TIPUTA (Rangiroa, Tuamotu Islands)
⊕14°57'·59S 147°37'·23W WGS84

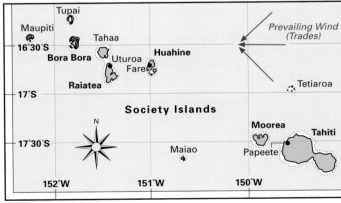

SOCIETY ISLANDS

Tuamotus

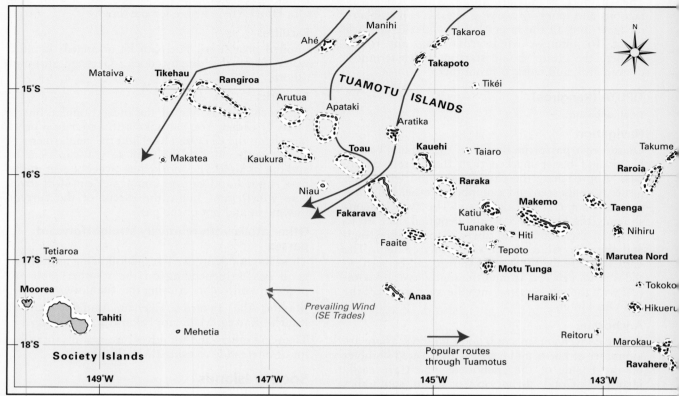

TUAMOTU ISLANDS

There are 79 atolls in the group with around 40 of the atolls populated. The population overall is not large and in some cases we are talking just a few families on an atoll. Rangiroa is the only atoll with a Gendarmerie where you need to check in.

Depending on your source the word Tuamotus means a lot of things: 'Islands Under the Clouds', 'Islands on the Ocean's Back', 'Low Islands', 'Many Islands' … take your pick. 'Motu' means a low island and I'd plump for 'Many'. The group has long been called the 'Dangerous Archipelago' by European navigators and despite modern navigation aids like radar, chart plotters and the like, they still are dangerous. SHOM charts (French Hydrographic Office) are the most reliable around the group, but even so caution is called for using any charts around the archipelago. Some of the larger and more populated atolls are better charted than the smaller less populated or deserted atolls. The immediate approaches anywhere in the Tuamotus must be made in daylight and with some care.

The islands generally won't be seen until five miles off and then you will see the coconut palms first. You can get a bit of an inkling of where they are from the clouds that form over the shallower and warmer water inside the atolls. The islands have passes through them of varying difficulty and you must time your transit for around slack water (see below). Have someone up front conning you in and wear polarised sunglasses to get the best contrast. On cloudy overcast days it is more difficult to pick up dangers under water and if in doubt slow right down and be prepared for a crash stop. Low-powered yachts may have difficulty powering through some of the passes against the current streaming out.

Pearl Farms

Many of the atolls have pearl farms growing black pearls in the Pacific black lipped oyster. Manihi had one of the first pearl farms and is still known as the black pearl centre of the Tuamotus although other atolls have large farms as well. You should stay well clear of the buoys limiting

Heading into a pass in the Tuamotus

the pearl farms. Most of the operators of the pearl farms are friendly to visiting yachts and you can get guided tours to many of them and, of course, the opportunity to buy black pearls. They are not cheap anywhere, but you are likely to get better quality pearls at a cheaper price than in Tahiti or the other Society Islands.

Cruising strategies

Which atolls you visit will depend on the time you have allotted for the Tuamotus and quite possibly some pressing need to get to Tahiti to do with visas, supplies and often friends coming out to visit. Everyone likes the sound of Tahiti and the idea of South Pacific Islands.

In general you should visit the most easterly islands first so you can cruise W-NW through the other atolls in the group with the E–SE Trades behind you. You will need to consult your pilot and a good chart of the Tuamotus to work out a route which suits your time and passages between the group. Sailing at night through the Tuamotus is not to be recommended, but is difficult to avoid in some instances depending on your itinerary. There are enough wrecks around the reefs in the Tuamotus to give anyone cause for concern and many of them date from the era of GPS.

A number of yachts have begun cruising around the atolls at the SE end of the archipelago that were formerly off-limits when the French used them as bases for the nuclear tests on Muraroa and Fangataufa. The French stopped nuclear testing in 1996 and several boats that have visited nearby atolls (not Muraroa or Fangataufa) showed no evidence of glowing green at night.

Passes

Around Tahiti and the Iles Sous le Vent you can use most of the main passes through the reef without regard to tides. There can be currents up to a couple of knots through some of the passes and in parts of the channel behind the barrier reef, but none of that will be too worrying when entering except to very low powered craft.

In the Tuamotus care is needed when timing your entry through a pass, especially for low-powered craft, although everyone needs to pay attention because there can be severe standing waves at times. There are two commonly used options for timing your entry and exit through a pass.

1. Slack water will be 12 hours from moonrise or moonset. Most GPS units have moonrise and moonset programmed into the unit and you can look it up there. Alternatively make a rough calculation from the actual moonrise or moonset (easily done when on passage). Or if you have an Almanac look in there.

2. Use tide tables to find slack water. A lot of yachts have tide tables for the world either on the laptop or sometimes on a chartplotter. We use Wxtide (www.wxtide32.com) and Tide Comp (see www.pangolin.co.nz). Using the 12 hour moonrise/set system you may find that the time for slack water does not exactly coincide with the tide tables, but it will be close.

It should be remembered that much of the flood out of the passes is from the trade wind swell crashing over the windward side of the atoll and exiting through the passes which are often on the leeward side of the atoll. If the trades have been boisterous and the swell high then the current out of the passes is likely to be strong because of the amount of water sloshed over the reefs into the lagoon. If the trades have not been boisterous then the current will be less. But remember there is still a tidal element to be considered and with boisterous trades you just need to be a lot more diligent about working out the time for entry and exit from the passes.

Dinghy Dock off the Kia Ora Hotel on Rangiroa

Getting the oysters ready for black pearl cultivation

Implanting the oysters so the itch grows a pearl

Rangiroa. When the wind blows across the lagoon a bit of chop develops, more uncomfortable than dangerous

PAPEETE (Tahiti)

Tidal range 0.3m

Navigation

All yachts must call Papeete Port Control on VHF Ch. 12 and obtain permission to enter the harbour. Papeete is a busy commercial harbour and there are always ferries and small coasters coming and going as well as larger ships. Arrival should be in daylight for a first time entry into the commercial harbour. The harbour is well lit for a night entry but for a first time approach the loom of lights in the town can make it confusing. The pass is straightforward at any state of tide.

Berths

25 berths. Visitors' berths. Max LOA 100m (by arrangement). Charge band 3.

Two pontoons can accommodate yachts here in the heart of Papeete. Good shelter although there is a bit of wash from boats using the harbour. Although there is a night watchman theft is still a problem here.

Facilities

Water and electricity on the pontoons. Fuel quay near the naval dock. Wi-Fi and internet cafés. Several boatyards on the outer quay near the entrance. Good yacht repair facilities including GRP and engineering work. Several chandlers on the E side of the commercial harbour.

Remarks

Right in the heart of the city with good shopping and market nearby. Noisy and care needed over theft.

Formalities

The Yacht Clearance Office is a one-stop dedicated office for yachts with customs and harbourmaster in the one building. It is efficient and friendly. You must clear in here as the final stage of formalities. You must also clear out before you leave and this is the final clearance you will need before leaving French Polynesia. Make sure you ask for your duty free fuel papers here and you can then take on duty free fuel in the commercial docks, at Marina Taina, or the Tahiti Yacht Club. You only need to present the duty free papers at the fuel dock to the attendant who will stamp it and charge you the duty free price.

Chenal Faaa

The channel which runs around from Papeete port to Marina Taina and the anchorage is well buoyed and easy to transit by day. All craft five metres or more high must call Papeete Port Control on VHF Ch 12 when they get to the airport perimeter. There is a large sign in English and French here. Port Control will give you permission to pass or if any large planes are landing or taking off will tell you to wait until it is clear. When you get to the end of the airport you must call again to inform Port Control you are clear.

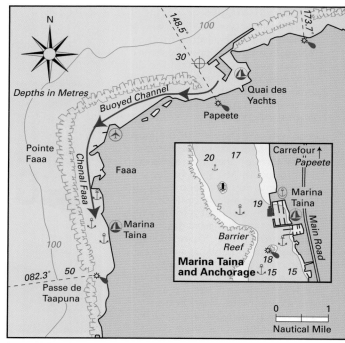

PAPEETE AND CHENAL FAAA
⊕17°32'·05S 149°35'·17W WGS84

Marina Taina and anchorage

Using Chenal Faaa you can get to Marina Taina and the anchorage off it (around 5M from Papeete port). VHF Ch 09 and 16

c.150 berths. Visitors' berths. Max LOA c.80m. Charge band 3.

Berth stern-to or alongside where directed. On the outside berths use your anchor and then supply a long line (or two) for the diver to take to a mooring

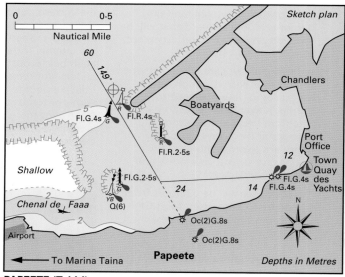

PAPEETE (Tahiti)
⊕17°32'·05S 149°35'·17W WGS84

on the bottom. Good shelter if a little bumpy at times. In the high season (July/August) you may have to wait for a day or two to get a berth.
Email marinataina@mail.pf

Anchorage

The anchorage behind the barrier reef off the marina is the most popular place for yachts to be, although it is now somewhat encumbered with permanent moorings. Anchor in 4–20 metres (depending how close you are to the reef) on sand and a bit of mud near the coast. Good holding. Excellent shelter in flat water. There is a dinghy dock at the marina.

Facilities

Water and electricity in the marina. Fuel dock. Yacht services. Small chandlers. Laundromat. Large Carrefour supermarket about five minutes walk away. Wi-Fi. Restaurants and bars. Mini-buses or Le Truck into downtown Papeete.

Remarks

It is clean enough to swim and snorkel over the reef. The marina is friendly towards visiting cruisers and it is about 15 minutes on the bus to Papeete. The airport is nearby.

RAIATEA

Navigation

Entry through Passe Teavapiti is straightforward. The channels behind the reefs are clearly marked.

Berths

Utuaroa
Go alongside. Fuel and water. Supermarket nearby.
Marina Apoiti Limited berths. Moorings. Water and electricity. Wi-Fi.

Raiatea Carenage
Moorings or anchor off. 25 ton travel hoist. Most yacht repairs. Chandlers. Wi-Fi.
www.raiatea.com/carenage

Remarks

The boatyard here is the last comprehensive yard before you get to New Zealand or New Caledonia.

Austral Islands

The group has all high islands and should be seen long before approaching the reefs. There are four islands with ports of entry: Rurutu, Raivavae, Tubuai and Rapa. Navigation between islands is easy.

RAIRUA (Raivavae)

Tidal range 0.5m

Navigation

Raivavae is surrounded by a lagoon, which can easily be entered by the well-marked pass. The alternative pass has several dangerous coral heads.

Anchorage

A calm and well-protected anchorage is near the wharf. Beware of coral close by.

Facilities

Supplies are limited. Piped water available at the wharf.

Remarks

Port of Entry. Rairua is one of the ports at the end of the semi-southern route from the W South Pacific to the E.

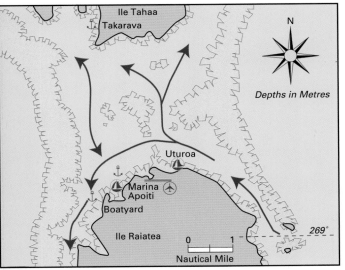

RAIATEA AND TAHAA

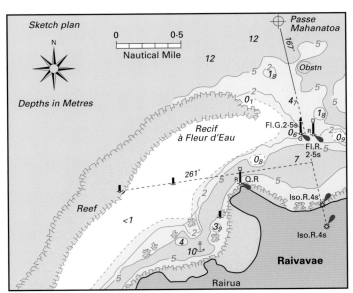

RAIRUA (Raivavae)
⊕23°50′·0S 147°40′·56W

Cook Islands

General The Cook Islands are self-governing but have close ties with New Zealand. The most populous island is Rarotonga.

Formalities The ports of entry are Rarotonga, Aitutaki and Penrhyn. It is not necessary to visit a port of entry before visiting Suvarov. There is a $25 departure tax at Rarotonga.

Telecom IDD +682.

Currency New Zealand dollar. There are banks in Rarotonga but banking elsewhere is minimal. ATMs available.

Sailing season May to October.

Routes and harbours Most yachts arrive sailing downwind from French Polynesia. Going N or S the passage is a reach. The landfall at Rarotonga is no problem since this is a high island without off-lying reefs. Aitutaki, which is a lovely island but has little water in the pass, is a moderately high island with a barrier reef and islets some miles offshore and requires caution in the approach, which should be made from the NE. The N Cook Islands are atolls, but only two, Suvarov and Penrhyn, have passes into the lagoon suitable for a yacht, the latter has few islets on the surrounding reef and can be difficult to pick up until very close.

RAROTONGA

Tidal range 0.8m

Navigation

VHF Ch 16. Contact *Port Control* for permission to enter the harbour.

Avatiu is the only viable place for a yacht.

Entrance should be made by day and in onshore winds care is needed.

Berths

The basin is very small and you must squeeze in wherever you can. Yachts anchor and take a long line ashore. Shelter is adequate with the trade winds. Yachts are not encouraged to stay during the cyclone season as this is not a safe harbour with strong winds.

Facilities

Water on the quay. Fuel by jerry can or large amounts by tanker. Internet café. Good shopping for provisions and fruit and vegetables. Most goods are shipped in from New Zealand.

Remarks

Despite the harbour most cruisers love this friendly town and the islanders are a fun-loving lot. More Cook Islanders live in New Zealand than on the islands.

SUVAROV (SUWARROW)

Tidal range 0.6m

Navigation

The pass is easily entered, but the current can be quite strong, up to 3kn.

Anchorage

The main anchorage is on the W of Anchorage Island which lies to the W of the pass. The holding is not good.

Remarks

The atoll of Suvarov is uninhabited except for a national park ranger and his family, who have been most welcoming. A charge is made for visiting here

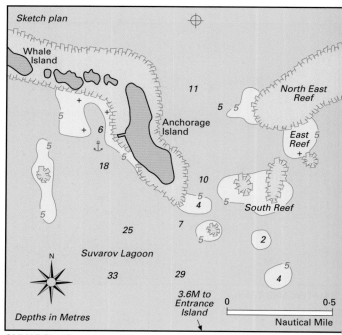

AVATIU (Rarotonga)
⊕21°12'·0S 159°47'·0W (0·2M N of entrance - not shown)

SUVAROV (Cook Islands)
⊕13°14'·4S 163°06'·0W

payable to the rangers. The park headquarters is on Entrance Island. The rangers control yachts and determine their length of stay.

PALMERSTON ATOLL

Palmerston Atoll anchorage (and moorings) 18°02'·84S 163°11'·57W

This atoll can be visited in settled trade wind conditions. The approach is best made in daylight where the reef and *motus* will be clearly seen from around 4–5 miles off. The anchorage off the reef is exposed to any winds except easterlies and should not be used in bad weather. Six moorings here can be used by visiting yachts and are generally in reasonable condition (they have been known to break). If you have not cleared into the Cook Islands you will need to do so here. A small charge is made for the moorings.

Yachts are welcomed here and often locals who need to leave will hitch a lift west. There is around one supply ship a year. Ashore the welcome is overwhelming.

 ## American Samoa

General This is an overseas territory of the USA.

Formalities There is a US$25 clearance fee both at entry and again at exit. Clearance is at the rough customs jetty. US visas are required.

Telecom IDD +684. Overseas calls are made at the Communications Office. Phones and internet are also available at the seamen's mission.

Currency US dollar. There are ATM machines.

Routes and harbours Landfall is easy since Tutuila is a high island. There are banks well offshore in the approach to Pago Pago, over which there can be dangerous waves. There are a number of anchorages on the N coast, but Pago Pago is the only one on the S.

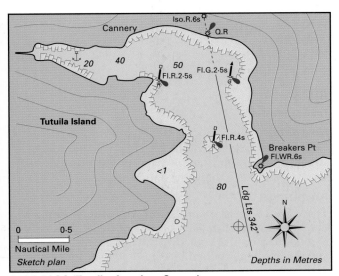

PAGO PAGO (Tutuila, American Samoa)
⊕14°18'·0S 170°40'·0W

PAGO PAGO (Tutuila)

Tidal range 1m

Anchorage

Holding is poor, expect the anchor to drag in any wind. Though the anchorage is sheltered strong gusts can drop from the surrounding hills.

Facilities

There are a few shops and supplies available.

 ## Samoa

General The Samoan Islands are high, beautiful and heavily populated. Savaii is the largest but Upoli has most of the population. By far the majority of the population are Samoan. The Polynesian hospitality tradition is still strong in areas where there are few visitors.

Formalities The port of entry is Apia. Initial contact should be made on VHF Ch 16. Permission must be sought from the Prime Minister's and Customs Departments before visiting other ports and anchorages. Clearance is at the wharf. The Samoa Ports Authority levies charges; Charge band 2 for seven days.

Telecom IDD +685. Overseas calls at the International Telephone Bureau.

Currency Tala. There is a bank in Apia.

Routes and harbours Landfalls are not a problem,

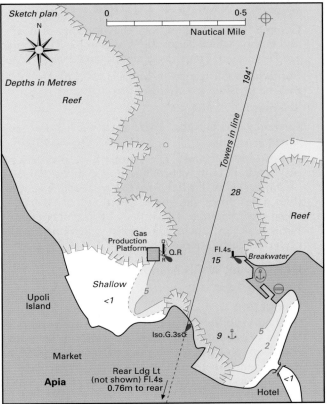

APIA (Upoli, Samoa)
⊕13°48'·5S 171°45'·6W

with the islands being so high that they will be seen visually or on radar long before the reefs are encountered. A circumnavigation of one or both major islands will enable visits to many beautiful and attractive anchorages. There can be strong currents in different directions in the strait between Upoli and Savaii. Exceptionally there can be a 4-knot current to the W outside Apia Harbour. The current on the S coast of Upoli is to the E. The principle anchorages are Apia and Asau, but there are rarely many yachts at either.

APIA (Upoli)

Tidal range 1.2m

Anchorage

There is good holding, protected from the prevailing weather but open to the N, but N winds are very rare in season.

Facilities

There is an excellent large market with a great variety of cheap vegetables and fruit. There is a good range of shops and mechanical facilities, but not much specifically for yachts. The yacht club welcomes visiting crews.

Remarks

Apia is the biggest town between Tahiti and Fiji and makes a good base for exploring Samoa, with adequate bus services to all parts of Upoli and bus and ferry to the villages on Savaii.

Wallis & Futuna

General France administers the territory of Wallis and Futuna which lies to the W of Samoa. The people are Polynesian. French is generally understood.

Formalities Clearance at Wallis is at Mata Ua but it may be possible to organise it from Gahi.

Telecom IDD +681.

Currency Pacific franc. There are no ATM machines. There is a bank.

Routes and harbours The Futuna Group makes an easy landfall, with reefs extending no more than ½M offshore, but Wallis has a barrier reef, which is up to four miles from the main island. Care is needed when approaching. The only tenable anchorage at Futuna is an open roadstead so Wallis is the preferred destination.

GAHI (Uvea, Wallis Islands)

Tidal range 1.5m

Navigation

In good visibility the approach to the anchorages at Wallis is not difficult. There are tidal currents and eddies up to 6kn in the Honikulu Pass into the Wallis lagoon, and up to 4kn in the inner, Faioa Pass. It may be necessary to wait for slack water, which occurs 30 minutes to two hours before HW and 15 to 45 minutes after LW. The time differences are

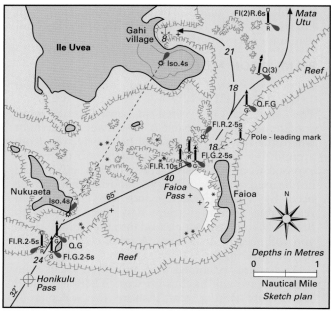

GAHI (Uvea, Wallis Islands)
⊕13°24′S 176°13′·4W

greatest at spring tides but are much influenced by the amount of sea breaking over the reef. The leading line for the pass is not easily seen. It consists of a white rock just off the SE point of Nukuaeta Island, and a white triangle on a grey wall on top of a hill on the main island (Uvea).

Once inside the pass there is another leading line. There should also be other beacons on the track to Gahi. The track to Mata Utu also has some beacons. In good visibility the lagoon is a delight to navigate.

Anchorage

The anchorage at the main village, Mata Utu, is exposed to the prevailing wind and is uncomfortable. The recommended anchorage is at Gahi.

Facilities

At Mata Utu there are a bank, Post Office, government offices, a supermarket and other services.

Niue

Niue is an independent country with close associations with NZ. Currency is NZ$.

ALOFI

Tidal range 0.6m

Navigation

Call *Niue Radio* on VHF Ch 16. The approach is straightforward and free of dangers but the approach should be made in daylight only.

Anchorage

There are 18 yacht moorings off Alofi administered by the Niue Yacht Club. Pick up one of these. This is not a good place to use your own anchor as it is very deep and the holding is poor. Once moored wait for customs to contact you or call *Niue Radio* on Ch 16 for instructions.

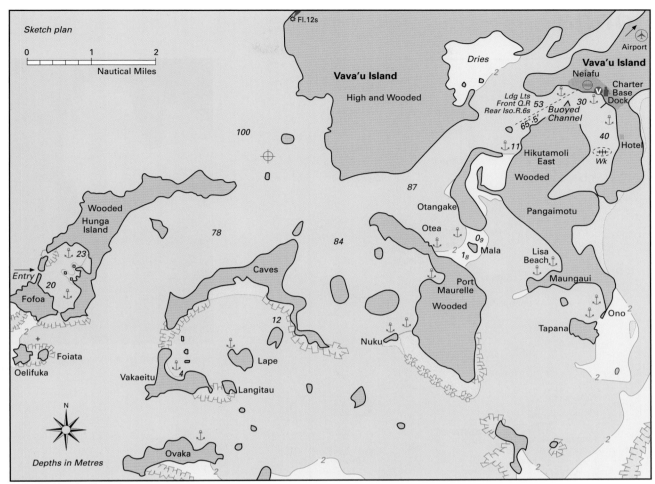

NEIAFU (Vava'u, Tonga)
⊕18°39'·88S 174°04'·42W WGS84

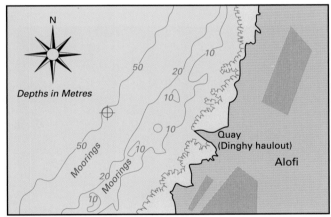

NIUE (ALOFI)
⊕19°03'·1S 169°55'·4W

Shelter here is adequate in settled trade wind conditions although you will roll around a bit. You take your dinghy over to the quay and use the small crane here to haul it out of the water. You will need a suitable strop to do this.

Facilities

Water and fuel by jerry can. Laundry and WC/showers. Wi-Fi. Some provisions and restaurants and bars.

Remarks

The Niue Yacht Club welcomes cruising yachts to this little island and a stay here is well worth the inconvenient anchorage.

 # Tonga

General The people are Polynesians. These islands are much visited by yachts: the Vava'u group is usually included in the cruise of a yacht crossing the South Pacific and it is also a popular destination for New Zealand yachts.

Formalities The ports of entry (from N to S) are Niuatoputapu, Neiafu on Vava'u, Lifuka on Ha'apai and Nuku'alofa on Tongatapu.

Telecom IDD +853. The phone system is via a satellite link and is good, but expensive. Internet services available.

Currency Pa'anga. There are banks in Nuku'alofa, Lifuka and Neiafu. ATMs.

Routes and harbours The route S from Niuatoputapu is open ocean, but from the Vava'u group S to Nuku'alofa it is possible to cruise by day-sailing between the beautiful anchorages of the Ha'apai group.

Tonga

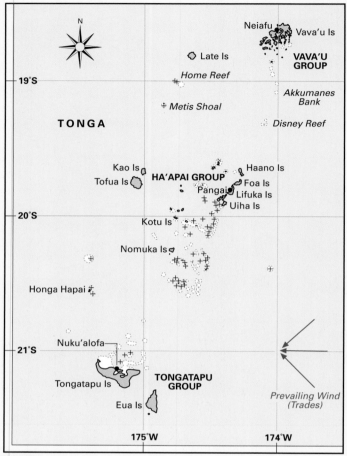

TONGA

Swallows Cave in the Vava'u group

Approach to Vava'u in the early morning

The Tongan archipelago stretches in a line more or less north to south over a distance of 500 miles from just north of 16°S for the northern Tongatapu group to 24°S at the Minerva Reefs. There are over 170 islands with around 50 inhabited. The island chain lies along the Tonga Trench (32,000 ft/9,900m), mostly just to the east of the trench, which is where three tectonic plates, the Pacific Plate, Tonga Plate and Australian Plate grind into each other. The edges of the plate grinding together let magma through which gives rise to a lot of underwater volcanic activity and if you look at the chart you will see volcanic activity reported all around the Tonga chain.

'Coral Garden' in the Vava'u group

The volcanoes include Tofua off the Ha'apai group where Bligh and some of his crew were put in a gig by the mutineers on The Bounty. The Ha'apai Islands are also where Captain Cook came close to being killed except, so the story goes, that the Tongans couldn't agree on the spoils so never actually got around to killing him.

Cruising strategies

Most cruisers will head for Neiafu on the Vava'u group which is an easy landfall with steep land and good depths off it when approaching around the north of the main island. Yachts which want to visit the northern Tongatapu group will usually visit Niuatoputapu (commonly referred to as 'new potatoes') first before dropping down to the Vava'u group. This is also the logical route from Samoa.

Anchorage off Big Mamas Yacht Club in Nuku'alofa

Many yachts heading west on the Coconut Milk Run will visit Niue first before heading for the Vava'u group or less commonly the southern Tongatapu group.

From the Vava'u group yachts can head down through the Ha'apai group (arguably the most beautiful part of Tonga) and then down to Nuku'alofa on Tongatapu. Some yachts will head directly to New Zealand from Neiafu though most leave from Nuku'alofa. Depending on the weather yachts can stop at Minerva Reef, usually North Minerva.

Seasons and winds

Cruising here is in the southern winter. Most yachts will head for New Zealand or west to Australia in October and November to be out of the area for the summer cyclone season (November to May). Historically there have been few

Yacht basin at Nuku'alofa

Vava'u Yacht Club in Neiafu

Friday evening race in Neiafu
Katrina Sewell

Cricket match in a village on Vava'u

cyclones through Tonga in November and early December with January through till March the worst months.

In the southern winter temperatures are tropical throughout the group. There can be more rain than most people appreciate and the Southern Pacific Convergence Zone (SPCZ) will often shift down over the group, particularly the northern group including the Vava'u group, bringing unsettled squally overcast weather with rain, sometimes with lots of rain. You tend to get 3–4 days of nice sunny weather and then 3–4 days where it is overcast and it rains.

Formalities
You need to call up Port Control on VHF Ch 16 to advise them of your arrival.

Clearing into Tonga is relatively simple and low-key, though you must play by the rules. In Neiafu you go alongside the commercial dock and the authorities will come to the boat (the offices are all just behind the commercial quay). The only problem with this is that the commercial quay has huge rubber fenders for commercial ships and at low tide these are at stanchion height. Try to time it for high tide and have all your fenders out. With even moderate winds from the SE a slop is set up on the quay. If you can go on the shorter western end where there are sufficient depths and you will be partially blown off.

The officials generally arrive promptly. There are a number of forms to fill in and mostly you will do this yourself, though not necessarily all.

Immigration Will want your passports, crew list, boat papers and exit papers from the last port. You can be fined if you don't have your exit papers.

Customs Passports and boat papers.

Health You need to fill in a form and pay a fee (30 pa'angas in 2009)

MAF You need to fill in a form and pay a fee (28 pa'angas in 2009). He will take away your old garbage.

If you don't have the local currency they are happy for you to bring it in later when you have been ashore to the ATM. In general it was all very amicable and they all sat below with coffee and cookies while we shot the breeze and filled in forms.

In Nuku'alofa you can anchor off and clear in and out without presenting your boat. The harbourmaster is in town, but all the other offices are on the commercial docks (Queen Salote Wharf). The entrance is just E of the yacht harbour.

Ashore
In Neiafu and Nuku'alofa things are pretty well set up for cruising boats.

Neiafu Most of the bars and restaurants in Neiafu are reliant on the annual migration of yachties arriving here and they provide a good service at a reasonable cost. Neiafu is quite deep to anchor in and mooring buoys are scattered all around the bay (US$6–8 per day).

There are also services like an internet café, Wi-Fi over the anchorage, laundry, water (sometimes brackish), and fuel. Provisions are limited although the fresh fruit and vegetable market is good.

Nuku'alofa Most yachts anchor off Big Mama's Yacht Club. Bar and restaurant ashore. Most things can be organised through the club (laundry, fuel, etc.), but in fact its better to go in the harbour at Nuku'alofa for fuel and water. Shopping in Nuku'alofa town is good and there is an excellent fresh fruit and vegetable market. Big Mama's YC runs a regular ferry service over to the main dock and back.

Facilities

Yachts can be hauled on a primitive sledge at Neiafu or craned onto the hard by arrangement in Nuku'alofa. Yacht spares are few and far between and while there are basic skills for engines and mechanical work, there is little else. Most spares can be flown in from NZ.

Reading

Cruising Guide to the Vava'u Island Group in the Kingdom of Tonga The Moorings. You can also download an older version of this guide from www.tongasailing.com/tonga_charters.htm

Sailingbird's Guide to the Kingdom of Tonga Charles Paul & Katherine Pham-Paul. (Sailingbird Publications)

My gem

Mutiny on the Bounty (the older movie with Marlon Brando).

Market in Neiafu

Weaving in Pangaimotu in the Ha'apai group

Local shop in Pangai in the Ha'apai group

Vavau Tonga

Vava'u is a high island and there are no off-lying reefs to the NE, N or NW. It is therefore an easy landfall if approached from these directions. The E coast of Tongatapu is also fairly steep-to but not high.

The approach from the E through Piha Passage has currents of up to 4kn. Passages through the barrier reef in Ha'apai Group can have tidal currents of up to 5kn and these are up to 2kn off the N point of the Group. There are very many coral reefs. These are marked or there are leading lines on the approaches to the three main ports. Elsewhere adequate visibility and care is needed.

The main base is at Neiafu in Vava'u, with both charter and visiting yachts.

NEIAFU (Vava'u)

Tidal range 1.2m

Navigation

Vava'u is a favoured place to clear into Tonga because the approaches around the N side of Vava'u Island are deep and clear of dangers. While it is possible to make a night approach it is best to heave-to and approach by day. If you arrive on a weekend when the authorities have closed anchor in Port Maurelle until Monday and then go into Neiafu.

Berths

Moorings in Neiafu. If you want to anchor it is mostly very deep at around 20 metres plus. The holding is uncertain in places with loose coral blocks on the bottom. Good shelter in flat water.

NUKU'ALOFA (Tongatapu)

Tidal range 1.2m

Navigation

Passage through the Northern Channel or through the E Piha Channel should be made by day. Most of the navigation aids are in place though not all. In the Piha Channel tides can run at 3–4 knots in the narrow section coming into Nuku'alofa so consult some tide tables so you come in on the stream.

Berths

Nuku'alofa small craft basin Around 15 berths. Anchor in mud and take a long line ashore to the outer breakwater. Good shelter.

Big Mamas Yacht Club Anchor off Big Mamas on Pangaimotu. It is quite deep here and you will be anchoring in 15–20 metres in most places. Good holding and good shelter from the trades.

Facilities

Water on the fishermans wharf opposite and diesel by arrangement with the BP station or by jerry can. Supermarkets a block behind the main road running into the town centre. Internet, Post Office and ATMs in town.

Big Mamas operates a ferry service into the small craft basin and can arrange for water, fuel and laundry. Good restaurant and bar.

Remarks

Big Mamas is the favoured place as it is secure and you can swim off the boat and clean the bottom for the passage down to New Zealand. Nuku'alofa town is a pleasant enough place and functions as normal after the 2006 riots against the monarchy.

MINERVA REEF

North Minerva Reef is a useful anchorage to get a 250 mile start on the Tonga or Fiji to New Zealand passage. The passage through the pass on the NW side is straightforward by day although there can be up to three knots of current. Most of the reef appears to be free of coral heads inside the reef but proceed with care. Anchor on sand and coral in 8–15 metres under the reef depending on wind direction. Good holding on sand and coral. Good protection although at high tide there can be some slop from the swell washing over the top of the reef.

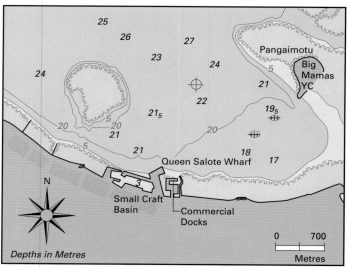

PANGAIMOTU
⊕21°07'·5S 175°10'·4W

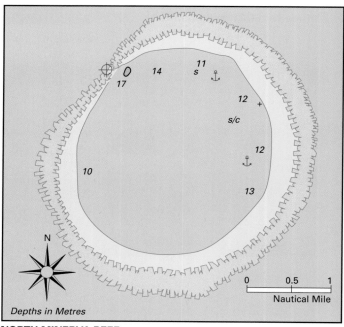

NORTH MINERVA REEF
⊕ 23°37'·33S 178°55'·85W WGS84

The following waypoints should be useful but use with care.

Approaches: 23°37'·00S 178°56'·20W
               23°37'·28S 178°56'·00W
Pass: 23°37'·33S 178°55'·85W

South Minerva Reef can also be used but is a little more tricky to enter with a dog-leg entrance through the coral.

Fiji

General Fiji is a friendly and beautiful country. The outer islands have preserved their traditions and lifestyle far better than many other Pacific destinations. Unfortunately, it has been politically unstable and governments have been changed by force. Previous instability has had only minimal effects on visiting yachtsmen.

Coastline There are two main islands, Viti Levu, the largest, and Vanua Levu to the NE. To the NW of Viti Levu and the SE of Vanua Levu are extensive island groups. There are many other islands. Coral reefs fringe most islands and the whole is a fascinating, if challenging, cruising ground.

Formalities Yachts must now notify Fiji Customs at least 48 hours before arrival. Notification can be by Form C2C on the Fijian Customs website www.frca.org.fj. The form can be emailed to yachtsreport@frca.org.fj.

A fine up to F$20,000 and even a term of imprisonment can be demanded for non-compliance.

Masters are required to enter the yacht within 24 hours. Expect to pay for service from customs officers after 1600 on weekdays and at weekends and holidays. The yacht must get an outward clearance before going to another port of entry or cruising the coast. In addition, documentary approval from the appropriate Provincial Authority must be carried. Ports of entry are Suva, Lautoka, Levuka and Savusavu. The more usual entry ports are Suva and Lautoka. Despite the reefs both are sufficiently lit to allow entry at night.

Telecom IDD +679. GSM network. Internet access in most towns.

Currency Fiji dollar. There are ATM machines at Suva and Lautoka. There are banks in all sizeable towns.

Routes and harbours The most popular route is from Suva to Nadi Waters and its resorts, either direct or by way of Kandavu Island. Other popular routes are a circle of the Lau group from Suva, the route N past Savusavu to Samoa or Wallis, and the circuit of the Yasawa Islands from Nadi Waters. Coming downwind from Vava'u, Savusavu is a very convenient entry point as it allows a downwind cruise through much of Fiji's waters. The main sailing bases are Suva (including the Trade Winds Hotel), Lautoka (including resorts in Nadi Waters such as Malololailai) and Savusavu.

Resources In several areas, the Fiji Navy has produced excellent new charts. These are available at the main sailing centres. The only detail charts of the Yasawa Islands are the Pickmere charts (available in New Zealand).

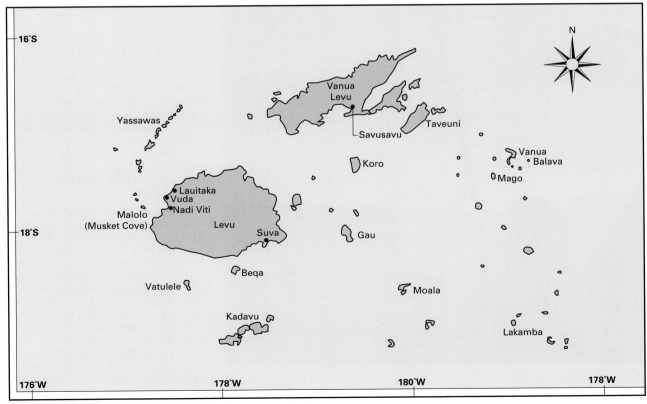

FIJI

Passage from the Tropics to New Zealand

Traversing the front

And motoring through the high

The passage from Tonga (or Fiji or New Caledonia/Vanuatu) to NZ is the great lemming leap from the Tropics and settled Trade Wind weather into the sub-Tropics and unsettled Spring weather. Hours, days, weeks are spent analysing weather, signing up for weather routing, downloading shed-loads of GRIB files and generally just worrying about it. This is the time for what NZ weather guru Bob McDavitt calls 'Analysis Paralysis'.

One of the problems for the Tonga to Opua passage is that lows come across from Australia every 6–7 days. Given that most yachts can't maintain a sufficient speed to do the 1,100–1,200 mile passage in six days, the likelihood is that you will hit a low somewhere on passage. So it's a matter of judging how low a low is and how dirty the associated front is going to be. This is where getting weather routing from someone like Bob McDavitt helps make sense of GRIB files. While GRIBS are great for the general picture, they don't give you much of an idea what fronts, troughs and ridges are going to be like and how strong squalls will likely be.

In settled weather for the sub-Tropics the general advice is that you leave on the back of a low and keep to the west of the rhumb line, heading for somewhere around 30°S and 175°E before turning south for Opua or other ports on the east coast of NZ. The thinking here is that when the next low comes along you will likely have SW winds and getting a bit of westing in will help you lay a course for Opua and other destinations with the SW winds.

There is another consideration not too often thought about. When the lows are not around there will generally be a high and motoring through the high can take a couple of days assuming you are not going to be sitting around waiting for wind. At this time of year most boats have been in the Tropics for some time and the antifouling has lost a lot of its 'anti'. Boats are pretty fouled up on the bottom. The prop also fouls up badly and you need to try to get it as clean as possible. The

All fouled up on arrival in NZ

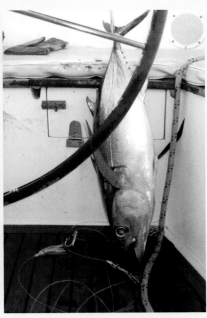

Good fishing coming into NZ waters

Tail-end of a front on passage to NZ

result of all this is that you are going to be a lot slower motoring through the high in whatever leftover swell there is compared to when the boat is clean. This all increases the passage time to NZ.

A lot of yachts head for North Minerva Reef before setting off for NZ and this gives you a 250-odd mile start on the passage. You can then sit here and wait for a weather window for the passage from Minerva Reef to NZ.

One other thing that cruisers in the Tropics encounter here is that it is cold after Tropical days and nights. All the woollies come out of the locker where they have been consigned for nearly a year and wet weather gear keeps the wind chill out. It's only Spring in NZ and sitting here in Opua it's definitely a lot more chilly than up north in the Tropics.

Bob McDavitt: More info at www.pangolin.co.nz/yotreps/list–manager.php
Feedback: Email bob.mcdavitt@metservice.com
Bob costs out his service to the NZ Met Service and it will typically be around NZ$50–80.

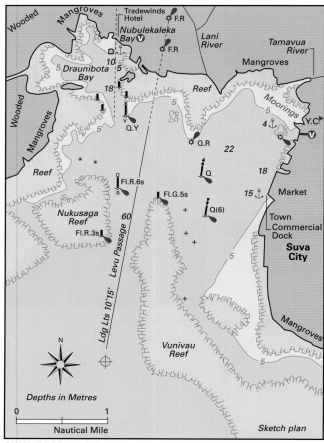

SUVA (Viti Levu, Fiji)
⊕18°10'·0S 178°23'·6E

SUVA (Viti Levu)

Tidal range 1.8m

Navigation

The harbour is well marked and easy to enter.

Berths

The club's marina may have room for visitors. There is greater security from thieves alongside the Trade Winds Hotel in Nubulekaleka Bay. Charge band 2.

Anchorage

Off the Royal Suva Yacht Club, good holding in mud. Sometimes the authorities may require the yacht to anchor where shown to the N of the commercial dock while awaiting clearance. Nubulekaleka Bay is an enclosed and safe anchorage.

Facilities

There is a slipway for haulouts. Fuel, water and limited yacht supplies are available. All marine engineering facilities are available and the town can supply most needs. The club is very friendly, with a restaurant, barbecues and hot showers.

Remarks

Suva is a port of entry. There have been thefts from boats.

SAVUSAVU HARBOUR (Vanua Levu)

Tidal range 1.5m

Berths

The Copra Shed Marina, near the town centre, provides berthing alongside or mooring hire. Charge band 2.

Anchorage

Moorings take up most of the available space. It is possible to anchor further up the creek, some distance from town.

Facilities

Hot showers, fuel, chandlery, charts, a restaurant and bar at the friendly and helpful marina. The town has supermarkets, banks and a good fresh produce market.

Remarks

Savusavu Harbour is a port of entry.

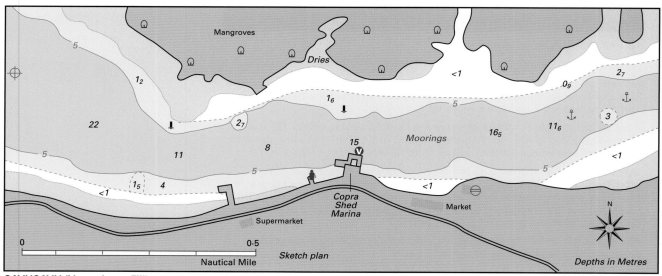

SAVUSAVU (Vanua Levu, Fiji)
⊕16°46'·6S 179°19'·6E

New Zealand

General A high proportion of all the yachts cruising the South Pacific arrive here at some time. It is not exaggerating to say that New Zealand is a yachtsman's paradise with excellent facilities, competitive prices, friendly people and much to see and do on land.

Coastline The North and South Islands (crossing the latitudes from sub-tropical to cool temperate) and off-lying islands provide a long and varied coast. With the exception of Fiordland, in the S, the W coast is exposed, with few ports. The E coast is more hospitable but there are still long stretches between ports. The primary cruising areas are the NE coast of North Island and the N coast of South Island.

Formalities Ports of entry (from N to S) are Opua (Bay of Islands), Whangarei, Auckland, Tauranga, Napier, New Plymouth, Wellington, Nelson, Christchurch (Lyttleton), Timaru, Dunedin, and Bluff. Unless written permission is obtained yachts must arrive and depart at a port of entry. Nationals of some countries need to obtain visas prior to arrival. US, Australian and EU citizens are exempt. It is a requirement that the master gives 48 hours' notice of arrival and port of entry. This can be done by calling Taupo *Maritime Radio* on 4125Khz or online by emailing yachts@customs.govt.nz . For more information go to www.customs.govt.nz/Visiting+craft/ . Advice will be given as to the clearance jetty. There is a separate quarantine (MAF) clearance. This can be done 24 hours a day, seven days a week. It is illegal for anyone except customs and police to board the yacht or for anything to leave until this is done.

Telecom IDD +64. There are both analogue and GSM systems. Internet service available everywhere.

Currency New Zealand dollar. ATMs which accept most but not all credit cards.

Sailing season All year but mostly in the summer months. There are no cyclones but the aftermath of a cyclone, a deep depression, may cause storm force winds. There is plenty of warning.

Routes and harbours Approaching the ports listed below from the N is straightforward. On the Trans-Tasman routes Pandora Bank, SW of Cape Reinga, is especially dangerous as steep and breaking seas occur on this bank with a heavy SW sea or swell and a confused sea may extend 10 miles to the W. At the Three Kings Islands there are tidal currents of up to 3kn and tidal races. Tidal currents from the islands S to Cape Reinga can reach 4kn in places.

Most visiting yachts visit the many harbours and anchorages on the Northland E coast and the Hauraki Gulf and some get to the Bay of Plenty. Not many sail further S but if a circumnavigation of New Zealand or North Island is planned, the usual route is S along the W coast and N along the SE coast.

There are yachting facilities at all entry ports. In addition there are popular sailing bases or anchorages at Whangaroa and Tutukaka Harbours, Bon Accord Harbour at Kawau Island, Port Fitzroy and Tryphena at Great Barrier Island, Mayor Island in the Bay of Plenty, and Picton and Havelock in the Marlborough Sounds.

NORTHLAND

Opua, in the Bay of Islands, and Whangarei are often the arrival and departure points for New Zealand. There is usually only a low swell on the E coast and a lot of sheltered anchorages along the indented coast.

OPUA

Tidal range 2.5m

Navigation

The bay can be entered in any weather and shelter found. A directional green/white/red light at Waitangi leads in from the open sea.

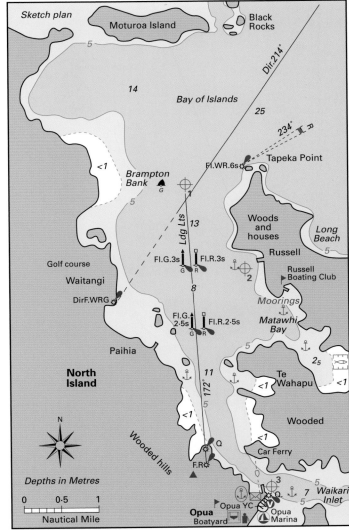

APPROACHES TO OPUA
1 ⊕ 35°14'·6S 174°06'E
2 ⊕ 35°15'·75S 174°07'E
3 ⊕ 35°18'·75S 174°07'·33E WGS84

Cruising New Zealand

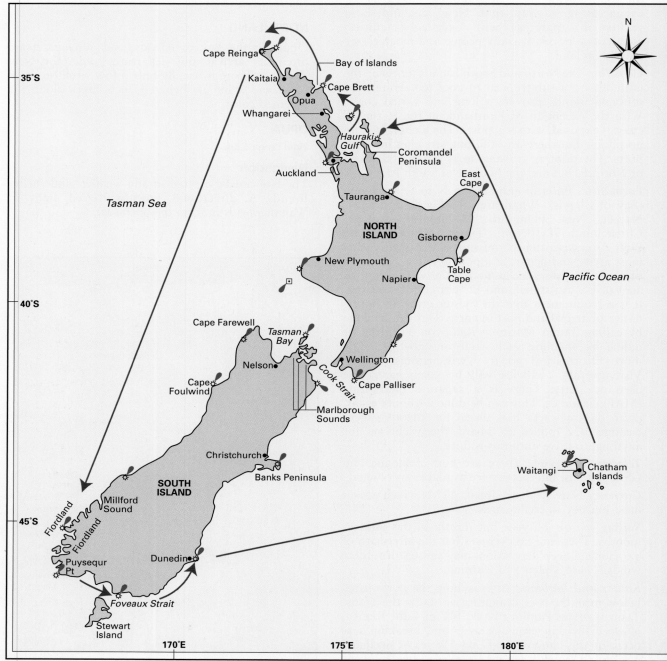

NEW ZEALAND

In New Zealand the vast majority of cruisers never venture further than the beautiful NE waters between Tauranga and the Bay of Islands. A small number make it to Nelson and the Tasman Bay area. However there are several other outstanding cruising grounds where peace and solitude is the rule. Of these the most easily accessible are the Marlborough Sounds, just across Cook Straight from the capital Wellington. The most thrilling is Fiordland with over a dozen long and totally unspoilt sounds to explore. Stewart Island and the Chatham Islands are the most remote and are rarely visited.

Stewart Island

Opua Marina

Opua

Bay of Islands

With sheltered anchorages, a subtropical climate, pleasant breezes and lots of sunshine, the Bay of Islands is idyllic. Hundreds of long distance cruising boats flock here every year to escape the South Pacific cyclone season. Opua with its marina and boatyards is the hub from which charter boats, local yachts and ocean voyagers cruise. Nearby Russell was the first capital of New Zealand and is a very popular anchorage where long distance cruisers tend to congregate and socialise.

The true allure of the Bay of Islands is out on the water; navigating up winding rivers and inlets, floating past green, hilly islands, picking mussels or diving for scallops and to end the day choosing a snug anchorage off a deserted, sandy beach. The Bay can be crowded in January and February but outside these months the sailing is just as good and much more peaceful.

Marlborough Sounds

This area is a drowned mountain range with forest clad peaks and ridges towering over plunging depths and crystal clear water.

Sailing is exciting with channels that seem to wind and twist upon themselves. Considering the number of bays and inlets, good anchorages are relatively scarce as the water is so deep and winds, often funnelled in strange directions by the ranges, can be very strong. However, the rewards are great as the weather is often sunny and warm and the area offers many excellent walking tracks.

Fiordland

There are 14 sounds, or fjords, that open to the sea and several others that branch out amongst the mountains. These are true fjords bearing unmistakable signs of glaciation and often have near vertical rock walls falling from a thousand metres above the mast to hundreds of metres below the keel. Where trees can cling to the cliffs they form an almost impenetrable forest that has not changed appreciably since man arrived on the island only a thousand years ago. Milford Sound is the only place with direct road access and a sizeable tourist presence. Doubtful Sound has a few sightseeing boats. Otherwise, apart from a few fishermen and the occasional yacht, it is rare to meet anyone and it is easy to see why this is considered one of the last great wilderness areas on earth, easily on a par with the canales of Chile or Fjords of Greenland. Sailing here is

Great Mercury Island *Graham Sewell*

Great Mercury Island *Graham Sewell*

Fiordland

Blue Cod Fiordland

Rain in Milford Sound, Fiordland

challenging because there are few natural anchorages and the crew has to learn to read the fjords and judge where the water is sufficiently shallow to drop an anchor and take stern lines into the overhanging trees.

Stewart Island

The whole island is a national park. The W coast is windswept with golden beaches and almost no vegetation, while the E has several fine waterways and sheltered anchorages amongst dense temperate rain forest. Port Pegasus near the SE tip has several good anchorages and, because the vegetation is so scanty, offers great walking with views over the southern ocean.

Port Pegasus, Stewart Island

Chatham Islands

Only 380M from Napier on the N Island, Chatham Island and its neighbour Pitt Island is one of the least visited parts of New Zealand. There are only a few anchorages, something for every wind direction, though nowhere you would want to leave your boat unattended longer than a few hours. However, the visitor is rewarded by fine wild scenery and a friendly little population of fishermen and farmers.

Weather and sailing season

The North Island

The climate is subtropical with plenty of sunshine all year round and N of Auckland frosts are very rare. Winds are usually fresh and variable in direction, often influenced by depressions passing to the S, particularly in winter. Land and sea breezes are the norm on the northland coast in summer. In summer tropical low pressure systems can occasionally bring E gales or storms, torrential rain and heavy seas to the E coast as far S as the Cook Strait area. Because temperatures are mild and winter days are not particularly short the cruising season is year round. I (AOG) have a strong preference for winter sailing when anchorages are tranquil and the colours often intense.

The South Island

The southern part of New Zealand juts into the Southern Ocean and the weather is dominated by the depressions that constantly sweep from W to E. Stable high pressure systems form from time to time and there can be spells of several weeks with still sunny weather. However, typical frontal weather with rain and winds backing from NW to SW followed by a period of fine weather lasting a few hours to a couple of days is the norm. Sometimes, particularly in the winter months the fronts can bring storms of unparalleled ferocity. Local influences are profound in the Cook Strait and between Puyseguer Point and Foveaux Strait where winds are accelerated as they pass around and between mountain systems. The Nelson and Golden Bay area is in a rain shadow formed by mountains to the W and enjoys the most sunshine in the country. Likewise, in Fiordland the weather tends to be a little more settled and drier deep in the sounds.

Because the latitude is not particularly high, Stewart Island is at 47°S (the same distance from the

Ponui Island in the Hauraki Gulf *Graham Sewell*

equator as Brittany in France) and the ocean has a stabilising effect on temperatures, winters are not particularly harsh or dark. So sailing is practical at any time of year, though most people prefer summer.

Cruising Strategies

Most of the country experiences a high proportion of W wind with the N having the most variables and the S the most regular westerlies. Inshore, especially on the E coast land and sea breezes can dominate when the weather is stable and sunny. It is possible to sail in any direction around the NZ coasts, but there are a few ideas that make it simpler. Both Foveaux Strait and Cook Strait are more easily sailed from W to E with the prevailing wind. Because of mountains to windward and the land effect, winds on the E coast tend to be less dependable so passage making is easier off the W coast in the Tasman Sea – the passages here being effectively ocean sailing. On both sides of the islands there are long stretches with no ports of refuge, many of the harbours shown on the chart have dangerous bars and are only navigable with local knowledge, fair weather and a good deal of courage. On the E coast shallows and an irregular bottom extend far from land, making for notoriously irregular and rough seas in bad weather. Whereas in deep water off the W coast the prevailing W swell, though often huge, is less dangerous.

From the coast N of Auckland, if making for Nelson, the Marlborough Sounds or Fiordland, the best route is to sail around Cape Reinga and then down the W coast, well offshore, to the latitude of the destination. After visiting these areas it is generally

fastest to sail back along the outward route, but those wanting to make a circumnavigation can run through one of the straits and up the E coast. Stewart Island is best reached from Fiordland and the Chathams can easily be reached from anywhere on the E coast, though returning from there it will be easiest to make for a destination at the N of the N island. On the sketch I have outlined a possible route for a circumnavigation of NZ.

Ashore

All areas offer a variety of interesting walks and opportunities for viewing wildlife with Chatham and Stewart Islands being particularly good spots to meet the flightless Weka and see Kiwis. Sadly, Fiordland offers the least possibilities as the forest is too dense for easy walking except on the few accessible public walking tracks.

Facilities

There are no yachting facilities, in Fiordland and Stewart Island. There are shops and fuel docks at Milford Sound in Fjordland, Waitangi in the Chathams and Half Moon Bay in Stewart Island.

Reading

Coastal Cruising Handbook, ninth edition by the Royal Akarana Yacht Club,
New Zealand Cruising Guide – Central Area, eighth edition 2006 by Murray & Von Kohorn.
A Boaties Guide to Fiordland Published by Mana Cruising Club
Stewart Island Cruising Guide Published By Mana Cruising Club

My gem

The Life of Captain James Cook J. C. Beaglehole. 1974

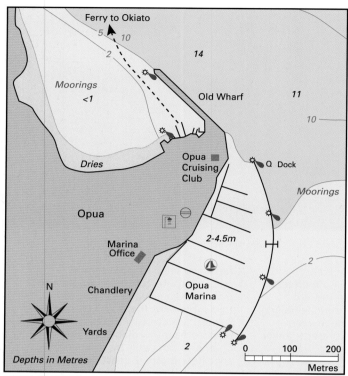

OPUA MARINA

Berths

Opua Marina VHF Ch 12. New Zealand Coastguard VHF Ch 16.

Yachts clearing into New Zealand must go alongside the first half of the detached pontoon off the marina. There are large signs saying this is the quarantine dock. Stay here until customs and MAF have checked you in. They will come over to the boat.

Opua Marina 235 berths. Visitors' berths. Max LOA 27m. Charge band 2.

Anchorage

1. Anchor east of the Opua wharf and in Waikari Inlet.
2. A mile SE of Russell is Matawhi Bay with depths of 2–3m, which is popular with longer-stay yachts.
3. There are many usable anchorages in the bay and its long estuary arms, which provide good shelter.

Facilities

Chandlery, engineers, boatyards and fuel are all available. The marina has all the usual amenities and there is the friendly Opua Cruising Club. www.opuamarina.co.nz

WHANGAREI HARBOUR

Tidal range 2.5m

Navigation

The harbour is easy to enter in fair weather. Tidal currents can be noticeable and with a gale from W or S there can be a nasty sea if the current is against the wind. Passage as far up harbour as Port

Whangarei is straightforward at any tide by observing the channel beacons. Beyond Port Whangarei to the Town Basin the channel is tidal and narrow. It is best to go on a rising tide about three quarters full, and to keep 12m off the beacons taking the corners gradually.

Berths

1. *Marsden Cove Marina* At the entrance to Whangerai inlet and all-tide access. Port of Entry with relevant officials. 230 berths. Visitors' berths. Max LOA 25m. Charge band 2/3. www.marsdencove.co.nz
2. *Whangerai Marina* In Whangerai at the head of the inlet. Also has fore and aft post moorings. 300 berths. Visitors' berths. Max LOA c.20 metres. Charge band 2. Good facilities nearby. www.whangareimarina.com
3. *Riverside Drive Marina* Small marina associated with a boatyard. 30 berths. Visitors' berths. Charge band 2. www.riversidedrivemarina.com

Anchorage

There are several pleasant anchorages near the entrance. Otherwise it is possible to find anchorages in the harbour to await a favourable tide.

Facilities

There are excellent yacht supplies and repair facilities plus all the usual facilities of a large town. www.whangarimarine.co.nz

HAURAKI GULF

The Hauraki Gulf is sheltered from the ocean by Great and Little Barrier Islands. The combination of lack of ocean swell, the proximity of Auckland and many attractive anchorages means boating of all descriptions is very popular in this area.

AUCKLAND

Tidal range 3.2m

Navigation

Tidal currents are strong in narrows. Commercial traffic is frequent; it is wise to stay well clear of the marked big ship channel. The W side of the channel between the 10m and 5m lines is safe from dangers.

Berths

Customs clearances are given at a landing in the centre of the city. VHF Ch 16 or 12. The following are the main marinas in order of distance from the centre of Auckland. Charge band 3–4.

1. *The Viaduct Basin* in downtown Auckland was set up for America's Cup bases and for mega-yachts. It has berths for yachts of all types. www.viaduct.co.nz
2. *Westhaven* is a very large marina at the W edge of the centre of Auckland. 1432 berths. Visitors' berths. Max LOA 30m. Charge band 2 www.westhaven.co.nz
3. *Hobson West Marina* Part of Viaduct Basin administered by Westhaven. 22 berths. Visitors' berths. 16–50 metres LOA. Charge band 2/3.
4. *Bayswater Marina* Popular marina on Aucklands

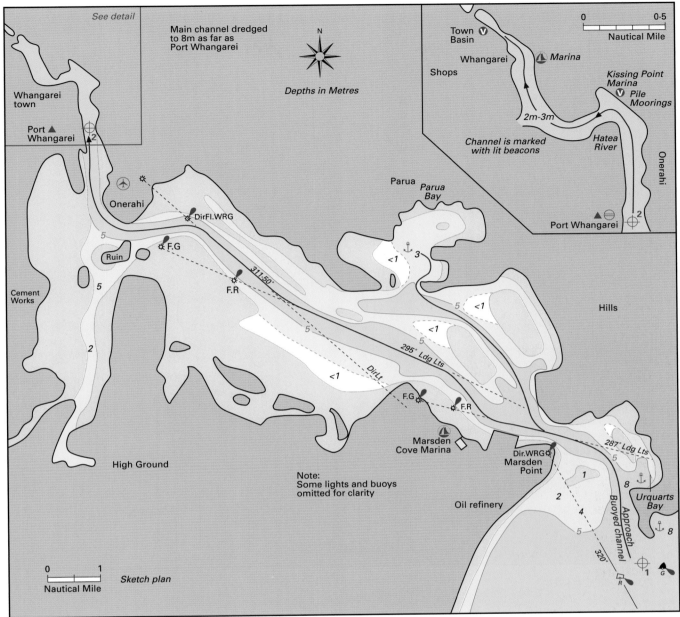

Depths in Metres

Main channel dredged
to 8m as far as
Port Whangarei

Whangarei
town

Port ▲
Whangarei

See detail

Onerahi

DirFl.WRG

F.G

Ruin

F.R

5

Cement
Works

5

2

311.50°

DirLt

<1

High Ground

Note:
Some lights and buoys
omitted for clarity

5

<1

Parua
Parua
Bay

<1

3

<1

5

5

295° Ldg Lts

Hills

F.G

F.R

Marsden
Cove Marina

Dir.WRG
Marsden
Point

Oil refinery

287° Ldg Lts

5

8

1

2

4

5

320°

Approach
Buoyed channel

1

Urquarts
Bay

8

8

R

G

Town
Basin

Whangarei

Shops

Marina

Kissing Point
Marina
Pile
Moorings

2m-3m

Channel is marked
with lit beacons

Hatea
River

Onerahi

Port Whangarei

2

0   0·5
Nautical Mile

0   1
Nautical Mile   Sketch plan

WHANGAREI
1⊕ 35°52'·7S 174°32'·5E
2⊕ 35°45'S 174°21'E

Northshore. 415 berths. Visitors' berths. Max LOA 45 metres. Access channel dredged to 2.4 metres at LAT. Charge band 2. www.bayswater.co.nz

5. *Westpark Marina* is towards the head of the harbour in a far western suburb. It is about 25km by road from the centre. There is a travel-lift and limited shopping. Public transport and other shops are not close. 590 berths. Visitors' berths. Max LOA 34m. Charge band 2. Dredged access channel. www.westpark.co.nz

6. *Half Moon Bay Marina* is near the mouth of the Tamaki Estuary to the E. It is about 30km by road from the centre. It has a travel lift, chandlery and a basic food shop. There is a ferry from Half Moon Bay to downtown Auckland. 500 berths.

Visitors' berths. Max LOA 15m. Charge band 2. www.hmbmarina.co.nz

7. *Pine Harbour Marina* is near Beachlands, 40km east. There are no nearby shops. There is infrequent public transport. www.pineharbour.co.nz

8. *Gulf Harbour Marina* is on the S side of Whangaparoa Peninsula. It is about 50km north of Auckland. There is a travel-lift and limited chandlery. There is a fast ferry from the marina to Auckland, and an infrequent bus. This marina has been popular with visiting yachts because berths are often available. 600+ berths. Visitors' berths. Max LOA c.35m. Charge band 2. www.gulf-harbour.co.nz

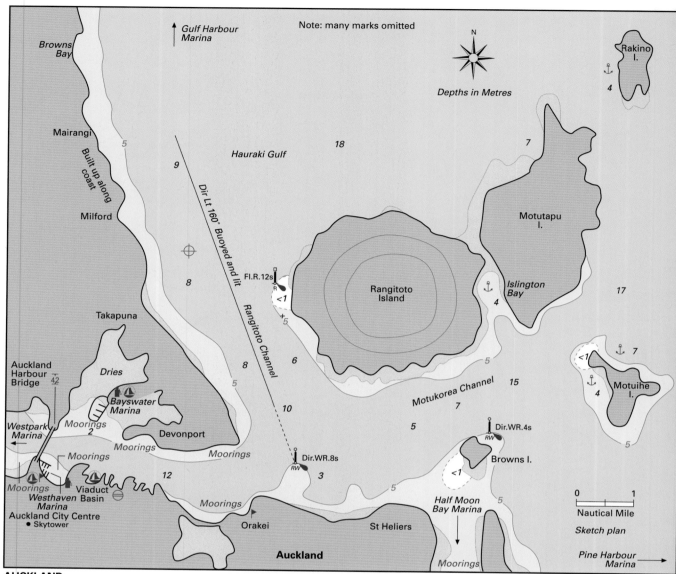

AUCKLAND
⊕36°46'·6S 174°48'E

Facilities

Ship chandlers and repair facilities are readily available. With so many yachts the range of yacht construction and servicing is very wide. All the facilities and amenities of a city.

Remarks

Auckland is a major city with over a million inhabitants. It claims to have the most yachts per head of population of any city in the world. It is the logical place to organise flights and trips around New Zealand.

BAY OF PLENTY

This area includes the port of Tauranga, where some cruising yachts make their landfall in New Zealand.

The W side is the main cruising area. There are a number of attractive anchorages along this coast.

TAURANGA HARBOUR

Tidal range 2.2m

Navigation

There is a bar at the entrance that can cause the sea to break in N and E gales. The tidal streams are strong, with currents of 5kn at neaps and 7kn at springs near the S point of Mount Maunganui peninsula. Swell can cause standing waves in the channel. When there is significant swell, it is best to enter on a rising tide towards high water slack, and to follow the main shipping channel.

Berths

VHF Ch 73. Tauranga Bridge marina is near the bridge and close to the city centre. The older marina near the yacht club has two visitors' berths just inside the entrance. This marina is a long distance from supplies.

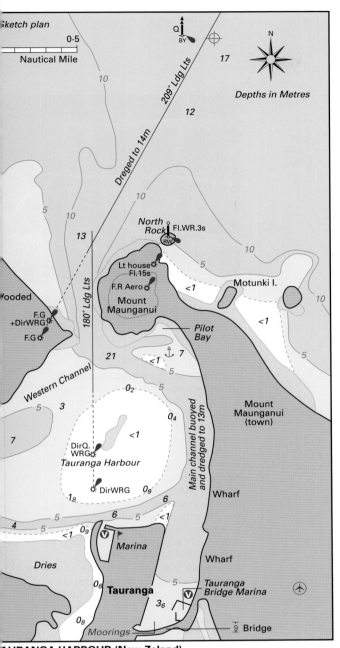

Depths in Metres

Sketch plan
0·5
Nautical Mile

Dreged to 14m

209° Ldg Lts

North Rock Fl.WR.3s

Lt house Fl.15s

F.R Aero
Mount Maunganui

Motunki I.

Pilot Bay

Western Channel

180° Ldg Lts

Wooded

F.G +DirWRG
F.G

21

DirQ. WRG
Tauranga Harbour

DirWRG

Mount Maunganui (town)

Main channel buoyed and dredged to 13m

Wharf

Marina

Dries

Wharf

Tauranga

Tauranga Bridge Marina

Moorings

Bridge

AURANGA HARBOUR (New Zeland)
37°36'·0S 176°11'·0E

Tauranga Bridge Marina 500 berths. Visitors' berths. Max LOA 37m. Charge band 2. www.marina.co.nz

Anchorage

There is anchorage on the S side of Mount Maunganui peninsula at Pilot Bay. Near the bridge, moorings may be available; anchoring is very difficult close to town as there is little space.

Facilities

There are facilities for all yacht repairs and needs. All the facilities of a large town are present.

Note See Chapter 7 Southern Ocean for comments on South Island and details of Nelson.

Vanuatu

General Malaria is present. Precautions are necessary. The islands are all high, originally or actively volcanic. They are well clothed in forest and the population is small.

The people of Vanuatu (Ni-Vanatu) are almost all Melanesian, but there are some people of Chinese and European descent. Vanuatu has a curious history: it was previously ruled simultaneously by France and Britain with two different systems of justice and education.

Formalities Harbour charges apply from entry to exit regardless of where you are cruising. The Ports of Entry are Lenakel on Tanna, Vila on Efate, Luganville on Espiritu Santo and Sola on Vanua Lava in the Banks Islands. At Luganville visitors use moorings at Aore resort, from where there is a boat shuttle to town. See separate section guide for more detail.

Telecom IDD +678. Internet in main centres.

Currency Vatu. ATM machines in main centres. There are banks in Port Vila and Santos and a few smaller places.

Routes and harbours There are few dangerous coral reefs in Vanuatu and the islands are high, so navigation is rather simple despite the inadequate charting. Port Vila is a very popular stopover for cruising yachts and Havannah Harbour is commonly visited. S Vanuatu is most visited because of the popularity of Port Resolution on Tanna, with its nearby active volcano.

Tidal currents flow quite strongly around the islands and rips form off headlands and in narrow channels.

PORT VILA (Efate)

Tidal range 1.6m

Navigation

The approach from Mele Bay has a leading line and directional light (Oc.10s). Large yachts are restricted to the outer harbour. The inner harbour is restricted by shoal water (3 metres least depth) and by an overhead cable (30 metres max air height at low tide). Yachting World can advise on navigation and tides.

Berths

Yachting World (VHF Ch 16) have sea wall tie-up with power and water. c.25 berths. Visitors' berths. Charge band 2. Laid moorings in the inner harbour which are the best option as it is 30–40 metres deep and so anchoring is not a great option. Charge band 2 for moorings. www.yachtingworld-vanuatu.com

Anchorage

The Q area has reasonable holding and adequate protection from the prevailing easterlies, but is open W. It is possible to anchor but the holding is poor. The harbour is well sheltered except in a cyclone.

Facilities

Water on the fuel quay (boats on moorings can fill up here). Fuel dock in inner harbour. Fuel by tanker in outer harbour. Wi-Fi. Laundry. Some yacht repairs and limited chandlery. Provisions and restaurants and bars.

Vanuatu

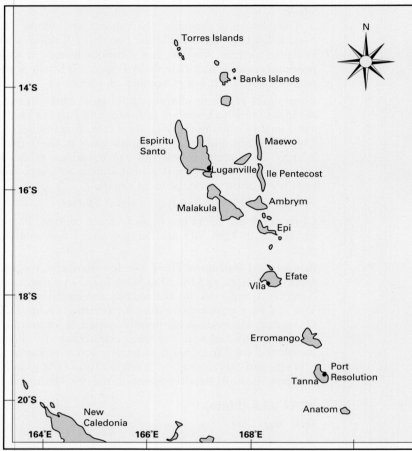

VANUATU

The locals will often come out to boats around islands offering to trade or just to say 'Hi'

Also called 'The Great Cyclades' (Bougainville in 1768) and 'The New Hebrides' (Cook in 1774). This chain of islands is something of a crossroads in the SW Pacific with boats from New Zealand on the Barefoot Circuit coming across from Tonga and Fiji before curving down to New Caledonia and then back to NZ and boats en route to Australia and SE Asia leaving from here to Cairns or up to the Solomons.

The island chain has never been a homogeneous group and although basically Melanesian, different languages were spoken on different islands and even between different villages. The islands had a reputation for cannibalism and savagery right up into the 20th century, but today the inhabitants of the different islands are a remarkably gentle and approachable people.
The recent history of the islands was a bizarre rule by both the French and the English who established different institutions to govern the islands in a complicated bipartisan way. The islands became independent in 1980 and the establishment of a common language, Bislama, a variation on Pidgin English, united the villages and islands under a common thread that soothed over old feuds and disputes. The language is quite easy to get a handle on once you hear it and I include some of my favourite phrases below.

Thank you *Tankyu tumas*
To hit *Killem*
To hit and kill something *Killem ded finis*
To ruin *Baggerap*
Piano *Wan bigfala bokis, I gat tith, sam I waet, sam I blak, taim yu killem I singaot*

Cruising strategies

Yachts on the Barefoot Circuit will often head for Vila on Efate from Fiji or Tonga. Yachts heading up from New Caledonia will often clear in at Tanna to see the live volcano there before heading on up to Vila. Yachts must clear in first at a port of entry which are currently Lenakel on Tanna, Vila on Efate, Luganville on Espiritu Santo and Sola on Vanua Lava in the Banks Islands. If you are heading for Tanna then you can go to Port Resolution and a pick-up truck will take you over the island to Lenakel (for a fee) to clear in. Outside of Vila and Luganville ensure you get receipts for all clearances to present at Vila or Luganville. Yachts must also clear out from a Port of Entry and also get permission to cruise in the different groups of islands. Clearing in and out and permits cost close to $US200 in 2009. Despite these costs these islands are a huge cruising area and most yachts will be lucky to see a tenth of the anchorages in a cruising season. These are places that take you back in time and the heavily wooded islands and outlying reefs are just stunning. Many of the villages are isolated places where the locals welcome any cruising yachts and will want to trade for fruit and vegetables. Trading goods vary from place to place, but exercise books and pencils, T-shirts, oil, fish hooks and line, balloons (for the kids) and just about anything you have will be welcome. The villagers are not offended if you don't have items.

Seasons and weather

Weather patterns here are much as for New Caledonia except being further N temperatures are more tropical. The islands lie in the cyclone belt and are hit by cyclones so most yachts leave for the cyclone season from November to May, although the boatyard in Vila has tie-downs and is reported to be a secure place to leave a yacht in the cyclone season – check with your insurer.

Like New Caledonia you do get depressions producing westerlies in the normal cruising season and you need to plan ahead to find shelter if westerlies are forecast.

Ashore

Port Vila on Efate has by far the best shopping and yacht facilities in Vanuatu. There is laundry, Wi-Fi, supermarket and fresh fruit and veggie market, yacht repair facilities and a boatyard. There is also a fuel dock and a gas filling plant. After that Luganville is virtually the only other place where you will be able to get provisions and fuel and water. Around the islands you can always find fruit and vegetables and the locals will often row out in their outrigger canoes to trade. There are a few local shops in places, but don't count on getting too much in these.

Behind Iririki Island in Vila

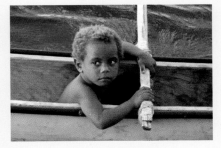
Pikanini in kanu in Malakula

Negotiation for vegetables in Havannah

One thing you must try when you are here is the Vanuatu beef – the fillet steak I had here was one of the very best I have tasted anywhere.

Facilities

Vila is the centre for yacht repairs and also has the only viable yard for hauling. In Luganville basic repairs can be made and there are a few hardware shops. Spare parts can be flown in from NZ or Australia.

Reading

Rocket Guide to Vanuatu (CD)
Yacht Miz Mae's Guide to Vanuatu Nicola Rhind
Vanuatu Bob Tiews & Thalia Hearne South Pacific Cruising Series

My gem

Doctor in Vanuatu: A Memoir Dr. E A (Ted) Freeman (Institute of Pacific Studies)

Vanuatu fast food in the market in Vila. Baked fish and chicken wrapped in banana leaves is popular and good

Market in Vila

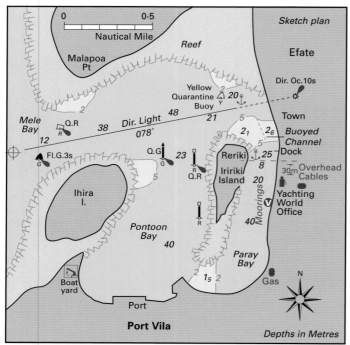

PORT VILA (Efate, Vanuatu)

⊕17°44'·48S 168°17'·49E WGS84

Remarks

Port Vila is the chief town of Vanuatu. It is not big but is surprisingly sophisticated, perhaps due to French influence.

New Caledonia

General The islands are overseas French territory. As well as golden beaches and some of the best reef diving in the world, they also have a magnificent backdrop of mountains and good sailing breezes. In addition fish are easy to catch, and, in town, it is possible to enjoy French cuisine. The temperatures in the cruising season are never too hot.

Coastline New Caledonia is a long thin island with an almost continuous off-lying reef and some interesting islands.

Formalities Noumea is the only port of entry and yachts must proceed directly there. Yachts are allowed to stay one month in New Caledonia. After that they are considered to be resident here and taxes apply. If departing for Vanuatu, prior permission must be obtained for a stop at the Loyalty Islands on route.

Telecom IDD +687. GSM network. Good internet access in the centres.

Currency Pacific franc. ATMs in the centres.

Routes and harbours New Caledonia is mostly surrounded by coral reefs, which makes for delightful yacht cruising. Despite the numerous reefs, navigating around New Caledonia in good visibility is easy; this also applies to the Loyalty Islands. However, tidal flows can be strong in the

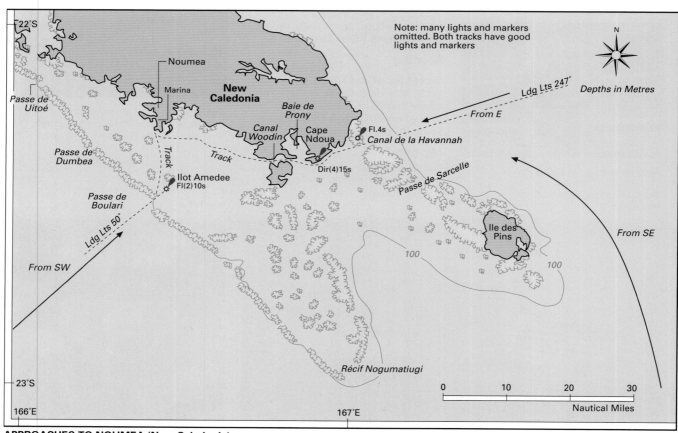

APPROACHES TO NOUMEA (New Caledonia)

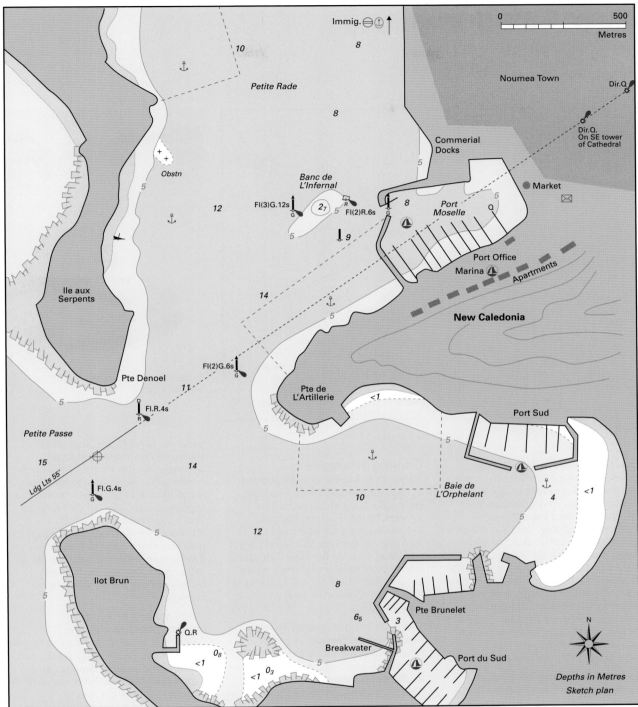

NOUMEA (New Caledonia)
⊕22°17'·10S 166°25'·15E WGS84

passages and passes with currents of up to 5kn with eddies and breaking seas. Violent eddies occur in Havanna Passage at the turn of the tide.

A circumnavigation of New Caledonia with extensions to Ile des Pins and Ouvea, and perhaps Beautemp- Beaupre is best undertaken in a clockwise direction. Then the seas will be astern on the short section of open ocean on the W coast. The main sailing base is Noumea.

NOUMEA

Tidal range 1.7m

Navigation

Landfall from the SW is the 53m high Amedee lighthouse, which is easily seen in the approaches to Passe du Boulari. There are a series of leading lines into the harbour. Ideally, this should be a daytime entry. Landfall from the E is into the Canal de la Havannah. This has lit marks leading to Cape

New Caledonia

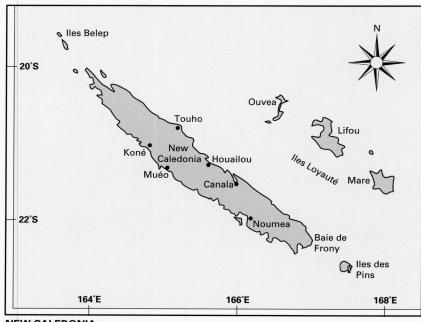

NEW CALEDONIA

Squeaky white sand beach on Isle des Pins

New Caledonia along with French Polynesia is the other French Territoire d'outre-Mer in the Pacific. It is something of a question mark for many cruisers though not to Australian and New Zealand cruisers who regularly use it as a stepping stone around the SW Pacific. Although in the Tropics it is some 20 degrees south of the equator so has a slightly cooler climate than islands closer to the equator, though its seascape conforms to ideas of the Tropics: coral reefs, coconut palms and white sandy beaches with temperatures in the low 20's C.

New Caledonia also has a large resident population of yachts and the best yacht repair facilities outside of New Zealand and Australia in this part of the world. If you have problems around the islands or en route to them then New Caledonia is the place to head for. Add to this French patisseries and baguettes, some half decent restaurants and French supermarkets with a selection of French cheeses and other goodies and New Caledonia takes on a whole new perspective.

Cruising Strategies

Yachts that have spent the summer in New Zealand will often include New Caledonia as part of a tour around Tonga, Fiji, and Vanuatu before heading for northern Australia or back to NZ. Some yachts will head directly for New Caledonia from New Zealand and then cruise around the island before heading for Vanuatu and then on to Australia or New Zealand.

There are various passes into the lagoon inside the barrier reef extending some 40 miles south of the island. Most yachts will use Passe de Boulari on the west side which has the iconic lighthouse Phare Amedee (53 metres high) with a leading mark in front showing the way in on 050° true. If you are late getting in you can anchor off under the islet Phare Amedee is on. The lighthouse was designed by Eiffel: he of the Parisian tower. Passage through the lagoon should be made in daylight and although electronic charts are reasonably accurate they should not be relied on absolutely. You will need a detailed paper chart as well. You can also use the main ship pass further up from Boulari, or

Passe de Sarcelle or Canal de la Havannah on the east side or between Isle des Pins and the reefs to the west. Again you must have good detailed charts and transit the lagoon in daylight. All yachts must first go to Noumea to clear in although the authorities helpfully give you three days to leave New Caledonian waters so you can do a little cruise around the lagoon before setting off to Vanuatu or elsewhere.

There are ample cruising opportunities around New Caledonia, which is the fourth largest island in the Pacific after North and South Island in New Zealand and Papua New Guinea. A barrier reef encloses most of the island encompassing a large body of water to the north and south. Its said it is the largest lagoon in the world though this bit of PR is difficult to reconcile when you have huge lagoons in the Tuamotus and the body of water enclosed by the Great Barrier Reef off the east coast of Australia. There are also lots of bays and harbours along the west and east coast of the main island and also good cruising around the Loyalty group to the east. There is enough here to keep many occupied for a season or more.

Port Moselle Marina

Seasons and weather

New Caledonia conforms to the seasons for the other South Pacific islands with the cyclone season running from November to May in the southern hemisphere summer. A lot of local boats stay in New Caledonia for this season with pretty good shelter in the inner harbour at Port Moselle and a possible hurricane hole at Baie de Prony. Most yachts will be cruising New Caledonia in the southern hemisphere winter from May to November.

Although the trades blow over New Caledonia in the winter, you also get a fair number of westerlies. You also get small depressions (yes, you do get depressions outside of the cyclone season although they do not develop into Tropical Storms) which can bring gales and rain to New Caledonia.

Ashore

Noumea has several large supermarkets and an excellent local market with fresh fruit and vegetables and good fish and prawns close to Port Moselle. There are other smaller shops and all the infrastructure you would expect of a small city of 100,000. There are laundries nearby and internet cafes in Noumea. You can refill gas bottles (including Camping Gaz). There is a large hospital and good local clinics.

New Caledonia is not a malaria area. There are flights from Australia, New Zealand and Fiji to New Caledonia and flights to Paris.

Facilities

Good yacht repair facilities and a yard at Noumea. You can get stainless steel welding done, engine repairs and sail and canvas work. Good chandlers in Noumea and at the boatyard and also good hardware shops. Spares can be quickly flown in from NZ and Australia. Outside of Noumea there is a large Zone Industriale where there are a whole range of services and shops including large hardware shops like Mr Bricolage. Here you source hard to get items although you will need to take a taxi or get a hire car or use the local bus service.

Reading

Nautical Rocket Guide to New Caledonia (CD)
The Cruising Guide to New Caledonia (Guide de Croisiere en Nouvelle Caledonie in French) by Joel Marc, Marc Rambeau and Ross Blackman. Available locally.
Migrant Cruising Notes: Southern New Caledonia Phil Cregreen (Boat Books NZ)

My gem

Transit of Venus: Travels in the Pacific Jeremy Evans (Secker & Warburg)

Market near Port Moselle

Ndoua at the W end of the passage. There are reefs at the entrance to the passage two miles before any land and there is a submerged reef with about 9m over it five miles from any land: this could be a danger in heavy seas. From Cape Ndoua the track is through Canal Woodin on leading lines, and then on leading lines and a course marked by lit beacons inside the barrier reef to Noumea.

The natural landfall from the SE is unsatisfactory, as it is into unmarked reefs extending 40 miles SE of New Caledonia. Unless the visibility is very good, it is safest either to sail SW of the barrier reef to pick up the SW landfall, or to sail NE of Ile de Pins to pick up the E landfall. In general the buoyage within the lagoon is well maintained (IALA 'A').

Berths

VHF Ch 67. Yachts arriving from abroad should call *Capitainerie, Port Moselle* (marina staff – English spoken) on the final approach to the harbour to advise their arrival and go to the visitors' pontoon of the marina to await clearance. The marina will arrange for the authorities to visit the boat.

Port Moselle
VHF Ch 67. Max LOA 30m. Depths 4.5–7.5m. Charge band 3.

Port du Sud
(In Orphelina Bay). Max LOA 40m. Charge band 3.

www.cruising-newcaledonia.com

Anchorage

In Baie de la Moselle, just off the marina, or in Baie de l'Orphelant.

Facilities

There are good repair facilities and yacht supplies. This is the best-equipped yachting base in the tropical South Pacific.

Remarks

Noumea is the most sophisticated city in the SW South Pacific outside New Zealand.

See the separate section for more information.

Solomon Islands

See plan on page 212

General Malaria is present so precautions are necessary. The NW Solomon Islands offer an (albeit rather hot and humid) alternative area to escape the S Pacific hurricane season.

Formalities There are entry ports at Late, Graciosa Bay in the Santa Cruz islands, Honiara on Guadalcanal, and in the Western Solomons at Munda, Noro (a commercial port on Hawthorne Sound) and Gizo. There is a Light Dues Fee of $S100 plus 10c per net registered ton. Once cleared, yachts can move around freely.

Telecom IDD +677.

Currency Solomons dollar. ATMs in Honiara.

Sailing season Mid-May to November but all year from Gizo to the W.

Routes and harbours The approach through the Bougainville Strait requires care because of the reefs, shoals and tidal currents with the possibility of steep waves or overfalls. A typical route in either direction through the Solomon Islands is through the centre of the group. However, the S coast of Cristobal is more beautiful and has better anchorages than the N coast, and likewise the NE coasts of Isabel and Choiseul are much preferable to their SW coasts. The best sailing base is Gizo.

HONIARA (Guadalcanal)

Tidal range 0.9m

Anchorage

The anchorage is uncomfortable in trade wind conditions in the afternoon due to the onshore waves.

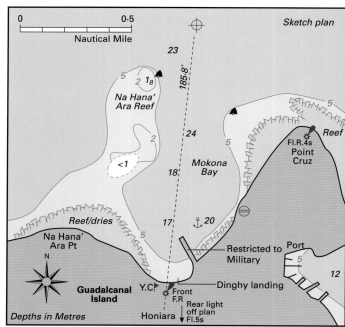

HONIARA (Guadalcanal, Solomon Islands)
⊕09°25'·4S 159°57'·3E

Facilities

A good range of everyday items.

Remarks

Honiara is the capital of the Solomon Islands.

GIZO

Tidal range 0.9m

Anchorage

The anchorage in the upper harbour is very well protected with excellent holding and is convenient to the town. It is necessary to leave room for the fuel ships to manoeuvre in and out.

Facilities

A sizeable township for such a small island. Besides the shops in the main street there are a shipbuilder, hotel, post office, market, banks and a hospital. This is the best place to refuel NW of Noumea. Sometimes drinking water may be taken from a tank near the fuel wharf. Town water is considered unsafe without boiling.

Remarks

This is the South Pacific of yesteryear, somewhat seedy but with character. Gizo was once the capital of the W British Solomon Islands Protectorate.

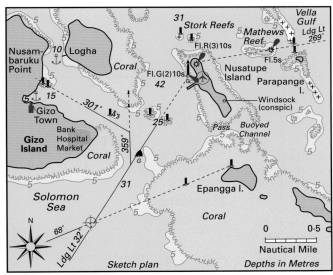

GIZO (Western Solomon Islands)
⊕08°06'·4S 156°50'·8E

Papua New Guinea

General Malaria is present so precautions are necessary. Violent crime is a major problem in Port Moresby and Lae. This is not the case in smaller places and one author (AO'G) considers some villages in the Louisiade Islands to be the closest thing he has experienced to the Garden of Eden. New Ireland and Bougainville are cyclone free and can be used to escape the S Pacific cyclone season.

Formalities High visa fees are charged. Visas must be obtained before arrival. Papua New Guinea has consulates in Australia, New Zealand, Fiji, Vanuatu and Solomon Islands. Ports of Entry: Port Moresby (don't go there), Samarai Island (SE of Milne Bay at the E end of the main island), Bwagoia on the SE coast of Misima Island, Kavieng at the N end of New Ireland.

Telecom IDD +675

Currency Kina. There are banks in main settlements.

Routes and harbours

Louisiade Archipelago

This is a very attractive cruising area, much of it in easily navigated and pretty lagoons. The islands in the lagoons are high, have many anchorages and the Melanesian people are pleasant. The usual route is from Bwagoia through the Deboyne Lagoon, a possible visit to the Conflict group, then S into the Louisiade Lagoon through the Cormorant Channel. After this, cruise the islands as far as Samarai from where you can clear out.

New Ireland

The islands off the NE coast of New Ireland are fascinating and seldom visited. The anchorages provide pleasant stopovers on a cruise between the E Caroline Islands and the Solomon Islands. New Ireland and the outlying islands, except Green Island, are high islands, making them easy landfalls. Green Island rises to 30m. The most interesting route to the SE is along the chain of outlying islands to the E.

Bougainville Group

Bougainville is in the process of becoming independent but this may be very drawn out. Meanwhile there are peacekeepers from Australia and New Zealand there. Cyclones do not occur. While Bougainville is a high island, there are outlying reefs up to six miles off shore to be avoided. The normal route is along the E coast in either direction and through the Buka Passage to Queen Carola harbour. There are anchorages suitably spaced for day sailing but the Buka Passage should only be used with suitable or no tidal currents. Kieta is a port of entry and is on the E side of Bougainville towards the S end.

Papua New Guinea

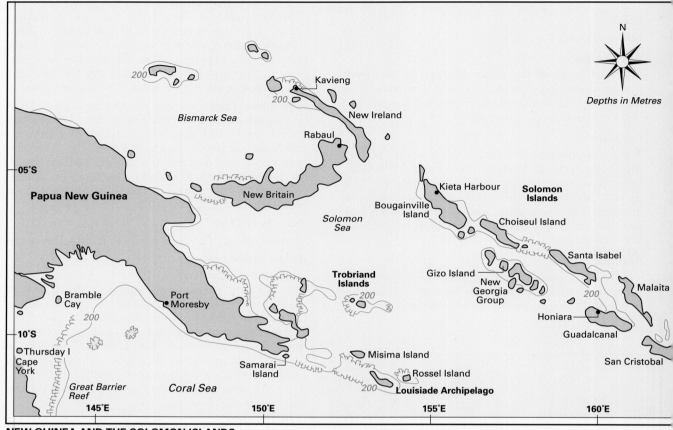

NEW GUINEA AND THE SOLOMON ISLANDS

When I hear people talk about the Garden of Eden my mind immediately returns to the island of Misima in the Louisiades. Here Balæna anchored off a village where the children were totally unused to the sight of white people, where most of the homes were constructed from natural materials and there were even a few ladies wearing grass skirts. The people made a subsistence living from the surrounding jungle and seas and were happy, friendly and welcoming. Cruising through the group we encountered many other delightful spots including many white sandy beaches and excellent diving in crystal clear waters. Surprisingly few yachts visit New Guinea, perhaps put off by the stories of violence, which is a problem in the bigger towns but unusual in the remote islands.

Weather

New Guinea is on the boundary between the SE trade winds and the doldrums. The ITCZ lies over Papua New Guinea in the southern summer. Tropical cyclones just reach the southern area, though are rare and do not occur further N. In the winter SE winds predominate over the whole group, though are less reliable to the N. In summer winds are variable, often light with squalls and NW tends to be a bit more common.

Cruising strategies

The Louisiade archipelago is a logical cruising area when heading towards the Torres Strait from the South Pacific and is best cruised E to W with the prevailing winds. The E end of the group can also be reached by setting a course across the wind from the S to mid Queensland coast. Instead of heading to New Zealand or Australia for the cyclone season it is possible to cruise safely in the

northern part of New Guinea, perhaps working N from the S Pacific towards Micronesia and SE Asia or Japan.

Practicalities

There are no yachting facilities, though there is a considerable amount of local small boat activity so slips are fairly frequent and basic work could be carried out without major difficulty. Fuel and staple provisions are available in the regional centres. Charts are old and coral reefs may have grown appreciably since they were drawn.

Reading

Cruising Papua New Guinea Alan Lucas

My gem

Isles of illusion, edited by Bohun Lynch; with an Introduction by Gavin Young (Asterisk) .

BWAGOIA (Misima, Louisiade Islands)

Tidal range 0.8m

Navigation

The island makes a good landfall as it is high.

Warning Many yachts have reported that heat haze, especially in the afternoon, can obscure high land in this area, even from as little as 5M offshore.

The harbour entrance may look fearsome with a narrow entrance and perhaps a rough sea, but it is in fact quite easy.

Anchorage

The harbour is small and narrow but there is room for a number of yachts in excellent shelter. Swell may come in from a SSE sea.

Facilities

Everyday supplies are available in Bwagoia. It is a government centre, and there is a Post Office, hospital and an airport with occasional charter flights to Australia.

Remarks

Bwagoia is the township for the Louisiades, although Misima Island is not strictly a Louisiade island.

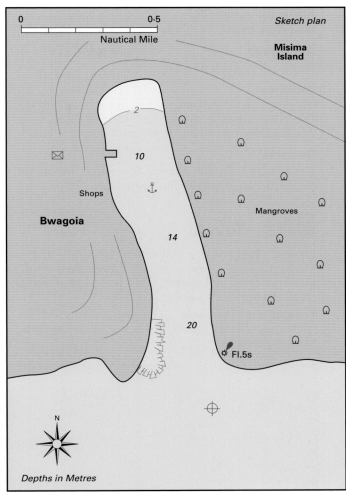

BWAGOIA (Misima, Louisiade Islands)
⊕10°42'·0S 152°51'·0E

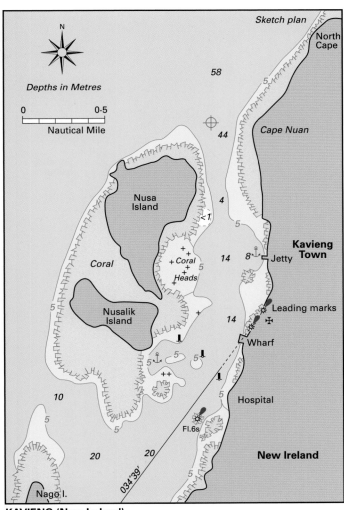

KAVIENG (New Ireland)
⊕02°32'·5S 150°47'·3E

KAVIENG (New Ireland)

Tidal range 1m

Navigation

The N approach to the harbour should be straightforward unless there is a N swell. The depths in the fairway are 6m but there are isolated depths of 4m and these are liable to change during the NW monsoon, so approach with caution. The SW approach, along the leading line shown, is S of Nago Island and is deeper, but, to the NW of the channel, there is a series of shoals from Nago Island in a SW arc towards Emago Island, about two miles WSW.

Anchorage

Shelter is poor and depths in the harbour are variable.

Facilities

A small town with a customs office, bank, hospital and a reasonable range of supplies including diesel delivered to the yacht. Gas is available.

Remarks

Kavieng is the chief town of New Ireland.

KIETA (Bougainville)

Tidal range 1.4m

Anchorage

Reasonably sheltered.

Facilities

There is a shopping centre adjacent to the anchorage. Everyday supplies should be available here or in Arawa. Diesel may have to be carried in jerry cans.

Remarks

Kieta, with adjacent Arawa, constitutes by far the largest urban centre on Bougainville.

Tuvalu

General Tuvalu is a Polynesian kingdom, and is proud that it is not a republic even though the monarch lives in London. This is an unbelievably small independent country.

Formalities The port of entry is at Funafuti. Clearance is at the wharf. There is a A$20 departure tax per person.

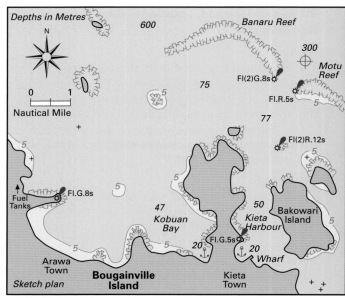

KIETA (Bougainville)
⊕06°08'·0S 155°39'·6E

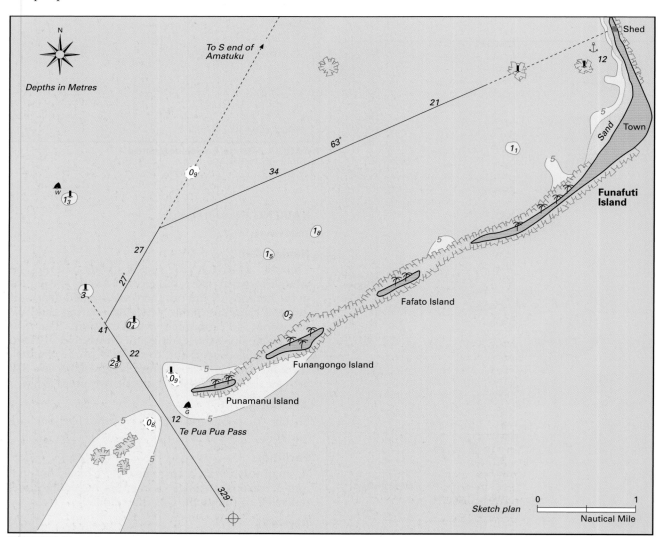

FUNAFUTI (Tuvalu)
⊕08°35'·0S 179°08'·0E

Telecom IDD +688.

Currency Australian dollar. There are no ATM machines. There is a bank.

Routes and harbours Several of the atolls may be visited; the most interesting is Nukufetau (8°00'S 179°20'E)

FUNAFUTI

Tidal range 1.2m

Navigation

Funafuti is an atoll but there are islets on all sides and most have palms that should be seen from some miles away. The approach to Te Pua Pua pass in the SE is best, with lengthy islets helping to identify the reefs. (The most difficult approach is from the N towards Te Ava I Te Lape pass where it is possible to be in danger before any sighting visually or on radar, particularly if approaching from the NE). Te Pua Pua faces the SE swell, which makes the banks either side dangerous because there is probably no more than 4m over them. The pass itself is narrow and should have 12m depth. The course is to a leaning steel post, two miles into the lagoon. There is another nearer post, which will be more obvious and is misleading. The next course is towards the S end of Amatuku, and the last course towards a conspicuous shed behind the wharf. Closer in it is necessary to deviate past a reef, which should be beaconed.

Anchorage

The most convenient anchorage is near the wharf, where there are some steps to land by dinghy.

Facilities

There are a few shops in the centre and further on a bank, hotel and airport.

Remarks

This is the main atoll and has more people than it can support.

Resources

PILOTS, GUIDES AND CHARTS
Charlie's Charts of Polynesia Charles & Margo Wood. (Charlie's Charts)
Landfalls of Paradise: Cruising Guide to the Pacific Islands Earl R. Hinz. (Latitude 20 Books)
Australian Cruising Guide Alan Lucas. (Imray)
Cruising the Coral Coast Alan Lucas. (Alan Lucas Cruising Guides)
South Pacific Anchorages Warwick Clay (Imray)
South Pacific Crossing Guide RCCPF / Michael Pocock, Ros Hogbin (Adlard Coles Nautical)
Coastal Cruising Handbook (Royal Akarana Yacht Club)
New Zealand Cruising Guide Central Area Murray and Von Kohorn (Steven William)
Boaties Guide to Fiordland (Mana Cruising Club)
Stewart Island Cruising Guide (Mana Cruising Club)
Downwind around Australia and Africa Warwick Clay (available from Imray)
All available from www.boatbooks.co.nz
All New Zealand Charts can be viewed on the internet on www.hydro.linz.govt.nz
There are many detailed guides to particular areas of the South Pacific.

Australia (E Coast)

General This is a huge country and is the only one in this book that is represented in three different chapters (Indian and Southern Ocean). It is a popular destination and has a large home-based yachting community. The people give travellers a great welcome. Most overseas yachtsmen think of Australia as a tropical destination; however, it also has temperate cruising grounds to compare with the best in the world.

Coastline The east coast of Australia is fairly uninteresting S of Brisbane, with the exception of a few wonderful natural harbours such as Sydney. N of Brisbane is the Great Barrier Reef upon which lie many islands and within which is a sheltered and popular cruising ground.

Formalities All nationals (except New Zealand) arriving in Australia require a visa. This can be easily obtained on the internet. Go to www.immi.gov.au

All yachts must advise Australian customs of their arrival 96 hours in advance. This can be done in a number of ways:

- Sending an *email* to yachtreport@customs.gov.au
- Sending a *fax* to +61 2 6275 5078
- Phoning the Australian Customs National Communications Centre on ☎ +61 3 9244 8973

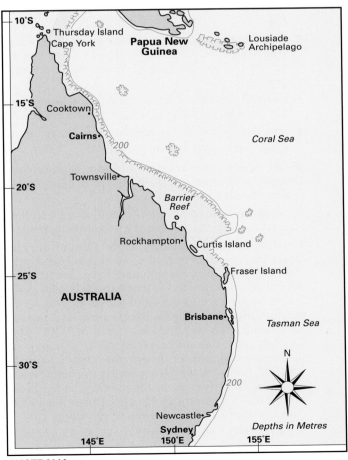

AUSTRALIA

You will need to provide the following information:
- The name of your craft
- Craft's Country and Port of Registration
- Your intended first port of arrival
- Your estimated arrival time
- Your last four ports
- The details of people on board including name, date of birth, nationality and passport number
- Details of any illness or disease recently encountered
- If you have any animals on board
- If you have any firearms on board

Yachts must clear in at a port of entry first. Ports of entry on the east coast are: Sydney, Port Kembla, Newcastle, Lord Howe Island, Eden, Coffs Harbour, Brisbane, Bundaberg, Gladstone, Mackay, Townsville, Cairns and Thursday Island.

Customs, Quarantine and Immigration clearance must be completed prior to going ashore.

- Please stay on board. No persons other than a Quarantine or Customs officer is allowed to board your craft, nor can any person, animal or article leave the craft until you have been given full clearance
- Depending on your arrival time, Customs and Quarantine may require all persons to remain on board overnight before clearing you the following day
- Don't throw any waste or foodstuffs overboard while you're in Australian waters or while you are moored. Use designated quarantine disposal points
- Keep all food and animals secure until your vessel has been inspected by Quarantine officers
- Don't trade foodstuffs with other overseas vessels
- Keep your vessel free of insects.

To go ashore without prior clearance is an offence. Contact with other vessels in port prior to clearance is also prohibited.

All of this information can be found on the excellent Australian customs website www.customs.gov.au

Cruising Permits are issued at the time of inwards clearance for yachts transiting Australia. The skipper must report to customs upon arrival at every major port or where requested in sensitive areas such as the Torres Strait. Permits are valid for 12 months or the length of the master's visa, whichever is less, but can be extended on application. Costs in 2009 were $Au330 (you can use a credit card) although on weekends and out of hours the cost is around $Au500. It may be worth anchoring overnight if you are going to arrive out of office hours and proceed into port in the morning. Do check with Australian customs whether this is permitted (it usually is).

Telecom IDD +61. GSM network. Wi-Fi available almost everywhere in larger centres.

Currency Australian dollar. ATM machines are common.

Sailing season All year in the S and May to October in mid to N Queensland

Routes and harbours

Queensland This coast is very popular with Australians. However, for yachts coming from the South Pacific and/or going to the Indian Ocean, their time may be better spent in the less developed tropical islands in those places. The exception is the S, which is clear of cyclones and where visiting yachts are likely to spend the cyclone season.

There are many sailing bases along the coast. The main ones are Brisbane, Mooloolaba, Gladstone, Hamilton Island, Townsville, and Cairns. There are many other ports and anchorages and yachts planning to sail this route are strongly advised to use one of the excellent guides available.

BRISBANE (MORETON BAY)

Tidal range 2.3m

Navigation

Moreton Bay is the approach to Brisbane and it has extensive banks across its entrance. Visitors should only enter via one of the marked channels to the NW of Moreton Island. There are two marked ship entry channels. The NE Channel is six miles NW of Cape

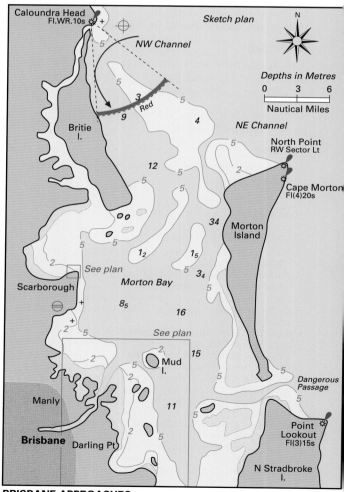

BRISBANE APPROACHES
⊕ 26°48'·7S 153°10'·6E

Moreton and the NW Channel is 21 miles NW of Cape Moreton near Caloundra Head. It has many shoals and the tidal streams can be strong near the shoals. The approach from Moreton Bay to the Manly Boat Harbour has a lit leading line and lit beacons marking the dredged channel into the Boat Harbour. There is a depth of about 3m.

Berths

1. *Scarborough Marina*

VHF Ch 75. This marina has a designated Customs and Quarantine Berth which yachts must use if clearing in at Brisbane. The marina is towards the N end of Moreton Bay on the W shore. There is reported to be 2.2m depth on the approach. Berths to 25m.

2. *Manly*

Manly Boat Harbour has three marinas. It is usually easiest to get into the commercial one, but the Royal Queensland Yacht Squadron may have room.

Anchorage

Many possibilities with good shelter. It is possible to find moorings up the Brisbane river.

Facilities

Hauling out, fuel and water are widely available. There is a small shopping centre close to Manly. All facilities and supplies are available in the Brisbane area.

Remarks

Brisbane is an attractive large city of about one million people. The main yachting centre is on the coast of Moreton Bay at the suburb of Manly. Manly is connected to the centre of Brisbane by a fast electric train service.

TOWNSVILLE

Tidal range 2.8m

Navigation

The approach from the open sea is via Palm passage, passing Pith Reef light, Rib Reef light, and Magnetic Island. Approach from N or S inside the barrier reef is straightforward and well marked.

Note there is some doubt as to the depth in the approach channel, the chart shows that it is dredged to 3m, but we have received reports of less water and shoaling may have occurred. The depth is far more into the commercial harbour.

Berths

VHF Ch 16 for Customs, Port Authority and the marinas. The clearance place is the fuel dock at the Breakwater Marina (immediately inside the marina entrance to starboard). The Motor Boat Club Marina is the most convenient for town but may be full. It is approached through the commercial harbour.

Facilities

There are facilities and supplies in Townsville for hauling out, repairs and yacht equipment. Fuel and water are available.

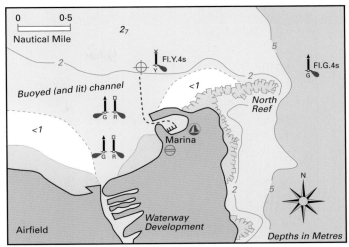

SCARBOROUGH
⊕ 27°11′.0S 153°06′.0E

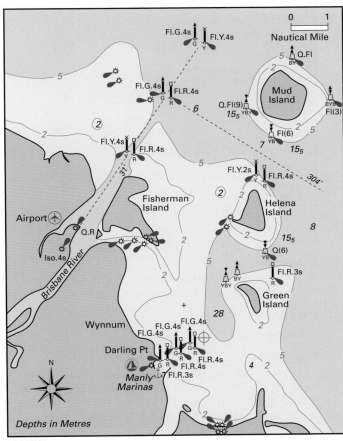

MANLY
⊕ 27°26′.4S 153°13′.0E

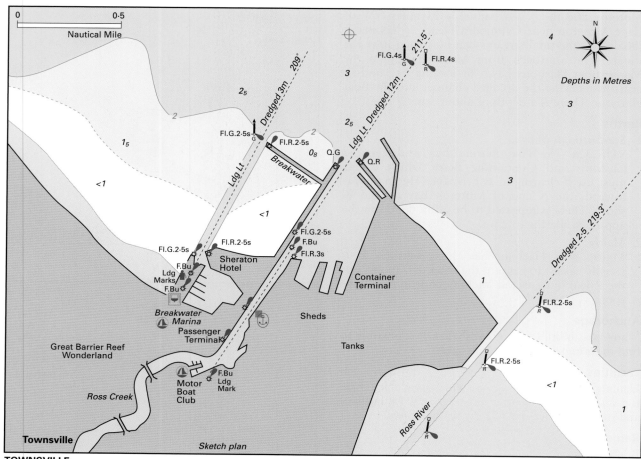

TOWNSVILLE
⊕19°14'·0S 146°50'·0E

Remarks

Townsville is the second largest city in Queensland and a common port of entry for yachts.

CAIRNS

Tidal range 2.3m

Navigation

The recommended approach from seaward is via the Grafton Passage, passing Euston Reef light, Fitzroy Island directional light, Cape Grafton and arriving at the leading line; from the S it is the last three; and from the N it is the leading line. There is a long dredged approach channel with leading lights and lateral beacons. The light is very bright even in daylight. The channel eventually turns towards the port. There is a back leading line and other marks to guide vessels in this section. The marina is at the W side of the entry to the port.

Berths

Cairns Marlin Marina
VHF Ch 16 during working hours. 125 berths. Visitors' berths. Max LOA c.50m. Depths 2.5-5m. Charge band 3.
Good shelter on finger pontoons.

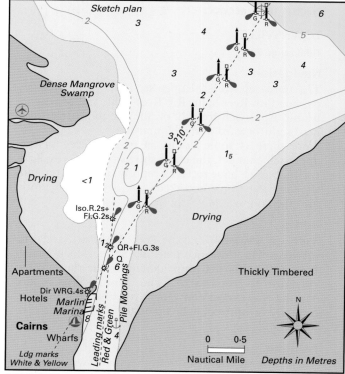

CAIRNS (Queensland)
⊕16°51'·3S 145°49'·1E

Anchorage

Yachts can anchor across from the marina on the E side of the channel. Good holding in mud and good shelter from the Trades. Dinghies can be left in the marina (usually pontoon 'E').

Facilities

Water and electricity. Showers and laundry. The marina is close to the centre of Cairns with supermarkets and restaurants and bars close by. Fuel dock. Yards and hauling facilities further upriver. Chandlers and yacht repair facilities.

Remarks

A friendly and welcoming marina close to everything that is going on.
www.cairnsport.com.au marina@cairnsport.com.au

CAPE YORK AREA

The navigator has to take account of many reefs and shoals, and the effects of strong currents and tides. However the passes and channels are well marked. It is a picturesque area, largely uninhabited. The winds are generally favourable but may be strong. The whole area is protected by the Great Barrier Reef and other reefs further N so there are no ocean waves or swell but the wind can whip up quite a chop. This is not a recommended swimming area because of the dangerous salt-water crocodiles in murky water.

THURSDAY ISLAND

Tides 3m

Navigation

The deep shipping channel is N of Wednesday Island and Hammond Island and NW of Goods Island. It is lit and should be used if not anchoring in this group of islands. However, account must be taken of the tidal currents. The approach through the channel between Horn Island and Prince of Wales Island has the advantage of little tidal current, which is unusual in this area. The main dangers are marked and there is a least depth of 3.4m at the bar at the SE end of the channel. The channel is N of Jardine Rock and SW of the marks on the drying bank. The shoal SE of Jardine Rock is very shallow but the isolated shoal a mile E has 1.8m over it. Care is needed at the exit from the channel into Thursday Island Harbour in order not to get swept into danger by the harbour current. Currents in the harbour can be up to 4kn.

The passage on the N side of Horne Island is shallower, has currents of up to 5kn and may have overfalls NE of Horn Island.

The exit to the W is S of Thursday Island and N of Friday Island. Currents can be up to 8kn from astern, which can make the passage quite exciting, particularly in light winds. Beyond Goods Island is the deep shipping channel.

Anchorage

VHF Ch 16 for customs. Yachts clearing in should anchor off the main wharf or between Madge Reef and Horn Island where it is calmer. In SE winds the

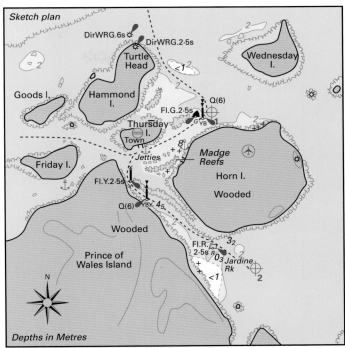

THURSDAY ISLAND (Queensland)
⊕₁10°34'·0S 142°15'·7E
⊕₂10°39'·5S 142°18'·0E

Horn Island anchorage provides greater protection. Anchorage off the township is exposed to strong tidal streams and the prevailing wind.

Facilities

Haul out, fuel, water and limited supplies are available. From Horn Island, it is possible to visit Thursday Island by ferry.

Remarks

Thursday Island is one of the smallest islands in the Prince of Wales Group, but it has the township on it. It is the port of entry likely to be used by yachts from the Solomon Islands and the Louisiades and those sailing N of Australia.

4

NORTH PACIFIC OCEAN

Hawaii coastline at Maui
© *Iofoto | Dreamstime.com*

General

For many circumnavigators the North Pacific is not directly on any of the obvious routes. However, there are large numbers of ocean voyaging yachts on the W seaboard of North America, in Hawaii and increasing numbers in Japan. In addition, more and more yachts are finding it worthwhile to visit these shores. Japan offers excellent cruising and yachting facilities and a very warm welcome. The archipelagos off the coasts of British Columbia and Alaska form one of the world's great temperate wilderness cruising grounds.

Cruising routes are divided into those to or from the ocean and those within the ocean. Only the main destinations have been dealt with, as the authors have no information on places such as Kamchatka or the Bering Strait.

Weather and sea

PREVAILING WINDS

Note To fully understand the rather complex weather for the ocean, reference should be made to the sketches, relevant pilot charts (or software) and the relevant route descriptions.

The principal circulation is clockwise around the N Pacific High. This is at its greatest extent and stability in summer. In winter the High is not confluent and generally consists of several cells of high pressure separated by troughs originating from depressions to the N. The high-pressure cells and troughs regularly cross the ocean from W to E.

To the N of the high pressure is a zone of W winds. In summer these are generated by low pressure to the N of 50°N and high pressure centred to the S of 40°N, giving rise to fairly steady westerlies. In winter depressions regularly pass across the N of the ocean and their passage is associated with far more variable winds, frequent severe gales and overcast weather.

To the S of the High lies the NE Trade wind. This is a very reliable wind and lies mainly between 30°N and 8°N in summer and in winter mainly between 20°N and the equator. There is a large variation over the ocean so refer to the pilot charts.

To the E of the High the general trend is for winds from the N quarter following the clockwise oceanic circulation. To the W the clockwise circulation is predominant in summer giving S winds. In the SE portion of the ocean this pattern is modified in summer, and in the W portion in winter. See seasonal winds below.

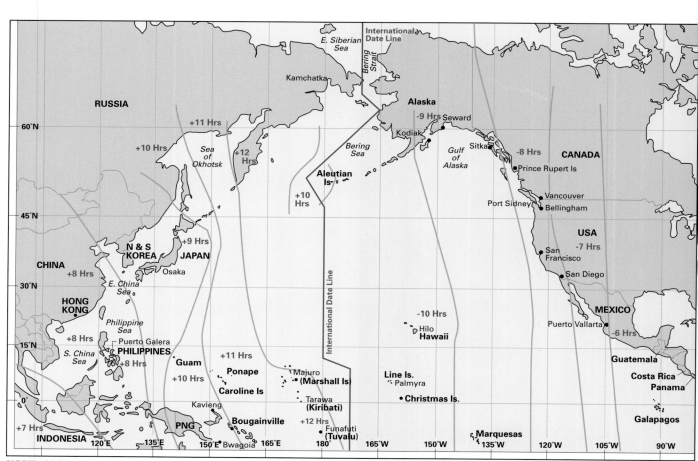

NORTH PACIFIC COUNTRIES, PORTS AND TIME DIFFERENCES ON GMT

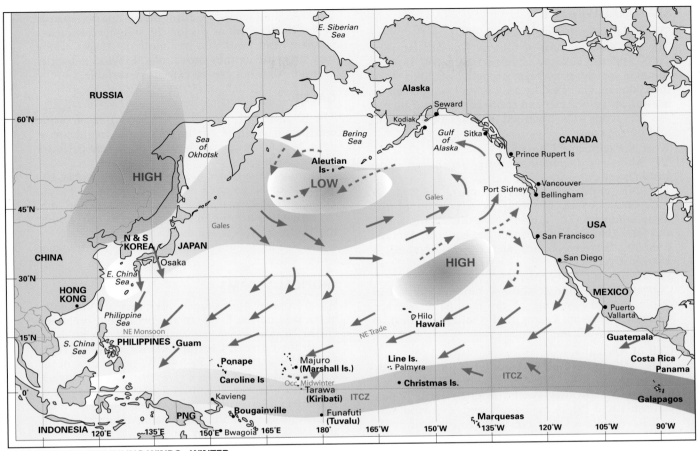

NORTH PACIFIC PREVAILING WINDS - WINTER

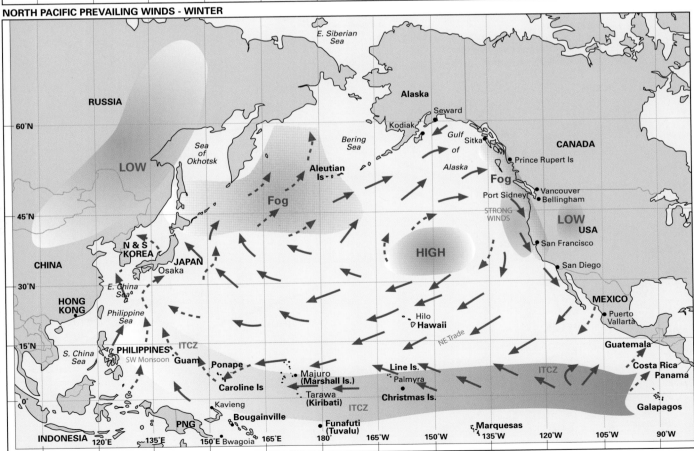

NORTH PACIFIC PREVAILING WINDS - SUMMER

SEASONAL WINDS

SE of N Pacific (June–October)

The area off the coast of Central America between 10°N and the equator is subject to a SW flow in summer (reaching average strengths of 20kn N of the Galapagos) caused by an intense low, formed by heating of the N American continent. The weather in this area tends to be unsettled with squalls at sea and rain on the coast.

W of N Pacific and China Sea

NE Monsoon (September–April, depending upon latitude)

The NE winds over this area are caused by anticyclonic winds resulting from cooling of the Asian landmass. The time of onset is earlier in the N and later (November) towards the equator. Average strength (between Guam and the Philippines) is 25kn in December.

SW Monsoon (May–September)

Conversely, in summer, the SW monsoon blows in response to the heating of the landmass. Average strength (between Guam and the Philippines) is 15–20kn in August.

Gulf of Alaska

N of 55°N, in the Gulf of Alaska, the summer winds are predominantly NE–SE. Leaving Kodiak and heading N towards Anchorage, Seward, Kenai Peninsula and Prince William Sound, the wind may well have quite a lot of NE in it. To the S of 55°N the prevailing winds are from the W quarter, mainly NW. The depressions during the summer are of less intensity and head into the Gulf of Alaska where they dissipate as they move inland. Wind velocities average 20kn but can be extremely variable.

GALES

The N part of the ocean is relatively free of severe weather in summer but in winter the frequency of gales N of 40°N can reach 50%. Elsewhere gales are far less common.

During the summer months, June–September, the W coast of N America is affected by the N Pacific High and the Low that builds on the mainland, due to continental heating, resulting in occasional strong to gale force N–NW winds offshore.

The China Sea and Taiwan are subject to frequent winter gales.

TROPICAL STORMS

When tropical storms reach 64kn they are known as hurricanes on the E side of the ocean and typhoons on the W side.

Off the coast of Central America, between 10°N and 30°N and E of 130–140°W, hurricanes occur between May and November. Most occur between June and October and the greatest frequency is in September. Sometimes these reach the Hawaiian Islands (in the last 55 years five have hit the islands and seven passed close by).

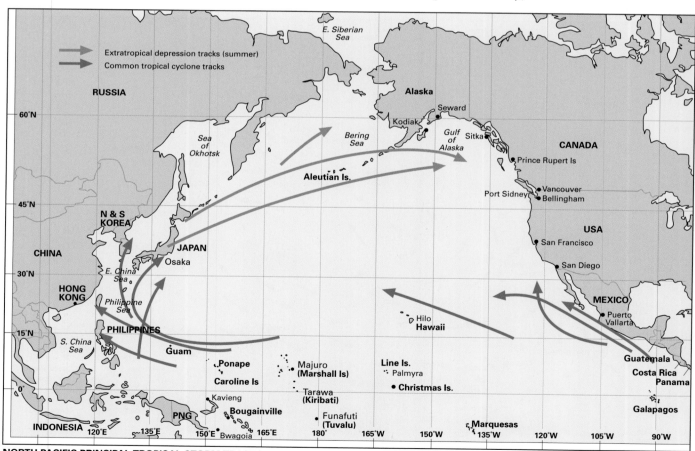

NORTH PACIFIC PRINCIPAL TROPICAL STORM TRACKS AND PRINCIPAL DEPRESSION TRACKS

Typhoons occur in the area between the N Philippines, N Vietnam, the coasts of China, Taiwan, S Korea and the S of Japan and extend into the oceanic islands S of Japan.

Typhoons do not follow such a predictable season as tropical storms in other areas and may occur at any time of year. The majority of storms occur in the summer months, 90% between May and December and 50% between July and October. September is the worst month. No typhoons have been recorded on the Chinese coast between December and April.

OCEAN CURRENTS

These follow the same clockwise circulation as the winds.

North Equatorial Current flows W in the trade winds.

Kuro Shio is the current on the W side of the ocean that flows NE past Japan and becomes the North Pacific Current.

North Pacific Current flows towards N America and turns S.

California Current is the part of the circulation flowing S down the N American coast.

There are a few exceptions to the general flow:

The Kamchatka Current flows in a SW direction from the W side of the Bering Sea towards the N coast of Japan, where it is known as the Oya Shio.

TROPICAL STORMS AND HURRICANES BY MONTH

Month	Tropical storms >35k Annual average		Hurricanes >64k Annual average	
	East	West	East	West
Jan	0	0.4	0	0.3
Feb	0	0.4	0	0.2
Mar	0.03	0.5	0	0.2
Apr	0	0.9	0	0.7
May	0.3	1.3	0.3	0.9
Jun	2	1.8	0.6	1.2
Jul	3.6	3.9	0.9	2.7
Aug	4.5	5.8	2	4
Sep	4.1	5.6	1.8	4.1
Oct	2.2	4.3	1	3.3
Nov	0.3	2.9	0	2.1
Dec	1 in 28 years	1.3	1 in 28 years	0.7

(Data from DMA)

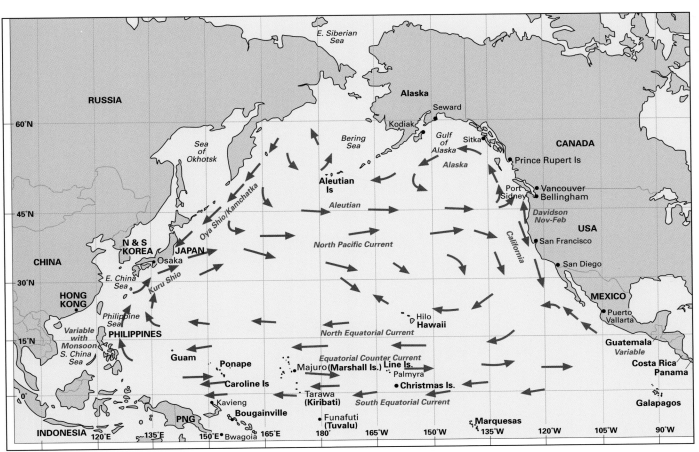

NORTH PACIFIC CURRENTS

Where this meets the Kuro Shio and is deflected to the E, it is known as the Aleutian Current.

The Aleutian Current flows in a NE direction towards the Aleutian chain and forms a colder N portion of the North Pacific Current.

Alaska Current In the vicinity of the Queen Charlotte Islands the Aleutian Current turns N and then W in the Gulf of Alaska and is known as the Alaska Current.

In the China Sea and to the W of the main circulation the currents tend to follow the seasonal monsoons described above.

Davidson Current The California Current does not meet the coast. S of Vancouver Island the inshore current is irregular in strength and direction except for mid-winter when there is a N-going inshore stream, known as the Davidson Current.

Off the Central American coast currents are variable and to some extent seasonal.

The Equatorial Counter-current is E-going. It is created by the return of surface water that originally flowed W with the trade wind. It lies between 2°N and 10°N depending upon longitude and season. S of this the South Equatorial Current lies to the S of the equator.

EL NIÑO

In the N Pacific El Niño usually dampens the normal trade winds and brings storms to California and Mexico. In a normal year Mexico's winter weather is so benign that cruisers often don't bother to monitor the weather. In an El Niño year that would be a mistake: the hurricane season may well start earlier.

FOG

Fog is frequently encountered in the W part of the ocean, especially in summer when the warm and moist, SW monsoon blows over the cold Oya Shio current.

Off the Aleutian chain, thanks to the cold Alaska Current, summer fog occurs 30% of the time.

Likewise, when the warmer W wind meets the cold S-going California Current, fog results. Fog affects coastal waters between Vancouver Island and San Diego during the summer, the worst month being August.

ROUTES AND PASSAGES

TRANS-EQUATORIAL ROUTES BETWEEN THE SOUTH AND NORTH PACIFIC

NP1 From French Polynesia (and S America) to Hawaii

Papeete to Honolulu 2,370M

Season May–November

Tropical storms Both French Polynesia (November–May) and Hawaii (May–November) are affected by cyclones, but the risk is far greater in the French islands, with the exception of the Marquesas

Try to make as much easting as possible. For this reason, the best place to depart from is the Marquesas. Sailing via the Line Islands is possible, but means that the course will be harder on the wind after crossing the equator.

NP2 From French Polynesia to Japan

Papeete to Inland Sea of Japan (Osaka), via Majuro 5,330M

Season and Best time See notes below.

Tropical storms Both French Polynesia (November–May) and Japan (max risk May–November) are affected by cyclones, but the risk is far greater in the French islands with the exception of the Marquesas, where it is lower

The most direct route is via Kiribati (Gilbert Island group) or the Marshall Islands. Much consideration needs to be given to the cyclone risk on the route. Probably the best option is to leave French Polynesia late in the season (October–November), spend several months in the equatorial island groups and then head for Japan early in summer (April–May). See notes for NPW2.

*NP3 From SE Australia and New Zealand to Hawaii or reverse

Auckland to Palmyra 2,860M
Palmyra to Honolulu 950M

Season May–November

Tropical storms November–May in S Pacific

Follow S Pacific routes SPN1 and SPN7 (via Tonga) or SPN3 and SPN8 (via French Polynesia) to the Line Islands. Christmas Island (Kiribati), where there is a small community, and further E uninhabited Palmyra, are popular stopping places. From the Line Islands sail N making as much easting as possible. If motoring through the doldrums, keep to the E of the direct course. Once in the NE Trades, steer for the destination, making allowance for leeway and the W-going current. This route is a close reach heading north and a broad reach heading S.

See *SPS1

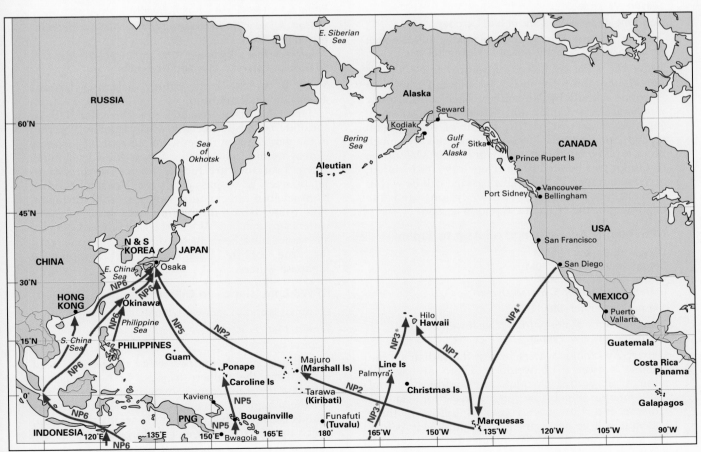

ROUTES TO AND FROM NORTH PACIFIC

*NP4 From W coast of N or Central America to French Polynesia

San Diego to Nuka Hiva 2,810M

Season November–May (later departures have less risk of tropical storms in S Pacific)

Best time March and April

Tropical storms Majority May to November (off Central America)

From the USA and Mexico yachts will head for around 05°N 130°W to cross the ITCZ. Once you hit the ITCZ head S until you pick up the SE Trades and then shape a course for your destination. This 'S'-shaped course will generally get you there faster than a direct rhumb line course. The Marquesas Islands are the usual destination. These islands are only occasionally affected by tropical storms but other parts of French Polynesia regularly suffer severe cyclones (see Chapter 3, South Pacific Ocean).

See separate section guide 'The Coconut Milk Run' in Chapter 3.

See *SPW3

NP5 From SE Australia and New Zealand to Japan

Brisbane to Gizo 1,200M
Gizo to Guam 1,500M
Guam to Osaka 1,400M

Season Variable

Best time Leave SW Pacific in late October

Tropical storms The majority are in May to November for S Japan, but S Pacific season is November–May

Leave the S Pacific before November (see S Pacific notes), and aim to be in the N Solomon Islands or Caroline Islands by November. Then work slowly northward via Guam and Okinawa to arrive in Japanese waters before the height of the typhoon season. Some vessels choose to make this trip much more rapidly, notably participants in the Melbourne to Osaka two-handed Race. They leave mid-March, arriving in Japan in May. This passage will be within the tail end of the S Pacific cyclone and the beginning of the N Pacific typhoon season.

NP6 From N Australia and SE Asia to Japan

Darwin to Batam 1,900M
Batam to Okinawa 2,050M
Okinawa to Osaka 650M
(Batam see Chapter 5, Indian Ocean)

Season November–May

Tropical storms Majority from May–November for Philippine Sea and S Japan

Depart Australian waters before the Indian Ocean cyclone season in November. There are several choices of route, through the Indonesian and Philippine archipelagos (piracy risk) or via the Chinese and Taiwanese coasts. If following these routes it will be necessary to wait until May before leaving SE Asia or the Philippines because the NE monsoon would be against you until then (see NPN1 and IW2). A yacht could also work to the N

of New Guinea and then to the Caroline Islands and follow the route described above (NP7).

ROUTES WITHIN THE NORTH PACIFIC

The circulation of winds and oceanic currents means that these routes are primarily clockwise around the ocean with a few N–S or S–N ones crossing it. Hawaii is centrally located near the N border of the NE Trade winds so it is a hub for many routes.

West-going passages

NPW1 West Coast of N America to Hawaii

San Diego to Hilo 2,200M

Season N of 30°N all year

Tropical cyclones May–November (S of 30°N)

Follow the coast S to the latitude of San Francisco or San Diego and then steer directly for Hawaii. The Transpac race is sailed in July, biennially on odd numbered years, between Los Angeles and Honolulu.

From Central America (winter only) steer direct in the NE Trades.

NPW2 Hawaii to W side of the N Pacific, Japan and the Far East

Honolulu to Ponape 2,680M
Ponape to Inland Sea (Osaka) 2,050M

Season All year for destinations below 10°N, otherwise November–May

Tropical cyclones Between 10°N and 35°N – all year, but 90% occur between May and December

Steer W in the trade winds, selecting latitude according to destination.

Japan is often reached via the Marshall or Caroline Islands, especially when departing Hawaii in the winter when there is time to spare if Japanese waters are not to be reached before May. In summer, when the trades are further N, to sail directly to Japan steer W to pass N of the Marshall Islands, from where a direct course can be steered for Japan. This route avoids the cyclone area until Japanese waters are reached. When steering towards Japan, allowance must be made for the Kuro Shio (current), fog, and for the huge amount of shipping in Japanese waters.

NPW3 Line Islands to Gilbert Islands

Christmas Island to Tarawa: 1,780M

Season March–October

Tropical cyclones None

This timing avoids the possibility of westerly head winds near the Gilbert Islands. In November to February the convergence zones of the Southern and Northern hemispheres may separate near the Gilbert Islands causing a belt of westerly winds to develop, which may be strong, even gale force. This does not happen every year and is not dangerous for a well set-up yacht, but it makes for hard windward sailing. At other times expect light following winds with the odd squall.

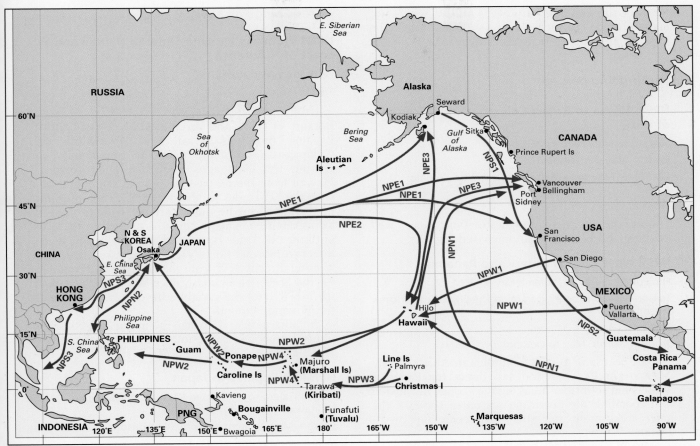

ROUTES WITHIN NORTH PACIFIC

NPW4 Gilbert Islands to the Marshall Islands & Micronesia

Tarawa to Majuro: 370M.
Majuro to Ponape: 800M

Season December–May

Best time April–May (in the vicinity of the Gilbert Islands)

Tropical cyclones Majority May to November, low risk in the Marshall Islands, higher in Carolines

The usual wind on this route is a moderate, occasionally fresh, NE but lighter near the Gilbert Islands. Expect a close reach to the Marshall Islands and broad reach thereafter.

East-going Passages

NPE1 Far East and Japan to Aleutian Islands, Alaska or W coast of N America.

Osaka to Kodiak 3,300M
Osaka to Straits of Vancouver 5,000M

Season May–September

Best time May–June

Tropical storms (S of 35°N) majority May to November

A course should be steered to get above 40°N and then steer to the destination. The ideal latitude is around 44°N, but this may prove to be too foggy and cold. Further S the weather will be better but the winds not quite so reliable. If heading for destinations S of 40°N, the vessel should reach at least 150°W before turning for the destination. Fog is the main navigational hazard if heading for the more northern destinations.

NPE2 Japan to Hawaii

Osaka to 40°N 155°W to Hilo 4,400M

Season May–August

Best time May–June

Tropical cyclones In Japanese waters, all year but 90% occur between May and December. Hawaii: hurricanes are infrequent and are most likely between June and October

Stay N of 40°N until N of the Hawaii group (sailing further N will give more favourable winds but also a higher incidence of fog). Then steer SE towards the E of the islands. Once the NE Trade is met steer for the destination, making due allowance for leeway and a W-going current.

NPE3 Hawaii to Alaska, British Columbia or W coast of USA

Hilo to Kodiak 2,280M
Hilo to Vancouver 2,600M

Season All year to California, May–September to Vancouver, May–August to Alaska

Tropical storms Hawaii occasionally affected in late summer.

Steer N through the variables until W winds are encountered (further N in summer) and the appropriate latitude is reached, then steer E for the destination

South-going passages

NPS1 Alaska to British Columbia and W coast of USA

Seward to San Francisco 1,670M

Season May–September

Best time May to September, see section on gales above

Tropical storms Nil

Follow the coast to the destination. Keep well offshore and beware of shipping and fog.

NPS2 West coast N America to Panama

San Francisco Bay to Panama City 3,430M

Season Variable, bearing in mind the E Pacific hurricane season

Best time April or October

Tropical storms May to October

Depart Seattle or British Columbia in April to early May or in October and sail direct for Panama. Vessels may consider breaking the voyage in Mexico and spending the hurricane season in some of the safer areas there and afterwards coast-hop on to Panama.

The W coast of USA in June–September can be very windy (see section on gales above).

Beware of strong winds in the Gulf of Tehuantepec during January; take local advice; watch weather sources carefully. Alternatives are to hug the coast for some shelter from offshore winds, or make passages under power during calm periods. Although Tehuantepec winds are less fierce from May to September the risk of hurricanes is present.

NPS3 Japan to SE Asia

Inland Sea (Osaka) to Hong Kong 1,300M
Hong Kong to Singapore 1,400M

Season November–April

Best time March and April

Tropical storms Majority May to November

This is a tricky passage at any time of year. To make the passage in summer is almost out of the question as the SW monsoon dictates a very circuitous course around the Philippines and the typhoon risk is high. In winter the NE monsoon is favourable, the typhoon risk much reduced but gales are very likely along the course. March and April have the least incidence of winter gales and a low probability of typhoons. The usual course is between Japan and Korea and then inside Taiwan.

Yachts wishing to cruise in SE Asia or transit the Suez Canal will want to leave Japan in November to be in SE Asia outside the typhoon season or reach the Red Sea by February when conditions are favourable for a N-bound passage.

North-Going Passages

NPN1 From the Panama Canal to Hawaii and W coast of N America

Balboa to Hilo 4,910M

Season All year

Tropical storms May–November (low risk)

Because of calms and variable winds in the Gulf of Panama, most vessels sail S of W towards the Galapagos (and many take the opportunity of visiting the Galapagos and then head towards Hawaii from there), passing close to them, and sail with the SE Trades to about 105°W. The doldrums in this area can be quite variable with prolonged calms reported. Then a course is shaped to the NW until the NE Trade is met and a course can be made direct to Hawaii. Some yachts have fared better by steering directly NW from the Galapagos. If making for the N American coast, once W of 135°W sail to the NNW until the variables have been crossed and the W wind is found.

An alternative is to sail N along the coast of Central America (see section on El Niño and passage NPS2 above).

NPN2 Philippines to Japan

Puerto Galera to Inland Sea (Osaka) 1,500M (via Okinawa)

Season May–November (with SW monsoon)

Best time May and June

Tropical storms All year, majority May to November

This passage would be impractical in winter (when the typhoon risk is lower) as it would be directly into the NE monsoon. The typhoon risk is highest from July to September so a passage in May or June is the best option. Typhoon reports should be carefully monitored, with Okinawa being a potential stopping point. (The authors have no recent information on this landfall but understand that there are several well-sheltered harbours here). In winter this passage could be reversed.

COUNTRY AND PORT GUIDE

 ## Alaska

See Chapter 1 North Atlantic for USA country information (with particular reference to post 9/11 entry requirements)

General All through Alaska, and especially in the more remote parts, the people are extraordinarily friendly. Fishermen are generous with advice and the occasional fish as well. There are many small places that have a free public pontoon. In many of the settlements and villages there is water and fuel available and occasionally power. The best time to cruise is between May and September.

Coastline This is long and mostly deeply indented; spectacular scenery is the rule in the Gulf of Alaska where glaciers carve into some of the fjords and in the myriad islands on the inside passage of the 'panhandle'.

Formalities There is a requirement for a special cruising permit to visit Glacier Bay in the inside passage, in order to stop it becoming overcrowded. Fishing licences are required, The current price is $100 (2004) for a season's permit. There is a large fine if you are caught without one. A fishing licence covers salmon, oysters, clams and crab.

Routes and harbours From Hawaii, plan to arrive in Kodiak or Dutch Harbour. Best to plan arrival after the beginning of June. Prince William Sound (PWS) is a fabulous summer cruising area. For those who want to spend more time in the area, to overwinter or leave their boat up north, these are two good places: Valdez or Cordova.

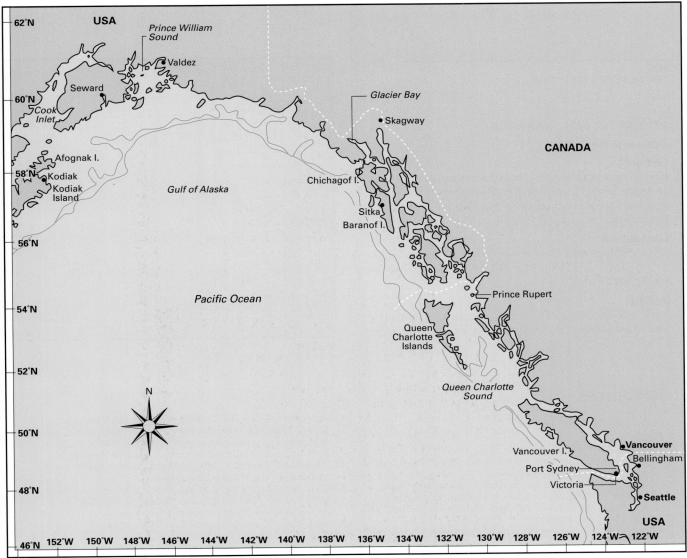

NORTHWEST COAST OF NORTH AMERICA

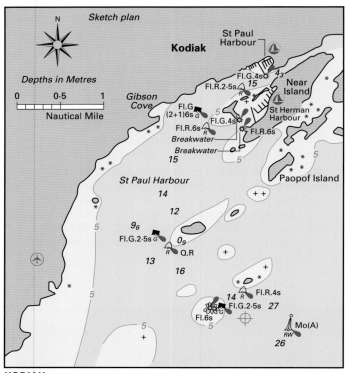

KODIAK
⊕57°44'·2N 152°25'·0W WGS84

(8m–20m) and another on Near Island (St Herman Harbour) of 325 slips (6m–50m). Most slips have access to water and power.

Facilities
Laundry and showers available. There are two grids, but they are normally in use by the commercial fishing fleet. No lift. Basic repair facilities. The town has a marine shop, a bank and a food store. For restocking with a wide choice, go to Eagle or Safeway – about five minutes by bus. Plane and ferry to Seward and Anchorage.

Remarks
This is a commercial fishing port, but the welcome for visiting yachts is warm.
www.city.kodiak.ak.us/harbor

SEWARD

Tidal range 5.5m

Navigation
Straightforward, without dangers, from Resurrection Bay.

KODIAK (ST PAUL HARBOUR)

Tidal range 4m

General
Kodiak is a port of entry and is a natural port to stop en route from Hawaii or the Aleutian Islands. Good starting point for cruising the Kenai or Alaska Peninsulas.

Navigation
Enter Chiniak Bay N of the port lateral mark (Green 57°42'·80N 152°14'·19W WGS84) to the NE of Humpback Rock.

Berths
VHF Ch 16 or 12. The city operates two marinas, one downtown (St Paul Harbour) of 250 slips

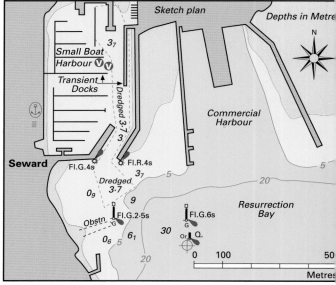

SEWARD
⊕60°06'·7N 149°20'·7W

Resources

PILOTS, GUIDES AND CHARTS
Alaska
Charlie's Charts. North to Alaska Charles E Wood. Good for passage-making with quite a fair number of ports and anchorages. (charliescharts.com)
Exploring the Inside Passage to Alaska Don Douglas and Reanne Hemingway-Douglass (Fire Edge Productions). This has many more anchorages than Charlie's Charts and is strongly recommended.
Alaskan Harbour and Boating Facilities Directory Published by the Alaska Department of Transport and public facilities

Canada chart book 3313 Canadian Hydrographic Service (Chart agencies). Every marine hardware shop, some groceries or even a garage will have local charts, from Alaska all the way down through the Inside Passage
Cruising Guide to Prince William Sound Jim and Nancy Lethcoe (Prince William Sound Books).
There is no guide for the Kodiak, Alaska & Kenai peninsulas but *US Coast Pilot No 9* covers these. Don Douglas is currently writing a guide for the Kodiak area
Dreamspeaker Cruising Guides (Rain Coast Books)
Vol 1 Gulf Islands and Vancouver I
Vol 2 Desolation Sound and Discovery Is
Vol 3 Vancouver, Howe Sound and Sunshine Coast. Anne and Laurence Yeadon-Jones

Berths

For vessels up to 25m. The visitor pontoon is on the fuel dock. Harbourmaster at head of pier ✆ 224-3138.

Facilities

50-ton lift in harbour and bigger one also available. Good shops, launderette, medical facilities and restaurants.

Remarks

Good transportation for crew changes.
www.cityofseward.net/harbor

SITKA

Tidal range 5m

Navigation

Western Channel and Eastern Channel are well marked and entrance is straightforward. There is a fixed bridge crossing the harbour with 15.8m clearance.

Berths

Three marinas with all facilities. (Transient berths at New Thomson Harbor and Crescent Harbor).

Facilities

Good access to transport and all facilities.

Remarks

Port of entry. Convenient first port when arriving from Hawaii. Winter climate said to be reasonable for live-aboards with heating.
www.cityofsitka.com/new_harbors_website/harbor.html

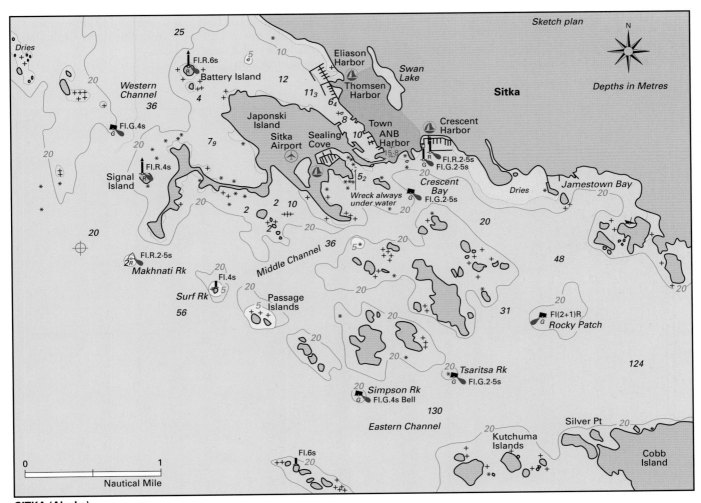

SITKA (Alaska)
⊕57°02'·2N 135°25'·3W

Canada (British Columbia)

General Canada is a member of the British Commonwealth. It has a federal system of government.

Coastline In British Columbia, mountains coming down into the sea, densely forested islands and deep inlets make this one of the most interesting cruising areas in the world. The outer coast is wild but islands provide sheltered waterways for almost the whole coastline. The East Coast is dealt with separately.

Formalities Call customs at the port of entry (☎ 1-800-CAN-PASS). They will be pleasant and efficient but will require a detailed declaration of alcohol aboard. Once formalities are completed you are unlikely to see them again before leaving the country. If planning to lay-up a boat in Canada, it is essential to obtain a permit from customs. Visas not required for US, Commonwealth and EU citizens. Fishing permits are required by law and are available from most hardware shops, marinas and the like.

Telecom IDD +1. GSM network. Internet facilities widespread, generally in public libraries.

Currency Canadian dollar. Credit cards universally accepted. ATMs widespread.

Sailing season Mid-April to October.

Routes and harbours This area is excellent for cruising, with many sheltered anchorages, even on the seaward coasts, and good facilities for the yachtsman. The inside passage between Vancouver and Prince Rupert is very popular.

PRINCE RUPERT (Kaien Island)

Tidal range 8m

Berths

The Prince Rupert Rowing and Yacht Club has a well developed marina in Cow Bay at the N end of town which welcomes visitors. Contact them on Ch 73. (www.prryc.com) Moorings may also be available in the fishing boat marina, S of the ferry terminal.

Anchorage

It is possible to anchor in the bay in front of the Yacht Club (to the NE of area shown on sketch).

Facilities

Full marina facilities and a friendly and helpful yacht club. Very good shops.

Remarks

Port of entry for Canada. Customs and immigration are in the town. Call them from the Yacht Club after which they will visit the boat.
www.prryc.com

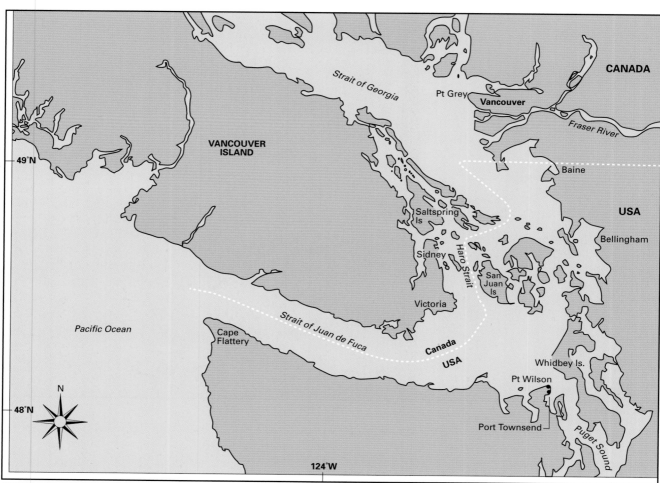

STRAIT OF JUAN DE FUCA

VANCOUVER VICTORIA AREA

At the S end of Vancouver Island and the adjacent coast of BC, two well situated ports are described. However, there are numerous excellent harbours and marinas and every yachting facility is easily available. Except for Port Sidney and Vancouver, which are expensive, Canadian prices match or are lower than those in the States. There is a big difference between summer and winter prices.

PORT SIDNEY

Tidal range 4m

Berths

There are numerous marinas, some public and some belonging to YCs. Most are in Tsehum Harbour, which is a little distance from the town. Port Sidney marina is conveniently located close to the centre of town. VHF Ch 66a. Van Isle Marina has all facilities including a fuel dock and 538 berths for boats up to 130m. Reservations are recommended during the summer.

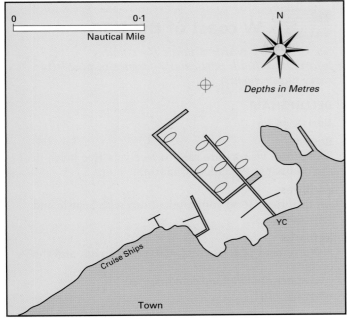

PRINCE RUPERT HARBOUR
⊕54°19′·15N 130°19′·09W

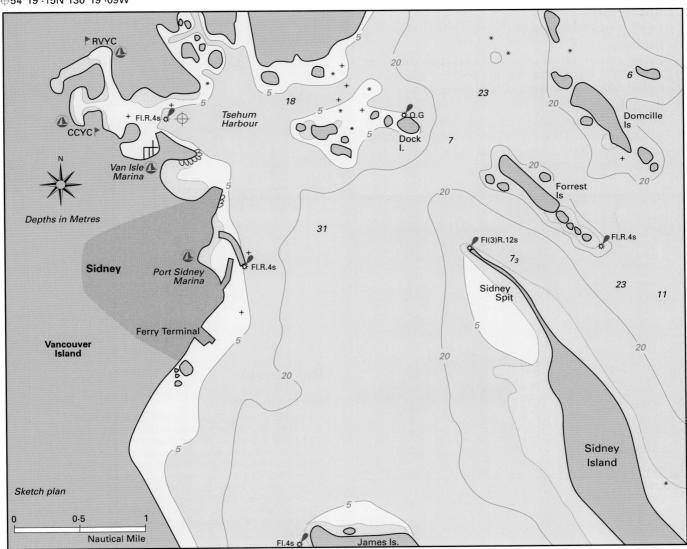

SIDNEY (Vancouver Island)
⊕48°40′·3N 123°24′W

Facilities

It is possible to lay up a yacht here for the winter ashore or afloat. There is a small travel-lift and several marine railway slips. The local store has limited supplies and bigger shops are quite a way away. Several ferries, plus airport, close by.

Remarks

Port of entry.
www.vanislemarina.com www.portsidney.com

VANCOUVER

Tidal range 5m

Navigation

There are strong currents in the approach and entrance to Coal Harbour.

Berths

False Creek has several marinas. Coal Harbour Marina in Vancouver City (49°17'·5N 123°07'·5W) VHF Ch 66a has 238 slips ranging from 9m–60m. Walking distance from the city centre. Very secure but expensive. There are also other marinas close to the town. Reservations are recommended during the summer season.

Anchorage

Possible to anchor free further up False Creek.

Facilities

Every conceivable facility is available. Excellent shops and restaurants for all pockets and tastes. Cyber cafés within easy reach of the marinas.

Remarks

A large cosmopolitan city. A visit is highly recommended. The city is on a tongue of land between Vancouver harbour and False Creek.
www.coalharbourmarina.com

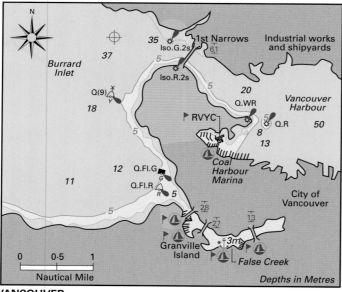

VANCOUVER
⊕49°19'·2N 123°10'·0W

 ## W coast of the USA

See Chapter 1 North Atlantic for country information (with particular reference to post 9/11 entry requirements)

BELLINGHAM

Tidal range 4m

Berths

Short-term visitors are said to receive a free berth in the municipal (Squalicum) marina.

Facilities

All facilities. Good communications with Seattle and Vancouver.

Remarks

A convenient port of entry, close to Canada and the ocean.
www.portofbellingham.com/marinas
www.byc.org

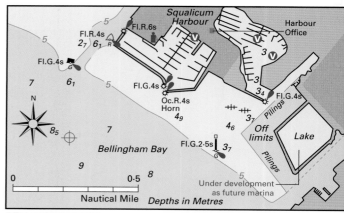

BELLINGHAM BAY
⊕48°45'·0N 122°31'·0W

Resources

PILOTS AND GUIDES

Waggoner Cruising Guide: Puget Sound, San Juan Islands, Gulf Islands, Inside passage North to Prince Rupert. B.C. Editor Robert Hale (Robert Hale & Co Publishers) www.waggonerguide.com

Exploring Vancouver Island's West Coast Don Douglass and Reanne Hemingway-Douglass. There may be a new edition of the Douglass guide covering all the BC waters (Fine Edge Productions)

Canadian tide tables or *Reed's Almanac* A must for going up the inside of Vancouver Island and Juan de Fuca Strait

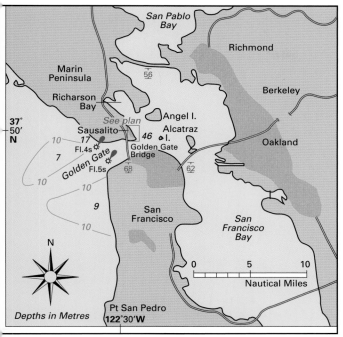

SAN FRANCISCO BAY

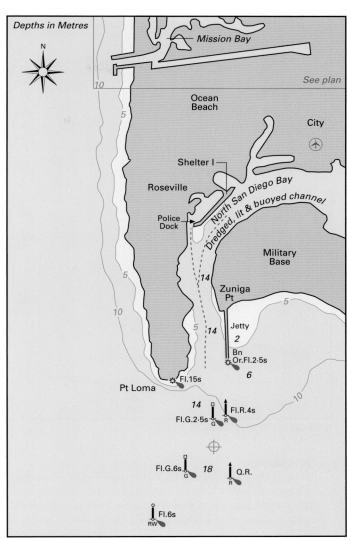

SAN DIEGO AREA
⊕32°38'·5N 117°13'·7W

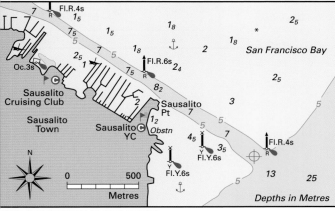

SAN FRANCISCO (SAUSALITO)
⊕37°51'·3N 122°28'·2W

SAN FRANCISCO (SAUSALITO)

Tidal range 2.5m.

Berths

There are several marinas. There appears to be a problem for yachts more than 13m to find a berth for more than a couple of weeks at a time. Maybe this is because the marinas are full of live-aboards.

Anchorage

There is an anchorage off Sausalito.

Facilities

All facilities available. Hoists and repairs.

Remarks

Port of Entry. San Francisco Bay is one of the world's great sailing areas.
www.boatingsf.com

SAN DIEGO (MISSION BAY)

Tidal range 2.5m

Navigation

Straightforward in settled weather. In the unlikely event of bad conditions it may be safer to enter the main harbour, which is safe to enter in all weather. The port office is at the entrance to Quivera Basin, to starboard. The Mission Bay Harbour Patrol/San Diego Lifeguard offers assistance 24 hours a day and can be reached on VHF 16. Their HQ is open weekdays from 0800 to 1700 hours. Because of fixed bridges, only the Quivera and Mariners Basin are usable by cruising yachts. Foreign flagged yachts must clear in with the authorities in the main harbour after which you can anchor out.

Berths

Several marinas, including Driscoll, with visitors' berths are located in Quivera basin. Charge band 5.

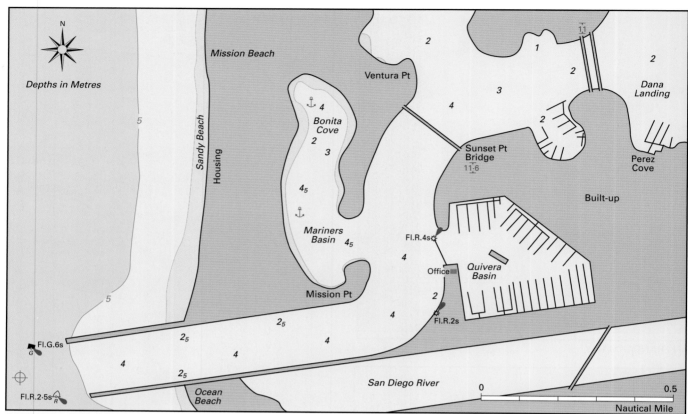

SAN DIEGO (MISSION BAY)
⊕32°45′·4N 117°15′·8W

Anchorage

Free anchorage for up to 72hrs per 7-day period in Mariners Basin. Dinghy landings on beaches around the basin with local stores nearby. Free dinghy dock and pump-out at Lifeguard HQ in Quivera Basin.

Facilities

Every conceivable facility, including fuel, water, electricity and pump-outs. The airport is very conveniently located close to the yachting centres.

Remarks

Port of Entry. Boats that have entered the US elsewhere and obtained immigration clearance and a cruising permit may proceed directly to whichever anchorage or marina they choose. Note: all vessels entering from foreign ports must tie up first at the Police Dock on the S end of Shelter Island in the main harbour. It is not permitted to enter US territorial waters and bypass San Diego for ports further N. There are numerous marinas and some anchorages (police permits generally required) in the main harbour of San Diego. Mission Bay is recommended as it is a quieter area and anchoring is simpler.
www.sailorschoice.com/Harbors.htm
(useful information on marinas and facilities in Southern California).
www.driscoll-boats.com

Mexico

General The W coast of Mexico is a popular and economical cruising area.

Coastline Mexico has long coasts on the Pacific and Caribbean shores. Both are more famous for their beaches than their harbours. The major ports should be avoided.

Formalities Entry/exit into and out of the country is now more streamlined with one-stop shops in Ensenada and Cabo San Lucas, where all the formalities of immigration, customs, clearing your crew list with the Port Captain can be carried out under one roof. It is normal if entering by sea to be given a 180 day Tourist Card.

There are strict controls on importing food. Fishing licences are required for all crew members, and all boats including dinghies, kayaks and life rafts.

Once a boat and its crew have entered formally into the country, all that is required is for the boat skipper to notify the port captain that the boat and crew is leaving or entering each new port.

Telecom IDD +52, GSM network. Internet in main towns.

Currency Peso. ATMs available.

Sailing season This is during the winter months (November to April) as both coasts are subject to tropical storms.

ENSENADA

Tidal Range 1.9m

Navigation

Approaching Ensenada from the north it is advisable to take a wide sweep entering Bahia de Todos Santos due to kelp beds. The entrance to the harbour is well lit at night, but entry into any port in Mexico at night is not advised, as maintenance of lights is poor.

Berths

There are five marinas in Ensenada. Banditos is a single slip affair, with no security, close to the town centre, with water and power. Marina Ensenada has only slips no power, security or water. Marina Baja Naval, Marina Coral and Cruiseport Village Marina are all full service. Fuel is available from Baja Naval. www.bajanaval.com www.ecpvmarina.com

Anchorage

Is located in the main basin, off Baja Naval Marina. The Port Captain charges boats to anchor.

Facilities

Haul out is available from several yards. Baja Naval has an excellent reputation.

There are a few chandleries, although they have limited stocks.

There are two Gigantes supermarkets within walking distance. The well stocked fish market is a must see. The La Palapa Loca Sports Bar welcomes

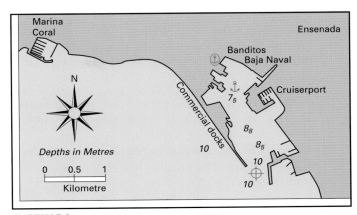

ENSENADA
⊕ 31°50'·5N 116°37'·4W

cruisers.

Remarks

This small working harbour is a home from home to many cruisers who arrive and never leave. Most people heading south from the Pacific West Coast of the USA make this their first port of call, primarily because the Mexican authorities have set up a one stop shop for cruisers to carry out the required complex entry/exit procedures, which is within walking distance of most of the marinas.

PUERTO VALLARTA

Tidal range 1.6m

Navigation

Approaching Banderas Bay from the north, it is advisable to travel south of Punta Mieta, and enter the bay south of Los Morros rocks, and the Islas Marietas. Cabo Corrientes is known for its cape effect currents that flow from the Ocean into the bay. There are numerous anchorages around the Bay, which make attractive day sails from Puerto Vallarta.

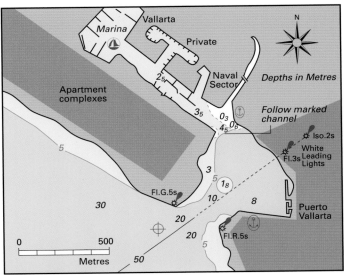

PUERTO VALLARTA
⊕ 20°39'·20N 105°14'·85W WGS84

Berths

Port clearance has to be with the Port Captain. This function is not delegated to the local marinas. If this is your first port of entry in Mexico then you must also go to the airport and clear customs and immigration, likewise if you are leaving the country.

There are several marinas in and around Puerto Vallarta. It's advisable to book ahead to ensure a berth.

Marina Vallarta is closest to town.

Paradise Village Marina is in Nueva Vallarta. Upmarket facility.

Nueva Vallarta close to Paradise Village. Care is needed with depths over the bar at Nueva Vallarta.

Marina Riviera Nayarit 350 berths. Visitors' berths. Max LOA 100m.
www.marinarivieranayarit.com

Anchorage

There is an anchorage in the entrance to Marina Vallarta, but it is not safe during a hurricane or tropical storm. Banderas Bay has many anchorages although the holding is reported to be poor.

Facilities

There are facilities for haul out, sail and engine repair, plus canvas work, and chandlers. Several large supermarkets including Wal-Mart, Sam's Club and Gigante, all reachable by bus or taxi.

Remarks

Puerto Vallarta is located in the centre of Bahia Banderas on the same latitude as Hawaii and therefore an important leaping off point for cruisers heading west. An attractive town, under a great deal of construction, as the tourism boom continues. International Airport with connections to Europe and North America. Recognised as a hurricane hole, although it has had one hit in 150 years.

Note For Panama, (country information and canal) see Chapter 1 North Atlantic Ocean and for Balboa, see Chapter 3 South Pacific Ocean.

Thanks to Rosemary Ralph for info on Mexico.

Nicaragua

General The coast of Nicaragua is little cruised, but by all accounts the locals are friendly and it is a relatively safe country to travel in. There is one small marina just S of the border with Honduras.

Formalities All boats and crew arriving from, or departing to foreign ports must be cleared by immigration, customs, and port authorities. The marina at Puesta del Sol can arrange all formalities.

Telecom IDD +505. GSM network. Internet at Puesta del Sol.

Currency Cordoba. US$ universally accepted.

Sailing season Winter months (November to April).

PUESTA DEL SOL

Tidal range 2.5m

Navigation

VHF Ch 16. The small marina is situated in a lagoon, El Estero de Aserradores, connected by a buoyed channel (least depth 2.5m) to the Pacific. The marina gives the following co-ordinates to locate the lagoon and marina:

5 miles off coast: 12°35'·65N 87°25'·56W
Lagoon entrance: 12°36'·57N 87°22'·43W
Channel entrance: 12°36'·83N 87°20'·93W
Marina: 12°37'·28N 87°20'·5W

The marina is reached by a buoyed channel 1.5M long.

Berths

c.30 berths. Visitors' berths. Max LOA 19m. Charge band 2.

Facilities

Water and electricity. Fuel berth. Restaurant and bar. Internet. Taxis arranged to El Viejo for shopping.
www.marinapuestadelsol.com

Hawaii

See Chapter 1 North Atlantic Ocean for USA country information (with particular reference to post 9/11 entry requirements)

General
Honolulu is the state capital and 80% of the Hawaiian population lives on the island of Oahu.

HILO (Hawaii Island)

Tidal range 1m

Navigation
Straightforward. Night-time entry is possible but leading lights are difficult to pick out against the background of city lights.

Berths
Call the Harbourmaster on VHF Ch 16, ask permission to moor in Radio Bay, the small boat harbour at the E extremity of the breakwater. Anchor off the quay and take sternlines. Surge can sometimes be a problem here (less in summer) so it pays to stay well clear of the wall and use the dinghy. Charge band 2–3.

Anchorage
If space permits, vessels may swing to an anchor in Radio Bay.

Facilities
At the basin there are showers, WC, book swap and a barbecue area. Shopping mall, fresh food market and supermarkets nearby in town. Internet and laundry at walking distance.

Remarks
Port of entry. Harbourmaster will arrange for a visit by quarantine, after which it is a 5-minute walk to customs and immigration. There is generally a fair amount of commercial activity in the port. Fantastic island to visit with the National Park and volcanoes easily accessible from Hilo.

ALA WAI BOAT HARBOUR (HONOLULU) (Oahu Island)

Tidal range 1m

Navigation
Separating Oahu from Molokai is the 22-mile wide Kaiwi channel. The trade winds accelerate through this channel, but the strongest effects occur near Molokai where the deflection of winds causes them

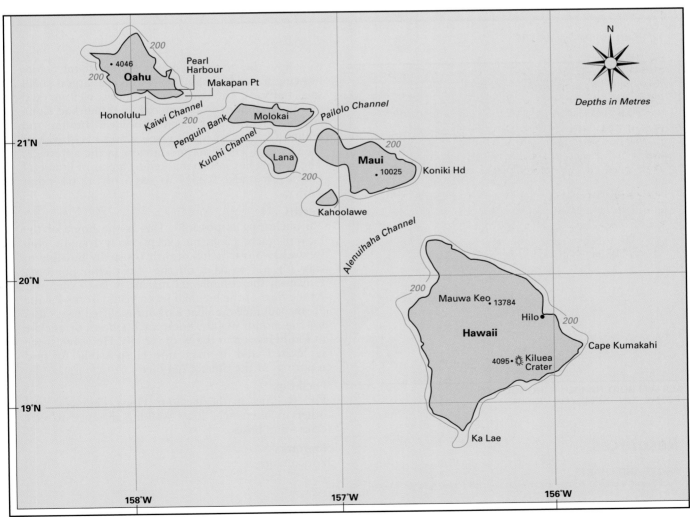

MAIN ISLANDS OF HAWAII GROUP

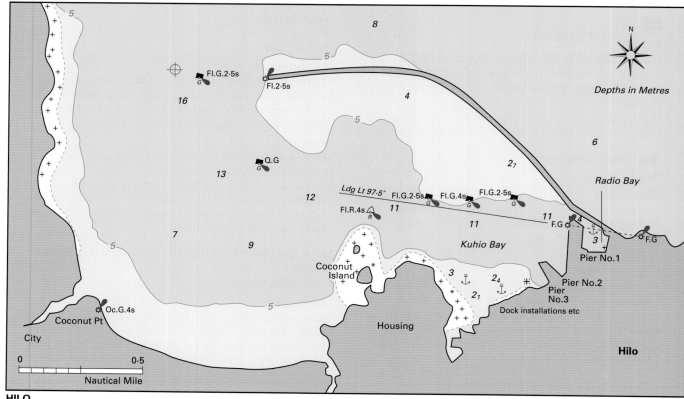

HILO
⊕ 19°44'·6N 155°04'·9W WGS84

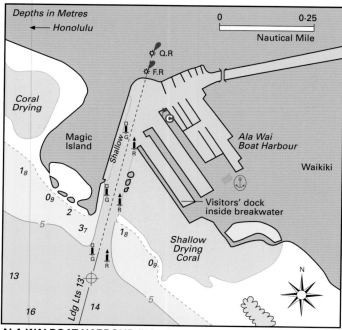

ALA WAI BOAT HARBOUR (HONOLULU)
⊕ 21°16'·73N 157°50'·76W WGS84

Resources

PILOTS AND CHARTS
Charlie's charts of the Hawaiian Islands (charliescharts.com)

to follow the N and S shores of the island before blowing towards Oahu. Ala Wai is the largest small boat harbour. The entrance channel is well marked and the harbour can be entered in all but bad Kona storms (S storms that generally occur in autumn and winter, October to April) when waves may break in the channel. There are no dangers in the approach. The leading line is also marked by a pair of lit lateral buoys just under 0.25M to the S of the waypoint shown.

Berths
No anchoring is possible. This is the home of the Hawaii Yacht Club, an exceptionally friendly club (www.hawaiiyachtclub.org). It is usually possible to stay for a few days on the yacht club pontoon. However, the commercial marina is less expensive. At the time of the biennial (even years) Trans-Pacific (Transpac) race the boat harbour is closed to visitors for the month of July. Some yachts berth or anchor in Kalihi lagoon to the W of the city. However, space is limited and it may not be possible to find moorings at the time of the race.

Facilities
Full facilities in the harbour. Hoist, engineers and other maintenance. Easy walking distance to city centre and buses.

Remarks
Port of entry.

Kiribati

(pronounced 'Kiribas')

General Kiribati is composed of three widely dispersed island groups in the central Pacific Ocean: from west to east these are the Gilbert, Phoenix, and Line islands (excluding three of the Northern Line group, which are territories of the United States). Banaba (formerly Ocean Island), an outlier from the Gilbert Islands, is also part of Kiribati. The Gilbert Islands are peopled by Micronesians and they differ in appearance to the Polynesians, who live on the islands to the south.

Formalities There are ports of entry at Tarawa in the Gilbert Islands and Christmas (Kiritimati) and Fanning (Tabuaeran) Islands in the Line Islands, and Canton (Kanton) in the Phoenix group. Citizens of most countries, in particular EU countries except Spain, Sweden and UK, USA and Australian citizens, need a visa to visit Kiribati; Canadians and New Zealanders do not for stays of less than 28 days. Visas should be obtained from a Kiribati consulate. 'In the case of somewhat difficult circumstances' the Principal Immigration Officer may accept a visa application on arrival. Yachts should call the Marine Guard on VHF Ch 16 to avoid unnecessary delays on arrival. The marine guard works around the clock at Tarawa and Kiritimati. Anchorage fees are charged, charge band 2, but if the yacht berths alongside the jetty it is charge band 4. Anchorage fees for Kanton, Kiritimati, and Tabuaeran for the duration of the stay are charge band 2.

Telecom IDD +686.

Currency Australian dollar. There are no ATM machines. There is a bank on Tarawa.

Sailing season All year, but in the Gilbert Islands it is best from March to October, which avoids the possibility of strong to gale force westerly winds that occur some years.

Routes and harbours It is usual to sail from E to W; distances are vast. Although the islands of the Gilbert group are atolls there are islets on the reef, particularly on their south and eastern sides, making them visible from a distance. The two Line Islands and Canton Island are low lying but have little in the way of off-lying reef. Tarawa lagoon is a minor base and has a haulout facility.

LONDON (Christmas Island (Kiritimati), Line Islands)

Tidal range 1.2m

Navigation

The channel and the anchorage require good light to avoid dangers. A NW swell breaks across the entrance to the passage. Ship Passage south of London Passage leads into a lagoon. The lagoon is generally very shallow with many dangers.

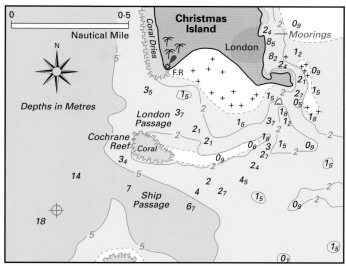

CHRISTMAS ISLAND (KIRITIMATI) (Line Islands)
⊕01°58'·4N 157°29'·4W

Anchorage

There are yacht moorings in the lagoon and anchoring is possible.

Remarks

Christmas Island is the largest of the Line Islands and has been quite recently settled by Micronesians from the Gilbert Islands. Port of entry.

 ## PALMYRA (USA)

Tidal range 1.2m

Navigation

The dredged channel is very narrow and was marked with beacons through the reef. (It is believed that the beacons have recently been replaced.) Approach through the dredged channel should be made on an ingoing tide with light winds so that the edges of the channel can be seen. The depth in the channel was over 7m.

Anchorage

The anchorage is well sheltered.

Remarks

Palmyra was a war base and the dredging in the lagoon and other works were done at that time. It is not part of Kiribati, but is one of the Line Islands. Yachts often visit Palmyra on passage. The island is privately owned and there have been plans to develop it for tourism for many years; however, no reports of such development have been received. Latest (2004), unconfirmed, reports are that the island is being administered by the US Conservation Department who are severely restricting yacht visits and charging exorbitant daily fees to those they permit.

Neighbouring Kingman Reef is used by the US Navy and is a restricted area.

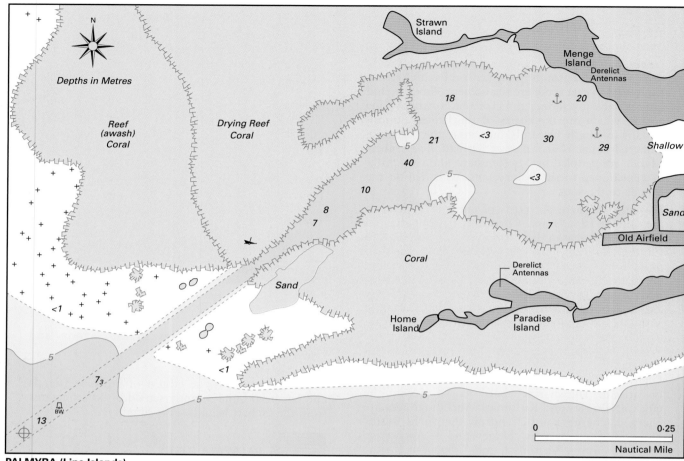

PALMYRA (Line Islands)
⊕05°51'·8N 162°07'·4W

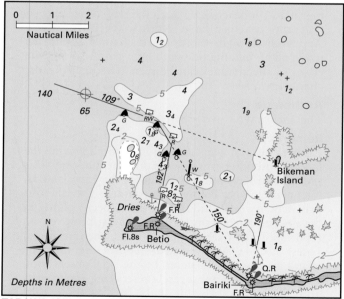

TARAWA (Gilbert Islands)
⊕01°25'N 172°54'·8E

TARAWA (Gilbert Islands)

Tidal range 2.5m

Navigation

The lagoon is quite easily entered but does not provide all-round shelter and it has many coral heads and shoals so that long passages are difficult.

Anchorage

Betio is not well sheltered but is normally tolerable; dinghy trips may be a bit rough. The anchorage at Bairiki is nearer some government departments and banks than Betio, but is less suited for most purposes.

Facilities

It is possible to slip a yacht at Betio. Supplies ashore are limited but well ahead of a typical island village. Diesel is available near the landing and gas bottles can be filled.

Remarks

Tarawa is the most populated atoll of the Gilbert Islands and is the capital of Kiribati.

Marshall Islands

General The Marshall Islands have been governed and used (or abused) by many foreign governments: Spain, Germany, Japan, and USA. Perhaps because of this they seem unwelcoming to strangers. Some atolls will not permit visits by yachts at all. Some impose a very high deterrent charge, which effectively stops visits. Majuro has not levied these fees.

Formalities Prior approval is required before visiting certain islands and a large charge may be made.

Telecom IDD +692 011.

Currency US dollar. There are no ATM machines. There are banks in Majuro.

Sailing season December to June.

Routes and harbours The Marshall Islands are usually visited as stepping-stones from the Gilbert Islands to the Caroline Islands. Although the islands are atolls there are islets on the reef, particularly on their SE sides, making them visible from a distance. There are only three atolls normally visited by cruising yachts. These are Majuro, Jaluit and Ebon.

MAJURO

Tidal range 2m

Navigation
The pass is deep and marked. The dangers on the track in the lagoon are also marked.

Anchorage
The anchorage off the centre of the township is not very protected but it may be possible to get into a confined artificial mooring area. The beach in the NE corner of the lagoon near the so-called 'yacht club' (there are no yachts) provides good protection from the prevailing wind and the sandy beach is suitable for beaching a yacht.

Facilities
Majuro is the chief island and has reasonably good (if stale) supplies and two banks. Diesel and hardware are available

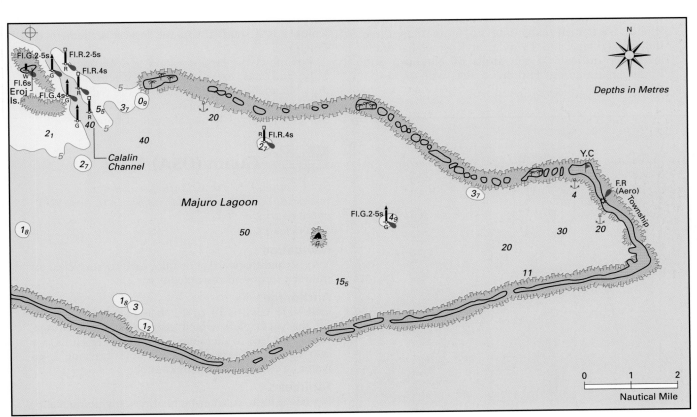

MAJURO (Marshall Islands)
⊕07°10'·5N 171°11'·75E

Resources

PILOTS AND GUIDES FOR KIRIBATI, MARSHALL ISLANDS AND MICRONESIA
South Pacific Anchorages Warwick Clay (Imray)
Hawaiian Islands (charliescharts.com)

Federated States of Micronesia (Caroline Is)

General The Caroline Islands have only been subject to three occupying powers – Spain, Japan and USA – compared with four in the Marshall Islands. It is perhaps for this reason, and the fact they have not been used for nuclear bomb and rocket testing, that they are friendlier to strangers. However they still officially feel threatened by them and you may need to obtain a permit before taking your yacht there.

Formalities Check if it is still necessary to apply for permission from the immigration service before visiting. Expect to have to clear in and out of each state and pay substantial charges.

Telecom IDD +691 011. There are card phones.

Currency US dollar. There are no ATM machines. There are money exchange facilities in main settlements.

Sailing season December to May.

Routes and harbours A normal route is from Kosrae W to Ponape and then either continuing W or turning S to New Guinea with the possibility of visiting Nukuoro and Kapingamarangi. The high islands have reefs extending no more than three miles at Ponape and 1½ miles at Kosrae. Landfalls are more difficult at the atolls of Nukuoro and Kapingamarangi but both have islets with palms on

the NE side, which is the side to approach. The trees may start to become visible 10 miles away.

A cruise from the northern Gilbert Islands through the Marshall Islands, the eastern Caroline Islands, New Ireland, and the western Solomon Islands, can be made during the South Pacific cyclone season as an alternative to spending the season in New Zealand or southern Australia. If heading N, such a cruise may also be a good way to spend the period between the beginning of the S Pacific cyclone season (November) and the Japanese summer (May).

PONAPE HARBOUR, KOLONIA (Ponape)

Tidal range 1.3m

Berths
A high charge is made if you tie up to the wharf even briefly.

Anchorage
At the head of the harbour, off a hotel. Well sheltered.

Facilities
Diesel can be obtained by a long dinghy ride.

Remarks
Kolonia is a small town, the largest settlement on Ponape.

Ponape is the largest island in Micronesia. It is hilly and has extensive reefs. There are many possible anchorages protected by the reefs. There is also anchorage at neighbouring Ant Atoll.

Port of entry. Charges for out of hours.

Guam (USA)

See Chapter 1 North Atlantic for country information (with particular reference to post 9/11 entry requirements)

Tidal range 1.3m

Navigation
Very straightforward, but take care to stay clear of military ships and restricted areas.

Anchorage
Call VHF Ch 16, 13 or 12. It is possible to anchor off the yacht club, which also has some moorings, which are free to members of other yacht clubs, for two weeks. There is a hurricane hole, carrying 2.4m water, accessed via the Piti channel.

Facilities
Big naval base. All marine facilities, including a slip, though not necessarily appropriate for yachts. Mail is delivered quickly from the USA. Friendly Yacht Club.

Remarks
This is US territory, so visas are required. It may make entry simpler if prior notice is given to the authorities. The best stop between Hawaii and Japan.

www.guam-online.com/myc/visitinfo.htm

PONAPE (Caroline Islands)
⊕07°00′.4N 158°10′.4E

(Map) Jokaj Passage · Coral · 12 · 30 · 8 · 60 · 10 · Fl.R.4s · .60 · Fl.4s · 30 · Fl.4s · Fl.4s · 18 · 21 · 17 · Fl.4s · Fl.4s · 14 · Airfield · Takatik Low · (Mangroves) · Q.Fl · 18 · Iso.6s · 10 · Aero Alt. WG · Coral · Wharf · 10 · 8 · Jokaj · 275m · 7 · 4 · 03 · 5 · Kolonia · 5 · N · Hotel · 6 · 5 · **Ponape** · 0 · 0·5 · Nautical Mile · Depths in Metres

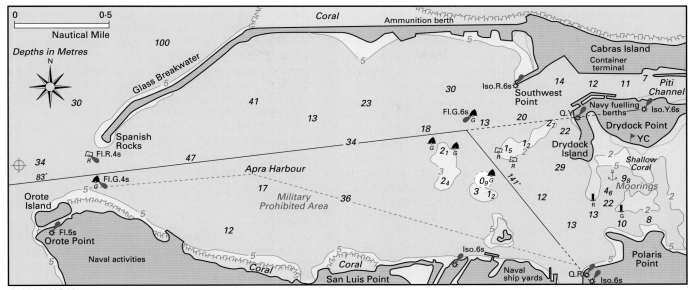

GUAM (USA)
⊕13°27'·1N 144°37'E

 ## Japan

General Overseas cruising yachts do not frequently visit this country, hence the limited information we can provide. However, from the available accounts, which speak of the outstandingly warm welcome given to foreign yachts, one wonders why it is not more frequently visited. Prices in Japan are high, but most visitors have found that free berths have been available to them for short stays.

Coastline Japan has four main islands that are all high and steep-to with few coastal plains. The coast is much indented in places, especially S of Tokyo Bay, and there are numerous natural harbours. In the N the island of Hokkaido has several active volcanoes. On the S side of Honshu Island is the Inland Sea with the islands of Shikoku and Kyushu sheltering it from the worst swell of the Pacific.

Formalities Enter at a port with a customs office (i.e. a major port). Visa exemption granted on arrival for short stays (varies from 3–6 months) to citizens of EU, USA and major Commonwealth countries. Formalities can be long-winded, best to enlist the help of a marina. Usually have to clear in and out of all ports.

Telecom IDD +81. GSM network. Internet cafés in larger centres.

Currency Yen. ATMs common. Major credit cards accepted everywhere.

Sailing season The season is in the summer from May to September, although this is also the typhoon season (June to October) so vigilance is called for. Most typhoons occur in late summer, in August and September. The southern islands have a mild almost sub-tropical climate and a mild winter where snow is

uncommon. The SE monsoon affects the southern part of Japan, lending a heavy humidity to the air. Despite its effects winds are variable, with sea breezes playing an important role. The northern islands have severe winters with blizzards and snow

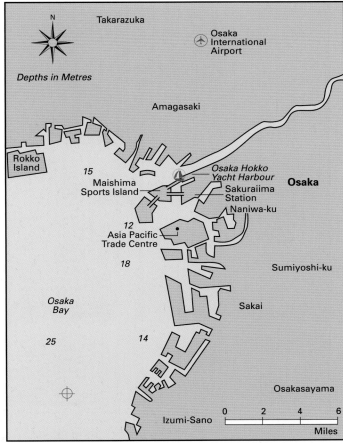

APPROACHES TO OSAKA HOKKO YACHT HARBOUR (Japan)
⊕ 34°30'·0N 135°15'·0E

so cruising in the N is really confined to the summer months. Weather forecasts for typhoons are sophisticated and you will know well in advance if and where a typhoon is going to hit the island chain. Fog is prevalent in some areas and gales are common in the winter all around Japan.

Routes and harbours Most yachts visiting Japan will cruise the southern islands and then head S towards Hong Kong or across the Pacific to the W coast of America. From Australia a typical route takes in the Louisiades (Papua New Guinea), the northern Solomon Islands, Guam and on to Japan. Once in Japan, local yacht clubs are only too willing to help and point out marinas and fishing harbours to visit. Some marinas are very expensive in Japan, but many give up to two weeks free to visiting yachts and fishing harbours make no charge. When cruising the coast great care is needed of fish traps and nets, shellfish and pearl farms, fishing boats and commercial shipping. Yachts that have cruised the coast recommend not doing overnight passages near the coast if at all possible.

OSAKA

Tidal range 1.0m. Strong tidal streams up to 5kn run through the narrow channels between the islands.

Navigation
The approaches to Osaka Harbour on the E side of the Inland Sea are beset by large numbers of ships coming and going and at anchor. This is a very busy roadstead and a good lookout is essential. Once up to the main channel for Amagasaki Harbour (34°40'N 135°22'E), the reclaimed land on which Maishima Sports Island is built will be seen. The yacht harbour sits 'behind' it and should be approached around the N side of Maishima.

Berths
120 berths. Visitors' berths. You will be directed to a berth on one of the three pontoons here. Good shelter. Port of entry.

Facilities
All the usual amenities including convivial clubhouse. Some repairs can be organised. Fuel in Japan is untaxed for fishermen and foreign vessels. Provisions and restaurants in Osaka, which is easily reached by train.

Remarks
The end point of the arduous Melbourne–Osaka two-handed race March–May.
www.ohyc.gr.jp

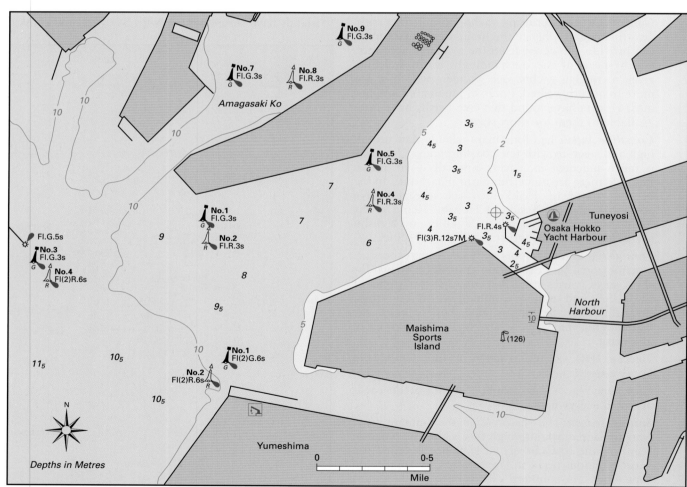

IMMEDIATE APPROACHES TO OSAKA HOKKO YACHT HARBOUR (Japan)
⊕34°40'·5N 135°24'·4E

Hong Kong

General Hong Kong consists of three different areas: the island of Hong Kong, Kowloon on the mainland peninsula and the New Territories. The British 99-year lease on the island expired in 1997 and the Crown Colony became a Special Administrative Region of China. Although many feared that things would change dramatically with the handover to China (there was a large exodus of Hong Kong Chinese and British expatriots), things seem to have settled down and business goes on as usual in the ex-colony. Hong Kong is home to a large fleet of cruising and racing yachts, with active yacht clubs and world class racing yachts which regularly contest the races in SE Asia and Australasia.

Formalities Yachts must clear in at the Marine Department Office in central Hong Kong within 24 hours of arrival. Take the yacht's registration document, passports and insurance papers and complete the necessary paperwork. You are usually given six months, renewable for another six months. When leaving take all papers back to the Marine Department Office to get your clearance papers.

Telecom IDD +852. GSM network. Internet cafés.

Currency Hong Kong dollar. ATMs everywhere. Major credit cards widely accepted.

Sailing season The season is pretty much all year round although the NE monsoon can blow strongly at times, often at gale force especially when channelled between islands, and making your way N is a very wet and bruising affair. Typhoons can occur in any month, though May to December are the common months and July to September the most likely for typhoons to develop.

Routes and harbours There is very little local sailing to do around Hong Kong itself. Several races run to the Philippines, including the well-known China Sea Race (every two years).

HONG KONG HARBOUR

Tidal range 1.3m springs. Strong tidal streams up to 5kn run through the narrow channels between the islands.

Navigation

The approaches to Hong Kong are congested with commercial shipping, ferries, fishing boats and local trading craft. You will need to be alert and keep an eye on all the traffic whizzing around. Yachts should have made prior arrangements for a berth if possible. Most cruising yachts head for Hebe Haven in the New Territories.

Berths

There are numerous marinas and we mention only the ones cruising yachts might find a berth in.

Discovery Bay Marina
On Lantau Island. Berths possible and a friendly club. Good yard and repair services.

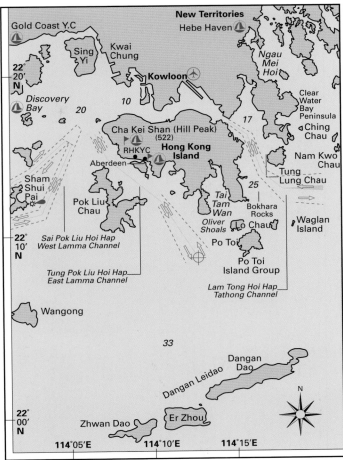

APPROACHES TO HONG KONG
⊕22°09'·2N 114°12'·7E

Gold Coast Yacht and Country Club
(22°22'·5N 113°59'·4E)
Marina with all facilities and a yard. Ferry to downtown Hong Kong.

Aberdeen Marina Club (22°14'·5N 114°09'·5E)
Berths available. Good yard and repair services.

RHKYC (22°17'·14N 114°10'·8E)
Moorings. Uncomfortable and dirty polluted water. The RHKYC has moorings and a clubhouse in Shelter Cove (near Hebe Haven) that are sometimes available to visiting yachts.

Hebe Haven YC (22°21'·85N 114°15'·65E)
Most cruising yachts head for here. Moorings. Amenities ashore. Bus to the MTR to downtown Hong Kong.

Facilities

Usual amenities at the marinas. Yards and yacht repairs at Discovery Bay, Gold Coast Yacht Club, Aberdeen and Clearwater Bay. Provisions in Kowloon and Hong Kong and also near Hebe. Restaurants and bars in most places.

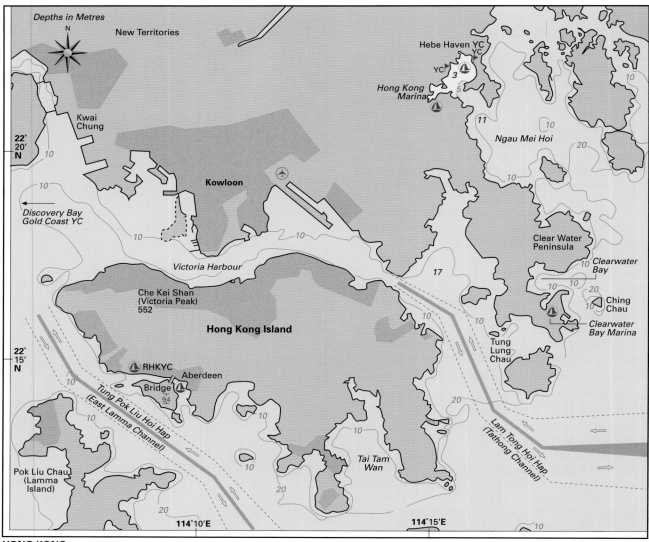

HONG KONG

Remarks

Most reports are that it is better to be somewhere like Hebe or Discovery Bay rather than in the thick of it on Hong Kong Island. If you want to visit China proper then various companies organise tours and this is really the best way for short visits. www.rhkyc.org.hk

 Philippines

General The islands are all part of a high volcanic chain of mountains (there are 20 active volcanoes) with little flat land, except around the larger islands of Luzon and Mindanao which have some coastal plains. Cruising around the Philippines is complicated by the unrest in southern Mindanao and the adjoining Sulu Sea on the W coast, which has a reputation for piracy and of late some politically motivated kidnappings of tourists by Muslim groups fighting for an independent state in the region. The Sulu Sea is one area that needs to be treated with caution although yachts have cruised the area in the past.

Coastline The Philippines has almost as many islands (estimated at around 2,700) as Indonesia although some are very small. It is a vast archipelago and poorly charted in places. Most yachts on passage will touch on just one or two places en route. Subic Bay on Luzon is the finish of the China Sea Race and Puerto Galera on Mindoro is popular with cruisers.

Formalities All nationalities must obtain a visa in advance. Entry formailies can be completed at Puerto Galera. On Luzon ports of entry are San Fernando, Subic Bay, and Manila. Marina staff at Subic Bay and Manila will complete formalities for you. Once you have cleared in with customs and immigration you will get a visa, usually for 20 days. At subsequent ports and even off small villages any officials (including the local policeman) may want to check that you have a visa. The coastguard may also check up on you. You will need to check out at a port of entry to get clearance papers for the next destination.

Telecom IDD +63. GSM network. Internet cafés.

Currency Philippines peso. US dollars are widely accepted. ATMs in cities and larger centres. Major credit cards accepted in cities and tourist areas.

Sailing season The season is normally during the NE monsoon from November to April (Amihan winds). It is generally channelled E through the islands and can blow briskly at times. The SW monsoon period (Hagabat winds) is the typhoon season from May to November. In fact, tropical storms can brew up in any month of the year though July to September are the worst months. The Philippines is regularly hit by typhoons and it is important to keep a constant check on the development of tropical storms.

Routes and harbours Most yachts will head towards Luzon to keep clear of the troubles in Mindanao and the possibility of piracy in the Sulu Sea. From the W (usually the Caroline Islands or Guam) yachts will head up through the San Bernardino Strait and onto Puerto Galera or harbours on Luzon. Local yachtsmen are enthusiastic about the rich and varied cruising around the many islands and happily help cruising yachts that put in here.

PUERTO GALERA (Mindoro)

Tidal range 1.0m springs. Strong tidal streams up to 7kn run through the narrow channels between the islands.

Navigation

The approach and entrance into the bay should be made in daylight. Local advice is to anchor off W of

PUERTO GALERA (Mindro, Philippines)
⊕13°31'·5N 120°56'·5E

Paniquian Island during the NE monsoon or in Varadero Bay during the SW monsoon and wait for daylight before entering. By day Manila Channel is the most straightforward. Batangas Channel can be used but care is needed once around the dogleg of a reef in the middle of the channel.

Anchorage

VHF Ch 68 for PGYC. Puerto Galera Yacht Club has 28 moorings in Muelle Bay suitable for yachts up to 50ft and one of these is usually free for short to medium term stays. If you want to leave the boat here it is best to contact the Yacht Club to reserve a mooring in advance. The bay is a recognised typhoon shelter. Yachts can also anchor in Dalaruan Bay or Boquette Bay though the club urges yachts to be careful of coral and the associated ecosystem.

Facilities

PGYC is situated in the SW corner of the bay and has a dinghy dock. There is also a boat boy who operates during club hours. Potable water and fuel. Usual facilities of a good club. Minor yacht repairs at the club workshop. For anything else, and to haul, the nearest boatyard is at the Maya Maya Yacht Club, which is on the W coast of Luzon about 40M to the NW. Most provisions can be found and there are restaurants nearby. For better shopping Batangas City is a ferry ride away.

Remarks

Popular stopover for cruising yachts. The anchorage has been used for shelter and provisioning since early Chinese times up through the Spanish occupation to the present. The club can arrange a caretaker if you want to leave the boat here for a while. The club can also arrange entry/exit formalities even though this is not an official port of entry.

www.pgyc.org www.mmyc.com

5

INDIAN OCEAN

Malaysian fishing boats

General

The Indian Ocean is relatively little cruised compared to the Atlantic and Pacific although it has its aficionados, generally based in Thailand and Malaysia and in South Africa. Yachts on a circumnavigation often spend time in SE Asia and then hurry across this ocean to get to the Mediterranean or South Africa. Those who cruise extensively here do so on two main circuits. From SE Asia boats cross to India and Sri Lanka and then drop down to the Seychelles and the Chagos group. To return, boats take a northern route when the SW monsoon starts to kick in. From South Africa boats coast up to Madagascar and then on to the Seychelles and Chagos group.

In general the northern Indian Ocean is gentler than the southern Indian Ocean. Passages across the Bay of Bengal and the Arabian Sea are often rated as the most enjoyable ocean passages of the three large oceans. In the southern Indian Ocean the trades are generally stronger and wave heights bigger, especially down towards the SW corner around Madagascar and South Africa.

2004 TSUNAMI

On 26 December 2004 a massive undersea earthquake triggered a tsunami that devastated coastal areas in the Indian Ocean. The epicentre of the earthquake off the northern tip of Sumatra affected Sumatra and other parts of Indonesia, Malaysia, Thailand, the Nicobar and Andaman Islands, Sri Lanka and India. It even reached East Africa, though its effect there was not as devastating. The death toll will probably never be known, but is estimated to be well over 250,000. Harbours and coastal facilities were damaged and yachts were lost, although the loss of life to cruising yachtsmen here was surprisingly small. The rebuilding of the yachting infrastructure was remarkably quick and yachts should expect to find most facilities back in place. Any further changes from the information detailed here and any major corrections will go on the Imray website www.imray.com

Weather and sea

PREVAILING WINDS

Northern Indian Ocean

The northern Indian Ocean is dominated by the NE and SW monsoons. The word monsoon applies equally to the prevailing winds and to the characteristics of the season in terms of rainfall, cloud cover and temperature. The NE monsoon is known as the cool season and is generally dry with clear skies and moderate temperatures, making it the

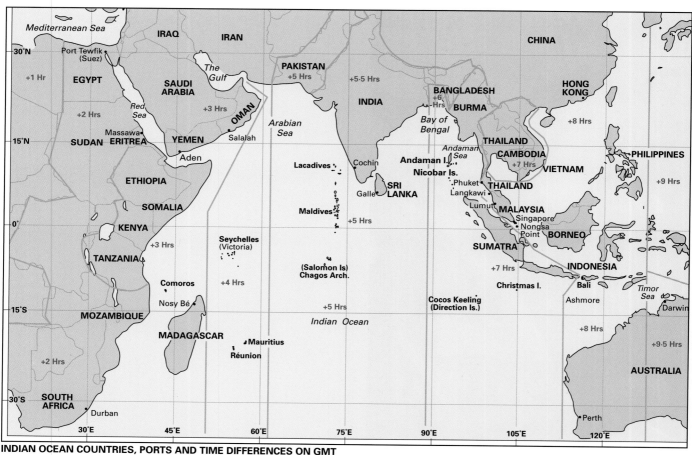

INDIAN OCEAN COUNTRIES, PORTS AND TIME DIFFERENCES ON GMT

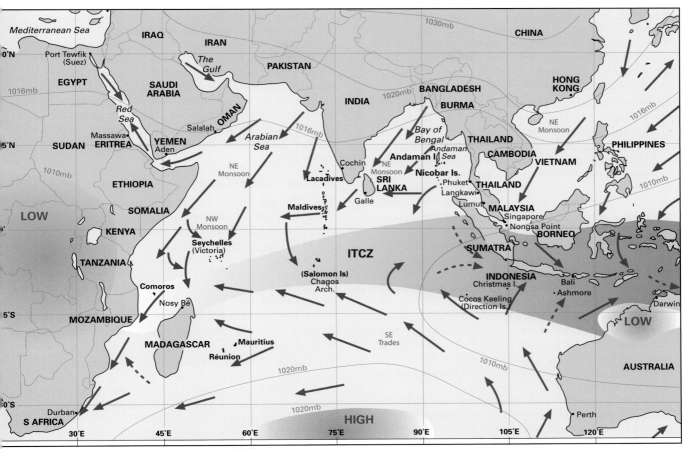

REVAILING WINDS IN THE INDIAN OCEAN - JANUARY

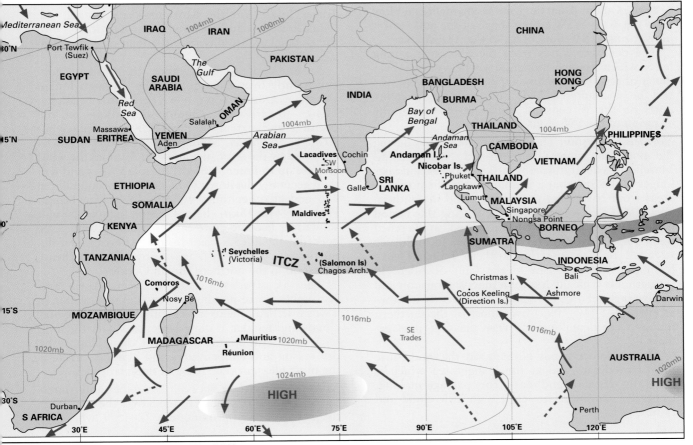

REVAILING WINDS IN THE INDIAN OCEAN - JULY

best time to be in the area. The SW monsoon is known as the rainy season and brings rain (often torrential) and moist humid conditions, which can be oppressive at times. The transitional period from April to May is known as the hot season until the relief of the rain in the SW monsoon arrives.

Southwest monsoon The SW monsoon blows during the northern summer from around June to August. During this period it blows with great constancy and can be relied upon for 90% or more of the time. Its influence stretches right across the northern Indian Ocean from the Andaman Sea to the Gulf of Aden. In strength it is typically stronger in the Arabian Sea than it is in the Bay of Bengal. In July it often blows at Force 7 or more for long periods in the Arabian Sea.

In the Bay of Bengal wind speeds over the open sea in July are generally Force 4–6 (10–25kn) although there will be occasional days of Force 7 and possibly 8 (30–40kn). In June and August wind speeds are a little less.

In the Arabian Sea wind speeds over the open sea in July are generally Force 5–7 (18–32kn) although there will often be days of Force 7–8 (30–40kn). In June and August wind speeds are a little less but still substantial and there is more than enough wind to shift you along.

In the Andaman Sea and along the coasts of Thailand and Malaysia the SW monsoon lifts over the land and the constancy and direction of the wind is less marked, although a heavy swell will still set onto any exposed coast.

In the Gulf of Aden the wind is channelled to blow from the W to WSW by the shape of the gulf until it joins the main SW flow of air in the Arabian Sea.

The constant winds from the SW have a long fetch which creates moderate to heavy seas over much of the area. On any exposed coast heavy seas will be encountered and, not surprisingly, many ports on the W coast of India are closed for the duration of the SW monsoon.

Northeast monsoon The NE monsoon blows during the northern winter from around November to March. In general it occurs earlier in the N and lasts longer in the S so that it is dominant in the northern areas from November to February and in southern areas from December to March. During this period it blows with reasonable constancy and can be relied upon for 75% or more of the time. Its influence stretches right across the northern Indian Ocean from the Andaman Sea to the Gulf of Aden. In strength it is typically less than the SW monsoon and rarely reaches Force 6–7 (25–30kn). Mostly it blows at Force 4–5 (10–20kn) over most of the northern Indian Ocean, making for very pleasant passage-making.

The moderate winds blowing off the land cause only a moderate and at times slight sea which is generally regular and easy for passage-making. Generally conditions are clear with little cloud and rain.

Transition periods Between the two monsoons there are transitional periods in April to May and September to November. During these periods the wind direction becomes variable and there may be some days when the wind changes between monsoon directions or goes light and variable. There are also more days of calm. Before the arrival of the SW monsoon there can be violent thunderstorms accompanied by strong squalls and heavy rain. At the end of the SW monsoon there will be similar conditions.

Southern Indian Ocean

The southern Indian Ocean is dominated by the SE Trades. These blow across most of the southern Indian Ocean all year round between approximately 5° and 25°S, although the extent of the SE Trades recedes over the top half of this area between the equator and 12°–15°S during the NW monsoon. In the far S after 30° S the prevailing winds are the westerlies of the Southern Ocean which become progressively stronger the further S you go to the Roaring Forties, Furious Fifties and Screaming Sixties.

SE Trades The SE Trades blow consistently and often at some strength over most of the Indian Ocean outside the wind shadow of the surrounding continents. Clear of the wind shadow of Australia and Sumatra the SE Trades kick in. On the western side the African continent stops the wind or the influence of the NE monsoon makes itself felt. Where land masses funnel the wind (such as in the Torres Strait and the Mozambique Channel) the wind direction can be altered and winds forced into the channel are usually stronger than over the open sea.

From April to November the trades blow consistently over the whole of the southern Indian Ocean at around Force 4–6 (12–25kn), becoming lighter towards the equator depending on the position and extent of the ITCZ and somewhat stronger towards Madagascar as the wind is deflected by the African continent. At times the wind will get up to Force 7 (30kn) for a few days and will then generally die down to its norm of around Force 4–6 and at other times will die down to a benign Force 4 (12–15kn) before rising again. It will sometimes become more easterly than SE, but never goes into the north except for the sea area under the northwest monsoon caused by the northeast monsoon in the northern Indian Ocean.

The SE Trades season between April and November, corresponding to the southern winter, is a warm settled time to travel with typical trade wind clouds and regular, if quite large, seas over the long fetch across the southern Indian Ocean. This is the dry season and temperatures and humidity make it the most pleasant time to be in these latitudes.

Northwest monsoon Between December and March the SE Trades are pushed to the S over the area from the equator to approximately 12–15°S when the northwest monsoon prevails. The northwest monsoon is something of a misnomer because although the prevailing wind is NW, it is not a consistent wind like the NE monsoon in the northern Indian Ocean and you can expect to have variable winds on many days and unsettled weather with fluky winds and thunderstorms. The NW monsoon is an extension of the NE monsoon in the north, which is deflected to the NW by the African continent and the retreat of the winter high pressure over the southern Indian Ocean. The influence of the NW monsoon is along the west coast of Africa and from the equator down to 12–15°S to about 80–90°E. In the same band under the equator winds from around 90°E to Sumatra and Australia are predominantly from the S, usually SW, although some W–NW winds will blow as well.

ITCZ

In general the ITCZ hovers around the equator or just below it during the southern winter/northern summer and then moves S and expands over a wider area across the top of Madagascar, extending in an arc to the top of Sumatra and down to 20°S over Australia for the southern summer/northern winter. These two generalised positions are shown on the accompanying maps. It must be stressed that these are average positions and the ITCZ moves about all over the place either side of the equator. The ITCZ also extends across land masses so it affects coastal regions as well, although thermal winds may dissipate its effects at times.

A northern convergence zone, often quite well defined, also separates winds in the Red Sea and over the Persian Gulf area. The Red Sea convergence zone is usually located around 12°–18°N in July and over the top of Somalia in January. However, one of the authors (RJH) has encountered it as a clearly defined zone at around 15°N in January and others report similar experiences, so it is likely to sit around here even in January when it is supposed to be much further S.

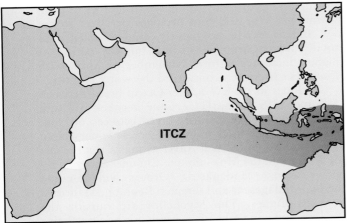

ITCZ - JANUARY

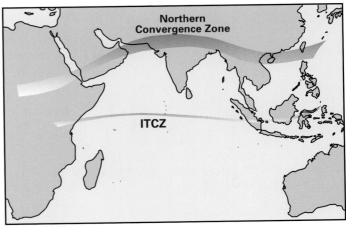

ITCZ - JULY

In the Indian Ocean ITCZ there is nearly always rain, often torrential, and sometimes continuous for days on end. One of the authors (RJH) has experienced two days of solid torrential rain and, along with the almost continuous cloud cover, the effects on morale of sailing in the ITCZ zone should not be underestimated. The lightning displays can be dramatic and scary. This is the region where St Elmo's fire was reported in days of yore.

GALES

Gales resulting from depressions passing through are confined to the northern and southern limits of the Indian Ocean and are rare. In the northern areas around Oman, Pakistan, and northern India depressions may track close to the northern sea area, but this is again unusual. Gale force winds can blow, often for days or even a week, when the SW monsoon is at its height. This occurs mostly around the African and Arabian coasts.

In the southern limits of the Indian Ocean depressions travel from W to E and gales are common at all times of year, but much more so in winter when the depressions also tend to be further N. These gales can be as severe as it is possible to find anywhere. Off the SE coast of South Africa the incidence of gales in the area between Port Elizabeth and East London reaches 8%. In summer the frequency of gales is down to around 3% in the same area, but the weather is still strongly influenced by passing depressions.

Most gale force winds in this area result from tropical storms.

TROPICAL STORMS

Northern Indian Ocean

Bay of Bengal In the northern Indian Ocean the Bay of Bengal has the highest incidence of cyclones, experiencing an average of 5–6 tropical storms and two cyclones a year. The cyclone season runs from late April to early December although the most dangerous months are May, October and November.

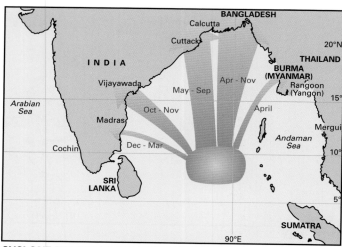

CYCLONE TRACKS IN THE BAY OF BENGAL

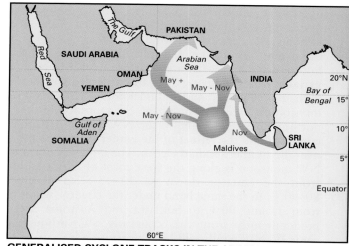

GENERALISED CYCLONE TRACKS IN THE ARABIAN SEA

FREQUENCY OF TROPICAL STORMS AND CYCLONES OVER A 50-YEAR PERIOD – BAY OF BENGAL

Month	Tropical Storms	Cyclones
Jan	4	1
Feb	1	0
Mar	6	3
Apr	14	8
May	21	13
Jun	24	3
Jul	23	5
Aug	16	2
Sep	22	7
Oct	32	14
Nov	39	16
Dec	20	5
Total	222	77

FREQUENCY OF TROPICAL STORMS AND CYCLONES – ARABIAN SEA

Month	Tropical Storms	Cyclones
Jan	5	5
Feb	0	0
Mar	3	1
Apr	9	8
May	32	25
Jun	24	12
Jul	7	0
Aug	11	3
Sep	10	5
Oct	54	30
Nov	70	36
Dec	29	13
Total	254	134

Note To roughly compare the frequency with the table for the Bay of Bengal reduce these figures by one third.

Cyclones in the Bay of Bengal typically originate in the sea area between 88°E and 94°E and around 10°N, except for the later season cyclones in October or November which can originate around 5°N. The cyclones typically move off in a northerly direction towards Bangladesh except for late season (October–November) cyclones which may curve NW to the Indian coast around the region of Andurapesh in the crook of the E coast or curve NE across to Burma.

Arabian Sea The Arabian Sea has a much smaller incidence of tropical storms at just 1–2 tropical storms a year. Some of these will develop into cyclones, but the incidence is much less than in the Bay of Bengal. There are two distinct periods for tropical storms in the Arabian Sea. The first is from May to June. In this period tropical storms originate in the general area around the Lacadives and move off to the N or NW. Occasionally these storms will curve back to the NE. The second period is from October to November and these tropical storms originate in the Bay of Bengal and move W or NW across India into the Arabian Sea.

Southern Indian Ocean

SW Indian Ocean The SW Indian Ocean has the highest incidence of tropical storms and cyclones for the Indian Ocean. The average is around 11 tropical storms per year and four cyclones per year. In the SW Indian Ocean no month can be regarded as totally free of tropical storms, but the period of highest incidence is from November to April, with December to March considered the worst months.

Cyclones in the SW Indian Ocean breed between 5°S and 13°S in the ITCZ zone between 50° and 95°E, although the majority breed between 60° and 80°E. They then track to the SW before re-curving to the S and SE. Some will travel as far as the E coast of Africa and the Mozambique Channel and may re-curve across Madagascar. Others will re-curve before Madagascar and threaten Réunion, Mauritius and Rodrigues. The Seychelles are outside the cyclone zone and Chagos is rarely hit by destructive winds.

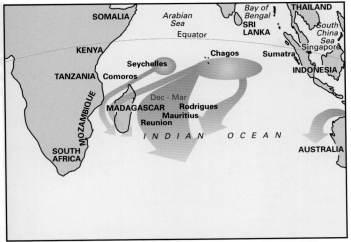

GENERALISED CYCLONE TRACKS IN THE S INDIAN OCEAN

FREQUENCY OF TROPICAL STORMS AND CYCLONES – SW INDIAN OCEAN

Month	Tropical Storms	Cyclones
Jan	3–4	1–2
Feb	3–4	1
Mar	2–3	1
Apr	1	0.4
May	0.2	rare
Jun	rare	rare
Jul	rare	rare
Aug	rare	rare
Sep	rare	rare
Oct	0.33	rare
Nov	0.4	rare
Dec	1.2	0.5
Total	11	4

Note Figures are averages per year

SE Indian Ocean In the Timor Sea and off the NW coast of Australia tropical cyclones occur between December and April.

CURRENTS

Northern Indian Ocean

Bay of Bengal The pattern of currents in the Bay of Bengal changes radically between the NE and SW monsoons. Basically, the NE monsoon sets up a W-flowing current with a clockwise circulation in the northern half of the Bay of Bengal. The SW monsoon sets up an E-going current with an anticlockwise circulation in the northern half of the Bay of Bengal. In the southern half of the bay, which is the bit that concerns most cruising yachts, the currents are reasonably strong and consistent.

If you are on passage against the prevailing currents it pays to get down towards the equator where there is less current and towards the end of the NE monsoon you can even pick up favourable counter-currents.

Arabian Sea As for the Bay of Bengal, current patterns change radically between the NE and SW monsoons. The NE monsoon sets up a predominantly W-going current although in the early stages the current around the bottom of India and Sri Lanka tends to flow NW up the coast before being pushed W. The SW monsoon sets up an E-going current which tends to curve around the top of the Arabian Sea and flow SE down the W coast of India. During the SW monsoon there is generally a weak southerly flow around the equator, although the current may reverse to a weak W-going flow in places.

In the intervening periods between the monsoons the currents die, become variable in places, and then pick up as the new monsoon wind takes over.

Gulf of Aden With the NE monsoon the W-going current is squeezed into the gulf and can be strong in places, up to 1–2kn in the Gulf of Aden and 2–4kn through Bab El Mandeb and the very S of the Red Sea. With the SW monsoon the current is predominantly E-going out of the Gulf of Aden and S–SSE out of the bottom of the Red Sea.

Southern Indian Ocean

Current patterns in the southern Indian Ocean are somewhat more complex than in the north.

South Equatorial Current In general there is a W-going current between 10°S and 25°S throughout the year, known as the South Equatorial Current. The N limit of this current butts onto the S limit of the SW Monsoon Current or the Equatorial Counter-current according to the season (see below). Its S limit is the E-going Southern Ocean Current. Out of the Timor Sea and across through Christmas Island, Cocos, to the top of Madagascar, this current flows strongly with rates up to one knot and more at times. Generally it is stronger and less variable in the N than in the S. During the southern hemisphere winter it flows around the bottom of Chagos and the Outer Islands of the Seychelles. In the southern winter it is pushed up around the top of Madagascar into the Somali Current and the Mozambique Current. In the southern summer it divides at Madagascar to flow S down the E coast of Madagascar and across to the African coast.

Equatorial Counter-current When the NE monsoon is blowing in the northern Indian Ocean, a counter-current is set up between the equator and between 8°S to 10°S. Its S limit is the South Equatorial Current. This current flows to the E during the southern summer (northern winter) while the NE monsoon is blowing. At this time it affects the Seychelles, Chagos and right across to Sumatra where it is deflected SE by the coast of Sumatra. It is a solid current with rates around 1–2kn with the higher rate usually found at the beginning and end of the season. Rates of 4kn have been reported.

SW Monsoon Current When the SW monsoon is blowing in the northern Indian Ocean an E-going current is set up between the equator and 5°S–8°S.

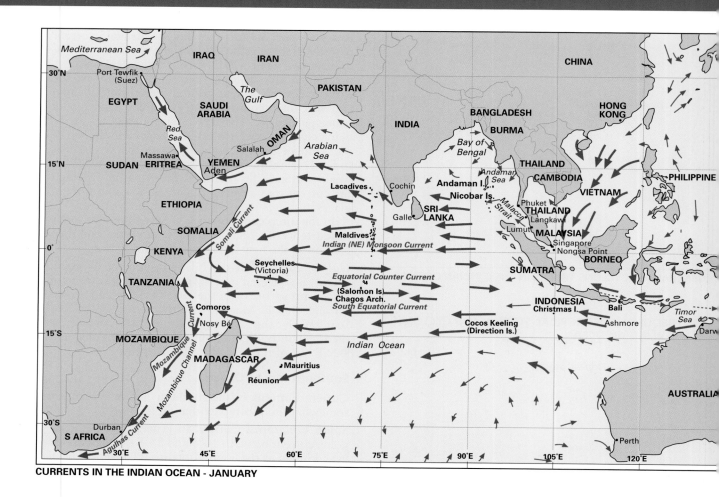

CURRENTS IN THE INDIAN OCEAN - JANUARY

This effectively replaces the Equatorial Counter-current during the southern winter (northern summer) and although the direction is basically the same, it has important implications around the region of the Seychelles. The Equatorial Counter-current is fed from the N in an anticlockwise direction while the SW monsoon is fed from the S in a clockwise direction. If you are on passage in this area the two contrary 'feeds' to the two currents can be important. The SW Monsoon Current is consistent and strong with rates around 1–2kn. Like the Equatorial Counter-current it is most consistent and strong at the beginning and end of the season.

Southern Ocean Current Also known as the Circumpolar Current. This current flows eastwards around the Southern Ocean propelled by the continuous westerlies that circulate here unhindered by any land mass. In the southern winter there is a SE to SW anticlockwise flow between 30°S and 40°S, while in the southern summer there is predominantly a SW flow between 30°S and 40°S except where the current is deflected back around the SW tip of Australia. Below 40°S the flow is to the E.

Mozambique Current The Mozambique Current runs S along the E coast of Africa from around the top of Madagascar where the South Equatorial Current divides. It is a strong current with rates of up to 4kn recorded. Usually it runs at around 1½–2kn, less in the southern winter. Up the W coast of Madagascar a weaker N-going current runs at around ½–1½kn. It is useful for yachts headed N up the Mozambique Channel.

Agulhas Current Around the tip of Africa there is a continuation of the Mozambique Current, augmented by the South Equatorial Current and known as the Agulhas Current. It has a strong SW flow curving W and then NW following the coastline. The current is always strong and rates of 5kn have been regularly recorded at all times of the year. Rates of at least 2kn can be expected, although in places rates are around 1½kn. The inside boundary of the current is said to be the 200 metre line so yachts wishing to get out of the current should go inside 200 metres. Around East London the current divides and one arm circulates anticlockwise to join the Southern Ocean Current. The Agulhas Current is known and feared by many

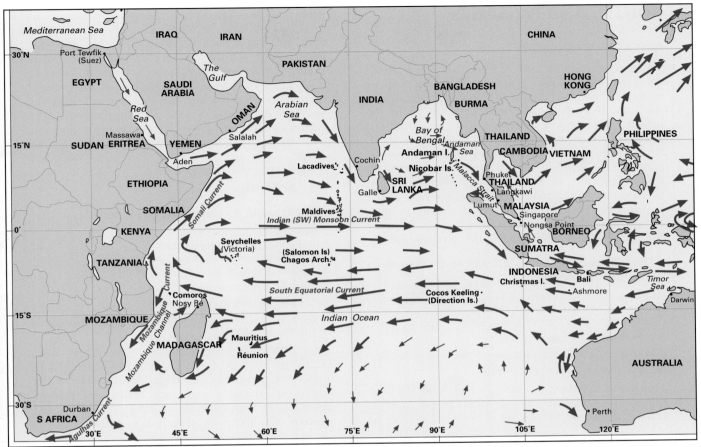

CURRENTS IN THE INDIAN OCEAN - JULY

as it can give rise to exceptionally steep seas with a short period when a SW blow comes through. Yachts should listen carefully to weather forecasts in the area when on passage around the tip of Africa.

Somali Current This current runs up or down the coast of Somalia and Kenya depending on the season. When the NE monsoon is blowing in the northern Indian Ocean it flows SW down the coast. It is a strong current, running at 2kn with 3–4kn not unusual at certain times. When the SW monsoon is blowing it flows NE up the coast and often attains rates of 3kn with 4kn not unusual.

ROUTES AND PASSAGES

PASSAGES WESTABOUT

Passages westabout take the normal trade winds route and this is the most common direction for yachts to go as part of a circumnavigation or starting off from Australasia for a cruise of the Indian Ocean region. There are a lot of variations, but for the most part yachts will travel through SE Asia and then across to Sri Lanka/India and then on across to the Red Sea and up to the Mediterranean. The alternative is to Christmas Island, Cocos, Chagos, Sri Lanka/India and on across to the Red Sea and the Mediterranean. An increasing number of yachts go down around Africa, but the majority still take the Red Sea option to the Mediterranean.

**IW1 Torres Strait and Darwin to Christmas Island/Cocos Keeling

Thursday Island to Darwin 725M
Darwin to Christmas Island 1,490M
Christmas Island to Cocos Keeling 530M

Season May to October

Best time July to September

Tropical storms December to April

This is the standard fast way out of Australia into the southern Indian Ocean. Most people stop in Darwin on the way. Once out of the wind shadow of

Australia the SE Trades blow consistently at 12–25kn, although in May and again in November they are less consistent. Generally this is a fast passage with a relatively easy landfall at Christmas Island. Some yachts break the passage at Ashmore Reef. From Christmas Island yachts usually proceed on to Cocos Keeling and some yachts will make the passage direct to Cocos Keeling because the anchorage at Christmas Island is uncomfortable with the swell pushed around into it with the SE Trades. The anchorage at Cocos is safe and comfortable with the SE Trades.

See *IW2 *IW6

*IW2 Darwin to Langkawi or Phuket

Darwin to Bali (Benoa) 970M
Bali (Benoa) to Singapore 985M
Singapore to Langkawi (Kuah) 420M
Langkawi (Kuah) to Phuket (Ao Chalong) 135M

Season May to December

Best time June to August

Tropical storms December to April. (A small chance only in the Timor Sea.)

This is the more leisurely route when going west. Many yachts follow the Darwin to Ambon Rally, proceeding on to the Raja Muda. There are numerous regattas and race series in between, finishing up with the King's Cup at Phuket in early December. There will be periods of calms once you

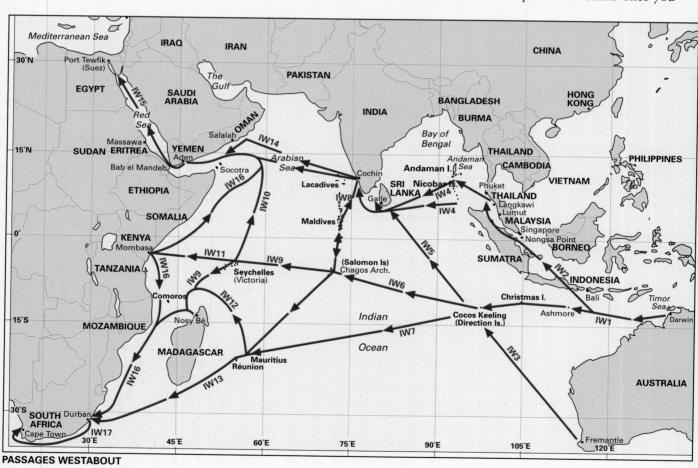

PASSAGES WESTABOUT

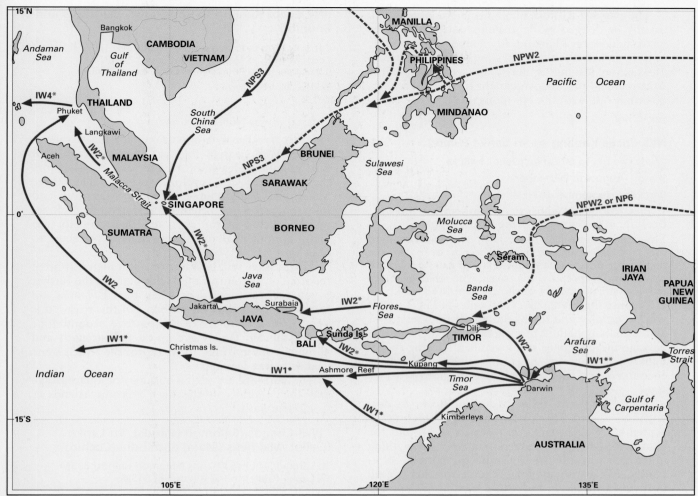

INDONESIA ROUTES

are amongst the Indonesian archipelago and in the Malacca Straits. The likelihood of tropical storms is very low and the only bad weather is likely to be squalls associated with thunderstorms, including the notorious Sumatra in the Malacca Straits. This route take some people a year or two to do as there are a lot of places to explore along the way. Yachts going west will normally leave from Langkawi or Phuket.

See *IW4

IW3 Fremantle to Cocos Keeling

Fremantle to Cocos Keeling 1,585M

Season May to October

Best time July to September

Tropical storms November to April

This is the quick route to the northern Indian Ocean during the SE Trades. The passage will normally be a fast one and at times a wet and rolly passage. Some yachts coast up the W coast of Australia before setting out for Cocos.

*IW4 Phuket to Sri Lanka (Galle) and via the Andamans (Port Blair)

Phuket to Sri Lanka (Galle) 1,100M
Phuket to Andamans (Port Blair) 410M
Andamans (Port Blair) to Sri Lanka (Galle) 850M

Season January to March, although yachts sometimes leave in December

Best time January to February

Tropical storms May to December

Once clear of the wind shadow of Thailand the NE monsoon blowing at 12–20kn gives a fast passage to Sri Lanka. Yachts normally pass through the Great Channel between Great Nicobar Island and the N end of Sumatra, but can also pass through the Sombrero Channel between Katchall Island and Little Nicobar which is free of dangers. It is prohibited to approach or anchor off the Nicobars. In the approaches to Dondra Head, the southern end of Sri Lanka, traffic is squeezed into narrow separation lanes and there will be a significant increase in shipping. The best option is to go between the inside lane and the coast and, although large numbers of fishing boats will be encountered, especially at night, this is a better option than mixing it with ships in the separation lanes further out.

The passage to Port Blair in the Andamans will usually be dogged by light winds until clear of the wind shadow off Thailand. Remember it is advisable to have an Indian visa with a stamp to visit restricted areas before leaving for Port Blair (see section on the Andamans). From the Andamans to Sri Lanka it is a downhill ride with the NE monsoon.

See *IW8

IW5 Cocos Keeling to Sri Lanka (Galle)

Cocos Keeling to Sri Lanka (Galle) 1,480M

Season August to December

Best time September to November

Tropical storms November to April in southern Indian Ocean/April to December in the Bay of Bengal.

This trans-equatorial route is pretty much clear of the tropical storm zones, although even on the fringes the effects of a tropical storm can be felt with winds and especially big seas. The chances of a tropical storm once N of the equator are small.

Because the route passes through the ITCZ winds will be variable and the likelihood of thunderstorms and squalls is high. Most yachts tend to make the passage in September to November. Closing on Sri Lanka a fair amount of commercial traffic will be encountered and a good lookout must be kept at this stage.

There are three different current flows to deal with here, but the overwhelming direction in September to November is towards the E and the Southwest Monsoon Current can flow at anything up to 2kn towards the E around the bottom of Sri Lanka. Allowance should be made for this overall push towards the E and while leaving the passage until December is an option, it doesn't seem to make a great deal of difference when compared to making an earlier passage.

*IW6 Cocos Keeling to Chagos (Salomon Islands)

Cocos Keeling to Chagos (Salomon Islands) 1,520M

Season May to October

Best time September to October

Tropical storms November to April

Most boats make this passage around September to October when the SE Trades have died down a bit, but are still consistent and strong enough to make for a speedy passage. The currents during this time are mostly W-going with the South Equatorial Current although the further N you get, the more likely the current will slow or even reverse towards the E as the Southwest Monsoon Current takes over. For most yachts this is a pleasant fast passage, if occasionally a bit rolly when the trades go into the E.

See *IW9

IW7 Cocos Keeling to Rodriguez, Mauritius and Réunion

Cocos Keeling to Rodriguez (Port Mathurin) 1,985M
Cocos Keeling to Mauritius (Port Louis) 2,330M
Cocos Keeling to Réunion (Port des Galets) 2,460M

Season May to October

Best time June to July

Tropical storms November to April

For this passage it is important that the voyage is planned well clear of the cyclone season and with time in hand to leave the area for east Africa before the onset of the cyclone season. The three Mascarene Islands of Rodriguez, Mauritius and Réunion have a good chance of being hit by cyclones which develop in the area and there are not too many options available if a cyclone is predicted to pass by.

The passage will be a fast one although it is often reported as uncomfortable, with big seas the further S you go and some days when the SE Trades are somewhat more than boisterous. For this reason it is not a bad idea to make the passage around June before the SE Trades get up to full strength and allowing some time to explore the Mascarene Islands before leaving.

The currents are all favourable for this passage and the landfall on the high volcanic islands is straightforward.

*IW8 Chagos (Salomon Islands), Sri Lanka (Galle), Maldives (Male) and India (Cochin)

Sri Lanka (Galle) to Chagos (Salomon Islands) 835M
Sri Lanka (Galle) to India (Cochin) 355M
India (Cochin) to Maldives (Male) 390M
Maldives (Male) to Chagos (Salomon Islands) 595M

Season January to April

Best time February to March

Tropical storms May to December

The rough triangle of routes here are mostly used during the NE monsoon period. Yachts en route to the Red Sea will often cross from Galle to the Maldives and a good number now go up to Cochin. Some yachts head down to Chagos and likewise some head from Cochin to the Maldives and then on to the Red Sea or down to Chagos. Winds can vary dramatically depending on the route.

From Galle to Chagos winds will initially be NE–E with the NE monsoon and then become variable in the ITCZ with a good chance of thunderstorms and squalls. You will also have to do a bit of motoring. Many yachts leave this passage until later in the season, around March or April.

From Galle to Cochin the passage will be boisterous where the NE monsoon is funnelled down through the gap between the bottom of India and Sri Lanka, with winds of Force 7 (30kn) not uncommon for a day or so. Once up to the coast there will be land and sea breezes to Cochin.

From Cochin to Male there is a good breeze from the NE monsoon once you are clear of the wind shadow off India, although this tends to weaken as you get towards the Maldives.

From Male to Chagos the winds will be variable with thunderstorms and squalls in the ITCZ zone as for the Galle to Chagos passage.

See *IW14

*IW9 Chagos (Salomon Islands) to the Seychelles (Victoria), Comoros, Madagascar (Nosy Be)

Chagos (Salomon Islands) to Seychelles (Victoria) 1,010M
Seychelles (Victoria) to Comoros (Moroni) 860M
Comoros (Moroni) to Madagascar (Nosy Be) 320M

Season May to October

Best time June to July

Tropical storms November to April

The passage from Chagos to the Seychelles is usually a pleasant one with the SE Trades providing a moderate breeze and hardly ever getting blustery. The seas are not too big and the current is going in the right direction. The approach to the Seychelles needs to be made with caution and the final approach to Victoria should be by day.

The passage to the Comoros tends to get more windy as you go S and the seas start to get bigger and less pleasant.

The passage from Moroni to Nosy Be tends to be sheltered from the worst of the swell by the bulk of Madagascar and the closer you get, the less sea there is.

See *IW16

IW10 Seychelles (Victoria) to the Red Sea

Seychelles (Victoria) to Red Sea (Bab el Mandeb) 1,720M

Season June to October

Best time September to October

Tropical storms May to June (small risk)

For this passage yachts need to hitch into the SW monsoon period which gives favourable winds and current. The problem is that when the SW monsoon is blowing at full strength there will often be gale force winds around the Horn of Africa and in the entrance to the Gulf of Aden. For this reason yachts normally make the passage in September to October when the SW monsoon has died down a bit, but there is still sufficient wind to shift you along and a favourable current.

Yachts should go well outside Socotra before heading into the Gulf of Aden because of the piracy risk around Somalia and Socotra. Yachts will probably head for Mukalla or Aden to break the voyage before tackling the Red Sea.

In the NE monsoon yachts will usually find light and variable winds from the NW–NE in October–November when heading towards the Gulf of Aden and when the NE monsoon is established there will be E winds in the Gulf of Aden itself.

IW11 Seychelles (Victoria) to East Africa (Mombasa)

Seychelles (Victoria) to East Africa (Mombasa) 950M

Season May to September

Tropical storms none

With the SE Trades this is a fast and pleasant passage. The currents are favourable until you hit the Somali Current which flows strongly to the N up the coast of Kenya and Somalia. The width of the current is around 100 miles for the worst of the current and this has been recorded at 4–5kn at times. By all accounts getting through the current is a wet business and there seems little to be done except to expect a loss to the N. If this can be compensated for by keeping as far S as possible in the approaches then so much the better. The current usually finishes around 30–50 miles off the coast.

IW12 Mauritius (Port Louis) to the Comoros (Moroni) and Madagascar (Nosy Be)

Mauritius (Port Louis) to Comoros (Moroni) 1,065M
Mauritius (Port Louis) to Madagascar (Nosy Be) 825M

Season May to October

Best time July to August

Tropical storms November to April

During the SE Trades this is a downwind run that will be fast, if a bit wet and furious at times. At the northern tip of Madagascar the wind tends to be particularly heavy although once around the top things get better. The seas up to Madagascar can be fairly big at times and it will not always be a comfortable trip. The currents are all favourable except for the counter-current running up the W coast of Madagascar.

The voyage can be broken at a number of places around Madagascar or at Mayotte.

IW13 Mauritius (Port Louis) to South Africa (Durban or Richards Bay)

Mauritius (Port Louis) to Durban 1,555M

Season May to October

Tropical storms November to April

This is the fast way out of the Indian Ocean around the southern end of Madagascar and to Durban/Richards Bay or a yacht can continue on to the Cape of Good Hope and into the Atlantic. The SE Trades die down towards the bottom of Africa and some SW winds and a SW blow will be likely.

*IW14 India (Cochin) to Oman (Mina Raysut), Yemen (Aden) and the Red Sea

India (Cochin) to Oman (Mina Raysut) 1,360M
India (Cochin) to Yemen (Aden) 1,850M
India (Cochin) to the Red Sea (Bab el Mandeb) 1,940M
Sri Lanka (Galle) to the Red Sea (Bab el Mandeb) 2,240M

Season January to April

Best time February to April

Tropical storms May to December

Yachts normally leave Galle, the Maldives and Cochin around January to February for the passage across to Mina Raysut (Salalah) or Aden when the NE monsoon is firmly established. Yachts can also leave in December when the risk of tropical storms is very low. Yachts heading for Aden or the Red Sea directly should not aim to make too much northing at first as the NE monsoon will be mostly N at first, gradually turning to NE and E at the entrance to the Gulf of Aden. This allows you to make the passage with the wind just aft of the beam all the way to the Gulf of Aden rather than going N and then rolling downwind to the Gulf of Aden. In addition the W-going current is strongest around 11°–12°N, giving a useful boost to daily averages.

Likewise, going to Mina Raysut it pays to curve gradually up to the north rather than trying to make a lot of northing in the beginning.

This passage is considered to be one of the gentler ocean passages with only a moderate swell and winds hardly ever above Force 5 (20kn) and clear skies with few thunderstorms and squalls.

See *IW15

*IW15 Red Sea passages

Bab el Mandeb to Port Tewfiq 1,200M

Season December to April

Best time May-April

Tropical storms None

Getting up the Red Sea is complicated by the fact that the preailing winds blow down the Red Sea from the N for most of the year. At the bottom of the Red Sea there will be southerlies from December to March/April blowing for anything up to 100-150 miles N of Bab el Mandeb. After that it is likely the convergence zone will be encountered and N of Massawa there will be northerlies. For the rest of the way up the Red Sea northerlies will blow, often quite strongly at Force 6–7 (23–35kn) with few days of calm. The short steep seas kicked up by the wind make going to windward a wet and bumpy business and the whole thing will come as a bit of shock to those who have been on passage downwind for some time. Unless you are in a hurry (in which case it will all just be wet and uncomfortable) it is best to take some time over the Red Sea passage.

See *MED1

*IW16 East Africa passages

Kenya (Mombasa) to the Red Sea (Bab el Mandeb) 2,150M (outside Socotra)
Kenya (Mombasa) to South Africa (Durban) 1,750 M

Season October to December

Best time November to December

Tropical storms May to October

The passage from Mombasa to the Red Sea is best made in October to December when the SW monsoon is dying out and the Somali current is still favourable. Late November to December are best, as then the NE monsoon can be caught in the Gulf of Aden and southerlies are more likely in the bottom of the Red Sea. Yachts need to keep well clear of Somalia and Socotra because of the piracy risk there.

Yachts will often break the passage at Mukalla or Aden.

The passage from Mombasa to Durban is rarely a direct one as there are lots of places to stop off en route. Yachts normally cruise down the coast of Tanzania to Mozambique and Madagascar in July to August, aiming to be going down the Mozambique Channel in September to October.

See *IW17

*IW17 Durban to Cape Town and the Atlantic

Durban to Cape Town 775M

Season December to April

Best time January to March

The passage round the Cape of Good Hope can be a challenging one, but with attention to planning and constant monitoring of the weather forecasts there should be few problems in the southern summer. The main danger is of SW gales coming in and causing steep and potentially dangerous waves when it blows against the SW-going Agulhas Current. Wave heights of 20 metres have been recorded and the waves are very steep. Choosing your time and monitoring the weather forecasts, it is possible to coast around here without encountering bad weather.

See *SAN1

PASSAGES EASTABOUT

Passages eastabout are less common than the westabout trade winds route. Yachts will choose an eastabout passage if they want to get directly from the Mediterranean to the Indian Ocean, to get from East Africa to other cruising grounds, or to get quickly back to Australasia and the Pacific from the bottom of South Africa. *See Chapter 7 Southern Ocean.*

IE1 Red Sea Passages

Port Tewfiq to Bab el Mandeb 1,200M

Season All year

Best time July-August

Tropical storms None

Getting down the Red Sea is easier than getting up. The prevailing winds are northerly for all of the year at least down as far as the bottom of Sudan. You can potter down the Red Sea or pick up a brisk northerly blow and fly down for as long as it lasts. For the southern end of the Red Sea the situation is somewhat different. With the NE monsoon blowing there will be strong southerlies, up to gale force, anywhere just S of Massawa to Bab el Mandeb. Add to these headwinds a current of anything from 1–3kn and it can be hard work getting out of the bottom of the Red Sea. When the SW monsoon is blowing northerlies extend further down the Red Sea and often there will be just a patch of variable wind or light southerlies at the bottom of the Red Sea.

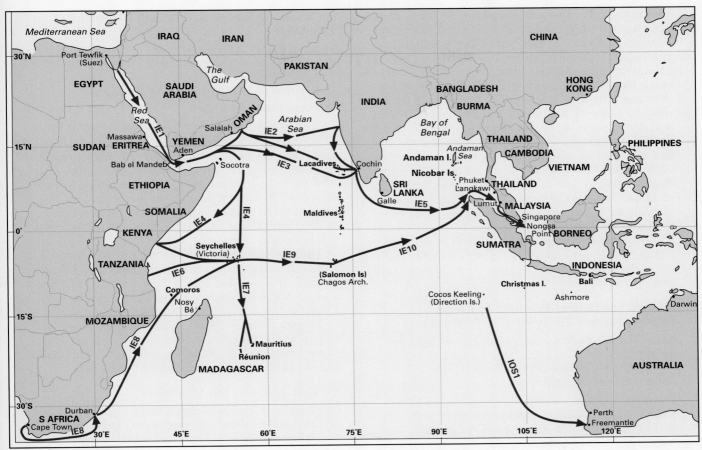

PASSAGES EASTABOUT

The favoured time to make the passage is in July-August when you can pop out of the bottom of the Red Sea and catch the last of the SW monsoon up to Mukalla or Mina Raysut before continuing on across to India or Sri Lanka. The only disadvantage to this is that it is very hot at this time in the bottom of the Red Sea and around the Arabian peninsula, often up to 40°C.

IE2 Red Sea (Bab el Mandeb) to Yemen (Aden), Oman (Mina Raysut), and India (Bombay and Cochin)

Bab el Mandeb to Aden 100M
Bab el Mandeb to Mukalla 370M
Bab el Mandeb to Mina Raysut (Salalah) 690M
Mina Raysut to Bombay 1,080M
Mina Raysut to Cochin 1,360M

Season December to March and August to October

Best time August to October

Tropical storms May to December (incidence in August to September is virtually nil)

Yachts normally try to exit out of the Red Sea into the Gulf of Aden around late July and through August and then proceed around the coast via Aden and Mukalla to Mina Raysut. The trick here is to avoid the SW monsoon when it is blowing strongest in July in the Arabian Sea and catch the tail end of the SW monsoon as it dies down in late August/September. Yachts normally cross to Mumbai, Goa (Panajim) or Cochin in late August and through September. Although this is theoretically the cyclone season, the incidence of cyclones is very low.

It is possible to cross from the Gulf of Aden to India during the NE monsoon although a yacht must be able to go efficiently to windward. (See IE3 below).

Care must be taken to keep well clear of the coast of Somalia and Socotra because of the risk of piracy.

IE3 Red Sea (Bab el Mandeb) to India (Cochin) and Sri Lanka (Galle)

Bab el Mandeb to Mukalla 370M
Bab el Mandeb to Ras Fartak 550M
Mukalla to Cochin 1,615M
Ras Fartak to Cochin 1,450M
Mukalla to Galle 1,910M
Ras Fartak to Galle 1,750M

Season December to March and August to September

Best time August to September

Tropical storms May to December (incidence in August to September is virtually nil)

During the NE monsoon getting out of the Gulf of Aden against the prevailing easterlies and against the W-going current (2–4kn) can take some doing, although it is possible to coast along Yemen until a good slant can be obtained from Ras Fartak. Around longitude 55°E the worst of the current should be over and it is then a matter of sailing hard on the wind to India or Sri Lanka. Initially it will not be possible to point in the right direction, but bit by bit the NE monsoon will turn to the NNE and then N and you will be able to pull around to Cochin or Galle. Although you are hard on the wind, the moderate breeze and moderate seas do not make this an unduly arduous passage.

With the SW monsoon it is a matter of catching the tail of the monsoon in August to September. It will be a rapid passage across to India or Sri Lanka and fairly wet at times. Although this is theoretically the cyclone season, the incidence of cyclones is very low.

IE4 Red Sea (Bab el Mandeb) to Kenya (Mombasa) and the Seychelles (Victoria)

Bab el Mandeb to Kenya (Mombasa) 2,150M (outside Socotra)
Bab el Mandeb to Seychelles (Victoria) 1,720M

Season November to March

Best time December to February

Tropical storms May to December in Arabian Sea (incidence in August to September is virtually nil)

This passage should be made in the NE monsoon when there will be favourable winds and current once you get out of the Gulf of Aden. The latter can be a bit of a struggle and most yachts go up to Mukalla.

Yachts on passage to Kenya should not be tempted to squeeze through the passage between Socotra and Somalia, because of the risk of piracy. Some yachts do take this short cut, but there have been more than enough incidents to make this a very risky business. Once out from Socotra it is a downwind passage to Kenya, with the Somali Current providing a useful increment to daily runs.

The passage from the Gulf of Aden to the Seychelles is straightforward once out of the Gulf of Aden, although yachts usually run out of wind for longish periods and a good supply of diesel will be necessary if you are not to take a long time over the passage.

IE5 Sri Lanka (Galle) to Thailand (Phuket) and Singapore

Sri Lanka (Galle) to Phuket 1,100M
Sri Lanka (Galle) to Malaysia (Kuah) 1,180M
Kuah to Singapore 420M

Season January to March and June to August

Best time February to March

Tropical storms April to December (June to August has a low incidence of cyclones)

This passage can be made during the NE monsoon although, like the passage eastabout across the Arabian Sea, it means going to windward to get to SE Asia. It is not unduly arduous and in the approaches to Sumatra and Thailand there may well be long periods of calm or light winds where you will have to motor.

The passage can be made during the SW monsoon in June to August and although there is a risk of tropical storms, the risk is low and by keeping around 10°N or lower you should be able to take avoiding action if a tropical storm threatens.

Passage from Phuket or Langkawi down to Singapore is best made with the NE monsoon, although the winds are much affected by the land and sea breeze pattern and there will be calms.

IE6 East Africa to the Seychelles

Mombasa to Seychelles (Victoria) 950M
Tanzania (Dar es Salaam) to Seychelles (Victoria) 975M

Season All year

Best time October to March

Tropical storms None

Although it is possible to make this passage all year round, the best time is during the NE monsoon when the wind is likely to be NNW–NW once across the Somali Current. You will also pick up the Equatorial Counter-current about halfway across. Winds are likely to be light and variable with some squalls as you get towards the Seychelles.

IE7 Seychelles to Mauritius and Réunion

Seychelles (Victoria) to Mauritius (Port Louis) 945M
Seychelles (Victoria) to Réunion (Port des Galets) 985M

Season May to October

Tropical storms November to April

This is a windward route which cannot be made when the SE Trades are partially displaced by the NW monsoon because of the risk of cyclones. Most yachts will tend to voyage down the coast of East Africa and then across to the Comoros and Mayotte before the final bash to Mauritius and Réunion.

IE8 South Africa to Seychelles

Cape Town to Durban 775M

Durban to Seychelles (Victoria) 2,100M

Season May to October

Best time May to June

Tropical storms November to April

Yachts proceeding round the bottom of Africa will have a hard job against the Agulhas Current. The usual way of making this passage is by coast-hopping and staying close inshore out of the Agulhas current. Passage up the Mozambique Channel should be in May or June as the chance of SW gales is highest in July and August. Once up towards Tanzania yachts can follow the passage as for IE6.

IE9 Seychelles (Victoria) to Chagos (Salomon Islands)

Seychelles (Victoria) to Chagos (Salomon Islands) 1,010M

Season November to December and April

Best time November and April

Tropical storms November to April

This passage is against the prevailing winds, so a yacht should attempt to make it at the beginning or end of the NW monsoon, which coincides with the cyclone season. In November and again in April the likelihood of a cyclone is low and in any case a yacht will be pretty much out of the sea area affected by keeping N of 5°S. Just because you are not in the actual path of a cyclone does not mean that the weather and seas will not impede progress and any cyclone developing in the area will send a considerable swell up to 5°S and the weather can be squally with impressive thunderstorms.

To make the passage during the SE monsoon between May to October would mean you would have to beat to windward to get there, but there would be a negligible risk of tropical storms.

IE10 Chagos (Salomon Islands) to Thailand (Phuket) and Malaysia (Langkawi)

Chagos (Salomon Islands) to Thailand (Phuket) 1,760M
Chagos (Salomon Islands) to Langkawi (Kuah) 1,815M

Season All year

Best time April to May

Tropical storms None

On this trans-equatorial route the incidence of tropical storms is rare, although (like IE9) the effects of a cyclone to the N or S can produce big seas and unsettled weather. The best time to make this passage is at the beginning of the SW monsoon period when with luck you will pick up good SW winds once across the ITCZ.

ROUTES TO THE SOUTHERN OCEAN

IOS1 Cocos Keeling to Fremantle

Cocos Keeling to Fremantle 2,025M

Season May to November

Best time October and November

Tropical storms December to April (in N)

This is a useful route for yachts circumnavigating Australia and wishing to avoid the very hard slog to windward when heading S along the W coast of Australia. Departing from Cocos Keeling the yacht may readily sail due S with the SE Trade wind on port tack. The trade wind tends to lessen in intensity as the latitude increases and a pleasant sail in regular seas is common. Once the variables are reached it is wise to plug on S until about 30°S. At that latitude moderate westerlies start to predominate and an easy course may be steered towards Fremantle. Avoid the temptation to turn E too soon, as the winds tend to be more southerly and stronger near the coast.

Resources

PILOTS AND GUIDES

Indian Ocean Cruising Guide Rod Heikell (Imray)
Red Sea Pilot Elaine Morgan and Stephen Davies (Imray)
East Africa Pilot Delwyn McPhun (Imray)
Downwind around Australia and Africa Warwick Clay
(available from Imray)

WEBSITES

Sail Africa/cruising connections www.cruiser.co.za
Cyclones www.taifun.org
Tropical storms and cyclones www.supertyphoon.com

SSB

Thailand: Mobile Maritime Net (Asia) 14323 MHz 0025
Zulu
SA Maritime Mobile Ham Net 14316kHz at 1130 UT
Eastern African Marine Radio Net (Kiore) 14316kHz at
0500 UT

Monsoon to Med Run

Fishing proa on the beach in Sri Lanka

Across the northern Indian Ocean yachts will leave Thailand and Malaysia to head west for Sri Lanka, India and the Maldives and then across to the Gulf of Aden and up the Red Sea to the Mediterranean. Most yachts will celebrate Christmas and New Year in Thailand or Malaysia and then head west aiming to arrive at the bottom of the Red Sea around March sometime.

Routes to the Red Sea and the Mediterranean

From Thailand (usually Phuket) and Malaysia (usually Langkawi) yachts will head to:
Galle in Sri Lanka (some will go via the Andamans)
India (usually Cochin)
Maldives (Male or Uligan)
Oman (Salalah)
Yemen (Mukalla and Aden)
Djibouti
Eritrea
Sudan
Egypt
Mediterranean

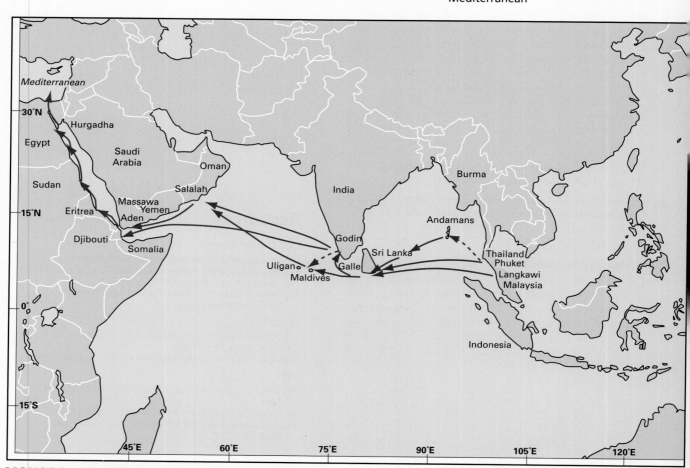

MONSOON TO MEDITERRANEAN

The piracy question

Foremost on most cruisers minds is piracy in the Gulf of Aden. At the outset it is important to stress there have been no reliable reported cases of piracy on yachts in India/Maldives or the Red Sea. Piracy is an issue in the Gulf of Aden and specifically off Somalia. There has been a lot of uninformed reportage on yacht piracy in the Gulf of Aden (and elsewhere), much of it is just plain wrong. While there is a risk in the Gulf of Aden, there are higher risks of yacht piracy in other parts of the world, notably Venezuela. In 2008 29 yachts were attacked in Venezuela, three people were killed and five badly injured (data from the Caribbean Security and Safety Net). In 2008 there were three incidents of yacht piracy off Somalia and none off the Yemen with no-one killed or injured (according to MAIB statistics). In 2009 the skipper of a French yacht off the east coast of Somalia was killed when the French Navy stormed the yacht to release those on board. It's also interesting to note that two of these yachts were close to the Somali coast which has been a big no-no in this area for fifty years and more. There have been other incidents in the Gulf of Aden in previous years and it is a worry for anyone transiting the area. That said there needs to be more objective assessment of the situation rather than the scare mongering so evident in the yachting press and on internet sites.

There are problems making these sort of comparisons. Some of these are outlined in the section on Piracy in the Introduction. Basically piracy is armed robbery in international waters as opposed to armed robbery at, say, an anchorage. The distinction is to some extent irrelevant as the outcome can be the same: injury, death and loss of possessions. It's not much help talking about piracy in this theoretical sense when the outcome can be so dire for yachts on passage and at anchor. None of us want to be the victim of piracy and for most the chances are slim. Some 250–300 yachts transit the Red Sea every year and for most the real concerns are the age old ones of cruising sailors, namely wind, sea and weather in general.

Some yachts will get together in Salalah and sail in convoy down into the Gulf of Aden to Aden or Djibouti or sometimes straight through to Eritrea. Yachts wanting to sail in a convoy with other yachts must be able to do a similar speed under sail and power. Generally a diamond-shaped convoy with a yacht at each corner is favoured. There can be real problems here when yachts cannot make the same speed as others in the convoy and the group must slow down. General rules are that yachts do not show lights at night, VHF communication is kept to low power only, and some even take down the radar reflector. It's also a good idea for at least one yacht in the convoy to have a satellite phone so MARLO or other authorities can be called direct.

Recently the increased piracy against merchant shipping (the real targets for pirates) in the Gulf of Aden and off the east coast of Africa has prompted the EU, USA, Russia, China and India to increase the naval presence in the area. A safe corridor has been established where the chances of a naval vessel being nearby is increased when using the corridor. The joint command cannot guarantee you will be safe in the corridor, but the odds are that you will be. The safe corridor is described below and west bound ships will use the northern side and east bound ships the southern side of the corridor. Each separation lane is five miles wide and the two separation lanes are separated by a two mile buffer zone.

The location of the corridors is as follows:

West bound northern corridor:
14°30'N 53°E   14°25'N 53°E
course 252° to
12°00'N 45°E   11°55'N 45°E

East bound southern corridor:
11°53'N 45°E 11°48'N 45°E
course 072° to
14°23'N 53°E   14°18'N 53°E

Recommended communication procedures are:

- Call for help on VHF Ch 16 and MF/HF DSC.

- Contact UKMTO ☎ +971 50 552 3215 *Email* ukmto@eim.ae

- If no answer call Marlo Bahrain ☎ +973 3940 1395
  Email marlo.bahrain@me.navy.mil

Check for the latest infor at www.cusnc.navy.mil/marlo/

Local fishermen may look like extras from a pirate movie, but are more often than not just curious and after food, water, booze and fags

Radio nets

Informal nets run every year and it is a matter of checking around to see what frequencies and times are used. These are often the best nets as the people on them will generally be in your vicinity and crossing at around your pace.

The following are long standing nets in the Indian Ocean and approaches.

- *Brunei Bay Radio* Daily broadcasts of weather and Maritime Safety Information warnings for all of SE Asia and eastern Indian Ocean. Brunei Bay Radio is also the regional Sailmail hub. www.bruneibay.net

- *Mobile Maritime Net* Richard Donaldson-Alves. Covers Japan to Seychelles – Hong Kong to Northern & Western Australia. (Specifically: Philippines, Malaysia, Indonesia, Northern Australia, Thailand, Sri Lanka, The Andamans & Nicobars, Chagos). **14.323Mhz @ 0025hrs zulu. At 0055hrs, Weather forecasts are relayed.** Wx @ 0055 Z daily

- *Roy's Net* Perth, W.Australia. Wx warnings & then covers boats in N & W Indian Ocean. **14320 kHz @ 1115hrs zulu.**

- *South Africa Maritime Mobile Net* S Africa. Covers Indian Ocean & S Atlantic. **14316 kHz & moves to 7045 kHz @ 0630hrs and also @ 1130hrs (both frequencies).**

- *Radio 'Peri-Peri'* East Africa. Covers Indian Ocean & S Atlantic. **8101 kHz @ 0500hrs zulu (weather) & then 12353 kHz after the weather. Again (both freqs) @ 1500hrs zulu.**

- **German Maritime Mobile Net** Covers the Atlantic, Pacific, Indian Ocean, Med, (worldwide). Ham, Echolink & Winlink. **14313 kHz @ 1630hrs zulu.**

Gentle sailing in the NE monsoon

Provisioning

Malaysia Langkawi is a duty free island and there are few who don't stock up with alcohol here. This is probably the best place to buy alcohol until you get to the Mediterranean. Reasonable shopping for staples and not too bad for fresh fruit and vegetables. Meat and fish is often frozen although you can find fresh fish as well.

Thailand Phuket town has good supermarket type shops for stocking up on staples. Good fresh fruit and veggie stalls around Ao Chalong and in Phuket town. Meat and fish is generally frozen.

Sri Lanka Shopping for staples in Galle is poor. You can order food items from several of the 'agents' otherwise try the shops in Galle. Fresh fruit and veggies are adequate in Galle or from the 'agents'. You may be warned off shopping in town by the 'agents' but in fact there is no problem there and prices are generally better.

India Reasonable shopping for staples in Cochin although you may have to search around for some items. Excellent fruit and vegetable market in Cochin with all sorts of goodies at cheap prices including spices and nuts like cashews and macadamias. Also good plum cake in the bakeries. The beer is OK but spirits are dire.

Maldives A few staples and some locally grown fruit, but that is about it. No alcohol.

Oman Reasonable shopping for some staples in Salalah. Good fresh fruit and veggie market in town. Meat and fish is often frozen. No alcohol.

Yemen Reasonable shopping for staples in the supermarket in Aden. Surprisingly good fresh fruit and vegetables that are long lasting on board in Aden and Mukalla. Meat often frozen. No alcohol.

Djibouti Good shopping for staples and all sorts of French foodstuffs you won't have seen for a while, but at a price. Most things are imported and the cost reflects this.

Eritrea Very basic shopping with only a few staples available. Poor fruit and veggie shopping.

Sudan Basic shopping for staples in Port Sudan. Surprisingly good fresh fruit and vegetable market.

Egypt Adequate shopping for most staples in larger places like Safaga, Hurgadha and Port Said. Adequate

You get better fresh fruit and veg than you might imagine on the edge of the desert. Here in Aden

fresh fruit and veggies depending on your luck. Some days shopping will be good and others not. Hurgadha is a good place to stock up.

Fuel

Malaysia Duty free diesel quays at Royal Langkawi Yacht Club, Rebak Marina and Telaga Marina.

Thailand Fuel quays at Boat Lagoon and Yacht Haven. Fuel barge in Ao Chalong.

Sri Lanka Fuel quay in Galle.

India Cochin. Fuel by jerry can or large amounts by tanker by arrangement.

Oman Salalah. Diesel from the Shell depot by tanker for large amounts. Smaller amounts by jerry can from the service station. Relatively cheap.

Yemen Fuel quay in Aden. Diesel can be contaminated. Paperwork required to get diesel. Relatively cheap.

Djibouti Can be arranged to be brought out, usually in jerry cans. Reasonably cheap.

Eritrea Supplies can be patchy and diesel contaminated. Relatively cheap.

Sudan Fuel quay in Port Sudan. Otherwise by jerry cans. Relatively cheap.

Egypt Fuel quay in Port Ghalib, Hurgadha and Port Suez. Diesel relatively cheap.

Yacht facilities are virtually non-existent along much of the Monsoon to Med run, though you can get some basics done. Here blacksmiths in Mukalla in the Yemen

Changing crew

Malaysia International flights from all over the world to Kuala Lumpur and some international flights to Penang. Connecting flights to Langkawi. One of the easiest places to put crew on the ships papers.

Thailand International flights from all over the world to Bangkok and connecting flights to Phuket. Some international flights direct to Phuket. Some paperwork involved putting crew on the ships papers.

Sri Lanka International flights to Colombo. Train or bus to Galle. Paperwork involved with putting crew on the ships papers and its best to use an agent for this.

India International flights to Bombay and Delhi. Connecting flights to Cochin. Paperwork involved to put crew on the ships papers.

Oman UK flights to Muscat. Flights from Dubai and Bahrain (with lots of international flights) to Muscat. Internal flights to Salalah.

Yemen UK flights to Saana. Flights from Dubai to Saana. Internal flights to Aden.

Egypt International flights to Hurgadha and Cairo.

Reading

Indian Ocean Cruising Guide Rod Heikell (Imray)
Red Sea Pilot Elaine Morgan and Steven Davies (Imray)

My gem

Empires of the Monsoon Richard Hall (Harper Collins)

Gas

Malaysia Some gas bottles can be filled, but not all. The situation is a bit fluid and in places like Port Klang you can get bottles filled while in others bottles will be refused. You may have to resort to filling bottles by gravity from a Malaysian bottle. Most gas is propane.

Thailand Most bottles can be filled in Phuket town. Ask around. Gas is propane.

Sri Lanka Gas filling station in the harbour at Galle. Propane and butane.

India Difficulties getting bottles filled in Cochin. You may have to resort to filling bottles by gravity from an Indian bottle.

Oman Bottles can be filled at the Shell station in Salalah. Gas is propane.

Yemen Bottles can be filled in Little Aden. Get one of the taxi drivers to arrange it. Propane and butane.

Eritrea Bottles can be filled in Asmara. Get one of the 'agents' to help you.

Sudan Most bottles can be filled in Port Sudan. Arrange with the agent.

Egypt Some gas bottles can be filled in Hurgadha and Port Suez. Some types of bottles will be refused.

Mediterranean Propane and butane bottles can be filled in Cyprus and Turkey.

Hauling out and repairs

Malaysia Yachts can be hauled at Lumut (large travel hoist at the naval base), Wavemaster in Langkawi (450 and 150-ton travel hoists), Telaga Marina (65-ton travel hoist) and Rebak Marina (60-ton travel hoist). Wavemaster has good repair facilities. Elsewhere there are local mechanical and engineering repairs. Duty free spares can be imported into Langkawi.

Thailand Yachts can be hauled at Boat Lagoon and Royal Phuket Marina (60-ton travel hoists). Some yacht repair facilities in Phuket. Basic chandlery.

Sri Lanka In an emergency yachts can be craned out at the fishing harbour in Galle. Mechanical and engineering repairs. No chandlery and importing items via an agent can be laborious.

India Small yard in Cochin. Mechanical and engineering repairs. No chandlery but good hardware shops.

Eritrea Emergency haul out by crane possible in Massawa. No facilities.

Egypt Limited repairs at Port Ghalib (no haul out). Basic repairs at Hurgadha and a slipway. Haulout facilities also at Abydos Marina.

Mukalla on Yemen coast

COUNTRY AND PORT GUIDE

Northern Indian Ocean

Singapore

General Singapore is used as a base in SE Asia as it is a stable and ordered society and most facilities can be found here. There are good worldwide communications and good facilities such as banks and hospitals. From Singapore you can cruise to nearby islands in the Indonesian archipelago or up the Malacca Strait to Malaysia and Thailand.

Entry Formalities can be carried out for a fee (currently around S$40–50/€20–25 per yacht) at Raffles Marina, Republic of Singapore Yacht Club or Changi Yacht Club. This is the easiest way to clear in. The alternative is to anchor in the designated small craft anchorage on the SE side of Singapore Island (01°17'·8N 103°55'·8E). There is a time limit on how long yachts can anchor here (between two to four days usually) and it is enforced. You may be able to get a mooring at Changi (book ahead) or there may be space to squeeze in and anchor to the W of the moorings. Another alternative is Johor Bahru (01°27'·5N 103°46'·5E) on the Malaysian side where you can get a bus across to Singapore. If you anchor in the quarantine area you will need to call on VHF Ch 16 and then go ashore to immigration and then to the port office. This is no longer easy and it is recommended you go to either Raffles or the RSYC.

Telecom IDD +65. GSM network. Internet cafés.

Currency Singapore dollar. Major credit cards widely accepted. ATMs. Money-changers (mostly located in Change Alley near the major banks) will change cash and traveller's cheques. They also deal in restricted currencies such as Indian rupees and it is useful to obtain some rupees here if headed for India.

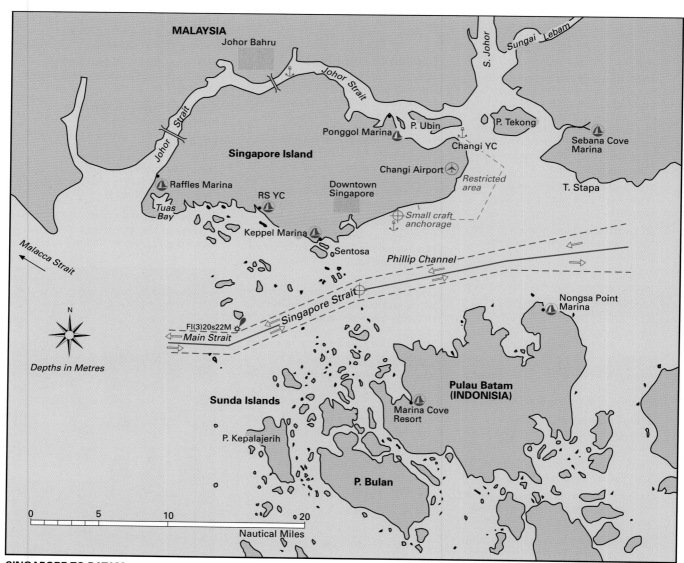

SINGAPORE TO BATAM
⊕01°17'·8N 103°55'·8E (Small craft anchorage)

Notes

1. The Singapore Strait is one of the busiest shipping channels in the world, with ships at anchor and proceeding through the straits in both directions. There are also ferries, workboats and tugs towing barges. It can be nerve-wracking keeping an eye on everything that is going on. Yachts should cross the shipping channels at a right angle to the channel and stay outside the channels when proceeding E or W.

2. *Small Craft Anchorage* The small craft anchorage at 01°17'·8N 103°55'·8E is now the only designated area for yachts to anchor off around Singapore island. The anchorage is off the East Coast Park and there are no facilities nearby. To even get to downtown Singapore for clearance procedures is a long and arduous trip. The anchorage itself is exposed to the swell and also wash from shipping and smaller craft. It cannot be recommended and the best policy is to head to either Raffles Marina, RSYC marina or Changi. Yachts anchored anywhere else around Singapore will be directed to this designated anchorage or to one of the marinas.

CHANGI

Tidal range 3.1m

Navigation

Restricted area off Changi Airport for yachts with masts over 49m. Otherwise approach is straightforward though care is needed of shipping and numerous coastal and coastguard vessels.

Anchorage

Off Changi Sailing Club (a mooring may be available) or anchored in Loyang Bay. Adequate but often rolly from the wash of passing vessels.

Berths

VHF Ch 16, 69 for Changi Sailing Club. 160 moorings. 300 dry berths ashore.

Facilities

Water. Slipway to 10m/6 tons. Some provisions. Restaurants and local stalls. Temporary membership of the club available which gives access to showers and toilets, bar, BBQ area and the library.

Remarks

No. 29 bus runs to Tampines where you can transfer to the MRT for downtown Singapore.

RAFFLES MARINA

01°20'·53N 104°05'·7E
Tidal range 2.6m

Navigation

Lies on the SW of Singapore Island a short distance up the Johor Strait. Night approach not recommended.

Berths

VHF Ch 77. 165 berths. Visitors' berths. Max LOA 20m plus. Eight super yacht berths. Charge band 3. You will be directed to a berth. Good shelter.

Facilities

All normal facilities. 70-ton hoist and repair facilities. Chandlers. Mini-market and restaurant and bar.

Remarks

Downtown Singapore can be reached by taxi or bus.
Email ahoy@rafflesmarina.com.sg
www.rafflesmarina.com.sg

Note Craft moving between ports in Singapore are reported to need an AIS Class B transponder. These can be hired for craft movement if required.

Malaysia

General Malaysia is a stable and well developed country with a useful number of harbours and anchorages along its coast.

Coastline The long skinny peninsula is bordered by flat coastal plains and off these the water is comparatively shallow. One thing you have to get used to in Malaysian waters is sailing around in less than 5m – if you get to 20m depths, that is deep water.

Formalities Proceed to the nearest port of entry. From S to N the ports of entry commonly used are Port Klang, Lumut, Penang and Kuah at Langkawi. You can also clear in at Malacca, Port Dickson and Sebana Cove Marina. Go to the Marine Department to register your arrival, to Immigration to be stamped into the country, to Customs and the Health Office, and finally to the harbourmaster. Customs ☎ 0345 231110 (national number).

Most visitors to Malaysia from Europe, the USA and Commonwealth countries will automatically get a visa on entry for 60 days. This is extendable up to three months and after that period you can go to Singapore or Thailand by road or air and on your return you will automatically be granted another 60 days, extendable to three months.

Note **It is a serious crime to bring illegal drugs (of any sort, but especially heroin) and firearms into Malaysia. Firearms must be declared on entry. Smuggling illegal drugs into the country can carry the death penalty on conviction.**

Telecom IDD +60. GSM network. Internet cafés in larger centres.

Currency Ringgit or Malaysian dollar. Major credit cards accepted in larger towns. ATMs in larger towns and tourist areas.

Sailing season The season is all year round, although the favoured time of year for the W coast is during the NE monsoon, with the best months in December, January and February. The NE monsoon lasts from about November to April. This is the dry season and consequently the least humid time of the year.

The SW monsoon brings rain and a high humidity. It is also the season when you are most likely to encounter squalls, including the sumatra in the Malacca Strait.

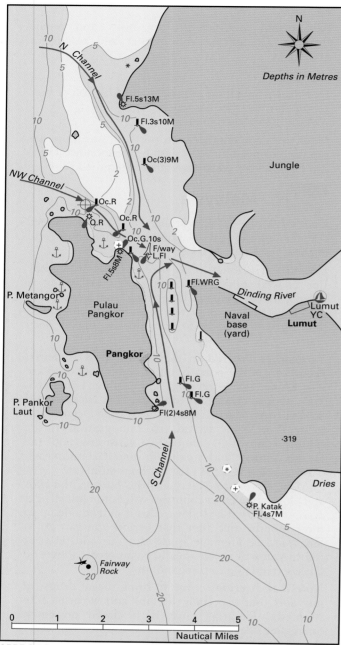

APPROACHES TO LUMUT AND DINDING RIVER (Malaysia)
⊕ 04°16'·10N 100°33'·05E WGS84

Piracy

The area around Singapore and the Malacca Strait is often mentioned in articles and official publications as a noted piracy area. For yachts the risk is very small here and the piracy risk is pretty much confined to commercial shipping. Yachts sailing from Singapore up the Malaysian coast to Langkawi and on to Thailand have a small risk factor. There is a fair amount of smuggling going on between Sumatra and Malaysia, most of it involved with bringing illegal immigrants over to Malaysia, but for the most part if you leave them alone they will not bother you. Local yachts based in Singapore regularly transit up and down the Malacca Strait without incident.

Routes and harbours Hemmed in by the Malacca Strait, routes are straightforward proceeding either N or S between Langkawi and Singapore. During the NE monsoon and the transition periods yachts will often anchor off the coast wherever there are convenient depths when the weather is calm. If you are sailing through the night then care is needed of the large volume of commercial traffic and local fishing boats. For most of the coast you can sit on the 20-metre line, which keeps you away from the shipping lanes further out and outside of the range of smaller inshore fishing boats. A lot of yachts join the Raja Muda race from Port Klang to Langkawi and this is a very social way to sail up the coast in company. The Langkawi archipelago near the border with Thailand is the most popular area, with a useful number of anchorages around the islands and the bonus of duty-free shopping so spares can be imported without duty. Langkawi is a favourite spot for yachts staying for longer periods with excellent anchorages and three marinas with good facilities.

LUMUT
Tidal range 3.2m

Navigation
Three channels lead into Dinding River around the island of Pulau Pangkor. Lumut is on the S bank of the river just inside the entrance. The NW Channel is easiest although the S Channel is buoyed and straightforward by day. The tide runs strongly through the channels and if you don't have tide tables then watch what the local trawlers are doing. A night entrance is not recommended.

Berths
VHF Ch 69 for anyone listening on a yacht upriver. Ch 16 for harbourmaster at Lumut.

Lumut International YC. Two pontoons. Visitors' berths. Max LOA 30m approx. Depths 2–5m. Charge band 2. Good shelter although there can be some wash from passing craft.

Anchorage
Around 2½ miles up the river is Changs Yard and a little further on is Kamphong Bahru. The channel has good depths. A new road bridge across the river before Kamphong Bahru has a reported air height of 15–18 metres. Check with the authorities in Lumut.

Facilities
Water and 220V at Lumut IYC. Fuel by cans. Limited yacht repairs at the naval yard by arrangement. Provisioning in Lumut town or Sitiwan, about 20 minutes by bus from Kamphong Bahru and Lumut. Restaurants in Lumut and just two simple restaurants in Kamphong Bahru.

KUAH (LANGKAWI)
Tidal range 3.2m

Navigation
The approach can be made from the SW through the islands or from the SSE through Selat Kuah. Care is

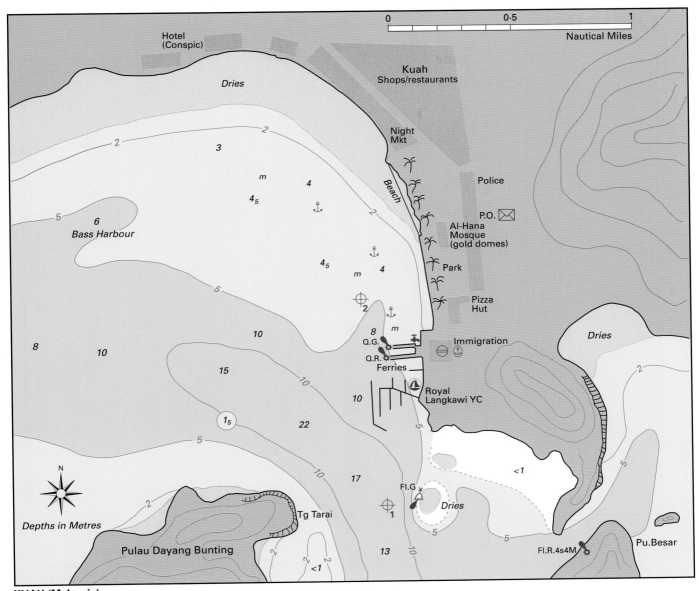

KUAH (Malaysia)
⊕1 06°17'·52N 99°50'·98E WGS84
⊕2 06°18'·58N 99°50'·95E WGS84

needed over patches of shoal water in the approaches from both channels.

Berths
VHF Ch 16 for port authorities. Ch 69, 72 for Langkawi Yacht Club and other yachts in the vicinity.
Royal Langkawi Yacht Club VHF Ch 69. 200 berths. Visitors' berths. Max LOA 60m. Depths 3–10m. Charge band 2/3. Shelter here is much improved with the outer breakwater which stops much of the wash from the ferries.
www.langkawiyachtclub.com

Anchorage
Anchor off to the N of Kuah pier where convenient in 4–8m leaving the approaches to Kuah pier clear for the ferries. The bottom is mud and excellent

holding. Good shelter and close to town. There is a pontoon on the pier for yacht tenders.

Facilities
Water, 220V and fuel at Langkawi Yacht Club. Wi-Fi. For large amounts of fuel there is a fuel barge moored in the anchorage. Good shopping for provisions including a 'night market' with fresh produce. Restaurants and a few bars. PO. Banks. ATMs. Internet cafés. Laundries.

Remarks
Langkawi is a duty-free zone and spares can be imported without duty. Most yachts choose to use Seaspeed as they are used to handling packages arriving for yachts.

Malaysia

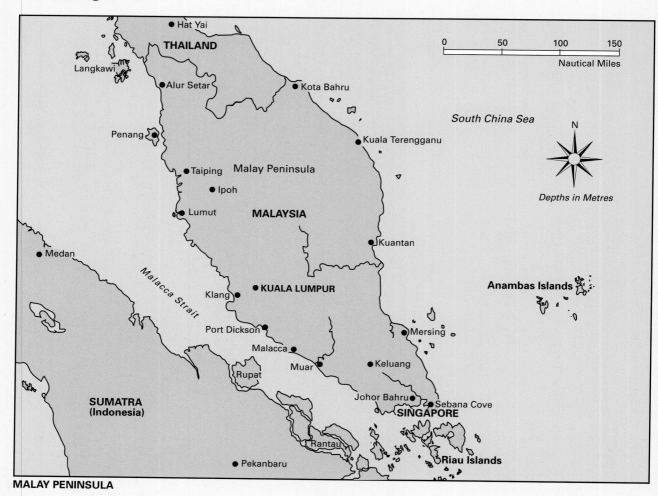

MALAY PENINSULA

Idyllic cruising around the limestone islands in the Langkawi archipelago

Malaysia is a bit of a mystery to most cruisers. Indonesia and Thailand are better known in many ways and so Malaysia comes as a surprise package, a wonderfully diverse country with a mix of cultures, food, topography and history with a modern infrastructure that all works. The coast is a mix of mangrove flats split by large rivers, some of them navigable, to rocky limestone islands covered in rain forest. Malaysia has some of the most ancient rain forest in the world and its biodiversity is astounding, from sea eagles and fruit bats that darken the evening sky as they fly back to roost, to the world's highest tree (the tualang) and the world's largest flower (the rafflesia). There are tropical fruits and strange fruits like the durian and the rambutan.

As a well developed country Malaysia has an infrastructure which makes it easy to pick up crew, arrange visas (for India), and get duty free items sent too. Langkawi is a duty free island and one of the few duty free places in the world that really is seamless. Pick up your West Marine Catalogue, get in touch and pay, and then pick it up when it arrives in Langkawi.

Cruising strategies

Most yachts will be coming from Indonesia and will cruise up the Malacca Strait to Penang and onto Langkawi. The Malacca Straits used to have a reputation for piracy, but for decades there has been minimal or no risk to sailing yachts and recently the area was removed from Lloyds List as a high risk piracy area. There are still some attacks on shipping here, but the risk to yachts sailing up the west coast of Malaysia is very low and none of the resident yachts in Malaysia know of any attack in the last two decades.

The problems of sailing up the Malacca Straits come from the fact that it is a narrow strait with heavy commercial shipping traversing it, along with local fishing boats, extensive shallows and considerable tides. One strategy for cruising up the coast is to roughly follow the 20 metre line which should keep you outside the local fishing boats, or at least most of them, and inside the main shipping channel.

There are a number of anchorages and harbours up the west coast that can be used and yachts will often hop from Singapore or the Riau Islands in Indonesia to Port Dickson or Port Klang to clear in and then on to Lumut, Penang and Langkawi. Some yachts will clear in at Sebana Cove Marina before continuing on.

Yachts spending some time around Malaysia can cruise around to the east coast of peninsular Malaysia, usually in the late winter and spring, and those that have done so rave about the cruising area.

Seasons and winds

There are two distinct seasons corresponding to the two monsoon periods. The favoured season is during the northern winter with the northeast monsoon between November and April and the less favoured is the summer with southwest monsoon between May and October. Winter and summer are relative terms this close to the equator and it makes more sense to talk about the monsoon periods. Along this coast the large land mass of Asia affects winds along the coast modifying the sort of wind you will find further out to sea.

The islands around the coast are often sheer limestone cliffs rising straight out of the water with top-knots of dense jungle

Malaysian fishing boats

Along the Malaysian coast there are good anchorages up some of the rivers. Here two miles up the Dinding River

Royal Langkawi Marina

Telaga Marina – a popular cruisers choice in Langkawi

Food, lovely food in Malaysia

The prevailing winds in the area are basically determined by the monsoon season, but the enclosed waters give rise to some variation. The wind blows from the northeast during the northeast monsoon and this is the favoured time to sail in this area when the wind is blowing off the land. However, there is a distinct diurnal component promoted by sea and land breeze effects. The NE monsoon will often be held up in the afternoon by the sea breeze and augmented at night by the land breeze. For this reason the Raja Muda Race does the longer legs at night when there is generally more consistent wind. By day you will often have to motor to get anywhere or there may be a NW or even W sea breeze when the NE monsoon is not fully developed.

During the NE monsoon the diurnal effect of calm days and windy nights means it is worthwhile taking some care over where you anchor as although it may be calm or light NW-W in the late afternoon, the wind can get up in the night from the NE and there can be gusts off any high land.

During the SW monsoon there can be little wind in the Malacca Strait or strong southerlies blowing up the strait depending on the strength of the SW monsoon. When it is blowing strongly there are often squalls in the strait, especially around the N entrance. Throughout the strait this is the time when a Sumatra is most likely.

Ashore

Malaysia charms the visitor and there is lots to do ashore. In most places restaurants are open throughout the year and are little affected by high and low season tourist flows. In fact for many of the places cruisers visit there is little in the way of tourism until you get to Langkawi. One of the features of the coast is that there are a number of rivers that you can safely navigate up and here you wind through the jungle to small villages (kampongs) on the banks that you can anchor off. Up these rivers and off the islands there is wildlife galore from monkeys and lizards to sea eagles and fruit bats.

Malaysian food is a remarkable miscellany of Chinese, Indian and Malay flavours and seldom disappoints. In the larger towns you will also get more international fare as well as the ubiquitous pizza and hamburgers, though Malay fast food

Some of the fishing methods off the coast are hard to work out. Here in the Malacca Strait

is so good you have to wonder why anyone bothers. There are often night markets (pasar malam), so-called because they open in the cool of the evening, where you can get all sorts of fast food like satay beef and chicken, fresh fruit and vegetables, nuts and dried fruit and lots of other things you probably don't need.

Shopping in the larger centres varies from adequate to good while fresh fruit vegetables are excellent. In Langkawi you can stock up on most things you need in the supermarkets in Kuah and also duty free alcohol.

Facilities

Yacht facilities are not well developed until you get to Langkawi. Yachts can be hauled at Lumut in the naval base, but you are better off going up to Langkawi where Wavemaster (450 and 150-ton travel hoists) has a yard with dedicated yacht repair facilities. Smaller yachts are probably better off going to Telaga Marina (65-ton travel hoist) or Rebak Marina (60-ton travel hoist). At Rebak you are a bit out of it so take most of what you need with you. In Langkawi there are local

Local trawler off Penang

mechanical and engineering repair facilities and duty free spares can be imported into Langkawi.

Reading

Indian Ocean Cruising Guide Rod Heikell (Imray)
Andaman Sea Pilot Bill O'Leary & Andy Dowden (Image Asia)

My gem

Lord Jim: A Tale Joseph Conrad (Penguin)

Transport around Penang

Thailand

General In recent years facilities in Thailand have much improved, with a cluster of facilities around Phuket and a relaxation of the swingeing import taxes that were in place. There is a resident yachting population around Phuket which really comes alive during the King's Cup when yachts from all over SE Asia and further abroad arrive for a week's racing.

Coastline Like peninsular Malaysia, much of the coast and the islands off the coast are bordered by shallow water and you will frequently be sailing in 5–10m. Parts of the coast are fringed by mangrove and in other places the limestone islands rise steeply out of the water in a dramatic way, so much so that they are often used for films that need a spectacular tropical location.

Formalities On entering territorial waters you must proceed to the nearest port of entry and clear in within 24 hours on arrival. Yachts do not normally fly a Q flag but a courtesy flag should be flown. Most yachts clear in at Ao Chalong on Phuket, but it is also possible to clear in at Krabi.

You must visit the immigration office, customs and the harbourmaster. Clearing out entails going

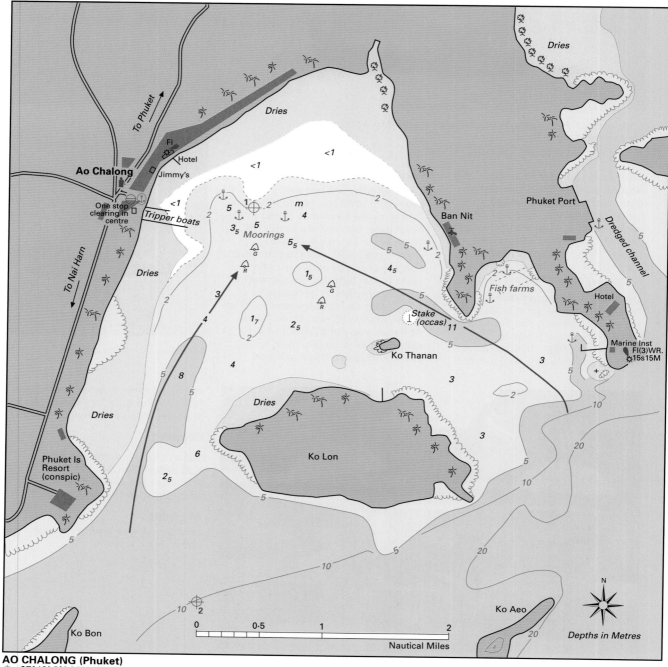

AO CHALONG (Phuket)
⊕1 07°49'·3N 98°21'·1E WGS84
⊕2 07°48'·2N 98°22'·8E WGS84

back to immigration and customs. Yachts are given a one-month visa from the time of clearing in. It is important to know that this visa is different to the tourist visa normally issued when you arrive by plane and this can cause complications if you want to leave other than by the boat you arrived on. If crew want to leave then it is best to clear them in as passengers rather than crew and they will then be free to leave.

Telecom IDD +66. Phuket code 076. GSM network. Internet cafés in larger centres.

Currency Thai baht. Major credit cards accepted in larger towns. ATMs in larger towns and tourist areas.

Sailing season The season is all year round, although the favoured time of year for the W coast is during the NE monsoon with the best months in December, January and February. The NE monsoon lasts from about November to April. This is the dry season and consequently the least humid time of the year. The SW monsoon brings rain and a high humidity. On the western coast of Thailand around Phuket there is a double rainy period with most rain falling in May and again in October. On average it will rain for more than 20 days in the month during these two months.

Routes and harbours Routes are pretty much N or S down the coast, stopping at shorter or longer intervals depending on inclination. Except for the passage to the Similan and Surin Islands, there are enough secure anchorages to be able to day sail along the coast and islands. There are several all season sailing bases around Phuket Island. Ao Chalong is used, although a significant chop is set up with strong NE and SW monsoons. Boat Lagoon, Royal Phuket Marina and Yacht Haven offer better protection and walk-on comforts. During the NE monsoon boats also base themselves at Patong and Ao Nang (Krabi) and to a lesser extent Nai Harn and Phi Phi.

AO CHALONG

Tidal range 2.3m

Navigation

Care is needed in the approaches of shallow patches and coral fringing the bay. W Channel is the more straightforward into the bay. Night approach not recommended.

Formalities There is a one-stop clearing in office at Ao Chalong with customs, immigration and harbourmaster all housed in the same block near the root of the pier.

Anchorage

Yachts listen on VHF Ch 69. Pick up one of the yellow mooring buoys if free or anchor where convenient off Ao Chalong. Alternatively anchor off Ban Nit on the E side of the bay. Excellent holding in mud. It can be wet getting ashore in the dinghy (usually left on the beach outside Jimmy's Bar).

Facilities

Authorities ashore for clearing in. Water and fuel by barge (Ch 69). Some yacht repairs and sailmaker. Good shopping in Phuket. Restaurants and bars.

Remarks

Secure anchorage and meeting place for yachts.

BOAT LAGOON

Tidal range 2.3m

Navigation

The marina is in the mangroves, with a 2km winding channel to it marked by beacons. The entrance to the channel is not easy to make out but nose in and you will come to it. Depths in the channel are c.2–2.5m at HW neaps (go in on a rising tide).

Berths

VHF Ch 67, 71 for Boat Lagoon. 180 berths. Visitors' berths. Max LOA 40m. Charge band 2/3. You will be directed to a berth. Excellent shelter.

Facilities

Water. 220V. Wi-Fi. Fuel quay. 40/80-ton travel hoists. Good repair facilities mostly through service agencies. Provisions in Phuket.

Remarks

Boat Lagoon is surrounded by apartments and a hotel and can get a little sticky in the humidity. Popular place to leave a boat.
www.phuketboatlagoon.com

ROYAL PHUKET MARINA

Situated adjacent to Boat Lagoon and reached by the same access channel.
www.royalphuketmarina.com

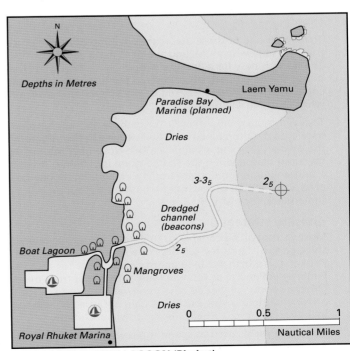

APPROACH TO BOAT LAGOON (Phuket)
⊕07°58′·67N 98°24′·95E WGS84

Thailand

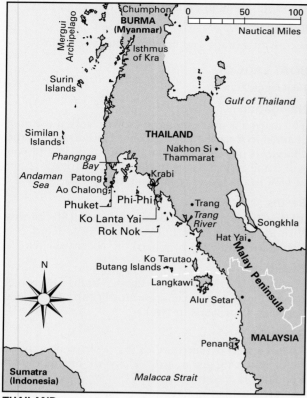

THAILAND

The almost surreal limestone seascape around the Thai coast

Thailand and especially Phuket have long been on the radar of cruisers and land-based tourists. Parts of Phuket are touristy, but get away from the island and head into Phang Nga Bay and further south to the off-lying islands and coast and it is remarkably easy to get off the beaten track away from the crowds.

Thailand is one of those places that cruising boats get stuck in. They arrive en route to somewhere else and the next thing you know five years has passed. The living is easy here and the people gentle and kind. Thailand is effectively out of the direct path of cyclones in the Bay of Bengal and if a cyclone does come close, as Cyclone Gay did in 1989, there are hurricane holes nearby where you can shelter.

Thailand has a good infrastructure ashore and has become a popular place to base a boat. Often a boat will be left here in the SW monsoon season with the owner returning around October–November in time for the more favoured season when the NE monsoon is blowing. There are now three marinas up and running around Phuket with more planned and there is always the option of leaving the boat on a mooring in Ao Chalong with someone to look after it.

Cruising strategies

Most yachts will be coming up to Phuket from Langkawi and will cruise up through the islands for 4–5 days or so before clearing in at Ao Chalong on Phuket. It is worth thinking about getting visas for all crew at the Thai Embassy in Penang as you will then get 90 days from the date of arrival. Otherwise you will get 30 days, renewable twice for a total of 90 days if arriving without a visa, but it is a pain because you will have to renew it at an immigration office (usually Phuket town) each time.

Previously yachts used to spend three weeks to a month cruising up to Phuket and then a similar period cruising back down to Langkawi, but it is not now advisable to do this and customs will check your passport to see when you

Cruising around Phang Nga Bay

Jimmy's Lighthouse Bar in Ao Chalong, a place for swapping information and some salty stories

Boat Lagoon Phuket *Boat Lagoon*

left. About 4–5 days is now acceptable, but check with other cruisers around the area.

Piracy

Thailand has been refreshingly free of piracy up until 2009 when a yacht was attacked off Koh Adang in the Butang Group (just N of the Malay-Thai border) and the owner murdered. This is an isolated incident allegedly carried out by illegal Burmese immigrants, but care is needed in this area.

Seasons and winds

See the section on Malaysia concerning monsoon winds and the effect of the Asian land mass on these close to the shore.

Ashore

Most yachts will hang around Phuket for a while or at least return here after pottering around the nearby islands. On Phuket there are all the facilities you would expect to find in a large tourist area. Around Ao Chalong where most cruising boats bring up in Phuket you are far enough away from the main tourist centres, especially sin-city Patong, to escape the worst of the trinket shops and touts. Ashore there are good little restaurants and bars catering for yachties including the well known Jimmy's Bar. To get into Phuket town jump on one of the buses at the market nearby or get one of the tuk-tuks on the roundabout. There are good fresh fruit and vegetables at the nearby market and good shopping in Phuket town for provisions.

Facilities

Yacht facilities have come on in leaps and bounds in Phuket and there are now a number of yacht service companies with a range of services from GRP repairs, engineering and mechanical repairs, woodwork, electrical and electronic repairs, and a good long-standing sailmaker. There are 60-ton travel hoists at Boat Lagoon and Royal Phuket Marina and more traditional yards over on the mainland. Start at Ao Chalong for yacht services and then check in Phuket town, at Boat Lagoon and Yacht Haven. Spares can be brought in but really its better to organise getting spares in Langkawi.

Reading

Indian Ocean Cruising Guide Rod Heikell. Imray
Andaman Sea Pilot Bill O'Leary & Andy Dowden. Image Asia
Sail Thailand Thai Marine & Leisure. Colin Piprell. Artasia Press

My gem

God's Dust Ian Buruma. Vintage

Ao Chalong on Phuket is a cruisers' waiting room before the migration west

Long-tail boat

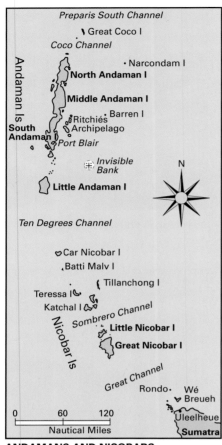

ANDAMANS AND NICOBARS

Andaman Islands

The Andamans are an island chain running more or less in a N-S direction for 200 miles from 13°40'N to 10°30'N. The Andamans are part of India and it is necessary to get an Indian visa with the required permit to visit a restricted area in advance before arriving here. Visas are most easily obtained in Kuala Lumpur.

PORT BLAIR

Navigation
In the approaches care is needed of Invisible Bank and then leave Ross Island to port. A night approach is not recommended.

Anchorage
Anchor W of Chatham Island and take the dinghy in to one of the jetties off Chatham Island. Reasonable shelter from the NE monsoon although it can be a bit rolly.

Facilities
Water and fuel by jerry can. Good market for fresh fruit and veggies and most staples. Butchers and bakers. Restaurants with good fish and venison in a number of styles including South India style, Chinese and Burmese.

Remarks
Yachts can get permission to cruise locally around Ross Island and nearby anchorages.

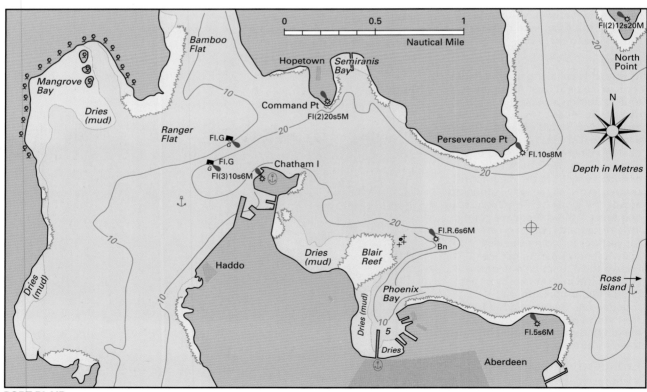

PORT BLAIR
⊕11°41'·0N 92°44'·7E

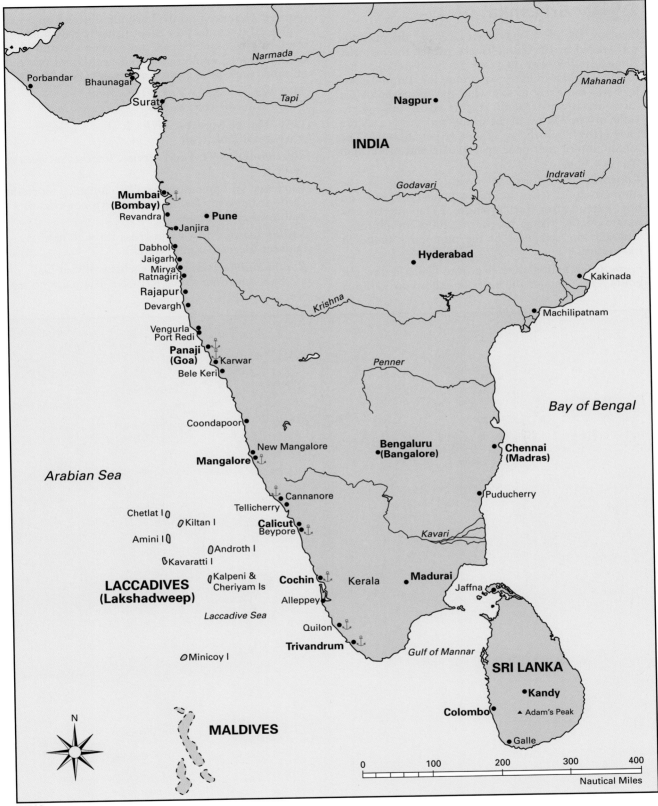

INDIA

Sri Lanka

General The island has been riven by the guerrilla war waged by the Tamil Tigers against the majority Singhalese for over 30 years and only recently has the Sri Lankan military overcome the Tamil Tigers. It is still too early to say what the future holds for this once divided island. Yachts really only go to Galle on the SW tip of the island and this is a secure base from which to take trips inland. The mountainous interior is spectacular and more than repays a tour.

Coastline The coast is mostly steep-to in the southern approaches and most of the coral reefs do not extend too far offshore. The interior is mountainous, rising to over 2,500m in places – although the steepness of the mountains makes it look more.

Formalities Yachts must clear into Galle in daylight hours. Once outside the harbour call up on VHF Ch 16 (working 12) so the navy can come out to clear you for entrance into the harbour. Once cleared you will need to contact an agent (usually the Windsors or GAC) to complete all the paperwork and clear with customs, immigration and health and pay one month's port dues. Costs are around US$175–200.

Don Windsor & Co Ltd. *VHF* Ch 69.
Email windsorreef@wow.lk

GAC Marine Services. *VHF* Ch 16, 71 (24/24). www.gacsrilanka.com

Telecom IDD +94. GSM service. Internet services at Galle.

Currency Sri Lankan rupee. Cash advance on credit cards at Bank of Ceylon in Galle. Money-changers and touts everywhere.

Sailing season Most yachts pass through here between December and March.

Routes and harbours Most yachts will visit Galle on a westabout route to the Red Sea. There are no real

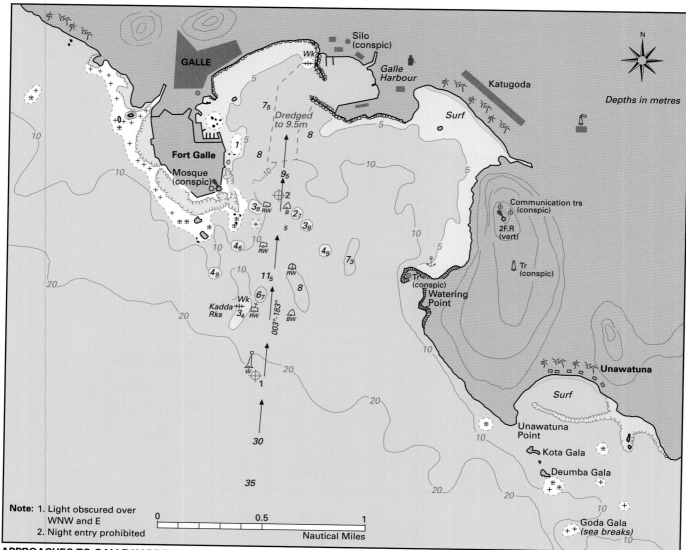

Note:
1. Light obscured over WNW and E
2. Night entry prohibited

0   0.5   1
Nautical Miles

APPROACHES TO GALLE HARBOUR (Sri Lanka)
⊕1 06°00'·4N 80°13'·3E WGS84
⊕2 06°01'·4N 80°13'·4E WGS84

problems in the approaches and the only real worry is shaping a course between the fishing boats just off the coast and ships cutting the corner around Sri Lanka on the way to the Red Sea and the Suez Canal.

GALLE

Tidal range 0.8m

Navigation

Entrance in daylight hours only (see *Formalities* above). Approach straightforward although there will be numerous fishing boats around and a large swell rolling in. Yachts must now anchor off outside the harbour entrance to await clearance by the navy. This is very uncomfortable and yachts are reported to go across to the E side of the bay and anchor under the headland with a conspic tower on it (Watering Point) to get a decent night's sleep. Once cleared with the navy proceed into the harbour.

Berths

VHF Ch 16, 12 for harbourmaster and navy; Ch 71 for GAC Agency and Ch 16 for Windsors. The harbourmaster will direct you to a berth. This will be either alongside the N side of the new pier or on one of the pontoons on the N side (Med moor). Depending on the surge in the harbour these berths can be uncomfortable at times. It is also possible to anchor out.

Note It is reported the navy no longer depth-charges the harbour to deter Tamil Tiger frogmen.

Facilities

Water on the shore. Fuel can be delivered. One of the agents can arrange some repairs and obtain other items. Provisioning at the harbour or in Galle. Most yachties go to Unawatuna to eat.

Remarks

Take a trip inland where there is magnificent tropical forest, old tea plantations and faded elegance in the old hill station settlements. Around the coast there are long sandy beaches though some have fierce tidal rips so care is needed when swimming. Proas are still used for fishing off the beach though nearly all are powered by outboards these days.

 # India

General Few yachts visit India except for those putting in at Cochin on a westabout route and into Mumbai (Bombay) on an eastabout route. This is partly because it lies off the direct westabout routes and partially because the formalities are so onerous. It is worth persevering and visiting Cochin at the very least.

Coastline Peninsular India is mostly bordered by low coastal flats behind which rise up the ghats, the central plateau of the country. The low-lying coast and the haze (mostly from cooking fires and charcoal production) means that it can be difficult to identify the coastline until closer in. The water around much of the coast is murky from silt brought down by the major rivers, although this silt enriches the water and attract a lot of fish and consequently fishing boats which work the coastal waters.

Formalities All crew members must have a valid visa before arriving in India. These can be obtained in Malaysia, Thailand or Sri Lanka when coming from the E or in Greece, Turkey, Cyprus and Egypt (including Port Said) when coming from the W. When 10M off call up the coastguard or port control on Ch 16 and follow their instructions. Anchor off in the designated area and customs will come to the boat. Then go to the harbourmaster (you will need Indian rupees), back to customs and then to immigration. This can easily take a day. Movements within the harbour must be authorised by the harbourmaster.

Telecom IDD +91. GSM service. Internet cafés in major towns and cities.

Currency Indian rupee. Money changers everywhere. Cash advances against credit cards in cities, though it is time-consuming. Only up-market shops and restaurants take credit cards.

Sailing season Yachts on a westabout passage will mostly be here between December and March. Yachts on eastabout passages will be here between August and December. When the SW monsoon is blowing a heavy swell is pushed onto the W coast and some harbours are closed during the SW monsoon period.

Routes and harbours The coast is fairly straight with few natural indentations, but nonetheless there are enough bays and natural harbours to be able to cruise this coast. During the NE monsoon a sea breeze blows for up to 20–30M off the coast, generally getting up around 1200 and dying down at dusk. At night a land breeze will often blow from midnight until dawn. These breezes are consistent and can be relied on during the NE monsoon period when sailing along the coast.

COCHIN

Tidal range 1.4m

Navigation

Call up coastguard on Ch 16 when 10M off. Once into the harbour anchor off the Taj Malabar Hotel at Willingdon Island and clear in. The bottom is mud and good holding although it can be uncomfortable with the wash from ships and local ferries.

Anchorage

With permission from the harbourmaster yachts can then proceed to the anchorage off the Bolgatty Hotel. Around 2.5m least depth in the winding channel into the Bolgatty Hotel anchorage. Good holding on mud although there is a strong current (ebb 9 hours). You may also be able to find a berth at the boatyard or on the W side of Willingdon Island.

Facilities

A number of bum-boats operate here and this can be the easiest way to get things done (including water, fuel, gas and laundry and getting ashore). Basic repairs of an engineering or mechanical kind. Little in the way of dedicated yacht repairs. Excellent provisioning and restaurants and bars. An excellent market in Cochin (you can take the dinghy up the canal to load up).

Remarks

One of the authors (RJH) left his yacht here for a 3-week tour inland and encountered no problems.

Resources

PILOTS AND GUIDES

Indian Ocean Cruising Guide Rod Heikell (Imray)
Andaman Sea Pilot Bill O'Leary & Andy Dowden (Image Asia). Available through Imray
Cruising Guide to Southeast Asia Vol II Stephen Davies & Elaine Morgan (Imray)

WEBSITES

www.asianyachting.com
www.eightnorth.com

Maldives

Entry formalities On arrival at Male call up the coastguard on VHP Ch 16 or 06 to obtain a security clearance. Once you have been cleared then you must appoint an agent within 72 hours for the rest of the clearing in procedure. This is a requirement and yachts which have attempted to get around this procedure have in the past encountered problems with the authorities. In effect the agent is your 'guarantor' in the Maldives. At present the agents fee is somewhere around $US150 to $US200 for yachts up to 15 metres (50ft). The agent will arrange inward and outward clearance and tourist visas for all the crew. The visas are valid for 30 days and an

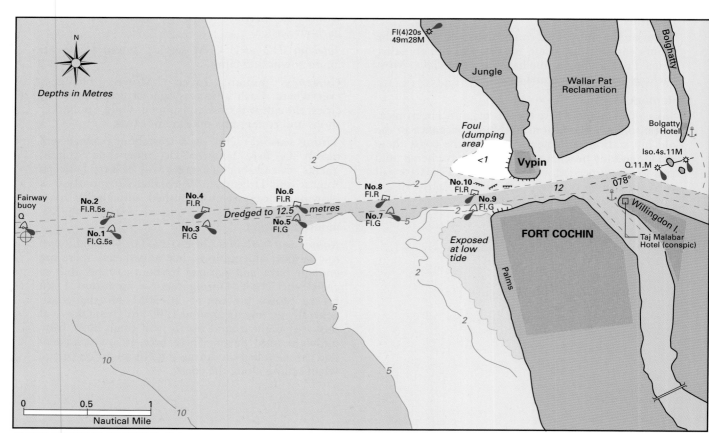

APPROACHES TO COCHIN (India)
⊕09°57'·70N 76°09'·40E WGS84 (Fairway buoy)

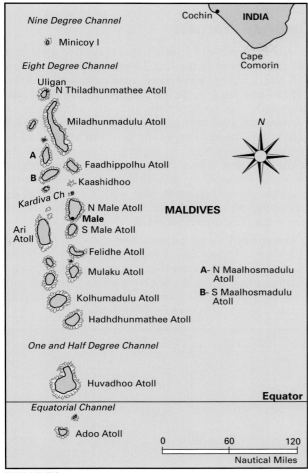

MALDIVES

Formalities All crew must have valid passports. Call up the navy on Ch 16 when five miles off. Once into the harbour you will be visited by customs, immigration, health and the harbourmaster. Ships papers and passports will be retained until you leave. Offices closed on Thursday and Friday.

Telecom IDD +968. GSM service.

Currency Omani riyal. Banks and money-changers will change cash.

MINA RAYSUT (SALALAH)

Tidal range 3.3m

Navigation

Call up the harbourmaster on Ch 16. The approach to the harbour is straightforward. A night approach is possible with care.

Anchorage

Anchor off under the headland. Good holding and good shelter. Dinghies can be left in the basin.

Facilities

Water from the shower block on the quay. Fuel by tanker or jerry cans from town. Limited repairs. Provisions and a few restaurants in Salalah.

Remarks

Salalah town is around 11km away. There is no public transport so it's a taxi or hitch-hiking.

extension for another 60 days can be arranged (around $US75 per person).

Several agents have been recommended.

AMSCO. VHP Ch 16, 67. PO Box 2086, Male, Maldives. ✆ +960 338 788 *Fax* +960 338 688 *Email* amsco@dhivehinet.net.mv

Silver & Co. VHP Ch 16, 13.

An increasing number of yachts stop at one of the northernmost islands, usually Uligan. Here there are the relevant officials to clear you in and out. Uligan is a simpler place with none of the facilities found in Male, but in many ways a more convivial stop than the capital.

Oman

General Oman is one of the more stable countries on the edge of the Arabian peninsula and Mina Raysut is a popular place to make for on a westabout or eastabout passage. There is virtually no chance of piracy here.

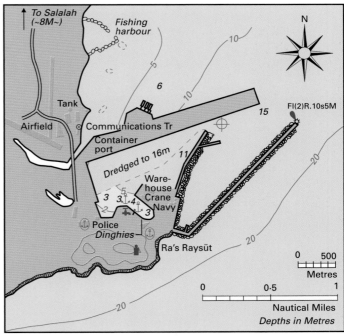

MINA RAYSUT
⊕ 16°56'·9N 54°00'·9E

Piracy

The island of Socotra and the Somali coast have long been a danger area for piracy, well before the present troubles around the Arabian peninsula and in Afghanistan and Iraq. The advice for the last 25 years has been to stay well away from Socotra and the Somali Coast and never use the passage between Socotra and the Somali coast as a short cut. Recently there have been problems off the Yemen coast as well. All these things need to be put into perspective given the number of yachts heading through the Gulf of Aden and up into the Red Sea. Certainly, the experience of one of the authors (RJH) leads him to conclude that curious and impoverished fishermen are often confused for pirates when they are nothing of the sort, however raggle-taggle and piratical they may look. Nonetheless there is some risk and some yachts now travel in a loose V-shaped convoy for protection. See the section in *Monsoon to Med Run* at the beginning of the chapter.

Yemen

General North and South Yemen have had a number of civil wars over the last 25 years, but for the last 15 years things have been relatively settled here. There has been some piracy off the Yemen coast although the government and the authorities in Yemen say they are committed to stopping piracy around the coast. Part of the problem appears to be from Somalian boats smuggling refugees across the Gulf of Aden. There have also been a number of terrorist attempts by Al Qaida operatives in Yemen, though the government also seems committed to stamping down on these. Monitor the airwaves to see what the current situation is.

Formalities Call up port control on VHF Ch 16 or 13 when 10 miles off. A night entrance to harbours is prohibited. On arrival go to customs, health and immigration. If you do not have a visa your passport will be retained by immigration and a shore pass issued. Small 'gifts' are frequently asked for.

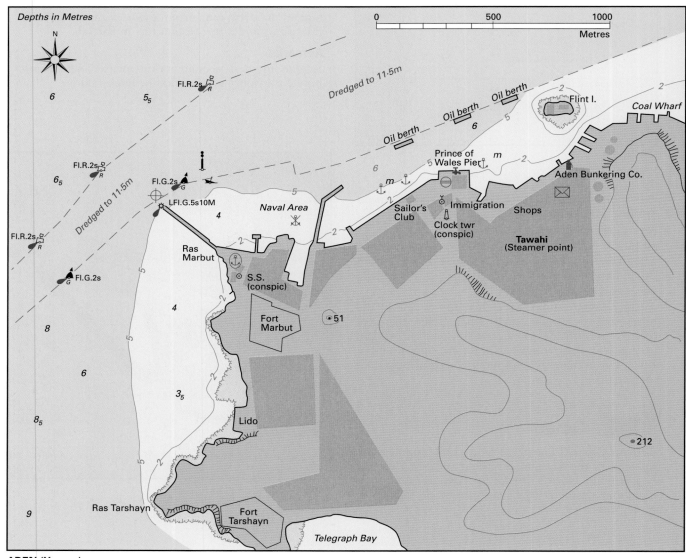

ADEN (Yemen)
⊕12°47'·5N 44°58'·0E WGS84

Telecom IDD +967. Bureaus that offer fax and telephone services.

Currency Yemeni riyal. The US dollar is the most common form of foreign currency accepted and most places will not accept other currencies. US dollars can be changed at banks or by money changers.

ADEN

Tidal range 2.6m

Navigation

The high jagged outcrop of Aden can be recognised from some way off. The oil refinery on Little Aden is conspicuous. Proceed to the anchorage and clear in.

Anchorage

VHF Ch 16 or 13 for port authorities.
Anchor off the Prince of Wales Pier. The bottom is mud and excellent holding. In the past there have been problems with oil slicks from broken pipes fouling the topsides of boat, but recent reports say there have been no such problems recently.

Facilities

Omar and several other drivers will help you find things in Aden. Water on the Prince of Wales Pier. Fuel at the Aden Bunkering Company. It should be possible to haul out in an emergency but otherwise there are no dedicated facilities. Basic provisions in Tawahi and Krater and a supermarket in Khormaksar. Simple restaurants.

General

Aden is a fascinating and little visited place.

DJIBOUTI

Navigation

There are numerous off-lying reefs in the approaches. Make the approach through Passe Est. There are leading marks. A night approach is not recommended.
VHF Ch 16 for capitainerie.

Berths

Anchor off where shown. The old yacht club pontoons may still be here and it may be possible to berth there. Good protection except for strong westerlies.

Facilities

Water and fuel by jerry can. Good shopping for provisions although prices are not cheap as everything is imported.

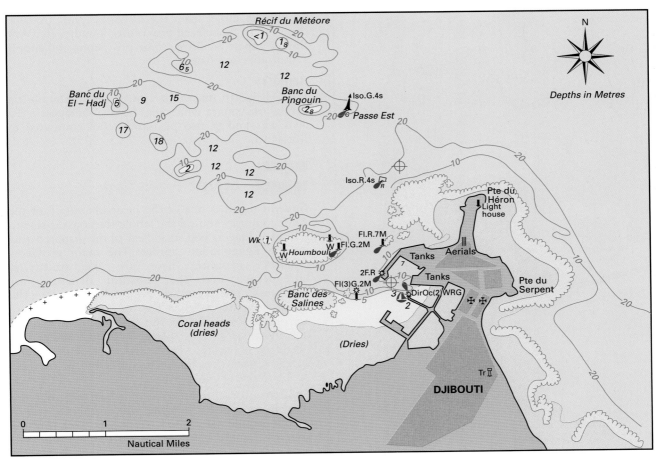

DJIBOUTI ⊕11°37′·7N 43°07′·8E

Red Sea

Eritrea

General Eritrea fought a 30-year war against the Ethiopians and was only recognised as a country in 1991. It is a stable and welcoming place though it has become a little authoritarian of late and you should make sure you abide strictly by the formalities detailed below. Most people enjoy their visit to Eritrea and find it a welcoming and friendly place despite the poverty. If you do cruise around the coast and islands there is some of the best diving to be had anywhere. The whole sea is like a marine soup after 30 years of civil war in which few boats ventured out to go fishing.

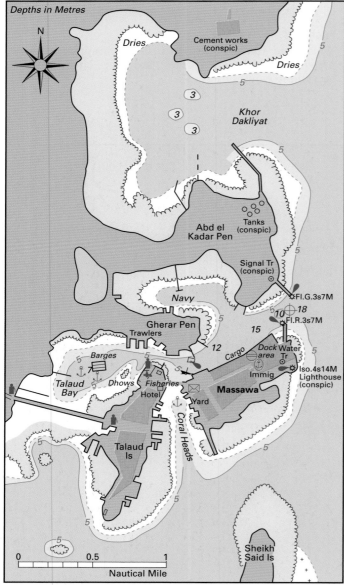

MASSAWA (Eritrea)
⊕15°36′·90N 39°28′·70E WGS84

Formalities Yachts must enter at Assab or Massawa and not stop anywhere else in Eritrean waters. When 10M off call up port control on Ch 16 (working 12). You will be directed to a berth and visited by customs, harbourmaster and health. You then go ashore to immigration and pay for tourist and visa taxes.

Telecom IDD +968.

Currency Eritrean nacfa. The US dollar accepted in most places. Banks will change cash.

MASSAWA
Tidal range 0.9m

Navigation

The approach through the low-lying islands and reefs is difficult and you will need large scale charts. The final approach is well lit and although a night approach is not recommended, you should be able to creep in at dusk.

Anchorage

After berthing on the cargo quay to clear in (and you may be here overnight) proceed into Talaud Bay and anchor clear of the barges and shoal water. Yachts have also been allowed to anchor on the S side of the bridge off the Dahlak Hotel. Good holding and shelter.

Facilities

Water and diesel from the Fisheries quay. 'Agents' can get gas, specialised provisions, laundry, etc. Very limited repair facilities. Some provisions and simple restaurants and bars.

Remarks

It's well worth making a visit to the mountain-top capital of Asmara which was hardly damaged in the civil war and is also pleasantly cool compared to Massawa.

Egypt

General Egypt is one of the most liberalised of the Arab countries and on the whole the coast is safe to sail up as long as you steer clear of the disputed area on the Egypt/Sudan border. The main problems cruisers encounter here are the stultifying bureaucracy and the constant demands for baksheesh. Yachts tend to wend their way along the coast, stopping at just a few harbours where there are officials and for the rest of the time anchoring out in more remote places without officialdom intruding on things. There are a lot of wonderful anchorages among the reefs and some of the best diving in the world.

Formalities Yachts must clear in and out of every port. In most ports an agent will do this for you at an often quite substantial fee. If you elect to do it yourself, some baksheesh speeds things up. You need to see the health officer, harbourmaster, customs and immigration. In most anchorages you will not be bothered and many yachts elect just to cruise from anchorage to anchorage. At Suez you will need to engage an agent for the canal transit.

Telecom IDD code +20. GSM supported in towns and cities.

Currency Egyptian pound. Banks will exchange cash. ATMs in cities. Some larger establishments in the cities take major credit cards.

PORT GHALIB MARINA

Navigation

The apartments and construction around the marina will be seen and there is a fairway buoy at the co-ordinates given on the plan. A buoyed channel leads into the marina. There are lights but a night approach is not recommended.
VHF Ch 16, 10.

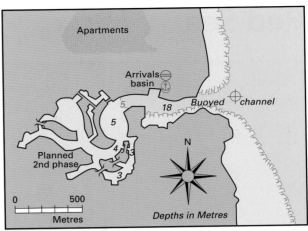

PORT GHALIB MARINA
⊕25°32'·00N 34°38'·71E WGS84

Berths

500 berths. Visitors' berths. Max LOA 50m. Depths 5–6m in outer basin.
Go where directed, normally in the basin on the N side near the entrance.

Facilities

Water and electricity. Fuel quay. Restaurant and café.

Remarks

The marina has immigration and customs and for a small fee (compared to elsewhere) will clear yachts in. It is the most useful first port of call in Egypt.
www.portghalibmarina.com

SUEZ (PORT TEWFIK)

Tidal range 2.5m

Navigation

The approach is well buoyed and busy with the coming and going of ships in and out of the Suez Canal. There are always numerous ships at anchor in the roadstead outside the southern entrance to the canal. By night the lights are a little confusing with the ships at anchor, but a night approach is quite feasible. Call up the Suez Canal authorities on Ch 16 although you are more likely to be answered by an agent (usually the Prince of the Red Sea in the case of yachts).

Berths

Fore and aft to the buoys off the Suez Yacht Club. A boatman will usually assist.

Facilities

Yachts engage an agent to transit the canal. The Prince of the Red Sea has established himself as the main yacht agent and provides good service at a fair price. He can arrange for fuel, gas, laundry, etc. Water on the Yacht Club jetty and some provisions and restaurants in town.

Remarks

A secure place to leave a yacht for trips inland in Egypt.

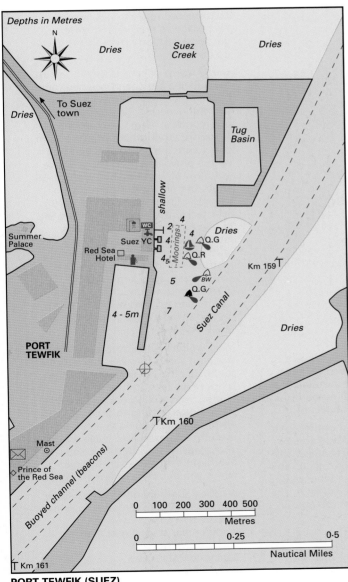

PORT TEWFIK (SUEZ)
⊕29°56'·5N 32°34'·3E

Red Sea

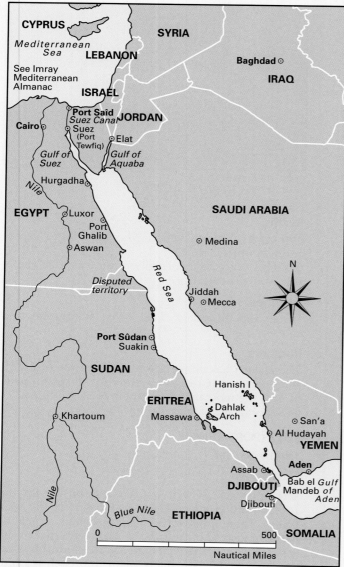

RED SEA

The Red Sea seems to engender bi-polar attitudes to it: you either love it or hate it. Largely this depends on how quickly or slowly you intend for the passage up the Red Sea (or down it). For many people, myself included, it was a revelation to cruise this area and in a hard-nosed way, literally when you are beating up it, to appreciate the landscape and the cultures along its coast.

The landscape is, not surprisingly, barren with barely a green shoot in sight and anywhere there is a clump of trees seems like a miracle. When you do come across vegetation the eyes feast on the unaccustomed greenness. The desert landscape itself varies and contrary to popular images of rolling sand dunes, much of the desert is rough rocky scree with some loose sand and shale. Night over the desert really does produce an azure blue sky with pinpoint stars that dazzle akin to the old fashioned blue velvet ceilings in cinemas with pin-hole lights to resemble stars.

Under the water the marine life is prolific, frighteningly so. In lots of places you will find hammerhead sharks congregating near the boat and if there is one type of shark that looks menacing it is the hammerhead. Add to this good coral that is not too damaged and just about every species of tropical fish you could wish to tick off the tropical fish list and its not surprising that divers rave about the diving.

Cruising strategies

Most of the coastline in the Red Sea is low-lying desert fringed by coral reefs. These reefs are extensive in places and you need to be careful over your navigation anywhere here. More yachts are lost on the reefs than are ever lost to piracy. Part of the reason for this is that after cruising downwind around the world, this is the first lengthy bit of windward work that yachts have to do and it comes as something of a shock to skipper and crew and is something of a test of boat equipment. Rigging and sail failures are common and engine and steering failures are not far behind. All boat gear should be rigorously overhauled before attempting this passage and there needs to be stern discipline over pilotage in and out of the reefs and anchorages. All too often yachts are tempted to try to get into an anchorage so skipper and crew can get some rest, and the yacht is piled up on a reef.

Going North Most yachts will sail up the Red Sea between December and May. In the bottom of the Red Sea you will generally get southerlies, often quite strong, up to around Massawa, where there will be a calm patch until a bit further N you pick up the prevailing northerlies. These can blow at anything between 10–30 knots and pretty much directly on the nose. Cruising yachts will hardly ever tackle the whole of the Red Sea in one go, though some do. The latter usually don't enjoy it very much. If you think it is possible to motorsail up the Red Sea then be advised that even large yachts (50–60ft and over) with large well maintained engines will not make great distances if the northerlies are really blowing.

Most cruisers will potter up the coast stopping along the way. It is possible to day sail the whole coast, but that is not really practical for most cruisers who will go out and spend several days getting to the next anchorage. One tactic that can be usefully employed is to leave an anchorage in the afternoon and sail overnight to the next anchorage which you enter in the late morning.

A typical itinerary going N would be:
Bab El Mandeb to Massawa in Eritrea
Massawa to Suakin in Sudan
    sometimes stopping at marsas
    along the way.
Suakin to Port Sudan
Port Sudan to Port Ghalib stopping
    at marsas and some island
    anchorages along the way.

Port Ghalib to Hurgadha stopping at marsas and island anchorages along the way.

Hurgadha to Port Suez stopping at anchorages along the way.

Suez Canal transit.

Going South Yachts heading down to the Indian Ocean will have a good run until around Massawa in Eritrea again. Getting out the bottom of the Red Sea can be a real battle as the wind tends to funnel up through Bab El Mandeb, often blowing at 30–35 knots. Have a look at the suggested timings in the Passage Notes at the beginning of this chapter.

The itinerary given above can simply be reversed although some cruisers will do longer legs when they have the prevailing wind with them until Eritrea.

Navigation

The coast has not been adequately surveyed since the 19th century and there are serious discrepancies and errors even on the modern metricated charts. In general I allowed a circle of probable error around my GPS position of at least 1M and in some cases, for example on the coast of Sudan and Eritrea, a circle of error (COE) of around 1.5M. There are also serious discrepancies over general descriptions such as whether or not an island has a reef around it, over the extent of reefs, over whether a reef is exposed at low tide or not, and over depths.

The moral here is very clear: keep a sharp eye on the depth sounder and when close to land or dangers to navigation augment the GPS with eyeball navigation and any fixes you can obtain. This is no place to rely on chart plotters. You must also be wary of GPS positions given out by other yachts as they may have just missed a danger to navigation which, within the known errors of GPS, you may hit. Remember there are no EGNOSS stations in the Red Sea so you cannot expect the accuracy you get in Europe or the USA (with WAAS). The final approach to an anchorage must be made with someone conning you in.

Ashore

Facilities for yachts are few and far between up the Red Sea. See the Monsoon to Med Run for the basics. Eating out ashore can be surprisingly good and you should try the fish restaurants in Massawa with fish baked in a banana and spice mixture and cooked in clay ovens, the pilaf anywhere, coffee and popcorn in

Mukalla on the Yemen coast was once an important port of the Hadhramout who explored much of the Indian Ocean from the 12th century on

Eritrea, some of the curries in Eritrea and Sudan, mezes and kebabs and meatballs in Egypt, fresh fruit juices anywhere, mukhbaza, a sweet pastry stuffed with fruit mush in Sudan, and salad anywhere you can get it.

Alcohol is hard to come by, even in countries where it is not banned, but you can get good local beer in Eritrea and Egypt and wine in more up-market restaurants in Egypt. Sharia Law and hence no alcohol or toleration of alcohol rules in Sudan.

Reading

Red Sea Pilot Elaine Morgan & Stephen Davies (Imray)
Indian Ocean Cruising Guide Rod Heikell (Imray)

My gem

Motoring With Mohammed Eric Hansen (Abacus)

Looking out from the yacht basin in Port Said across the Suez Canal to Port Said city

Southern Indian Ocean

Australia

See Chapter 3 South Pacific for country information

Coastline The Northern Territory comprises the very N of Australia, with the port of Darwin the chief interest for cruisers. There is a lot of good, if somewhat adventurous, cruising to be had around the Northern Territory though most cruising yachts will do longish legs to Gove and then on to Darwin without stopping in many places. This sea area abuts a number of seas: principally the Arafura Sea and the Timor Sea, with the Gulf of Carpentaria and the Torres Strait more or less seas in themselves.

Sailing season The weather here is dictated by the monsoons. The SE Trades blow during the dry season from April to November and NW winds during the wet season from December to March. During the wet season there is a possibility of cyclones in the area. Cyclone Tracy on Christmas day 1974 wreaked havoc in the area and destroyed buildings in Darwin. Most yachts will head W during the SE Trades, which get channelled through the Torres Strait to become more of an easterly.

Routes and harbours Most yachts will follow IW1 to Ashmore Reef, Christmas Island and on through Cocos and the Chagos, or IW2 up through Indonesia to Malaysia and Thailand.

A number of yachts now cruise around to Western Australia, where the Kimberley area is said to offer the best cruising grounds in Western Australia with numerous deeply indented sounds and well sheltered bays. For yachts headed W it is possible to cruise the Kimberley coast and then clear customs at Broome to head for Christmas Island.

DARWIN
Tidal range 8m

Navigation
Some care is needed entering Van Diemen Gulf because of strong tidal currents, and negotiating Clarence Strait through the Vernon Islands. The strait is well marked but also subject to strong tides. Once through the Clarence Strait the approach is straightforward. A night approach through Clarence Strait is possible with care.

At springs the tidal streams run at up to 3.5kn through the Dundas Passage and the Clarence Strait, so it is worth timing your passage through here. Approaching Cape Don at around 4.5 hours before HW Darwin will give you four hours of S-going current down into the gulf. Faster yachts can make it through the light adverse stream to Cape Hotham (at the E end of Clarence Strait) in time to pick up the start of the W-going stream through the strait. This W-going stream begins at Cape Hotham at four hours after HW Darwin, and this flood tide will carry all the way around and into Darwin harbour for the next eight hours.

Berths
VHF Ch 16 for port authorities. Ch 11 for Cullen Bay Marina. Ch 68 for Bayview Marina.

These marinas have locks to maintain the water level inside and you will need to lock in and out around 1½hours either side of high tide. Contact the marina for exact times.

Cullen Bay Marina 250 berths. Visitors' berths. Max LOA 32m. Draught max 4m. Entry through lock.

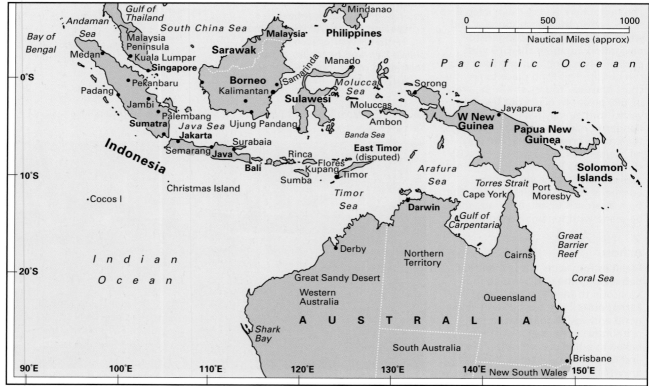

AUSTRALIA TO THE MALACCA STRAIT

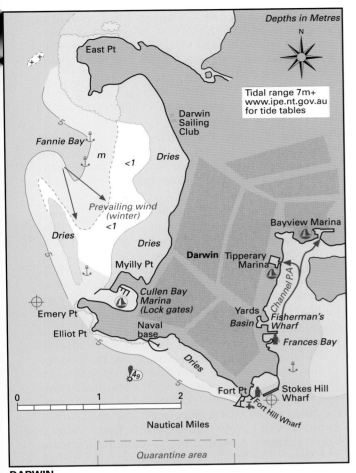

DARWIN
⊕12°27'·2S 130°48'·4E

Charge band 3. One-off lock entry fee currently Aus $240 up to 12m LOA and Aus $430 over 12m LOA.
www.cullenbaymarina.com.au

Bayview Marina Visitors' berths. Max LOA 26m. Draught max. 2.5m. Entry through Sadgroves Creek and lock. Charge band 3.
www.bayviewmarina.com.au

Tipperary Waters Marina New marina asociated with apartment complex. You are locked into the basin in common with the other marinas. Access via Sadgroves Creek. *Email* dermoudy@hotmail.com

Anchorage

Anchor off in Fannie Bay clear of the drying mudflats which extend for some distance out from the beach. The bottom is mostly mud, good holding. Good shelter in the dry season although there may be some swell causing yachts to roll at anchor – more uncomfortable than untenable. Darwin Sailing Club on the beach has a bar and you can often get a

Resources

PILOTS AND GUIDES
Indian Ocean Cruising Guide Rod Heikell (Imray)
Downwind around Australia and Africa Warwick Clay
   (available from Imray)

lift into town. Locals dry out yachts on the beach to clean the bottom and antifoul. Yachts can also anchor clear of the entrance to Cullen Bay Marina behind the drying sandbank and in Frances Bay.

Facilities
Water. Fuel dock. Most yacht repairs. Slipway in Cullen Bay Marina. Provisions and restaurants and bars.

Remarks
Darwin is really the last place before South Africa where you will be able to carry out extensive repairs and provisioning when setting out across the southern Indian Ocean

Indonesia

General Indonesia is the fourth most populated country in the world, a huge archipelago of islands made up of some 360 tribal and ethnic groups with a huge diversity of religions and associated cultures. It has the largest Muslim population in the world. In the late 1990s Indonesia experienced civil unrest under the Suharto regime, and despite his resignation in 1998, there is still civil unrest and some internal security problems, such as those in Irian Jaya (Western New Guinea) and Aceh on the northern tip of Sumatra. East Timor is now independent.

Coastline Indonesia consists of a massive archipelago (some 13,660 islands of which around 3,000 are inhabited) in the sea area between the land mass of SE Asia and Australia. The islands can be divided into northern and southern groups separated by the Java, Flores and Banda Seas. The northern group consists of the 'fat' islands, principally Borneo (Kalimantan, southern half), Sulawesi, the Moluccas and Irian Jaya (Western New Guinea). The southern group consists of long 'skinny' islands running in a crescent arc, principally Sumatra, Java, the Sunda Islands, West Timor and others. This southern chain is an active plate and has a large number of volcanic peaks, some of them active (including Krakatoa).

Formalities A cruising permit (CAIT) and a social visa (Budaya visa) must be obtained in advance. The CAIT is valid for 90 days. The social visa is valid for 60 days and can be renewed monthly up to six

Piracy

Indonesia is often cited as a piracy area, but this is mostly to do with commercial shipping and there have been very few incidents affecting yachts in the last ten years. It pays to stay away from any areas where internal conflict is going on (Irian Jaya, Aceh) or at least take local advice. Yachts going through the archipelago on an organised race will usually check in on SSB every day. Other yachts can sail in company with anyone else going the same way. There are a lot of rumours flying around, but the number of reported incidents is low.

months. For yachts not on the Sail Indonesia Rally it is best to use an agent. Charges for an agent vary but are in the region of $US150. Some charge more and some less. Choosing an agent is an area fraught with concerns and in general you should use an agent that has a track record. The sources given below are a starting point and not an endorsement.

The social visa will be issued for 60 days at the nearest Indonesian Consulate and is renewable each month for a total of six months. The social visa can be obtained at the Indonesian Consulate in Darwin. For stays of less than 30 days a social visa is not required and a tourist visa can be issued on arrival. It takes at least four weeks to process the CAIT so prepare well in advance. The CAIT can be renewed for another 90 days in Indonesia.

Once in Indonesian waters you must first go to a port of entry where you must obtain a tourist visa valid for 30 days. (You can obtain the tourist visa in Indonesia if you are a national of the USA, Australia, South Africa, Argentina, Brazil, Denmark, UAE, Finland, Hungary, UK, Italy, Japan, Germany, Canada, South Korea, Norway, France, Poland, Switzerland, New Zealand or Thailand. If not you must obtain the tourist visa before you arrive in Indonesia).

www.balimarina.com
www.josc.org
http://cruisingindonesia.blogspot.com

Note It is no longer necessary to clear in and out of every port in Indonesia.

This whole process sounds labyrinthine, but in practice it is not that bad. Some choose to go on one of the rallies such as the Sail Indonesia Rally to Ambon where the paperwork is processed for the whole group, though you will still have to deal with some paperwork yourself.

Temporary Importation Duty There has been much uninformed speculation and rumour mongering over Temporary Importation Duty in Indonesia. There is a 2004 regulation that states foreign flagged yachts must pay an import duty on arrival in Indonesia based on a percentage of the value of the yacht which is refundable when the yacht leaves Indonesia. Yachts must pay this at the first port of entry and get the refund when they check out of Indonesia. Yachts with a CAIT and intending to leave Indonesia do not have to pay this duty and to date (2009) have not paid it.

It is likely that the situation and consequent scare mongering was based on some officials demanding a bit of unofficial tourist tax. My (RJH) attitude is

Resources

PILOTS AND GUIDES
Cruising Guide to SE Asia Vol II Stephen Davies and Elaine Morgan (Imray)

WEBSITES
www.asianyachting.com
www.sailindonesia.net

that it is worth paying a relatively small amount to an agent to smooth things over. Whatever you have heard on forums or read in the press, in 2009 yachts were sorting out their own CAIT's and clearing in at Bali, Kupang and Ambon.

Telecom IDD +62. GSM coverage in the more populated areas. Internet cafés in tourist areas and larger towns and cities.

Currency Rupiah. US dollars widely accepted. ATMs in larger centres or banks will give cash advances on major credit cards. Credit cards accepted in a few of the larger and more expensive shops and restaurants.

Sailing season Essentially all year round. Yachts going W (the most common route by far) will cruise during the SE Trades from April to November. This is the dry season and the best time to sail here. During the wet season, when NW winds predominate, there can be violent thunderstorms and also long periods of calm weather and the high humidity makes life difficult.

Routes and harbours Most yachts will be travelling E to W through the islands, heading for Singapore and Malaysia. Some yachts now make the passage around the W side of Sumatra directly up to Phuket. This is not an easy passage with some headwinds and often confused seas. Yachts headed up through the group from Darwin or points E will often stop at Ambon, Dili (now independent East Timor), Kupang, Flores, Komodo, Benoa (Bali), Kalimantan, and Nongsa on Batam. The best facilities are at Bali International Marina and to a lesser extent on Java and at Nongsa. In general it is best to wait until you get to Singapore where there are good repair facilities and chandlers.

BENOA (Bali)
Tidal range 2.6m

Navigation
There are strong currents and tidal sets in the channels between the islands so care is needed. The harbour is approached along a buoyed channel on 255° through the fringing reef. Local advice is to keep closer to port hand marks. A night approach should not be made.

Berths
VHF Ch 77 Bali International Marina. Ch 11 Bali Yacht Services. c.75 berths. Visitors' berths (first come, first served basis). Charge band 2. Berth where directed in the marina.

Anchorage
Anchor of to the E or S of the docks. It is very tight in here and can get crowded. Bali Marina has a number of moorings you may be able to use. You can also anchor or pick up a mooring on the N side of Pulau Serangan.

Call TC Marine Services on *VHF* Ch 68 to arrange a mooring. *Email* Al@travelcomarine.com

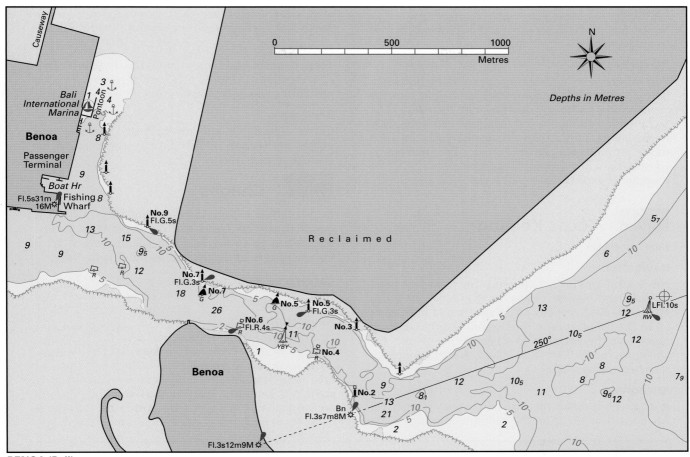

BENOA (Bali)
⊕08°45′·25S 115°14′·1E

Facilities

Usual amenities. Fuel quay. Some repairs by Bali Yacht Services. Some provisions and restaurants. Better shopping in Denpasar.

Remarks

Bali Marina will process your CAIT and entry and exit formalities. All the relevant officials are close by. TC Marine (see above) will also help with clearance. www.balimarina.com

NONGSA POINT MARINA (Batam)

Tidal range 3m

Navigation

The marina lies on the NE tip of Batam on the S side of the Singapore Strait. There is shoal water on the E of the immediate approaches marked by several buoys. The entrance to the marina is a tricky narrow pass through the fringing reef. There are beacons at the entrance though care is needed not to confuse these with the beacons marking the channel to the ferry terminal at Nongsa which is immediately W of the marina channel.

Berths

VHF Ch 72. 178 berths. Visitors' berths. Max LOA c.18m. Max. draught 2.5m. Charge band 2. Berth where directed. It can be bumpy in here but shelter is generally good.

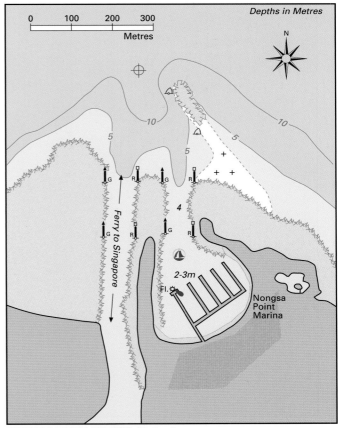

NONGSA POINT MARINA (Batam)
⊕01°12′·15N 104°05′·70E

Facilities

Water. Fuel quay. Restaurant and bar ashore. Ferries to Singapore.

Remarks

Port of entry so yachts can clear out of Indonesia here. Sometimes uncomfortable in the marina though most yachts are satisfied with their stay here. Some yachts choose to stay here and catch the ferry to Singapore rather than taking the yacht into the mêleé around Singapore Island. The marina is cheaper than any around Singapore.
www.nongsaresorts.com

Cocos Keeling

Tidal range 0.5m

Navigation

An Australian visa is required prior to arrival here. Contact the marine officer on VHF Ch 20 when about 10–20M off. No off-lying dangers until right up to the N entrance to the lagoon. Depths come up quickly at the entrance to <10m. Proceed into the anchorage under Direction Island. A night approach is not recommended.

Anchorage

If necessary contact the authorities on VHF Ch 20. Anchor off or tie up to the yellow quarantine buoy

until cleared in. Once cleared move closer to the beach and anchor. Good shelter from the SE Trades.

Facilities

Treated water on Home Island. Toilets ashore. Fuel at West Island. Limited mechanical repairs. Limited provisions which are expensive.

Remarks

Cocos Keeling is administered by Australia and yachts must clear in first before going ashore or visiting another yacht.

Chagos

British Indian Ocean Territory, but Diego Garcia is leased to the US Navy and is off limits to yachts. Yachts can go to the Salomon Islands, which are a marine reserve and patrolled by the British Navy.

SALOMON ISLANDS

Tidal range <1m

Navigation

Deep water in the approaches. Use the NW Pass between Ile de la Passe and Ile Anglaise. Depths come up quickly at the entrance to <10m. Although the tidal range is small, strong tidal currents run obliquely across the entrance. Tidal currents within the lagoon are negligible. Care is needed within the lagoon of coral heads and eyeball navigation is necessary.

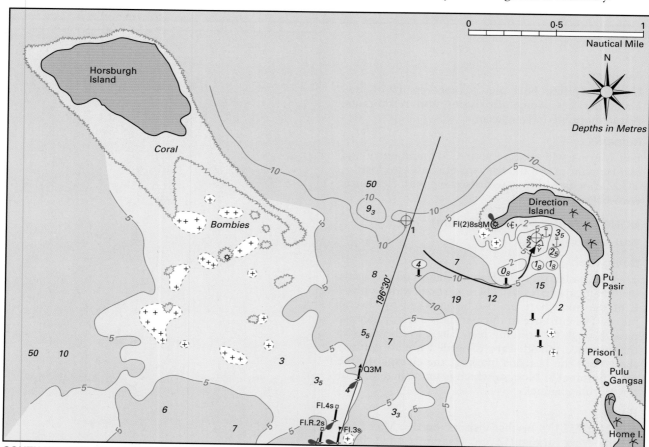

SOUTH KEELING: DIRECTION ISLAND ANCHORAGE
⊕1 12°05'·3S 96°52'·3E
⊕2 12°05'·5S 96°53'·0E

CHAGOS REGULATIONS

In 2007 new regulations were introduced for yachts intending to stop in the Chagos archipelago. At the time of writing the following regulations are to be implemented, though things may change in the future.

1. All yachts must obtain a permit IN ADVANCE from the British Indian Ocean Territory Administration (BIOTA) in London.

2. Mooring fees for the Chagos Archipelago have been raised from $100 per month to £GBP100 per month.

3. On application for a permit a Visitor Permit Request will be sent. This must be filled in with the dates that a yacht will be in the reserve and sent back with the mooring fee to BIOTA. At present there is no way of paying over the internet but it is hoped that in the future a system will be in place so credit card payments can be made.

4. Once the form has been completed and payment made then the BIOTA Permit, the regulations governing the reserve and the co-ordinates showing where yachts can moor will be sent. It is expected that moorings will be laid at some time in the future.

5. Yachts attempting to enter the Chagos area without a permit may be liable for a term of imprisonment up to three years and/or a fine of up to £GBP3,000.

6. Regular patrols of the Chagos area will be made and visitors must abide by the regulations concerning the marine reserve (no fishing, fires, damaging coral, harming native species, etc.), must keep pets on board and must conform to customs regulations regarding illegal drugs, firearms, etc.

British Indian Ocean Territory Administration,
King Charles Street, London, SW1A 2AH, UK
☏ + 44 (0) 20 7008 2890 or 2691
Fax + 44 (0) 20 7008 1589
Email BIOTadmin@fco.gov.uk
www.fco.gov.uk/en/about-the-fco/country-profiles/asia-oceania/british-indian-ocean-territory

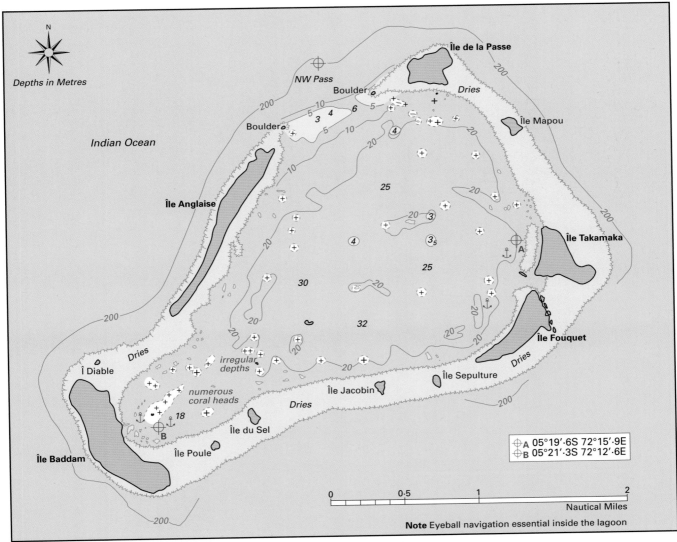

SALOMON ISLANDS
⊕05°18′·2S 72°14′·25E

Anchorage

The preferred anchorage is off Ile Fouquet. Good shelter from the SE Trades. Yachts also anchor under Ile Takamaka and Ile Baddam.

Facilities

None. Yachties usually help each other out and yachts talk on an SSB net may be able to bring spares and essential provisions from other places like India or the Seychelles.

Remarks

This is a marine reserve and there are legal and unwritten rules governing yachts stopping here. Yachts should not stay more than one month, should not dispose of waste in the lagoon, spear-fishing is illegal and the habitat must be left as you found it.

Seychelles

General The Seychelles became independent in 1976 and for a number of years imposed strict bureaucratic controls over cruising the islands, coupled with high charges for a cruising permit. Today the charges are more reasonable and more yachts visit the main group.

Coastline The Seychelles covers more sea area than any other group. In the N the Mahe group is high with fringing coral reefs. The S group is mostly low atolls and is comparatively little-populated.

Formalities All yachts must enter and leave the Seychelles at Victoria on Mahe which is the only port of entry and exit. When 10–12M off call up port control on VHP Ch 16 or 2182kHz and advise them of your intended arrival. Call sign is *Seychelles Radio*. Yachts must fly a Q flag and on arrival anchor off where indicated by the port authority (usually E of Victoria lighthouse) until entry

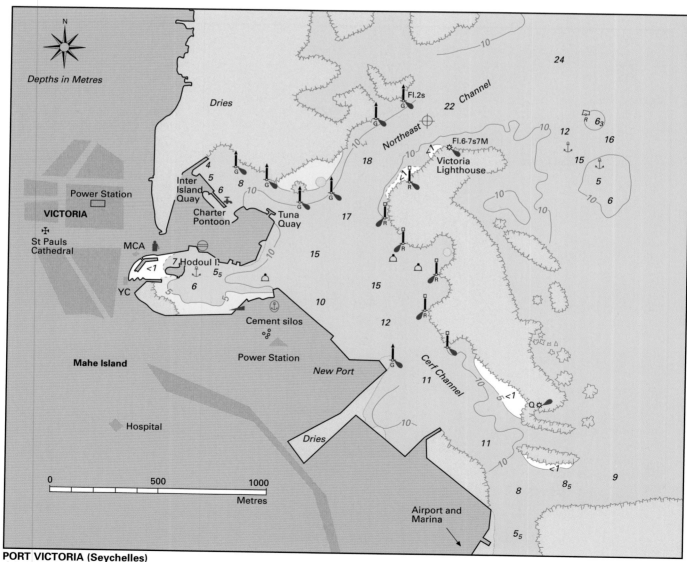

PORT VICTORIA (Seychelles)
⊕04°37'·01S 55°28'·16E WGS84

formalities have been carried out. Yachts must not proceed into the harbour unless advised to do so by the port authorities. The quarantine officer will arrange for the yacht to be fumigated which is mandatory for all new arrivals. Once the paperwork and fumigation has been carried out a yacht will be directed to berth in the harbour, usually at Victoria Yacht Club. Within 24 hours (except weekends) the captain must report to the port office and complete an arrival form and hand over the ship's papers which are kept until departure.

Fees All fees are in Seychelles Rupees. 6SR = $US1 approx. official exchange rate. A charge of 100SR is made for quarantine inspection and 200SR for spraying.

Cruising fees are calculated on a daily basis and are as follows.

Gross tons	First 5 days	5-10 days	Over 10 days
>20	50SR	40SR	30SR
20–100	75SR	50SR	40SR
100–30	150SR	125SR	100SR

Charges in marine parks are 50SR per person from 0900–1700 and 50SR per yacht overnight. If you arrive after 1700 and leave before 0900 you pay only the 50SR per yacht fee.

These taxes apply for all anchorages around the Seychelles and must be paid before you can redeem the ship's papers from the port office at Victoria.

Telecom IDD +248. GSM network.

Currency Seychelles rupee. Major credit cards accepted in only a few places. ATM in Victoria.

Cruising routes and harbours Most yachts visit the northern Mahe group and cruise the nearby islands like Praslin. One of the authors (RJH) recommends the anchorages on the W side of Mahe, which are often overlooked.

VICTORIA

Tidal range 1.1m

Navigation

Yachts should make for the NE Channel. The approach through the islands and reefs should preferably be made by day. Get a large-scale chart of the islands and approaches. Although the approach to Victoria is well lit, a night approach is not recommended.

Berths

You may find room on the old charter quay, depending on whether charter boats are in or not. Eden Island Marina has opened nearby.

Eden Island Marina Visitors' berths. Max LOA c.70m. Depths 5m in the approach channel. www.edenislandmarina.sc

Wharf Hotel Marina 40 berths. Max LOA c.45m. Depths 11.5m. www.wharfseychelles.com

Anchorage

Once cleared in yachts can anchor off under Hodoul Island. It is tight in here so you need to anchor with care.

Facilities

Water and 220V at the charter pontoon, Eden Island Marina and Wharf Hotel. Fuel at the charter pontoon. Limited yacht repairs. Most provisions in Victoria. Restaurants and bars.

 # Mauritius

Mauritius is a high volcanic island with a well developed infrastructure. Yachts should clear in at Port Louis on the W coast where there is a large commercial harbour and yacht basin of sorts. The channel through the coral is buoyed and more straightforward than that for Port Mathurin on Rodrigues.

Once cleared in most yachts move around to Grande Baie on the NW tip where there is good shelter and more convivial surroundings.

 # Reunion

Reunion is the last high volcanic island in this chain. It is a French dependency and has a good infrastructure ashore. Yachts head for Port-des-Galets on the NW side where there is a large commercial harbour with a yacht basin.

RODRIGUES ISLAND

Rodrigues is a high volcanic island lying some 300M E of Mauritius. It is surrounded by a coral reef with the only useable harbour of Port Mathurin on the NW side. The channel through the reef is marked by beacons and buoys and leads to a commercial quay and fishing harbour. Yachts berth on the covered jetty at the NE end of the commercial quay. Entrance to the channel: 19°40'·25S 63°25'·6E

For more information on Rodrigues, Mauritius and Reunion see *Indian Ocean Cruising Guide* Rod Heikell published by Imray.

 # Madagascar

Formalities A yacht must go to a port of entry: Diego Suarez (Antisiranana), Hell-ville (Adoany) on Nosy Be, Maharjanga, and Toliara. When 10M off call up port control on Ch 16. The clearing in procedure appears to vary depending on the port, but at Hell-ville it is best to arrive with a visa rather than attempting to get one here. Go to customs and immigration, the harbourmaster and the *dispensaire* for health clearance. You must leave your ship's papers (or a copy) at the customs and immigration office. You will need at least eight copies of a crew list. Total fees are around £25 GBP ($40US), which includes a cruising permit for one month.

Telecom IDD +261.

Currency Malagassy franc. Banks will change cash. Some banks in larger centres will give a cash advance on major credit cards.

Seychelles

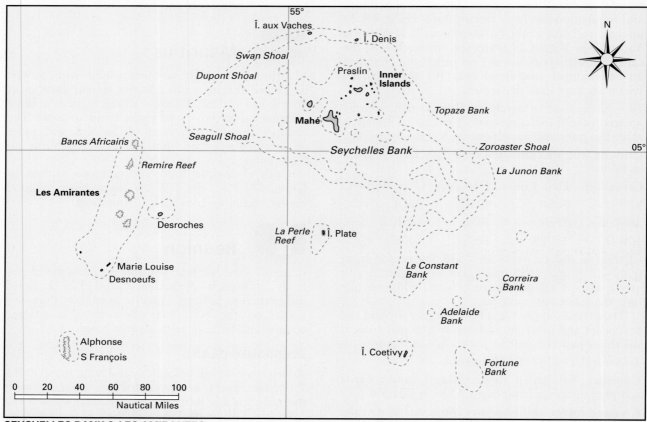

SEYCHELLES BANK & LES AMIRANTES

The Seychelles used to be a difficult place to cruise around in the troubled years after independence in 1976, but in the last decade and things have got a lot better. Most yachts arriving here will only cruise the Inner Islands comprising the main island Mahe and nearby islands. Even here a number of islands are off limits to yachts. If you want to visit the Outer Islands including the atolls in Les Amirantes you need to get special permission from Victoria on Mahe and really it is only worth doing if you are into diving in a big way.

The inner islands are all granite, very old granite that is thought to have made up part of the original continent of Gondwanaland from 150 million years ago, and as such are very different from the volcanic islands that pepper the oceans. The fauna and flora is also unique and foremost amongst the oddities is the Coco de Mer that grows only in the Vallee de Mai on Praslin. The female seed is the largest of any plant in the world, but it is it's shape, suggestive of the female pelvis, that excites interest by non-botanists. Likewise the male catkin is a long phallic shape suggestive of .... General Gordon, he of Khartoum, visited the island in 1881 and thought it to be the original Garden of Eden and the Coco de Mer the forbidden fruit that Adam tasted. Whatever theology you subscribe to, a wander around the Vallee de Mai is worth it for the cool under the forest canopy and, yes, for those suggestive giant seeds.

Much of the Seychelles is national park and conservation is important. On Ile Curiese there is a large colony of giant tortoises and a breeding programme because like the tortoises on Galapagos, ships of old decimated the tortoise population by carting them off for victuals on board. These leftovers from the dinosaur age are massive, can live up to 150 years old, and are endearingly clumsy. If the grunts from the forest are anything to go by, the breeding programme seems to be working.

The 'Granite Islands'

Cruising Strategies

The islands are a bit off the usual west-going routes to the Red Sea or South Africa. Yachts will usually call here on a W-going route before curving up to the Red Sea. On this route it is essential to keep well off the coast of Africa and Socotra before entering the Gulf of Aden close to the Yemen shore. At the time of writing a yacht on passage from the Seychelles to Madagascar was seized by Somali pirates, though exact details are scarce.

The Seychelles are also a useful stop on the E-going route from East Africa or Madagascar towards SE Asia.

See the section on *Passages* at the beginning of this chapter.

Seasons and winds

The climate over the Inner Islands is equatorial and air temperatures are around 27°–31°C all year around. Sea temperatures are likewise a blessed 24°–29°C which means that swimming is just about a necessity, not a duty. Rainfall is highest during the wet season from December to February. The dry season runs from May to August.

The wind direction varies between the NE monsoon season and the SE trades. Winds over the Inner Islands are predominantly NW-NE during the NE monsoon season from December to March and SE from April to November when the southern ocean SE trades blow in. Winds normally blow at an ideal Force 3–6 (10–25 knots) and it is rare to get gale force winds with just a 1–2% chance in July to September. The Inner Islands are not affected by Cyclones.

Praslin

Ashore

There is not a huge amount of life ashore and many restaurants seem to open only at lunch-time and close in the late afternoon. In and around Victoria and at the tourist hotels, restaurants and bars will open in the evening, though visiting yachties will not always be welcome at some of the resort hotels.

For provisioning Victoria is the only place to go with most things available in the general stores and a good fish and fruit and vegetable market in the morning.

Facilities

Yacht facilities are limited though the development of Eden Marina may improve things. In Victoria you can get water on the charter pontoon if you can negotiate a space

Giant tortoise on Curiese

to do so. Elsewhere it is a matter of carrying water in jerry cans. You can get fuel on the pontoon at MCA, but depths are a problem and you will need to check the tides. Alternatively you can get fuel by jerry can.

Elsewhere in the islands you may be able to get water and fuel at Praslin.

Eden Island Marina has water, electricity (including three phase) at all berths. Pump-out station. Also Wi-Fi, phone and TV connections. There are plans for a fuel dock and ancillary services, but at present these do not exist. See www.edenislandmarina.sc

Reading

Les Iles Seychelles Alain Rondeau (Pilote Cotier Bateau)
Indian Ocean Cruising Guide Rod Heikell (Imray)

My gem

Long John Silver Bjorn Larsson. (Vintage)

Charter pontoon in Victoria

Note In 2009 Madagascar was in political upheaval with the old Prime Minister ousted with the help of the army. Most of the rioting and strife was in and around Antananarivo on the E coast and it remains to be seen what the effect will be around Nosy Be.

HELL-VILLE (Nosy Bé)

Tidal range 1.2m

Navigation

Care needed of the large area of shoal water on the W side of Hell-ville final approaches. Yachts should head for the anchorage on the E side of Hell-ville or Crater Bay.

Anchorage

Anchor off in 10–15m. The bottom is mud and good holding.

Facilities

Water reported unpotable. Fuel on the quay. Basic mechanical repairs only. Most provisions and some local restaurants and bars.

Remarks

This is the most popular place for yachts to head for and there will usually be a fair number of other yachts here. Tenders and outboards should be locked up. This is a malarial area.

South Africa

See Chapter 2 South Atlantic for country information.

DURBAN

Navigation

Entrance is straightforward. Do not enter without permission. Call Port Control on Ch 16. In addition observe the following traffic signals displayed on the signal tower:

- NO LIGHT – Channel clear for use
- RED LIGHT – Ship leaving harbour; keep clear of the entrance channel
- GREEN LIGHT – Ship entering harbour, keep clear.

Harbour authorities will direct the yacht to a berth in the Yacht Basin (via Silburn Channel) for clearance. Generally this is at the outer berth of the RNYC or the 'international jetty'.

Berths

There is generally space at the Royal Natal, Point or Bluff Yacht Clubs. Good shelter.

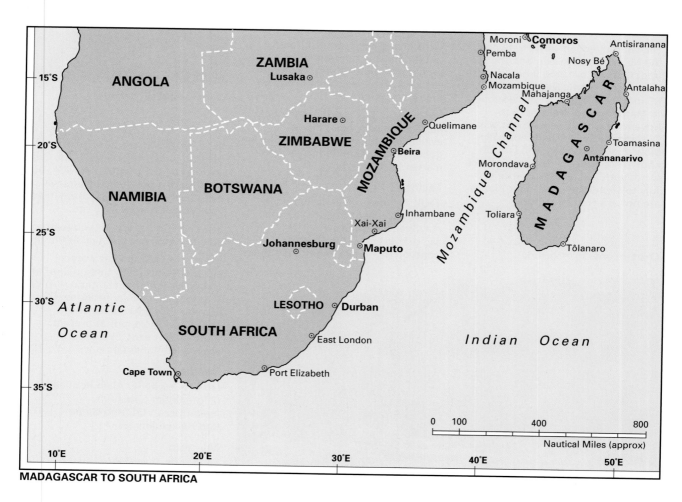

MADAGASCAR TO SOUTH AFRICA

Facilities

The clubs provide excellent facilities. Yachts of any size can be slipped. All repairs to the hull, rig and sails can be carried out.

Remarks

Durban is well known as a friendly destination where a yacht can refit after crossing the Indian Ocean. Perhaps the only disadvantage, for some, is that the facilities are in the centre of a bustling city. Those wishing to have a quieter stay may prefer Richards Bay, up the coast to the N. Durban is a good place in which to leave the boat and visit some of South Africa's inland attractions. Up-to-date information on facilities is available at: www.cruiser.co.za

Resources

PILOTS AND GUIDES

Indian Ocean Cruising Guide Rod Heikell (Imray)
East Africa Pilot Delwyn McPhun (Imray)
South African Cruising Notes Tony Herrick (Cruising Connections)
Downwind around Australia and Africa Warwick Clay (available from Imray)

WEBSITES

Sail Africa/Cruising Connections www.cruiser.co.za

SSB

SA Maritime Mobile Ham Net: 14316kHz at 1130 UT
Eastern African Marine Radio Net (Kiore): 14316kHz at 0500 UT

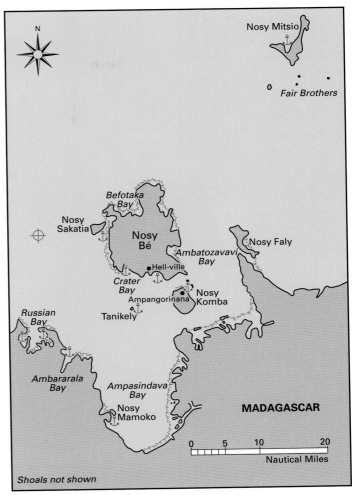

NOSY BE (Madagascar)
⊕13°20´·0S 48°00´·0E

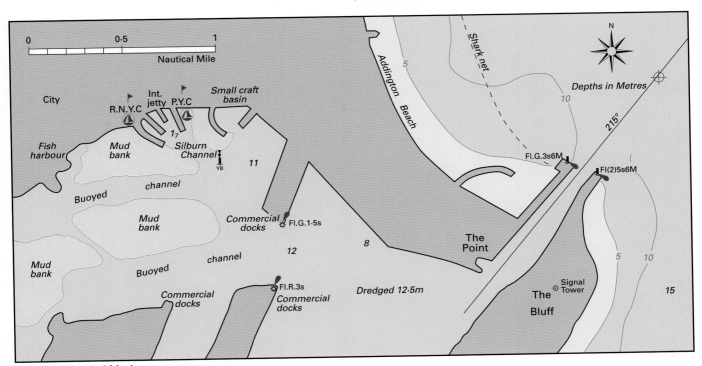

DURBAN (South Africa)
⊕29°51´·5S 31°04´·0E WGS84

6

MEDITERRANEAN SEA

Anchorage on the Turkish coast

General

The Mediterranean is more of a cruising area than one for making passages. Bits of land and islands obstruct direct passages and most yachts will plan cruises and passages around and between the different countries depending on time and inclination. I detail just three of the main passages between the western and eastern end of the Mediterranean. These are very generalised passages and variations on this theme and other passages can be put together on an ad hoc basis from other sources.

Note This chapter is briefer than the others as it is the only 'sea' in a book about ocean passages. It is included because it is the joining link between ocean passages to the E and W and because many yachts cruise the Mediterranean before setting off on an ocean passage.

Weather and sea

PREVAILING WINDS

In the Mediterranean most of the prevailing winds in the summer are sea breezes. There are a number of special cases and a few interruptions from depressions passing over Europe or unseasonably through the Mediterranean, but for most observations the sea breeze prevails and can be relied upon for over 50% of the time for most places and for up to 75% of the time in a few places during the summer months.

The following should be noted in relation to the sea breeze:

1. The relatively high temperatures of the Mediterranean mean that sea breezes are not the gentle zephyrs encountered in more temperate climes. In many places the temperature differences generate winds up to Force 5–6 and can reach up to 50 miles off the coast.

2. There is a fairly accurate wind clock for the sea breeze. As the land warms up in the morning the sea breeze will begin to blow at 1100–1200 local time at around Force 2–3. Usually within an hour the wind will get up to Force 4–6 and will blow through the afternoon until early evening. The wind will die off fairly quickly around 1900–2000 local time. The abruptness of the change is linked to the air temperatures and geography of a region. In general the higher the temperature, the more abrupt the transition between morning calm and the onset of the full force of the sea breeze. The terrain affects the sea breeze according to altitude: low-lying plains or gentle S-facing slopes will heat up more quickly than mountain ranges with valleys in shadow for much of the day and so generate greater pressure differences and stronger winds.

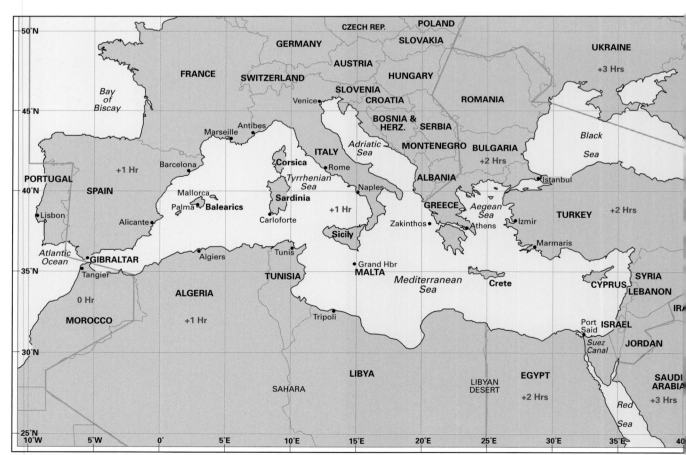

MEDITERRANEAN SEA COUNTRIES, PORTS AND TIME DIFFERENCES ON GMT

3. The direction the coast faces will affect the sea breeze clock. In general S-facing coasts will have an earlier sea breeze than N-facing coasts. Likewise, E-facing coasts will have an earlier sea breeze than W-facing coasts.

The *meltemi* is a special case in that it is the prevailing wind over the Aegean caused by pressure differences at a macro level. It blows throughout most of the summer, starting gently in June and ending around the end of September. It can blow at Force 6–7 and although there may be a slight thermal component lessening its strength in the late evening, it usually blows night and day for anything from 2–3 days up to a week or more before there is a brief respite for a few days. It is caused by a pressure gradient between the Azores high and the monsoon low over Pakistan. Only in the Aegean is the pressure gradient pronounced enough to produce these constant summer winds. From the Dardanelles it blows from the NE, curving down through the Aegean to blow from the N and NW before curving to blow from the W around Rhodes.

GALES

Between summer and winter there is a marked difference in weather patterns. In the summer pressure gradients are relatively stable and there are few cyclonic changes. In the winter nearly all weather is from disturbed cyclonic patterns, with depressions entering the Mediterranean and directly causing bad weather or passing over Europe or North Africa and indirectly causing bad weather. The following points are general observations on gales in the Mediterranean.

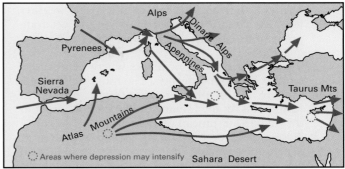

PRINCIPAL DEPRESSION TRACKS INTO THE MEDITERRANEAN

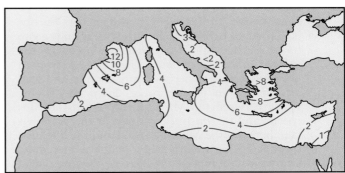

PERCENTAGE FREQUENCY OF GALES IN THE WINTER

1. Depressions from the Atlantic tend to enter the Mediterranean directly through the Strait of Gibraltar, drop down from Europe into the Golfe du Lion or Gulf of Genoa, or swing up from North Africa across the east coast of Tunisia. Because depressions passing through the Mediterranean follow an erratic path at an erratic speed compared to the fairly predictable tracks and plodding speed of depressions across the

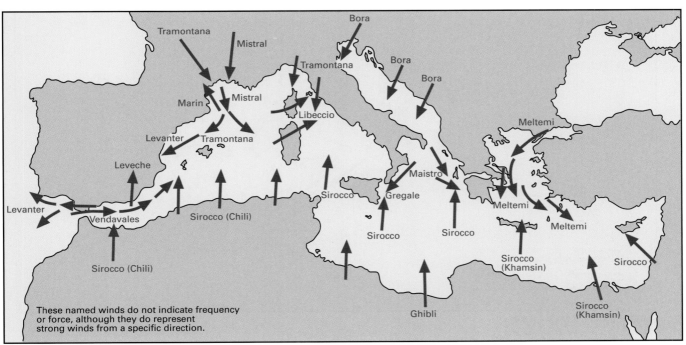

These named winds do not indicate frequency or force, although they do represent strong winds from a specific direction.

NAMED WINDS

Atlantic, they are difficult to track and weather forecasts cannot be relied upon to give accurate predictions of the speed and direction of a depression.

2. There are a number of places where depressions tend to linger and deepen. The most well known are the Gulf of Genoa, around the Atlas Mountains, in the Ionian, and to a lesser extent in the SE Mediterranean off Cyprus.

3. A lot of gale force winds are the indirect result of depressions passing over Europe from mountain gap or coastal slope winds and are not from actual depressions in the Mediterranean itself.

4. *Mountain gap winds* These winds result when cold air from a depression passing across Europe is bottled up behind mountains until it finds a gap to escape through. The classic examples are the *mistral* and *tramontana*. These result from a depression passing across central France and cold air finding an escape route down the Rhône valley between the Massif Central and the Alps (producing the *mistral*) or through the Toulouse Gap between the Massif Central and the Pyrenees (producing the *tramontana*). In the winter these two winds are much to be feared, blowing out of a clear sky with little warning and often reaching gale force and sometimes Force 10–11. The *levanter* blowing in the Strait of Gibraltar is another example of a mountain gap wind.

5. *Coastal slope winds* These result when cold air from an unstable airstream falls off plateaux and coastal slopes onto a warm sea. The classic example is the *bora* in the Adriatic which can blow at gale force and up to Force 10–11 out of a clear sky with little warning.

6. *Desert winds* These blow off the hot desert when a depression passes through the Mediterranean. The classic example is the *sirocco* which blows off the North African coast. It is dry and dusty but is more often sultry and humid by the time it passes over the sea and reaches Europe. It will often blow at gale force, though rarely more.

CURRENTS

Although there are virtually no tides of consequence in most of the Mediterranean, there is a complex hydrology at work. Evaporation from the Mediterranean is the driving force for the roughly anticlockwise circulation of water around the basin. Rivers and rainfall replace around 50% of this loss and the 50% deficit flows in through the Strait of Gibraltar. This surface current is predominantly into the Strait, with a reverse current of heavier salty water flowing out on the sea bottom. There is a tidal angle on all this although the upshot is more of a lessening of the inflowing surface current rather than a reversing of it.

For more information see Gibraltar.

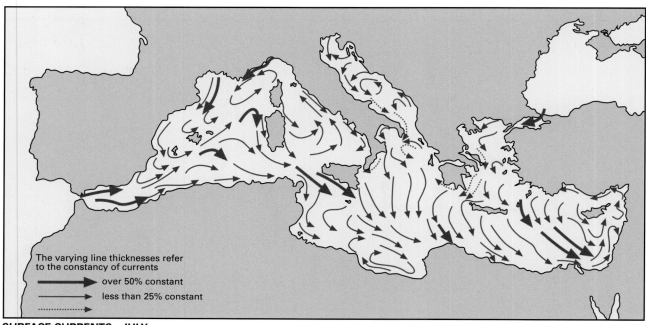

The varying line thicknesses refer to the constancy of currents

→ over 50% constant

→ less than 25% constant

SURFACE CURRENTS - JULY

Routes and passages

The passages shown are for either westabout or eastabout routes. The prevailing westerlies in the Mediterranean would appear to favour the eastabout routes although in practice actual weather patterns vary so much that it makes little difference. It is important to remember weather changes a great deal more quickly in the Mediterranean than over larger oceans and it can very quickly go from a gentle Force 3 to a sustained Force 7 in under an hour. Yachts in a hurry can motor through the night in settled conditions when it is often calm. Yachts intent on sailing will need to have good light airs performance for some parts of the sea and good heavy weather sails for other parts.

Yachts tend to make these longer passages in the summer months, with June to September the most settled months in weather terms. However, the large number of possible ports of refuge mean that passages can be taken in any season, though in the winter months you cannot rely on good weather for the whole passage from one end to the other.

Yachts heading across the Atlantic will usually want to be in Spain or Gibraltar by August or September so that the passage to the Canaries is undertaken in relatively settled weather. Yachts arriving later at the Strait of Gibraltar (in October and November) will have to watch the weather more carefully for the passage to the Canaries.

Yachts heading down the Red Sea should aim to be going through the Suez Canal in July–August so they can get down the Red Sea and catch the tail-end of the SW monsoon to cross the Arabian Sea or drop down to the Seychelles.

Incoming yachts from the Atlantic and Red Sea will usually be entering the Mediterranean in the spring, so they have the whole settled summer season in front of them.

* MED1 Port Said to Malta and on to Gibraltar

Port Said to Malta 1,025M
Malta to Gibraltar 995M

Best time May to September

This is the quickest route through the Mediterranean between Port Said and Gibraltar. Only a few large yachts use this route, usually taking on fuel at Malta before continuing E or W. In the early and late season and in the winter you will probably have to divert to somewhere for shelter, so ports of refuge should be planned in advance. Care needs to be taken to keep a reasonable distance off the Moroccan and Algerian coasts (suggested 25M) so you are not mistaken for a smuggling vessel. You can close the coast at Tunisia without problems. There are numerous variations on this route depending on weather and time. Some care is needed of the large amount of shipping using this direct route and a good watch should be kept at all times.

*See *NAW1*

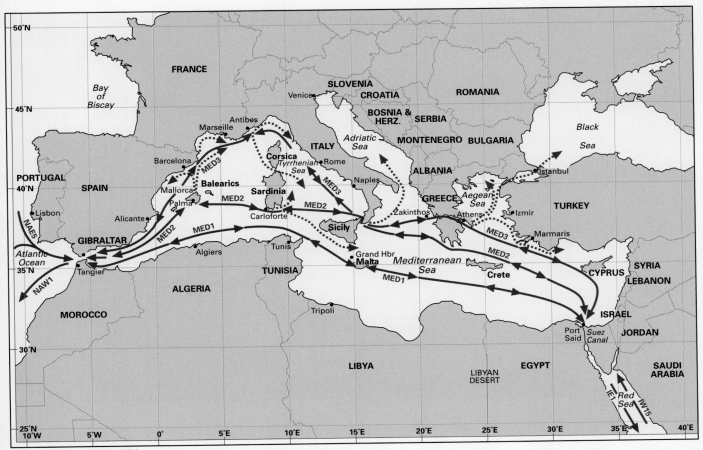

MEDITERRANEAN ROUTES

MED2 Gibraltar to the Balearics, Sardinia, Strait of Messina, Ionian/Crete and Port Said (or reverse route)

Gibraltar to Palma (Mallorca) 455M
Palma to Carloforte (Sardinia) 280M
Carloforte to Strait of Messina 345M
Strait of Messina to Zakinthos (Greece) 280M
Zakinthos to Khania (Crete) 210M
Khania to Port Said 500M

Best time May to October

This route is reasonably direct between Gibraltar and Port Said, but with shorter passages between ports. In the summer months of July and August, when most Europeans go on holiday en masse, some of the harbours, especially in Spain and Italy, will be crowded, and you should either book ahead or plan alternatives if there is not a secure anchorage nearby. As above, there are numerous variations on this route.

MED3 Gibraltar around the coasts of Spain, France, Italy, Strait of Messina, Corinth Canal and Aegean to Cyprus and Port Said (or reverse route)

Gibraltar to Barcelona (Spain) 430M
Barcelona to Antibes (France) 260M
Antibes to Livorno (Italy) 135M
Livorno to Strait of Messina 405M
Strait of Messina to Corinth Canal 385M
Corinth Canal to Marmaris (Turkey) 285M
Marmaris to Larnaca (Cyprus) 315M
Larnaca to Port Said 230M

Best time May to October

This route allows for a lot of sightseeing along the way and is really just an illustration on which there are a large number of variations. In general weather in the western Mediterranean settles down more slowly than weather in the eastern Mediterranean, so those at the eastern end can start the season earlier.

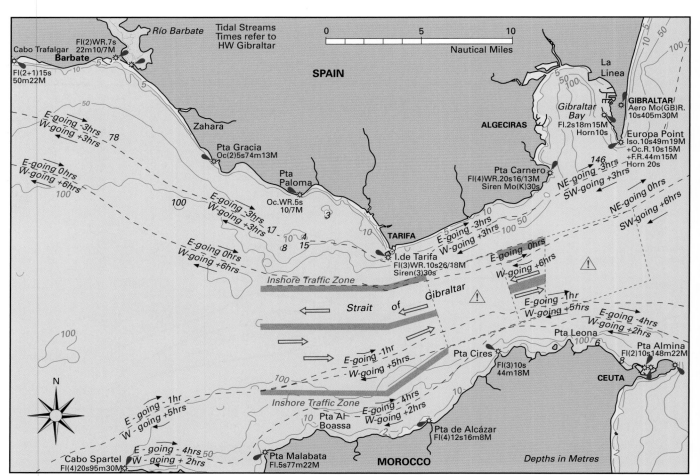

GIBRALTAR STRAIT

COUNTRY AND PORT GUIDE

EU COUNTRIES

The relevant EU countries in this sea area are:
Spain, France, Italy, Slovenia, Greece, Cyprus and Malta.
For EU regulations pertaining to the Mediterranean EU countries see Chapter 1 North Atlantic.

Port information

Information is eastabout from Gibraltar to Port Said. For most entries no tidal range is given as it is negligible for most of the Mediterranean.
See Chapter 1 North Atlantic for country information.

 ## Gibraltar

General Gibraltar is somewhere you stop at when on passage in or out of the Mediterranean as it has good communications, good provisioning and good chandlers. It is also used as a base by some yachts to cruise the nearby Spanish and Moroccan coasts.

Formalities All yachts can complete formalities from one of the marinas.

Telecom IDD +350. GSM network. Internet cafés.

Currency Pound sterling (GBP) or Gibraltar pound. Major credit cards widely accepted. ATMs ashore.

GIBRALTAR PORT

Tidal range 0.9m

Navigation

The approach is straightforward although care is needed of the large amount of shipping in the vicinity and of numerous ferries and supply boats. A night approach is possible though with all the lights ashore and afloat there is room for confusion.

There is currently no facility for yachts at anchor to clear into Gibraltar.

Yachts are not permitted to enter Marina Bay (or the fuel station) when the runway lights are flashing.

Berths

VHF Port authorities Ch 06, 12, 13, 14. Pilots Ch 16, 12, 14. Sheppards Marina Ch 68, 69, 71. Marina Bay Ch 71. Queensway Ch 71.

Ocean Village Marina Part of the Ocean Village waterside apartment development. It is likely that many berths will be for apartment owners. Limited visitors' berths. Max LOA 30m.

Resources

PILOTS AND GUIDES

Imray Mediterranean Almanac Ed. Rod Heikell and Lucinda Michell (Imray) Biennial publication
Mediterranean Cruising Handbook Rod Heikell (Imray)
RYA Book of Mediterranean Cruising Rod Heikell (Adlard Coles Nautical)

SSB

Mediterranean net: 7085kHz at 0700 zulu

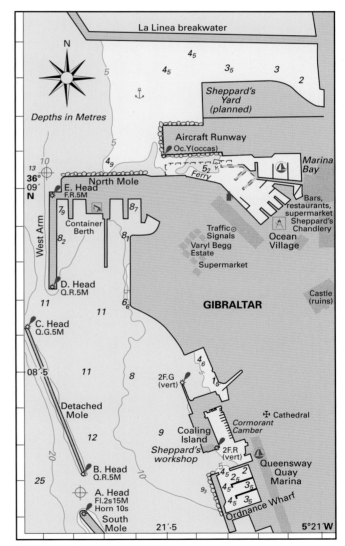

GIBRALTAR YACHT HARBOUR

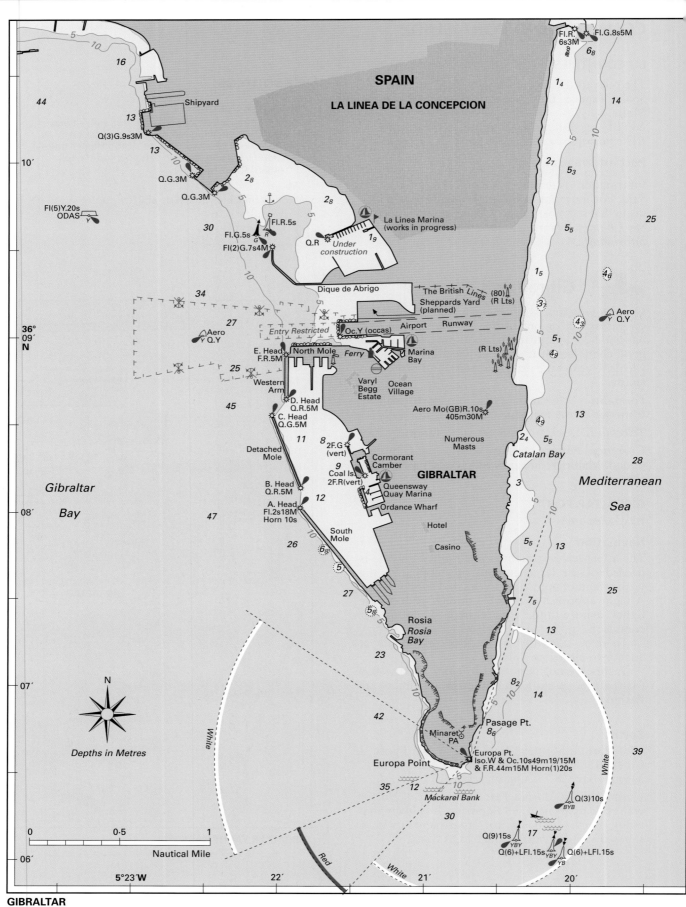

SPAIN

LA LINEA DE LA CONCEPCION

16

44

13

Shipyard

Q(3)G.9s3M

13

Q.G.3M

10′

2₈

Q.G.3M

FI(5)Y.20s
ODAS

2₈

anchor

La Linea Marina
(works in progress)

30

FI.R.5s

FI.G.5s

FI(2)G.7s4M

Q.R

1₉

Under
construction

Dique de Abrigo

The British Lines (80)
Sheppards Yard (R Lts)
(planned)

34

Airport   Runway

27

Entry Restricted

Aero
Y Q.Y

Oc.Y (occas)

1₅

4₆

3₇

4₇

Aero
Y Q.Y

36°
09′
N

E. Head
F.R.5M

North Mole   Ferry

Marina
Bay

(R Lts)

5₁

25

Western
Arm

Varyl
Begg
Estate

Ocean
Village

4₉

Aero Mo(GB)R.10s
405m30M

45

D. Head
Q.R.5M

C. Head
Q.G.5M

Numerous
Masts

4₉

5₅

13

Catalan Bay

28

11

Detached
Mole

8   2F.G
(vert)

9

Coal Is.
2F.R(vert)

Cormorant
Camber

GIBRALTAR

2₄

5₅

Mediterranean

Sea

08′

B. Head
Q.R.5M

12

Queensway
Quay Marina

3

47

A. Head
FI.2s18M
Horn 10s

Ordance Wharf

26

South
Mole

Hotel

Casino

6₈

5₅

13

5

27

5₈

Rosia
Rosia
Bay

7₅

25

Gibraltar

Bay

N

07′

23

42

8₂

14

Pasage Pt.

Minaret
PA

8₆

Depths in Metres

White

Europa Point

Europa Pt.
Iso.W & Oc.10s49m19/15M
& F.R.44m15M Horn(1)20s

39

35

12

Mackarel Bank

White

30

Q(3)10s
BYB

0   0.5   1

Nautical Mile

Q(9)15s
YBY

17

Q(6)+LFI.15s
YBY   YB

Q(6)+LFI.15s

06′

Red

White

5°23′W   22′   21′   20′

Marina Bay
209 berths. Visitors' berths. Max LOA 65m. Depths min. 3–4m. Charge band 2.
www.marinabay.gi pieroffice@marinabay.gi

Queensway Quay Marina
150 berths. Visitors' berths. Max LOA 50m. Depths 4-7m. Charge band 2/3.
Email qqmarina@gibnet.gi

Call up one of the marinas for a berth. During the autumn exodus to the Canaries for the E to W Atlantic crossing the marinas are often full.

Anchorage

If anchoring in Gibraltar waters you are requested to obtain permission from the Port Captain. Anchoring near the runway is discouraged due to height restrictions, and yachts are advised to anchor N of La Linea breakwater (in Spanish waters). A new marina is under construction here and will be the logical alternative to berths in Gibraltar.

Facilities

Usual amenities. Fuel quay near Marina Bay. Good chandlers and most repairs afloat. Limited yard capacity. Reasonable shopping for provisions.

Remarks

Gibraltar is pretty much a traditional stop when entering or leaving the Med. It is a good place to provision for English specialities in the supermarkets here. Regular flights to the UK.

Morocco

Formalities Yachts must clear in at a port of entry. Somewhere like Marina Smir is used to dealing with yachts and is a good place to clear into. You may be checked by the coastguard who regularly patrols the coast to stop illegal smuggling of immigrants and *kif* (marijuana).

Telecom IDD +212. GSM network. Internet cafés in larger centres.

Currency Moroccan Dirham (Dh). Euros widely accepted. ATMs in larger centres.

MARINA SMIR

Navigation

Make the approach from seawards and don't stray too close to the coast.

Berths

Marina Smir VHF Ch 09, 16.
450 berths. 100 visitors' berths. Max LOA 60m. Charge band 3.

Facilities

Water and electricity. Fuel. 150-ton travel hoist. Some yacht repairs. Limited provisions and restaurants.

Remarks

Duty free port. Bus into town for shopping.

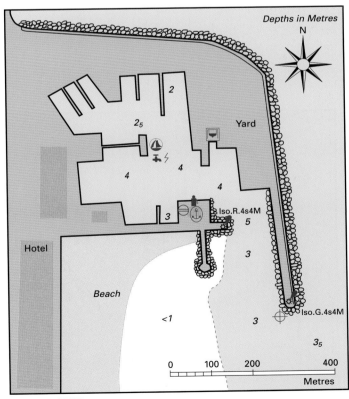

MARINA SMIR
⊕35°45´·2N 05°20´·2E WGS84

Spain

See Chapter 1 North Atlantic for country details.

ALMERIMAR

Navigation

Straightforward although difficult with strong SW winds when a swell piles up in the entrance. Buoyed channel into the marina.

Berths

VHF Ch 09, 16, 74. 1,000 berths. 200 visitors' berths. Max LOA 60m. Depths 2.5–6m. Charge band 2.

Facilities

Water and electricity. Fuel quay. 60/110-ton travel hoist. Chandlers. Wi-Fi. Laundry. Supermarket and bars and restaurants.

Remarks

Popular marina for wintering over. You will need a car to get out to see some Spanish life.
www.almerimarpuerto.com

PALMA DE MALLORCA

Navigation

Straightforward into the large bay. Planes constantly come and go from the airport on the E side of the bay. Closer in the large commercial harbour will be seen. Care needed of ferries and other craft entering and leaving at speed. Approach by night straightforward with care.

Berths

VHF Ch 16, 06 for port authorities. Ch 09, 16 for Real Club Nautico, Pier 46, Club de Mar and Marina Puerto de Mallorca.
Réal Club Nautico 750 berths. Max LOA 20m. Depths 3–10m. Charge band 5.
Club de Mar 610 berths. Max LOA 110m. Depths 3–10m. Charge band 5.
Marina Port de Mallorca (occupies the old public quay on the Paseo.) 150 berths. 30 visitors' berths. Max LOA 30m. Depths 3–6m. Charge band 4.
www.portdemallorca.com

Anchorage

No well sheltered anchorages nearby. There are a limited number of laid moorings outside the E pier which yachts can pick up if one is available. In the summer months you can anchor off in some of the coves nearby though there is a lot of wash from passing craft.

Facilities

Usual amenities. Fuel quay at Club de Mar. All yacht repairs. Good shopping for provisions and restaurants and bars everywhere.

Remarks

One of the super-yacht capitals of the Mediterranean. In high season you will need to book ahead to secure a berth.

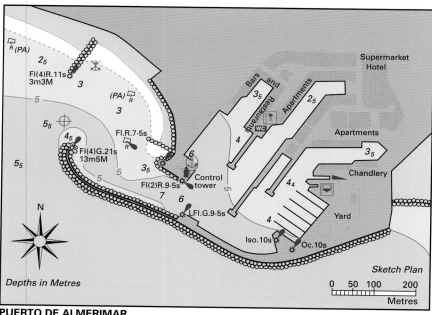

PUERTO DE ALMERIMAR
⊕36°41′·68N 02°47′·92E WGS84

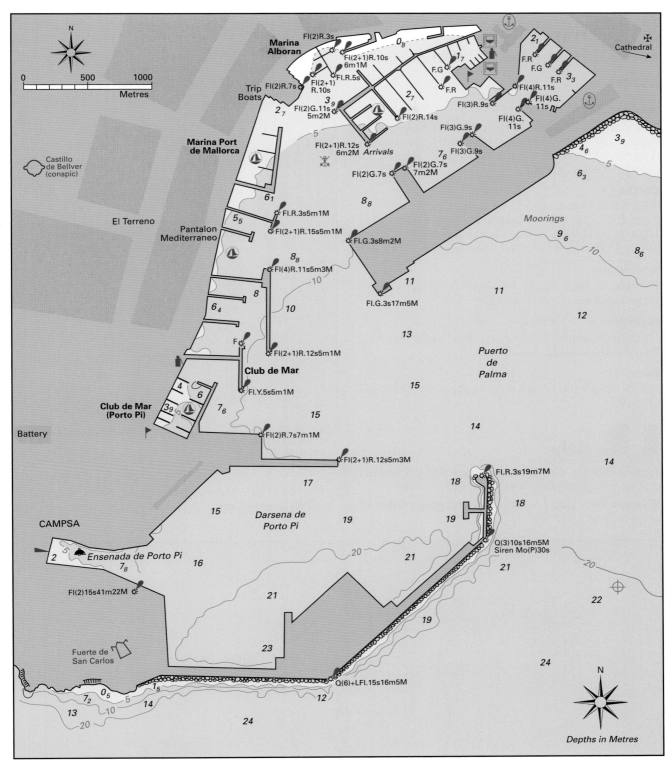

PUERTO DE PALMA DE MALLORCA
⊕39°32´.92N 02°38´.67E WGS84

France

See Chapter 1 North Atlantic for country information.

ANTIBES

Navigation

No dangers in the approaches. La Garoupe lighthouse and Fort Carre easily recognised. Approach by night straightforward. Report to capitainerie for a berth.

Berths

VHF Ch 09 for marina (24/24) and IYCA.
Port de Plaisance 1700 berths. Visitors' berths. Max LOA 65m. Depths 2–7m. Charge band 3/4.
IYCA 19 berths. LOA 70–165m. Depths 5–7m.

Anchorage

Possible in Anse de la Salis just S of the port in settled weather. Open S and E.

Facilities

Usual amenities. Fuel quay. All yacht repairs. Provisions, restaurants and bars.

Remarks

A popular port although it is usually possible to find a berth.

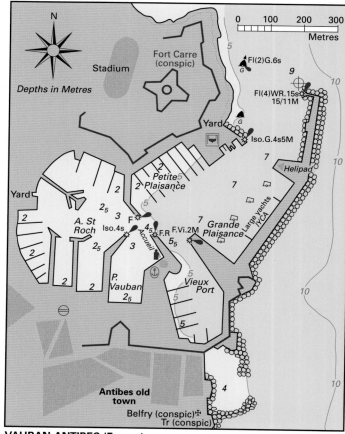

VAUBAN-ANTIBES (France)
⊕43°35´.4N 07°08´.0E

Italy

Formalities EU formalities. Registration documents and insurance papers must be carried.

Telecom IDD code +39. GSM network. Internet cafés in larger centres.

Currency Euro. Major credit cards widely accepted. ATMs everywhere.

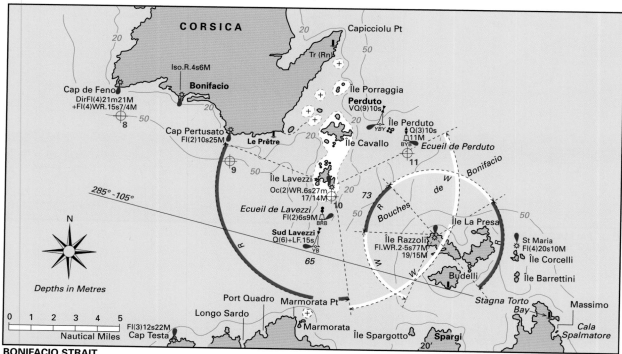

BONIFACIO STRAIT

BONIFACIO STRAIT

The middle route through the Western Mediterranean uses the Bonifacio Strait to get E or W. There are lots of good anchorages, harbours and marinas on either side of the strait and there are also good yacht facilities.

See Imray *Mediterranean Almanac* or more detailed pilots for pilotage information.

CARLOFORTE (Sardinia)

Navigation

Situated on the E side of Isola di S. Pietro on the SW corner of Sardinia. Care needed of shoal water in the channel between Isola di S. Pietro and Sardinia. Night approach possible with care.

Berths

VHF Ch 11, 16 for port authorities. Ch 09 for Marina Sifredi.
Marine Sifredi 160 berths. Visitors' berths. Max LOA 50m. Depths 2–5m. Charge band 3.
www.marinesifredi.it
Marine Service Carloforte 100 berths. Max LOA 40m. Depths 2–6m. Charge band 3.

Facilities

Some amenities on pontoon berths. Fuel quay in fishing harbour. Limited repairs. Provisions and restaurants and bars ashore.

Remarks

Convivial and useful port for MED2 route.

STRAIT OF MESSINA

Yachts heading to or from the Eastern Mediterranean will often choose to transit the Strait of Messina to explore cruising areas like the west coast of Italy, northern Sardinia and Corsica or to explore northern Sicily rather than taking the route around southern Sicily. The Strait of Messina is used by a lot of commercial shipping and also has a lot of ferries running back and forth between the mainland and Sicily, so some care is needed and the transit is best made by day.

See Imray *Mediterranean Almanac* or more detailed pilots for pilotage information.

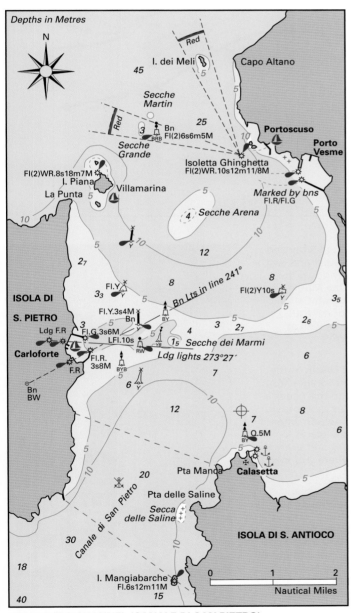

**SAN PIETRO CHANNEL (CANALE DI SAN PIETRO)
AND APPROACHES TO CARLOFORTE (Sardinia)**
⊕39°07′·22N 08°22′·00E WGS84

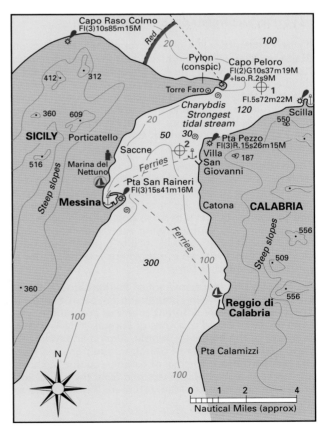

STRAIT OF MESSINA

Western Mediterranean

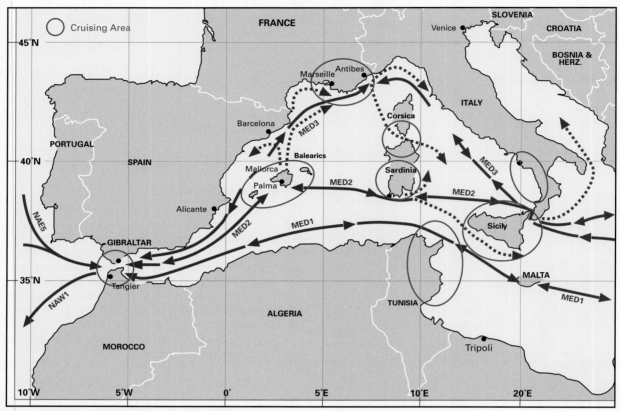

WESTERN MEDITERRANEAN CRUISING ROUTES

It's handy to take a line down through Italy and then on through Sicily and Malta to Libya which roughly divides the Mediterranean into west and east. It's as much a cultural line as a geographical one, splitting Italy down the middle and enclosing the Orthodox Balkans and Greece and the Muslim countries of Turkey around to Libya in an eastern bloc and Roman Catholic Spain, France and Italy and the Maghreb into the western bloc. Like all dividing lines it can obscure as much as it reveals, sailing-wise as well as culturally, but it's a convenient start for looking at the western Mediterranean.

The western Mediterranean to Italy is the more sophisticated cousin of the eastern Mediterranean with a lot more marinas and fewer anchorages. You will likely have to make more use of marinas and harbours and this needs a bit of planning in relation to costs, some of the marinas are very expensive, and to ensure you get a berth in popular marinas in the high season when it can get very busy. With planning you can anchor in quite a few places in settled weather, but you will need to research options carefully and study the charts and pilots with an eye to where you can anchor and where you might run to if the weather turns.

On the plus side there are a lot of marinas around the coast of mainland Europe and the off-lying islands and not all of them will be over-budget. There are seven very different countries around the western basin ranging from the Latin-based countries of Europe, Italy, France and Spain, to the countries of the Maghreb, Tunisia, Algeria and Morocco. At the western end there is also the enclave of Gibraltar, traditionally a stop-over into and out of the Mediterranean. The mix of cultures, cuisine, architecture and history are all interwoven in complex ways and from the Islamic influences in Spain to the French influence on the Maghreb there is much to do and see ashore.

Cruising strategies

Cruising yachts coming from the eastern Mediterranean will often leave in the late summer and potter through parts of the western Mediterranean until

Gibraltar. The 'Rock' looking up from Marina Bay

they get to somewhere around the Strait of Gibraltar. The fast route will take you north or south of Sicily and then up to the bottom of Sardinia where you can wait for a weather window to hop across to the Balearics and then on along the Spanish coast to around Gibraltar. A slower route might head up the west coast of Italy to around Naples or Rome before heading off across to the Strait of Bonifacio and then on across to the Balearics and Spain. Alternatively yachts can head further north either around the west coast of Italy or more usually across to Corsica and then around the French coast to Spain and onwards.

Yachts coming into the Mediterranean from the Atlantic will usually be going to spend a season or more here and there is a mixed bag of routes they can take. Some will stay in the western Mediterranean and others will cruise through to the eastern Mediterranean to spend the winter there. In Spain popular areas to spend the winter are along the Costa del Sol, Costa Brava and around the Balearics. In France cruisers will usually opt to spend the winter in the Côte d'Azur or Riviera where winter temperatures are milder than around the coast of Languedoc Roussillon and Provence. In Italy most cruisers opt for somewhere around Rome or south of Rome or in Sardinia or Sicily. Across the water Malta is popular and an increasing number of cruisers are wintering in Tunisia where marinas like El Kantaoui and Monastir are popular.

Seasons and winds

The western Mediterranean has settled summer weather and quite boisterous winters and the normal sailing season is from April through to October. In the summer once the Azores high and the relatively stationary high over the Tyrrhenian Sea in Italy are established winds are predominantly thermal winds with quite strong sea breezes blowing onto the land in the afternoon. Pressure variations over Europe and northern Africa will also have an influence, but by and large sea breezes and light land breezes at night dominate the weather patterns.

In the spring and autumn depressions moving over the Mediterranean and over Europe and northern Africa can bring unsettled weather and gales, though normally these will be over in three days or so.

Collioure in France

In the winter any passages through the western Mediterranean need to be planned carefully as there can be severe weather with winds up to storm force. Several areas are renowned for strong gales and big seas with the Strait of Gibraltar, Golfe du Lion and the Gulf of Genoa areas where special care must be taken.

Weather forecasts for the western Mediterranean are good with 5-day forecasts available over the internet from the various met offices around the basin and GRIB files available for up to seven days. Care needs to be taken interpreting GRIB files in the Mediterranean as the effects of large land areas influencing thermal winds and the erratic paths of depressions

through the sea or over the land make forecasting particularly difficult in the area. Shorter 48 hour forecasts are available on Navtex, VHF and SSB.

The Mediterranean has its own special climate and geographers refer to the Mediterranean climate as the region between the olive tree in the north and the large palm groves in the south. Temperatures in the summer are in the region of 22°–30°C range although heat waves are known where the temperature can get up over 40°C. Humidity is low compared to the Tropics which means the heat is dryer and easier on the body. Although temperatures are high, you are at comparatively high latitudes so in the summer you get

Etrusca Marina on the Tuscany coast in Italy

Msida Marina at Ta 'Xbiex on Malta *Malta Tourist Board*

Erice on Sicily

long evenings before the sun goes down. In the spring and autumn temperatures are less and in the winter there can be snow at sea level in some areas and it is colder than you might be led to believe. Look at some temperature charts for the winter when you are thinking of where to spend the winter.

Ashore

In the summer the western Mediterranean is a popular place for land-based tourists and in fact the first packaged tours were to the Spanish 'costas'. Everywhere you will find restaurants and bars of all types and prices. Local restaurants in Spain, France and Italy can provide

Boatyard at Marina Baie des Anges in France

excellent value and you will often find there is a set menu, a *menu del dia*, *menu du jour* or *menu del giorno*, which can be excellent and budget beating. Many of the restaurants and bars in the tourist spots will close in the winter so if wintering over somewhere it's important to choose one that doesn't become a ghost town in the winter. Along the coast of North Africa there is less tourism than along the European coast, but still enough in Tunisia and Morocco to keep most happy.

Shopping is good all along the coast of Europe and you will have no difficulty in finding everything you want. There are also lots of local markets where fresh fruit and vegetables and other local produce will be found.

Provisioning for the Atlantic

Cruisers leaving the Mediterranean for an Atlantic crossing used to provision up in Gibraltar where there were excellent supermarkets which catered for cruisers with stores like 'strong' flour for bread-making and Fray Bentos pies. In recent years Gibraltar has become less cruiser-orientated and along with others I think there are better places nearby to stock up for the crossing.

Try Almerimar where there is a good supermarket and chandlers within the marina and you can trundle the supermarket trolley to the boat. Ceuta has good supermarkets and local markets and is a duty free port

as well. After provisioning in one of these harbours you can still put in at Gibraltar for some last minute shopping or when the new marina at La Linea on the border with Gibraltar is complete this may be a better place to stop before the passage through the Straits of Gibraltar and into the Atlantic.

Facilities

Yacht facilities are well developed all along the European coast and you will not have problems finding somewhere to leave it afloat or ashore. The caveat to this is that in some popular marinas and yards you will need to book ahead for a berth or hard standing space. You can also leave a boat or haul in Malta and Tunisia although again these have become popular of late and it would be wise to book ahead. Some marinas and yards are more favoured by the cruising community than others with places like Malta, southern and western Sardinia, Port Napoleon and nearby yards in Languedoc-Roussillon in France, and around Barcelona and Almerimar in Spain all popular. There are of course lots more places.

In the northern European countries and Malta you won't have any problems finding spares and getting specialist repairs done. Communications are also good from Spain, France and Italy with budget flights flying to many European airports where you can get onward long-haul flights.

Strait of Gibraltar

There is a constant surface current flowing into the Strait of Gibraltar from the Atlantic of between 1–2kn and this must be taken into account when calculating the duration, set and rate of the tidal streams. What it in effect means is that the overall tide/current equation is most favourable for a W to E passage and least favourable for an E to W passage.

The Strait of Gibraltar has in effect three tidal streams: N, middle and S. The rate and direction of these streams varies and times are based on HW Gibraltar. Gibraltar tide tables can be found in a number of publications, including the current edition of the Imray *Mediterranean Almanac*.

Northern stream
E-going -3 to +3hrs
W-going +3 to -3hrs

Middle stream
E-going HW to +6hrs
W-going -6hrs to HW

Southern stream
E-going -4 to +2hrs
W-going +2 to -4hrs

By playing the three different streams it is possible to get through the Strait even if you are not precisely on time for the favourable stream. The different streams can be recognised if there is any wind by the usual 'wind against tide' or 'wind with tide' sea conditions. Any yacht moving across the Strait of Gibraltar must remember that there is a large volume of commercial shipping both in and out of this narrow waterway and that large ships cannot alter course quickly or easily. The overall tidal stream strength and direction can also be altered by surface drift currents set up by strong winds blowing consistently from one direction for several days.

Note If in doubt one of the authors (RJH) usually sticks to the northern side of the Strait. Leaving the Strait this is always the best option, aiming to be off Punta Carnero approximately 1½ hours before the W-going stream and then sticking very tight in under the N side. Keep going to Tarifa and then continue due W for another 10M before attempting to cut across and head on a course for the Canaries or head up around the Spanish coast towards Cape Trafalgar.

Almerimar. A popular place for cruisers to gather before leaving for an Atlantic leg

Reading

Imray Mediterranean Almanac
Ed. Rod Heikell & Lucinda Michell
(Imray) Biennial publication
Mediterranean Cruising Handbook
Rod Heikell (Imray)
Costas del Sol & Blanca (RCCPF /
John Marchment (Imray)
Costas del Azahar, Dorada & Brava
RCCPF / John Marchment (Imray)
Islas Baleares RCCPF /
John Marchment (Imray)

Mediterranean France & Corsica
Rod Heikell (Imray)
Italian Waters Pilot Rod Heikell
(Imray)
North Africa RCCPF / Graham Hutt
(Imray)

My gem
The French Theodore Zeldin (Harvill)

Savona on the Italian Riviera

Malta

Formalities EU formalities. Registration documents and insurance papers must be carried. Yachts should head for the customs office at Msida Marina, Grand Harbour or Mgarr on Gozo to clear in.

Telecom IDD +356. GSM network. Internet cafés.

Currency Euro. Major credit cards widely accepted. ATMs everywhere.

GRAND HARBOUR AND MARSAMXETT

Navigation

From the distance it is difficult to identify what is where. The Hilton tower at St Julian's and St Paul's dome in Valletta show up well. A night approach can be made with care.

Berths

VHF Ch 09, 12, 16 for Valletta port control. Ch 09 for Msida Marina, Ch 13 for Grand Harbour Marina.

Msida Marina
700 berths. Visitors' berths. Max LOA 18m. Depths 4-14m. Charge band 2/3.

Grand Harbour Marina
285 berths. Max LOA 85m. Depths 4–15m.
www.cnmarinas.com

Anchorage

Limited space on N side of Manoel Island.

Facilities

Usual amenities. Most yacht repairs and spares are readily available or can be ordered. Provisions and restaurants and bars.

Remarks

Popular wintering spot.

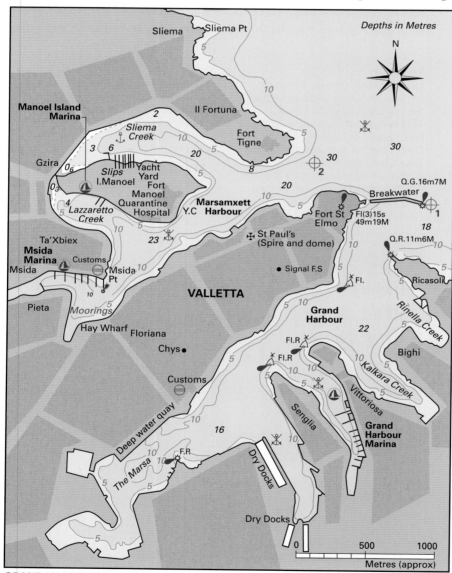

GRAND HARBOUR AND MARSAMXETT (Malta)
⊕1 35°54'·17N 14°31'·58E WGS84
⊕2 35°54'·30N 14°30'·98E WGS84

Greece

Formalities EU formalities. Registration documents and insurance papers must be carried. Yachts should head for a port of entry and obtain a cruising log.

Telecom IDD +30. GSM network. Internet cafés common.

Currency Euro. Major credit cards widely accepted. ATMs everywhere.

LIMIN ZAKINTHOU (Zakinthos)

Navigation

Situated on E side of Zakinthos Island in the Ionian Sea. Approach straightforward by day or night. Care needed of large ferries entering and leaving.

Berths

On the yacht quay or on the N end of the town quay. Good shelter.

Anchorage

Sometimes possible in the SW corner.

Facilities

Water. Fuel truck. Minor repairs. Provisions and restaurants and bars.

Remarks

Marina under construction on S side of harbour. Useful first port of call, with the option of heading through to the Corinth Canal or around the Peloponnese into the Aegean.

If you need to go to Athens for any reason it should be kept in mind that although there are numbers of marinas along the coast of Piraeus and the adjacent suburbs of Athens, these are all busy with Athens based boats and getting a berth is not always easy. It is best to try to book a berth before arriving. Zea Marina, Marina Faliron and Kalamaki

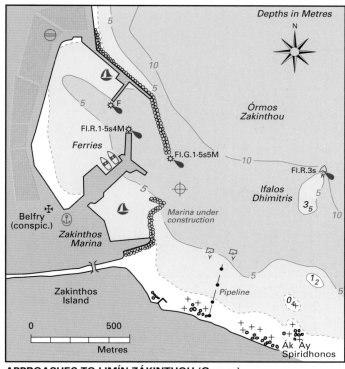

APPROACHES TO LIMÍN ZÁKINTHOU (Greece)
⊕37°46′·69N 20°54′·36E WGS84

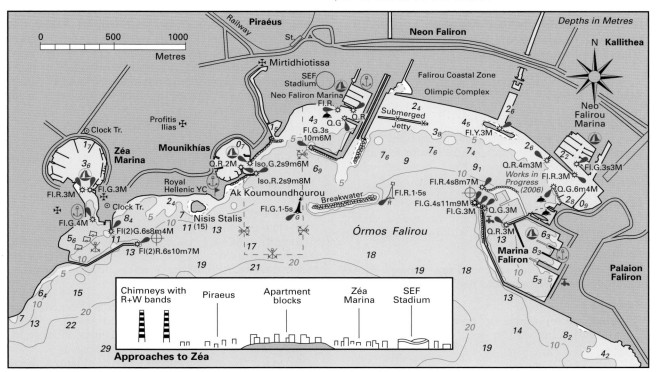

ORMOS FALIROU
⊕ Zéa Marina 37°55′·93N 23°39′·22E WGS84

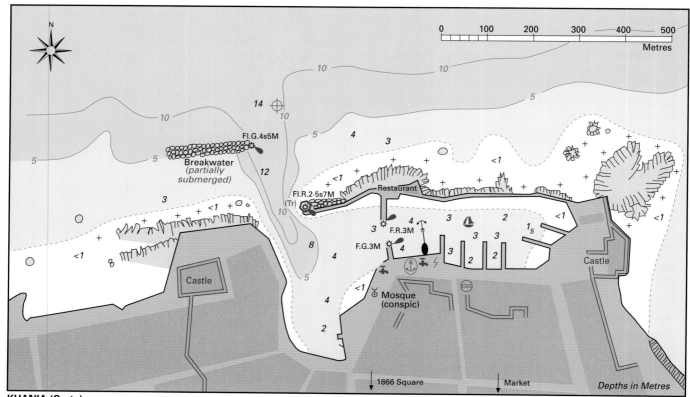

KHANIA (Crete)
⊕35°31'·35N 24°01'·09E WGS84

Marina are the likely choices for a berth. One other option is to go to one of the nearby islands like Aigina or Poros and get one of the fast ferries into Piraeus.

Zea Marina www.medmarinas.com

Faliron Marina www.faliro-marina.com

See Imray *Mediterranean Almanac* or more detailed pilots for pilotage information.

KHANIA (Crete)

Navigation

The city is easily identified. Care needed of the detached breakwater which is now 1m or less above water. Care needed with strong onshore winds which heap up big seas in the entrance.

Berths

Go stern or bows-to where shown. Good shelter although there can be a surge with onshore winds.

Facilities

Water. Fuel by mini-tanker. Minor repairs. Good shopping for provisions and restaurants nearby.

Remarks

Often used as a jumping-off point down to the Suez Canal if not going via Cyprus.

Turkey

Formalities Go first to a port of entry. Clear in with customs, health, harbourmaster and coastguard. A transit log valid for one year will be issued. New regulations may mean you need an agent to obtain a transit log. Most passport holders get a 90 day visa so if you are staying longer it will be necessary to hop on a ferry to Greece for the day and get another 90 days on your return. Yachts can then cruise freely around the coast.

Telecom IDD +90. GSM network. Internet cafés.

Currency Yeni Turkish lira (YTL). Major credit cards widely accepted in larger centres. ATMs everywhere.

MARMARIS

Navigation

Marmaris is situated inside a large enclosed bay across from Rhodes. Approach straightforward by day and night. Yachts usually use Sark Bogazi, the E channel into the bay. A night approach is straightforward.

Berths

VHF Ch 06, 16 for Marmaris Marina (Port Marmaris) Ch 72, 73 for Marmaris Yacht Marine.

Marmaris Marina 700 berths. Visitors' berths. Max LOA 40m. Depths 2–15m. Charge band 3.

Marmaris Yacht Marine 600 berths. Visitors' berths. Max LOA 60m. Depths 1.5–8m. Charge band 2–3.

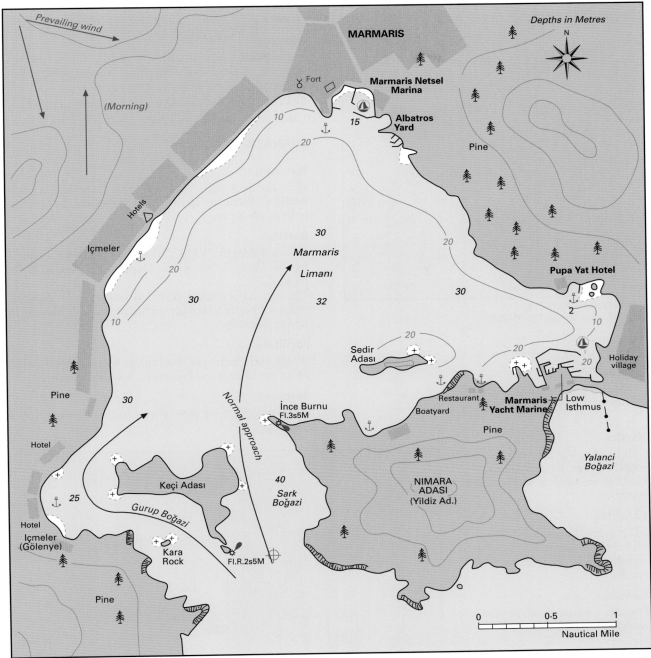

APPROACHES TO MARMARIS
⊕36°47′·83N 28°15′·84E WGS84

You need to take a minibus to get into town (about 15 minutes). www.yachtmarin.com

Anchorage
Off Marmaris Marina, around the NW side of the bay and off Pupa Yacht Hotel. The latter has the best shelter but is some distance from town.

Facilities
Usual amenities in marinas. Fuel quay. Most yacht repairs. Good shopping for provisions and restaurants and bars.

Remarks
Marmaris Marina is close to Marmaris town. Marmaris Yacht Marine is on the isthmus joining Nimara to the mainland in the SE corner of the bay.

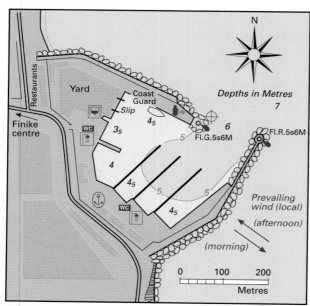

SETUR FINIKE MARINA
⊕36°17'·69N 30°09'·11E WGS84

FINIKE

Navigation
The approach is straightforward and free of dangers. VHF Ch 73.

Berths
350 berths. Visitors' berths. Depths 3-6m. Charge band 2. Call the marina to be allotted a berth.

Facilities
All the usual amenities. 80 ton travel hoist. Large hardstanding area. Provisions and restaurants.

Remarks
Popular marina to winter over. www.seturmarinas.com

Cyprus

Formalities Clear in with the authorities at Larnaca who are all close to the marina. Overtime charged at weekends and outside working hours.

Telecom IDD +357. GSM network. Internet cafés.

Currency Euro. Major credit cards accepted. ATMs.

LARNACA MARINA

Navigation
Give the reef and shoal water of Cape Kiti a wide berth. Difficult to identify exactly where the marina is until closer in.

Berths
Larnaca Marina VHF Ch 08. 350 berths. Visitors' berths. Max LOA 40m. Depths 1.5–5m. Charge band 2.

The marina is usually crowded and it can be difficult to find a berth although yachts are usually slotted in where possible.

Facilities
Water and electricity. Fuel quay. 40-ton travel hoist. Most yacht repairs. Provisions and restaurants.

Remarks
Good provisioning stop when heading down into the Red Sea.

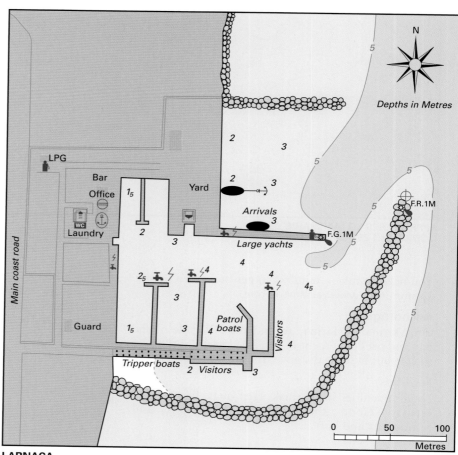

LARNACA
⊕34°55'·1N 33°38'·6E

Egypt

General Egypt is one of the most liberalised of the Arab countries and on the whole the coast is safe to sail up as long as you steer clear of the disputed area on the Egypt/Sudan border. The main problems cruisers encounter here are the stultifying bureaucracy and the constant demands for baksheesh. Yachts tend to wend their way along the coast, stopping at just a few harbours where there are officials and for the rest of the time anchoring out in more remote places without officialdom intruding on things. There are a lot of wonderful anchorages among the reefs and some of the best diving in the world.

Formalities Yachts must clear in and out of every port. In most ports an agent will do this for you at an often quite substantial fee. If you elect to do it yourself, some baksheesh speeds things up. You need to see the health officer, harbourmaster, customs and immigration. In most anchorages you will not be bothered and many yachts elect just to cruise from anchorage to anchorage. At Port Said you will need to engage an agent for the canal transit.

Telecom IDD code +20. GSM supported in towns and cities.

Currency Egyptian pound. Banks will exchange cash. ATMs in cities. Some larger establishments in the cities take major credit cards.

PORT SAID

Navigation

Numerous ships are always underway entering or leaving the canal and at anchor in the roadstead. Follow the buoyed channel into the harbour. Do not go outside the channel as the W breakwater is underwater for a considerable length. Night approach possible but not straightforward. VHF Ch 16 for port authorities. Often you will get a reply from an agent on this channel.

Berths

Stern-to in Port Fouad Yacht Centre. Good shelter although there is a lot of wash from the pilot boats and ships.

Facilities

Water. Fuel by arrangement. Limited yacht repairs. Provisions and restaurants.

Remarks

You need to come here either as the end-point of a transit through the Suez Canal or to arrange for a N to S transit. A lot of yachts use the Felix Agency to arrange a transit.
www.felix-eg.com

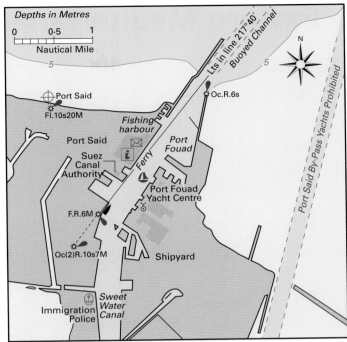

PORT SAID (Egypt)
⊕31°18´·1N 32°21´·5E

Resources

PILOTS AND GUIDES

Imray Mediterranean Almanac Ed. Rod Heikell and Lucinda Michell (Imray) Biennial publication
Italian Waters Pilot Rod Heikell (Imray)
Adriatic Pilot T & D Thompson (Imray)
Greek Waters Pilot Rod Heikell (Imray)
Turkish Waters & Cyprus Pilot Rod Heikell (Imray)
North Africa RCCPF/Graham Hutt (Imray)

Eastern Mediterranean

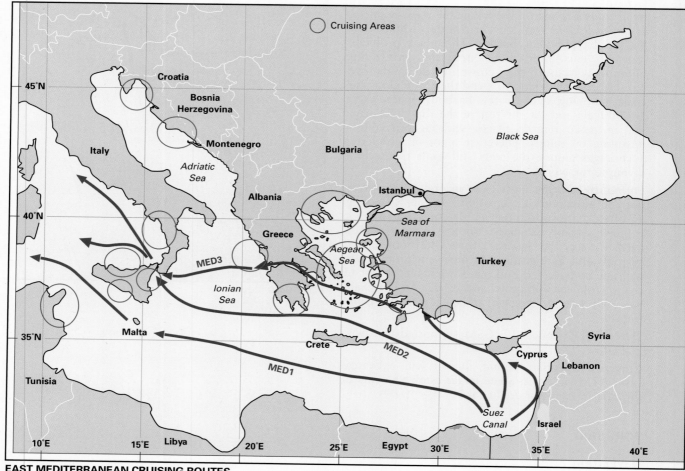

EAST MEDITERRANEAN CRUISING ROUTES

Around the eastern basin there are 14 countries and a millennia of accumulated history and culture. All around the coast the vestiges of past civilizations can be seen, from the Phoenicians through the Greeks, Romans, Byzantines, Selçuks, Ottomans, and other Muslim nations as well as adventurers like the Venetians, Genoese, the French and the British. Visitors should make some effort to venture inland and not just touch on the coast.

Cruising-wise you have a lot more options for anchoring out and getting away from it all on this side of the Mediterranean. Between the archipelagos scattered around the coasts of Croatia and Greece and the much indented coastlines of Italy, Croatia, Greece and Turkey there are a lot of small harbours and anchorages and fewer marinas than in the western Mediterranean. The coast of the Levant from Syria to Egypt is a lot straighter with fewer safe harbours and good anchorages.

Cruising strategies

Yachts coming up from the Red Sea will usually potter up some of the Israeli coast or head directly across to Turkey. Southern Cyprus has only a couple of marinas which are notoriously hard to find a berth in and likewise Northern Cyprus also has little space for visiting yachts. Yachts cruise the Turkish coast and the Greek islands before heading west to Italy and the western Mediterranean before crossing the Atlantic.

Cruising folk often dally in this part of the world seduced by the easy day-sailing from one destination to the next and also by the relatively modern

Simi in the Dodecanese

Meganisi Island in the Ionian

western-orientated cultures that make it easy to refit, travel and fit into things ashore. Some never leave. There is a lot of cruising to be had here and you can easily spend a season in Turkey and then another season in Greece before heading up the Adriatic or dawdling around Italy.

EMYR The Eastern Mediterranean Yacht Rally is a cruise in company around the southeast corner of the Mediterranean taking just over a month. There is a feeder rally earlier from Istanbul. The rally usually starts mid-May in Kemer Marina in Turkey and visits Syria, Northern Cyprus, Lebanon, Israel and Egypt depending on the political situation. It is a popular way to visit this part of the world and for yachts heading down the Red Sea in late July and August makes a convenient and very social start before going through Suez and onwards.
www.emyr.org

Seasons and winds

The normal sailing season here is from April through to October. The summer has a settled weather pattern that is predictable from year to year. In the spring and autumn

depressions move over the area or over the land masses to the north or south causing gales over the area. These are well forecast and there are safe anchorages and harbours everywhere.

In the summer the *meltemi* blows briskly down through the Aegean at anything from 15 to 30 knots. In the spring and autumn winds are generally less. Sea areas outside the Aegean are mostly subject to sea breezes in the summer which can be anything from a lazy 5–10 knots to brisker winds of 15–20 knots depending on the area.

Meltemi blowing in the Aegean

Weather forecasts for the eastern Mediterranean are good with five day forecasts available over the internet from official met offices and other sources and GRIB files are available for up to seven days. Shorter range 48-hour forecasts are available on Navtex, VHF and SSB.

Temperatures in the summer are in the 25°–30°C range though unlike the Tropics the humidity is very low so it is a dry heat. Although the climate is benign you are in comparatively high latitudes so you get light until late into the evening and not the abrupt darkness early on

of the Tropics. In the spring and autumn temperatures are less and in the winter temperatures drop to 10°–18°C except in the Adriatic where it can be a lot colder in winter. Greece and Turkey are popular places for yachts to winter over and there are numerous marinas offering good winter rates. Malta and southern Italy are also popular for the winter.

Ashore

The eastern Mediterranean is a popular place for people to visit both land-based and on the water. This means that in spring through to late autumn there are enough restaurants, bars and cafés to satisfy everyone. Eating out is a national sport in the Mediterranean and an evening stroll (the *volta* in Greece, *passaregio* in Italy) after the sun has gone down is a national pastime.

Shopping is good throughout the northern countries from Italy to Turkey where you can buy just about everything and local markets for fruit and veggies are excellent. In the south the shopping is less international apart from Israel and Cyprus. Larnaca in southern Cyprus is an excellent place to stock up in if heading down the Red Sea.

If you are living aboard through the winter it pays to make a few enquiries about how many of the restaurants, bars and shops stay open through the winter as in some places you will find more than 50% of them will close for the off season. Some marinas provide additional facilities to make life more social for liveaboards during the winter and its worth listening in to the grapevine to find out what's going on.

Methoni on the Peloponnese

Astipalaia in the Aegean

Turkish markets are a shoppers delight

Boatyard in Turkey

Facilities

Yacht facilities are well developed in all the northern countries and you won't have much trouble finding somewhere to leave the boat for the winter afloat or ashore. Deals can be done in some places though not everywhere. Most spares are readily available in the EU countries and can be ordered in the others although customs procedures can be bothersome. On the southern side yacht facilities are sparse and you will struggle to get most things.

Reading

Mediterranean Almanac Ed. Rod Heikell and Lucinda Michell (Imray) Biennial publication
Italian Waters Pilot Rod Heikell (Imray)
Adriatic Pilot T & D Thompson (Imray)
Greek Waters Pilot Rod Heikell (Imray)
Ionian Rod Heikell (Imray)
West Aegean Rod Heikell (Imray)
East Aegean Rod Heikell (Imray)
Turkish Waters & Cyprus Pilot Rod Heikell (Imray)
North Africa Pilot Graham Hutt. (Imray)

My gem

The Colossus of Maroussi Henry Miller (Penguin)

The Byzantine village on the 'rock' at Monemvasia and local transport

Kasos in the Aegean

7

SOUTHERN OCEAN

High latitude cruising (35°S to 55°S)

Caleta Sur, Isla Chair, NW arm of Beagle Canal

General

At these latitudes there is relatively little land. The world is encircled by ocean, broken only by the southern parts of South Africa and Australia, the narrow wedge of Patagonia and the islands of Tasmania and New Zealand. In this aquatic environment are to be found the great whales, albatross, penguins and a great abundance of seabirds and marine life. The seas build up to magnificent proportions. To see another vessel of any type is a rare occurrence.

Each year more yachts are choosing to visit destinations in high southern latitudes which have been given a fearful reputation by earlier mariners who had to weather the southern capes in whatever weather they encountered. They were on the other side of the world from home and lacked the sophisticated weather information, motors and navigation gear that is now common on yachts. In fact, these places are not so different from similar latitudes in the Northern Hemisphere, which have bred so many yachtsmen. What is more, they offer unspoilt and uncrowded cruising. Guides that have appeared in recent years make the cruising grounds more accessible but leave thousands of little-known anchorages for those who wish to explore further.

The four main cruising destinations are Fiordland and Stewart Island in New Zealand, the vast waterways of Southern Patagonia (mainly in Chile), the SW coast of Western Australia and the shores of Tasmania. All these places can be reached from more temperate climes by coastal hops of varying length. However, many skippers have correctly reasoned that if their vessel is tough enough to withstand the weather once there, they can make a southern ocean passage to reach the chosen cruising ground.

Preparation

Earlier sailors in these waters had a tough time; the lack of man-made landmarks, poor charts and frequent spells of bad visibility complicate navigation. Reliable motors, GPS, updated charts, yachtsmen's guides and radar have all played their part in reducing these problems to an enormous extent. It is possible to sail without them but they do make cruising far more pleasant and safer. The yacht should be exceptionally sound and well equipped with every spare needed to make running repairs that will be able to stand the test of ocean sailing. Insulation and some form of heating that will dry the boat out are virtually a necessity, even in summer. And most important of all is the preparation of the crew. They must be hardy enough to withstand wet and cold, patient enough to wait for good weather and absolutely determined to see the voyage through without external assistance (which generally will not be available). The reward for all this is wonderful cruising and surprisingly frequent spells of superb weather.

Weather and sea

PREVAILING WINDS

In a word, they are westerly. However, along coasts there are often considerable local variations brought about by land and sea breezes, katabatic winds falling from mountain chains, and winds directed by narrow channels and mountains that sometimes blow in quite surprising directions. On the coast of Chile N of Valdivia (39°50'S) the winds are predominately from the S. S of this point they are more changeable with NW preceding the passage of fronts and SW following. The border between frontal weather and steady southerlies tends to lie further S in summer and further N in winter.

At sea, especially in January and February, there can be a lot of E winds in the Roaring Forties; at times this can be an advantage, such as for vessels crossing the Tasman, the Great Australian Bight or returning to South America from the Falkland Islands, but it is often a disappointment to those expecting to make a fast downwind passage. Some skippers prefer to cross the Roaring Forties in late spring or early autumn in the hope of more reliable westerlies.

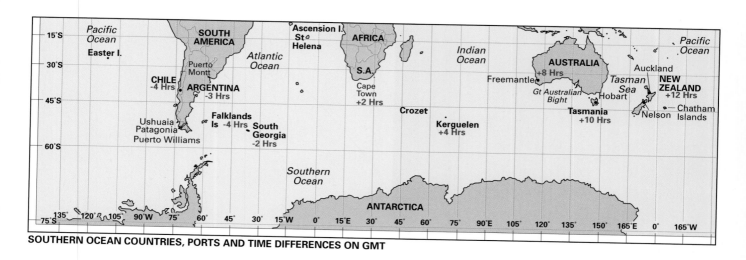

SOUTHERN OCEAN COUNTRIES, PORTS AND TIME DIFFERENCES ON GMT

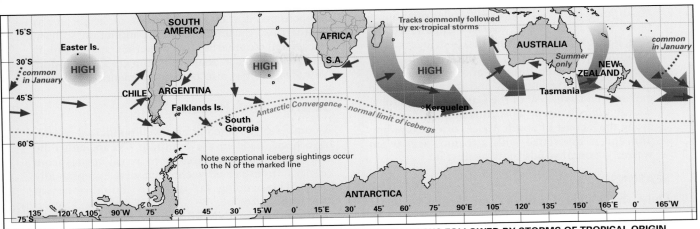

SOUTHERN OCEAN - PREVAILING SUMMER WINDS, NORMAL LIMIT OF ICEBERGS, TRACKS FOLLOWED BY STORMS OF TROPICAL ORIGIN

GALES

These travel from W to E and are common at all times of year, but much more so in winter when the depressions also tend to be further N. Luckily coastal sailing in the most visited spots is made safe by the presence of many exceptionally well sheltered anchorages. In the S of Chile, where a yacht has no problem in finding safe anchorages, many reckon that winter is the best time to cruise. The presence of a large high over the frigid Patagonian interior often keep gales offshore, resulting in settled spells all the way S to Cape Horn.

At any time of year a gale in the Southern Ocean can be violent and develop into a survival storm.

TROPICAL STORMS

During the peak of the tropical storm season (January–April) storms in the SW Pacific often travel down to below 40°S. They rarely maintain their original violence, but can link up with Southern Ocean depressions to form severe gales. It is well worth watching activity in the tropics when making a Tasman crossing or on the first half of a W–E Pacific crossing.

ICE

Ice is not common N of 50°S except in the South Atlantic Ocean where the Antarctic Peninsula pushes the E-setting current to the N. Here the Antarctic Convergence reaches 50°S and quite large bergs are regularly sighted to the N of the convergence. Very occasionally bergs have been sighted near the coasts of New Zealand, S Africa and S America.

CURRENTS

The Southern Ocean Current or the west wind drift predominates. Throughout most of the region there is approximately 0.5 knot of E-going current at all times of year. There are small local variations and prolonged periods of E wind can temporarily reverse the direction. Important exceptions are as follows:

1. *The Great Australian Bight* Between February and April the current, up to 300 miles offshore, runs in an E direction.
2. *The Tasman Sea* Currents here vary throughout the year, pilot charts should be carefully consulted when planning a passage.
3. *The Peru or Humboldt Current* This runs up the W coast of South America from approximately 46°S. It has strength of about ½ knot, however, it is frequently augmented by local weather

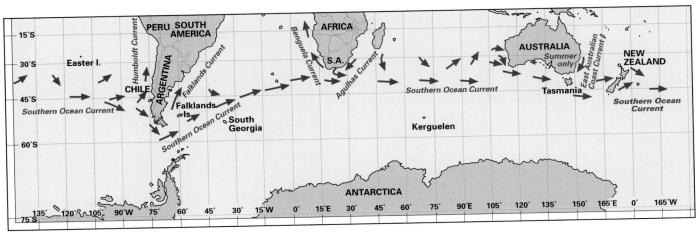

SOUTHERN OCEAN CURRENTS

conditions. It extends up to 600 miles offshore. S of 46°S the trend is SSE, towards Cape Horn.

4. *The Benguela Current* On the N fringe of the Atlantic Southern Ocean, this current runs N up the W coasts of South Africa and Namibia. It can attain rates exceeding 2kn and its influence can extend well to the SW of the Cape of Good Hope.

5. *The Agulhas Current* This runs in a SE direction along the S coast of South Africa, often exceeding 2kn and is associated with atrocious seas when westerly frontal winds blow against it.

SEASONS

Only the toughest sailors and strongest boats venture into the ocean in the winter months. The season for ordinary mortals is between October and April. However, on the coasts the situation is different. Most who know the waters of Chilean Patagonia and the Canal Beagle recommend winter as the best time for cruising. The cold is more than compensated for by long periods of bright sunny weather and outstanding winter mountain scenery. Occasional southerlies or easterlies make sailing northwards easier than in summer. Fiordland in New Zealand has also been recommended in winter.

Search and Rescue

A number of spectacular and well publicised rescues have been made in the Southern Ocean, either by other competitors in races or by naval vessels from nearby nations. These yachtsmen were exceptionally lucky. Those going far offshore should entertain little hope of rescue.

406 EPIRB or INMARSAT are probably the best ways of summoning help. Distances are so great that MF and HF radio propagation is not to be relied upon.

ROUTES AND PASSAGES

Not surprisingly, these are primarily W to E with the prevailing winds.

Note Distances given are for Great Circle courses on shorter routes, but are for composite Great Circle courses on longer routes in order to avoid going too far S.

SO1 New Zealand to South America

Auckland to Puerto Montt, staying above 50°S 5,260M

Season November to March

Best time Possibly late November early December

This is the longest continuous stretch of ocean anywhere. An interesting break on the trip is to visit the Chatham Islands off the E coast of New Zealand. Some yachts make intermediate breaks in the trip by visiting the Austral Islands, S of Tahiti, Pitcairn or Easter islands. The latter options all involve leaving the zone of W winds, crossing the variables and add considerably to the time on passage. Swell at Pitcairn or Easter islands can make landing impossible.

On the W side of the ocean the prevailing winds between mid-December and mid-February are not invariably from the W. Between 40°S and 50°S and New Zealand and 140°W there are a fairly high proportion of winds from N and E. (In January 2000 one of the authors (AO'G) experienced E winds for the first half of this crossing; a friend who crossed two months earlier had fair winds all the way.) Many of these winds are due to weather systems originating in the tropics so a close watch on the weather reports to the N is of use. E of 140°W the winds are more reliable due to the presence of the SE Pacific High.

The fastest route is to follow a great circle course, which lies entirely in the belt of westerly winds. This will take a vessel S of the Antarctic Convergence and into icebergs. It is definitely not recommended for ordinary cruising yachts. Most cruisers cross in a latitude between 40°S and 50°S. Around mid-summer it is usually necessary to head further S to catch westerlies.

If wishing to cruise in Chile, then Puerto Montt is a good destination. Further S a yacht could consider making for the Straits of Magellan. This would probably mean a trip to Punta Arenas to enter the country and that is not a good port to visit. Otherwise the yacht should round the Horn and then work N across Bahía Nassau (there are many secure anchorages in this area and the seas are relatively sheltered) to the Canal Beagle and make for the good ports of Puerto Williams (Chile) or Ushuaia (Argentina).

SO2 South America to South Africa (via Falkland Islands)

Strait of Le Maire to Cape Town, avoiding the Antarctic Convergence and passing S of Tristan da Cunha. 3,820M

Season November to March

Best time January and February

The S Atlantic has reliable westerlies between 40°S and 50°S. Because of the higher ice risk than other oceans at comparable latitudes, it is wise to stay N of 45°S. Leaving from Tierra del Fuego it will be necessary to steer N at first, perhaps calling at the Falkland Islands on the way. Ice has occasionally been known to drift onto the direct course between Estrecho le Maire and the Falkland Islands.

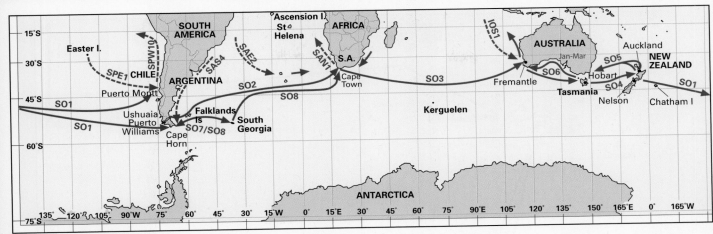

SOUTHERN OCEAN ROUTES

The area to the S of Tristan da Cunha and Gough Island has a well-earned reputation for strong winds and high irregular seas. It may be prudent to keep north of 40°S between 30°W and Cape Town.

SO3 South Africa to Australia (via Crozet and Kerguelen)

Cape Town to Fremantle reaching 45°S mid-passage 4,670M
Fremantle to Bass Strait 1,730M

Season November to March

Best time January and February

Once again the great circle course is not recommended as ice may be encountered south of 50°S. S of 40°S the westerly winds are reliable. The French islands of Crozet and Kerguelen both lie near the route and can be visited without a serious ice risk. If making for the Bass Strait and E coast of Australia a yacht should stay S of 40°S to avoid the heavy coastal traffic and, in the summer months, the easterlies that occasionally blow in the Great Australian Bight.

SO4 Australia to New Zealand

Hobart to Nelson 1,160M

Season November to March

Best time January and February

Most of the Tasman has variable winds. The great circle course between New South Wales or Tasmania and the Cook Strait, which separates the N and S islands of New Zealand, has a reasonably high proportion of W winds.

SO5 New Zealand to Australia

Auckland to Sydney 1,290M

Season November to March

Best time January and February

The direct route between the north of New Zealand and Sydney is through an area of variable winds so the course can be laid much of the time. Yachts departing from Cook Strait or heading for Tasmania may find better conditions by steering N of the great circle route and keeping N of 40°S.

SO6 E coast of Australia to the W coast via the S coast

Bass Strait to Freemantle following the coast 1,800M

Season January to March

Best time January and February

In summer, the intense heat of the Australian interior creates low pressure and causes SE winds off the S coast. Several yachts have reported good passages by staying within 100M of the coast when crossing the Australian Bight from E to W. The advantage of this route is that it offers an alternative route to the Indian Ocean when the cyclone season is closing the route around the N. There is also some excellent cruising to be had along the way.

With the exceptions of Bass Strait and Cape Leuwin (both of which may be negotiated in shorter hops between ports when the weather is favourable) this route has a low incidence of gales and adverse weather.

SO7 Falkland Islands or South Georgia to South America

Stanley to Strait of Le Maire 340M
South Georgia to Stanley 800M
South Georgia to Strait of Le Maire 1,010M

Season November to March

Best time January and February

Charter yachts regularly make the passage back from South Georgia and the Falklands to the Beagle Channel. This is not an easy passage and heavy weather and ice are always a possibility (*see SO8*). From South Georgia it is probably best to head first towards the Falklands before turning SW again.

There is a weak adverse current on this trip. Winds will vary mainly between NW and SW. Weatherly yachts will be able to take the most favourable tack and go directly to windward. Those that find beating difficult may be advised to sail WNW for the Argentinian coast and then turn S in more sheltered waters with predominantly beam winds.

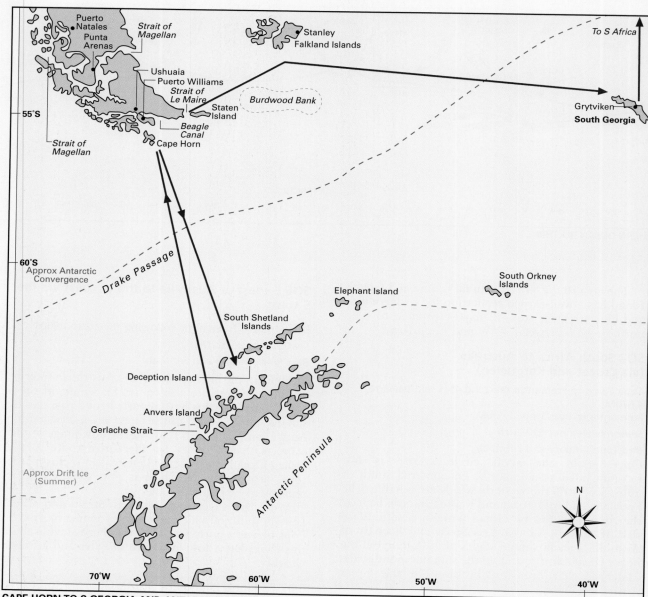

CAPE HORN TO S GEORGIA AND ANTARCTIC PENINSULA

SO8 Tierra del Fuego to South Africa (via South Georgia)

Strait of Le Maire to South Georgia 1,010M
South Georgia to Tristan da Cunha 1,440M
Tristan da Cunha to Cape Town 1,290M

Season November to March

Best time January and February

Around a dozen yachts make the trip to South Georgia each year, with the numbers steadily growing. Several of these will be charterers who make the trip regularly. It is not an easy passage and many yachts have been capsized or run into ice. (In the year that one author (AO'G) visited, he heard of three boats that hit ice, two of which abandoned the trip).

As ice is the greatest danger, it is advisable to lessen the distance within the Antarctic Convergence by steering N of the Burwood Bank, passing S of the Falklands and approaching South Georgia from the WNW. Likewise, if departing for South Africa, it is wise to steer N until clear of the Antarctic Convergence before heading towards Cape Town.

Some routes to the Southern Ocean

IOS1 Cocos Keeling to Fremantle
See Chapter 5 Indian Ocean

SPE1 Easter Island to Puerto Montt
See Chapter 3 South Pacific Ocean

SAN1 Cape Town North
See Chapter 2 South Atlantic Ocean

SAS4 Rio de la Plata to Tierra del Fuego
See Chapter 2 South Atlantic Ocean

COUNTRY AND PORT GUIDE

 New Zealand

See Chapter 3 South Pacific for country information

NELSON

Tidal range 4.2m

Navigation

Beware of entering on a strong ebbing tide against a fresh N wind. The yacht harbour is in Dixon Basin in the E part of the harbour. The depth in the outer part of the basin is maintained at 4m but drops to 1.8 at the S end.

Anchorage

There are a few private moorings near the entrance but this is not a practical option for visiting yachts.

Berths

Currently there are 500 berths and the number is growing. Visitors are given a vacant berth and there are usually plenty available. Charge band 2.

Facilities

Fuel and water alongside at the marina. Yacht builders and repairs; any size of yacht can be slipped (larger vessels in the commercial dockyard, which is very close to the yacht facilities). Sailmakers, chandlers, all mechanical and electrical services. Good shopping in the city.

Remarks

Nelson provides an exceptionally good stopover for any vessel voyaging in the Southern Ocean. Nearby are the outstanding cruising grounds of Tasman Bay and Marlborough Sounds. Wellington, the capital of New Zealand, is a short sail away with all the attractions of a major city. Fiordland and Stewart Island, two of the world's most pristine wildernesses and exciting cruising grounds, are a few days away.
www.nelsoncitycouncil.co.nz/sports/facilities/
boating/marina/marina.htm

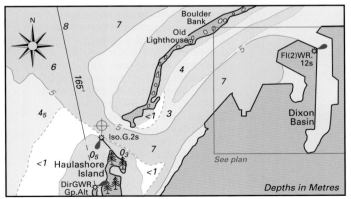

PORT NELSON (New Zealand)
⊕41°15´·44S 173°17´·17E

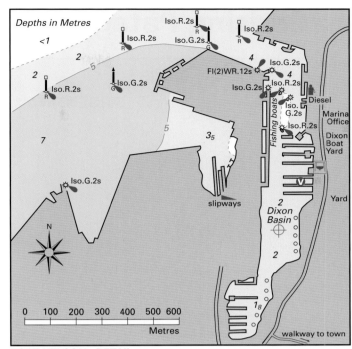

PORT NELSON - DETAIL
⊕41°15´·7S 173°16´·9E

 Chile

General Chile is a marvellous cruising destination. It has a well developed infrastructure and institutions and is a safe, friendly and interesting country to visit. (One author (AO'G) considers the cruising here to be the very best he has experienced in the world.) More and more yachts are choosing to cruise here so facilities can be expected to continue improving over the next few years.

Coastline N of Canal Chacao (41°48'S 73°54'W) the coast has few indentations and natural harbours. S of this point lie thousands of islands, channels and superb natural harbours. This area offers one of the world's greatest wilderness experiences.

Formalities Do not land before checking in at a port of entry. Contact the navy (*Armada de Chile*) who are responsible for all maritime affairs. They will generally visit and organise the other authorities (customs, immigration and agriculture). In addition to the normal papers for crew and ship, radio licenses and evidence of third party insurance are sometimes requested. Citizens of the US, EU, Australia and New Zealand do not require visas (2003).

Maritime disputes Chile is involved in a long-standing dispute with Argentina over three small islands at the E entrance to the Beagle Channel (Canal Beagle), the position of the frontier where it crosses Tierra del Fuego and rights of navigation through Canal Murray (which, were it not strictly closed to all but Chilean flagged vessels, would provide good access to Ushuaia from Bahía Nassau and Cape Horn). This situation creates a certain

Cruising Patagonia

Everyone seems to have their own definition of what constitutes Patagonia. For the purposes of this book I will call it all of South America lying S of a line between Puerto Montt on the Pacific coast and Península Valdes on the Atlantic at around 42°S. The area provides a huge variety of excellent cruising, from temperate farmland to rainforest, glaciated fjords, the storms of Cape Horn and the arid wastes of the Argentine Pampas. The area has some distinct regions:

Chiloé to Golfo de Penas

Chiloé is a large island at the northern end of Patagonia, the climate is mild and the soil fertile. Indigenous tribes and the Spaniards, who arrived early in the 1500s, have merged to breed fine people who have been caught in a time warp where language and traditions hark back to an earlier day. One can sail into a sheltered anchorage on a sunny evening and see apple-laden carts drawn by oxen to a wooden cider press. Fishermen will come by with fresh fish and oysters. Smoked salmon is plentiful and cheap at the markets.

The large island shelters an archipelago from the Pacific swells, and the winds tend to be moderate. One can visit town to hear traditional music, sail out to a rural island or in half a day sail across to the dramatic fjords that lie at the foot of the Andes, the snowcapped volcanic peaks which are hardly ever out of sight.

S of Chiloé in the canals (channels) of Patagonia the yacht enters a magnificent cruising ground. Though the climate can be harsh, this contrasts with some of the most secure and tranquil anchorages to be found anywhere. The crew can feel as though they are amongst the first to sail these waters. Indeed, information available covers only a tiny proportion of the available waterways and anchorages; the scope for exploration is almost unlimited. In the N are miles of delightful cruising: through the rugged, mountainous islands and canales of the Archipelago de los Chonos. On the coast at the S end, Península Taitao leads round to Golfo de Penas, where the first (or last when coming from the S) of more consistently difficult weather may be expected.

The South

Golfo de Penas to Cabo de Hornos is roughly a thousand miles to sail. The entire coast is a maze of offshore islands and sheltered inshore canales where a boat can sail at any time of year. Puerto Edén (49°S 74°W) is the only settlement of any size on the main canales. In the far S Punta Arenas is a major city but a poor yacht anchorage and Puerto Williams is a small naval and fishing settlement. Puerto Natales, an important tourist town and source of supplies, is 60M off the main route. The route passes through the Straits of Magellan and Beagle Canal. Rugged, wet, often extremely windy with *ráfagas* (williwaws) churning the water into flying spume and *rachas* (another term for williwaws) spinning yachts on their anchors, if

Seno Pia on Beagle Canal

A calm winter day in the Beagle Canal - *Balaena* encounters a little ice

they hold, the canales are awe-inspiring but quite delightful and incredibly scenic whatever the conditions. There are numerous anchorages where, with care, a yacht can be perfectly secure.

Argentine Patagonia

To the E of Cape Horn, with the exception of Staten island, the coastline becomes smoother, drier and less mountainous. Good anchorages are few and the winds blowing across the pampas are cruel and strong. However, the few destinations that are available are delightful: small towns with wonderfully warm people or isolated anchorages with clear blue water rich in marine life and almost desert conditions on shore. At the northern extremity of Argentine Patagonia lies Peninsula Valdez which is, from mid winter to early summer, home to a large number of breeding whales.

Weather

The two main factors are the position of the S Pacific High and the continuous stream of depressions that move from W to E in the Southern Ocean. Sandwiched between these two systems is a belt of usually strong W winds. Fronts associated with the depressions bring a change in wind from NW to SW. They also bring rain and snow to the Chilean coast but on the Argentinean side tend to be dry. Because the Chilean canales run from NNW to SSE, winds with a W component are usually funnelled from the N, though occasionally the passage of a front can bring a short lived but fierce S wind.

In winter, when the S Pacific High lies more to the N and the depressions may be expected to pass directly over the continent, it is not uncommon for a fairly stable high pressure to form over the Pampas of Southern Patagonia due to the intense cold. These highs, which often remain for several weeks on end, can bring splendid weather in the S with many days of cloudless skies, intense sunshine and little wind. In this situation the depressions are forced S of Cape Horn and isobars are squashed to give the weather that has earned the Drake Passage such a foul reputation.

Cruising strategies

On the Pacific side it is always preferable to sail from N to S with the prevailing winds. However, most boats arrive from the Atlantic and want to sail S to N. I strongly recommend that you do this in winter (July to September) as you are much less likely to spend your days fighting against fierce head winds in the rain.

To enjoy cruising in the far S, to visit Cape Horn or the glaciers, winter is also the best time. All the old hands are agreed: the southern winter is the best time to be in Southern Patagonia.

Winter also seems to be a good time to make a passage on the Argentinean coast as the average wind strength is considerably lower than in summer (though short days

Glacier on Beagle Canal

and tricky river entrances make reaching port a bit difficult). However, this passage is entirely practical at any time of year as the prevailing wind is W and therefore a reach in either direction.

Useful books

Chile RCCPF / Andy O'Grady (Imray)
Patagonia Cruising Guide Ardrizi
Argentina (RCCPF) Free download at rccpf.org.uk

My gem

Uttermost part of the earth
E. Lucas Bridges

Puerto Hoppner, Isle de los Estados, Argentina

amount of tension in the area and yachts are frequently challenged on VHF as to their identity, crew and destination. Naval officials on both sides are extremely polite and helpful and it pays to comply with all requirements. In the event that the skipper believes that it would endanger the vessel to comply with directions, to use a specific anchorage for instance, the authorities are invariably understanding.

Telecommunications IDD +56. GSM network in the vicinity of major centres.

Currency Chilean peso. ATMs common. Credit cards widely accepted.

Sailing season Within the Patagonian waterways, yachts can sail at any time of year. Winter in the far S is cold but has long spells of fine weather. In the open sea S of Valparaíso it is preferable to sail in summer only.

Routes and harbours Most yachts visiting Chile will be planning to cruise in the Patagonian waterways. Sailing from N to S is much the easiest option as the mountains and orientation of channels tends to make NW the predominant wind direction. Those wishing to sail S to N often choose to do so in winter when there are more periods of calm and occasional E or S winds. Some well-found yachts choose to make the passage N offshore where they can take advantage of the SW winds. The most popular choices for a sailing base are Valdivia and Puerto Montt, both of which have good marinas and adequate facilities. Puerto Williams, less than 100 miles N of Cape Horn, has an excellent little marina, often used to leave vessels for long periods.

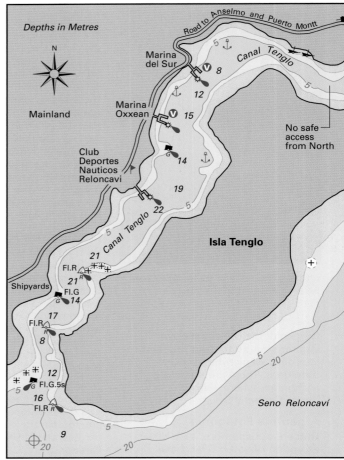

PUERTO MONTT (Chile)
⊕41°31′·0S 72°59′·9W

PUERTO MONTT

Tidal range 7m

Navigation

Enter Canal Tenglo from the SW (the north is very shallow at low water and the route is often encumbered by large ships and their mooring lines). Make certain to pass on the Isla Tenglo side of the green buoy which marks a reef off the N entrance point.

Berths

There are always berths at Marina Oxxean, Marina del Sur or Club Deportes Náuticos Reloncaví. Charge band 2.

Anchorage

On the mainland side between Marina Oxxean and Marina del Sur or on the Isla Tenglo side to the SW of Marina Oxxean. Neither anchorage is secure and there is no easy landing place.

Facilities

Port of entry. Fuel can be taken alongside at Marina Oxxean. Yacht repairs can be undertaken. There is a large travel-lift at Marina del Sur but no hard standing. Club Deportes Náuticos Reloncaví has a travel lift of 36-tons capacity and storage space ashore. Larger vessels could possibly be accommodated in one of several commercial shipyards. Sailmakers in nearby Valdivia, some chandlery, all mechanical and electrical services. Good supermarkets and shopping in the city.

Remarks

This is a good first port of call and officials and marina staff have a well-deserved reputation for helpfulness. Other yachts will almost certainly be in the port and able to advise about local conditions. www.oxxean.cl

Resources

PILOTS, GUIDES AND CHARTS
Chile RCC/Ed. Andy O'Grady (Imray)
Atlas Hidrográfico. (Servicio Hidrográfico y Oceanográfico de la Armada (SHOA). All Chilean charts in one volume produced by the Chilean navy, reduced to ¼ size.

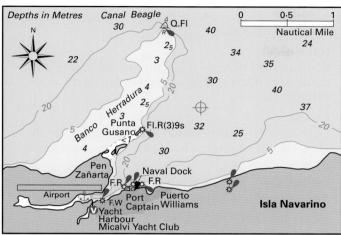

PUERTO WILLIAMS (Chile)
⊕54°55'·0S 67°35'·0W

PUERTO WILLIAMS

Tidal range 2m

Navigation

Yachts drawing over 2m must pass to the N of Banco Herradura (when approaching from the W). Those with less draught may pass 75–100m N of Punta Gusano, the NW entrance point, marked by a red tower.

Berths

Alongside the *Micalvi*, a hulk, used as a yacht club and mooring pier. Space is limited (to about 10 yachts) and in winter may all be used up unless prior arrangement has been made. Though less than 100M from Cape Horn, this is one of the securest berths in the area. Charge band 2.

Anchorage

The authorities are unlikely to allow a yacht to anchor here, but may allow one to moor to the large buoy N of the *Micalvi* with an anchor out to hold the yacht off.

Facilities

Port of entry. Showers, toilets and a bar on the *Micalvi*. No power. Simple repairs can be undertaken. The navy will try to help but their facilities are limited. Fuel must be fetched by jerrycan and is more expensive than in Ushuaia. There is a small supermarket with basic provisions, a bank, and internet café and airline office serving local flights. Those needing more should visit Ushuaia.

Remarks

This is a good first port of call if planning to cruise in Chile and officials are helpful. Other yachts will almost certainly be in the port and able to advise about local conditions.

Argentina

See Chapter 2 South Atlantic Ocean for country information.

USHUAIA

Tidal range 2m

Navigation

Entry is straightforward and dangers are well marked. The city lights may complicate entrance at night.

Berths

On the long pontoon of AFASyN, a busy yacht club. Visitors may need to raft up in summer when it is crowded. Charge band 2.

Anchorage

The W, more sheltered, part of the harbour is relatively shallow and occupied by yachts on moorings. It can be difficult to find an anchorage. Moorings are sometimes available for rent from AFASyN.

Facilities

Showers, toilets and a bar at the club. Repairs can be undertaken, there is a possibility of hauling at the club though there are no facilities installed. Engineering services and parts readily available. Fuel can be taken from alongside at the fuel depot just to the east of the main pier. No chandlery, though much can be obtained from Buenos Aires. The city has all supplies, banks, internet cafés and a major airport.

Remarks

The harbour is subject to strong W winds even though it blows off the land. E winds can be dangerous here. This is a poor place to leave a yacht unattended – Puerto Williams is far better. A good first port of call and for obtaining supplies. It is much used by charter vessels operating in the Cape Horn region and Antarctica.

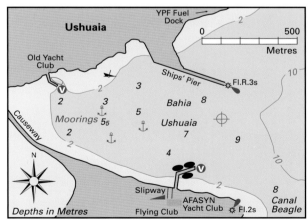

USHUAIA (Argentina)
⊕54°48'·7S 68°18'·0W

Falkland Islands

General The islands are British possessions. They have fascinating flora and fauna and are increasingly popular with tourists who come to see the prolific bird life, which includes several penguin colonies. There is no indigenous population; however, just under three thousand people live here, mainly in Stanley but with small settlements and isolated homesteads scattered about 'camp', as the country is called. Britain maintains a military presence of one to two thousand servicemen and women.

Coastline There are two main islands but over 200 individual islands. The total area exceeds 12,000km². Many off-lying dangers make for interesting navigation.

Formalities All visitors must have a valid passport. Visas are not required for visitors from the EU, Commonwealth or USA. A fee of £11 sterling is payable for all visitors over twelve years disembarking.

Maritime claims and disputes See notes on Argentina in *Chapter 2 South Atlantic*.

Telecommunications IDD +500. Internet and Email facilities and Facsimile are all available.

Currency Pound sterling. There is a bank in Stanley and credit cards are generally accepted.

Sailing season Weather is very changeable and can be very windy at any time of year. Most yachts visit in summer.

STANLEY

Tidal range (springs) 2m

Navigation
The coast is tortuous, tidal currents are strong and there are many off-lying reefs. Navigate with extreme caution.

Berths
Occasionally yachts have been allowed to lie alongside the commercial or naval berths. Neither of these is secure in a blow.

Anchorage
The anchorage is off the town and is sheltered from the seas but can be extremely windy.

Facilities
There are no facilities for yachts. Supplies can be obtained but fresh produce is very limited. Engineering work of moderate complexity can be undertaken and spare parts may be obtained from the UK.

Remarks
There is excellent cruising and many fascinating anchorages amongst the islands.

Resources

PILOTS AND GUIDES
Falkland Islands Shores (RCCPF)

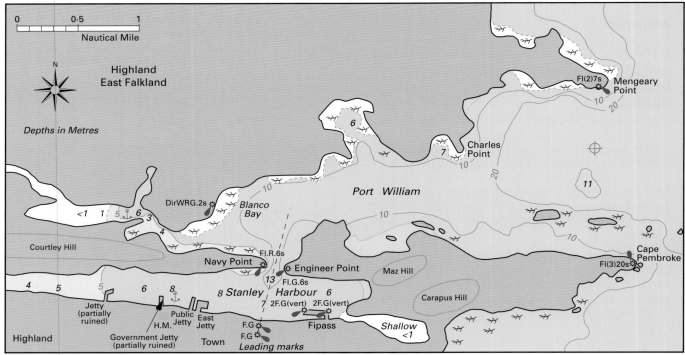

PORT STANLEY (Falkland Islands)
⊕51°39´·5S 57°44´·0W

South Africa

See Chapter 2 South Atlantic Ocean for country and port information (Cape Town).

Australia

See Chapter 3 South Pacific Ocean for country and more port information.

Coastline The South coast of Australia is mostly barren and inhospitable, but there are a few excellent natural harbours along the way, with the Great Australian Bight being the only stretch without refuge. Tasmania has many good harbours and some very rewarding cruising.

FREMANTLE

Tide 0.8m

Navigation

Do not enter the Swan River, which leads to Perth via busy commercial docks. There are three harbours at Fremantle – choose one of the two yacht harbours. Both are easy to enter.

Berths

There is a lack of formal visitors' berths but visitors are very welcome and will be allowed to use vacant berths. It may be possible to arrange with one of the clubs for a longer stay; a prior letter of introduction from the home club has been of assistance here.

Facilities

Fuel and water alongside. There are several large and very friendly clubs. Any size of vessel can be slipped or lifted out and all repairs can be undertaken. There is a range of excellent chandlers. Every possible facility and all provisions are available in Fremantle or Perth.

Remarks

The SW 'Fremantle Doctor', wind blows strongly here, especially in the summer months, so that manoeuvring in the harbour can be difficult. There is very good cruising in SW Australia.
Fremantle Sailing Club: www.fsc.com.au

HOBART

Tidal range 1.2m

Navigation

Approach and entrance are straightforward. If entering one of the docks, call port control on Ch 16 or 12 to request opening of the entrance bridge.

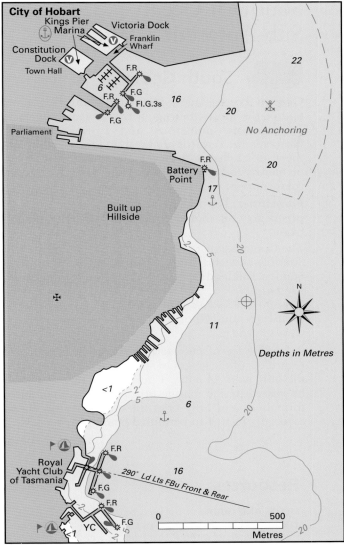

HOBART (Tasmania)
⊕42°53′·5S 177°20′·5E

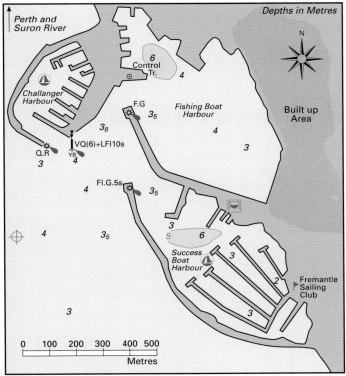

FREMANTLE (Australia)
⊕32°04′·0S 115°44′·3E

Berths

The clubs always have visitors' berths available and it is possible to find a berth in the marina in Constitution Dock or at King's Pier Marina (up to 17m).

Facilities

Fuel and water alongside. The clubs are very welcoming to visitors. There is a boatyard with slip and crane and all repairs can be undertaken. Every possible facility and all provisions are available in Hobart.

Remarks

Hobart is a major centre for sailing in southern latitudes and for yachts wishing to visit Australian Antarctic Territory. Tasmania, especially the nearby De Entrecasteaux Channel, has some fabulous cruising.
Kings pier: www.hpc.com.au
Royal Yacht Club of Tasmania: www.ryct.org.au

Southern Ocean
Sub-Antarctic Islands

South Georgia

General The passage to and from South Georgia is one of the most challenging that a yacht can face. Icebergs are numerous and storms frequent. However, the rewards are great and the island offers the visitor a chance to view a place where the impact of man is today minimal and the animal kingdom rules supreme.

Formalities The islands are British possessions. A permit to visit should be obtained prior to sailing, from:

The Commissioner for South Georgia and the South Sandwich Islands, Government House, Stanley, Falkland Islands, South Atlantic via United Kingdom
✆ +500 27433 *Fax* +500 27434
Email gov.house@horizon.co.fk
www.sgisland.gs

A landing fee of £60 sterling per yacht is collected regardless of the length of stay. King Edward Point is the only place of entry. Upon arrival the vessel will be visited by the marine officer who will complete formalities and fully brief the crew on procedures, especially related to permitted landing areas.

Resources

PILOTS AND GUIDES
The RCCPF publishes a guide to South Georgia, available for download without cost from its website www.rccpf.org.uk

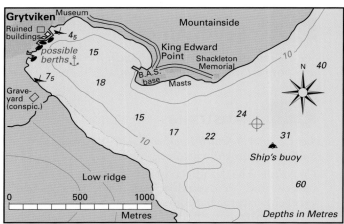

GRYTVIKEN (South Georgia)
⊕54°17'·25S 36°29'·0W

GRYTVIKEN

Tidal range 0.6m

Navigation

The coast is tortuous, ice floes are common and there are many off-lying reefs. Navigate with extreme caution.

Berths

It may be possible to use one of the old wharves and very occasionally yachts have been invited to use the wharf at the base. Neither of these is comfortable in a blow.

Anchorage

The anchorage is off the old whaling station, where holding and shelter are fairly good but conditions can be extreme.

Facilities

The only facilities of any sort are a post office and small gift shop. No food or supplies are available. The visitor must be entirely self-sufficient.

Crozet and Kerguelen

General The islands are French possessions. They are not far off the best route between S Africa and Australia and, though they are within the extreme limit for icebergs, the ice danger in their vicinity is low. Both groups of islands are interesting habitats for Antarctic wildlife and are protected.

Formalities It is believed that a permit to visit should be obtained prior to sailing. However, a French yachtsman made repeated enquiries in Paris and Réunion on our behalf and failed to obtain a response. It is reported that some yachts have been allowed to make limited cruises after arriving without a permit and reporting to the administrative centres at Crique de Navire, Île de la Possession 46°26'·5S 51°52'·4E (Crozet) or Port-aux-Français 49°21'·7S 70°11'·8E (Kerguelen) (treat these GPS co-ordinates with extreme suspicion). However, it has also been reported that prohibitively high daily

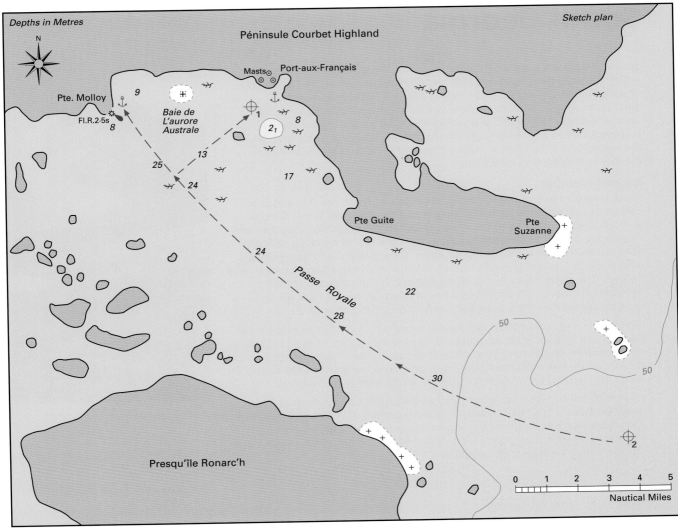

Depths in Metres

Péninsule Courbet Highland

Sketch plan

N

Pte. Molloy

Masts○

Port-aux-Français

9

Fl.R.2·5s 8

Baie de
L'aurore
Australe

1

8

13

2 1

25

24

17

Pte Guite

Pte
Suzanne

24

Passe Royale

22

28

50

30

50

2

Presqu'île Ronarc'h

0   1   2   3   4   5

Nautical Miles

ILES KERGUELEN
⊕1 49°22′S 70°12′W
⊕2 49°33′S 70°30′W

charges are made. Note that the waypoints on the sketch are for the seaward approach and the anchorage off Port aux Français.

Tidal range 2m (Kerguelen).

Anchorages

Crozet has little in the way of suitable anchorages. Kerguelen has a number in its many fjords, though Port-aux-Français, the administrative centre, is very exposed (behind Pte Molloy is probably more sheltered, but is 5M from the base). The weather is severe in both places, with gale force winds likely to occur much more frequently that the 10% reported for Kerguelen in January.

 ## Campbell and Auckland Islands

General The islands are a part of New Zealand.
Formalities A permit to visit should be obtained prior to sailing, from Ranger (Concessions Management),

Southern Islands Area, Department of Conservation, PO Box 743, Invercargill ① (03) 214 7536.
Or make contact via the DOC website:
www.doc.govt.nz

A large fee will be required and it is stated that a National Park Ranger must be taken aboard if landings are to be made. A small yacht may be able to negotiate over the need to carry a ranger.

Tidal range 1m

Navigation

Both islands are rugged, with many indentations and off-lying dangers.

Anchorage

Several good anchorages are available.

Facilities

No food or supplies are available. The visitor must be entirely self-sufficient.

South Georgia

South Georgia is a magnificent destination for the experienced cruiser. The sailing is challenging, requiring skill and thorough preparation. The scenery, often glimpsed through snow or rolling cloud, is marvellous beyond description. The wildlife, in its unbelievable abundance and variety, offers a unique feeling of viewing the world as it was before the presence of mankind. Indeed the beaches are almost entirely occupied by fur seals and in the earlier part of summer it is almost impossible to land because of their number and aggressive reception.

Ice and Weather

South Georgia lies S of the Antarctic convergence. Therefore the islands are bathed in cold Antarctic water flowing in an ENE direction. In this flow are numerous icebergs, some of them enormous tabular bergs. At times they are clustered together, presumably resulting from the recent break up of larger ones, at others they are scattered far apart. If bergs are sited there will be smaller bergy bits and growlers in the vicinity and an extra good lookout must be kept. The outer limit of ice is about 400 miles in the direction of the Falklands, further in the direction of South Africa. In winter, pack ice occasionally reaches the S coast but rarely, if ever, progresses to the N.

A continuous stream of deep depressions moving from W to E dominates the weather. An occasional depression originates in the vicinity of the Falklands and crosses South Georgia. Most often they pass to the S giving winds from the W quarter but occasionally they pass over or to the N with cyclonic and E winds. Precipitation is often in the form of snow, even in mid summer.

All year round the weather is unsettled and variable. Long periods of unsettled weather can be followed by superb periods of anticyclonic weather. The barometer is often little help in predicting weather, which is strongly influenced by local topography. Visitors should be prepared for the worst and can then often be pleasantly surprised.

Fortuna glacier

St Andrews Bay, South Georgia

Getting there

The majority of yachts arrive from Stanley, Ushuaia or Puerto Williams. Leaving is more difficult than arriving. By choosing a weather window some vessels succeed in making a good passage back to Stanley. Others head N to Uruguay, which usually involves facing a lot of N wind. Charter yachts regularly slog back to Ushuaia but this requires time, luck and a large diesel. A few vessels take the downwind, but rough, route to Cape Town.

Anchoring

There is no anchorage in South Georgia totally protected from all winds. The vessel must be capable of putting to sea in extreme conditions and have gear considerably heavier than normally used to withstand wind and sea blowing onshore. Be prepared to take lines ashore to rocky outcrops.

Stores and facilities

Freshwater, ice, and dandelion leaves are the only commodities available locally. Everything else must be carried on-board. Total self sufficiency is expected by the authorities. There are absolutely no Search and Rescue facilities and no facilities to aid yachts. In the event of being shipwrecked, a yacht's crew would need to be able to survive for weeks in an inhospitable environment and would need radio communications to attract assistance. Grytviken has a post office but mail is infrequent. The facilities of the British Antarctic Survey base are unavailable to yachtsmen.

Ashore

Apart from a few scientific reserves the yachtsman is free to make short trips ashore and there are many fascinating walks and climbs and countless opportunities for observing the wildlife close to. Sometimes too close, as in the case of aggressive fur seals. Special permits are required for overnight stays on shore. In any case, it would be unwise to leave the boat unattended for more than a few hours. Many people are interested in the abandoned whaling stations. All the stations and jetties, other than Grytviken, are off limits. The stations were closed due to the risks the visitor faces from asbestos and chemicals in the industrial installations and from flying sheet iron and other debris.

South Georgia

Useful books

Antarctic Oasis T. Carr, and P. W.W. Norton 1998. Beautifully illustrated account of the yacht *Curlew's* cruises 1992–1997 in South Georgia.

The Totorore Voyage: An Antarctic Adventure G. Clark. (Century Hutchinson 1988 and Homelands Publications, Kerikeri, New Zealand.) Ornithological expedition of the yacht Totorore that included two winter cruises to South Georgia, 1984 and 1985.

Website (with lots of information and forms to download – look under visitors and applications): www.sgisland.gs

Free notes by Pete Hill and Andy O'Grady at rccpf.org.uk

My gem

South: The Story of Shackleton's Last Expedition, 1914–17, Sir Ernest Shackleton

Southern Ocean gale with sea anchor

Handling lines in the snow can be cold work

Melchoir Islands, a perfect anchorage

Meet the locals

Leopard seals seem to spend most of the day resting

Setting shore lines in the snow

Sailing to Antarctica

The Drake Passage between Cape Horn and the South Shetland Islands is probably the most feared stretch of water on earth. A constant stream of depressions pass around the globe and are squeezed through this narrow gap between the land masses of S America and the Antarctic Peninsula. Isobars already tight together get even tighter and the wind can blow with hurricane force or more! During our crossing the barograph aboard Balæna hovered around 960, even with relatively light winds of 30–40 knots, we were all sick as dogs in these 'good' conditions. Nearing Antarctica there is the added danger of ice and the uncertainty as to whether the centre of the depressions will pass to the N or the S and if the trip will end with a sudden E gale blowing against the huge W swells generated by the same depression a little to the N. Having arrived in Antarctica there are very few truly safe anchorages, holding is often poor, winds strong and bits of ice float around constantly to keep you on your toes. I don't want to encourage anyone to make this trip because it is dangerous and yachts are lost regularly in this area. Add to this the bureaucratic hurdles that each yacht must go through to obtain a permit from the Antarctic authority in their home country, the lack of cruising guides, the poor detail of charts and the total absence of any support facilities. I recommend that you sail on one of the charter boats that make this trip several times a year. Just a look at these boats will demonstrate why I make this recommendation, they define the words: strong, seaworthy and well prepared!

However, there are those of us crazy enough to take our little cockleshells into these waters and the rewards are enormous. Wildlife is not as awe inspiring as in South Georgia, but there are sufficient penguins and seals to keep everyone amused, whales are a daily sighting and there are many fascinating sea birds. But it is the scenery of the frozen continent which is so amazing. Nothing can prepare you for the sight of ice that covers virtually every bit of land, usually to hundreds of metres in thickness. A normal anchorage is just a cleft in massive walls of ice and snow that tower above the boat and make ominous rumblings all day and night. Every now and then hundreds or thousands of tons of ice crash into the water and set the boat shaking. And when the sun shines the scenery is quite beyond description and the vastness of the view cannot be captured on camera.

Practicalities

There is no guide book. Those that take the trouble to befriend the skippers of charter boats working in the area will often receive much advice and help. But these experienced seamen will want to have confidence in your ability not to cause a problem for everyone. Don't expect to show up in the middle of their busy summer season and receive a package of information from professionals who are hard pressed to meet all the demands of their own vessels and guests.

All vessels must obtain a permit prior to departure from the authorities in their home country and comply with the requirements during the visit, potential penalties for not doing so are great and the damage done to the interests of other yachts and visitors by not complying with the regulations may eventually result in a total prohibition of yacht visits.

Most vessels choose to leave from Chilean waters, thus shortening the journey a little and allowing for a departure anchorage near to Cape Horn. It makes most sense to sail for the South Shetland Islands first, a course that is E of S, making the winds a little more favourable. Don't linger too long in these islands as the weather is better and scenery more interesting on the Peninsula, especially in the area of the Strait of Lemaire. When returning to S America, it is common practice to depart from the Melchoir Islands, thus being a little more to the W and gaining a little distance to windward for the return crossing.

Sunset and penguins

The availability of grib files downloaded as email attachments has made the crossing much less hazardous. It is usually possible to pick a spell of 3–4 days with lighter winds. However, most sailors in the area estimate that you can add 10 knots to the predicted wind strengths and anything over 20 knots can turn out to be a gale.

An afterthought

In early March 2009 when *Balæna* was sheltering in tranquil waters near Cape Horn, several charter yachts had to ride out a 120 knot gale in Deception Island. When I consider the size of the motors and rigging on these vessels and depth of experience of the skippers I have serious doubts that we would have been able to keep Balæna off the rocks.

Flippers? *Magnus O'Grady*

Reading

Southern Ocean Cruising, Sally and Jerome Poncet.
Free download from http://www.era.gs/resources/soc/index.shtml.
This is a guide to the rules and regulations and responsible environmental behaviour it provides little practical information for sailing.

Antarctica (Lonely Planet). This is a good source of information of a touristic type. RCCPF, some notes available for free download at www.rccpf.org.uk

Night near the Antarctic circle

My gem
Scott and Amundsen, Roland Huntford

Ice can be very beautiful

APPENDIX

1. Resources

Note that all the chapters also have a Resources list of books and websites at the end of each relevant section. These resources are not meant to be definitive and often relate to books and websites the authors and others have used and found useful.

BOOKS

Planning

Ocean Passages of the World UKHO NP136
The Mariner's Handbook UKHO NP100
Admiralty World Catalogue UKHO NP131
World Cruising Routes Jimmy Cornell (Adlard Coles Nautical)
World Cruising Handbook Jimmy Cornell (Adlard Coles Nautical)
Circumnavigator's Handbook Steve & Linda Dashew (Beowulf Inc)
Offshore Cruising Encyclopaedia Steve & Linda Dashew (Beowulf Inc)
Mariner's Weather Handbook Steve & Linda Dashew (Beowulf Inc)
Tropical Cruising Handbook Mark Smaalders & Kim des Rochers (International Marine)
Cruising in Tropical Waters & Coral Alan Lucas (Adlard Coles Nautical).

Boat

Cruising Under Sail E Hiscock (International Marine)
Celestial Navigation for Yachtsmen M Blewitt (McGraw-Hill)
How to sail around the world H Roth (International Marine)
Seaworthiness. The Forgotten Factor C A Marchaj. (Adlard Coles Nautical)
Voyaging on a Small Income Annie & Pete Hill (Waterline/Adlard Coles Nautical)
Blue Water Countdown Geoff Pack (Yachting Monthly)
Sensible Cruising: The Thoreau Approach Don Casey & Lew Hackler (International Marine)
Heavy Weather Sailing K Adlard Coles (Adlard Coles Nautical).

On-board manuals

West Marine Catalogue Annual commercial catalogue for West Marine shops, with helpful pages analysing what sort of equipment is needed and how to fit it
This old boat Don Casey (International Marine/McGraw Hill)
Boat Owner's Mechanical and Electrical Manual Nigel Calder (Adlard Coles Nautical)
RYA Book of Diesel Engines Tim Bartlett (Adlard Coles Nautical)
Electrics Afloat Alastair Garod (Adlard Coles Nautical)
Fibreglass Boats Hugo de Plessis (Adlard Coles Nautical)

Practical Sail Care & Repair Lisa Car (Adlard Coles Nautical)
Dangerous Marine Animals Bruce Halstead
First Aid at Sea Douglas Justins & Colin Berry (Adlard Coles Nautical).

Wider reading

Oceanography & Seamanship William G van Dorn (Cornell Maritime Press)
Oceanography R Gordon Pirie (Oxford University Press)
A Sailor's Guide to Wind, Waves & Tides Alex Simpson (Adlard Coles Nautical)
The Long Summer Brian Fagan (Granta)
Sealife: A Guide to the Marine Environment Ed. Geoffrey Walle
The Natural History of Whales & Dolphins Peter G H Evans (Christopher Helm)
Seabirds of the World Peter Harrison (Christopher Helm)
Collins Photo Guide to Tropical Plants W Lotschert & G Beese (Harper Collins).

SOFTWARE

Visual Passage Planner 2 (Digital Wave) Excellent routeing software (both authors use it). www.digwave.com
Raytech Navigator (Raymarine) (displays grib files). www.raymarine.com
Maxsea Navigation software (displays grib files) and raster charts. www.maxsea.com
Offshore Navigator (Maptech) www.maptech.com
SeaPro (Euronav) www.euronav.co.uk
C-map Vector charts www.c-map.com
Navionics Vector charts www.navionics.com
Garmin Mapsource www.garmin.com
Yotreps Voyager. Position-reporting software www.pangolin.co.nz
Wxtide Freeware world tide software (uses old tidal differences) www.wxtide32.com

WEBSITES

Sailmail www.sailmail.com
Armchair Sailor www.bluewaterweb.com/armchair_info.asp
Noonsite www.noonsite.com
Setsail www.setsail.com
Long passages www.longpassages.org
Sailnet www.sailnet.com
Cruising Association www.cruising.org.uk
Seven Seas Cruising Association www.ssca.org
RCC Pilotage Foundation www.rccpf.org.uk
Imray www.imray.com
UKHO www.ukho.gov.uk
West Marine www.westmarine.com
Marine radio nets www.marinenet.net
US National Weather Service www.nws.noaa.gov
Rod Heikell www.tell-tales.info

2. A selection of radio and weather fax services

Corrected to March 2005 – fax details change often.
(All frequencies are in kHz and times are UTC. Transmissions are 24hrs unless stated.)

North Atlantic

VHF Continuous broadcasts of local weather information on VHF Wx channels in USA and Canada.

Weather Fax
Northwood, United Kingdom
2618.5, 4610, 8040, 11086.5. Schedule broadcast at 0100, 1300
Halifax, Nova Scotia, Canada
122.5, 4271, 6496.4, 10536, 13510. Schedule broadcast at 1100
New Orleans, Louisiana, USA
4317.9, 8503.9, 12789.9, 17146.4, 1200–2045
Schedule broadcast at 0825/2025
Boston, Massachusetts, USA
4235 (0230–1015), 6340.5, 9110, 12750 (1400–2215).
Schedule broadcast 1405 and 1420 (Micronesia)

Other radio services
Ham nets

Trans Atlantic Net	21400	1300
Italian M/M Net Italian & English (IK6IJF)	14297	2000
'Le Réseau Du Capitain' Net (French)	14118	1200 +2330
(One hour earlier during Canada daylight time)		
UK M/M Net	14303+/–	0800 & 1800
Caribbean M/M Net Saint Croix	7241	1100
Northwest Caribbean Cruisers Net	8188	1400

South Pacific

Weather information
Weather forecasts are available from coast stations around Australia, the Fiji Meteorological service, New Zealand, Tahiti and Chile (For Easter Island).

Weather Fax
Australia
Australia broadcasts a huge array of weather information covering Australian waters, the E Indian Ocean, W Pacific and a large part of the Southern Ocean.

VMC (Queensland)

2628	0900–1900
5100	
11030	
13920	
20469	1900–0900

VMW (Western Australia)

5755	1100–2100
7535	
10555	
15615	
18060	2100–1100

A schedule of Australian faxes is broadcast daily, 0015/1215, 0030/1230.

New Zealand
Weather Faxes are broadcast throughout the 24 hours on the following frequencies. There is an excellent chart of the S Pacific.

3247.4	0945–1700
5807	
9459	
13550.5	
16340.1	2145–0500

Schedule broadcasts at 1100/2300.

Chile

Chile broadcasts an excellent weather chart for its coast and the SE Pacific from Valparaíso Radio.
4228
8677
17146.4.

Other radio services
Marine Radio SSB
New Zealand – Russell Radio:

4445	0730–0800	1900–2015
13137	0800–0900	1600–1645
Also		
12359	0830 & 1630 (NZ time)	
12353	0915.& 1600 (NZ time)	

Russell Radio often sets up a special time for yachts in the Southern Ocean and has managed to provide communications as far away as Brazil, and South Georgia, in the S Atlantic.

Chile - Patagonia Cruising Net

8164	0800 (Chilean time)

Amateur Radio

Maritime Mobile Service Net	14313/14300	0000/1600
Pacific Inter Island Net	14.315	0800 (Micronesia)
Pacific Seafarers Net.	14.313	0200–0325
Pacific Maritime Mobile Service Net	21.412	2130, 2200
Robby's Net, Australia	14.315	1000 and 2300
Tony's Net New Zealand ZL1ATE	14.315	2100

North Pacific

VHF
Continuous weather information is broadcast in the USA and Canada on VHF weather channels.

Weather Faxes
Kodiak, Alaska, USA

2054	1000–1159, 1600–1748
4298	Continuous
8459	Continuous
12412.5	0400–0548, 2200–0018

Schedules are broadcast at: 0527/1727
Pt Reyes, California, USA

4346.0	Night
8682	
12590.5	
17151.2	
22527.0	Day

Schedules at the following times:
1104 broadcast schedule (part 1)
1115 broadcast schedule (part 2)
2324 broadcast schedule (part 1)
2335 broadcast schedule (part 2)
KVM70, Honolulu, Hawaii, USA

9982.5	1030–1630
11090.0	0000–2400 except 2345–0345
16135.0	0000-2400 except 1030–1630
23331.5	2345-0345

Schedule broadcast at 1045

TOKYO, JAPAN
3622.5
7305
13597
18220

Amateur Radio

Maritime Mobile Service Net	14313/14300	0000/1600
Pacific Inter Island Net	14.315	0800
		(Micronesia)
Pacific Seafarers Net	14.313	0200–0325
Pacific Maritime Mobile		
Service Net	21.412	2130, 2200

Indian Ocean

Nairobi, Kenya
9044.9
17447.5 continuous

New Delhi, India
7404.9   1430-0230
14842.0   0230-1430
Schedule broadcast at 0340

Amateur Radio

SA Maritime Mobile Ham Net	7045 &14316	0630/1130
Eastern African Marine		
Radio Net (Kiore)	14316	0500

Mediterranean

Athens, Greece
4481
8105
Mediterranean M/M Net   7.085   0700

South Atlantic

Weather Fax
South Africa, Cape Naval Radio - ZSJ
4 014   1600–0600 (When TX available)
7 508
13 538
18 238   0600–1600 (When TX available)

Amateur Radio
South Africa – Maritime Net
7045 & 14316   0630 &1130
Italy – M/M Net (Italian & English spoken)
14.297   2000 (1900 between 30 Mar & 20 Oct)
SSB
South Africa Piri-piri net
8180   1500
8297   1500
12353   1500
16528   1500

Southern Ocean

Weather information
Chile, South Africa, Australia and New Zealand offer regular faxes and weather forecasts on HF. The weather nets in the relevant ocean cover the southern section of each ocean well. See above under S Pacific, Indian and S Atlantic oceans.

3. Conversions

S.I. - BRITISH UNITS
* Indicates a conversion factor which is exact.

LENGTH

	British units to S.I		S.I. units to British	
millimetre (mm)	1 in	= 25·4 mm*	1 mm	= 0·039 370in
centimetre (cm)	1 in	= 2.54 cm*	1 m	= 3·280 83ft
metre (m)	1 yd	= 0·9144 m*	1 m	= 1·093 61yd
kilometre (km)	1 N Mile	= 1.852 km	1km	= 0.539 N Mile (approx)
kilometre (km)	1 mile	= 1·609 34 km	1 km	= 0·621 371 Mile

OTHER COMMON CONVERSIONS

Nautical Mile	1 N Mile	= 1.151 M	1M	= 0.868 N Mile (approx)
Yard (Yd)	1 Mile	= 1760 Yds	1 N Mile	= 2000 Yds (approx)
Cable	1 Cable	= 200 Yds	1 N Mile	= 10 Cables (approx)
Fathom	1 Fathom	= 1.8288m*	1 Fathom	= 2 yards (6 feet)

AREA

square millimetre (mm²)	1 in²	= 645·16 mm²*	1 mm²	= 0·001 550 in²
square centimetre (cm²)	1 ft²	= 0·092 903 m²	1 m²	= 10·7639 ft²
square metre (m²)	1 yd²	= 0·836 127 m²	1 m²	= 1·195 99 yd²
square kilometre (km²)	1 acre	= 4046.86 m²		
hectare (ha) = 10000m²	1 acre	= 0·404 686 ha	1 ha	= 2·471 05 acre

VOLUME

cubic millimetre (mm³)	1 in³	= 16387·1 mm³	1 mm³	= 0·000 061 0237 in³
cubic centimetre (cm³)	1 ft³	= 0·028 3168 m³	1 m³	= 35·3147 ft³
cubic metre (m³)	1 yd³	= 0·764 555 m³	1 m³	= 1·307 95 yd³
litre (l) = 0·001m³	1 gal	= 0·004 546 09 m³	1 m³	= 219·969 gal
	1 pint	= 0·568 26 1 litre	1 litre	= 1·759 75 pint
	1 gal	= 4·546 09 litre	1 litre	= 0·219 969 gal
	1 gal	= 1·2 US gal	1 litre	= 0.26 US gal
	1 freight ton (40ft³)	= 1·1327 m³		

MASS

gramme (g)	1 oz (avdp)	= 28·3495 g	1 g	= 0·035 274 oz (avdp)
kilogramme (kg)	1 lb	= 0·453 592 37 kg*	1 kg	= 2·204 62 lb
	1 cwt	= 50·8023 kg	1t (tonne)	= 0·984 207 ton
tonne (t) = 1000 kg	1 ton	= 1016·05 kg	1t (tonne)	= 2204·62 lb
	1 ton	= 1·016 05t (tonne)		

DENSITY

kilogramme/cubic metre (kg/m³)	1 lb/ft³	= 16·0185 kg/m³	1 kg/m³	= 0·062 428 lb/ft³
gramme/cubic centimetre (g/cm³)	1 lb/in³	= 27·6799 g/cm³	1 g/cm³	=0·036 127 lb/in³
tonne/cubic metre (t/m³)	1 ton/yd³	= 1·328 94 t/m³	1 t/m³	=0·752 479 ton/yd³

FORCE

newton (N)	1 tonf	= 9·964 02 kN	1 kN	= 0·100 361 tonf
kilonewton (kN)	1 lbf	= 4·448 22 N	1 N	= 0·224 809 lbf
meganewton (MN)	1 poundal	= 0·138 255 N	1 N	= 7·233 01 poundal

VELOCITY

metre/second (m/s)
kilometre/second (km/s)
knot International = 1,852·0 m/h

1 in/s	= 25·4 mm/s*	1 mm/s	= 0·039 3701 in/s
1 ft/min	= 5·08 mm/s	1 mm/s	= 0·196 85 ft/min
1 ft/s	= 0·30348 m/s*	1 m/s	= 3·280 84 ft/s
1 mph	= 0·447 040 m/s	1 km/h	= 2·236 94 m/s
1 mph	= 1·609 34 km/h	1 km/h	= 0·621 371 mph
1 knot (British)	= 1·000 64 knot (inter)	1 knot (inter)	= 0·999 36 knot (British)
1 knot	= 1·152 mph		
1 knot	= 1·85 km/h	1m/s	=1·94 N Miles/hr

VOLUME FLOW RATE

cubic metres/second (m³/s)	1 ft³/s	= 0·028 3168 m³/s	1 m³/s	= 35·3147 ft³/s
cubic metres/hour (m³/h)	1 gal/h	= 0·004 546 09 m³/h	1 m³/h	= 219·969 gal/h
litres/hour (1/h)	1 gal/h	4·456 09 l/h	1 l/h	= 0·219 969 gal/h
litres/second (l/s)	1 gal/min	= 0·272 765 m³/h	1 m³/h	= 3·666 16 gal/min
	1 gal/min	= 0·075 768 2 l/s	1 l/s	= 13·1981 gal/min

ENERGY

joule (J)	1 kWh	= 3·6 MJ*	1 MJ	= 0·277 778 kWh
kilojoule (kJ)	1 ftlbf	= 1·355 82 J	1 J	= 0·737 562 ftlbf
megajoule (MJ)	1 ftpdl	= 0·042 1401 J	1 J	= 23·7304 ftpdl
	1 therm	= 105·506 MJ	1 MJ	= 0·009 478 13 therm
	1 Btu	= 1·055 06 kJ	1 kJ	= 0·947 813 Btu

POWER

watt (W)	1 hp	= 745·700 W	1W	= 0·001 341 02 hp
kilowatt (kW)	1 ftlbf/s	= 1·355 82 W	1W	= 0·737 561 ftlbf/s
megawatt (MW)				

TORQUE CONVERSION

1 lb ft = 1·356 Newton metres (Nm)
1 Nm = 0·737 lb ft

TEMPERATURE CONVERSION

Centigrade to Fahrenheit: (°C x 9/5) + 32 = °F

Fahrenheit to Centigrade: (°F – 32) x 5/9 = °C

0°C = 32°F
0°F = −17·8°C

4. Reader's voyages

Dear Ocean Voyager,

For the next edition of *Ocean Passages and Landfalls* we would like to include your passages in our section on actual passages made. We would be very grateful if you would fill in details on the form below for passages that you have made (make as many copies as you like). We will be particularly interested in passages made outside the 'usual season' or by unusual routes. If the original plan or advice given in this book or other pilots was not followed, we would be interested to hear the reasons.

Please return forms to Imray:

Imray Laurie Norie & Wilson Ltd
Wych House
The Broadway
St Ives
Cambridgeshire
PE27 5BT
England

Fax 00 44 1480 496109
Email ilnw@imray.com

Thanks from Andy O'Grady and Rod Heikell

Name of vessel:

Type and length overall (if not a well-known class please include a short description):

Skippers name:

Size of crew (including skipper):

From:

To:

Date of departure:

Date of arrival:

Distance sailed (nautical miles):

Route taken (ie: details of individual legs if not a direct course between two points):

Conditions encountered (storms, calms, shipping ice...):

Comments (such as whether it was a good choice of time and route):

Details of actual passages made by a variety of yachts

Here are some passages that we have made over the years plus some that have been contributed by readers. We hope that these will give an idea of actual passage times

Departure	Destination	Yacht	Crew	Departure date	Days at sea	Distance sailed	Comments
NORTH ATLANTIC							
Yarmouth IOW, UK	Luara, Cantabrica, Spain	*Skugga*	3	16 Sep 82	9	670	Two major gales – set 100M to leeward in Biscay
Bayona, Spain	Funchal Madeira	*Skugga*	3	9 Oct 82	11	800	Much calm, engine not used
Funchal, Madeira	Los Cristianos, Tenerife	*Skugga*	3	24 Oct 82	2.5	300	Steady NE breeze
Gomera, Canary Islands	Bridgetown, Barbados	*Skugga*	3	12 Nov 82	26	2710	Picked up steady NE trades after 2 days
St Georges, Grenada	San Blas Is, Panamá	*Skugga*	2	26 Feb 83	9	1021	Strong trades and big seas off Colombian coast
Sint Maarten	Horta, Azores	*Seven tenths*	3	13 May 99	21	2302	N towards Bermuda and then rhumb line. Light wind passage
Ponta Delgada	Gibraltar	*Seven tenths*	4	16 Jun 99	9	1040	Rhumb line. Heavy windward passage
Ponta Delgado	Lisbon	*Skylax*	2	10 Jun 05	6	798	S and then rhumb line. Changed route from Gib to Lisbon
Gibraltar	Porto Santo	*Sanyassa*	2	11 Oct 97	5	551	Huge seas although winds were only around 30kns Lay a-hull at 34°40'N 10°37'E for 12hrs. Resumed sailing at 34°30'N 10°51'E
Gibraltar	Lanzarote	*Seven tenths*	2	11 Nov 03	5	637	W and then rhumb line. Light trade winds
Gran Canaria	Point a Pitre Guadeloupe	*Seven tenths*	3	29 Nov 03	24	2915	Rhumb line and then S and W Tropical storm *Peter* on 07/12/03
Antigua	Horta/Azores	*Skylax*	2	08 May 05	23	2860	Beating and driven S by weather
Forteau, Canada	Sisimut, Greenland	*Balæna*	2	27 May 05	13	1000	Mainly S and SE wind several days calm and NW gale – no ice
Prins Cristian Sound, Greenland	Bere Is. Eire	*Balæna*	2	16 Aug 05	11	1210	Rescued yacht W of Ireland – one day hove-to and one day towing
Cherbourg, France	Muros, Spain	*Balæna*	2	10 Oct 07	3	620	Mod E winds all the way
Lisbon, Portugal	Porto Santo, Madeira	*Balæna*	2	6 Oct 07	4	520	Light winds
Lanzarote	Mindelo, Cape Verdes	*Skylax*	2	22 Nov 07	6	968	Rhumb line. Blustery trades
Santa Cruz de La Palma, Canaries	Mindelo, Cabo Verde	*Balæna*	2	23 Nov 07	5	850	Fresh N-NE winds
Mindelo Cape Verdes	Falmouth Antigua	*Skylax*	3	07 Dec 07	14	2173	Great Circle. Easy trades. Few squalls
Sint Maarten	Panama	*Skylax*	2	10 May 08	7	1177	Rhumb line. Easy trade wind passage
SOUTH ATLANTIC							
South Georgia	Cape Town	*Terra Nova*	2	15 Feb 03	26	2800	Ice encountered as far N as 42°S. Very rough
Cape Town	Tobago	*Balæna*	2	3 Dec 03	35	5577	Steady SE almost all the way, sailed close to 100m line off Amazon
Mindelo, Cabo Verde	Salvador, Brazil	*Balæna*	2	5 Dec 07	16	1950	Very rough time in ITCZ, crossed equator at 27°23'W

Appendix

Departure	Destination	Yacht	Crew	Departure date	Days at sea	Distance sailed	Comments
SOUTH PACIFIC OCEAN							
Islas Perlas, Panamá	Wreck Bay, San Cristobal, Galapagos	*Skugga*	2	5 Apr 83	16	900	Much calm, little use of engine
Wreck Bay, San Cristobal, Galapagos	Hiva Oa, Marquisas	*Skugga*	2	26 Apr 83	32	3113	Much calm at beginning of trip
Maeva Beach, Moorea	Aitutaki, Cook Islands	*Skugga*	2	18 Apr 83	7	550	Gale in SE trades
Aitutaki, Cook Islands	Nuie	*Skugga*	2	3 Sep 83	6	500	Strong SE trades
Suva, Fiji	BOI, NZ	*Skugga*	2	24 Oct 83	15	1072	Variable winds – no engine
Hobart, Aus.	Port Taranaki, NZ	*Balæna*	3	30 Dec 91	11.5	1463	Gales and calms, cyclone passing over N of NZ
BOI, NZ	Fiordland NZ	*Balæna*	2	24 Jan 97	6.5	776	Variable winds, mainly E quadrant
BOI, NZ	Ha'upai, Tonga	*Balæna*	5	3 Jul 98	10	1200	Variable winds, up to 40 knots, confused sea at times
Va'vau, Tonga	Savusavu, Fiji	*Balæna*	5	7 Aug 98	3	405	Nice trade winds
Lautoka, Fiji	BOI, NZ	*Balæna*	5	19 Sep 98	7.5	1024	Easy sail, mainly E and occasionally strong
Chatham Is, NZ	Puerto Montt, Chile	*Balæna*	2	24 Dec 99	37.5	4578	Much E wind for first part of trip, sailed to 50ºS to find W wind
Easter Island	Valdivia, Chile	*Terra Nova*	2	12 Nov 01	24	1940	Much calm and head wind, should have curved more to south
Port Villa, Vanuatu	Wellington, NZ	*Cape Resolution*		20 Aug 07	12	1400	Heavy weather in S part of route
Balboa	Santa Cruz, Galapagos	*Skylax*	2	30 May 08	9	1135	S and then rhumb line – headwinds
Galapagos	Atuona Marquesas	*Skylax*	2	14 Jun 08	19	3116	Great circle – steady trades
Hiva Oa Marquesas	Rangiroa Tuamotus	*Skylax*	2	21 Jul 08	5	545	Rhumb line – light winds
Raiatea Society Is.	Neiafu Tonga	*Skylax*	2	10 Sep 08	11	1362	Diversion to Palmerston – SPCZ, squalls and trades
Nukualofu Tonga	Opua NZ	*Skylax*	2	02 Nov 08	7	1064	Rhumb line – 2 fronts encountered
Opua NZ	Port Resolution, Vanuatu	*Pateke*	3	26 May 01	9	960	Rhumb line – winds NW-SW
Vanuatu	Cairns	*Pateke*	3	17 Aug 01	8	1287	Rhumb line – trades
Opua	Sydney	*Pateke*	3	19 Jan 05	10	1225	Rhumb line once clear of NZ N-NE wind with S going current
Sydney	Hobart	*Pateke*	4	07 Feb 05	4	400	Coast to Tasman Strait mainl NW-SW
Opua NZ	Suva, Fiji	*Sanyassa*	2	08 May 09	12	1052	We had waited several days along with many other crews for a good weather window. Signs were good yet within 36hrs we were getting forecasts of 40kns northerlies. Once again the value of our parachute anchor was proven. In 10 years we have only used it twice and both were in this area.
NORTH PACIFIC OCEAN							
Galapagos	Hawaii	*Seabiscuit II*	2	12 Jun 08	25	4763	Good trade winds (15–25k) for the most part in the S Pacific. Approaching the ITCZ wind steadily dropped

Departure	Destination	Yacht	Crew	Departure date	Days at sea	Distance sailed	Comments
Hawaii	Victoria BC	*Seabiscuit II*	2	31 Aug 08	20	2628	Started out trying to make as close to N as we could but the NE winds kept us W until we reached 37°N. From here course changed to S shape.
Marquises Is	Hawaii	*Cahoots*	2	25 Oct 04	13	2150	NE trades were well aft
Hawaii	Straits of Juan de Fuca	*Cahoots*	2	29 May 05	16	2500	Early in season – encountered two gales

INDIAN OCEAN

Departure	Destination	Yacht	Crew	Departure date	Days at sea	Distance sailed	Comments
Benoa, Bali	Christmas Is	*Balæna*	4	26 Sep 91	3.5	509	Steady trade wind all the way
Christmas Is	Cocos Keeling Atoll	*Balæna*	4	3 Oct 91	3	434	Trade wind strong – up to 30 knots
Cocos Keeling Atoll	Fremantle – Australia	*Balæna*	3	12 Oct 91	17	1875	S to 30° then SE. Mostly sailing fast on the wind
Fremantle	Melbourne	*Balæna*	1	9 Nov 91	17	1950	Steady westerlies and regular seas
Mukalla	Cochin	*Tetranora*	2	02 Jan 96	21	2100 (great circle 1300)	Hard on wind in route down to ITCZ and back up
Galle, Sri Lanka	Phuket Thailand	*Tetranora*	2	10 Mar 96	13	1332	S and then rhumb line NE monsoon.
Cochin, India	Mukalla	*Tetranora*	2	23 Jan 97	13	1300	S of rhumb line NE monsoon
Cape Town, RSA	Fremantle – Australia	*Terra Nova*	2	12 Jan 04	49	5100	Rough, knocked down in storm
Cocos Keeling	Rodrigues	*Pateke*	2	28 Sep 05	15	2058	Great circle 20–25 knot SE trades
Mauritius	Durban	*Pateke*	2	05 Nov 05	14	1750	Kept well S of S end Madagascar. Mostly 10–15 knot SE trades
Kilifi Kenya	Mahe Seychelles	*Pateke*	2	18 Feb 07	8	1000	NE 10–15 knot trades
Mahe Seychelles	Maldives	*Pateke*	2		–	1250	Light SE trades
Maldives	Langkawi Malaysia	*Pateke*	2	10 Oct 07	18	1800	Light S-SE winds

MEDITERRANEAN

Departure	Destination	Yacht	Crew	Departure date	Days at sea	Distance sailed	Comments
Port Said	Kas ,Turkey	*Tetranora*	1	24 Mar 97	4	335	Rhumb line. W-NW and calms. Hove-to 12 hours in gale
Gibraltar	Palma, Mallorca	*Seven tenths*	1	13 Oct 99	3	470	Coastal. Light NW and SW. Some calms
Andraitx, Mallorca	Levkas, Greece	*Skylax*	2	11 Jul 05	7	918	Sardinia – Messina – Levkas. Wind mostly NW-NE some light
Trapani, Sicily	Palma, Mallorca	*Skylax*	2	11 Oct 07	3	495	Winds variable and strong from N quad

DETAILS OF VESSELS

Name of vessel	Owner/skipper	LOA – metres	Rig	Design	Comments
Tetranora	Rod Heikell	9.5	Berm. sloop	Cheverton New Campaigner	Long keel
Balæna	Andy O'Grady	12.5	Gaff cutter	Colin archer type	Long keel
Cape Resolution	John Beaglehole	12	Berm. sloop	Mummery	Fin and skeg
Cahoots	John Renwick	13	Berm. cutter	Cartwright 44'	Modified fin and skeg
Terra Nova	Willem Stein	12	Berm. Ketch	Colin Archer type – Joshua class	Long keel
Skugga	Andy O'Grady	8	Berm. sloop	Colin Archer type	Long keel
Skylax	Rod Heikell	14	Berm. sloop	Warwick	Fin and skeg
Seven tenths	Rod Heikell	11	Berm. sloop	Pedrick 36	Mod keel
Pateke	Fenton Hamlin	9	Berm. cutter	Lyall Hess	Long keel
Sanyassa				Prout Snowgoose Elite	Catamaran
Seabiscuit II	Allan Poole	12		Saga 409	

5. Southeast Asia regattas

There is now an extensive series of regattas in Southeast Asia, many of which are aimed at cruising yachts heading up to Thailand from Darwin. Many of these regattas are well established events and are a lot of fun. The social side is often hectic and if you can survive the parties ashore and the racing on the water, you will survive just about anything.

Note on Indonesian Rallies
Rallies come and go according to the political situation in Indonesia. The various rallies running in Indonesia have now been amalgamated into just one: Sail Indonesia. The exact route of the rally can change so check the website www.sailindonesia.net for information. It may be that in the future new rallies will run from Darwin depending on demand and the situation in Indonesia.

Sail Indonesia Rally

This is now the most popular of the rallies and leaves Darwin in late July. The rally used to go to Kupang on the W end of Timor, but after problems with the officials in Kupang it now goes to Samulaki on Jamdena or Ambon (Eirie). The distance to Samulaki is around 200 miles most yachts complete it within 2–3 days depending on the winds. On arrival at Samulaki rally participants are cleared in and the social events begin. This is now a substantial rally with 200 yachts expressing interest for 2009. www.sailindonesia.net

Darwin to Ambon Rally

This is now part of the Sail Indonesia circuit. Go to www.sailindonesia.net

Oz Med Rally

Run by Blue Water Rallies. Yachts can join in the Round the World Blue Water Rally in Australia and complete the second half of the rally to the Mediterranean. www.yachtrallies.co.uk

Sail Malaysia

Picks up where Sail Indonesia leaves off and the rally goes from Danga Bay on Johor to Langkawi. It leaves mid-November and takes around 5–6 days visiting Lumut and Penang en route.
Go to www.sailmalaysia.net

Raja Muda (late November)

A week of races up the west coast of peninsular Malaysia from Port Klang to Langkawi including several Olympic triangles. Several of the early legs are sailed at night to take advantage of the land breeze augmented by the NE monsoon.

The regatta is run under the IRC Handicap System and is open to racing and cruising yachts with different divisions. www.rsyc.com.my

King's Cup (early December)

The race week is in early December with around six races over seven days (one lay day). The courses are a mix of triangle, windward/leeward and passage races. There are ten divisions: Racing, Premier Cruising, IRC 1, IRC 2, IRC 3, Ocean Rover, Ocean Multihull, Classic, Beach Catamarans and Sports Boats. It is run under the IRC Handicap System and measurement can take place before the race in Phuket. www.kingscup.com

Andaman Sea Rally (early January)

Gentle racing to Port Blair in the Andamans from Phuket and back again. Its future is not certain at the moment and the website is not running.

Phang Nga Bay Regatta

Takes place around Phuket and Phang Nga Bay in February. Go to www.bayregatta.com

Envoi

A lot of cruising yachts decline to enter these races for reasons which range from an inverse snobbery to mutterings about the expense. In truth they are not expensive and the amount of fun to be had is vast. In 1996 I entered the venerable old *Tetra* in the classic class of the King's Cup and to my own and a few locals' surprise won the classic division. In 2009 *Skylax* will be in the Raja Muda and the Kings Cup. The racing on the water is adrenaline buzzing stuff, even in the classic class, and the entertainment ashore makes you wish for a quiet night on board – except you might miss some of the fun, not to mention the booze and food, so you don't. At the end of the whole affair there is a wonderful calm as you realise that today you don't have to get up and party or race. I'm going back for more. For Asian Regattas see www.sailing-asia.com

INDEX